Christian Stadler · Michael Wieser · Kate Kirk (Eds.)

Psychodrama.
Empirical Research and Science 2

Psychodrama.

Empirische Forschung und Wissenschaft 2

Zeitschrift für Psychodrama und Soziometrie

Sonderheft 7 | 2016

Christian Stadler · Michael Wieser ·
Kate Kirk (Eds.)

Psychodrama. Empirical Research and Science 2

Psychodrama.

Empirische Forschung und Wissenschaft 2

Springer VS

ZPS

www.zps-digital.de

Zeitschrift für Psychodrama und Soziometrie

Anschrift: Redaktion ZPS, Konrad-Adenauer-Str. 27, 85221 Dachau, e-mail: praxisstadler@arcor.de

Springer VS | Springer Fachmedien Wiesbaden GmbH
Abraham-Lincoln-Straße 46 | D-65189 Wiesbaden
Amtsgericht Wiesbaden, HRB 9754 | USt-IdNr. DE811148419

Geschäftsführer: Peter Hendriks
Joachim Krieger

Editorial Director Psychology & Reference Works:
Dr. Andreas Beierwaltes
Gesamtleitung Anzeigen und Märkte: Volker Hesedenz
Gesamtleitung Marketing: Rolf-Günther Hobbeling
Gesamtleitung Produktion: Olga Chiarcos

AbonnentInnenbetreuung: Springer Customer Service Center GmbH; Service VS Verlag; Haberstr. 7, D-69126 Heidelberg; Telefon: +49 (0)6221/345-4303; Telefax: +49 (0)6221/345-4229; Montag bis Freitag 8.00 Uhr bis 18.00 Uhr
E-Mail: springervs-service@springer.com
Marketing: Ronald Schmidt-Serrière M.A.; Telefon: (06 11) 78 78-280; Telefax: (06 11) 78 78-439
E-Mail: Ronald.Schmidt-Serriere@springer.com
Mediaberatung: Yvonne Guderjahn; Telefon: (06 11) 78 78-155; Telefax: (06 11) 78 78-430
E-Mail: Yvonne.Guderjahn@springer.com
Anzeigendisposition: Nicole Frohnweiler; Telefon: (06 11) 78 78-147; Telefax: (06 11) 78 78-443
E-Mail: Nicole.Frohnweiler@springer.com
Anzeigenpreise: Es gelten die Mediadaten vom 1.1.2016
Produktion/Layout: Marina Litterer; Telefon: (0 62 21) 48 78-755
E-Mail: marina.litterer@springer.com

Jährlich können Sonderhefte erscheinen, die nach Umfang berechnet und den Abonnenten des laufenden Jahrgangs mit einem Nachlass von 25% Rabatt des jeweiligen Ladenpreises geliefert werden. Bei Nichtgefallen können die Sonderhefte innerhalb einer Frist von 3 Wochen zurückgegeben werden.

Gedruckt auf säurefreiem und chlorfrei gebleichtem Papier

ISBN 978-3-658-13014-5 ISSN 1619-5507 (Print) ISSN 1862-2526 (Online)

Zeitschrift für Psychodrama und Soziometrie

Editorial

Hauptbeiträge

1. Research instruments, methods, and network research

2. Clinical research with adults

Epilogue

Z Psychodrama Soziometr (2016) (Suppl) 15:1–4
DOI 10.1007/s11620-016-0316-2

EDITORIAL

Zeitschrift für Psychodrama
und Soziometrie

Psychodrama

Empirical research and science 2

Kate Kirk · Michael Wieser · Christian Stadler

Published online: 3 February 2016

It is with great pleasure that we welcome you to this edition of Zeitschrift für Psychodrama und Soziometrie that is dedicated to research undertaken in many forms and places. Kate Kirk was honoured to be asked to be part of the editorial team by Michael Wieser and Christian Stadler. We must not forget someone who was present though more behind the scenes, Konrad Schnabel in a supportive role of reviewer of statistics. This edition's content is much more than simply a German or even European journal, it is international. This project demonstrates the breadth of psychodrama research taking place in parts of the world.

Of course, we cannot have a journal dedicated to psychodrama psychotherapy research without mentioning the influence, role and support of the Society for Psychotherapy Research (SPR). Psychodrama researchers have been active in presenting at SPR annual international conferences—look out for details for SPR Jerusalem 2016. Some of the co-authored studies are evidence of SPR collaboration across modalities, as well as countries. One exciting aspect of this journal is to see the studies that have been conceived and observed through their gestational process at meetings of the Federation of European Psychodrama Training Organisations (FEPTO) research committee. Here is the delivery of these FEPTO babies for the scrutiny of the psychodrama research community and they demonstrate the liveliness of European psychodrama studies.

So without further ado let us give you a flavour of the contents held within this edition full of riches related to psychodrama research influencing theory and practice.

The contents are divided into four sections:

✉ Kate Kirk
Kate.Kirk@gov.im

[1] CAMHS Noble's Hospital, IM4 4DG British Isles, Braddan, Douglas, Isle of Man

1 Research instruments, methods, and network research

The opening article is drawn from an original unpublished manuscript from the late David Kipper. In Factor Analysis of the Revised Spontaneity Assessment Inventory (SAI-R) Kipper and Beasley use this scale designed to assess spontaneity; they highlight three factors that support theoretical views on spontaneity. The use of SAI-R is described in the following two articles. The first is a comparative study across two countries (Testoni et al.): Austria and Italy; whereby levels of spontaneity are correlated with levels of psychological well-being using SAI-R and CORE-OM and Beck's Depression Inventory. This study is seen as a helpful pre-cursor to a study of clinical population.

The next article, by Rabung et al., that uses SAI-R is Psychometric Evaluation of the German Version of the SAI-R. In a development of SAI-R, a German translation was applied in two settings: non- clinical and clinical populations. The findings reveal the reliability, acceptability and validity of this German SAI-R.

From Portugal, Pio-Abreu and Villares Oliviera's article introduce readers to their method of measuring *tele* in material derived from sociometric tests. They describe the four indices that comprise the measure and describe its application and analysis to both real world and virtual groups. A second Portuguese article entitled Towards the Development of Helpful Aspects of Morenian Psychodrama Content Analysis System (HAMPCAS) by Cruz et al. demonstrates the innovation and development of a psychodrama specific data collection method, based in previously validated instruments. It has been exciting to watch the process of this research from conception and delivery in the arena of FEPTO research committee through to dissemination in this journal.

Dima and Bucuta represent Romania with their article entitled 'The method of interpretative phenomenological analysis (IPA) in psychodrama research'. Their article takes the reader through the theory and practice of IPA in a simple instructive way. The final article in this section is both geographically broad and culturally sensitive. Drawing on new material from Hong Kong and Hungary the results were compared by Stadler et al. with a 2009 study from Germany/Austria, Israel and Nigeria the focus was not surprisingly on 'Intercultural network-research: Cross-cultural analysis of social network characteristics and life satisfaction'.

2 Clinical research with adults

Debus and Ahrens present their psychodrama research from the toughest corner of clinical work: inpatient psychiatric ward with violent patients and situations. In a sensitive exploration they demonstrate ways of using psychodramas of conflicted and difficult situations to inform and promote alternatives to other more oppressive ways of managing challenging patients; if, it seems, the therapist is willing to undertake the role reversal required to gain understanding. The setting for Fingerhut's research was in a psychiatric outpatient clinic with material drawn from two psychodrama groups. Changes are demonstrated through case studies and the presentation of post-group evaluation of patients over 2 years.

The final article in this section is from Slovenia, Prosen's psychodrama research follows 7 years of clinical psychodrama with clients who have eating disorders. She presents not only the themes but tentatively suggests a degree of effects and the relevance of psychodrama with this client group.

3 Clinical research with children and young people

In an appropriately playful entitled article, which highlights role expansion from shark to bank teller, Uschold-Meier and Wagner's research takes place in a German children's home. They use a psychodrama specific tool (RDI) to measure change, in conjunction with other tools, from different perspectives. They found the method effective in practice and that it supported therapists' own reflections. The next article is from Austria. Köfeler and Krall's study has been followed with keen interest in the FEPTO research committee; it focuses on promoting social interaction with children who have selective mutism. This study uses multiple collection methods: specially designed questionnaires and video analysis; importantly they include the children's views. They found that some psychodrama interventions were directly related to an improvement in social interaction.

Scheuffgen et al.'s study population are boys who are in a specialised unit for trauma and sexually abusive behaviours where psychodrama is an intrinsic part of treatment. This long-term study from 2010 has been evaluating the boys' progress at 6 monthly intervals from three perspectives: their own, their therapists and their pedagogues. When there is agreement across the three perspectives this is viewed a success; differences are explored further through supervision for the therapist involved. Results are also given from an interview survey of previous clients who were asked about their experiences of psychodrama group psychotherapy.

In the final article in this section, Gstrein's study focuses on a specific, and unusual, application of psychodrama; i.e. with young people (17–19 years) who have mathematics anxiety. She ran ten psychodrama sessions for students and evaluated the changes in their presenting problems using a number of tools. The results, gained from combined qualitative and quantitative data collection tools, demonstrated the positive impact of psychodrama on their struggles.

4 Research in supervision, education, and training

From Hungary, Marlok et al. test Krüger's technique of self-supervision with role reversal (SSRR) in promoting the relationship between the client and therapist. They compared SSRR with a modified writing exercise. Their results demonstrated both methods effective in dissolving blocks and containing therapists' feelings; however SSRR promoted more empathy and helpfulness towards clients.

Daniel's Australian phenomenological study sought to replicate a previous study and further to explore the experiences that supervisees had of role reversal in one-to-one supervision. Her findings revealed similar themes to those noted in the earlier study: increase in spontaneity and confidence and a decrease in anxiety. She reflects on the dynamic of holding multiple roles in relation to her research participants, with a side effect of causing some anxiety in the beginning.

Çam's study explores the role psychodrama plays in promoting self-disclosure in Turkish university students who, as a consequence, recognised the need to improve their communication and social skills.

Fürst and Krall describe one snapshot of their work training trainee psychotherapists in research skills and awareness alongside their psychotherapy training. TRAIN (Towards Research Applied in an International Network of Trainees) has been in development in FEPTO research committee for some years, instigated and continued by the Austrian authors. This article reveals the results from interviews with trainees who have been on the receiving end of psychotherapy training that is steeped in research from the beginning. The findings reveal what has been helpful and hindering in the process and also the students' recommendations for future training.

From Germany, Schnabel and Reif's article 'Ways to Evaluate Psychodrama Training' aims to fill a gap in the research literature, i.e. research into the effects and quality of psychodrama training. An interesting finding from their study suggests that the earlier trainees engage in psychodrama enactment predicts the likelihood of them continuing their training. They recommend self and observer feedback as part of evaluation in training and as a way of measuring the long term effects of training.

In the final article of this section we return to Austria and Hintermeier presents 8 years worth of psychodrama psychotherapy master's theses. In a detailed description she lays out not only the subjects under exploration by students' but also the research methods they have used. What emerges is a wealth of material that could be a great resource for other students and researchers, so as not to reinvent the wheel but to use as a starting platform for their own studies. We are sad that it is in German and so not accessible to other students in other countries.

By way of closing the circle, in some way, you find that Kirk has written the Epilogue. It is a reprint and updating of a letter written in surplus reality to Dr Moreno. We are pleased that things have moved on since the original letter was written.

So here you are, a progression from Stadler and Wieser (2011), 4 years on and a second issue focussing on research. Will we have to wait another 4 years? Or, will you submit snapshots of your own research studies, works in progress and results? Please do submit proposals to the editorial board of the ZPS: praxisstadler@arcor.de. On another but related matter, there are moves afoot to start a European Psychodrama Research Journal. So look out for information on this development.

Happy reading and good luck with any of your own research projects.

Z Psychodrama Soziometr (2016) (Suppl) 15:5–10
DOI 10.1007/s11620-015-0301-1

HAUPTBEITRÄGE

Zeitschrift für Psychodrama und Soziometrie

Factor analysis of the Revised Spontaneity Assessment Inventory (SAI-R)

David A. Kipper · Christopher R. Beasley

Published online: 27 November 2015

Abstract The present study describes a factor analysis of the Revised Spontaneity Assessment Inventory (SAI-R), an original scale design to measure spontaneity. The analysis revealed three factors underlying the inventory. The first, titled vigor/pleasure, suggests that spontaneity is a pleasurable and dynamic experience. The second factor, titled freedom, indicates that spontaneity is characterized by a sense of free expression and actions unhindered by conventions. The third factor, titled involvement/focus, indicates that spontaneity is focused experience a characteristics that separates it from impulsivity. These factors seemed consistent with the theoretical understanding of spontaneity.

Keywords Spontaneity · Factor analysis · Measurement · Psychodrama

Faktorenanalyse des Revidierten Spontaneität Assessment Inventars

Zusammenfassung Faktorenanalyse des Revidierten Spontaneität Assessment Inventars (SAI-R) Diese Studie beschreibt die Faktorenanalyse des Revidierten Spontaneität Assessment Inventars (SAI-R), eine Originalskala, die entwickelt wurde, um Spontaneität zu messen. Die Analyse zeigte drei Faktoren, die dem Inventar zu Grunde liegen. Der erste mit dem Titel Vitalität/Behagen, legt nahe, dass die Spontaneität eine angenehme und dynamische Erfahrung ist. Der zweite Faktor, betitelt mit Freiheit, besagt, dass Spontaneität im Sinne des freien Ausdrucks und Handlung sich von Konventionen nicht behindern lässt. Der dritte Faktor, mit dem

Translated by Michael Wieser.

Assist. Prof. C. R. Beasley, Ph.D. (✉) · D. A. Kipper
Department of Psychology, Washington College,
300 Washington Avenue,
21620 Chestertown, MD, USA
e-mail: cbeasley2@washcoll.edu

Titel Beteiligtsein/Fokus, zeigt an, dass Spontaneität eine Eigenschaft des Erlebens ist, die anders als Impulsivität zu verstehen ist. Diese Faktoren sind konsistent mit dem theoretischen Verständnis der Spontaneität.

Schlüsselwörter Spontaneität · Faktorenanalyse · Test · Psychodrama

The concept of spontaneity was first introduced to psychotherapy by Moreno (1953) who considered it a major contributor to well-being. His theory and the kind of group therapy (psychodrama) he created are based on the notion that a spontaneous person is a mentally healthy one. Moreno's (1953, 1964) theory held that the process leading to well-being begins with spontaneity which triggers creativity that ends in action. Interestingly, both Moreno (1953), an opponent of psychoanalysis, and Fiumara, (2009), a psychoanalyst, are in agreement on one point, that is, the importance of spontaneity and its relation to creativity. In a recent psychoanalytic exploration of the nature of spontaneity the latter argues that spontaneity is a personality factor critical to the development of the self. Spontaneity, therefore, serves as an agency affecting the creative action. Other than Moreno and his followers (e.g., Baim et al. 2007; Blatner 2000) and Fiumara's (2009) theories regarding spontaneity, the literature on the place of spontaneity in psychotherapy is scant. Further, except for one attempt to operationally define spontaneity by designing a scale measuring it (Kellar et al. 2002), empirical investigations of spontaneity are practically non-existent.

Recently, Kipper and colleagues (e.g. Kipper and Shemer 2006; Kipper et al. 2010) developed a paper-and-pencil, self-report inventory designed to measure spontaneity. Twenty-five internationally known psychotherapists; psychodrama experts, contributed the characteristics of spontaneity featured in the inventory. The rationale for seeking the input of these experts was that since they conduct psychotherapeutic treatments that promote spontaneity, they are in the best position to describe it. They were asked to provide five adjectives that describe the feelings and thoughts that characterized the state of spontaneity. An item-analysis of these descriptions resulted in a scale titled: the Revised Spontaneity Assessment Inventory (SAI-R).

Previous studies showed that the SAI-R scores correlated positively with measures of well-being, self-efficacy, self-esteem, intrinsic motivation, and the executive function of the brain. Further, the SAI-R correlated negatively with stress, anxiety, avoidance, obsessive-compulsive tendency, impulsivity, and inhibition (e.g., Davelaar et al. 2008; Kipper et al. 2009, 2010; Kipper and Shemer 2006). These results, both the positive and the negative correlations, are congruent with the theoretical predictions regarding the meaning of spontaneity and as such they lend some validity to the SAI-R. Also, the fact that from the outset the adjectives comprising the items of the SAI-R were selected because they were deemed fair descriptions of spontaneity provides a face-validity to the measure. Still, we thought that unraveling the factors underlying the measure might shed further light on what elements of spontaneity are addressed in the SAI-R and are these elements congruent with the theoretical characterization of spontaneity.

1 Method

1.1 Participants

Participants were 351 graduate students at an independent urban university in the Upper Midwest United States; 82 (24 %) males and 269 (76 %) females. Their age ranged from18 to 57 (*M*=21.60, *SD*=6.85) with a level of education of *M*=16.36, (*SD*=1.99). Participation was voluntary. To encourage honesty the participants were asked not to reveal their names and provide only their age, gender, and years of education.

1.2 Measure

The Revised Spontaneity Assessment Inventory (SAI-R) (Kipper and Shemer 2006) is a paper- and-pencil, self-report inventory designed to measure spontaneity. It poses the question "How strongly do you have these feelings or thoughts in a typical day?" The question is followed by a list of 18 adjectives describing various moods, feelings and thoughts (e.g., happy, uninhibited, light and living, energized, in control). Participants are asked to rate themselves on each of the 18 adjectives using a 5-point Likert scale that range from 1=very weak to 5=very strong. The sum total of all the ratings represents the total SAI-R score. Previous studies with the SAI-R showed satisfactory Cronbach's alphas. In the present study the alpha was .89.

1.3 Procedure

Participants took the inventory in small groups either before or immediately after the end of their classes. They were read an informed consent and were assured that the university Institutional Review Board approved the study. They were also told that that they could withdraw from the study at any point without penalty. Completing the SAIR took 10 min. Participants did not receive any reward; credit or otherwise compensated, for taking part in the study.

2 Results and discussion

The average SAI-R score was *M*=63.33 (*SD*=9.71), results consistent with those reported in earlier studies using the SAI-R. Also, consistent with the earlier studies there was no statistically significant gender difference on the SAI-R results (males: *M=63.24, SD*=9.71; females: *M=63.35, SD=9.73;* $t(349)=0.089$, n.s.). The SAI-R scores did not correlate significantly with the gender of the participants ($r=.01$, *n.s.*), their age ($r=-.03$, *n.s.*), or their level of education ($r=-.05$, *n.s.*).

We conducted a principle axis factor analysis (Costello and Osborne 2005) on the 18 SAI-R items using direct oblimin oblique rotation (quartimin). The Kaiser-Meyer-Olkin measure verified the sampling adequacy for the analysis with *KMO*=0.91 (Kaiser 1970). Bartlett's test of sphericity revealed $\chi^2=0.15$, $p<.01$, indicating that

Table 1 SAI-R items: pattern Matrix

	Factor		
	1	2	3
Joyful	**0.795**	0.045	−0.006
Happy	**0.779**	−0.051	−0.019
Light and loving	**0.588**	−0.050	0.134
Pleasure	**0.534**	0.020	0.226
Exhilarated	**0.530**	0.469	−0.134
Fulfilled	**0.463**	−0.046	0.393
Alive	**0.462**	0.134	0.174
Energized	**0.442**	0.057	0.276
Free to invent	−0.053	**0.680**	0.075
Free to act, even outrageously	0.139	**0.569**	−0.001
Creative	−0.136	**0.500**	0.072
Uninhibited	0.093	**0.476**	−0.068
Do whatever, within limits	0.130	**0.322**	0.198
In control	0.147	−0.147	**0.686**
Successful	−0.003	0.127	**0.665**
Powerful	−0.013	0.329	**0.490**
Things seem to flow	0.092	0.040	**0.447**
Living fully with balance	0.324	0.116	**0.434**

The bold loadings denote the items that comprise the three factors

the correlations between the items were large enough to conduct a principle axis factor analysis.

Using Kaiser's (1960) criterion of eigenvalues of 1 or above the result revealed three factors that included all 18 items explaining 44.93 % of the variance. Table 1 shows the pattern matrix of the factors' loading after the rotation. Factor 1, titled vigor/pleasure, includes eight items (the original items nos. 2, 5, 7, 10, 12, 13, 14, and 18). Factor 2, titled freedom, includes five items (the original items nos.1, 3, 6, 8, and 17). Factor three, titled involvement/focus, includes five items (the original items nos. 4. 9, 11, 15, and 16). The Cronbach's alphas for the first, second and third factors were 0.88, 0.69, and, 0.79 respectively.

We also conducted a scree plot that showed an inflexion that suggested two factors. However, we chose to adopt the three factors solution derived from the eigenvalues because it better fit the theory that led to the construction of the measure. According to Moreno (1964) spontaneity is an innate drive or energy that is pleasurable. It features deep involvement accompanied by a sense of freedom. Indeed, the etymology of the word *spontaneity* is: a free will. It has a directionally in the sense that it aims at triggering the creative process. The three-factor solution we adopted appears to capture the essence of spontaneity as characterized in the theory.

The first factor is by far the largest of all three and explains 34.65 % of the variance. The eight items included in this factor suggest that spontaneity is a pleasantly exciting experience and that it is forceful. Such a characterization is congruent with Moreno's (1964) consistent claim that spontaneity is energy. It is also consistent with the finding that spontaneity correlates positively with well-being and negatively with stress (e.g., Kipper and Shemer 2006). The second factor is small and contains five items that explain 6.79 % of the variance. It addresses one of the most important characteristics of spontaneity. Not only is spontaneity a pleasurable experience, it is also characterized by a sense of freedom of actions and expressions and an attitude of being unhindered by conventional boundaries. The five items comprising the third factor explain 3.49 % of the variance. Although small this factor speaks to the distinction between spontaneity and impulsivity. It suggests that spontaneity is a more focused and deliberate state of mind as opposed to impulsivity, a form of expression marked by emotional, unfocussed, and uncontrolled out-busts typically associated often unpleasant feelings. This facet of spontaneity is consistent with the findings by Kipper et al. (2010) who reported that the SAI-R correlated negatively with impulsivity, specifically as reflected in the measures of urgency, i.e., the inability to effectively cope with negative effects and consequently react rapidly, and the lack of perseverance, i.e., the failure to focus or consistently commit to an activity.

The present findings raise two issues that deserve to be addressed in future studies. First, the majority of the participants were females. Although study after study with the SAI-R, including the present one, did not show statistically significant gender difference in scoring the inventory, it might be advisable to use a gender-balanced sample. Second, all the participants in the present study were students. Administering the SAI-R to a wider population will allow a greater generalization of the findings.

Acknowledgments We thank Barbara Kipper for permission of publishing this original manuscript.

References

Baim, C., Burmeister, J., & Marciel, M. (Eds.). (2007). *Psychodrama: Advances in theory and practice*. New York: Routledge.

Blatner, A. (2000). *Foundations of psychodrama* (4th ed.). New York: Springer.

Costello, A. B., & Osborne, J. W. (2005). Best practices in exploratory factor analysis: Four recommendations for getting the most from your analysis. *Practical Assessment Research and Evaluation, 10,* 1–9.

Davelaar, P. M., Araujo, F. S., & Kipper, D. A. (2008). The Revised Spontaneity Assessment Inventory (SAI-R): Relationship to goal orientation, motivation, perceived self-efficacy, and self-esteem. *The Arts in Psychotherapy, 35,* 117–128.

Fiumara, G. C. (2009). *Spontaneity: A psychoanalytic Inquiry*. New York: Routlege.

Kaiser, H. F. (1960). The application of electronic computers to factor analysis. *Educational and Psychological Measurement, 20,* 141–151.

Kaiser, H. F. (1970). A second-generation little jiffy. *Psychometrika, 35,* 401–415.

Kellar, H., Treadwell, T. W., Kumar, V. A., & Leach, E. S. (2002). The Personal Attitude Scale-II: A revised measure of spontaneity. *Journal of Action Methods Psychodrama, Skill Training and Role Playing, 55,* 35–46.

Kipper, D. A., & Shemer, H. (2006). The Revised Spontaneity Assessment Inventory (SAI-R): Spontaneity, well-being, and stress. *Journal of Group Psychotherapy, Psychodrama & Sociometry, 59,* 127–136.

Kipper, D. A., Davelaar, P. S., & Herst, S. (2009). The relationship between spontaneity and inhibition. *The Arts in Psychotherapy, 36,* 329–334.

Kipper, D. A., Green, D. J., & Prorak, A. (2010). The relationship among spontaneity, impulsivity, and creativity. *Journal of Creativity and Mental Health, 5,* 39–53.

Moreno, J. L. (1953). *Who shall survive?* Beacon: Beacon House.

Moreno, J. L. (1964). *Psychodrama* Vol. 1. Beacon: Beacon House.

David A. Kipper was Prof. at Department of Psychology Roosevelt University in Chicago and passed away in 2010.

Christopher R. Beasley, Ph.D., Assistant Professor, Washington College, Department of Psychology.

Z Psychodrama Soziometr (2016) (Suppl) 15:11–23
DOI 10.1007/s11620-015-0307-8

HAUPTBEITRÄGE

Zeitschrift für Psychodrama
und Soziometrie

Spontaneity as predictive factor for well-being

Instruments for psychodrama—the validation of Spontaneity Assessment Inventory—Revised (SAI-R) and its relationship with psychological suffering and depression in Italy and Austria

Ines Testoni · Michael Wieser · Alessandra Armenti · Lucia Ronconi · Maria Silvia Guglielmin · Paolo Cottone · Adriano Zamperini

Published online: 3 December 2015

Abstract The study discusses the construct of spontaneity and its causal relationship with psychological well-being. It develops a preview phase of validation of the SAI-R and its correlation with the Clinical Outcomes for Routine Evaluation-Outcome Measure (CORE-OM) and the Beck Depression Inventory (BDI-II) and assumes the hypothesis that a high level of spontaneity is correlated negatively with low level of well-being and positively with depression. The research involved Italian and Austrian participants, consisting of 166 Italian and 146 Austrian university students. The findings suggested a causal relationship between low spontaneity and psychological suffering. The results obtained confirm the hypothesized model, showing significant negative causal relationship. The verification of this theoretical model on non-clinical samples allows us to set the ground for future use in clinical samples. Furthermore, this result encourages the development of further research into the use of SAI-R.

Keywords Psychodrama · SAI-R · CORE-OM · Spontaneity · Depression · Psychological well-being

Prof. I. Testoni (✉) · A. Armenti, Ph.D. · L. Ronconi · M. S. Guglielmin · P. Cottone · A. Zamperini
Department of Philosophy, Sociology, Education & Applied Psychology (FISPPA), Section of Applied Psychology, University of Padua (Italy),
via Venezia 8,
35131 Padua, Italy
e-mail: ines.testoni@unipd.it

Mag. Dr. phil. M. Wieser
Department of Psychology, Alpen-Adria-Universitaet Klagenfurt,
Universitätsstr. 65,
9020 Klagenfurt, Austria
e-mail: Michael.wieser@aau.at

Spontaneität als prädiktiver Faktor für das Wohlbefinden
Instrumente für das Psychodrama – die Validierung des Spontaneität Assessment Inventar – Revidiert (SAI-R) und seine Beziehung zu psychischen Belastungen und Depression in Italien und Österreich

Zusammenfassung Die Studie diskutiert das Konstrukt der Spontaneität und ihre ursächliche Beziehung mit psychischem Wohlbefinden. Nach einer Validierung von SAI-R mit „Clinical Outcomes for Routine Evaluation-Outcome Measure (CORE-OM)“ und Beck Depression Inventar (BDI-II) wird die Hypothese aufgestellt, dass hohe Spontaneität negativ korreliert mit Depression und geringem Wohlbefinden. Die Forschung umfasste italienische und österreichische TeilnehmerInnen, bestehend aus 166 italienischen und 146 österreichischen UniversitätsstudentInnen. Die Ergebnisse zeigen eine ursächliche Beziehung zwischen geringer Spontaneität und psychischen Beschwerden. Die erzielten Resultate bestätigen die Hypothesen der signifikant negativen ursächlichen Beziehungen. Die Verifikation des theoretischen Modells mit einer nicht-klinischen Stichprobe gibt uns die Basis der zukünftigen Anwendung bei klinischen Stichproben. Die Ergebnisse ermutigen zu weiterer Forschung in der Anwendung von SAI-R.

Schlüsselwörter Psychodrama · SAI-R · CORE-OM · Spontaneität · Depression · Psychisches Wohlbefinden

1 Introduction

Spontaneity has been considered an ambiguous and theoretically elusive concept. David Kipper describes it as “a human quality whose exact origin is not known” (Kipper 1986, p. 12). Many authors define it as a philosophical concept, analyzed by philosophers like Spinoza, Descartes, Hume, Kant, Hegel, Peirce, Bergson and many others, in ways that can hardly be translated into psychological terms. Actually, Moreno also tried to define this, he was as much a philosopher as a psychologist. Indeed, it is said that Moreno told Freud: “You analyze people’s dreams, I make their dreams come true” (see Fox 1987). In the philosophical opinion of the psychodrama father, this is the main duty of humans, whose major challenge is living creatively because their spontaneity makes them co-creators of their own universe and the world at large. This titanic task implies the development of the individual’s capacity to be flexible and adaptive instead of rigid and stiff.

Indeed, early on Moreno defined the origin of this quality, and it is simply arduous to find a better kind of meaning in any other psychological way. So much so that he states that the idea of giving a place to dreams in the “theatre of spontaneity” (Das Stegreiftheater 1947/1983) derived from his observation of the creative and free behaviour of children, by which he developed his theories of spontaneity and creativity, where the first is the opening to the second (Moreno 1947/1983). This axis is the human essential nature, which, whether it is not clipped, is normally recognizable by observing the free flow behaviour. Indeed, self-expression is an important channel for developing the relationship between these two factors and, from this early understanding, psychodrama sprung as a complex of concepts and practices, within the larger fields of psychotherapy and applied psychology, whose methods and ideas promote spontaneity in the service of creativity.

The term spontaneity often indicates human imagination, versatility, intuition, responsiveness, which cannot be confused with mere impulsivity, improvisation or instinctiveness. Despite this, it is not only an expression of naturalness, it carries the exploration of extreme alternatives, some of which contain the seeds of breaking insights. This is the reason why it is important in any psychodramatic intervention. The "psychological truth" of the realm of play, which develops as drama, represents the innate tendency towards imagination and pretending. Moreno called such a dimension where spontaneity releases creativity "surplus reality".

In the surplus reality, it is possible to live in a dreamlike dimension, activating spontaneity and resolving the problems surrounding it. When human spontaneity is blocked, individuals become anxious and the anguish may generate psychopathological symptoms. In his clinical observation, Moreno (1946/1980) stated that spontaneity and anxiety are inversely related, and the action in the surplus reality increases the first and reduces the second. The resulting action in the psychodramatic scene liberates the potential capacity of people to learn and heal. In fact, this playful contest activates the childlike parts of the psyche, which releases energy for the learning and healing process.

However, it remains difficult to define the exact structure of spontaneity. The distinction of this construct from related concepts, such as instinct, improvisation, impulsivity and intuition, is not enough. This inadequacy requires further empirical studies, which can describe the psychological functioning of its structure. This article aims at further developing the studies of Kipper and collaborators (Kipper and Ritchie 2003; Kipper et al. 2010), which go along such a path.

2 The psychodramatic research on spontaneity

Although spontaneity is a concept that appears to be understood intuitively, it is not easy to define empirically. However, in the psychodramatic field, the importance of measuring this factor is increasingly recognized (Kipper and Ritchie 2003). Moreno treated the problem of measuring spontaneity in some early papers (Moreno 1941, 1944; Moreno et al. 1955; Jennings and Moreno 1936). Following this indication some further studies, among which the Meyer's (1941) and the Steitzel and Hughey's (1994) derived; this followed by the more recent research of Kipper and collaborators emerges (Kipper et al. 2010; Davelaar et al. 2008; Christoforou and Kipper 2006a, 2006b; Kipper 2000; Kipper and Hundal 2005). In their opinion, this construct on the one hand retains the idea of acting from natural free will and, on the other, the lack of premeditation while containing the direction and the constraint implied by realistic and efficacious actions. Starting from such standpoints, these authors explored the concept and proposed the innovative idea of the separation of spontaneity and non-spontaneity, which represent two separate continua rather than opposite states of mind. They proposed that spontaneity is an entirely positive quality. This means that individuals can be spontaneous to various degrees and the absence of spontaneity does not signify the presence of pathology. Non-spontaneity represents something else, for instance, characteristics associated with routine behavior.

These authors measured the cogency of such constructs by means of a newly designed Spontaneity Assessment Inventory (SAI) and the Spontaneity Deficit Inventory (SDI) (Kipper and Hundal 2005). On this basis, they administered the SAI and the SDI and investigated correlations with the Friedman Well-Being Scale (FWBS) and the Marlowe-Crowne Social Desirability Scale (MCSDS). The results confirmed the overall notion that spontaneity and non-spontaneity cannot coexist, because they are negatively correlated. Besides, both the SAI and SDI showed a satisfactory split-half reliability, correlated in the expected direction with the FWBS scores, and correlated positively with the MCSDS. Further results have confirmed the positive correlation between spontaneity and well-being, since spontaneity is a form of intrinsic motivation that precedes the process of taking action (Kipper and Shemer 2006); it is then closely related to personal well-being, and a precursor to feeling joy and deep satisfaction (Davelaar et al. 2008). In further studies, Bengston et al. (1985) and Catz and Felton (2002), Kipper and Shemer (2006) confirmed the positive correlation between spontaneity and individual well-being, and a negative correlation between levels of spontaneity and stress. Thus, empirical evidence confirms the idea of Moreno that spontaneity plays a significant role in mental health and that the lack of spontaneity does not mean pathology (Kipper and Shemer 2006).

In our research, we wanted to consider the possibility that spontaneity causes well-being and reduces pathological symptoms. If this hypothesis is confirmed, it will be possible to further conjecture that spontaneity is a predictive factor with respect to psychological well-being, and so that any experience that threatens this quality is potentially dangerous for mental health.

3 Method

3.1 Aims and hypothesis

As indicated by Kipper and Hundal (2005) and by Kipper and Shemer (2006), the SAI and the SAI-R (which is the revised version of the SAI) are positively correlated with well-being. In our research, we want develop a single aspect of these studies, focusing our attention on the relationship between spontaneity and the inverse condition of well-being: suffering and depression. Our work is divided in two parts: in the first, we have already analyzed the relationship between SAI-R and the Clinical Outcomes for Routine Evaluation-Outcome Measure (CORE-OM) for well-being, and Beck Depression Inventory (BDI-II) for the worst condition in which anxiety may precipitate, that is to say the depression. Since high scores on the CORE-OM ad BDI-II are indicative of severe problems, while high scores on the SAI-R indicate a high level of spontaneity, in a preliminary study (Testoni et al. 2013) we found the inverse correlation between aspects of spontaneity (SAI-R) and severity of symptoms (CORE-OM) and depression (BDI-II).

In this research, we wanted to verify if it is possible to consider spontaneity as a predictive factor against suffering and depression. The main hypothesis of this second phase of the analysis is the definition of the causal relationship among the instruments formerly described. The central aim is the description of the causality of spontaneity against psychological distress.

3.2 Participants and procedure

A total of 312 Italian and Austrian University students participated in the study; 156 females and 156 males, between the age of 18 and 24 years (*M*=20.85; *SD*=1.39). The Italian sample consisted of 166 university students (*N*=166), 83 females and 83 males between the age of 19 to 24 years (*M*=20.99; *SD*=1.38), while the Austrian sample was made up of 146 university students (*N*=146), 73 females and 73 males, between the ages of 18 and 24 years (*M*=20.68; *SD*=1.38). All participants took part in the study voluntarily. They did not receive any type of compensation for their participation in the study. Participants were administered the three instruments (SAI-R, CORE-OM and BDI-II) individually and anonymously. The questionnaire included a socio-demographic form (age, gender, occupation) together with the three assessment tools. The analysis of the Austrian and Italian groups are held separately in order to make the results usable for further research in the two countries.

3.3 Measures

Spontaneity Assessment Inventory—Revised (SAI-R) is the revised version of the original SAI that had already proved to be a valid clinical instrument (Christoforou and Kipper 2006; Kipper and Shemer 2006). Similar to the original version, the SAI-R poses just one initial question: "How strongly do you have these feelings and thoughts during a typical day?" The question is followed by a list consisting of 18 items, some are adjectives and other phrases that describe different feelings and thoughts. The participants respond by expressing an opinion on a five-point Likert scale, ranging from 1 (very weak) to 5 (very strong).

Clinical Outcomes for Routine Evaluation-Outcome Measure (CORE-OM). This instrument is used as an assessment tool during routine provision of psychotherapy, in large-scale population studies and assessing treatment outcomes in primary care and specialist settings (Barkham et al. 2005; Evans et al. 2002; Evans et al. 2003) in the United Kingdom. The scoring system is made up of three interdependent instruments. Specifically, we utilized the CORE-OM scale (34 items) that focused on psychological well-being. Every statement is evaluated on a 5-point Likert scale, based on how frequently they experienced a certain mood during the last week (Palmieri et al. 2009). The level of psychological distress is quantified by the total score on the test.

Beck Depression Inventory—II (BDI-II). It is a self-assessment tool for measuring the severity of depression in adults and adolescents (Beck and Steer 1987; Beck et al. 1996). It was developed to assess symptoms corresponding to diagnostic criteria of depressive disorders listed in the Diagnostic and Statistical Manual of Mental Disorder (DSM-IV, American Psychiatric Association 1994). It consists of 21 groups of affirmations about symptoms and depressive attitudes. Each group is followed by five response options, from 0 to 4, indicating how much that symptom or behaviour has increased or decreased over the past 2 weeks. The total score is calculated by summing up the scores on the 21 items.

4 Analysis and results

Multiple analyses were carried out using SPSS 18.0 and LISREL 8.70. Firstly, the internal consistency of instruments (SAI-R, CORE-OM and BDI-II), was assessed. Secondly, confirmatory factor analysis was conducted to examine the one-factor model of SAI-R. Since the observed variables were ordinal, a weighted least squares robust method based on polychromic correlations was used. In this study, the goodness-of-fit was evacuate using multiple criteria: chi-square, goodness-of-fit, Root-Mean-Square-Error of Approximation (RMSEA), Non-Normed Fit Index (NNFI) and Comparative Fit Index (CFI); the cut-off point of RMSEA was below .08, and CFI and NNFI values were above .90 (MacCallum et al. 1996). Thirdly, correlations analysis among instruments was analysed. Finally, path analysis was conducted to evaluate the impact of SAI-R on CORE-OM and BDI-II.

4.1 Internal consistency and scores

SAI-R. In the Italian sample, the internal consistency of the SAI-R was .81 (Cronbach's Alpha), a value greater than that reported in the literature of .79 (Kipper and Shemer 2006). The average score on the SAI-R was 57.05 ($SD=8.09$); a value that is less than that reported by Kipper and Shemer ($M=66.41$, $SD=10.16$) that corresponds to a good level of spontaneity according to the criteria for a non-clinical sample, such as the sample investigated.

In the Austrian sample, the internal consistency of the SAI-R was .91 (Cronbach's Alpha), a value that indicates a high reliability and higher than both the Italian scores and that reported in the literature (Kipper and Shemer 2006). The average on the total score was 63.70 ($SD=9.83$), a value somewhat smaller than reported in the literature and greater than the score obtained by the Italian sample.

CORE-OM. In the Italian sample, the internal consistency of the CORE-OM was 0.90 (Cronbach's Alpha), a score very similar to that reported by Evans et al. (2002), of 0.94. The average of the total score of the CORE-OM was 0.99 ($SD=0.45$); a value which is slightly higher than that found by Evans and collaborators ($M=0.76$, $SD=0.59$) and corresponds to a good level of psychological well-being according to the criteria for a non-clinical sample, like the sample investigated.

In the Austrian sample, the internal consistency was 0.93 (Cronbach's Alpha), a value very similar that reported in studies by Evans et al. (2002). The average of the total scores of the CORE-OM was 0.74 ($SD=0.49$); a value that is similar to that found by Evans et al. (2002) and that corresponds to a good level of psychological well-being according to criteria for non-clinical samples.

BDI-II. In the Italian sample, the internal consistency of the test was 0.86 (Cronbach's Alpha), which is greater than that found by Ghisi et al. (2006) equal to 0.80. The average of the total score of the BDI-II was 8.59 ($SD=6.69$), which corresponds to a minimum level of depression, according to criteria relative to a non-clinical

Table 1 Confirmatory factor analysis of SAI-R

Country	Model	*N*	Chi-square	df	RMSEA	NNFI	CFI
Austria	Baseline	146	238.54	135	0.073	0.971	0.974
Italy	Baseline	166	616.73	135	0.147	0.743	0.774
Italy	Modified	166	605.88	134	0.106	0.909	0.921

Table 2 Pearson's correlations, Italy

	SAI-R	CORE-OM	Well-being	Symptoms	Functioning	Risk	Item NoRisk	BDI-II
SAI-R	–	−0.47**	−0.50**	−0.39**	−0.46**	−0.01	−0.49**	−0.33**
CORE-OM		–	0.81**	0.92**	0.87**	0.42**	0.99**	0.74**
Well-being			–	0.74**	0.62**	0.16*	0.83**	0.64**
Symptoms				–	0.66**	0.27**	0.93**	0.71**
Functioning					–	0.34**	0.87**	0.62**
Risk						–	0.36**	0.26**
Item NoRisk							–	0.74**
BDI-II								–

*$p < .05$; **$p < .01$; ***$p < .001$

sample, such as the sample in question (Beck et al. 1996). In the Austrian sample, the internal consistency was 0.87 (Cronbach's Alpha), even in this case a higher score in respect to that found in the literature. The average score of the BDI-II was 5.96 (SD=4.97), which corresponds to a minimum level of depression according to the criteria for a no-clinical sample (Beck et al. 1996).

4.2 Confirmatory factor analysis of SAI-R

In order to test a one-factorial structure of SAI-R also in Italian and Austrian samples, were used a Confirmatory Factor Analysis (CFA).

Contrary to goodness-of-fit in Austrian sample, the goodness-of-fit in Italian sample was not acceptable: $\chi2(166)=616.73$, df=135; RMSEA=0.147, NNFI=0.743, CFI=0.774 (Table 1). To improve the model, standardized residuals and correlations between error terms were taken into account, following guidelines in the literature (e.g., modification index>3.84; Byrne 1998; Jöreskog and Sörbom 1996). Once detected, through the test of modification indexes and the introduction of the correlation between errors measurement of the items 18 and 12, it was possible to obtain at a good fit indexes model also in Italy (Modified Model).

4.3 Correlations

Second, was tested the general hypothesis underlying the existence of a negative correlation between spontaneity (SAI-R) and the dimensions of psychological sufferance and depression (CORE-OM and BDI-II). Indeed, statistically positive correlations were observed between BDI-II and CORE-OM, and negative correlations between SAI-R and BDI-II/CORE-OM. In Tables 2 and 3 were illustrated the Pearson correlation coefficients between the instruments in Italy and in Austria.

Table 4 presents the Pearson's correlation coefficients between SAI-R, BDI-II and CORE-OM of the three instruments on the total sample.

Table 3 Pearson's correlations, Austria

	SAI-R	CORE-OM	Well-being	Symptoms	Functioning	Risk	Item NoRisk	BDI-II
SAI-R	–	−0.54**	−0.51**	−0.48**	−0.51**	−0.18*	−0.54**	−0.58**
CORE-OM		–	0.87**	0.94	0.91**	0.47**	0.99**	0.66**
Well-being			–	0.77**	0.78**	0.31**	0.88**	0.55**
Symptoms				–	0.72**	0.36**	0.94**	0.64**
Functioning					–	0.41**	0.90**	0.56**
Risk						–	0.40**	0.36**
Item NoRisk							–	0.65**
BDI-II								–

*$p < .05$; **$p < .01$; ***$p < .001$

Table 4 Pearson's correlation in total sample

	SAI-R	CORE-OM	Well-being	Symptoms	Functioning	Risk	Item NoRisk	BDI-II
SAI-R	–	−0.54**	−0.55**	−0.46**	−0.54**	−0.12*	−0.55**	−0.47**
CORE-OM		–	0.85**	0.93**	0.90**	0.45**	0.99**	0.71**
Well-being			–	0.75**	0.71**	0.24**	0.86**	0.63**
Symptoms				–	0.70**	0.32**	0.94**	0.67**
Functioning					–	0.38**	0.89**	0.61**
Risk						–	0.36**	0.31**
Item NoRisk							–	0.71**
BDI-II								–

*$p < .05$; **$p < .01$; ***$p < .001$

Since a high score on the BDI-II is indicative of a greater number of aspects related to depression, the negative correlation with the SAI-R indicates that with a decrease in the levels of spontaneity, there is an increase in aspects of depression. Finally, we hypothesized significant positive correlations between the BDI-II and the CORE-OM. The results show significant positive correlations between the two instruments both in Italy and Austria, $r = .742$, $p < .001$ in Italy and $r = .655$, $p < .001$ in Austria. The positive correlation between the BDI-II and CORE-OM establishes a direct proportionality between levels of depression and general conditions of psychological distress. Table 4 presents the Pearson correlation coefficients between SAI-R, BDI-II and CORE-OM (total) of the three instruments in the total sample.

4.4 Regression analysis

Regression analysis was performed considering spontaneity (SAI-R) as independent variable (or predictor) and well-being (CORE-OM) and depression (BDI-II) as dependent variables.

As showed in Table 5, considering the total sample, the best predictor of well-being turned out to be spontaneity, namely well-being is higher for people with a higher level of spontaneity. However, the best impact is only on 'well-being' and 'functioning', contrary on 'risk'. Generally, the percentage of explained variance is good level. However, considering the results by country were observed some differences. First, in Austrian sample, SAI-R explained variance index greater than in

Table 5 Regression analysis results with SAI-R as predictor

Dependent Variable	Total		Austria		Italy	
	R-square	Beta	R-square	Beta	R-square	Beta
CORE-OM						
Total score	.29***	−.54***	.29***	−.54***	.22***	−.47***
Well-being	.30***	−.55***	.26***	−.51***	.25***	−.50***
Symptoms	.21***	−.46***	.23***	−.48***	.15***	−.39***
Functioning	.28***	−.54***	.26***	−.51***	.21***	−.46***
Risk	.01*	−.12*	.03*	−.18*	.00	−.01
BDI-II						
Total score	.22***	−.47***	.33***	−.58***	.11***	−.33***

*$p<.05$; **$p<.01$; ***$p<.001$

Italy. Second, the variance index on CORE-OM and BDI-II are similar. Finally, in Italy sample, the SAI-R does not explain a significant variance portion of 'Risk' dimension.

Discussion

The objective of this study was to develop the validation of the SAI-R, showing its relationship with CORE-OM and BDI-II. In the Italian sample, the internal consistency obtained a greater value than that reported in the literature, meanwhile in the Austrian one, the internal consistency indicated a higher reliability than both the Italian scores and the one reported in literature (Kipper and Shemer 2006). In the confirmatory one-factorial test, the SAI-R produced better results in Austria then in Italy, where the goodness-of-fit was not acceptable and the standardization of residuals and correlations between error terms was required in order to obtain a good fit indexes. First, the research demonstrated that the German and the Italian versions of the SAI-R are acceptable as instruments for assessing spontaneity in the respective countries.

Second, results for the SAI-R confirmed the hypothesis that the construct of spontaneity is negatively correlated with the dimensions of psychological sufferance and depression (CORE-OM and BDI-II), meanwhile a statistically positive correlation between depression (BDI-II) and psychological sufferance was confirmed. Indeed, the regression analysis establishes that well-being (CORE-OM) and depression (BDI-II) are dependent variables by spontaneity (SAI-R), when the latter considered as independent variable. These results provide valuable support to the original theories, namely that spontaneity is related to personal well-being. In this sense, it would be useful to further develop research in order to reconsider and better specify the Kipper model, which conversely presented the possibility that a low level of spontaneity is not necessarily a symptom of psychological sufferance, as we also hypothesized. However, following Moreno, it is also conceivable the mediation between these two instances, saying that low level of spontaneity indicates a bad relationship with world and life, which is so widespread that is not necessarily psychopathological. In light of these results, we believe that an intervention based on a psychodramatic approach that aimed at increasing levels of spontaneity, could indeed have a strong influence in helping depressed and severely stressed individuals increase their levels of psychological well-being.

References

American Psychiatric Association. (1994). *Diagnostic and statistical manual of mental disorders -DSM-IV* (4th edn.). Washington DC: American Psychiatric Association.

Barkham, M., Culverwell, A., Spindler, K., Twigg, E., & Connell, J. (2005). The CORE-OM in an older adult population: Psychometric status, acceptability, and feasibility. *Aging and Mental Health, 9*, 235–245.

Beck, A. T., & Steer, R. A. (1987). *Manual for the Beck depression inventory*. San Antonio: The Psychological Corporation.

Beck, A. T., Steer, R. A., & Brown, G. K. (1996). *Manual for the Beck Depression Inventory, Second Edition (BDI-II)*. San Antonio: Psychological Corporation.

Bengston, V. I., Reedy, M. N., & Gordon, C. (1985). *Aging and self conceptions, personality processes and social contexts. Handbook of psychology and aging*. New York: Van Nostrand Reinhold.

Byrne, B. M. (1998). *Structural equation modelling with LISREL, PRELIS and SIMPLIS: Basic concepts, applications and programming*. Mahwah: Erlbaum.

Catz, S. L., & Felton, C. G. (2002). Psychological distress among minority and low-income women living with HIV. *Behavioral Medicine, 28*, 53–60.

Christoforou, A., & Kipper, D. A. (2006). The spontaneity assessment inventory (SAI), anxiety, obsessive compulsive tendencies and temporal orientation. *Journal of Group Psychotherapy, Psychodrama & Sociometry, 58*, 119–129.

Davelaar, M. A., Araujo, M. A., & Kipper, D. A. (2008). The revised spontaneity assessment inventory (SAI-R): Relationship to goal orientation, motivation, perceived self-efficay, and self-esteem. *The Arts in Psychotherapy, 35*(2), 117–128.

Evans, C., Connell, J., Barkham, M., Margison, F., McGrath, G., Mellor-Klark, J., & Audin, K. (2002). Towards a standardised brief outcome measure: Psychometric properties and utility of the CORE-OM. *British Journal of Psychiatry, 180*, 51–60.

Evans, C., Connell, J., Barkham, M., Marshall, C., & Mellor-Clark, J. (2003). Practice-based evidence: Benchmarking NHS primary care counselling services at national and local levels. *Journal of Clinical Psychology and Psychotherapy, 10*, 374–388.

Fox, J. (1987). *The essential Moreno: Writings on psychodrama, group method and spontaneity*. New York: Springer.

Ghisi, M., Flebus, G. B., Montano, A., Sanavio, E., & Sica, C. (2006). *Beck depression inventory-II: Edizione Italiana*. Firenze: Giunti Editore.

Jennings, H. H., & Moreno, J. L. (1936). *Spontaneity training: a method of personality development. Sociometric Review*, New York State Training School for Girls, Hudson, NY.

Jöreskog, K. J., & Sörbom, D. (1996). *LISREL 8: User's reference guide*. Chicago: Scientific Software International.

Kipper, D. A. (1986). *Psychotherapy through clinical role playing*. New York: Brunner Mazel Publishers.

Kipper, D. A. (2000). Spontaneity: Does the experience match the theory? *Action Methods*, Spring: 33–47.

Kipper, D., & Hundal, J. (2005). The Spontaneity assessment inventory: The relationship between spontaneity and nonspontaneity. *Journal of Group Psychotherapy Psychodrama & Sociometry, 58*, 119–129.

Kipper, D. A., & Ritchie, T. D. (2003). The effectiveness of psychodramatic techniques: A meta-analysis. *Group Dynamics: Theory, Research, and Practice, 7*(1), 13.

Kipper, D. A., & Shemer, H. (2006). The Spontaneity assessment inventory-revised (SAI-R): Spontaneity, well-being and stress. *Journal of Group Psychotherapy, Psychodrama & Sociometry, 59*, 127–136.

Kipper, D. A., Green, D. J., & Prorak, A. (2010). The relationship among spontaneity, impulsivity, and creativity. *Journal of Creativity in Mental Health, 5*(1), 39–53.

MacCallum, R. C., Browne, M. W., & Sugawara, H. M. (1996). Power analysis and determination of sample size for covariance structural modeling. *Psychological Methods, 1*, 130–149.

Meyer, A. (1941). Spontaneity. *Sociometry, 4*(2), 150–157.

Moreno, J. L. (1941). The philosophy of the moment and the spontaneity theater. *Sociometry, 4*, 205–226.

Moreno, J. L. (1944). *Spontaneity test and spontaneity training*. Beacon: Beacon House (Psychodrama Monograph 4).

Moreno, J. L. (1946/1980). *Psychodrama* (6th edn., Vol. 1). Beacon: Beacon House.

Moreno, J. L. (1947/1983). *The Theatre of Spontaneity*. (3rd edn.). Amber: Beacon House.

Moreno, J. L., Moreno, Z., & Moreno, J. (1955). The discovery of the spontaneous man. *Sociometry, 18*(4), 155–182.

Palmieri, G., Evans, C., Hansen, V., Brancaleoni, G., Ferrari, S., Porcelli, P., Reitano, F., & Rigatelli, M. (2009). Validation of the Italian version of the clinical outcomes in the routine evaluation outcome measure (CORE-OM). *Clinical Psychology and Psychotherapy, 16*, 444–449.

Steitzel, L. D., & Hughey, A. R. (1994). *Empowerment through spontaneity: A taste of psychodrama*. San Jose: Associates for Community Interaction Press.

Testoni, I., Armenti, A., Ronconi, L., Wieser, M., Zamperini, A., & Verdi, S. (2013). Violência de gênero. Testando um, modelo: espontaneidade bem-estar psicológio e depressão (Gender violence. Testing a model of assumptions: spontaneity, psychological well-being and depression). *Revista Brasileira de Psicodrama, XXI*(1), 95–110.

Ines Testoni is psychodramatist and Professor of Social Psychology at University of Padova. She is director of the Master "Death Studies And The End of Life" and author of many publications, among which ten books and fifty articles. She directed the European Daphne project "Empower", where the psychodramatic techniques were utilized in order to support women suffering from domestic violence.

Michael Wieser, (1962), Mag. Dr. phil., assistant professor; psychologist, psychodrama educator and psychotherapist. Member of board of directors of International Association of Group Psychotherapy and Group Processes; Consultative Assembly of Organizational Affiliates chair; vice-president of the Society Moreno Museum; associate editor of psychotherapie forum; member of editorial board Zeitschrift fuer Psychodrama und Soziometrie; maintain the international psychodrama bibliography; holder of the Zerka T. Moreno Award.

Alessandra Armenti, Ph.D. in Social and Personality Psychology (University of Padua, IT, 2013). Her main research interests concern applied psychology in social, economic and environmental field. She worked in several projects and networks at international, european and national level, funded by the European Commission (EU) and Ministry of Education, University and Research (MIUR). She collaborated with multiple U.S. and Spain research abroad programs at University Georgetown of Washington D.C. and University Complutense of Madrid. She is an expert of psychosocial research methods, research design, quantitative and qualitative analysis software packages and methodologies. She teaches courses in qualitative methods "TRANSANA Software" at University of Padua. She is a member of Italian Association of Psychology (AIP).

Lucia Ronconi is a Statistical Consultant and Analyst of the School of Psychology at University of Padua. Teaches courses in statistical packages. Her research interests are focused on statistical methods such as structural equation models and multilevel models.

Maria Silvia Guglielmin, Psychologist, psychotherapist and psychodramatist. I am director of Psychodrama Teatre in Treviso (Italy). I teach at the school of classical psychodrama of Giovanni Boria. I'm collaborating with the University of Padua and with AIPsiM in several European project.

Paolo Cottone is an assistant professor at the University of Padua. After obtaining his Ph.D. in Social Psychology and Personality, has worked, and now directs the activities of the laboratory Interaction and Culture. Teaches courses in Social Psychology and Intercultural Psychology and is a member of the Doctoral Committee of the Ph.D. School in Social Sciences at the University of Padua. Research interests are mostly in the field of Cultural Psychology and are focused on cooperation and communication, as social processes, with a special attention on new media and intercultural aspects.

Adriano Zamperini is Professor of Psychology in Interpersonal Relationships, Psychology of Violence and Psychology of Social Discomfort at University of Padua where he is also the Director of the Center of Research and Services for Migration and Intercultural Studies (CIRSIM). His field of research in Social Psychology includes: solidarity and indifference, social justice and human rights, social exclusion and ostracism, interpersonal and collective conflicts, war and peace, psychology of health.

Z Psychodrama Soziometr (2016) (Suppl) 15:25–39
DOI 10.1007/s11620-015-0313-x

HAUPTBEITRÄGE

Zeitschrift für Psychodrama und Soziometrie

Psychometric evaluation of the German version of the revised spontaneity assessment inventory (SAI-R)

Sven Rabung · Michael Wieser · Almut Thomas · Ines Testoni · Chris Evans

Published online: 4 January 2016

Abstract Spontaneity has been defined as an adaptive response to varying situational conditions. In this regard, it may be considered as a major contributor to well-being and mental health which could play an essential role within the context of psychotherapy. Despite its potential importance empirical research on spontaneity has been lacking until recently. As a remedy, the present paper introduces the German translation of the Revised Spontaneity Assessment Inventory (SAI-R; Kip-

Electronic supplementary material The online version of this article (doi: 10.1007/s11620-015-0313-x) contains supplementary material, which is available to authorized users.

S. Rabung (✉) · M. Wieser
Department of Psychology, Alpen-Adria-Universität Klagenfurt,
Universitätsstr. 65-67,
9020 Klagenfurt, Austria
e-mail: sven.rabung@aau.at

M. Wieser
e-mail: michael.wieser@aau.at

A. Thomas
Viktor Frankl, University College of Teacher Education Carinthia,
Hubertusstraße 1,
9020 Klagenfurt, Austria
e-mail: almut.thomas@ph-kaernten.ac.at

I. Testoni
Department of Philosophy, Sociology, Education & Applied Psychology (FISPPA),
Section of Applied Psychology, University of Padua (Italy),
via Venezia 8,
35131 Padua, Italy

C. Evans
East London NHS Foundation Trust,
9 Alie Street,
E1 8DE London, UK
e-mail: chris@psyctc.org

per and Shemer, Group Psychother Psychodrama Sociom, 59(3):127–136, 2006) as a qualified self-report measure of spontaneity.

The German version of the 18-items SAI-R has been applied both in a non-clinical (n=467 students) and in a clinical sample (n=40 female survivors of domestic violence) and has been psychometrically analysed. The total score of the questionnaire, which shows to be well accepted and feasible, reveals high reliability. Evidence of its validity and sensitivity to change are demonstrated. Thus, this study provides preliminary evidence indicating that the German version of the SAI-R may be a reliable and valid measure for the assessment of spontaneity.

Keywords Spontaneity · Psychodrama · Assessment · SAI-R

Psychometrische Überprüfung der deutschen Version des überarbeiteten Spontaneität Assessment Inventars (SAI-R)

Zusammenfassung Spontaneität kann als adäquate Antwort auf eine neue Situation oder als neue Antwort auf eine alte Situation definiert werden. In diesem Sinne sollte sie einen wichtigen Beitrag zu Wohlbefinden und psychischer Gesundheit leisten und könnte auch eine bedeutsame Rolle im Kontext von Psychotherapie spielen. Trotz ihrer theoretischen Relevanz mangelt es bislang jedoch an empirischer Forschung zu Spontaneität. Um diesem Missstand zu begegnen, stellt die vorliegende Arbeit die deutsche Übersetzung eines Selbstbeurteilungsinstruments zur Erfassung von Spontaneität, das überarbeitete Spontaneität Assessment Inventar (SAI-R; Kipper und Shemer, Group Psychother Psychodrama Sociom, 59(3):127–136, 2006), vor. Die deutsche Version des 18 Items umfassenden SAI-R wurde in einer nicht-klinischen (n=467 Studierende) und einer klinischen Stichprobe (n=40 weibliche Opfer häuslicher Gewalt) eingesetzt und psychometrisch überprüft. Der Fragebogen zeichnet sich durch hohe Akzeptanz und Praktikabilität aus. Die hohe Reliabilität sowie Hinweise auf Validität und Veränderungssensitivität der Skala lassen das deutsche SAI-R als geeignetes Instrument zur Erfassung von Spontaneität erscheinen.

Schlüsselwörter Spontaneität · Psychodrama · Selbstbeurteilung · SAI-R

1 Introduction

The concept of spontaneity has first been introduced to the field of psychotherapy by Moreno (1946). According to him, “spontaneity can be defined as the adequate response to a new situation or the novel response to an old situation” (Moreno 1934, p. 336). Moreno considered spontaneity (along with creativity) as a major contributor to well-being and mental health. Correspondingly, spontaneity plays a central role in the theory underlying his therapeutic approach (Moreno 1953). The activation and integration of spontaneity and creativity is a fundamental goal of psychodrama (Moreno 1959).

Moreno's concept of spontaneity is primarily related to the context of sociometry and psychodrama. Nonetheless, there are several similarities and connections to more widespread theoretical concepts (Ameln et al. 2009, pp. 209–210). Maybe most relevant, spontaneity can be regarded as a counterpart to the concept of *automatic action* (Waldow 2001) which plays an important role in cognitive and behavioural therapy (e.g. automatic thoughts) as well as in psychodynamic therapy (e.g. transference). Spontaneity can also be interpreted in terms of *self-organization* (e.g. concept of dissipative structures; Schacht 1992). Not least, there are certain parallels between the concepts of spontaneity and *emotional intelligence* (Goleman 1995; cf. Schaller 2001).

1.1 Measuring spontaneity

Despite its particular importance—especially with regard to psychodrama and sociometry—empirical research on spontaneity has been lacking until recently. After Moreno (1946) had introduced a first non-standardized, performance based *spontaneity test*, it wasn't until 50 years later that a standardized measure specifically dedicated to the assessment of spontaneity has been developed.

Collins et al. (1997) devised a 58-item self-report inventory entitled the *Personal Attitude Scale* (PAS) to measure the capacity for spontaneity in a variety of situations. The items of the inventory have been derived based on theory, i.e. the authors compiled various characteristics and definitions of spontaneity which they identified from the published literature. Collins et al. (1997) reported adequate reliability but somewhat limited construct validity of the PAS. Following a first examination, the authors revised the PAS by adding new items, modifying ambiguous items and removing improper items (Kellar et al. 2002). The resulting inventory, called the PAS-II, consists of 66 items which show improved reliability and a higher degree of construct validity. To our knowledge, however, except for the two papers describing the psychometric properties of the PAS no further studies have been published concerning this scale.

At about the same time, Kipper and colleagues adopted another approach of constructing a self-report measure of spontaneity. Unlike the PAS, which was based on theory, they based their scale, called the *Spontaneity Assessment Inventory*, on clinical expertise (SAI; Kipper and Hundal 2005; Kipper and Shemer 2006). To collect relevant items, the authors contacted 20 internationally renowned psychodrama therapists from the United States and Europe who had a minimum of 25 years of professional experience and specific expertise in both the theoretical and practical application of the concept of spontaneity. The experts were asked to write down five adjectives or characteristics that describe "the feeling of being in a spontaneous state" (Kipper and Hundal 2005, p. 122). Kipper and colleagues compiled their descriptions into a list of 79 items (e.g. "uninhibited", "energized", "powerful") which were to be rated according to their intensity on a 6-point Likert-type scale ranging from 1 ("none") to 6 ("very strong"). Based on pre-tests and item analyses the authors eliminated several items, resulting in the original 20-item version of the SAI (Kipper and Hundal 2005). First studies showed satisfactory to good reliability and construct validity of the scale (Christoforou and Kipper 2006; Kipper and Hundal 2005). However, two items representing American idioms that would restrict the opportunity of cross-cultural studies were eliminated from the SAI afterwards. In addition, the response scale was changed from a 6-point to a 5-point Likert scale. The resulting 18-item version of the measure has been introduced as the *Revised Spontaneity Assessment Inventory* (SAI-R; Kipper and Shemer 2006).

1.2 Studies using the revised spontaneity assessment inventory (SAI-R)

To our knowledge, the original version of the SAI-R has been used in seven published studies (Davelaar et al. 2008; Kipper and Buras 2009; Kipper et al. 2009; Kipper et al. 2010; Kipper and Shemer 2006). Most of these studies are based on graduate and undergraduate student populations, while only one study used a convenience sample from the general population (Kipper and Shemer 2006). The available studies, in sum including about 650 participants, show a satisfactory reliability of the scale with Cronbach's alpha ranging from.79 (Kipper and Shemer 2006) to.92 (Davelaar et al. 2008, study 2). The average SAI-R score across those studies using student samples is fairly consistent with means around 63 and standard deviations of about 10. In all these studies, there are no statistically significant gender differences or statistically significant correlations between SAI-R and age or level of education (Kipper 2011). In accordance with Moreno's theory (Moreno 1946, 1953), the studies report significant positive relationships between spontaneity and various parameters of well-being. Conversely, there are several studies showing negative correlations between spontaneity and measures of psychopathology (for more details see Kipper 2011). However, since the available studies using the SAI-R are mainly based on student populations, the validity of the SAI has not yet been satisfactorily established.

1.3 Aim of the present study

A first attempt to apply the SAI-R in a therapeutic setting has been made within the *EMPoWER* project, a research project on women survivors of domestic violence funded within the European Daphne III Program (Testoni et al. 2012; Testoni et al. 2013). Within this project the SAI-R has been translated into the languages of the six participating countries (Albania, Austria, Bulgaria, Italy, Portugal, and Romania). The project itself comprised two empirical components, i.e. a validation study (Testoni et al. 2013; Testoni et al. 2012; Testoni et al. 2013) and an intervention study (Testoni et al. 2013). It is the aim of the present paper to analyse the psychometric properties of the German version of the SAI-R based on the data collected in the context of these studies.

2 Methods

2.1 Samples

Two samples, one clinical and one non-clinical, participated in the study.

Sample 1 (non-clinical) comprised $N = 467$ students taking courses at the Alpen-Adria-Universität Klagenfurt, Austria. The age of students ranged between 17 and 67 years (M=26.6, SD=9.2) with an average of M=15.4 (SD=2.7) years of education completed; 73.3 % of the students were female.

Sample 2 (clinical) included $N=40$ women who were victims of domestic violence. Participants had been treated at a psychological counselling service in Klagenfurt, Austria, with either psychodramatic ($n=22$) or ecologically-integrated techniques ($n=18$) within the framework of the *EMPoWER* project (Testoni et al. 2012; Testoni et al. 2013). Treatment duration was about six months, comprising in Austria up to 15 2 h group sessions. Due to drop-out the sample size decreased to $n=33$ at the end of treatment. The age of the women in the clinical sample ranged between 16 and 68 years (M=39.7, SD=12.6) with an average of M=12.1 (SD=3.2) years of education completed.

2.2 Assessment procedure

Data assessment took place in the context of the *EMPoWER* study (see Testoni et al. 2012; Testoni et al. 2013). Participants of *sample 1* were asked to answer the test battery (see below) during their courses. Participants of *sample 2* answered the test battery at the beginning and at the end of their treatment in order to evaluate the effectiveness of the program. All participants took part in the study voluntarily. They did not receive any type of compensation.

2.3 Measures

The test battery consisted of three scales:

The *Revised Spontaneity Assessment Inventory* (SAI-R; Kipper and Shemer 2006) is an 18-item self-report inventory designed to measure the intensity of the presence of spontaneity. The occurrence of feelings or thoughts representing being in a spontaneous state on a typical day has to be judged on a 5-point Likert scale, ranging from 1 (“very weak”) to 5 (“very strong”).

The SAI-R has been adapted to the German language following the procedure recommended by Evans (2008), including forward and back translation (Amerstorfer et al. 2011). The original and translated wording of the items is presented in the Appendix at the end of this article. The whole questionnaire, both in English and in German, can be assessed online.

The *revised version of the Beck Depression Inventory* (BDI-II; Beck et al. 1996; German version, Hautzinger et al. 2010) is a widely used 21-questions self-report inventory measuring the severity of depression based on criteria of the Diagnostic and Statistical Manual of Mental Disorders (DSM). This second version of the BDI reflects revisions made to the definitions of depression in the fourth edition of the DSM (DSM-IV; American Psychiatric Association 2000). Participants are asked to rate how they have been feeling for the past 2 weeks. Each item presents another symptom with four possible answers ranging in intensity (being coded 0 to 3).

The *Clinical Outcomes in Routine Evaluation Outcome Measure* (CORE-OM; Evans et al. 2000; German version, Sproll 2011) is a generic self-report measure of psychological distress or wellbeing, respectively. Thirty-four statements about how the participant has been over the last week have to be judged on a 5-point Likert scale, ranging from 0 (“not at all”) to 4 (“most or all the time”). In addition (or alternatively) to the total score, two subscales measuring "risk" and "psychological distress" (non-risk), respectively, can be scored (Lyne et al. 2006).

2.4 Statistical analyses

We assessed the *acceptability and practicability* of using the *SAI-R* via rates of missing data and by eliciting qualitative feedback from participants. To avoid bias due to missing data we imputed all *missing values* (max. 12.5 % per item/11.1 % per scale) using the expectation maximization algorithm (EM method; Little and Rubin 2002). We evaluated the *fairness* in terms of lack of confounding by other variables by relating the number of missing values and the total score to age, gender and education of the participants using Pearson correlations (age, education) or t-tests (gender). To test for *reliability* we assessed internal consistency (Cronbach's α). In addition, we calculated item discrimination coefficients (corrected item-total correlation) to identify particular items which may either diminish the reliability (very low correlations) or may be redundant (very high correlations), respectively. Regarding the *distribution* of item scores, we determined skewness and kurtosis as well as floor and ceiling effects (for a definition of skewness and kurtosis as adopted by the computing package SPSS see Joanes and Gill 1998). We scrutinized *construct validity* with regard to convergent and discriminant validity by calculating Pearson correlations between SAI-R and other measures (i.e. BDI-II, CORE-OM). As the theory of spontaneity predicts that it will be negatively associated with mental health problems, we compared the non-clinical and the clinical sample with regard to their SAI-R scores using t-tests. To examine the *predictive validity* of the SAI-R we tried to predict the outcome of treatment in the clinical sample, as measured with SAI-R, BDI-II and CORE-OM (dependent variables), by the SAI-R score at the beginning of treatment (independent variable). Regression analyses were used to simultaneously control for the pre-treatment scores in the respective outcome measures (additional independent variable). Finally, we calculated the standardized response mean (SRM) as the difference between SAI-R scores at the beginning and end of treatment divided by the pre-treatment standard deviation to analyse *sensitivity to change*. In addition to the parametric tests listed above we performed complementary non-parametric tests. However, since these tests did not change the results we restrict the presentation of results to the parametric analyses.

Statistical analyses were conducted using SPSS version 22.0. Due to the rather exploratory character of the analyses we used the conventional level of $p = 0.05$ when interpreting results as significant despite the multiple tests. In addition, we calculated 95 % Confidence Intervals (CIs) where reasonable. Furthermore, we used the following thresholds to interpret effect sizes as being small, medium, or large: 0.2/0.5/0.8 for d and 0.1/0.3/0.5 for r (Cohen 1988).

2.5 Predictions

Based on research with the original English version of the SAI-R (Kipper 2011) we were not to expect any effects of gender, age or education. The reliability of the German SAI-R was predicted to be at least satisfactory as it had been demonstrated for the original version (Kipper 2011). By definition, spontaneity should be directly or indirectly associated with well-being (Moreno 1953). As depression manifests itself in restrictions like sadness, negative self-concept or listlessness, which can be expected to interfere with the expression of spontaneity, it was predicted that depression as measured by the BDI-II would be negatively correlated with spontaneity as assessed with the SAI-R. The CORE-OM was used to scrutinize the hypothesized association between spontaneity and well-being more in general. It could be predicted that spontaneity as assessed with the SAI-R would be negatively correlated with psychological distress as measured with the CORE-OM. However, this should rather be true for the non-risk subscale than for the risk items of the CORE-OM as the latter "should not be regarded as a scale but as clinical flags" (CORE System Group 1999). Finally, as the concept of spontaneity is strongly related to Moreno's therapeutic approach (Moreno 1959), the SAI-R should also prove clinical relevance. Thus, first of all, the SAI-R should discriminate between the non-clinical and the clinical population under study with the former showing higher values. Secondly, spontaneity as measured with the SAI-R should be associated with therapeutic change in well-being or psychological distress as measured with BDI-II or CORE-OM, respectively. And finally, the SAI-R itself should be sensitive to change.

3 Results

3.1 Acceptability and practicability

Regarding the SAI-R, 95.7 % of the non-clinical sample (*sample 1*) and 97.5 % of the clinical sample (*sample 2*) returned complete data. Across all 18 items of the SAI-R there was a maximum of 2 ($M=0.05$, $SD=0.23$) missing values per participant in *sample 1* and a maximum of 1 missing ($M=0.03$, $SD=0.16$) in *sample 2*, respectively. The mean percentage of missing values per item of the SAI-R was 0.26 % (range 0.00–1.07 %) in the non-clinical sample (*sample 1*) and 0.14 % (range 0.00–2.50 %) in the clinical sample (*sample 2*). Some participants reported difficulties with the instruction ("*How strongly do you have these feelings or thoughts during a typical day?*") because the term "*typical day*" is not definite. In addition, some participants complained about the ambiguity of item 3 ("uninhibited"), item 4 ("things seem to flow"), item 7 ("exhilarated"), and item 12 ("light and loving"). This qualitative information corresponds with the finding that items 3 and 7 showed the highest rates of missing values (1.07 % each) in the student sample (*sample 1*). However, there were no missing values in items 4 and 12 in *sample 1* and no missing values across all four items in *sample 2*.

3.2 Fairness

With regard to missing values in the SAI-R, there was no significant effect of age and education across the two samples (all $r<0.07$ with $p>0.41$). However, there was a small but significant gender difference in *sample 1* with female students showing an average of $M=0.06$ ($SD=0.27$) missing values across the 18 items of the SAI-R while male students didn't show any missing values at all ($t_{464}=2.66$, $p=0.008$; $d=0.44$). Regarding the total score of the SAI-R, there again was no significant effect for age and education (all $r<0.16$ with $p>0.21$). Focusing on gender, however, the SAI-R total score showed a significant difference between male (M=65.09, SD=9.50) and female students (M=62.75, SD=11.39; $t_{464}=2.05$, $p=0.041$), corresponding to a small effect ($d=0.22$).

3.3 Reliability

Internal consistency coefficients (Cronbach's α) and mean corrected item-total correlations are presented in Table 1 as indicators for the reliability of the SAI-R. The SAI-R total score showed high internal consistency across both samples. Except for item 1 ("creative"; $r_{it}=0.25$), all item-total correlations showed medium to large coefficients in the non-clinical sample (*sample 1*; all remaining.74 $> r_{it} >$ 0.41). In *sample 2* all item-total correlations showed large coefficients (all.90 $> r_{it} >$ 0.51).

3.4 Distribution characteristics

The distribution characteristics of the SAI-R total score are depicted in Table 1, too. Apart from 0.2% of participants in the non-clinical sample (*sample 1*) achieving the highest possible total score no other indication could be found for a ceiling or floor effect. Also on the item level, there is no indication for any such effect. While the distribution of the total scores was lopsided to the left in the non-clinical sample (*sample 1*, negative skewness), it was positively skewed in the clinical sample (*sample 2*). In both samples, the distribution of the SAI-R total score was leptokurtic (positive kurtosis), i.e. it had a higher peak and longer tails around the mean than the normal distribution does.

3.5 Construct validity

Pearson correlations between SAI-R, BDI-II, and CORE-OM are presented in Table 2. There were significant and large negative correlations between the SAI-R

Table 1 Distribution characteristics of the SAI-R

	Internal consistency (Cronbach's α)	Mean corrected item-total correlation (r_{it})	Ceiling (%)	Floor (%)	Skewness	Kurtosis
Sample 1 (non-clinical, *N*=467)	0.93	0.60	0.20	0.00	−0.40	0.45
Sample 2 (clinical, *N*=40)	0.96	0.72	0.00	0.00	0.86	0.53

Ceiling: Percentage of participants achieving the highest possible total score. Floor: Percentage of participants achieving the lowest possible total score. Skewness: Measures the asymmetry of a distribution; a value of zero indicates a symmetric distribution of observations; positive skewness indicates a distribution with a long right tail, negative skewness indicates a distribution with a long left tail. Kurtosis: Measures the clustering of observations around a central point; a value of zero indicates a normal distribution of observations; positive kurtosis indicates the observations being more clustered about the center of the distribution, negative kurtosis indicates the observations cluster less than a normal distribution

Table 2 Pearson correlations (with 95 % confidence intervals) between SAI-R, BDI-II, and CORE-OM

r [95 % CI]	SAI-R	BDI-II total	CORE-OM psychological distress (non risk)	CORE-OM risk
SAI-R	1 [1; 1]	−0.64 [−0.70; −0.58]	−0.66 [−0.72;-0.58]	−0.23 [−0.34; −0.14]
BDI-II total	−0.70 [−0.85; −0.45]	1 [1;1]	0.76 [0.70; 0.80]	0.40 [0.29; 0.51]
CORE-OM non risk	−0.62 [−0.79; −0.35]	0.79 [0.64; 0.88]	1 [1;1]	0.38 [0.30; 0.48]
CORE-OM risk	−0.28 [−0.48; −0.04]	0.57 [0.29; 0.76]	0.52 [0.28; 0.72]	1 [1; 1]

Correlation coefficients in the non-clinical sample (Sample 1, $N=467$) are given above the diagonal (all $p<0.001$); coefficients in the clinical sample (Sample 2, $N=40$) are given below the diagonal (r(SAI-R;CORE-OM risk), $p=0.08$; all other $p\leq0.001$)

and the BDI-II as well as between the SAI-R and the psychological distress scale of the CORE-OM. In contrast, the negative correlation between SAI-R and the risk scale of the CORE-OM was small in both samples and was not even significant in *sample 2* ($p>0.05$).

The comparison of the two samples with regard to their mean SAI-R total scores showed significantly higher values in the non-clinical sample (*sample 1*; M = 63.35, SD = 10.96) than in the clinical sample (*sample 2*; M = 41.25, SD = 15.34; $t_{505}=11.81$, $p<0.001$), corresponding to a large effect (d = 1.68).

3.6 Predictive validity

To analyze the predictive capacity of the SAI-R we calculated regression analyses to predict the post-treatment scores of the SAI-R, BDI-II and CORE-OM (as the dependent variable) by using the pre-treatment score of the SAI-R (independent variable), controlling for the pre-treatment score of the predicted measure as an additional independent variable where applicable. The results are presented in Table 3. As could be shown, the SAI-R pre-treatment score allowed for the explanation of a considerable proportion of the variance of the outcome scores assessed at the end of treatment (R^2_{corr}). While the highest standardized regression coefficient (*Beta*) could be found for the post-treatment score of the SAI-R itself (Table 3, model 1) there were still medium to large coefficients for the BDI-II and the non-risk scale of the CORE-OM (Table 3, models 2a and 3a). Entering the pre-treatment score of the dependent variable into the regression model accounted for some part of the variance, however, the SAI-R throughout remained the strongest predictor (Table 3, models 2b and 3b). In contrast to these findings, no significant association could be found between SAI-R and the outcome on the CORE-OM risk scale (Table 3, models 4a and 4b).

3.7 Sensitivity to change

The standardized response mean (*SRM*) for the difference in SAI-R scores between the beginning and the end of treatment in the clinical sample (*sample 2*) was d = 0.42 ($t_{32}=2.90$, $p=0.01$), corresponding to a medium effect. In comparison, the *SRM* amounted d = 0.86 ($t_{32}=4.13$, $p<0.001$) for the BDI-II, d = 0.46 ($t_{32}=2.08$, $p=0.05$)

Table 3 Prediction of post-treatment scores of SAI-R, BDI-II and CORE-OM (clinical sample, $n=33$)

Model	Dependent variable	Independent variables	Beta	T	p	R^2_{corr} (%)
1	SAI-R post	SAI-R pre	0.66	4.95	<0.001	42.3
2a	BDI-II post	SAI-R pre	−0.48	−3.06	0.01	20.7
2b	BDI-II post	SAI-R pre	−0.44	−1.92	0.06	18.2
		BDI-II pre	0.05	0.23	0.82	
3a	CORE-OM non-risk post	SAI-R pre	−0.52	−3.43	0.002	25.2
3b	CORE-OM non-risk post	SAI-R pre	−0.39	−2.00	0.06	26.0
		CORE-OM non-risk pre	0.22	1.16	0.26	
4a	CORE-OM risk post	SAI-R pre	−0.17	−0.94	0.36	0.4
4b	CORE-OM risk post	SAI-R pre	−0.04	−0.23	0.82	10.1
		CORE-OM risk pre	0.38	2.15	0.04	

for the CORE-OM non-risk score and d=0.37 ($t_{32}=1.87, p=0.07$) for the CORE-OM risk score.

4 Discussion

This paper presents a first psychometric evaluation of the German version of the Revised Spontaneity Assessment Inventory (SAI-R). At the same time, to the best of our knowledge, it provides the first publicly documented application of the SAI-R in a clinical setting.

With response rates close to 100%, both in the clinical and non-clinical population, the German version of the SAI-R proves to be a practicable instrument that is highly accepted. In face of an overall almost perfect response rate, the small but statistically significant gender difference indicating slightly higher rates of missing data in female students than in male students may be classified as negligible. Another gender difference, however, in which male participants scored significantly higher on the SAI-R total score than did the female participants indicates that gender must be considered when analyzing SAI-R scores. While the same phenomenon had been found for the Personal Attitude Scale (PAS; Collins et al. 1997) and its revised version (PAS-II; Kellar et al. 2002) as well as for the original version of the Spontaneity Assessment Inventory (SAI; Kipper and Hundal 2005), no gender effect has been reported in earlier studies on the SAI-R. A closer look on these studies, though, reveals the same pattern with a similar size of effect in most of the studies (e.g. Davelaar et al. 2008, studies 2 and 3; Kipper et al. 2009; Kipper and Shemer 2006; etc.). Presumably, the non-significant findings reported earlier may originate from the limited power due to the small samples used in these studies. Nonetheless, it remains unclear why women score statistically significantly lower than men on the SAI-R in this study. Collins et al. (1997) argued that this "difference may be related to cultural factors that promote greater risk taking by men than by women" (p. 154). Indeed, this finding warrants further study.

Internal consistency for the German version of the SAI-R turned out to be even higher than the highest coefficients reported for the original version (Davelaar et al. 2008, study 2), indicating a very good reliability of the translated scale. The almost non-existent floor or ceiling effects across the two samples, together with the low rates of missed items, suggest the usability of the scale in both healthy and impaired populations. As expected, the SAI-R showed high correlations with the BDI-II as well as with the psychological distress scale of the CORE-OM providing first evidence for the construct validity of the German SAI-R. The markedly lower correlation between the SAI-R and the risk scale of the CORE-OM, however, needs further exploration. In addition, the SAI-R is capable to differentiate between clinical and non-clinical samples. In this context, it has to be highlighted that the mean and standard deviation of the SAI-R values in the German speaking student sample are very similar to the corresponding coefficients that have been consistently reported for the original English version across different student populations (Kipper 2011).

With regard to the clinical relevance of the SAI-R it can be demonstrated that the initial spontaneity level is suitable to explain a considerable proportion of the variance of therapy outcomes in the clinical sample across all measures (again with the expected exception of the risk subscale of the CORE-OM). It is of special note that the initial SAI-R score actually is a better predictor of outcome than the initial score of the respective outcome measure itself (which is generally regarded as the best predictor of outcome, e.g. Hamilton and Dobson 2002).

The SAI-R's sensitivity to change is comparable to the one of the CORE-OM and thus can be classified as satisfactory. The markedly higher treatment effects that were found for the BDI-II may be due to the higher problem specificity of the latter measure.

The present study includes several limitations that must be kept in mind when interpreting the findings, but that at the same time highlight the need for further research. First, the two samples under study restrict the generalizability of the results. With a first sample consisting of students only and a second sample consisting of women victims of domestic violence only, this study focuses on a very specific selection of the whole spectrum of possible non-clinical and clinical populations. Further studies should broaden the non-clinical perspective by including unselected samples from the general population or could include larger clinical samples with more sophisticated characteristics (e.g. patients suffering from specific disorders). With regard to treatment it would be of special interest if the findings concerning the predictive validity of the SAI-R are transferable to other psychotherapeutic approaches and settings. Another limitation concerns the measures applied for validation purposes. While the BDI-II and the CORE-OM focus solely on relatively generic aspects of psychological well-being or distress, respectively, further studies should include other instruments that are more closely related to the concept of spontaneity. Finally, it is important to underscore the correlational character of the present study. Whereas the results clearly point to a negative relationship between spontaneity and psychological distress they do not indicate causality. Thus, it cannot be claimed that low spontaneity causes distress and high spontaneity causes well-being. Instead, more differentiated statistical models including more measurement times and additional intervening variables would have to be realized in order to clarify the connection between spontaneity and well-being.

Within the above mentioned limitations, this study provides preliminary evidence indicating that the German version of the SAI-R may be a reliable and valid measure for the assessment of spontaneity. Further research should provide more information about the psychometric properties and the usefulness of this newly available German-language measure.

Acknowledgements The non-clinical sample reported in this paper (N=467) differs from the Austrian student sample of the EMPoWER project reported elsewhere (N=146; Testoni et al. 2013, 2013) as, for the present paper, we used the entire student convenience sample instead of applying specific selection criteria regarding age or gender.

We want to thank C. M. Amerstorfer, M. Berchtaler, H. Heaney, M. Hendel, Ph. Mayring, and G. Sigott for their support in the process of translation and back-translation. Further thanks go to the staff of Caritas Lebensberatung Kärnten (life counseling Carinthia) who worked with the women survivors of violence, S. Tillian who used her contacts to nursery school and psychodrama trainees, as well as J. Kadur and L. Fazakas who supported us as undergraduate research students.

This study has been conducted with the financial support of the DAPHNE III Programme of the European Union for the Project 'EMPoWER: Empowerment of Women - Environment Research'. The contents of this publication are the sole responsibility of the authors of this article and can in no way be taken to reflect the views of the European Commission. The publication itself has been supported with a grant of the research advisory board of the Alpen-Adria-Universität Klagenfurt provided through Private Foundation Kärntner Sparkasse.

Appendix: Instruction and items of the English and German version of the SAI-R

	Original English version	German version
Instruction	How strongly do you have these feelings and thoughts during a typical day?	Wie stark haben Sie diese Gefühle und Gedanken an einem typischen Tag?
Item 1	Creative	Kreativ
Item 2	Happy	Glücklich
Item 3	Uninhibited	Ungehemmt
Item 4	Things seem to flow	Alles läuft gut
Item 5	Alive	Lebendig
Item 6	Free to invent	Gestalterischen Freiraum haben
Item 7	Exhilarated	Heiter
Item 8	Free to act, even outrageously	Frei zu handeln, auch überschießend
Item 9	Living fully with balance	Voll und ausgeglichen im Leben stehend
Item 10	Energized	Energiegeladen
Item 11	In control	Die Dinge in der Hand haben
Item 12	Light and loving	Unbeschwert und liebevoll
Item 13	Fulfilled	Erfüllt
Item 14	Pleasure	Angenehm
Item 15	Powerful	Kraftvoll
Item 16	Successful	Erfolgreich
Item 17	Do whatever, within limits	Alles tun, aber in Grenzen
Item 18	Joyful	Freudig
5-Point Likert-Scale	1=very weak, 2=weak, 3=neither weak nor strong, 4=strong, 5=very strong	1=sehr schwach, 2=schwach, 3=weder noch, 4=stark 5=sehr stark

References

Ameln, F. v., Gerstmann, R., & Kramer, J. (2009). *Psychodrama* (2nd edn.). Heidelberg: Springer.

American Psychiatric Association. (2000). *Diagnostic and Statistical Manual of Mental disorders. DSM-IV-TR* (4th edn.). Washington DC: American Psychiatric Association.

Amerstorfer, C. M., Berchtaler, M., Heaney, H., Hendel, M., Mayring, P., Sigott, G., & Wieser, M. (2011). *Deutsche Version des Revised Spontaneity Assessment Inventory (SAI-R). Alpen-Adria-Universität* Klagenfurt: Unveröffentlichter Fragebogen.

Beck, A. T., Steer, R. A., & Brown, G. K. (1996). *Beck Depression Inventory–II* (2nd edn.). San Antonio: The Psychological Corporation.

Christoforou, A., & Kipper, D. A. (2006). The Spontaneity Assessment Inventory (SAI), anxiety, obsessive-compulsive tendency, and temporal orientation. *Journal of Group Psychotherapy, Psychodrama & Sociometry, 59*(1), 23–34.

Cohen, J. (1988). *Statistical power analysis for the behavioral sciences* (2nd edn.). In: Hillsdale, NJ. Hillsdale: Lawrence Erlbaum.

Collins, L. A., Kumar, V., Treadwell, T. W., & Leach, E. (1997). The personal attitude scale: a scale to measure spontaneity. *Journal of Group Psychotherapy, Psychodrama & Sociometry, 49*(4), 147–156.

CORE System Group. (1999). *CORE System User Manual.* Leeds: CSG.

Davelaar, P., Araujo, F., & Kipper, D. A. (2008). The Revised Spontaneity Assessment Inventory (SAI-R): Relationship to goal orientation, motivation, perceived self-efficacy, and self-esteem. *Arts in Psychotherapy, 35*(2), 117–128.

Evans, C. (2008). Translating and "normalising" CORE system. CORE System Trust (CST) position statement. Nottingham.

Evans, C., Mellor-Clark, J., Margison, F., Barkham, M., Audin, K., Connell, J., & McGrath, G. (2000). CORE: Clinical outcomes in routine evaluation. *Journal of Mental Health, 9*(3), 247–255.

Goleman, D. (1995). *Emotional intelligence*. New York: Bantam Books, Inc.

Hamilton, K. E., & Dobson, K. S. (2002). Cognitive therapy of depression: Pretreatment patient predictors of outcome. *Clinical psychology review, 22*(6), 875–893.

Hautzinger, M., Keller, F., & Kühner, C. (2010). *Das Beck Depressionsinventar II. Deutsche Bearbeitung und Handbuch zum BDI II.* Frankfurt a. M.: Pearson Assessment & Information GmbH.

Joanes, D., & Gill, C. (1998). Comparing measures of sample skewness and kurtosis. *The Statistician, 47*, 183–189.

Kellar, H., Treadwell, T. W., Kumar, V., & Leach, E. S. (2002). The Personal Attitude Scale-II: A Revised Measure of Spontaneity. *Journal of Group Psychotherapy, Psychodrama & Sociometry, 55*(1), 35–46.

Kipper, D. A. (2011). Empirische Studien zur Spontaneität: Eine Überprüfung. *Zeitschrift für Psychodrama und Soziometrie, 10*, 21–34.

Kipper, D. A., & Buras, E. (2009). Measurement of spontaneity: The relationship between Intensity and frequency of the spontaneous experience. *Perceptual and Motor Skills, 108*(2), 362–366.

Kipper, D. A., & Hundal, J. (2005). The spontaneity assessment inventory: The relationship between spontaneity and nonspontaneity. *Journal of Group Psychotherapy, Psychodrama & Sociometry, 58*(3), 119–129.

Kipper, D. A., & Shemer, H. (2006). The Revised Spontaneity Assessment Inventory (SAI-R): Spontaneity, well-being, and stress. *Journal of Group Psychotherapy, Psychodrama & Sociometry, 59*(3), 127–136.

Kipper, D. A., Davelaar, P. S., & Herst, S. (2009). The relationship between spontaneity and inhibition. *Arts in Psychotherapy, 36*(5), 329–334.

Kipper, D. A., Green, D. J., & Prorak, A. (2010). The relationship among spontaneity, impulsivity, and creativity. *Journal of Creativity in Mental Health, 5*, 39–53.

Little, R., & Rubin, D. (2002). *Statistical analysis with missing data.* New York: Wiley.

Lyne, K. J., Barrett, P., Evans, C., & Barkham, M. (2006). Dimensions of variation on the CORE-OM.. *British Journal of Clinical Psychology, 45*(Pt 2), 185–203.

Moreno, J. L. (1934). *Who shall survive? A new approach to the problem of human interrelations.* Washington, DC: Nervous & Mental Disease Publishing.

Moreno, J. L. (1946). *Psychodrama (Vol. 1)*. Beacon: Beacon House.

Moreno, J. L. (1953). *Who shall survive? Foundations of sociometry, group psychotherapy and sociodrama (2nd ed.).* Beacon: Beacon House.

Moreno, J. L. (1959). *Gruppenpsychotherapie und Psychodrama. Einleitung in die Theorie und Praxis.* Stuttgart: Thieme.

Schacht, M. (1992). Zwischen Ordnung und Chaos. Neue Aspekte zur theoretischen und praktischen Fundierung der Konzeption von Spontaneität und Kreativität. *Psychodrama, 5*(1), 95–130.

Schaller, R. (2001). *Das große Rollenspiel-Buch. Grundtechniken, Anwendungsformen, Praxisbeispiele.* Weinheim: Beltz.

Sproll, S. (2011). Ein kurzes Outcome-Maß zur routinemäßigen Datenerhebung im Kontext von Evidence-Based Practice und Practice-Based Evidence in der Psychotherapie - Übersetzung und psychometrische Eigenschaften des deutschen CORE-OM. Wien, Universität Konstanz: Unveröffentlichte Diplomarbeit.

Testoni, I., Armenti, A., Ronconi, L., Cottone, P., Wieser, M., & Verdi, S. (2012). Daphne European research project: Italian validation of hypothesis model (SAI-R, CORE-OM and BDI-II). *Interdisciplinary Journal of Family Studies, 17*(1), 207–218.

Testoni, I., Armenti, A., Evans, C., Guglielmin, M. S., Ronconi, L., Zamperini, A., & Bucuta, M. (2012). Empower: A Daphne III project, our mission, structure and results. *Interdisciplinary Journal of Family Studies, 17*(2), 119–129.

Testoni, I., Armenti, A., Ronconi, L., Wieser, M., Zamperini, A., Verdi, S., & Evans, C. (2013). Gender violence. Testing a model of assumptions: Spontaneity, psychological well-being and depression. *Revista Brasileira de Psicodrama, 21*(1), 95–110.

Testoni, I., Armenti, A., Ronconi, L., Verdi, S., Wieser, M., Bucuta, M., & Tarashoeva, G. (2013). Developing spontaneity and well-being in women victims of domestic violence. La camera blu. *Journal of gender studies, 10*, 186–201.

Testoni, I., Armenti, A., Bertoldo, A., Di L. S. D., Wieser, M., Moita, G., Cottone, P (2013). Assessing psychodramatic intervention on female victims on violence. The cross-cultural validation of CORE-OM and SAI-R for Project Empower Daphne. In C. Arcidiacono, I & Testoni A. G (Eds.), *Daphne and the centaurs – overcoming gender based violence* (pp. 161–178). Opladen: Barbara Budrich Publisher.

Waldow, M. (2001). Zur grundlagentheoretischen Kategorie der Spontaneitaet von J. L. Moreno. *Gruppenpsychotherapie und Gruppendynamik, 37*(1), 1–28.

Sven Rabung, (1973), Dr. phil., Dipl.-Psych., assistant professor at the Department of Psychology, Alpen-Adria-Universität Klagenfurt, Austria.

Michael Wieser, (1962), Mag. Dr. phil., assistant professor; psychologist, psychodrama educator and psychotherapist. Member of board of directors of International Association of Group Psychotherapy and Group Processes; Consultative Assembly of Organizational Affiliates chair; vice-president of the Society Moreno Museum; associate editor of psychotherapie forum; member of editorial board Zeitschrift fuer Psychodrama und Soziometrie; maintain the international psychodrama bibliography; holder of the Zerka T. Moreno Award.

Almut Thomas, (1967), Mag. Dr. rer. nat., lecturer, psychologist, teacher educator. She has published articles on various aspects of motivation and on diagnostic assessment.

Ines Testoni, is psychotherapist, psychodramatist, associate professor of Social psychology, psychology of groups and systems and director of the Master in Death Studies & The End of Life at Padua University. She is member of many scientific associations and directed the European Daphne project "Empower", against domestic violence. She is author of many scientific articles and books.

Chris Evans, MRCPsych, MSc, MInstGA, Honorary professor University of Nottingham, Division of Psychiatry and Applied Psychology, Institute of Mental Health; Consultant Medical Psychotherapist, East London NHS Foundation Trust; Trustee at CORE System Trust, London.

Z Psychodrama Soziometr (2016) (Suppl) 15:41–55
DOI 10.1007/s11620-015-0310-0

HAUPTBEITRÄGE

Zeitschrift für Psychodrama und Soziometrie

On measuring tele

José Luís Pio-Abreu · Cristina Villares Oliveira

Published online: 14 December 2015

Abstract The authors developed a method for measuring the *telic sensitivity* of individual members in a group, derived from the sociometric test, which has to be previously performed. Such a measure is subdivided into 4 indices: *composite indices of Positive* and *Negative Perception*, and *composite indices of Positive* and *Negative Mutuality*. Each index scores from 0 to 100. The indices have a normal distribution and, whenever the choices are randomized, an expected mean of 50 ($SD = 11.3$), irrespective of the size of the groups and the number of the received preferences and rejections. Young girls and boys (mean age 12 years) in actual school groups tend to have higher scores, especially for *Positive Perception* and *Positive Mutuality*, as opposed to randomized virtual groups. The authors identify other results in order to exemplify future research in clinical and organizational psychology settings

Keywords Sociometry · Sociodrama · Psychodrama · Tele · Mental health · Psychopathology · Human relationships

Die Messung von Tele

Zusammenfassung Die AutorInnen entwickelten eine Messmethode für das Tele von einzelnen Mitgliedern einer Gruppe, das sich in einem soziometrischen Test

Translated by Michael Wieser.

J. L. Pio-Abreu (✉) · C. V. Oliveira
Trav. da R. Padre Manuel da Nóbrega,
no. 6-5 Esq,
3000-323 Coimbra, Portugal
e-mail: pioabreu@netcabo.pt

C. V. Oliveira
e-mail: cvilares@clinic.ub.es

zeigt. Eine solche Messung ist unterteilt in vier Indikatoren: Verbundene Indikatoren für positive und negative Wahrnehmung und verbundene Indikatoren für die positive und negative Gegenseitigkeit. Jeder Index hat Werte von 0 bis 100. Die Indikatoren sind normalverteilt und wenn die Wahlen zufallsbestimmt sind, haben sie einen erwarteten Mittelwert von 50 (SD=11.3), das ist unabhängig von der Gruppengröße und der Anzahl an erhaltenen Wahlen und Ablehnungen. Junge Mädchen und Buben (Durchschnittsalter 12) in Schulgruppen haben höhere Werte besonders in positiver Wahrnehmung und positiver Gegenseitigkeit im Gegensatz zu zufällig zusammengestellten virtuellen Gruppen. Die AutorInnen identifizieren noch andere Ergebnisse um künftige Forschung in klinischer und Organisationpsychologie anzuregen.

Schlüsselwörter Soziometrie · Sociodrama · Psychodrama · Tele · Psychische Gesundheit · Psychopathologie · Menschliche Beziehungen

1 Introduction

Moreno's psychodrama and sociometry changed the scope of psychology, psychopathology and psychotherapy, shifting it from the individual to relationships. The concept of tele underpinned this change. However, the definition of tele is somewhat ambiguous. It varies from being a measure of relationships, either generic—"Tele is what sociometric test measures" (Moreno 1954, p. 219)—or specific—"Tele was defined as the elementary liaison between individuals and between individuals and objects" (Moreno 1959, p. 52), —to a personal performance—"We will use the term tele to express the simplest unit of feeling transmitted from one individual towards another" (Moreno 1954, p. 211)—or ability—"Tele is the set of perceptive processes which enable the individual to evaluate correctly the environmental world" (Rojas-Bermudez 1966, p. 60). On the other hand, the concept of tele refers not only to attraction between people, but also to repulsion between them (Kellerman 1992, p. 102; Blatner 1994), and includes what may be called "negative tele" (Moreno 1954, p. 215). It "is an extension of the innate tendencies of organisms to show selectivity" (Blatner 1994).

For Moreno, the concept of tele could be compared to Freudian transference (Moreno 1946, pp. 284–289). However, transference depend on the subject's previous relationships and was usually pathological. On the contrary, tele depend on the present reality and should correct pathological transference. Thus, tele is not an explanation of relationships, but the actual relationship in each context and at each moment in time. It is objective and can be measured by means of the sociogram. Ideally, it must be appropriate and not contaminated by transference. Such appropriateness is difficult to evaluate, but it always implies some reciprocity.

To deal with appropriateness, Moreno introduced the sociometric perception test (Moreno 1954, p. 217), which has been incorporated into routine sociometric testing (Bastin 1966). Moreno expected that this new test would explain discrepancies between transmitted and received choices. In fact, in spite of often being chosen themselves, some subjects chose the few people who did not choose them. In other words, their choices were not mutual. As a consequence, they felt abandoned and isolated: Tele did not happen. Moreno's hypothesis was that they did not perceive the effects of their choices on other people, nor were they aware of other people's choices. In Moreno's words, they had a "weak cognitive tele", which could be re-educated by means of psychodramatic techniques (Moreno 1954, pp. 216–218).

"Telic sensitivity" is crucial for psychotherapists (Blatner 1994) and, if we could assess it, such a measure would give us specific information about individual psychopathology and its evolution. In fact, as tele is sometimes distorted by transference or psychopathological states (social phobia, depression, mania, paranoia, schizophrenia), we find people who are aware of people who:

1) choose them but not of people who reject them;
2) reject them but not of people who choose them.

Moreover, some ambivalent people may think that they are

3) rejected by people who actually prefer them, and/or
4) chosen by people who actually reject them.

Finally, and regardless of their perceptions, people can even display mutual choices or rejections, or reject some people who choose them and choose people who reject them.

Although all this information seems complex, it is useful and it is contained in the sociometric test, providing this test includes questions about perception. The sociometric test, whose underlying concept is simple, gives information both about the informal structure of a human group and about each member in it, namely the distinction between *popular* (also called *stars*), *average, rejected* and *neglected* subjects (Bastin 1966; Newcomb et al. 1993). The sociometric matrix has been statistically studied (Moreno 1954) and it has undergone several developments, both graphical and numerical, which embrace reciprocities of choices and accuracy of perceptions (Bastin 1966; Bustos 1979; Moreno 1959). Generally, they are applied to the group for measuring social cohesiveness or, to specific individuals for measuring their psychological distance from the group or from another specific individual. Bustos (1979) proposed a "direct relationship index" and a "perception index". They describe the percentage of choices or perceptions which match the real choices of the receptors, including positive, negative and neutral choices. These indices may be comparable, but they can be distorted as long as neutral choices increase in large groups.

We could also count the number of correct perceived preferences or rejections as an index of accurate perception, in the same way that Moreno considered the importance of mutual choices in his sociogram. However, the probability of matching choices depends on the number of choices received. This index may therefore be biased by the status of the studied subject. On the one hand, a popular subject (preferred by most of the other members of the group), may display several perceptions which match the actual choices by pure chance. On the other hand, an isolated subject chosen by few other members may have the correct perception of all (the few) choices and have a smaller number of correct perceptions. Thus, there is not yet any way of studying individual telic sensitivity in a comparable and unbiased way (dependent neither on the sociometric status of the subject studied nor on the number of members in the group).

Composite index of Positive Perception: (cPP)
cPP=100: people who think they are only preferred by all people who actually prefer them.
cPP=0: people who think they are only preferred by all people who actually reject them.
Composite index of Negative Perception: (cNP)
cNP=100: people who think they are only rejected by all people who actually reject them.
cNP=0: people who think they are only rejected by all people who actually prefer them.
Composite index of Positive Mutuality: (cPM)
cPM=100: people who only prefer all people who actually prefer them.
cPM=0: people who only prefer all people who actually reject them.
Composite index of Negative Mutuality: (cNM)
cNM=100: people who only reject all people who actually reject them
cNM=0: people who only reject all people who actually prefer them.

Fig. 1 Extreme values and their putative meaning in the indices to develop

The goal of the present paper is to develop a method for measuring accurate perceptions and reciprocity of choices, both positive and negative, which permits individual comparisons irrespective of the number of members in a group and the number of received choices. We propose to derive four indices from the obtained sociometric data: (1) *index of Positive Perception (PP)*, to measure the accuracy of perception of preferences received by the subject; (2) *index of Negative Perception (NP)*, to measure the accuracy of perception of rejections; (3) *index of Positive Mutuality (PM)*, to measure transmitted preferences which match received preferences; (4) *index of Negative Mutuality (NM)*, to measure transmitted rejections which match received rejections. In order to include situations of misunderstanding (for instance, a subject who thinks he is chosen by people who actually reject him), we will try to develop composite indices.

The meaning of the extreme values of these indices is proposed in the Fig. 1. If these indices are displayed on a similar scale, we can compare the accuracy of perception for preferences versus rejections, and the mutuality of actual preferences or rejections. The indices for individuals belonging to the same or different groups, and the evolution of the indices in a subject belonging to several groups, can also be compared.

2 Mathematical development of the indices

In this section, we will develop the mathematical equations that allow us to have comparable indices not influenced by the size of the group and the status of each individual within the group. In order to have the raw data, we first need to perform a sociometric test and a sociometric matrix. An example of a sociometric matrix, after performing a sociometric test in a psychodrama group, will be displayed to illustrate the mathematical computation of each index.

2.1 Sociometric test

The sociometric test (Bastin 1966) consists of four simple questions asked to each member of a closed group. A specific task (the so-called sociometric criterion[1]) is

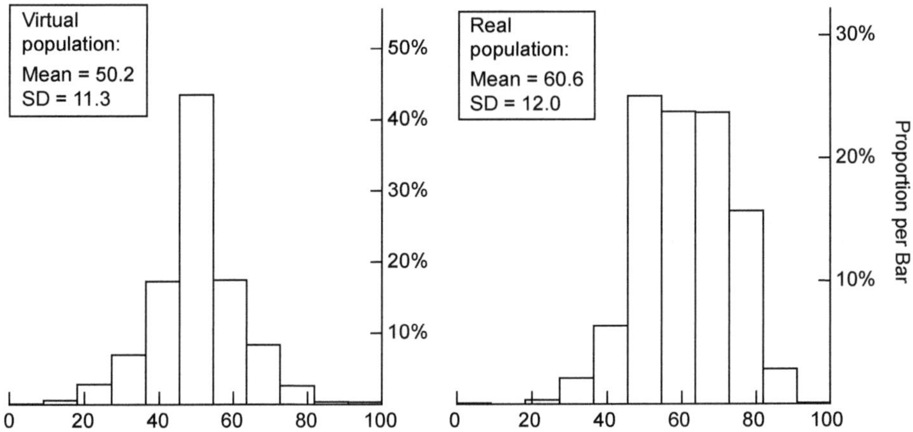

Fig. 2 Histograms of the composite indices in virtual population with randomized choices and real population

described, and then each member is asked about: (1) who will s/he choose to do this task with; (2) who will he reject; (3) who he thinks has chosen him; and (4) who he thinks has rejected him. There are several proposals to be found on the Internet for making a sociomatrix and a sociogram after performing a sociometric test[2]. These proposals frequently discard the perception questions (Q3 and Q4) and force choices and/or put limits on their number. In our current practice, the perception choices are optional although their absence makes the perception indices impossible) and we do not limit the number of choices or force them. However, the answers are sorted in order of preference.

Data are displayed in a squared matrix (see Fig. 2), where transmitters are displayed on the vertical axis (in columns) and the receivers on the horizontal axis (in rows). Since the choices are hierarchical, we labelled the first choice with the number five, the second with the number four, the third with the number three, the fourth with the number two, and the remaining with the number one. Preferences are labelled with positive numbers, and rejections with negative numbers. These values are important to develop the sociogram and to analyse leadership. In the context of the present work, we discard these values and only count the presence of a positive or negative number.

On the rows we can count the number of transmitted preferences (*tp*) and transmitted rejections (*tr*) for each subject. On the columns, received preferences (*rp*) and rejections (*rr*) can be counted. There are manual and computerized methods for finding reciprocal (mutual) preferences (*mp*) or rejections (*mr*). We also count the preferences which match rejections (inverse mutual preferences—*imp*), and the rejections which match preferences (inverse mutual rejections—*imr*). Perceived preferences or rejections can be displayed on the same matrix, as **p** or **r**, but in inverse order (from the horizontal to the vertical axis, or in columns instead of rows). It is thus easy to count the matched (correct) perceptions vertically, for both preferences (*cp*) and rejections (*cr*). In the same way, the number of transmitted perceptions, both of preferences (*pp*) and rejections (*pr*) can also be counted vertically.

Table 1 Sociometric matrix of a small psychodrama group

	A Anne	B Bob	C Clair	D Don	E Edna	F Fred	G Gary	Transmitted preferences *tp* (mutual/ inverse)	Transmitted rejections *tr* (mutual/inverse)
A (Anne)	**0**	**−5**	**3 r**	**5**	**0**	**0 p**	**4**	3 (*mp*=2/*imp*=0)	1 (mr=0/*imr*=1)
B (Bob)	**2 p**	**0**	**5**	**3 p**	**0 p**	**0**	**4 p**	4 (*mp*=3/*imp*=1)	0 (*mr*=0/*imr*=0)
C (Claire)	**0 p**	**4 p**	**0**	**5 p**	**0**	**−5 r**	**3 r**	3 (*mp*=1/*imp*=1)	1 (*mr*=0/*imr*=1)
D (Don)	**5 p**	**3 p**	**0 p**	**0**	**−4 r**	**−5 r**	**4 p**	3 (*mp*=3/*imp*=0)	2 (*mr*=0/*imr*=2)
E (Edna)	**1**	**4 r**	**5**	**1 r**	**0**	**2**	**3 r**	6 (*mp*=1/*imp*=2)	0 (*mr*=0/*imr*=0)
F (Fred)	**1 r**	**4**	**3 r**	**1 r**	**2**	**0**	**5 p**	6 (*mp*=2/*imp*=2)	0 (*mr*=0/*imr*=0)
G (Gary)	**3 p**	**2**	**−5 r**	**4 p**	**−4 p**	**5 p**	**0**	4 (*mp*=4/*imp*=0)	2 (*mr*=0/*imr*=2)
Received Preferences (*rp*)	5	5	4	6	1	2	6		
Received Rejections (*rr*)	0	1	1	0	2	2	0		
Perceived Preferences (*pp*)	4	2	1	3	2	2	3		
Correct (*cp*)	3	2	0	3	0	1	3		
Inverse (*ipp*)	0	0	0	0	1	0	0		
Perceived Rejections (*pr*)	1	1	3	2	1	2	2		
Correct (cr)	0	0	1	0	1	2	0		
Inverse (*ipr*)	1	1	2	2	0	0	2		

Table 1 shows a matrix resulting from a sociometric test applied to a psychodrama group, where every member was asked to choose playmates to play a competitive game. As an example, subject C (Claire) has chosen Don, Bob (who has chosen her), and Gary (who has rejected her) to belong to her team, and has rejected Fred (who has chosen her). It can be seen that her preferences and rejections are not strongly mutual. For her part, Claire was chosen by four subjects (Anne, Bob, Edna, Fred), two of whom she has perceived as rejecting her, and was rejected by Gary, a rejection which matched her own perception. Since Claire is a special case of misunderstanding relationships, we will take her as an example in future calculations. Her figures are: n (number of members in the group)$=7$; $tp=3$; $tr=1$; $rp=4$; $rr=1$; $mp=1$; $mr=0$; $pp=1$; $pr=3$; $cp=0$; $cr=1$. We also have to take into account the figures for misunderstanding: *inverse perceived preferences* (perceived preferences which match actual rejections—ipp)$=0$; *inverse perceived rejections* (perceived rejections which match actual preferences—ipr)$=2$; *inverse mutual preferences* (transmitted preferences which match received rejections—imp)$=1$; *inverse mutual rejections* (transmitted rejections which match received preferences—imr)$=1$.

These data are computed to create the sociogram, for which we only use the first few choices of each individual list. Furthermore, it has been suggested that each member of the group may have a distinct sociometric profile based on the number of preferences and rejections, actual or perceived, transmitted or received (Bastin 1966; Newcomb et al. 1993). We can also compute the extreme figures exceeding a given probability of occurrence (generally $p<0.5$). The classification of sociometric status is based on these extreme figures.

2.2 Measuring positive perception

We begin by measuring what we may call the *index of Positive Perception.* It was defined as a normalized and comparable index for detecting each member's ability to correctly perceive the preferences actually received from other members.

The starting numbers for measuring *Positive Perception* are:

pp—The number of displayed perceived preferences;

rp—The number of received preferences;

cp—The number of correct perceptions, the perceived preferences which match the received preferences.

This last number is the key one. However, we want to know the difference between this figure and the number of correct perceptions occurring by pure chance. Taking n as the number of members in the group, and the fact that a given member does not choose himself or herself, the probability of matching the received preferences, for each transmitted perception, is:

$$p = \frac{rp}{n-1}\left(p = \text{probability of matching for each transmission}\right). \tag{1}$$

However, since there is not just one, but *pp* transmitted perceptions of preferences, the expected mean matching for all the transmitted perceptions is:

$$X = \frac{pp\ .\ rp}{n-1}\left(X = \text{expected mean matching}\right). \tag{2}$$

Thus, the difference between actual *(cp)* and expected *(X)* correct perceptions is:

$$g_{am} = cp - \frac{pp\ .\ rp}{n-1}\left(g_{am} = \text{gain in the actual matching}\right). \tag{3}$$

For instance, in a group of $n=7$ members, C (Claire) receives $rp=4$ preferences, transmits $pp=1$ perceptions of preferences, and matches $cp=0$. We can thus compute:

$$g_{am\,(C)} = 0 - 1 * 4 / \left(7-1\right) = -0.666667$$

which is the gain in correct perception above the figure expected by chance (in this case, a negative gain).

However this number is only an indication, which must be compared with the chance a subject has of having the best matching. That is to say, if this member correctly perceived every received preference, he would have displayed four perceptions and matched all the received preferences. In this case, the best gain he could have would be:

$$g_{bm\,(C)} = 4 - 4 * 4 / (7-1) = 1.333333$$

or, in a generic formula:

$$g_{bm} = rp - \frac{rp.rp}{n-1} \left(g_{bm} = \text{gain in the best matching} \right) \tag{4}$$

Dividing *(3)* by *(4)*, we can finally arrive at a comparable *index of Positive Perception* (*PP*). In the above example, it would be $PP_{(C)} = -0.666667/1.333333 = -0.5$. Irrespective of starting data, this number will range between -1 and $+1$. The negative or positive signal depends on the correct perceptions being lower or higher than the expected figures. For practical purposes the transformation of the variable may be useful. We suggest the whole rounded number resulting from the multiplication by 50 and addition of 50. In this case we would have a whole number between 0 and 100. In the example above, it would be $(-0.5*50+50)=25$.

The general formula of the main equation ($g_{am}(3)/g_{bm}(4)$) is:

$$PP = \frac{cp - \frac{pp.rp}{n-1}}{rp - \frac{rp.rp}{n-1}} = \frac{(n-1).cp - pp.rp}{(n-1).rp - rp^2} \tag{5}$$

2.3 Extreme values and correction of zeros

In certain circumstances, the denominator of the fraction can be equal to zero, making the division impossible. This can happen in extreme and rare situations, when the number of received choices will be equal to zero (the neglected members) or equal $n-1$ (the most popular members, thus chosen from all the others). This problem can be solved by adding 0.001 to *rp*, whenever this variable is equal to $n-1$ or 0. In the case of $n-1$ choices, the index will vary between 1 and 0, depending on if all or less real choices are perceived. In the case of null choices, the index will be lesser the more perceptions are transmitted. If the neglected members emit 0 perceptions, there will be a division of 0 by 0, which will have to correspond to index 1. Computer programs can do this easily (see Appendix).

2.4 Developing composite indices

To get more information from the sociogram, we may also measure inverse perceptions. This is the case where a subject thinks that he is preferred by a member who actually rejects him. The key value will thus be the number of perceived preferences which match the actual rejections (*inverse perceived preferences* or *ipp*), also counted on the vertical axis of the matrix. Figures of formula *(5)* can be applied, but, besides using *ipp* instead of *cp*, received rejections (*rr*) should replace received preferences (*rp*). Thus, we can have the *inverse index of Positive Perception*:

$$iPP = \frac{(n-1).ipp - pp.rr}{(n-1).rr - rr^2} \tag{6}$$

By itself, this index only detects special situations of misunderstanding. Assuming that people do not misunderstand rejections as preferences, it can be expected to be negative, although it would theoretically range between −1 and +1. For an example, C (Claire) will have:

$$iPP(c) = ((7-1)*0 - 1*1)/((7-1)*1 - 1^2) = -1/5 = -0.25$$

This new index thus helps to correct the impression, given by the index of positive perception, that Claire is a bad perceiver of others' preferences. She cannot perceive preferences towards her, but she does not excessively misunderstand rejections as preferences. Therefore, if we subtract it from the index of Positive Perception, we get more information from the sociometric matrix, and have a better picture of perception accuracy. For Claire, it will be,

$$cPP(c) = [PP] - [iPP] = (5) - (9) = -0.5 - (-0.25) = -0.25$$

This is a composite index, theoretically ranging between −2 and +2, which we call the C*omposite index of Positive Perception*:

$$cPP = \frac{(n-1).cp - pp.rp}{(n-1).rp - rp^2} - \frac{(n-1).ipp - pp.rr}{(n-1).rr - rr^2} \quad (7)$$

2.5 Composite indices of negative perception and mutuality (positive and negative)

The above reasoning can be applied to other data where reciprocity may be measured. This is the case of *correctly perceived rejections* (*cr*), *mutual preferences* (*mp*) and *mutual rejections* (*mr*) which must replace *pp* (*perceived preferences*) for the first term of each equation, and the number of perceived rejections which match received preferences (*inverse perceived rejections—ipr*), of transmitted preferences which match received rejections (*inverse mutual preferences—imp*), and of transmitted rejections which match received preferences (*inverse mutual rejections—imr)* which must replace *ipp* (*inverse perceived preferences*) for the second term. For both the terms of equations, *perceived rejections* (*pr*), *transmitted preferences* (*tp*) and *transmitted rejections* (*tr*) must be counted instead of *perceived preferences* (*pp*). Also in the second term of each new equation, the same rules apply as for the equation *(6)*: received rejections *(rr)* must replace received preferences *(rp)* for positive indices and *vice-versa* for negative indices. The new indices and respective equations are the following:

a) Composite index of Negative Perception = NP—iNP:

$$cNP = \frac{(n-1).cr - pr.rr}{(n-1).rr - rr^2} - \frac{(n-1).ipr - pr.rp}{(n-1).rp - rp^2} \quad (8)$$

b) Composite index of Positive Mutuality = PM—iPM:

$$cPM = \frac{(n-1).mp - tp.rp}{(n-1).rp - rp^2} - \frac{(n-1).imp - tp.rr}{(n-1).rr - rr^2} \quad (9)$$

c) Composite index of Negative Mutuality = NM—iNM:

$$cNM = \frac{(n-1).mr - tr.rr}{(n-1).rr - rr^2} - \frac{(n-1).imr - tr.rp}{(n-1).rp - rp^2} \quad (10)$$

Each of these composite indices will range between −2 and +2. For practical purposes, we can transform the variable to give a figure of the same magnitude of the single indices. Thus, the whole rounded result of the multiplication by 25 and addition of 50 will give a number ranging between 0 and 100. Assuming a normal distribution, random responses will be expected to be around 50, which results from the transformation of 0.

Computing the data related to example C, we obtain:

$$\boldsymbol{cPP(c)} = \mathbf{-0.25}\,(\textit{as computed before})$$
$$\text{or}(-0.25*25+50) = 43.75 \approx \mathbf{44;}$$

$$\boldsymbol{cNP(c)} = ((7-1)*1-3*1)/((7-1)*1*1^2)-$$
$$((7-1)*2-3*4)/((7-1)*4-4^2) = 0.5-0 = 0.5$$
$$\text{or}(0.5*25+50) = 62.5 \approx \mathbf{63};$$

$$\boldsymbol{cPM_{(C)}} = ((7-1)*1-3*4)/((7-1)*4-4^2) - ((7-1)*1-3*1)/$$
$$((7-1)*1-1^2) = -0.75-0.6 = \mathbf{-1.35}$$
$$\text{or}(-1.35*25+50) = 16.25 \approx \mathbf{16};$$

$$\boldsymbol{cNM_{(C)}} = ((7-1)*0-1*1)/((7-1)*1*1^2) - ((7-1)*1-1*4)/$$
$$((7-1)*4-4^2) = -0.2-0.25 = \mathbf{-0.45}$$
$$\text{or } (-0.45*25+50) = 38.75 \approx \mathbf{39.}$$

2.6 Population

These composite indices were studied in virtual groups with randomized choices and with real groups where the sociometric test had been applied. The virtual groups consisted of 315 supposed individuals belonging to 21 groups, which ranged sequentially from 5 to 25 members in each group. After defining the number of members in each group, a computer program randomly decided the preferences, rejections and perceptions, within a mean of choices corresponding to the mean of real groups. The real groups consisted of 311 boys and girls belonging to 12 school classes, ranging from 19 to 30 members (Mean age = 12 years). The sociometric test was applied to each class in the context of another study carried out by one of the authors (Villares-Oliveira 1999). The students were asked who they would choose (or not) to go on a school trip with, and who they thought would choose (or not choose) them.

In each type of group we detected the *popular* and *rejected* members, by means of the number of received preferences or rejections out of the limit defined by the

Table 2 Number and percentage of all sociometric statuses in each population studied[a]

Population	Total	Popular	Average	Rejected	Neglected
Random	315[b]	24 (8%)	*251 (80%)*	30 (10%)	7 (2%)
Real	311	52 (18%)	*167 (54%)*	56 (18%)	36 (12%)

[a] $\chi^2 = 54.6$ (3df) $p < .0001$

[b] 2 members were controversial;

cumulative binomial probability ($p < 0.05$) in each group. The *neglected* members were defined by the social impact ($rp + rr$) under the limit defined by the cumulative binomial probability of $p < 0.05$ (Bahn 1972). The social impact above the limits defines *controversial* members. All remaining members were considered *average*. The number and status of the total members are shown in Table 2.

3 Results

Figure 2 shows the histogram of all the composite indices in the virtual population with randomized choices and in the real population. Normal distribution can be assumed. The standard deviation is nearly the same for both virtual ($SD = 11.3$) and real ($SD = 12.0$) populations. As it was expected, the mean of the indices, wherever the randomized choices were present (virtual population), is about 50. In real populations, the general mean is 60.6. The difference is highly significant ($t = 11.16$, $p < .0001$).

Table 3 compares the means for each composite index belonging to small ($n < 10$) and large ($n > 20$) groups of the virtual population, as well as the means for each sociometric status in this population. No mean is significantly different and, in every circumstance, the 95% confidence interval for mean (mean ± 1.96 x standard deviation divided by the square root of the sample size) includes the value of 50.0.

Finally, Table 4 compares the index means for each sociometric status in the real population. Interestingly, indices that match preferences (*cPP* and *cPM*) tend to be higher than indices that match rejections (*cNP* and *cNM*). All these differences are

Table 3 Mean, standard deviation and 95% confidence interval for mean for each composite index in small ($n < 10$) and large ($n > 20$) groups, and in each sociometric status of the virtual population with randomized choices

	Small groups	Large groups	Popular	Average	Rejected	Neglected
	$N=35$	$N=115$	$N=24$	$N=251$	$N=31$	$N=7$
cPP	48.0±14.7	51.3±9.2	50.4±9.3	49.4±10.9	50.1±8.3	56.0±19.1
	(43.0–53.1)	(49.6–53.0)	(46.4–54.3)	(48.1–50.8)	(47.1–53.2)	(38.3–73.7)
cNP	50.8±15.1	50.5±8.6	48.0±10.5	50.7±10.6	49.4±14.9	53.6±13.5
	(45.6–56.0)	(48.9–52.0)	(43.5–52.4)	(49.4–52.0)	(44.1–55.0)	(41.1–66.0)
cPM	52.6±15.6	48.9±8.6	48.9±11.1	49.8±12.0	50.1±10.7	44.3±18.1
	(47.3–58.0)	(47.3–50.5)	(44.2–53.6)	(48.3–51.3)	(46.3–54.2)	(28.4–59.9)
cNM	53.8±19.1	51.0±9.1	49.2±9.4	51.1±11.3	52.7±8.0	44.1±17.0
	(49.3–58.3)	(49.4–52.7)	(45.2–53.1)	(49.7–52.5)	(49.7–55.6)	(27.7–61.2)

Table 4 Mean and standard deviation of the composite indices in each sociometric status of the real population

	Popular	Average	Rejected	Neglected
	N=52	*N*=167	*N*=56	*N*=36
cPP	63.5±7.7	64.1±9.4	66.1±13.0	63.5±11.6
cNP	59.8±13.6	55.5±11.5	57.2±12.2	56.6±11.3
cPM	62.9±8.1	66.9±11.0	65.3±14.0	63.9±12.4
cNM	56.6±12.5	55.8±10.4	54.5±10.8	55.2±12.7

statistically significant [p(t-test) < .003], with the exception of the perception in *popular* members. No other pair of means is significantly different in each group, except for *average* members, where positive mutuality (*cPM*) is significantly higher than positive perception (*cPP*) (t=2.5, 332 df, $p < .013$), contrary to the general tendency in other groups. Moreover, the means are greater than in the virtual randomized population.

4 Discussion

The sociometric test is easily applied but difficult to decode into a readable form: sociometric matrix and sociogram. This problem may be overcome with computers. It is now time to gather and study all the information provided by this useful tool. This paper explored the concept of *tele* by acquiring individual measures of telic sensitivity, irrespective of the size of the group and the number of received preferences and rejections that define the sociometric status of each member. These measures were developed rationally, but we had to introduce a correction in order to deal with zero numbers.

Application of these measures to virtual populations with randomized choices (Table 2) showed they were effectively independent of the size of the groups and the sociometric status of the individuals. Composite indices are preferable to single indices, as they generate more information. Though in the past they were more difficult to process, this is overcome with computer software. Based on our global results, we can say that an index between 37 and 75 (61±2*12) is acceptable for real people. More or less than this indicates special and rare (less than 5 %) people, who are either extremely accurate regarding others' choices or they misunderstand these choices.

In fact, real people have a higher mutuality and accurate perception (mean=60.6, see Fig. 2) than does the virtual population with randomized choices (mean=50.2). Moreno (1959, p. 47) emphasized this phenomenon by comparing the number of reciprocal, "chain", "closed" and "leadership" structures in real groups, against asymmetrical relations in randomized choices. Furthermore, he tried to demonstrate graphically that schizophrenic patients misunderstand the choices that other people direct towards them (Moreno 1959, p. 59). Using these indices in subsequent research, we may expect to sustain such assumptions, and to detect special cases of individual misunderstanding within a group. These would, at least, be people at risk. Returning to our example, subject C (Claire) had three indices within the accepted range (*cPP*=44; *cNP*=63; *cNM*=39), but mutual preferences (*cPM*=16) were clearly low.

In fact, she was a married woman with an obsessive personality, experiencing a marital crisis. Her husband liked her very much, as did other men, but she complained about the difficulty she had in dealing with them. She conveyed to the psychodrama group her tendency to be attracted to those people who reject her.

The real people in our study are rather more attentive to preferences than to rejections (*cPP>cNP*, and *cPM>cNM*). This may either be a special characteristic of the youthful population studied or a generic tendency of the healthy human beings. Nevertheless, the difference in perception of positive and negative choices is not significant in *popular* members. This may be a feature of leadership. In fact, popular members have the highest perception indices of negative choices and the lowest positive mutuality, perhaps as a result of performing strategic choices. However, more research is clearly needed. It is interesting to see that indices of perception are generally higher than indices of actual mutuality (*cPP>cPM*, and *cNP>cNM*, see Table 4) except in *average* members, where the difference is opposite and significant for positive choices. This could mean that *average* people are well engaged in action but don't really think about other people's choices.

Since this is a preliminary study, the above speculations remain to be substantiated in subsequent research. However, they do point to the diagnostic and research possibilities that such comparable indices may have in organizational and clinical psychology. In spite of its susceptibility to conceptual ambiguity, and the lack of attention from psychodramatists, tele may be a central concept in Moreno's theory (Blatner 1994). In view of the fact that several psychodrama techniques rely on tele, this concept deserves further development and research.

Notes

1 The sociometric criterion is the task on which the choices are based. Some examples are: Who do you choose: "to keep a secret?"; "for support in taking risks?"; "to go on a trip with?"; "to generate creative ideas with?". These criteria may be adjusted to the group and be diverse in order to generate different choices in each test. Putatively, they do not influence the indices.

2 Some examples: http://www.hoopandtree.org/sociometry.htm, acceded in JAN/2015; http://www.simonecapretti.it/groupdynamics/, acceded in JAN/2015.

Acknowledgments The authors wish to thank Adam Blatner and Eberhard Scheiffele for comments and criticism on previous versions of the paper. They also thank Sarah Minnes for the English support.

Appendix

Program (in QBasic) to compute the indices

```
PRINT "For Positive Perception insert cp (Matching), pp (Transmitted), ipp (Inv. match)"
PRINT "For Negative Perception insert cr (Matching), pr (Transmitted), ipr (Inv. match)"
```

```
PRINT "For Positive Mutuality insert mp (Matching), tp (Transmitted), imp (Inv. match)"
PRINT "For Negative Mutuality insert mr (Matching), tr (Transmittes), imr (Inv. match)"
PRINT "For Positive Indices insert first rp (Received), then rr (Inverse received)"
PRINT "For Negative Indices insert first rr (Received), then rp (Inverse received)"
1 INPUT "Number of members "; n
2 INPUT "Matching (cp, cr, mp, mr)"; var1
3 INPUT "Transmitted (pp, pr, tp, tr)"; var2
4 INPUT "Received (rp, rr) "; var3: GOSUB 12
5 PRINT "single index"; index; "="; FIX(index * 50+50)
6 LET indice1=index
7 INPUT "Inverse matching (ipp, ipr, imp, imr)"; var1
8 INPUT "Inverse received (rr, rp) "; var3: GOSUB 12
9 PRINT "inverse "; index; "="; FIX(index * 50+50)
10 PRINT "composite"; index1 - index; "="; CINT((index1 - index) * 25+50)
11 STOP
12 indices
13 IF var3=0 AND var2=0 THEN LET index=1: GOTO 23
14 IF var3=0 THEN LET var3=.001
15 IF var3=n - 1 THEN LET var3=var3+0,001
16 LET numerator=(n - 1) * var1 - var2 * var3
17 LET denominator=(n - 1) * var3 - var3 ^ 2
18 LET index=numerador/denominator
19 RETURN
```

Note: This program is embedded in SOCIOM (http://195.22.18.186/sociom/Tabelas-Dados.aspx)

References

Bahn, A. K. (1972). *Basic medical statistics*. New York: Grune & Stratton.

Bastin, G. (1966). *Les techniques sociometriques*. Paris: P.U.F. (Portuguese translation: *As técnicas sociométricas*. Lisboa: Livraria Morais Editora).

Blatner, A. (1994). Tele: The dynamics of interpersonal preference. In P. Holmes, M. Karp, & M. Watson (Eds.), *Psychodrama since Moreno* (pp. 283–300). London: Routledge.

Bustos, D. M. (1979). *O teste sociométrico: fundamentos, técnica e aplicação*. São Paulo: Ed. Brasiliense.

Kellerman, P. F. (1992). *Focus ou Psychodrama*. London: Jessica Kingsley Publishers.

Moreno, J. L. (1946). *Psychodrama* (Vol. 1). São Paulo: Beacon House, Inc. (Portuguese translation: Psicodrama) (Cultrix, 1976).

Moreno, J. L. (1954). *Who shall survive?* New York: Beacon House Inc. (Spanish Translation: *Fundamentos de la sociometria*. Buenos Aires: Ed. Paidos).

Moreno, J. L. (1959). *Gruppenpsychotherapie und Psychodrama: Einleitung in die Theorie und Praxis*. Stuttgart: Georg Thieme Verlag. (Portuguese translation: *Psicoterapia de grupo e psicodrama*. São Paulo: Ed. Mestre Jou).

Newcomb, A. T., Bukowski, W. M., & Pattee, L. (1993). Children's peer relations: A meta-analytic review of popular, rejected, neglected, controversial, and average sociometric status. *Psychological Bulletin, 113*, 99–128.

Rojas-Bermudez, J. G. (1966). *Quê Es El Psicodrama?* (3rd edn). São Paulo: Ed. Mestre Jou (1980, Port. Translation: Introdução ao Psicodrama).

Villares-Oliveira, C. (1999). *Os jovens e os seus pares: Estudo sociométrico e psicopatológico de uma população escolar*. Coimbra: Tese de Doutoramento.

José Luís Pio-Abreu is a clinical Psychiatrist and Professor of Psychiatry at the Faculty of Medicine at Coimbra University. He is also a Psychodramatist and former President of the Portuguese Society of Psychodrama. Currently, he is a Member of the Center for Philosophy of Sciences of the University of Lisbon, Portugal. Email: pioabreu@netcabo.pt

Cristina Villares Oliveira is a Psychiatrist and Professor at the Faculty of Medicine of Coimbra. She is a Psychodramatist and former President of the Portuguese Society of Psychodrama. Currently, she develops her clinical and research work at the Barcelona Schizophrenia Clinic Unit, Neuroscience Institute, Hospital Clinic, University of Barcelona, Spain. Email: cvilares@clinic.ub.es

Z Psychodrama Soziometr (2016) (Suppl) 15:57–67
DOI 10.1007/s11620-015-0314-9

HAUPTBEITRÄGE

Zeitschrift für Psychodrama und Soziometrie

Towards the development of Helpful Aspects of Morenian Psychodrama Content Analysis System (HAMPCAS)

Ana Sofia Cruz[1] · Célia Maria Dias Sales[2] · Gabriela Moita[3] · Paula G. Alves[4]

Published online: 27 January 2016

Abstract The main goal of this study is to develop a system of categorizing what clients find helpful and hindering in psychodrama sessions using a patient-generated process measure, the Helpful Aspects of Therapy (HAT; Elliott, Helpful Aspects of Therapy Form. http://www.experiential-researchers.org/instruments/elliott/hat.html, 1993). An existing system, the Helpful Aspects of Experiential Therapy Content Analysis System (HAETCAS; Elliott, Helpful aspects of experiential therapy content analysis system (HAETCAS): Rating manual. Unpublished manuscript. Department of Psychology, University of Toledo, 1988), was adapted to psychodrama, by exploring to what extent its categories were applicable or not to this therapeutic approach. HAETCAS is meant to categorize each client identified therapeutic event from three aspects: action (to which the event refers to), impact (that the event had on the individual) and content (that the event is about). This study showed that the majority of impact and context categories of HAETCAS are potentially applicable to psychodrama. In relation to action, the results demonstrate the need for psychodrama specific categories, which would reveal theoretical aspects of this therapeutic model. An extended version of HAETCAS, which includes the categories of action specific to psychodrama was identified as HAMPCAS (Helpful Aspects of Morenian Psychodrama Content Analysis System). The implications of using it to analyze HAT data, for both therapists and clients will be addressed; highlighting the possibilities and drawbacks of routinely taking clients' perspectives on board.

✉ Ana Sofia Cruz
ana.s.dacruz@gmail.com

1 Universidade Fernando Pessoa, Praça 9 de Abril, 349, 4249–004 Porto, Portugal

2 Centro de Psicologia da Universidade do Porto, Portugal Cis/ISCTE-IUL, Lisbon, Portugal

3 Instituto Superior de Serviço Social do Porto|Cooperativa de Ensino Superior de Serviço Social, C.R.L., Av. Dr. Manuel Teixeira Ruela, 370, 4460-362 Senhora da Hora, Portugal

4 Instituto Universitário de Lisboa (ISCTE-IUL), CIS-IUL, Avenida das Forças Armadas, Edifício ISCTE-IUL, Sala 2w17, 1649-026 Lisbon, Portugal

This study is part of the IPHA Group (Sales et al., Counselling and Psychotherapy Research 14(3):181–191, 2014), an international practice-based research network dedicated to personalized assessment.

Keywords Morenian Psychodrama · HAMPCAS · Change process research · Client's perspective

Zur Entwicklung eines Inhaltsanalyse-Systems hilfreicher Aspekte des Psychodrama nach Moreno (HAMPCAS)

Zusammenfassung Hauptziel dieser Studie ist es, ein Kategoriensystem zu entwickeln, mit dem KlientInnen darstellen können, was für sie hilfreich und was hinderlich in Psychodrama-Sitzungen ist. Dafür wurde ein von PatientInnen generiertes Prozessinstrument, der *Helpful Aspects in Therapy* Fragebogen (HAT; Elliot, Helpful Aspects of Therapy Form. HYPERLINK "http://www.experiential-researchers.org/instruments/elliott/hat.html" http://www.experiential-researchers.org/instruments/elliott/hat.html, 1993) eingesetzt. Das *Helpful Aspects of Experiential Therapy Content Analysis System* (HAETCAS; Elliot, Helpful aspects of experiential therapy content analysis system (HAETCAS): Rating manual. Unpublished manuscript. Department of Psychology, University of Toledo, 1988) wurde an das Psychodrama angepasst, indem untersucht wurde, inwiefern das HAETCAS Kategoriensystem passend bzw. unpassend zu den psychodramatischen Kategorien ist. HAETCAS zielt auf die Kategorisierung jeder von den KlientInnen wahrgenommenen therapeutischen Interventionen aus drei Blickwinkeln: Aktion (auf die sich die Intervention bezieht), Wirkung (welche die Intervention auf die KlientInnen hat) und Inhalt (der Intervention). Die Studie konnte nachweisen, dass die Mehrheit der Wirkung- und Inhalt-Kategorien von HAETCAS für das Psychodrama potentiell anwendbar sind. In Bezug auf die Handlung hat sich gezeigt, dass psychodramaspezifische Kategorien entwickelt werden sollten, die theoretische Aspekte des psychodramatherapeutischen Modells einbeziehen. HAMPCAS (Helpful Aspects of Morenian Psychodrama Content Analysis System) ist die erweiterte Version von HAETCAS, welche die handlungsspezifischen Kategorien des Psychodrama berücksichtigt. Implikationen beim Gebrauch von HAMPCAS für die Auswertung der HAT-Daten, sowohl für TherapeutInnen als auch für KlientInnen werden beschrieben; dabei werden Vor- und Nachteile beschrieben, die entstehen, wenn routinemäßig die KlientInnenperspektive einbezogen wird. Diese Studie ist Teil des internationalen praxisorientierten Forschungsnetzwerks für personalisierte Beurteilung IPHA (Sales et al., Counselling and Psychotherapy Research 14(3):181–191, 2014).

Schlüsselwörter Psychodrama nach Moreno · HAMPCAS · Veränderungsforschung · KlientInnen-Perspektive

1 Introduction

Developed by Moreno in the late 1930s, Psychodrama is an individual psychotherapy conducted in a group format, where "instead of talking about problems, patients are helped to enact those problematic situations, and in the direct dialogue and associated physical energizing, patients often have powerful insights, emotional catharses, and even discover ways of working through those problems" (Blatner & Shaughnessy 2003, p. 137).

Despite the contribution of Psychodrama to the development of Group Psychotherapy as a whole, with the recognition and accreditation by the Austrian and Hungarian governments and the European Association of Psychotherapy, Psychodrama remains unrecognized in the scientific fields of psychology, psychiatry and psychotherapy (Wieser 2007). The scarcity of research is potentially a result of psychodramatists' self-image, who emphasize action instead of language (in the field of intervention) and practice over theory (in the field of research). This trend is rooted in the origins of psychodrama set in opposition to the Freudian theory, stating that the path to the human psyche would not be in the language but in action and interaction between people. This led to a withdrawal of Psychodrama from the academia, hindering the research in this field. How can this tendency be reversed?

In psychotherapy research in general, the term Change Process Research (CPR) emerged 30 years ago and refers to a paradigm that focuses on the identification, description, explanation and prediction of process factors that lead to therapeutic change, overcoming the old dichotomy between process and outcome (Greenberg 1986 cit. in Elliott 2010). Subsequently, in CPR, the study of the processes by which change occurs in psychotherapy came to include both the processes involved in therapy that produce change and the sequence in which these changes occur.

The emergence of CPR, in addition to the growing tendency to conduct practice-based research, has opened new doors to Psychodrama and stimulated research through the opportunity of reducing the gap between practitioners and researchers. Therefore, it is not surprising the fact that the majority of ongoing investigations in the field of psychodrama, are being carried out by researchers in dual role–practitioner/researcher. Moreover, these developments led to the introduction of research skills training in the curricula of various schools of Psychodrama; they have been using CPR to answer questions such as: "What generalizations can be made from the systematic study of client experiences? What are the basic domains of clients' therapeutic experiences? What are the varieties and underlying dimensions within and across these domains? What can the systematic study of client experiences tell us about the nature of therapy?" (Elliott and James 1989, p. 444). These authors also advocate, that understanding the potential of the wide range of client experiences is an important component to the therapeutic skills and leads to a better understanding of clients and therefore of more effective interventions. Therapists can also use this feedback to select, create and modify interventions by improving their performance and becoming more responsive to clients' needs (Hampson 2008). Finally, the development of this type of research responds to a generalized growing pressure by the international health services, contributing to the improvement of services and ensuring that clients of mental health services receive more appropriate treatment (Booth et al. 1997; Hampson 2008; Elliott 2008).

How can we study the clients' perspectives in Psychodrama? One of the strategies of analysis of clients' qualitative accounts is coding using observational category systems. In a literature review the authors found six standardized coding systems to analyze the clients' perspectives. These six systems can be grouped in three categories: transversal systems, whose categories can be found in most therapeutic modalities (Therapeutic Impacts Content Analysis System—TICAS- Elliott et al. 1985; Booth et al. 1997; Integrative corrective experiences coding system; Friedlander et al. 2011; Good moments in counselling and psychotherapy; Mahrer and Nadler 1986; Jones et al. 1986); systems that are adapted to certain theories, where categories refer exclusively to a certain type of therapy (Helpful Aspects of Experiential Therapy Content Analysis System—HAETCAS–Castonguay et al. 2010; Coding system for helpful and hindering aspects of CBT and IPT; Gershefski et al. 1996; Levy et al. 1996); and systems that refer to specific therapeutic phenomena, whereby the categories refer to phenomena that occur during the treatment (Empowerment Events System Timulak and Lietaer 2001; Timulak 2003). None of the systems mentioned above was considered appropriate to Morenian Psychodrama (MP), which lead us to develop the Helpful Aspects of Psychodrama Content Analysis System (HAMPCAS). In this paper we describe the preliminary steps of this development, namely the process of category generation, and its preliminary validation in a naturalistic psychodrama group.

2 Methods

2.1 Participants

This study looks at a group of MP in the context of private practice. The group was composed of seven females, mostly single and aged between 30 and 60 years old. With regard to the educational level, only one participant of the group is an undergraduate.

This was a weekly therapy group and each session lasted for approximately 2 hours. For most clients this was not their first time in therapy, although only one of the participants had been in a Psychodrama group with another therapist. Four of the participants were in Psychodrama training. From a clinical point of view, this was a heterogeneous group, which presented different diagnoses: bipolar disorder, suicidal ideation, depression, bereavement and relationship problems.

2.2 Therapists

This psychodrama group was run by two psychodramatists, one director (Gabriela M) and one auxiliary ego (João TS), both members of the Portuguese Psychodrama Society. The director was also one of the supervisors of the present study.

2.3 Research team

The research team was comprised of four researchers: Ana SC, PhD student and Psychodrama director (role: project design, data collection, development of the system, data analysis, HAMPCAS training package); Célia S, PhD, associate professor with expertise in psychotherapy research (role: project design, development of the system, data analysis, HAMPCAS training package); Gabriela M, PhD, associate professor with expertise in Psychodrama and Psychodrama director (role: project design, development of the system, data analysis, HAMPCAS training package, conductor) and Paula A, PhD student with expertise in psychotherapy research (role: development of the system, data analysis, HAMPCAS training package).

2.4 Measures

The HAT (Helpful Aspects of Therapy; Elliott 1993; Portuguese version by Sales et al. 2007) is an open-ended semi-structured self-report measure that asks clients for their perceptions of key change processes in therapy. Clients are asked to identify and describe, in their own words, the most helpful event in the session and to rate how helpful it was. They are asked about other helpful or hindering events in the session. The HAT form is usually administered immediately after each session, and sometimes in the intersession period: that is, immediately before the next session.

Besides HAT, two other instruments were used to double check the information provided in this instrument, to support the identification of the techniques used. These were: (1) HAT—Therapist version is an adaptation of the HAT that seeks to explore the significant events of therapy, for clients, from the perspective of the therapist. In this questionnaire, therapists are asked about the most significant events (helpful and hindering) of the session, to the protagonist, auxiliary egos and audience and why they were important; and (2) a Session Notes Form was completed by the auxiliary ego at the end of each session. It aimed to register attendance at the session, who was the protagonist and auxiliary egos, what techniques were used, who commented and the occurrence of other events as important moments of spontaneity, catharsis of integration, training role, and other aspects that the auxiliary ego considered relevant.

2.5 Procedure

Prior to entering in the study, the objectives and conditions of the study were explained to each participant so that they could give informed consent; the HAT was filled in weekly in the intersessional period. During the first 2 months, the instruments were completed by patients before the next session, in the office, on paper. Because of the difficulties presented by group members, related to the delays and the difficulty in remembering the content, we began to collect data with online surveys and between sessions. Data were collected between January 7 of 2011 and July 30 of 2012, when all the psychodrama group elements participating in the research, were clinically discharged.

2.6 Development of HAMPCAS

The content analysis system was developed by the principal researcher (Ana SC) in the context of her PhD (Cruz 2014) and discussed at three different times with the research team. In the first stage, the HAT material was coded following a grounded theory approach, in which each response given to HAT was considered a meaning unit. A constant comparison of the meaning units was made throughout the categorization procedure, to explore similarities between the data. Three domains emerged from this preliminary reading of the HAT materials: action, impact and context. This was in line with Elliott's proposal about HAT containing three types of information (action, impact and context), which are important to describe and study the significant moments of therapy from patients' point of view. As such, it was decided to follow Elliott's framework in the line with the three domains.

The second stage involved the definition of the categories in each of the three domains. Next, the HAT material was classified with these newly created categories, whose results were jointly discussed by the research team in two meetings. In these meetings, the research team proposed and defined the final list of the emergent categories.

Then, the list of the emergent action categories was sent to two Psychodrama experts, independent to the research team (Alfredo Soeiro and Rojas-Bermudez). These experts provided theoretical input to the preliminary system, to ensure the categories were in accordance with the constructs proposed by the Morenian theory of Psychodrama.

In relation to the impact and context domains a comparison with HAETCAS was made and correspondence for majority of categories was found. Due to differences concerning individual and group therapy some new categories were created mainly related with group factors and therapeutic alliance.

The final step involved the preparation of the coding manual for HAMPCAS. This manual was adapted from TICAS and HAETCAS manuals and included three sections: (1) an explanation of the coding procedure; (2) the theoretical definition of the categories of action, impact and context; and (3) HAT examples for each category.

2.7 Preliminary validation of HAMPCAS

The preliminary version was validated by two independent judges. With regards to the domains of impact and context, only the new categories were validated, considering that the other common categories had already been validated in previous studies (Castonguay et al. 2010; Hampson 2008; Booth et al. 1997). All categories were validated in the domain of action.

Validation of HAMPCAS involved the following steps:

1) Preparation of the Training Material: Choosing HAT events to be categorized by the raters, for training purposes.
2) First meeting with raters categoriztwo members of the Portuguese Society of Psychodrama were trained in using the Manual, which included coding initial examples together in the group

Table 1 Comparison between HAETCAS and HAMPCAS—action

Domain	Haetcas (Elliott 1988)	Hampcas
Action	1. Client expression 2. Client disclosure 3. Client discussion (extratherapy events) 4. Client exploration 5. Other client actions 6. Basic therapist techniques 7. Specialized therapist techniques 8. Other therapist techniques or actions	1. Self-sharing 2. Others' sharing 3. Therapeutic team sharing 4. Self-dramatization 5. Others dramatization 6. Role reversal 7. Soliloquy 8. Mirror 9. Double 10. Sculpture 11. Resistance interpolation 12. Social atom 13. Intermediate objects 14. Games 15. Sociometry 16. Role training 17. Other techniques or actions (symbolic representation; amplification; concretization; empty chair)

3) Raters rated 1/3 of the data, independently
4) Meeting to discuss discrepancies and difficulties
5) Raters coded another 1/3 of the data
6) The inter-rater reliability between raters was calculated for each new category (the reliability values ranged from 0.39 in the category Relational Weakening and 0.95 in Functional Unit Sharing).
7) The categories of action were discussed with the FEPTO Research Committee until a final version was reached.

3 Results

In the development of HAMPCAS, thirty-eight psychodrama sessions were studied during 2011, corresponding to 148 HATs. In 23 of these, patients reported that they did not have "any important event to mention", resulting in 125 HATs with 208 valid units of analysis.

In this study we developed a categorization system to analyze clients' accounts about Psychodrama. The content analysis variables are divided into three domains: Action/Technique: (what the client, therapists or group did in the event; and which gave rise to its impact), Impact (the effect the event had on the client. The categories are divided into Helpful and Hindering Impacts) and Content (what the event was about for the client). In relation to the impact and context domains, the majority of the categories were equal to HAETCAS. The Action domain of HAMPCAS has completely new categories. Of these, the first 5 categories refer to stages of the Psychodrama session, the next 5 are the basic techniques used in MP and the last 9 are Other Techniques or Model specificities (see Tables 1, 2 and 3).

Table 2 Comparison between HAETCAS and HAMPCAS—impact

Impact	Haetcas (Elliott 1988)	Hampcas
Helpful	1. Self insight	1. Self-insight
	2. Other insight	2. Other Insight
	3. Self-awareness	3. Self-awareness
	4. Other awareness	4. Other awareness
	5. Positive self	5. Positive self
	6. Positive other	6. Positive other
	7. Self metaperception	7. Self metaperception
	8. Other metaperception	8. Other metaperception
	9. Problem clarification	9. Problem clarification
	10. Problem solution	10. Problem solution
	11. Alliance strengthening	11. Problem relativization
	12. Relief	12. Alliance strengthening
	13. Other specific helpful impacts	13. Group alliance strengthening
		14. Self-forgiveness
		15. Other-forgiveness
		16. Relief
		17. Other specific helpful impacts
Hindering	14. Unwanted thoughts	18. Unwanted experiences
	15. Therapist omissions	19. Therapist omissions
	16. Digression	20. Digression
	17. Poor fit	21. Poor fit
	18. Other hindering impacts	22. Relational weakening
		23. Other hindering impacts

Table 3 Comparison between HAETCAS and HAMPCAS—content

Domain	Haetcas (Elliott 1988)	Hampcas
Content	1. Self only	1. Self only
	2. Family of origin	2. Family of origin
	3. Marital family	3. Marital family
	4. Work	4. Work
	5. Other relationships	5. Other relationships
	6. Therapy	6. Therapy
	7. Other specific content	7. Intragroup
		8. Other specific content

4 Conclusion

This study briefly describes the first steps towards the development of a system with which to categorize the significant therapeutic events identified by patients in Psychodrama. The system known as HAMPCAS can potentially be used in studies within the change-process research paradigm by interpreting the words of patients about their treatment experiences. All in all, we believe that further research using HAMPCAS can help us to strengthen Psychodrama theory, close the gap between what theory claims and what clients gain, from a clinical point of view, in psychodrama sessions. Importantly this research starts to place psychodrama research, in line with its other psychotherapy allies, creating an evidence base.

Acknowledgements The authors would like to thank FEPTO-RC, Alfredo Soeiro and Rojas-Bermudez for their contribution in the development of HAMPCAS. We would also like to express our gratitude to the researchers, that participated in the validation of HAMPCAS as judges, for their availability. One of the authors of this paper (PA) is a grant holder of the Portuguese Foundation for Science and Technology (FCT; SFRH/BD/87308/2012).

References

Blatner, A. & Shaughnessy, M.F. (2003). An Interview with Adam Blatner about Psychodrama. North American Journal of Psychology, 5(1), 137–146

Booth, H., Cushway, D., & Newnes, C. (1997). Counselling in general practice: Clients' perceptions of significant events and outcome. *Couns Psychol Q, 10*, 175187.

Castonguay, L. G., Boswell, J. F., Zack, S. E., Baker, S., Boutselis, M., Hemmelstein, N., Jackson, J., Morford, M., Ragusea, S., Roper, J., Spayd, C., Weiszer, T., Borkovec, T., & Holtforth, M. (2010). Helpful and hindering events in psychotherapy: A practice research network study. *Psychotherapy: Theory, Research, Practice, Training, 47*, 327–344.

Cruz, A. (2014). *Perspectivas Integradoras Sobre o Psicodrama Moreniano: os teóricos, os terapeutas e os clientes*. Tese de Doutoramento. Porto: Universidade Fernando Pessoa.

Elliott, R. (1988). *Helpful aspects of experiential therapy content analysis system (HAETCAS): Rating manual*. Unpublished manuscript. Department of Psychology, University of Toledo.

Elliott, R. (1993). *Helpful aspects of therapy form*. http://www.experiential-researchers.org/instruments/elliott/hat.html.

Elliott, R. (2008). Research on client experiences of therapy: Introduction to the special section. *Psychotherapy Research, 18*(3), 239–242.

Elliott, R. (2010). Psychotherapy change process research: Realizing the promise. *Psychotherapy research: journal of the Society for Psychotherapy Research, 20*(2), 123–135.

Elliott, R., & James, E. (1989). Varieties of client experience in psychotherapy: An analysis of the literature. *Clinical Psychology & Psychotherapy, 9*, 443–467.

Elliott, R., James, E., Reimschuessel, C., Cislo, D., & Sack, N. (1985). Significant events and the analysis of immediate therapeutic impacts. *Psychotherapy, 22*(3), 620–630.

Friedlander, M., Haetherington, L., Constantino, M., Messer, S., Kortz, L., & Shaffer, K. (2011). *What's therapy got to do with it? Clients' explanations of corrective change*. Paper presented at the 42nd Meeting of the Society for Psychotherapy Research, Bern, Switzerland.

Gershefski, J., Arnkoff, D., Glass, C., & Elkin, I. (1996). Clients' perceptions of treatment for depression: I. Helpful aspects. *Psychotherapy Research, 6*, 233–247.

Hampson, N. (2008). Helpful aspects of therapy: An evaluation of dewsbury adult psychology service and a comparison of three classification systems [PhD thesis]. Leeds. United Kingdom: University of Leeds.

Jones, E. E., Wynne, M. F., & Watson, D. D. (1986). Client perception of treatment in crisis intervention and longer-term psychotherapies. *Psychotherapy, 23*, 120–132.

Levy, J., Glass, C., Arnkoff, D., Gershefski, J., & Elkin, I. (1996). Clients' perceptions of treatment for depression: II. Problematic or hindering aspects. *Psychotherapy Research, 6*(4), 249–262.

Mahrer, A., & Nadler, W. (1986). Good Moments in Psychotherapy: A preliminary review, a list, and some promising research avenues. *Journal of Consulting and Clinical Psychology, 54*(1), 10–15.

Sales, C., et al. (2007). Formulário—Aspectos Úteis da Terapia (HAT). [Protocol—Helpful Aspects of Therapy]. Universidade Autónoma de Lisboa, Unpublished manuscript.

Sales, C. M. D., Alves, P. C. G., Evans, C., & Elliott, R. (2014). The individualised patient-progress system: A decade of international collaborative networking. *Counselling and Psychotherapy Research, 14*(3), 181–191.

Timulák, L. (2003). Empowerment events in process-experiential psychotherapy of depression: An exploratory qualitative analysis. *Psychotherapy Research, 13*(4), 443–460.

Timulák, L., & Lietaer, G. (2001). Moments of empowerment: A qualitative analysis of positively experienced episodes in brief person-centred counselling. *Counselling and Psychotherapy Research, 1*(1), 62–73.

Wieser, M. (2007). Studies on treatment effects of psychodrama psychotherapy. In C. Baim, J. Burmeister, & M. Maciel (Eds.), *Psychodrama: Advances in theory and practice* (pp. 271–292). New York: Routledge/Taylor & Francis Group.

Ana Sofia Cruz, (1976), PhD; psychodramatist and psychodance director, clinical psychologist at the Community Psychiatry Unit of Psychiatric and Mental Health Service of Porto's Hospital Centre. Member of FEPTO-RC (Federation of European Psychodrama Training Organizations–Research Committee); trainer member of the Portuguese Society of Psychodrama; founding member of the Iberian Association of Psychodance Jaime Rojas-Bermudez.

Célia Maria Dias Sales, (1969), Phd; Associate Professor in Psychology, Vice-President of the Portuguese Association of Family and Community Therapy, Researcher of the Center for Psychology at the University of Porto, Portugal.

Gabriela Moita, (1963), PhD; psychologist, psychodrama educator and psychotherapist. Auxiliar Professor at Instituto Superior de Serviço Social do Porto (ISSSP). Member of Tatcher Commission of Portuguese Society of Psychodrama (SPP). Former Co-President of Federation of European Psychodrama Training Organizations (FEPTO) (2011–2013).

Paula G. Alves, (1983), MSc, PhD grantholder, psychologist, researcher at the Centre for Research and Social Intervention of the Lisbon University Institute; member of various international organisations, such as the Society for Psychotherapy Research, the Cochrane Drugs and Alcohol Group and the Academic Network of the Global Drug Survey.

Z Psychodrama Soziometr (2016) (Suppl) 15:69–81
DOI 10.1007/s11620-015-0296-7

HAUPTBEITRÄGE

Zeitschrift für Psychodrama und Soziometrie

The method of Interpretative Phenomenological Analysis in psychodrama research

Gabriela Dima · Mihaela Dana Bucuţă

Published online: 19 January 2016

Abstract Research in the field of psychodrama is rich with descriptions of experiences and case illustrations; however viewed through the lens of research many prove to be methodologically weak. This paper aims to introduce and propose Interpretative Phenomenological Analysis (IPA) as a valuable instrument for psychodrama research. For the purposes of this paper, the method will be described as three broad elements: the epistemological position; some guidelines for conducting research and an example of using IPA in psychodrama research. Studies using IPA bring an in-depth understanding and sense-making of the experiences of participants in various psychodrama groups, they reveal the therapeutic change process and the personal meaning of therapeutic outcomes.

The paper concludes with a discussion on the potential for IPA to contribute to the field of psychodrama research, directions for its use and its limitations. Whilst acknowledging that psychodrama research primarily needs experimentally conducted designs to achieve the mainstream standards of the scientific community, there is a need to increase the rigor of qualitative studies. Therefore this article is meant to act as a catalyst for more studies using Interpretative Phenomenological Analysis, the robustness of which will be useful for psychodrama research.

Keywords Psychodrama · Psychodrama research · Qualitative research · Interpretative Phenomenological Analysis

G. Dima (✉) · M. D. Bucuţă
Braşov, Romania
e-mail: dima.gabriela@unitbv.ro

M. D. Bucuţă
e-mail: mihaela.bucuta@ulbsibiu.ro

Die Methode der Interpretativ Phänomenologischen Analyse in der psychodramatischen Forschung

Zusammenfassung Im Bereich der Psychodrama-Forschung gibt es zahlreiche Fallstudien und Kasuistiken; betrachtet man diese jedoch durch deine reine Forschungsperspektive erscheinen sie methodologisch schwach zu sein. Der vorliegende Beitrag möchte die Interpretative Phänomenologische Analyse (IPA) als valides Instrument für die Psychodrama-Forschung vorstellen und vorschlagen. Zu diesem Zweck wird die Methode in Form dreier Elemente beschrieben: die erkenntnistheoretische Position, einige Richtlinien zur Durchführung von Forschung und ein konkretes Beispiel wie mithilfe von IPA Psychodrama-Forschung aussehen kann. Studien, die auf IPA basieren, fördern ein vertiefendes Verständnis und stellen einen Sinnzusammenhang der Erfahrungen der Teilnehmenden in unterschiedlichen Psychodramagruppen her; sie offenbaren außerdem den therapeutischen Prozess und die persönliche Bedeutung der therapeutischen Wirkung.

Der Beitrag schließt mit einer Diskussion, inwiefern das Potential der IPA zu Psychodrama-Forschung beitragen kann, wie sie angewandt werden kann und welche Beschränkungen es gibt. Auch wenn man anerkennt, dass Psychodrama-Forschung in erster Linie experimentell durchgeführte Forschungsdesigns benötigt, um den Mainstream-Standards der wissenschaftlichen Gemeinschaft zu genügen, gibt es auch einen steigenden Bedarf an qualitativen Studien. Aus diesem Grund ist dieser Beitrag auch als Katalysator für mehr Studien mit der IPA gedacht, deren Stärke für Psychodrama-Forschung im allgemeinen hilfreich sein kann.

Schlüsselwörter Psychodrama · Psychodrama-Forschung · Qualitative Forschung · Interpretativ Phänomenologische Analyse

1 The development of Interpretative Phenomenological Analysis (IPA)

The method of Interpretative Phenomenological Analysis (IPA) is a relatively recent addition to qualitative research methodology, introduced by Smith (1996) in the UK in the field of health psychology. Even though IPA is a young approach, a rapidly growing body of research has given it worldwide recognition with a steady increase in its application, particularly in clinical and counselling psychology and in related disciplines in human, social and health sciences (Smith et al. 2009; Brocki and Wearden 2006). IPA has three broad elements: an epistemological position, a set of guidelines for conducting research and a corpus of empirical research to date (Smith 2004).

1.1 Theoretical foundations

From the beginning IPA has been positioned as an integrative approach drawing on well-established philosophical positions. One important theoretical touchstone for IPA is phenomenology, which originated in Husserl's approach to constructing a philosophical science of consciousness (Smith 1996). IPA is phenomenological in that it is concerned with exploring experience and its perception. The second important theoretical foundation for IPA is hermeneutics, the theory of interpretation (Smith 1996; Smith et al. 2009). Heidegger's formulation of hermeneutic phenomenology as the study of person-in-context, and that person's relatedness to the "phenomena at hand", the 'Dasein' (literally 'there-being') implies a degree of reflexive awareness (Larkin et al. 2006). IPA implies a "*double hermeneutic*": in that participants make sense of their personal and social world, and the researcher tries to make sense of the participants' sense-making of their world (Smith and Osborn 2008, p. 53). The term '*interpretative phenomenological analysis*' signals the dual nature of the approach (Smith 1996, p. 264): the phenomenological requirement to understand and '*give voice*', exploring the participant's inside view on the phenomenon being studied, and the interpretative requirement to contextualise and '*make sense*' of these claims from a psychological perspective. Hence, a third significant influence for IPA is symbolic interactionism. Its central concern is the meanings individuals ascribe to events; however, those meanings are obtained through a process of social engagement and interpretation (Larkin et al. 2006).

Smith and his colleagues (Smith et al. 2009) positioned IPA among other qualitative approaches and not only discussed their epistemological connections and degree of overlap, but also what is distinctive about IPA. From the foundation of the method, Smith (1996) argues in his core paper "*Beyond the divide between cognition and discourse: Using interpretative phenomenological analysis in health psychology*" about IPA's concern with cognition and concepts of cognitive psychology and approaches of discourse analysis. IPA subscribes to social constructivism, but to a less strong form of it than discursive psychology or Foucauldian discourse analysis (Smith et al. 2009). There are more links between IPA and Foucauldian discourse analysis, because of their shared preoccupation with how the context contributes to the experiences of a person. Certainly IPA shares the basics of phenomenology with all phenomenological approaches among, which Van Manen (1990), Giorgi (1997), Ashworth (2003), Finlay (2008) in Smith et al. (2009); however, each of them articulates an approach in a different, specific way. Another important distinction has to be made between IPA and grounded theory, because there is a degree of overlap and it seems to be the main alternative method for researcher's considering IPA. Both approaches offer clear, systematic guidelines to conduct the study, however grounded theory aims to generate a theoretical level account of the phenomenon under study; by contrast, IPA focuses on the "micro analysis" of individual experience, which has the potential to contribute to more "macro accounts" (Smith et al. 2009, p. 202).

From a research perspective Smith (2004) defines IPA method in terms of three main characteristics: idiographic, inductive and interrogative. IPA is strongly *idiographic* with its focus on the study of the individual person, as opposed to nomothetic approaches allowing only group level claims; the commitment to the particular operates at the level of detail and depth of analysis, and understanding how particular experiences have been understood by particular people, in a particular context. IPA is an *inductive*, open and flexible approach to both, data collection and analysis. The analyst has to be able to engage with the data collected as much as possible with no preconceptions and predefined theoretical frameworks to allow for unanticipated themes to emerge during analysis. Furthermore, IPA is *interrogative* by engaging in a constructive dialogue with existing concepts and research. The in-depth analysis of case studies and its results are then discussed in relation to the existing psychological literature, interrogating and illuminating current research to make a contribution to psychology.

IPA studies are usually concerned with existential issues such as significant "*life transforming or life threatening*" moments (Smith 2004, p. 49), issues of significant consequence for the individual. It is considered to be particularly suited for "*unexplored territory where a theoretical pretext may be lacking*" enabling "*meaning and unexpected analysis*" of psychosocial issues to arise (Reid et al. 2005, p. 20).

1.2 Guidelines for conducting an IPA study

Smith et al. (1999) acknowledge that there is no single definitive way of doing IPA, but offer clear guidance and suggestions for the analysis, interpretation and writing up process, and also advice for researchers on how to adapt the method to their own particular way of working. Another helpful resource is the website (www.psyc.bbk.ac.uk/ipa)[1] set up to develop the community of IPA researchers, share knowledge, ensure support in planning and conducting IPA research projects, and provide answers to various questions and difficulties along the study.

In the following section some guiding principles are provided to help plan and conduct an IPA study.

1.2.1 Aims and research questions

Consistent with IPA theoretical foundations, research tends to focus on people's experiences and/or understandings of particular phenomena, on personal meaning and sense-making in a particular context for people who share a specific experience (Smith et al. 2009). Hence IPA is suitable to respond to broadly and openly framed research questions, which has been referred to in literature as 'big Q' research (Kidder and Fine 1987 cited in Smith and Eatough 2006). Some examples drawn from IPA studies in different fields are: How does a woman's sense of identity change during the transition to motherhood? (Smith 1999); How do gay men think about sex and sexuality? How do people who have complained about their medical treatment make sense of being angry? (Smith et al. 2009, p. 45); How do parents manage the challenge of living with an autistic child? What does jealousy feel like? How do people make a decision whether or not to have a genetic test? (Smith and Eatough 2006).

The psychodrama study using IPA reported in this paper was guided by following research questions: How do members of psychodrama therapy experience and make sense of therapeutic change? How do they experience and describe the group experience? (Dima and Bucuta 2012; Dima and Bucuta 2013).

1.2.2 Sampling and sample size

As an idiographic method, committed to bring depth, small sample sizes are the norm in IPA (Smith 2004). Brocki and Wearden's (2006) meta-analyses of IPA studies using interviews show ranges from one single case up to a number of 30 participants, higher number being reported when focus groups were used (Reid et al. 2005). The author of the method emphasized that "*there is no right answer to the question of the sample size*" (Smith et al. 2009, p. 51). However he observed that as the approach has matured and more studies were published, the sample sizes came down. Reid et al. (2005) asserted that "*less is more*" while also highlighting the power of single case studies. As a rough guide, a sample size of three to six or up to eight or ten can be reasonable (Smith and Eatough 2006; Smith et al. 2009).

IPA sampling tends to be purposive and broadly homogenous (Smith 2004; Smith et al. 2009). Purposive sampling enables to identify a more closely defined group for whom the research question has relevance and personal significance. Saturation is seen as a problematic concept in this context, as IPA studies are concerned with examining divergence and convergence in smaller samples (Brocki and Wearden's 2006, p. 94) trying to achieve both "*coherence and integration while preserving nuances*" as qualitative studies should strive for according to Elliott's guidelines for qualitative research studies (Elliot et al. 1999).

The IPA study described below was carried out on a sample of six research participants.

1.2.3 Data collection methods

Semi-structured face-to-face interviews are the preferred method for IPA (Brocki and Wearden 2006; Smith and Osborn 2008; Smith et al. 2009); they are capable of offering the rich and detailed data about personal experiences, thoughts, feelings related to the phenomenon under study. The IPA interview has to be "*participant-led in the fullest sense, yet guided by the researcher*" (Smith and Eatough 2006, p. 330). The interview guide is based on open and extensive questions, while the interviewer has to adopt a probing stance towards the participant's story. Close rapport and interviewing skills are essential. Smith et al. (2009) argue that unless the researcher has deeply engaged with the participant, listening actively and open to learning more about his life world, data will be too thin for analysis. Finlay (2008, p. 29) emphasises the crucial role of an appropriate "*phenomenological attitude*", defined as "*the process of retaining an emphatic openness to the world while reflexively identifying and restraining pre-understandings*".

Other methods of data collection used in published IPA studies were focus groups, electronic dialogue, postal questionnaires, diaries (Reid et al. 2005). IPA is suitable also for multi-perspectival studies, exploring one phenomenon from multiple perspectives (e.g. Clare 2002 in Smith et al. 2009), for comparison studies using comparison groups to study one phenomenon (Reid et al. 2005), or multiple interviews with the same participant (Flowers 2008).

1.2.4 Levels of data analysis

Similar to any qualitative analysis, IPA operates close to the text and involves a cyclical reading and re-reading of interview transcripts for a total immersing in the data. Smith et al. (2009) acknowledges the essence of IPA as being its analytic focus guided by a set of common processes (moving from the particular to the shared, from description to interpretation) and principles (understanding the participant's perspective and meaning-making of their experience in particular contexts). In empathy the researcher is required to put aside his/her own understandings in order to see the world anew, while still maintaining his/her position as researcher and being influenced by his/her biography. Finlay (2008, p. 3) compares this tension and contradictory motion to a dance between "*striving for reductive focus and being reflexively self-aware, between bracketing pre-understandings and exploiting them as a source of insight, between naive openness and sophisticated criticality*".

Smith et al. (1999) acknowledge that there is no single definitive way of doing IPA. They offer clear guidance, but also advice researchers to adapt the method to their own particular way of processing and doing interpretative work. The stages suggested are (Smith et al. 1999; Smith et al. 2009):

- Reading and re-reading;
- *Initial notes* written down first in the left-hand margin when reading line-by-line consisting of initial thoughts, possible codes, associations or connections that come in mind etc.;
- *Developing emergent themes, patterns* working through the initial notes and writing down in the right-hand margin themes that come forward, emphasizing both commonality and nuance; a dialogue between the coded text and the researcher's psychological knowledge is leading to the development of more interpretative accounts;
- *Searching for connections across emerging themes:* clusters of themes are produced by grouping together meaningful themes (righ-hand written notes are jotted down, to facilitate looking for connections) developing higher-order themes;
- A *master list* or *table of themes* (matrix) ordered coherently to illustrate the relationships between themes is developed;
- *Moving to the next cases*: a single respondent's transcript may be written up as a case-study, if not the analysis can be continued on a number of cases in different ways: either using the master-theme list from the first interview for the second interview and others, being open to identifying new arising themes and adding them; or beginning the process anew with the second interview producing a master-list for each interview and merging them into a consolidated list of master themes for the group of respondents.

The organization of all this material has to ensure that each theme is represented in the verbatim transcript and therefore analysis is a cyclical process of moving back and forward.

One of the current discussions in IPA is *levels of interpretation*. This is evidenced in the position between a "*hermeneutic of empathy*" and a "*hermeneutic of questioning, of critical engagement*" (Smith 2004). While the first level of analysis is more descriptive, the second level of analysis moves to more formal, theoretical connections, guided by the emerging themes. Good qualitative work clearly distinguishes between what the respondent said and the analyst's interpretation or account of it (Smith et al. 1999) *Writing up* is based on the master table of emerging themes and can be organized in two different ways:

Firstly, the analysis section is a substantial narrative account of all themes grounded in verbatim extracts, central to IPA to bring to the forefront participants' voices. A separate section is then devoted to make sense of the results from a theoretical position.

Secondly, each theme is taken in turn, described and linked to the existing literature at the same time (Smith et al. 1999).

The aim of IPA is to provide a detailed analysis of both convergence and divergence across cases, capturing the richness of each particular person investigated (Smith et al. 2009). Reflections on the research process and one's perceptions and conceptions are an essential part of IPA reporting (Brocki and Wearden 2006).

2 The development of psychodrama research

The method of psychodrama is based on theories of action, spontaneity and creativity (Moreno 2009). Wieser (2007, p. 272) comments on the status of psychodrama psychotherapy, which despite being well established in practice, has not yet been recognized by the scientific community mainly because studies have failed to attain mainstream standards.

Meta-analytical studies carried out on psychodrama research (Kipper and Ritchie 2003; Wieser 2007) found that psychodrama literature is abundant in ample description, case studies, clinical experiences, theoretical discussions, but little empirical evidence to demonstrate the efficiency of psychodrama psychotherapy. Another problem identified is the weak research designs and methodologies used. Consequently, the highest need for research in psychodrama is quantitative studies, especially using randomized control trials (RCT) to prove the treatment results.

In addition, a discussion about qualitative psychodrama research and its quality is also necessary. Hintermeier (2011) advises the use of already established methodological approaches for analyses of qualitative research data in order to meet scientific criteria. The author discusses a variety of qualitative methodologies used in psychotherapy research generally (e.g. content analysis, grounded theory, phenomenological analysis, conversational analysis etc.) and focuses on the contribution of the interpretative paradigm for psychodrama. Qualitative research is considered ideal to study psychodrama as it reflects the spontaneous and creative nature of psychodrama (Hintermeier 2011).

3 An example of IPA applied in psychodrama research

This section illustrates the use of Interpretative Phenomenological Analysis in a study on the experience and meaning-making of therapeutic change in psychodrama with participants preparing to become psychotherapists carried out by the authors (Dima and Bucuta 2012, 2013). The study sample was comprised of six adults, female, aged between 25 to 45 years. They participated in an average of 24 psychodrama sessions for personal therapy and had been part of two different groups. They were interviewed by the authors 2 to 4 months after ending of therapy.

The extensive matrix of themes is presented below, however for reasons of space only one theme will be presented and analysed in more detail.

3.1 The matrix of themes

Themes	Subthemes
The group experience	Acceptance and support
	Trust
	Identification: "I was not unique"
	Catharsis
	Feed-back
The therapeutic journey	The beginning: anxiety, uncertainty
	Holding back vs. openness
	Repression vs. emotional relief
	Judgemental vs. acceptance
	Self-knowledge
	Existential problems
	The ending
The experience of change	Transformation
	Self-worth and personal power
	Insight, clarification
	Experiential learning: 'I have learned…'
	Own rhythm
	Impact of change:
	'Me' before and after therapy
The authentic 'I'	I had the courage to be myself'
	'I regained myself'
	Self-acceptance
	Acting according to the authentic 'I'
The experience of therapy and psychodrama method	The experience of therapy
	The impact of techniques
	Playing
	Touching
	A 'unique' experience
The therapeutic relationship	The therapist
	Warmth, caring
	Trust
	Support and guidance

3.2 Phase one of IPA analysis: 'giving voice' to the experiences of participants

The theme '*The authentic I*' came to the forefront as one of the most significant therapeutic benefits for all participants and is described by the elements: '*I had the courage to be myself*', '*I regained myself*', '*self-acceptance*' and '*acting according to the authentic I*'.

The authentic encounter with the self and with others was possible after growing out of early group anxieties and defence mechanisms and a climate of emotional security, trust and mutual support developed: "*It is an honour to be trusted. I have also offered trust to my colleagues [...] There I could act and I could be seen as I really am [...] the memory of this, the fact that you can show yourself to people and discover the way you are together with them (crying)...*" (Maria)[2]. Psychodrama therapy encourages self-knowledge and self-development through encounters with other group participants and the use of its main technique of role reversal: "*I saw myself through their eyes and I realized that in fact I am the same person... me and myself seen through the eyes of others... and somehow this cheered me up and gave me the courage to be me, to not hide*" (Ioana).

The sub-theme '*I regained myself*' shows the significance of the feeling of congruency with oneself and the sense of fulfilment which derives from here. Liberating oneself from barriers and blockages developed over time and giving permission to be and manifest as they are brings people in touch with their deep, inner power put into motion: "*I can say that I am ME again [...] that brave person, with self-confidence, without fear of being judged [...] Now I am, I simply am, I feel free to say what I feel, what I live [...] I am simply ME. I think it was the greatest benefit, to accept myself as I am... without hiding from myself*" (Ioana). This is in fact one of the main aims of psychotherapy, helping people be in harmony with themselves. The way psychodrama method helps achieve this goal is by enacting life experiences on the scene and taking part in other group member's life scenes. One of the participants captured the process of becoming herself through psychodrama: "*I view it (therapy) as a way to see my life and become Me again, simply to relive my life or to live the feelings and thoughts and experiences of other colleagues*" (Maria).

In addition to discovering and getting in touch with the inner self, one important dimension to reveal the authentic 'I' is self-acceptance, mentioned by most participants and vividly expressed in Flavia's words: "*Something has changed and uh... it happened at one time (laughs)... I allowed myself to be me... Once my mother said at home: 'God, you're like a circus, you're like a spectacle on the street!' I was very lively dressed, very colourful and very relaxed [...] I think I have met ME in a new way and [...] I had the courage to be ME; I accepted ME in a much nicer way. It's what I felt.*" Part of the therapeutic change process for Flavia was the opportunity offered within the group to see herself from different perspectives, as perceived by others, enabling her to change self-perception, be more positive, accepting and loving of herself. All of this contributed to personal growth and gave her the courage to express her true self.

The last sub-theme, '*Acting according to the authentic 'I'*', comes as a corollary of the changes that have occurred during therapy. By enlargement of self-knowledge and regaining of oneself, one's power and sense of worth, participants were prepared to act in their lives more congruently with their own feelings and needs as was the case of Onelia: "*I gained once again the confidence that I somehow know what I am like and how I am on the inside [...] it gave me wings in a way... to do the things I want to do and make the changes that I want to make in my life and to develop myself the way I feel*".

Another research participant talks about her journey from being completely immersed and absorbed in her own situation, life problem, feeling constrained on a path to liberation and self-affirmation in the chosen direction: "*A former problem... which impacted on me ...like I wasn't me anymore, it was only this situation [...] I didn't know who I was [...] In a way I freed myself of much of the weight and... I now truly see myself as a free person and have my own way. My way is not that which somebody tries to impose to me; this is my path*" (Maria). It is recognized that finding personal meaning and direction in life and having the courage to assume one's own way equals self-actualization and self-fulfilment.

3.3 Phase two of IPA analysis: 'making-sense' of the experiences of participants

One of the main benefits of therapy mentioned by our participants was the authentic encounter with oneself and with others, the awareness, recuperation or acceptance of their authentic self.

Spontaneity and creativity, the basis of psychodrama (Moreno 2009) encourage the expression of the authentic self. Psychodrama is a positive, optimistic therapy in itself; the person is credited with being able to improve life in a creative way when freed from anxiety, manifesting themselves spontaneously and entering into authentic relationships with oneself and with others (Boria 1991). Boria (2005) believes that the person able to speak with freedom in a group context will live an experience of vital essence, of existence, 'to be'. This experience was found in all participants studied. They lived the freedom of expression, the courage to be 'I', exposing themselves unhidden within the group. Retrieving the 'I' lost in the face of life and suffering, recognition and recovery of those parts of their self, long forgotten or repudiated, had a profound liberating effect.

The feeling of self-recovery, a different way of encounter with oneself and authentic expression was possibly due to increased self-knowledge, self-understanding and self-acceptance, beyond weaknesses. For participants in this study 'accepting' meant more than just 'tolerating' and 'resigning to'; acceptance includes the courage to recognize and accept imperfection, as Christophe Andre (2009, p. 91) said: "*Not guilty, not pathetic, but imperfect!*". Discrepancies to the ideal image are tolerated and accepted without feelings of shame, anxiety, lack of value etc., and reality appears more clearly. Finally, human nature begins to be seen and accepted "*as it is, and not as they would like to be*" (Maslow 2007, p. 270). Self- actualization and authentic self-expression are reflected in a more natural and spontaneous behaviour, with more freedom, releasing participants from a conduct of limitations and sustained effort, as experienced before therapy (Maslow 2007).

Transformations described above reported by group participants could be seen as an emergent result of psychodrama mechanisms of change described by Boria (1997) as active in a psychodrama group and leading to changes in people's functioning. Among this mechanisms, which proved to have a significant impact for some of the participants are: playing as an expression of the holistic person and their complex inner world (e.g. Maria); the power of 'breaking scenario/pattern', especially by the use of role reversal, the interrelation between the 'actor' and 'observer' roles (e.g. Ioana); the restructuring of the way significant figures in the life's of the participants were internalized (their 'internal theater', e.g mother for Flavia). Role reversal, the main technique in psychodrama, appears to have had a huge impact on the participants. This reflects the finding of Kipper and Ritchie's (2003) meta-analysis of the effectiveness of psychodrama techniques, which demonstrate that role reversal is the most effective intervention.

According to the existential perspective, achieving the contact with and liberating the personal power of that regained 'I' is one of the sources of personal meaning. Yalom (2010) suggests that people should seek to accomplish self-actualization and devote themselves to realize their innate potential. It is the case of those who have completed therapy knowing and taking responsibility of the personal life path.

4 Appreciating the advantages and limitations of the IPA method in psychodrama research

This paper aims to introduce and propose the method of Interpretative Phenomenological Analysis as a valuable contribution to psychodrama research, despite its limitations. IPA seemed to be particularly attractive for applied psychologists due to its capacity to make links between understanding and sense-making of the person and theoretical frameworks of mainstream psychology (see Brocki and Wearden 2005; Reid et al. 2005; Smith et al. 2009, p. 186). Common to IPA and psychodrama is the commitment to, and value of, the 'subjective truth' of participants. Larkin et al. (2006) emphasize that phenomenology is important because it returns people's perspectives and experiences to the forefront of psychological study. Smith et al. (2009, p. 32) argue that "*there is a considerable ground for the development of phenomenological-informed models for the synthesis of multiple analyses from small studies and single cases*". Although psychodrama is studied mainly using qualitative approaches and case studies, IPA's contribution is its capacity to offer insights into experiences of personal events, the therapeutic process, and the personal meaning of therapeutic outcomes (Smith et al. 2009, p. 193). As a consequence the experiences of various psychodrama patient groups could be explored. The method is suitable for process-oriented psychotherapy research.

Another advantage of IPA is derived from its already established recognition and capacity to lead to good quality research data. Psychodrama research does not lack qualitative studies, but it is weak in terms of rigorous methodologies capable to meet scientific criteria. Elliott et al. (1999) developed specific criteria to evaluate qualitative research studies in psychology and related fields in order to ensure their validity and scientific standard. Seven criteria are presented: owning one's perspective, situating the sample, grounding in examples, providing credibility checks, coherence, accomplishing general versus specific research tasks, and resonating with readers. They suggest that authors should be able to address how they meet the intentions of the guidelines for reporting qualitative research, or their rationales for meeting alternative standards (Elliot et al. 1999, p. 221).

Methods for credibility checks are: use of research participants or others similar to them; use of multiple qualitative analysts, an external '*auditor*' or the original analysts undergoing a '*verification step*' and reviewing the data for discrepancies; overstatement or errors; comparing two or more different qualitative perspectives; and triangulation with external factors or quantitative data (Elliot et al. 1999). The study exemplified here made use of multiple qualitative analysts and a '*verification step*'.

While admitting that analysis is, unavoidably, an interpretative process, it tries to be as visible and recoverable as possible by use of the verbatim extracts (Smith et al. 2009). However, there are studies when the extension and depth of description and analysis is sacrificed, because of space and word limitations for publishing.

IPA is strongly connected to the interpretative or hermeneutic tradition for its recognition of the researcher's central role in analysis (Smith 2004). The concept of reflexivity and the need to critically interrogate the impact of the researcher's subjectivity is a vital facet of the Interpretative Phenomenological Analysis (Smith 2004; Finlay 2008), yet authors do not always explicitly or comfortably discuss such issues

(Brocki and Wearden 2006). Reflection does not undermine the value of the findings for the researched group but enriches it. Reflexivity may be assisted by acknowledgement of the researcher's particular perspectives, research interests, theoretical groundings and reasons for undertaking a particular study. This admits that qualitative research results "*reflect the researcher as much as the researched, but this remains tacitly rather than openly acknowledged in many cases*" (Salmon's in Brocki and Wearden 2006, p. 99).

Another issue in IPA is levels of interpretation. While novice researchers tend to be too descriptive, Smith (2004) illustrates ways to dig deeper and offer an increased depth of analyses (e.g. social comparison, temporal, metaphorical). However, one of IPA's strengths is its flexible and inductive approach, which is able to engage with new areas lacking a theoretical pretext (Reid et al. 2005).

To conclude, we believe that the research profile of psychodrama would significantly increase by using stronger research methodologies in qualitative studies and moving from a more descriptive level of analysis to a deeper and more interpretative one.

Notes

1 IPA website established by the founder of the method, Jonathan Smith to provide a corpus of data on published research studies, and UK and international contacts.

2 The name of research participants were changed for anonymity reasons.

References

Andre, C. (2009). *Imperfecţi, liberi şi fericiţi. Practici ale stimei de sine. (Imperfect, free and happy. Practices for self-esteem)*. Bucharest: Ed. Trei.

Boria, G. (1991). *Spontaneita e incontro nella vita e negli scritti di J.L. Moreno*. Padova: UPSEL.

Boria, G. (1997). *Lo psicodramma classico*. Milano: Franco Angeli.

Boria, G. (2005). *Psicoterapia psicodrammatica—Sviluppi del modello moreniano nel lavoro terapeutico con gruppi di adulti*. Milano: Franco Angeli.

Brocki, J. M., & Wearden, A. J. (2006). A critical evaluation of the use of interpretative phenomenological analysis (IPA) in health psychology. *Psychology and Health, 21*(1), 87–108.

Dima, G., & Bucuta, M. D. (2012). The experience of therapeutic change for psychologists preparing to become psychotherapists. Procedia—Social and Behavioral Sciences. Proceedings of the 2nd International Conference "Psychology and the Realities of the Contemporary World"- PSIWORLD 2011, vol. 33, 672–676.

Dima, G., & Bucuta, M. D. (2013). "Îmbrăţişând schimbarea": în căutarea sensului vieţii ("Embraching change": the search for life meaning]. In M. Milcu (Ed.), *Cercetarea aplicativă în psihologia modernă: Premise metodologice (Applied research in modern psychology: methodological premises)* (pp. 73–78). Bucharest: University Press.

Elliott, R., Fischer, C. T., & Rennie, D. L. (1999). Evolving guidelines for publication of qualitative research studies in psychology and related fields. *British Journal of Clinical Psychology, 38*, 215–229.

Finlay, L. (2008). A dance between the reduction and reflexivity: explicating the "Phenomenological Psychological Attitude". *Journal of Phenomenological Psychology, 39*, 1–32.

Flowers, P. (2008). Temporal tales: The use of multiple interviews with the same participant. *Qualitative Methods in Psychology Newsletter, 5*, 24–27.

Hintermeier, S. (2011). Qualitative Psychodramaforschung. In C. Stadler & M. Wieser (Eds.), *Psychodrama: Empirische Forschung und Wissenschaft*. Wiesbaden: VS Verlag.

Kipper, D. A., & Ritchie, T. D. (2003). The effectiveness of psychodramatic techniques: A meta-analysis. *Group Dynamics: Theory, Research and Practice*, *7*(1), 13–25.

Larkin, M., Watts, S., & Clifton, E. (2006). Giving voice and making sense in interpretative phenomenological analysis. *Qualitative Research in Psychology, 3,* 102–120.

Maslow, A. H. (2007). *Motivaţie şi Personalitate (Motivation and personality)*. Bucharest: Ed. Trei.

Moreno, J. L. (2009). *Scrieri fundamentale: despre psihodramă, metoda de grup şi spontaneitate. (Fundamental writings: About psychodrama, group method and spontaneity)*. Bucharest: Ed. Trei.

Reid, K., Flowers, P., & Larkin, M. (2005). Exploring lived experience. *The Psychologist, 18*(1), 20–23.

Smith, J. A. (1996). Beyond the divide between cognition and discourse: Using interpretative phenomenological analysis in health psychology. *Psychology and Health, 11,* 261–271.

Smith, J. A. (1999). Towards a relational self: Social engagement during pregnancy and psychological preparation for motherhood. *British Journal of Social Psychology, 38,* 409–426.

Smith, J. A. (2004). Reflecting on the development of interpretative phenomenological analysis and its contribution to qualitative research in psychology. *Qualitative Research in Psychology, 1,* 39–54.

Smith, J. A., & Eatough, V. (2006). Interpretative phenomenological analysis. In G. M. Breakwell, S. Hammond, C. Fife-Schaw, & J. A. Smith (Eds.), *Research methods in psychology* (3rd edn.). London: Sage Publications.

Smith, J., & Osborn, M. (2008). Interpretative phenomenological analysis. In J. Smith (Ed.), *Qualitative psychology: A practical guide to research methods* (2nd edn.). London: Sage Publications.

Smith, J. A., Jarman, M., & Osborn, M. (1999). Doing interpretative phenomenological analysis. In M. Murray & K. Chamberlain (Eds.), *Qualitative health psychology*. London: Sage Publications.

Smith, J. A., Flowers, P., & Larkin, M. (2009). *Interpretative phenomenological analysis: Theory, method and research*. London: Sage Publications.

Wieser, M. (2007). Studies on treatment effects of psychodrama psychotherapy. In C. Baim, J. Burmeister, & M. Maciel (Eds.), *Psychodrama: Advances in theory and practice*. London: Routledge.

Yalom, I. D. (2010). *Psihoterapia existenţială (Existential psychotherapy)*. Bucharest: Ed. Trei.

Gabriela Dima is a psychologist, psychodrama psychotherapist and supervisor within the Romanian Association of Classical Psychodrama. She received her PhD from Queen's University Belfast, School of Sociology, Social Policy and Social Work using Interpretative Phenomenological Analysis for the qualitative component of her research. Currently she is an associate professor at Transilvania University of Brasov.

Mihaela Dana Bucuţă is an associate professor at Lucian Blaga University of Sibiu and received her PhD from Babeş-Bolyai University with the thesis "The experience of depression and significance of psychosocial support: An interpretative phenomenological approach". She is teaching and supervising graduate and postgraduate students using IPA in their research. She is a psychodrama psychotherapist and supervisor within the Romanian Association of Classical Psychodrama.

Z Psychodrama Soziometr (2016) (Suppl) 15:83–100
DOI 10.1007/s11620-015-0312-y

HAUPTBEITRÄGE

Zeitschrift für Psychodrama und Soziometrie

Interkulturelle Netzwerkforschung. Kulturvergleichende Analyse sozialer Netzwerkcharakteristika und Lebenszufriedenheit

Christian Stadler · Michaela Pötscher-Gareiß · Michael Wieser · Claudia Otto · Zsuzsa Marlok

Online publiziert: 4. Januar 2016

Zusammenfassung Soziale Netzwerke und ihre Charakteristika in verschiedenen Kulturen wurden im Hinblick auf den Zusammenhang mit der Lebenszufriedenheit mithilfe eines Fragebogens untersucht. Netzwerktypen (zentralisiert, dezentral, verteilt) wurden, unterschieden nach Ländern (Hong Kong und Ungarn), mit der Lebenszufriedenheit anhand der Dienerskala (Diener et al., J Pers Assess 49:71–75, 1985) in Zusammenhang gebracht. Die Ergebnisse dieser explorativen Studie wurden mit den Ergebnissen einer Studie aus 2009 zusammengeführt, welche Deutschland/Österreich, Israel und Nigeria zu denselben Parametern untersuchte. Die einzelnen Kulturen unterscheiden sich signifikant hinsichtlich der Netzwerktypen und

C. Stadler (✉)
Konrad-Adenauer-Str. 27,
85221 Dachau, Deutschland
E-Mail: praxisstadler@arcor.de

M. Pötscher-Gareiß
Klagenfurter Straße 41,
9300 St. Veit an der Glan, Österreich
E-Mail: michaela.gareiss@aau.at

M. Wieser
Department of Psychology, Alpen-Adria-Universität Klagenfurt,
Universitätsstr. 65–67,
9020 Klagenfurt am Wörthersee, Österreich
E-Mail: michael.wieser@aau.at

C. Otto
Ernsberger Str. 19,
81241 München, Deutschland
E-Mail: praxis@psychotherapy-otto.com

Z. Marlok
Semmelweis Egyetem Egészségügyi Közszolgálati Kar Mentálhigiéné Intézet,
1428 Pf.: 370, Budapest, Ungarn
E-Mail: marlok.zsuzsa@public.semmelweis.univ.hu

der Lebenszufriedenheit. Die Erkenntnisse legen eine kultursensitive Psychotherapiepraxis nahe.

Schlüsselwörter Kultur · Soziale Netzwerke · Netzwerktypen · Lebenszufriedenheit · Soziometrie · Psychodrama · Kultursensitive Psychotherapie und Beratung

Intercultural network-research. Cross-cultural analysis of social network characteristics and life satisfaction

Abstract Social networks and their characteristics in different cultures were analyzed regarding their correlation with life satisfaction. Based on their questionnaire responses participants from Hong Kong and Hungary were assigned to one of three types of network (centralized, decentralized, distributed) and their life satisfaction was surveyed using Diener Scale (Diener et al., J Pers Assess 49:71–75, 1985). The outcome of our explorative study was combined with the results of a study from 2009, which explored samples from Germany/Austria, Israel and Nigeria focusing on the same issues. The individual cultures differ significantly in terms of network types and life satisfaction. The findings promote a culture-sensitive psychotherapy practice.

Keywords Culture · Social networks · Network characteristics · Life satisfaction · Sociometry · Psychodrama · Cross cultural psychotherapy and counselling

1 Lebenszufriedenheit und die Bedeutung sozialer Beziehungen im Kulturvergleich

In Anlehnung an Spörrle et al. (2009) orientiert sich unsere Untersuchung an der Kulturdefinition von Fiske et al. (1998). „Culture is defined as the belief systems and value orientations, that influence customs, norms, practices, and social institutions, including psychological processes (language, caretaking practices, media, educational systems) and organizations (media, educational systems)" (Fiske et al. 1998; zit. nach APA 2003, S. 380). Spörrle et al. (2009) machten die Relevanz kultureller Faktoren für die psychodramatische Praxis deutlich. Die explorative Studie in Ungarn sowie in Hong Kong erfolgte 2011 als weiterführende Datenerhebung. Damit konnten zusätzliche Aspekte aufgenommen und die bestehenden Erkenntnisse ergänzt bzw. erweitert werden. Globalisierung und Migrationsbewegungen machen die Welt multikultureller, so dass TherapeutInnen, BeraterInnen und Coaches in der täglichen Praxis mit KlientInnen bzw. PatientInnen aus verschiedenen Kulturen zu tun haben, und es damit von praktischer Relevanz sein kann, sich mit Zusammenhängen von Lebenszufriedenheit, kultureller Herkunft und sozialen Netzwerken zu beschäftigen.

Lebenszufriedenheit ist eine Kenngröße subjektiven Wohlbefindens und damit ein Faktor psychischer Gesundheit (vgl. Diener et al. 1998). Es besteht bei der Konzeptualisierung von Lebenszufriedenheit eine geringe Einschränkung, da sie vor allem den kognitiven Aspekt abbildet; sie muss durch affektive Qualitäten ergänzt werden. Was Lebenszufriedenheit angeht, stellten Diener et al. (1995) und Myers und Diener (1995) fest, dass die ausgeprägtesten interkulturellen Unterschiede hinsichtlich der Skala Kollektivismus-Individualismus bestehen. Aus diesem Grund haben wir uns entschlossen in der Untersuchung weiterhin die Netzwerkcharakteristika heranzuziehen, d. h. dasselbe Erhebungsinstrument wie bei der 2007er Datenerhebung zu verwenden.

Uchida et al. (2004) resümieren in ihrer Übersichtsarbeit zu kultureller Konstruktion von Wohlbefinden, dass sich das soziale Eingebundensein in kollektivistisch geprägten Kulturen, wie z. B. der ostasiatischen, stärker auf das subjektive Wohlbefinden auswirkt, als dies in individualistisch geprägten Kulturen, wie z. B. in der euro-amerikanischen Kultur der Fall ist.

Die Daten aus der Studie von Spörrle et al. konnten diese Hypothesen nicht eindeutig bestätigen (vgl. Spörrle et al. 2009, 312 ff.), haben jedoch zu folgenden soziometrischen Ergebnissen und neuen Hypothesen geführt (Soziometrie vgl. Stadler 2013):

1. In der deutsch-österreichischen Stichprobe war ein signifikant positiver Zusammenhang zwischen Netzwerkgröße und Lebenszufriedenheit nachzuweisen, während die Netzwerkstruktur, also die Art des Netzwerks, für die Lebenszufriedenheit keine Rolle zu spielen scheint.
2. In Israel werden verteilte Netzwerke eher funktional erlebt; zentralisierte und dezentrale eher dysfunktional.
3. In Nigeria besteht ein positiver Zusammenhang zwischen Lebenszufriedenheit und dezentralen Netzwerken.
4. Aus den Punkten 1–3 wurde die Hypothese formuliert, dass „in individualistischen Kulturen [...] die Struktur persönlicher sozialer Netzwerke weniger starken Einfluss [...] auf die Lebenszufriedenheit [hat], da hier insgesamt soziale Eingebundenheit [...] eine geringere Rolle für die Lebenszufriedenheit spielt als in kollektivistischen Kulturen." (Spörrle et al. 2009, S. 314)
5. Es wurde aufgrund der Datenlage die Vermutung formuliert, „dass eine bestimmte Struktur persönlicher sozialer Netzwerke gerade dann für das Individuum funktional und somit der Lebenszufriedenheit zuträglich ist, wenn sie der im betreffenden kulturellen Kontext üblicherweise anzutreffenden Netzwerkstruktur entspricht – möglicherweise, weil unter dieser Voraussetzung eine höhere Kompatibilität und erweiterte Anschlussfähigkeit an die sozialen Netzwerke anderer Personen besteht, die zum weiteren Ausbau des eigenen Netzwerks dann effizienter genutzt werden kann." (a. a. O., S. 314) Mit anderen Worten: Menschen fühlen sich mit den Netzwerken am wohlsten, die in ihrer Kultur am häufigsten vorkommen. Lebenszufriedenheit könnte unter diesem Blickwinkel stark mit Zugehörigkeit zu tun haben.

2 Methode

2.1 Stichprobe und Durchführung

Insgesamt haben an der Studie bislang 357 Personen zu zwei Untersuchungszeitpunkten teilgenommen (Länderverteilung siehe Tab. 1 und Abb. 1). Der Mittelwert des Alters liegt bei 33,45 Jahren mit einer Standardabweichung von 12,87 (siehe Abb. 2). Es sind 198 Männer in der Stichprobe (was einem prozentualen Anteil von 55,5 % entspricht) und 154 Frauen. 5 Personen haben keine Angabe zum Geschlecht gemacht (siehe Abb. 3). Die untersuchten Kulturen sowie die jeweils teilnehmenden Personen wurden nicht systematisch oder randomisiert, sondern nach Verfügbarkeit als Ad-hoc-Stichprobe ausgewählt.

Die Teilnehmenden füllten auf freiwilliger Basis und unentgeltlich einen Fragebogen aus. Sie wurden auf die Anonymität der Daten sowie die Beschränkung der Verwendung für wissenschaftliche Zwecke hingewiesen. Die Beantwortung des Fragebogens nahm in etwa zehn Minuten in Anspruch. Die Stichprobe Deutschland/Österreich, Israel und Nigeria wurde 2007 erhoben, die in Hong Kong und Ungarn 2011 und 2012.

Die Stichprobe verteilt sich aktuell auf fünf Kulturen.

3 Messinstrumente

3.1 Lebenszufriedenheit

Die Lebenszufriedenheit wurde mit der „Satisfaction with Life Scale" (SWLS) von Diener et al. (1985) gemessen (vgl. Spörrle et al. 2009, S. 306 f.). Mit fünf Items bildet das Instrument die subjektive Einschätzung der allgemeinen Lebenszufriedenheit auf einer siebenstufigen Likertskala ab. Dieses Verfahren zur Erfassung von Lebenszufriedenheit gilt bzgl. Messgenauigkeit und Validität als gesichert, selbst bei kulturvergleichenden Studien. Kuppens et al. (2008) wiesen über verschiedene Kulturen hinweg gute Reliabilitäten von durchschnittlich alpha = 0,78 für diese Skala nach. Auch in der vorliegenden Studie ergab die Reliabilitätsprüfung einen Wert von cronbachs alpha = 0,807.

Kang et al. (2003) erkannten in unterschiedlichen Kulturen Zusammenhänge zwischen dem Mittelwert der Diener-Skala und „kulturspezifisch für Lebenszufriedenheit bedeutsamen Variablen wie Selbstwert und Beziehungsqualität" (Spörrle et al. 2009, S. 307).

Tab. 1 Länderstichprobe

		Häufigkeit	Prozent
Gültig	Deutschland/Österreich	76	21,3
	Israel	31	8,7
	Nigeria	108	30,3
	Hong Kong	34	9,5
	Ungarn	108	30,3
	Gesamtsumme	357	100,0

Abb. 1 Länderverteilung

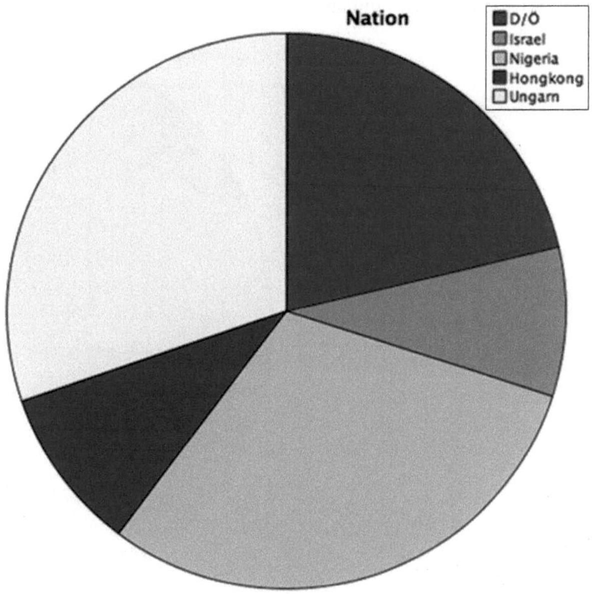

Abb. 2 Altersverteilung

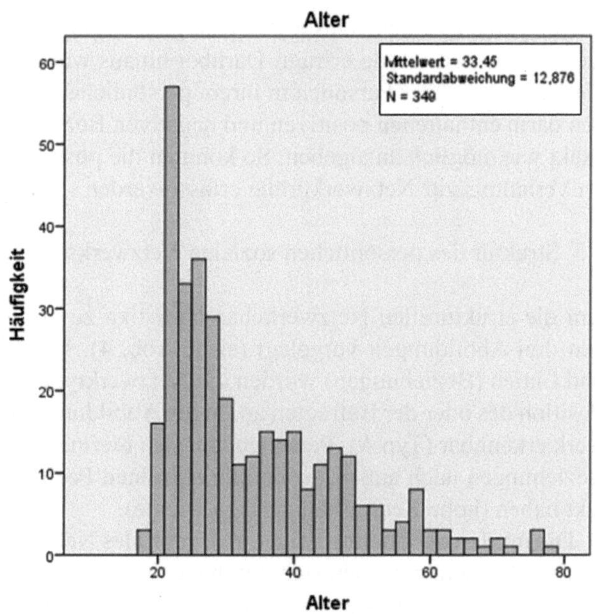

3.2 Größe des persönlichen sozialen Netzwerks und Valenz der Beziehungen innerhalb des Netzwerks

In einer kurzen Instruktion wurde den Teilnehmenden erläutert, dass das persönliche soziale Netzwerk aus denjenigen Personen besteht, „mit denen man selbst in regelmäßigem (auch medienvermitteltem) Kontakt steht, unabhängig von der (positiven

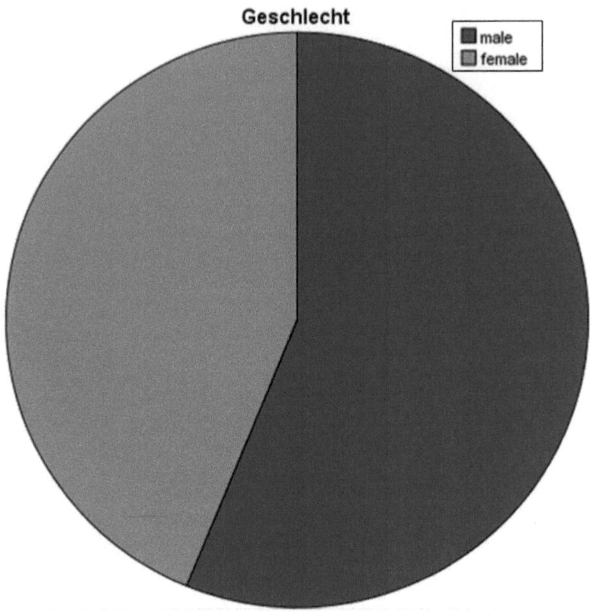

Abb. 3 Geschlechterverteilung

oder negativen) Valenz dieser Beziehungen." (Spörrle et al. 2009, S. 307). Die Anzahl dieser Personen wurde erfragt. Darüber hinaus wurden die Teilnehmenden gebeten, die Gesamtzahl der Personen in ihrem persönlichen sozialen Netzwerk getrennt nach den darin enthaltenen positiven und negativen Beziehungen als numerischen Wert so exakt wie möglich anzugeben. So konnten die positiven und negativen Beziehungen im Verhältnis zur Netzwerkgröße erfasst werden.

3.3 Struktur des persönlichen sozialen Netzwerks (Netzwerktypen)

Um die strukturellen Netzwerkcharakteristika zu erfassen, wurden den ProbandInnen drei Abbildungen vorgelegt (siehe Abb. 4). Mit Hilfe von Punkten (Personen) und Linien (Beziehungen) wurden die Netzwerktypen dargestellt. Der Pfeil zeigt die Position des oder der Befragten an. In der Abbildung links ist ein zentralisiertes Netzwerk erkennbar (Typ A). Personen, die sich hierin wiedererkennen, haben zahlreiche Beziehungen nach außen, wobei die einzelnen Personen untereinander keinen Kontakt haben (hohe Zentralität, geringe Dichte).

Die mittlere Abbildung zeigt ein dezentrales Netzwerk (Typ B). Personen, die sich hierin erkennen, zeichnen sich durch weniger direkte Kontakte aus; diese haben eine Reihe anderer Kontakte, die z. T. auch untereinander Kontakte haben (mittelhohe Zentralität, mittelhohe Dichte).

Die rechte Abbildung stellt ein verteiltes Netzwerk dar (Typ C). Die Personen haben nur wenige direkte Kontakte zu anderen, die aber alle auf ähnliche Weise wiederum mit Anderen vernetzt sind (geringe Zentralität und hohe Dichte).

Die Netzwerktypen wurden im Fragebogen insgesamt folgendermaßen dargestellt und erfragt (Spörrle et al. 2007):

Abb. 4 Netzwerktypen (Spörrle et al. 2007)

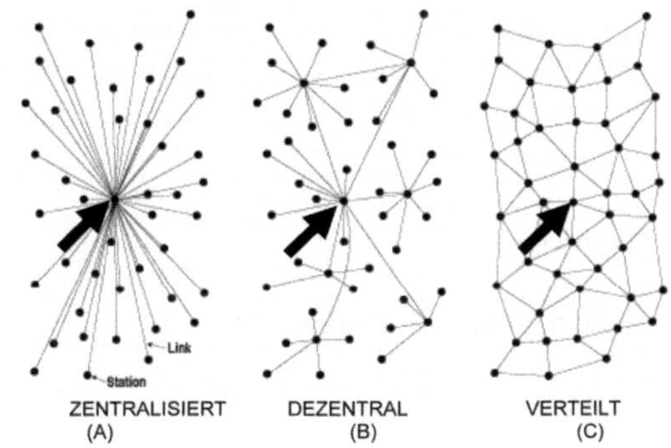

Wie sehr ähnelt Ihr Netzwerk einem der drei oben dargestellten Netzwerke?

Mein persönliches soziales Netzwerk ähnelt dem NETZWERK (A) ...

0	1	2	3	4	5	6	7	8	9	10
überhaupt nicht										sehr stark

Mein persönliches soziales Netzwerk ähnelt dem NETZWERK (B) ...

0	1	2	3	4	5	6	7	8	9	10
überhaupt nicht										sehr stark

Mein persönliches soziales Netzwerk ähnelt dem NETZWERK (C) ...

0	1	2	3	4	5	6	7	8	9	10
überhaupt nicht										sehr stark"

Kommen wir nun zur *Form Ihres persönlichen Netzwerks*:
Unten sehen Sie drei Arten von Netzwerken abgebildet. Die erste Abbildung (A) stellt ein zentralisiertes Netzwerk dar, in dem eine zentrale Person mit den anderen Netzwerkmitgliedern verbunden ist, diese aber nicht oder nur wenig untereinander verbunden sind.
Das zweite Netzwerk (B) ist ein dezentrales Netzwerk, in dem einige Personen zentrale Positionen einnehmen und mit einigen anderen Netzwerkmitgliedern verbunden sind.
Das dritte Bild (C) zeigt ein verteiltes Netzwerk, in dem es keine zentralen Positionen gibt, aber alle Netzwerkmitglieder Verbindungen zu einigen anderen haben, die ihrerseits wieder weitere Verbindungen haben.
Der Pfeil markiert die Position Ihrer Person innerhalb des jeweiligen Netzwerks. Selbstverständlich ist kein persönliches Netzwerk einem der drei dargestellten Typen genau gleich – dies sind jeweils nur sehr typische Beispiele für verschiedene Formen, die ein Netzwerk annehmen kann.

Der Netzwerktyp gibt auf der individuellen Ebene darüber Aufschluss, welche Art von Networking ein Individuum betreibt. Mit der Erhebung wird gleichzeitig deutlich, ob ein bestimmter Netzwerktyp für eine Kultur typisch ist. Um diesen Wert zu bestimmen, wurde zunächst erhoben, welcher Netzwerktyp dem Eigenen am ehesten ähnelt (Maximum aus den Ähnlichkeitsratings: wo wurde der höchste Wert vergeben? Bei gleich hohem Wert auf zwei Typen = Mischratings). Danach wurde für jede Kultur der prozentual häufigste vorkommende Wert berechnet.

Als Einschränkung für die Ergebnisse besteht, wie bereits bei der 2009-er Untersuchung, die Problematik, dass bei den Netzwerktypen zwei Kriterien gleichzeitig bedient wurden: Zentralität und Dichte (vgl. Spörrle et al. 2009, S. 314).

4 Ergebnisse

4.1 Netzwerkcharakteristika

4.1.1 Anteil positiver/negativer Beziehungen innerhalb der Netzwerke abhängig von Kulturen

Während in der ersten Studie (Länder: D/Ö, Israel, Nigeria) ein interpretierbarer Zusammenhang von Kultur und positiv bzw. negativ valenzierter Beziehungen erkennbar war, ist dies in der zweiten Studie (Ungarn und Hong Kong) statistisch nicht signifikant. In der Nigeria-Stichprobe waren signifikant mehr negative und weniger positive Valenzen im Netz angegeben worden als in Deutschland/Österreich und Israel (vgl. Spörrle et al. 2009, S. 308 f.)

4.1.2 Korrelation Lebenszufriedenheit und Netzwerktypen A/B/C sowie positive Einstellung zu den Netzwerken und negative Einstellung zu den Netzwerken über alle Kulturen

Für diese Fragestellung wurde das kulturelle Kriterium vernachlässigt; es wurden ausschließlich die Korrelationen zwischen Lebenszufriedenheit und den Netzwerktypen innerhalb der fünf untersuchten Kulturen berechnet. Die Korrelationen sind allesamt nicht besonders hoch, weisen eher auf Tendenzen hin.

Folgende Korrelationen konnten festgestellt werden (siehe Tab. 2):

1. Die Lebenszufriedenheit und der Netzwerktyp A weist einen mäßigen negativen Zusammenhang von $r = -0{,}212$ auf. Das bedeutet, je zentralisierter der Netzwerktyp, desto weniger Lebenszufriedenheit, bzw. je mehr Lebenszufriedenheit, desto weniger zentralisiert ist der Netzwerktyp. Es handelt sich um ein statistisch signifikantes Ergebnis; der Zusammenhang ist aber nicht sehr stark ausgeprägt.
2. Die Lebenszufriedenheit und der Netzwerktyp B weist keinen Zusammenhang auf $r = 0{,}049$.
3. Die Lebenszufriedenheit und der Netzwerktyp C weist keinen Zusammenhang auf $r = 0{,}012$

Tab. 2 Korrelationen Lebenszufriedenheit und Netzwerktypen

	Korrelation Spearman
Lebenszufriedenheit Netzwerk A $N=297$	$-0{,}212^{a}$
Lebenszufriedenheit Netzwerk B N309	0,049
Lebenszufriedenheit Netzwerk C $N=306$	0,012
Lebenszufriedenheit Positive Einstellung zur Netzwerknutzung $N=335$	$0{,}188^{a}$
Lebenszufriedenheit Negative Einstellung zur Netzwerknutzung $N=331$	$-0{,}142^{a}$

[a]Sign. Korrelationen

Tab. 3 Kultur und Netzwerktyp

	Netzwerk A		Netzwerk B		Netzwerk C	
Kultur	*N*	Gruppierter Median	*N*	Gruppierter Median	*N*	Gruppierter Median
D/Ö	59	2,80	64	5,82	63	5,00
Israel	29	2,13	30	*8,28*	29	*3,10*
Nigeria	78	*5,00*	83	5,52	85	*6,06*
Hong Kong	31	2,89	32	*7,00*	30	4,89
Ungarn	104	1,60	106	7,00	104	4,42

4. Positive Einstellung zur Netzwerknutzung und Lebenszufriedenheit $r=0{,}188$. Der Zusammenhang ist statistisch signifikant leicht positiv. Je positiver das eigene soziale Netzwerk valenziert wird, desto höher die Lebenszufriedenheit.
5. Negative Einstellung zur Netzwerknutzung und Lebenszufriedenheit ergeben einen mäßig negativen Zusammenhang von $r=-0{,}142$. Der Zusammenhang ist statistisch signifikant leicht negativ. Je negativer das eigene soziale Netzwerk valenziert wird, desto niederer die Lebenszufriedenheit.

4.1.3 Netzwerktypen und Kulturen

Hypothese 1 *Die einzelnen Kulturen unterscheiden sich intraindividuell hinsichtlich des Netzwerkes Typ A, B oder C (Tab. 3).*

Blickt man zunächst auf die Netzwerktypen, kann folgendes festgestellt werden:

Hinsichtlich der Nutzung *Netzwerk A (zentralisiert)* gibt es signifikante Unterschiede (p-Value$\leq$0,001, Chi^2=30.869, df=4) zwischen den Kulturen. Nigeria nutzt das Netzwerk A signifikant am häufigsten zu allen anderen Nationen (3.Spalte senkrecht).

Netzwerk B (dezentral) unterscheidet sich ebenfalls signifikant (p-Value$\leq$0,001, Chi^2=26.810, df=4) zwischen den Kulturen. Die Tabelle lässt erkennen, dass Israel diejenige der fünf Kulturen ist, die das dezentrale Netzwerk am häufigsten benutzt.

Bis auf Nigeria haben alle anderen Kulturen den Netzwerktyp B (dezentral) als den häufigsten genannt; der Unterschied zu den anderen Netzwerktypen A und C war jedoch nicht immer statistisch signifikant.

Bei Betrachtung des *Netzwerks C (verteilt)* kann man ebenfalls signifikante Unterschiede erkennen (p-Value=0,039, Chi^2=10.097, df=4). Hier ist erkennbar, dass Nigeria im Kulturenvergleich diese Form von Netzwerk am häufigsten nutzt, signifikant häufiger als alle anderen und Israel signifikant weniger als alle anderen. Zwischen D/Ö, Hong Kong und Ungarn gibt es nur geringe Unterschiede.

Wird der Blick auf die Länder gerichtet, fällt folgendes auf:

D/Ö nutzt den *Netzwerktyp A* (zentralisiert) deutlich weniger als die anderen beiden Netzwerktypen.

In Israel, Hong Kong und Ungarn wird statistisch signifikant besonders *Netzwerktyp B* (dezentral) genutzt.

In Nigeria werden alle drei Netzwerktypen in etwa gleich genutzt.

Tab. 4 Lebenszufriedenheit abhängig von Kultur

Kultur	Personen	Gruppierter Median
D/Ö	76	27,27
Israel	31	26,25
Nigeria	102	18,55
Hong Kong	34	21,67
Ungarn	107	25,82

In der Tab. ist der gruppierte Median auf der Diener Skala zu erkennen: Je höher dieser Wert umso höher die Lebenszufriedenheit.

Tab. 5 Ränge Geschlechtsunterschiede

	Geschlecht	*N*	Mittlerer Rang	Rangsumme
	Männer	192	146,64	28154,00
Dienerskala	Frauen	153	206,08	31531,00
	Gesamt	345		

Tab. 6 Dienerskala Geschlechtsunterschiede

Geschlecht	Mittelwert	*N*	Standardabweichung	Gruppierter Median
Männer	21,3958	192	5,94738	20,9167
Frauen	24,8627	153	5,47369	25,8889
Gesamt	22,9333	345	5,98775	23,6129

4.2 Assoziationen von Kulturen, Geschlecht und Alter bzgl. Lebenszufriedenheit

Neben den Ergebnissen zu den Netzwerktypen konnten verschiedene Zusammenhänge mit der Lebenszufriedenheit erfasst werden.

Hypothese 2 Verschiedene Kulturen unterscheiden sich hinsichtlich der subjektiven Einschätzung von Lebenszufriedenheit.

Die Berechnungen erfolgten mittels Kruskal Wallis; dies ist ein Verfahren für ordinalskalierte Variablen, da die Voraussetzungen für die Varianzanalyse (gleich große Gruppen; homogene Varianzen) nicht gegeben ist. Sie liefern ein signifikantes Ergebnis ($Chi^2=89{,}80$, df=4, p-Value$\leq 0{,}001$). Beim Vergleich der gruppierten Mediane über die Nationen lässt sich erkennen, dass die niedrigste Lebenszufriedenheit in Nigeria zu finden ist. Nigeria unterscheidet sich hinsichtlich der Lebenszufriedenheit von allen anderen Nationen. Danach folgt in diesem Vergleich Hong Kong, das sich hinsichtlich der Lebenszufriedenheit ebenfalls von allen anderen Nationen unterscheidet. Für Deutschland/Österreich wurde der höchste Zufriedenheitswert ermittelt.

Als Einschränkung der Aussage gilt hier die Tatsache, dass es sich um keine randomisierten Gruppen handelt.

Hypothese 3 Männer und Frauen unterscheiden sich hinsichtlich der Lebenszufriedenheit, unabhängig davon, welcher Nation sie angehören.

Frauen weisen mit einem gruppierten Median von 25,89 signifikant höhere Werte (p-Value$\leq 0{,}001$) auf als Männer, deren gruppierter Median bei 20,92 liegt (Tab. 5, 6).

Hypothese 4 Zusammenhang von Alter und Lebenszufriedenheit.

Der Korrelationskoeffizient von $r = 0{,}283$ weist hinsichtlich Lebensalter und Lebenszufriedenheit auf einen mittleren Zusammenhang hin.

5 Diskussion

Zur Hypothese 1 Die einzelnen Kulturen unterscheiden sich intraindividuell hinsichtlich des Netzwerktypus.

Entgegen unseren Ausgangsvermutungen scheint kein starker Zusammenhang zwischen Netzwerktypen und Lebenszufriedenheit über alle fünf untersuchten Kulturen hinweg zu bestehen. Einzig der zentralisierte Netzwerktypus scheint einen leicht negativen Zusammenhang mit Lebenszufriedenheit aufzuweisen. Es sei dahingestellt, ob aufgrund der nicht randomisierten Stichprobe hier eine weitere Variable wie z. B. Bildungsniveau oder gesellschaftliche Schicht das Ergebnis beeinflusst hat. Für die erhobene Stichprobe gilt eine leichte Tendenz, dass bei vorliegender Zentralisierung des individuellen Netzwerkes die subjektiv empfundene Lebenszufriedenheit eher leidet.

Ebenfalls ein leichter Zusammenhang besteht bei der Einstellung zum Netzwerk und der Lebenszufriedenheit: bei positiver Einstellung zum eigenen Netzwerk ist die Lebenszufriedenheit höher, bei negativer niederer. Dies kann als Beleg für die Bedeutung passend empfundener sozialer Eingebundenheit interpretiert werden: fühlt eine Person sich mit der Art der Netzwerkeingebundenheit wohl, trägt dies direkt zu subjektivem Wohlbefinden bei.

Wird der Zusammenhang der Netzwerktypen und Kulturen in den Fokus genommen, wird insgesamt deutlich, dass die Nutzung nur einer Form von Netzwerk für die Kulturen nicht vorliegt. Alle untersuchten Kulturen nutzen alle Formen von Netzwerken, auch wenn es einzelne Unterschiede gibt; so wird z. B. der zentralisierte Netzwerktyp (A) innerhalb der deutsch-österreichischen Stichprobe am seltensten gewählt.

Wird der Ländervergleich zugrunde gelegt, fällt auf, dass das zentralisierte Netzwerk (A) von den untersuchten Kulturen am häufigsten von Nigeria genutzt wird. Dies hat eine hohe Plausibilität, da Nigeria unter den Kulturen diejenige ist, die im Vergleich traditionell wahrscheinlich an zentralen Gesellschafts-, Familien- und Stammesstrukturen orientiert ist. Relativierend muss aber bei dieser Aussage berücksichtigt werden, dass in der nigerianischen Stichprobe alle Netzwerktypen (beinahe) gleichverteilt vorkamen.

Die höchsten Werte über alle Kulturen mit Ausnahme von Nigeria hat das dezentrale Netzwerk (B). Dies ist ein Ergebnis, das einerseits sehr gut zum psychodramatischen Rollenverständnis passt, und andererseits gut anschlussfähig ist an Konzepte von Patchwork-Konstellationen. Menschen erleben sich in unterschiedlichen Rollen je nach ihrer sozialen Situation. Die dezentralen Netzwerke bilden verschiedene Subgruppen (Cluster) ab, die in ihrer Gesamtheit für eine Person das gesamte soziale Netzwerk bilden. Hier könnten weitere differenzierende Untersuchungen folgen, welche die einzelnen Cluster in den dezentralen Netzwerken zum Ziel haben.

Hintergründe zur Erklärung der Ergebnisse in Ungarn Die Netzwerkcharakteristika in Ungarn (vgl. Fruzsina und Beáta 2012) haben sich in den letzten 30–35 Jahren stark verändert, weg vom Familizismus, hin zu mehr Wahlbeziehungen. In den 80er Jahren haben die Netzwerke eine relativ kleine Größe mit starker Instrumentalität und Dominanz der familiären Beziehungen, sowie wenig Freundschaften aufgewiesen. Die traditionelle ost-mitteleuropäische Form, für die meist nur eine oder keine Vertrauensperson, häufig der oder die EhepartnerIn, war typisch. In den 90er Jahren nach der Wende sind die Kontakte sogar noch weiter zurückgegangen. Dies hat zu tun mit der Veränderung der Familienstruktur: immer weniger Ehen, viele Scheidungen, häufige Partnerwechsel, kleiner werdende Familien. Dadurch sind Vertauenspersonen eher ein Freund, eine Freundin oder KollegIn geworden. Erst seit 2005 besteht wieder eine Tendenz zu mehr Kontakten, und neben oder statt den familiären Beziehungen immer mehr Gewicht auf den Freundschaften. Die Qualität der familiären und Freundschaftsbeziehungen hat sich auch stark verändert. Die familiären Beziehungen werden nicht mehr nur als Pflicht empfunden, sondern weisen immer häufiger Charakteristika von Freundschaft auf; man hat Kontakt mit Personen aus der Familie, auf die man Lust hat, und die eher als Freunde betrachtet werden können: es wird gewählt. Freunde helfen häufig in schwierigen Situationen, was früher eher die Aufgabe der Familie war.
Diese Sachverhalte kann die vorliegende Untersuchung nicht abbilden, da sie die Formen der Netzwerke (familiär oder freundschaftlich) nicht unterscheidet, aber es wäre eine lohnenswerte differenzierende Untersuchung. Auch Kohorteneffekte sind bei der großen Altersverteilung der Untersuchung nicht zu identifizieren: es ist bekannt, dass die Personen über 60 in Ungarn sehr wenig Kontakte haben, fast keine FreundInnen oder intime Beziehungen, nur die Familie.

Zur Hypothese 2 Verschiedene Kulturen unterscheiden sich hinsichtlich der subjektiven Einschätzung von Lebenszufriedenheit.

Deutschland/Österreich, Israel und Ungarn haben hier in etwa gleiche Werte, während Nigeria den niedersten Wert aufweist, gefolgt von Hong Kong. Betrachtet man sich den Reliabilitätskoeffizienten nur für die nigerianische Stichprobe so beträgt cronbachs alpha = 0,59, was einen möglichen Hinweis auf die Kultursensitivität des Messinstrumentes gibt.

Hier müsste eventuell mit einem anderen, weniger kultursensitiven, Instrument nachuntersucht werden, aber auf jeden Fall eine ausführliche soziologische Untersuchung erfolgen, welche diese Ergebnisse valide interpretieren kann. Möglicherweise hat das Ergebnis bei beiden Kulturen Nigeria und Hong Kong mit nicht passenden Messinstrumenten zu tun. Inhaltlich könnten wir die Hypothese aufstellen, dass beide Kulturen zum Erhebungszeitraum in einer gesellschaftlichen Umbruchsituation waren, die zu niederen Zufriedenheitswerten bei der untersuchten Population geführt haben. In Nigeria bestanden zum Untersuchungszeitpunkt starke Verwerfungen, die sich zwischen Norden und Süden, Islam und Christentum sowie armen und reichen

Bevölkerungsgruppen manifestierten. In Hong Kong erfolgte 1997 der Anschluss an China, so dass sich die Menschen in der Sonderverwaltungszone in einer Umbruchsituation mit erheblich mehr Einfluss der Volksrepublik China befinden.

Hintergründe zur Erklärung der Ergebnisse in Hong Kong Im Artikel von Spörrle et al. (2009) wurde bereits diskutiert, dass soziale Eingebundenheit im ostasiatischen (kollektivistisch geprägten) Kulturkreis bedeutsamer für subjektives Wohlbefinden ist als im westlich-amerikanischen (individualistisch geprägten) Kulturkreis. Es wird Bezug genommen auf den theoretische Rahmen von Markus und Kitayama (1991), die folgendes beschreiben: Das individuelle Wohlbefinden hängt bei interdependenter Selbstkonstruktion (im ostasiatischen Kulturkreis) stark von der Realisierung positiver sozialer Beziehungen ab, die als Teil des eigenen Selbst angesehen werden. Wohingegen bei unabhängiger Selbstkonstruktion (im euroamerikanischen Kulturkreis) die soziale Bestätigung positiver Attribute des eigenen Selbst besondere Bedeutung für das individuelle Wohlbefinden hat (Uchida et al. 2004). Soziale Eingebundenheit trägt also in kulturspezifisch unterschiedlicher Weise zum subjektiven Wohlbefinden bei. In der chinesischen Kultur besteht eine starke Bezogenheit auf die Familie und es bestehen Verbindlichkeiten bis hin zu starken Verpflichtungen innerhalb der Familie. Dies erfüllt Bedürfnisse nach Sicherheit, Stabilität sowie Zugehörigkeit. Yu-Chien Kuan und Häring-Kuan (2007) benennen die seit Jahrhunderten bestehende Sippenhaft in der chinesischen Gesellschaft als Ursache des starken Zusammenhaltes in den Familien. Dabei sind chinesische Familien bis zu mehreren Hundert Personen große Sippen. Selbst entfernt Verwandte werden in der Sippe herzlich aufgenommen und es wird mit ihrer Unterstützung in allen Lebensbereichen gerechnet. Es besteht eine starke Hierarchie im chinesischen Familiensystem mit dem Vater als Oberhaupt. Die Ein-Kind-Politik, die jedoch nicht für Hong Kong gilt, hat diese Hierarchie in den vergangenen Jahren verändert.

In Hong Kong besteht seit vielen Jahren neben der traditionell chinesischen Kultur ein großer Einfluss durch andere Kulturen, so dass die hier erfassten Ergebnisse nicht allgemein auf die chinesische Kultur übertragen werden können. Ganz davon abgesehen, dass auch innerhalb Chinas viele Minderheiten leben, und ca. 40 verschiedene Kulturen zusammenleben. Der Großteil der Hongkonger ImmigrantInnen kam aus der Provinz Kwangtung, Südchina (Siu-kai 1978) und sprach kantonesisch. Siu-kai (1978) betont, dass für die Anpassung an das neue Umfeld mit all den Unsicherheiten und psychologischen Anspannungen das Familiensystem eine wesentliche Rolle spielte.

Mit jeweils 133.000 (Zahl von 2011) Personen sind die bedeutendsten Minderheiten IndonesierInnen und PhilipinerInnen, beide vor allem als Hausangestellte tätig. Danach folgen InderInnen, PakistanerInnen, NepalesInnen, JapanerInnen und Thais. Es leben etwa 30.000 US-amerikanische, jeweils 20.000 kanadische, australische und britische StaatsbürgerInnen in dem Territorium, daneben auch ca. 10.000 Menschen aus Frankreich, ca. 3000 Deutsche, 1200 SchweizerInnen und 400 ÖsterreicherInnen. Einen großen Einfluss hatte die britische

Kultur während der Kolonialzeit (1843–1997). Ngo (1999) betont die positiven Aspekte der Kolonialisierung in Form der Entwicklung Hong Kongs von einer unbedeutenden Fischer-Insel zu einer Metropole. Aktuell gilt Hong Kong als Sonderverwaltungszone der Chinesischen Republik mit Beibehaltung der freien Marktwirtschaft. Das demokratisch-marktwirtschaftliche System soll mindestens für 50 Jahre bestehen bleiben (Ngo 1999). 95 % Prozent der EinwohnerInnen sind chinesischer Abstammung mit überwiegend kantonesischer Muttersprache (Wikipedia). Bei der vorliegenden Untersuchung wurden chinesisch-stämmige EinwohnerInnen Hong Kongs befragt. Nicht erfasst wurde dabei deren kultureller Hintergrund, was in einer weiteren Untersuchung zu differenzieren wäre. Einen Einfluss hätte zum Beispiel, ob es sich um ehemalige Flüchtlinge aus der Volksrepublik China oder deren Nachkommen handelt. Zusätzliche wäre interessant, ob die ProbandInnen Auslandserfahrungen in Form von mehrjähriger Schulausbildung oder Studienaufenthalten im westlichen Ausland haben. Vor allem letzteres ist in Hong Kong sehr üblich und hat sehr wahrscheinlich Auswirkungen auf die Lebenszufriedenheit und die sozialen Netzwerke.

Was die soziometrische Fragestellung in Abhängigkeit von den Netzwerken angeht, also den Zusammenhang von Netzwerktypus und Lebenszufriedenheit und von Netzwerktypus und Kultur, kann zusammenfassend festgehalten werden, dass je zentralisierter die Netzwerke sind, desto eher sinkt die Lebenszufriedenheit, und dass bis auf Nigeria der Netzwerktyp B, also die dezentralen Kontakte in den untersuchten Kulturen am häufigsten anzutreffen sind.

6 Implikationen für Forschung und Praxis

Vertiefend könnte den drei genannten Hypothesen im Bereich soziometrischer Forschung nachgegangen werden:

Zusammenhang von Netzwerkbildung und Kultur:

1. Anhand der Ergebnisse sind Ähnlichkeiten über die Kulturen bzgl. ihrer Netzwerk-Bildung deutlich geworden (z. B. Deutschland/Österreich, Israel, Hong Kong und Ungarn bei Wahl des Netzwerkes B). Vertiefende Fragestellungen ergeben sich aus den vorliegenden Daten vor allem für das dezentrale Netzwerk (B): Welche Subgruppen (Familie, FreundInnen, ArbeitskollegInnen, elektronische Kontakte wie Mail, Chat, Internet) verstecken sich hinter den einzelnen dezentralen Clustern? Ist es wichtig voneinander unabhängige Cluster zu haben, und ist das eine Entsprechung einer inneren Rollenpatchworklage? Welche Clustercharakteristika wirken salutogen (Größe, Nähe, Art), welche sind eher der psychischen Gesundheit abträglich? Wie wird die Clusterstruktur der dezentralen Netzwerke bewertet? Diese Fragestellung knüpft an Fragestellungen zur Identitätsbildung und innere wie äußere Patchwork-Konstellationen an (vgl. Keupp 1999; 2004; Seiffge-Krenke 2012; Stadler 2015; Stadler 2016).

2. Zusammenhang von Lebenszufriedenheit und Gender: Hier scheinen in den untersuchten Stichproben die Frauen vorne zu liegen. Die Ergebnisse einer allgemeinen Fragebogenuntersuchung wie der Dienerskala können hier weiter ausdifferenziert werden. Was sind die genauen Faktoren, die Frauen im Schnitt mehr Lebenszufriedenheit angeben lassen als Männer?
3. Auch der Zusammenhang von Lebenszufriedenheit und Kultur müsste näher untersucht werden, zum einen mit einer deutlich größeren Stichprobe, zum anderen mit weniger kultursensitiven Messinstrumenten.

Relevant für die Praxis ist es, wie bereits 2009 beschrieben (Spörrle et al.), den kulturellen Hintergrund bei der Beziehungsaufnahme und –gestaltung in der Therapie bzw. Beratung zu berücksichtigen. Besonders das dezentrale Netzwerk scheint in Deutschland/Österreich, Israel, Hong Kong und Ungarn das verbreitetste zu sein. Aber dieser Fakt darf nicht überbewertet werden, denn alle Kulturen nehmen alle Netzwerke; es scheint wichtiger für die Lebenszufriedenheit zu sein, dass man auch mit seiner Art des Netzwerks in die vorherrschende Kultur passt als dass man einen bestimmten Netzwerktypus präferiert. Das Netzwerk wird in der Regel in Beratungen und Therapie besonders dann als Ressource verstanden werden, wenn es dezentrale Strukturen aufweist.

Unabhängig von den festgestellten Ähnlichkeiten gilt nach wie vor, dass „kulturelle Unterschiede mit Unterschieden in psychischen Prozessen einhergehen und dass Unterschiede hinsichtlich der Selbstkonstruktion zur sozialen Umwelt eine Erklärung für diese psychischen Unterschiede bieten können. Sich solcher kulturellen Unterschiede bewusst zu sein und in der therapeutischen wie beraterischen Praxis zu berücksichtigen kann zur Verwirklichung einer kultursensitiven Psychotherapie beitragen (zu kultureller Kompetenz in psychologischer Beratung siehe: Sue 1998; Sue und Sue 2003)“ (Spörrle et al. 2009, S. 300). Aber es gilt auch als bestätigt (Pederson et al. 2008), dass die individualistische Perspektive in Beratungs-Settings geeigneter ist als die kollektivistische, unabhängig vom kulturellen Hintergrund. Die AutorInnen gehen sogar so weit, dass sie den Einfluss der jeweiligen historischen Wurzeln einer Person auf das Beratungssetting als minimal betrachten. Diese Feststellung dürfte zu einer weiteren soziometrischen Untersuchung provozieren.

Danksagung Anne-Christin Schmidt und Manuel Funk sei für die Mithilfe bei der Dateneingabe herzlich gedankt.

Literatur

American Psychological Association (APA). (2003). Guidelines on multicultural education, training, research, practice, and organizational change for psychologists. *American Psychologist, 58*, 377–402.

Diener, E., Emmons, R. A., Larsen, R. J., & Griffin, S. (1985). The satisfaction with life scale. *Journal of Personality Assessment, 49*, 71–75.

Diener, E., Diener, M., & Diener, C. (1995). Factors predicting the subjective well-being of nations. *Journal of Personality and Social Psychology, 69*, 851–851.

Diener, E., Sapyta, J. J., & Suh, E. (1998). Subjective well-being is essential to well-being. *Psychological Inquiry, 9*, 33–37.

Fiske, A., Kitayama, S., Markus, H. R., & Nisbett, R. E. (1998). The cultural matrix of social psychology. In D. Gilbert, S. Fiske & G. Lindzey (Hrsg.), *The handbook of social psychology* (4. Aufl., S. 915–981). San Francisco: McGraw-Hill.

Fruzsina, A., & Beáta, D. (2012). Az interperszonális kapcsolathálózati struktúra átrendeződése Magyarországon. In I. Kovách, C. Dupcsik, T. P. Tóth & J. Takács (Hrsg.), *Társadalmi integráció a jelenkori Magyarországon* (S. 343–356). Budapest: Argumentum Kiadó.

Kang, S. M., Shaver, P. R., Sue, S., Min, K. H., & Jing, H. (2003). Culture-specific patterns in the prediction of life satisfaction: Roles of emotion, relationship quality, and self-esteem. *Personality and Social Psychology Bulletin, 29*, 1596–1608.

Keupp, H. (2004). Fragmente oder Einheit? Wie Identität heute geschaffen wird. http://www.ipp-muenchen.de/texte. Zugegriffen: 14. Sept. 2004.

Keupp, H., Ahbe, T., Gmür, W., Höfer, R., Mitzscherlich, B., Kraus, W., & Straus, F. (1999). *Identitätskonstruktionen. Das Patchwork der Identitäten in der Spätmoderne*. Hamburg: Rowohlt.

Kuan, Y., & Häring-Kuan, P. (2007). *Der China Knigge*. Frankfurt a. M.: Fischer.

Kuppens, P., Realo, A., & Diener, E. (2008). The role of positive and negative emotions in life satisfaction judgement across nations. *Journal of Personality and Social Psychology, 95*, 66–75.

Markus, H. R., & Kitayama, S. (1991). Culture and the self: Implications for cognition, emotion, and motivation. *Psychological Review, 98*, 224–253.

Myers, D. G., & Diener, E. (1995). Who is happy? *Psychological Science, 6*, 10–19.

Ngo, T. W. (1999). *Hong Kongs History: State and Society under colonial rule*. London: Routledge.

Pederson, P. B., Draguns, J. G., Lonner, W. J., & Trimble, J. E. (2008). *Counselling across Cultures*. Los Angeles: Sage Publications.

Seiffge-Krenke, I. (2012). *Therapieziel Identität. Veränderte Beziehungen, Krankheitsbilder und Therapie*. Stuttgart: Klett-Cotta.

Siu-kai, L. (1978). *Utilitarianistic familism: the basis of political stability in Hong Kong*. Hong Kong: Social Research Center, Chinese University of Hong Kong.

Spörrle, M., Strobel, M., & Stadler, C. (2007). Netzwerkfragebogen.

Spörrle, M., Strobel, M., & Stadler, C. (2009). Netzwerkforschung im kulturellen Kontext: Eine kulturvergleichende Analyse des Zusammenhangs zwischen Merkmalen sozialer Netzwerke und Lebenszufriedenheit. *Zeitschrift für Psychodrama und Soziometrie, 8*(2), 297–319. doi:10.1007/s11620-009-0059-4.

Stadler, C. (Hrsg.). (2013). *Soziometrie. Messung, Darstellung, Analyse und Intervention in sozialen Beziehungen*. Wiesbaden: Springer VS.

Stadler, C. (2015). Wenn zwei, drei, vier… Atome aufeinandertreffen. Psychodramatherapie bei inneren und äußeren Patchwork-Lagen. *Zeitschrift für Psychodrama und Soziometrie, 14*(1), 15–27.

Stadler, C. (2016). *Ich bin viele. Umgang mit Rollen, Anteilen, States und Typen. Die Vielfalt verstehen und entwickeln*. München: ERV.

Sue, S. (1998). Search of cultural competency in psychotherapy and counseling. *American Psychologist, 53*, 440–448.

Sue, D. W., & Sue, D. (2003). *Counseling the culturally diverse: Theory and practice* (4. Aufl.). New York: Houghton Mifflin.

Uchida, Y., Norasakkunkit, V., & Kitayama, S. (2004). Cultural constructions of happiness: Theory and empirical evidence. *Journal of Happiness Studies, 5*, 223–239.

Claudia Otto, Diplom-Psychologin, Psychodrama-Therapeutin, in Weiterbildung zur Psychologischen Psychotherapeutin (Tiefenpsychologie/ Erwachsene/ Einzel und Gruppe), Trainerin für Autogenes Training, in eigener Praxis in München; Co-Leitung in Selbsterfahrungs- und Weiterbildungsgruppen am Moreno Institut Edenkoben/ Überlingen; Dozentin für Psychologie an der Berufsfachschule für Krankenpflege der Klinikum Freising GmbH (Lehrkrankenhaus).

Christian Stadler, Diplom-Psychologe, Psychologischer Psychotherapeut (TFP), Psychodrama-Therapeut (DFP, IAGP), Supervisor (PSR), EMDR-Therapeut, Praxis in Dachau (Psychotherapie, Supervision, Mediation, Coaching); akkreditiert bei der bayerischen Psychotherapeutenkammer für Weiterbildung, Supervision und Selbsterfahrung, als Weiterbildungsleiter und Supervisor beim Moreno Institut Edenkoben/ Überlingen und als Supervisor beim Institut für Bildung und Entwicklung (Caritasverband München und Freising).

Michaela Pötscher-Gareiß, Mag.a. Humanwissenschaftlerin an der Pädagogischen Hochschule Kärnten, Viktor Frankl Hochschule, an der Abteilung für Schulentwicklung. Kooperationspartnerin im FWF-Projekt LIFE „Lebensereignisse, Ressourcen und Weisheit". Ehemalige Universitätsassistentin für Entwicklungs- und Pädagogische Psychologie und an der Abteilung für Angewandte Psychologie und Methodenforschung an der Alpen-Adria Universität. Externe Lehrende an der Fachhochschule in Kärnten am Studiengang. „Gesundheit und Soziales" und an der Alpen-Adria Universität Klagenfurt „Psychologie".

Michael Wieser, Mag. Dr.phil., Ass.-Prof.; Psychologe, Psychodramatrainer und Psychodramatherapeut. Mitglied des Board of Directors der Internationalen Vereinigung für Gruppentherapie und Gruppenprozesse (IAGP); Vorsitzender der beratenden Versammlung der IAGP-Mitgliedsorganisationen; Vize-Präsident der Moreno Museum Gesellschaft; Mitherausgeber von Psychotherapie Forum; Redaktionsmitglied der Zeitschrift für Psychodrama und Soziometrie; Verwalter der internationalen Psychodrama Bibliographie; Träger des Zerka T. Moreno Preises.

Zsuzsa Marlok, Dr. (PhD Erziehungswissenschaft). Dozentin an der Semmelweis Universität Budapest im Institut für Mentalhygiene. Lehrerin, Fachfrau für Mentalhygiene, Psychodramaleiterin, Bibliodramaleiterin, Familientherapeutin. Seit 2013 Lehr-Psychodrama- und Lehrbibliodrama. Arbeitsschwerpunkte: Psychodrama Selbsterfahrungs- und Ausbildungsgruppen, Psychodrama im Einzelsetting, Beratung, Familientherapie, Fortbildungen und Workshops zum Thema Psychodrama in Gruppen und im Einzelsetting.

Z Psychodrama Soziometr (2016) (Suppl) 15:101–118
DOI 10.1007/s11620-015-0311-z

HAUPTBEITRÄGE

Zeitschrift für Psychodrama und Soziometrie

Das „Hilfs-Ich" jenseits der „Weißen Wand": Eine psychodramatische Kasuistik zur Simulation und Reduktion von Zwangsmaßnahmen in der Psychiatrie

Stephan Debus · Ullrich Ahrens

Online publiziert: 22. Dezember 2015

Zusammenfassung Psychiatrische Zwangsmaßnahmen (Fixierung, Zwangsmedikation, Isolation) beschränken die Freiheitsrechte, belasten alle Beteiligte und tragen zum negativen Bild der Psychiatrie in der Öffentlichkeit bei. In der medizinischen Literatur fehlen jedoch detaillierte Prozessanalysen von Zwangsanwendungen. Es wird eine Kasuistik aus dem Forschungsprojekt „Simulation und Reduktion von Zwangsmaßnahmen" präsentiert, in der Psychodrama als Methode der Reaktualisierung relevanter Szenen und zugleich als Erhebungsmethode qualitativer Interviewdaten verwendet wird. Der explorative Ansatz ermöglicht detaillierte Identifizierung von verbalen und nonverbalen Zeichenprozessen (sprechen, gestikulieren, Raum kontrollieren) innerhalb von Zwangsanwendungsstrategien und generiert empirisch begründbare Hypothesen über die beobachteten Interaktionsmuster. Die psychodramatische Reinszenierung einer Zwangsmaßnahme offenbart die Widerstände seitens der TherapeutInnen, einen inneren Rollentausch mit einem hochgradig erregten Patienten zu vollziehen. Dem Patienten als unterstürzendes „Hilfs-Ich" zur Seite zu stehen wird unter dieser Bedingung nahezu unmöglich auch wenn die Rolle in ihrem Potential noch nicht ausgeschöpft ist.

Schlüsselwörter Akutpsychiatrie · Gewalt · Zwangsmaßnahme · Filmanalyse · Regelanalyse · Gewaltreduktion · Symbolische Handlungsalternativen · Psychodrama als Untersuchungsmethode · Hilfs-Ich · Doppel

PD Dr. S. Debus (✉)
Klinik für Psychiatrie, Sozialpsychiatrie und Psychotherapie,
Medizinische Hochschule Hannover,
Carl-Neuberg-Str. 1,
30625 Hannover, Deutschland
E-Mail: Debus.Stephan@mh-hannover.de

Dr. U. Ahrens
Sozialpsychiatrische Kontaktstelle Hannover,
Fernroder Str. 9,
30161 Hannover, Deutschland

"Auxiliary Ego" beyond the "White Wall": a psychodramatic casuistry from simulation and reduction of coercive measures in psychiatry

Abstract The application of means of coercion (fixation, compulsory medication, isolation) in psychiatry is limiting rights of freedom, puts all participants under stress and contributes to the negative image of psychiatry in public perception. A case is presented from our research project "Simulation and Reduction of Coercive Measures in Psychiatry", in which psychodrama is used as a re-enactment method of relevant scenes and as a method of collecting qualitative interview data. The explorative approach ensures detailed identification of verbal and non-verbal communication (speaking, gesticulating, and spatial control) within coercive strategies and provides empirically founded hypotheses about patterns of interaction in psychiatric wards. A psychodramatic re-enactment of a violent situation reveals the resistance of therapists to perform an internal role reversal with a very excited and aggressive patient. Under this condition, helping an in-patient with an "auxiliary ego" is difficult but not impossible.

Keywords Psychiatry · Violence · Coercive measure · Video analysis · Rule analysis · Reduction of violence · Symbolic alternatives of action · Psychodrama as research method · Auxiliary ego · Double

1 Psychiatrische Zwangsanwendung als Gegenstand der semiotischen Milieuforschung

Die langfristige und arbeitsteilige Erforschung von Zwangsanwendungen sowie Gewaltentstehung und Gewaltprävention ist von hoher gesellschaftlicher Relevanz, denn die nach dem Psychisch-Kranken-Gesetz (PsychKG) nur unzureichend geregelte Ausübung von Zwang (Zwangseinweisung, Zwangsbehandlung, Zwangsfixierung und Zwangsmedikation) gehört in der Psychiatrie zu den freiheitsbeschränkenden Maßnahmen, die alle Beteiligten (PatientInnen, Angehörige und professionelle Teams) in hohem Maße belasten und die zum negativen Bild der Psychiatrie in der Öffentlichkeit beitragen. In diesem Beitrag geht es um eine Kasuistik aus dem Forschungsprojekt: „Simulation und Reduktion von Zwangsmaßnahmen in der Psychiatrie"[1], das die Relevanz psychodramatischer Methoden und Interpretationen für die Erforschung von psychiatrischen Zwangsanwendungen verdeutlichen soll.

Einige konservative Schätzungen belegen die – nicht notwendig krankheitsbedingte – Zunahme von Zwangsmaßnahmen in den letzten 10 bis 15 Jahren. In schätzungsweise 10% aller Akut-Behandlungsfälle wird Zwang angewendet. Weitere Outcome-Studien zeigen im Ergebnis, dass Zwangsausübung nicht allein eine Reaktion auf psychopathologische Verhaltensweisen von PatientInnen ist, sondern auch vom typischen Verlauf von der Therapeuten-Patienten-Interaktion und von verschiedenen Umweltfaktoren abhängt: Dazu zählen etwa soziale Atmosphären in kritischen und für ein psychiatrisches Milieu kennzeichnenden Situationen oder milieuübergreifenden bzw. milieutypischen Handlungsstrukturen. Es wird unterschieden nach

Abb. 1 Anlässe für Zwangsmaßnahmen auf vier akutpsychiatrischen Stationen in einem Beobachtungszeitraum von einem Jahr (n=200 Beobachtungsfälle)

Gefährlichkeit von Situationen

Anlässe von Fixierungen (n=200) mit abnehmender Relevanz)

psychomotorische Unruhe	(1)
Angriff auf Personal	(2)
verbale Aggression	(2)
Erregung bei Manie und Alkoholentzug	(1,2)
Selbstverletzung	(1)
Androhung von Tätlichkeiten	(2)
Desorientiertheit	(1)
Verweigerung der Medikamenteneinnahme	(1,2)
Zerstörung von Gegenständen	(2)
Wahnideen	(1,2)
Fluchtgefahr	(1,2)
Suizidgefahr	(1)
Zündeln	(2)
Aufstehen während Infusion	(1)

(1)=Therapeutisches Handeln bei Selbstgefährdung
(2)=Schutz-, Organisationshandeln bei Fremdgefährdung

psychopathologischen, interaktionistischen oder strukturellen Ursachen von Gewalt und Zwangsanwendung.

Aus eigenen Studien an der Medizinischen Hochschule Hannover, bei denen über einen Zeitraum von einem Jahr hinweg auf vier psychiatrischen Akutstationen 120 Fixierungen an 52 PatientInnen beobachtet wurden, ist bekannt (Bastiaan et al. 1998), dass die Ausübung von Zwang primär am ersten Tag der Aufnahme und hier in der ersten Nachthälfte (18:00 bis 24:00 Uhr) stattfindet. Die Anlässe für die Fixierungen sind in einem Fixierungsfragebogen dokumentiert und mit abnehmender Relevanz in Abb. 1 zusammengestellt. Es fallen zwei sehr unterschiedliche Anlasstypen auf: 1) Therapeutisches Handeln als Einsatz bei und Schutz vor Selbstgefährdung der Patienten, 2) Schutz- und Organisationshandeln der TherapeutInnen zur Aufrechterhaltung der Stationsorganisation, und 3) Anlässe, die sowohl dem einen als auch dem anderen Typen zugeordnet werden können.

Die Liste der Anlässe beantwortet nicht die Frage, wie es zu diesen Anlässen kommt. Beim zweiten Anlasstyp wissen wir nicht, welche Art von Stationsorganisation überhaupt aufrechterhalten werden muss. Beim „Zündeln“ etwa geht es meist relativ eindeutig um Gefahrenabwehr für Stationsmitglieder und um den Erhalt der baulichen Substanz der Station. Aber schon bei der Deutung von Handlungen wie „Zündeln“ und dem Verständnis der Symbolik des „Feuers“ versagt ein solcher Ansatz. Bei „Fluchtgefahr“ stehen die TherapeutInnenteams nach erfolgter Flucht hinsichtlich der Verletzung ihrer Aufsichtspflicht in der Verantwortung. Doch ist das alles? Welche Dimension der Stationsorganisation wird hier aufrechterhalten? Beim „Angriff auf das Personal“ geht es sowohl um Schutz vor Gefährdung der TherapeutInnen als auch um Schutz vor Selbstgefährdung der PatientInnen. Welches Verhalten aber fällt unter „verbale Aggression“ und welche Stationsorganisation muss durch Fixierung aufrechterhalten werden, wenn einE PatientIn laut wird. Geht es hier um medizinisch-therapeutische Interventionen oder um die Ausbalancierung einer gereizten Stationsatmosphäre durch Zwangsausübung als letztem Mittel oder um erzieherische oder strafende Versuche, die PatientInnen zum Schweigen zu bringen?

Die Analyse von Filmdokumenten verdeutlicht die Probleme (vgl. die Filmdokumente *Alltag in der Psychiatrie* von Ilan Klipper auf Youtube.com).

Im Bemühen um Gewaltreduktion führen moralisierende Forderungen nach Abschaffung von Zwangsmaßnahmen, deren stillschweigende Hinnahme oder sogar mystifizierende Umdeutungen zu ‚notwendigen therapeutischen' Maßnahmen nicht weiter. Die vorhandenen qualitativen Studien arbeiten häufig mit sehr vagen Begriffen, singulären Arbeitsmethoden und nicht übertragbaren Arbeitsergebnissen. Quantitative, klinische und epidemiologische Studien fokussieren demgegenüber auf die Abschätzung von Risikofaktoren, auf Korrelationen zwischen psychopathologischen Variablen und Inzidenz-/Prävalenzraten oder auf psychopharmakologische Wirkungen auf aggressives Verhalten von PatientInnen (Epidemiologie: z. B.: Laing 1994; Martin et al. 2007; Klinikvergleiche, z. B.: Martin et al. 2007; Ketelsen et al. 2011; Dokumentationsauswertung z. B.: Nitschke-Janssen und Brandik 2006; prospektive Studien z. B.: Klimitz et al. 1998). Aber die statistische Oberflächenbeschreibung der Phänomene von Gewalt und Zwang reicht nicht aus: Es fehlen systematische, institutionenübergreifende und verstehende Forschungsansätze, die die Phänomene in ihren sowohl diskursiven als auch strukturellen Aspekten ganz grundsätzlich untersuchen. Dazu aber werden arbeitsteilige und interdisziplinäre Studien innerhalb eines gemeinsamen Theorierahmens benötigt. Die Studien sollten hinsichtlich der Komplexität der zu behandelnden Sachfragen, Kontinuität, Kritik und Vergleich von Forschungsergebnissen, wenn nicht schon gewährleisten, so doch zumindest anstreben. Nur wie?

Eine in unserer Abteilung für Sozialpsychiatrie 2003 durchgeführte und von der DFG finanzierte Tagung „Semiotik und Sozialpsychiatrie – Über Sinn und Zeichen einer Fachsprache" (Debus et al. 2005; Debus und Eink 2003) brachte den entscheidenden Impuls, wissenschaftstheoretische Brücken und Anschlussstellen zwischen disparaten Ansätzen der qualitativ-psychiatrischen Forschung zu entwickeln. In der Arbeit „Formen psychiatrischer Milieus – semiotische Studien zur Methodologie der Milieuforschung" (Debus 2008) wird gezeigt, wie über die Semiotik eine gemeinsame theoretische Basis für phänomenologische (Wissens- und Rahmenanalyse), strukturalistische (Regelanalyse) und ethnomethodologische (Situations- und Handlungsanalyse) Forschungsansätze geschaffen wird, die für die empirische Prozessforschung genutzt werden kann.

Die theoretischen, methodischen und praktischen Vorbereitungen sind ab Frühjahr 2012 in das Pilotprojekt „Simulation und Reduktion von Zwangsmaßnahmen in der Psychiatrie" eingegangen, das in Kooperation mit den genannten niedersächsischen psychiatrischen Kliniken durchgeführt wurde. Die MitarbeiterInnen der Krankenpflege wurden mittels der Methode des Psychodramas angeleitet, typische Gewaltsituationen zu reinszenieren. In anschließenden ExpertInnen-Gruppen-Diskussionen wurden die MitarbeiterInnen befragt. Diese Reinszenierungen und Befragungen wurden gefilmt, die Filme transkribiert und exemplarisch ausgewertet. In dieser Pilotstudie konnten alle Methoden und das Arbeitsprogramm praktisch erprobt werden. Und es entstanden eine Reihe von Publikationen zum Forschungsprojekt (zur Rolle und Bedeutung psychodramatischer Re-Inszenierungen (Ahrens 2011); zum Einsatz von Videoanalysen als Instrument der semiotikbasierten Datenanalyse (Serenari 2011) zu

Grundbegriffen des Forschungsprogramms (Debus 2011; Debus und Posner 2011; Posner und Debus 2011).

2 Semiotische Milieuforschung

In unserem Forschungsprojekt wird die Milieuforschung als angewandte Semiotik aufgefasst. Semiotik ist die Lehre von Zeichen und ihrem Gebrauch. Zeichenprozesse sind alle Ereignisse, in denen z. B. Worte, Gesten, Mimik, Haltungen etc. zur Verständigung verwendet werden. Die folgende Kasuistik und ihre Interpretation stützt sich auf basale Begriffe wie: konstitutive und regulative Regel, Situationskontext, Deklaration und Anzeichen. Diese Begriffe im Sinne der Sprachakttheorie von Searle (Searle 1997) stehen zueinander in folgender Beziehung: Konstitutive und regulative Regeln gehören zum gemeinsam geteilten, meist konventionalisierten Wissensbestand der MitarbeiterInnen einer psychiatrischen Station. Die konstitutiven Regeln treten als soziale Festlegungen auf, die eine Institution, ein Team oder eine Handlungsroutine im Sinne einer internen „Verfassung" stabilisieren. Über regulative Regeln werden die strategischen Aspekte der Handlungssituation rekonstruiert. Konstitutive Regeln haben die Form: x gilt im Situationskontext C als y; Regulative Regeln haben die präskriptive Form: wenn x, tue y, wobei x und y jeweils Prozesse (Verhalten, Äußerungen etc.) sind. Zur Veranschaulichung: die FIFA-Regeln des Fußballspiels sind konstitutiv, die strategischen Regeln des Fußballteams (Spielzüge) sind regulativ (vgl. hierzu ausführlich in Debus 2008; Debus und Posner 2011). Wer eine regulative Regel bricht, handelt im weitesten Sinne falsch, wer eine konstitutive Regel bricht, handelt „absurd". Die Rekonstruktion von konstitutiven und regulativen Regeln liefern Einsichten in das jeweilige organisatorische und kommunikative Regelwerk von psychiatrischen Stationen, das das Verhalten der Akteure steuert. Mit Hilfe dieser Regeln lassen sich unterschiedliche Stationskonzepte differenzieren und damit Unterschiede in der mehr oder weniger bewussten Konsens- bzw. Dissenskultur beschreiben. Die Geltung der Regeln wird durch deklarative Akte geäußert. In Kenntnis einer konstitutiven Regel kann ein Ereignis y, durch das ein Ereignis x gedeutet wird, selbst als Anzeichen für das Vorliegen eines bestimmten Situationskontextes C dienen, d. h. am Deutungsschema „y steht für x", erkennen die Akteure, in welcher Situation sie sich befinden.

Dieser Zusammenhang von Regel, Situationskontext, Anzeichen und Deklaration, soll in Vorbereitung auf die Interpretation der folgenden Kasuistik verdeutlicht werden: So ist z. B. die Aufnahme auf eine psychiatrische Station ein Akt, der aus einer erkrankten Person einen Patienten oder eine Patientin des Gesundheitssystems macht, wobei die konstitutive Regel gilt:

R1: Person A wird im Situationskontext C „Aufnahme auf einer psychiatrischen Station" zum Patienten P_A.

Der Patientenstatus wird mittels formaler Regularien (z. B. ID-Nummer, Anlegen einer Patientenakte, Aufnahmediagnose) deklariert. Im Patientenstatus, insbesondere nach einer Zwangseinweisung, können bestimmte verfassungsmäßig garantierte Grundrechte durch Gerichtsbeschluss aufgehoben werden, damit im Rahmen des

Behandlungsauftrages Zwangsmaßnahmen durchgeführt werden dürfen. Eine ähnliche Regel gilt für MitarbeiterInnen:

R2: Person B wird im Kontext C2 eines Mitarbeitervertrages zu einem Klinik-Mitarbeiter M_B.

Durch die – häufig zeremoniell gefeierte – Unterschrift unter den Mitarbeitervertrag wird eine Person zum Mitarbeiter oder zur Mitarbeiterin der Klinik deklariert. Gemäß diesem Vertrag sind PflegemitarbeiterInnen nach ärztlicher Anweisung berechtigt und verpflichtet Zwang anzuwenden. Es gibt eine übergeordnete regulative Regel, die in den meisten Fällen sinnvoller Weise verhindert, dass der Status von Patiententypen P und Mitarbeitertypen M nicht vermischt oder getauscht werden darf.

R3: Wenn A den Status P_A innehat, dann darf dieser nicht vermischt oder getauscht werden mit dem Mitarbeiterstatus M_B von B.

Es soll Rollenklarheit herrschen, Rollendiffusion oder Köperberührungen sind zu vermeiden. Diese Regel zur Unterlassung des Rollentauschs hat zur Folge, dass die Kulturen von PflegemitarbeiterInnen und PatientInnen auf der Station strikt getrennt sind, was sich nicht nur architektonisch sondern z. B. auch durch symbolische Raumgrenzen manifestiert (wie etwa der symbolischen Hemm-Schwelle zum Dienstzimmer). Durch diese Regel werden Frage- und Antwortmuster, oder Muster von Beobachten und Beobachtet-Werden festgelegt. Die durch die Regel erzeugte binäre Verhaltensstruktur erschwert die wechselseitige Perspektivübernahmen oder den Aufbau eines gemeinsam geteilten WIR-Erfahrungsraumes. Dahin gehende Versuche müssen immer eine Ausnahme von dieser Regel einfordern oder den offenen Regelbruch riskieren.

Eine weitere für diese Kasuistik relevante Gruppe von konstitutiven und regulativen Regeln legt bestimmte Arten von Verhaltensinterpretationen fest, die auch schon im Hinblick auf die Fixierungsanlässe aus Abb. 1 aufgetreten sind: „Therapeutisches Handeln" versus „Organisationshandeln".

R4: Im Situations-Kontext C4 „Therapie" gilt eine Aufforderung (x) an einen P_A z. B. zur Medikamenteneinnahme oder zur Verlegung auf eine andere Station, als therapeutische Intervention (y) zum Wohle des Patienten.

R5: Im Situations-Kontext C5 „Gerichtsbeschluss" gilt eine Aufforderung an einen Patienten, z. B. zur Medikamenteneinnahme oder zur Verlegung auf eine andere Station, als unanfechtbare Verhaltensanweisung.

Nach Regel R4 wird eine MitarbeiterIn-Äußerung zu einer KANN-Aufforderung mit Empfehlungscharakter eines „Therapeutischen Handelns". Nach Regel R5 wird dieselbe Äußerung zu einer MUSS-Aufforderung mit Unbedingtheitscharakter eines „Organisationshandels". Den PatientenInnen ist der jeweilige Kontext C4 oder C5 häufig nicht klar und deklarative Akte des Teams zur Orientierung der PatientenInnen werden meist unterlassen. Auch können PatientInnen die Art und Weise, wie diese Aufforderung geäußert wird, nicht als Anzeichen für den jeweiligen Situationskontext deuten. Im Gegenteil, es geschieht sehr häufig, dass die Grenzen zwischen „Therapiehandeln" und „Organisationshandeln" durch übergroße Freundlichkeit, die eher dem Situationskontext „Therapie" zuzuordnen sind, verwischen, um den aggressiven Charakter einer Zwangsbehandlung im Kontext „Organisationshandeln" den Patient-

Innen gegenüber zu verdunkeln. In diesem Fall sprechen wir von der Mystifizierung (Verschleierung) der Regel R5. Wir formulieren hier eine Team-Regel R6:

R6: Wenn ein Patient orientierungslos ist, dann sind deklarative Akte zur Orientierung des Patienten sinnlos.

Mit den obigen Grundbegriffen geben wir folgende Arbeitsdefinition eines psychiatrisches Milieus: Ein psychiatrisches Milieu als Gegenstand der Milieuforschung ist eine mikrosoziale, vorwiegend binäre TherapeutInnen-PatientInnen-Gruppe, mit professionell tradierbaren regulativen und konstitutiven Regeln und gemeinsam geteilten Überzeugungen, die das therapeutische Team als eine spezielle und über lange Zeiträume sässige Untergruppe des Milieus charakterisieren und einer PatientInnengruppe, die durch Regeln ausgezeichnet ist, welche vorwiegend der Alltagsbewältigung dienen. Die Wahrnehmungs- und Handlungsstruktur als eine für bestimmte Zeiträume gültige und stabile rekonstruierbare Gesamtheit der gruppenspezifischen Regeln ist, im Sinne der Strukturationstheorie, eine Ressource zur Lösung der gruppenspezifischen Koordinations- und Kooperationsprobleme und zur Reproduktion der Gruppenstabilität. Sie eröffnet und begrenzt den Wahrnehmungs- und Handlungsspielraum der Akteurinnen und Akteure, das heißt den vorwiegend medizinisch-therapeutischen Spielraum der TherapeutInnen und den vorwiegend alltagspraktischen Spielraum der PatientInnen.

3 Fragestellungen

Im Rahmen des Forschungsprojektes sollen folgende Fragen beantwortet werden:

- In welchen interaktiven Sequenzen manifestiert sich der Einsatz von Zwangsmaßnahmen in allgemeinpsychiatrischen und forensischen Akutstationen? Welche Akteurinnen und Akteure sind daran beteiligt, welche Arten von Prozessen (kausale, manipulative, kommunikative – deklarative, direktive, assertive, expressive und kommissive) dominieren?
- Welche wechselseitigen Interaktionsmuster steuern den Interaktionsverlauf?
- Welche Handlungs- und Entscheidungsspielräume haben die Akteurinnen und Akteure?
- Welche konstitutiven und regulativen Regeln steuern den Interaktionsverlauf? Welche Unterschiede zwischen standardisierten Interaktionsstrategien und Improvisationshandlungen lassen sich nachweisen? Welche Regeln unterstützen bzw. begrenzen den Improvisationsspielraum?
- Lässt sich eine Regel-Hierarchie (Handlungsgrammatik) für bestimmte Situationen oder Stationen rekonstruieren?
- Welche Unterschiede und Gemeinsamkeiten weisen die Muster in verschiedenen Handlungssituationen und in verschiedenen psychiatrischen Stationen auf? Lassen sich gemeinsame Handlungsmuster für alle und/oder für typische Handlungssituationen rekonstruieren? Oder sind alle Situationen singulär, d. h. müssen alle Zwangssituationen je nach verschiedenen Mustern und Regeln unterschieden werden?

4 Kasuistik einer milieutypischen Situation mit Zwangsanwendung

Am Beispiel einer milieutypischen Androhung und Anwendung von Zwang sollen hier einige Forschungsfragen zur Entstehung und Prävention von Gewalt im Zusammenhang der Methode des Psychodramas konkretisiert werden.

Die folgenden vier Abb. (2a, b, c, d) charakterisieren eine unfreiwillige Situation auf einer psychiatrischen Akutstation eines hoch erregten Patienten, der seine Verlegung auf eine andere Station massiv verweigert und Drohungen gegen das Pflegepersonal äußert. Die Abbildungen illustrieren schematisch die unterschiedlichen Situationsdeutungen der PatientIn und des psychiatrischen Teams. Sobald sich PatientInnen in einer Aufnahmesituation nicht beruhigen und für das Team verschiedene objektive (Angriff) oder intersubjektiv geteilte (gemeinsam unterstellte Labilität des Patienten oder der Patientin) oder auch subjektive (Furcht) Gefährdungskriterien erfüllt, ruft ein Mitglied des Teams über die Notfallalarmanlage alle verfügbaren MitarbeiterInnen aller anderen Stationen in der Gefährdungssituation zusammen. Es entsteht eine Standard-Situation wie in Abb. 2a.

Die Situation besteht aus einer in nahezu allen Akutstationen bekannten und nur wenig variierenden Standard-Szene „Einer und Alle". Sie ist durch konstitutive und regulative Regeln festgelegt und variiert meist nur unter den architektonisch-räum-

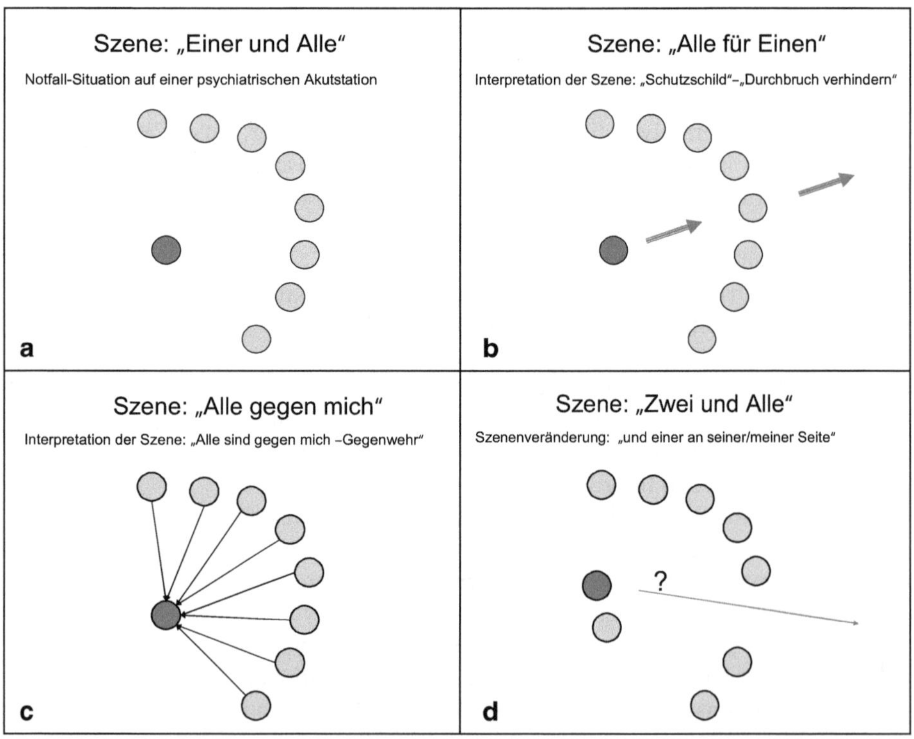

Abb. 2 a–d Unterschiedliche Interpretationen einer Szene, die erfahrungsgemäß kurz vor der physischen Anwendung von Zwang (Überwältigung und Fixierung) steht lichen Gegebenheiten der jeweiligen Klinik. Die per Alarm zusammen gerufene TherapeutInnengruppe hat im Sinne ihres eigenen professionellen Selbstverständnisses eine Situationsdeutung „Alle für Einen“ (Abb. 2b), indem sie sich als Schutzschild deutet, der den Patienten oder die Patientin vor sich selbst und für alle anderen schützt, etwa dadurch, dass sie einen Durchbruch oder körperliche Aggressionen verhindern will. Aus Sicht des Patienten oder der Patientin liegt eine Deutung „Alle gegen mich“ vor (Abb. 2c), die alle Kräfte der Gegenwehr in der betroffenen Person mobilisiert.

Ohne Schwierigkeiten lässt sich hier ein Handlungsablauf erkennen, der allzu leicht in Wehr und Gegenwehr eskaliert, bis eine Zwangsfixierung aus Sicht des therapeutischen Teams unumgänglich erscheint. Die dabei ablaufenden Handlungen und die sie organisierenden regulativen Regeln sind in vielfachen Übungssituationen auf Station simuliert und einstudiert worden. Konstitutive Regeln legen fest, wer, wann, was entscheidet und mit Hilfe welcher verbalen oder non-verbalen Äußerungen (meist Kommandos) diese Entscheidungen kundgetan werden. Die regulativen Regeln generieren standardisierte Handlungsabläufe mit bestimmen Körperhaltungen und Sicherheitsgriffen. Die jeweiligen Regeln sind in Dokumentationshandbüchern nachzulesen.

4.1 Das Hilfs-Ich jenseits der ‚Weißen Wand‘

In der kurzen Zeit vor dem Zugriff sieht sich der Patient einer ‚Weißen Wand‘ gegenüber, gebildet aus einer Übermacht von Mitgliedern des therapeutischen Teams. Die Frage, die sich stellt, wo und wie in dieser ‚Weißen Wand‘ sich noch ein Spielraum für Verständigungsprozesse öffnen könnte, der aus dem typischen ‚Tit for Tat‘[2] Handlungsablauf herausführen könnte? Wehr und Gegenwehr, Befehl und Gegenbefehl, Beleidigung und Gegenbeleidigung, Drohen und Gegen-Drohen sind in den Psychodramen der Zwangsmaßnahmen, die wir in dem Pilotprojekt reinszeniert haben, regelmäßige Kommunikationsstrukturen.

Die Inspiration und Reflexion für kreative therapeutische Interventionsstrategien haben wir in der psychiatrischen Praxis insbesondere Jakob Levy Moreno, dem Begründer des Psychodramas, zu verdanken. Im klinisch-psychiatrischen Kontext kreierte Moreno eine Technik zur Behandlung von Psychosen, die in den Annalen der Psychiatrie einmalig blieben (Moreno 2012, S. 241). Er schaffte ein theatrales Setting um die Bedürfnisse des Patienten herum – eben nicht umgekehrt. Im Zuge dieser Hilfs-Welt-Technik wird das gesamte Milieu des Patienten zur Bühne seines Psychodramas gestaltet. Moreno führte seine PatientInnen zu einer Performance in sein therapeutisches Theater, wobei diese anfänglich nicht selbst agierten, sondern als ZuschauerInnen im Auditorium Platz nahmen. Das in Frage stehende Problem wurde von Hilfs-Ich-TherapeutInnen auf der Bühne dargestellt, entweder spontan oder als geplantes therapeutisches Theater (Moreno 1959 und 1969). Dies ist nicht anderes als eine Form der Spiegeltechnik, die Moreno hier als eine erste Annäherung nutzte.

4.2 Die Weiße Wand

Die Frage, die wir uns im Rahmen des Forschungsprojektes gestellt haben, lautet, was passiert, wenn wir jenseits der ‚Weiße Wand‘ ein Hilfs-Ich in die Situation einführen (Abb. 2d), das als spiegelndes Doppel gleichsam als „DolmetscherIn" für den Patienten oder die Patientin agiert? Welche Regeln würden dabei verletzt und welche Regeln müssten eingeführt werden, damit die TherapeutInnen in einem solches Setting erfolgreich arbeiten können? Und wann kann man überhaupt von einem Erfolg sprechen?

Zunächst beinhaltet die ‚Weiße Wand' keinerlei therapeutische Funktion, auch wenn dies bis in 1990-iger behauptet worden ist. In den Aufsätzen aus dieser Zeit wird das Festbinden als wirksame Impulskontrolle bei psychotischen PatientInnen aufgeführt, Rastlosigkeit und Reizüberflutung würden nachlassen (Rytina 2012).

In dem Moment, wo es zu einer Zwangsanwendung kommt, herrscht aber auch heute noch eine Konfusion, was der Fall ist, bzw. was die Rollen sind, aus denen heraus agiert wird (Ahrens 2011). Die Mitglieder des ärztlichen Teams wechseln von der Rolle der Heilenden (Situationskontext „Therapie") in die Rolle von VollzugsbeamtInnen (Situationskontext „Organisationshandeln") und in der Folge mit ihm auch die Mitglieder des Pflegeteams. Aus der Rollenperspektive der PatientInnen wäre interessant zu erfahren, inwieweit ihnen in den Interaktionen des Klinikalltags deutlich ist, aus welcher Rolle heraus der Psychiater oder die Psychiaterin ihnen gegenüber intervenieren: Ist dieses Medikament und dessen Verordnung eine therapeutisch hilfreiche Maßnahme gegen meine Ängste und aus der Motivation verabreicht worden, zu helfen und zu schützen? Oder aber ist das Medikament zur inneren Fixierung verordnet worden? Und wenn ein und dasselbe Psychopharmakon in dem einen und zugleich in dem anderen Kontext verschrieben wird, wie wirkt dieses Mittel als psychisches Objekt in dem Patienten?

Wenn aber das Personal einer psychiatrischen Klinik Zwangsmaßnahmen nicht als das benennt, was sie sind, nämlich Maßnahmen der sozialen Kontrolle, sondern diese umdefiniert als therapeutisch motivierte Intervention zum Wohlergehen des Patienten, dann wird im Sinne Ronald Laings (Laing 1969; Laing 1971; Laing 1994) mystifiziert.

5 „Wir wollen den Arzt sprechen"

Den WorkshopteilnehmerInnen des Pilotprojektes haben wir die Idee der Einführung eines Hilfs-Ich jenseits der ‚Weiße Wand' vorgestellt und anhand eines Fallbeispieles erläutert. Die Reaktion daraufhin bestand im Widerstand, dies könne nicht funktionieren. Als Szene für das Experiment wurde dann auch folgerichtig eine aussichtslose Situation auf Station gewählt. Zunächst sollte es auch nicht funktionieren.

5.1 Die Ur-Szene

Die Ausgangssituation wurde wie folgt geschildert: ein männlicher Patient, 35 Jahre alt, kommt von seiner Ehefrau begleitet und wohl auch überredet, freiwillig in die psychiatrische Klinik und wird auf eine offene Station eingewiesen. Die Diagnose lautet paranoid-halluzinatorische Psychose. Nun aber soll er auf eine geschlossene Station verlegt werden, sein Zustand hat sich auf der offenen Station deutlich verschlechtert, er kann sich nicht an Absprachen (Medikamenteneinnahme, Verbot die

Station trotz offener Türen zu verlassen) halten, er wirkt sehr angespannt und verhält sich wiederholt offen aggressiv. Nun ist ein Beschluss erlassen worden, der besagt, dass der Patient auf eine geschlossene Station verlegt werden muss. Der Patient sagt ‚nein‘, er möchte nicht verlegt werden. Sogar das Teammitglied, welches die Situation schildert, versteht die Verlegungsmaßnahme als eine Art „Strafe“:

> Der kennt uns jetzt, wir haben angefangen und jetzt wird er wie zur Strafe auf ne Geschlossene verlegt, ne?

Der Patient empfindet es als eine Art ‚Herabstufung‘, auf jeden Fall als eine Verschlechterung seiner Situation. Er weigert sich seine Sachen zu packen und zeigt keinerlei Kooperationsbereitschaft, selbst als ein weibliches Teammitglied sein Zimmer betritt, um ihm beim Packen behilflich zu sein. Die Situation zwischen den Beteiligten eskaliert, der Alarm wird ausgelöst und eine Reihe von Pflegekräften reihen sich vor dem Patienten auf, um ihn zu fixieren.

In dem Moment, da die ‚Weiße Wand‘ aufgestellt ist, stehen die Zeichen auf Konfrontation. Auf beiden Seiten herrschen eine ängstliche Anspannung und nervöse Aggressivität. In diesem Zustand sind auch die Mitglieder eines erfahrenen Pflegeteams nur bedingt in der psychischen Verfassung, eine Verständigung herbeiführen zu können. Könnte es in dieser Situation hilfreich sein, ein Hilfs-Ich aus der ‚Weißen Wand‘ freizustellen, dem es erlaubt ist, aus seiner Rolle herauszutreten und die Perspektive des Patienten einzunehmen?

Aber – wie wir sehen werden – ist dies keine leichte Übung. Denn erstens verletzt es die konstitutiven Regel zur Unterlassung eines Rollentauschs (R3) und es bedarf verschiedener Fähigkeiten, um die Rolle des Hilfs-Ichs (Moreno 2006) mit Rollentausch einzunehmen, nämlich:

- der Fähigkeit zur markierten, d. h. spielerischen Imitation (Spiegeln)
- der Fähigkeit eine gemeinsame Perspektive auf ein Drittes einzunehmen (Doppeln)
- der Fähigkeit die Welt aus der Perspektive des Anderen zu sehen (Rollentausch)
- und der Fähigkeit mit einer bedrohlichen Realität spielen zu können.

In den folgenden experimentellen Spielen verabreden die Pflegeteams, wer von ihnen die Hilfs-Ich Rolle einnimmt und wer das Zeichen für den Zugriff gibt, wenn die Situation nicht länger verhandelbar erscheint (hier werden neue regulative und konstitutive Regeln erdacht).

5.2 Versuch I: ohne Perspektivenwechsel

Im Verlauf des ersten szenischen Versuchs verbleibt das Hilfs-Ich in der ‚Weißen Wand‘ und bewegt sich nicht aus der schützenden Reihe und Nähe des Pflegeteams. Von diesem für das Hilfs-Ich sicheren Ort werden folgende Worte an den Patienten gerichtet:

> Ja, aber ich denke mal, bei uns ist es auch ganz nett und die Kollegen sind ganz freundlich.

Das sind verführerische und einladend gemeinte Worte, aber diese – aus der Sicht des Patienten – sind gesprochen vom Ort der Bedrohung, der ‚Weißen Wand'. Räumlich bleibt das Hilfs-Ich ein Mitglied des Pflegeteams, welches die Aggression leugnet, die gerade geschieht. Es wird mystifiziert (d. h. Leugnung der Differenz zwischen Regel 4 und Regel 5): Wir sind ‚nett', wir sind keine Aggressoren, die Verlegung ist ein therapeutisch notwendiger, hilfreicher Akt, der ‚nett' gemeint ist. Es verbirgt, was ein anderes Teammitglied bereits ausgesprochen hat, dass die Verlegung des Patienten auch als Bestrafung empfunden werden könnte. Die Situation droht zu eskalieren und der Versuch des Hilfs-Ichs wird unterbrochen.

5.3 Versuch II: starke Rollenverhaftung

In einem zweiten Versuch nimmt das Hilfs-Ich eine Position neben dem Patienten ein, so dass sie nun gemeinsam auf die ‚Weiße Wand' blicken. Das Hilfs-Ich deklariert den ‚Rollentausch', allerdings ohne diesen dann auch im körperlich-emotionalen Verhalten zu vollziehen:

> Das kann ich gut nachvollziehen… mal sprechen

Das Hilfs-Ich hofft auf ein vernunftorientiertes Gespräch und gleitet nicht in die aggressive Erregung des Patienten hinein:

> … Sie haben Sorge, dass wir Sie verändern in Ihrer Persönlichkeit? Aufgrund der Medikamente?
> „Hä?" lautet die irritierte und ärgerliche Reaktion des Patienten.

Das Hilfs-Ich versucht den Patienten in seinen Sorgen zu verstehen und erntet Unverständnis. Auch in dieser Spielsituation wagt es das Hilfs-Ich nicht, den Patienten in seiner Wut zu spiegeln. Als das Hilfs-Ich bemerkt, dass der Patient wieder nicht auf das angebotene Verständnis reagiert, verfällt es wieder in das bekannte Muster der Mystifizierung:

> Also, ich denke mal, wir versuchen Sie zu unterstützen, …

Der Patient fühlt sich gerade in keiner Weise unterstützt. Die Situation steht wieder kurz vor der Eskalation. Mittlerweile sind das spielende Pflegeteam und der Patient derartig für ihre Rollen angewärmt, dass es bei einem letzten Versuch des Hilfs-Ichs zu einem gewaltsamen Zugriff auf den Patienten kommt.

5.4 Ein allerletzter Versuch „Wir wollen den Arzt sprechen"

Die Gruppe erkennt in einer kurzen Reflexion des Geschehens, dass es ein wesentliches Merkmal des Hilfs-Ichs sein könnte, ebenso aggressiv wie laut sein zu können wie der Patient. Es soll seinen eigenen Rollentausch auch körperlich-emotional dem Patienten gegenüber kommunizieren. Ein anderes männliches Hilfs-Ich wird bestimmt. Die Szene, die folgt, entwickelt sich entscheidend anders als die vorhergegangenen.

Mit dem Eintreten des Pflegeteams in den Raum des Patienten platziert sich das neue Hilfs-Ich neben den Patienten. Es stellt unvermittelt gestisch eine gemeinsame Perspektive mit dem Patienten her, indem es beide Hände abwehrend gegen die ‚Weiße Wand‘ streckt. Stellvertretend für den Patienten schafft er einen durch Gesten angezeigten Schutzraum für diesen und gegen das Pflegeteam. Der Patient kann hoffen, dass er sich in einer therapeutischen Situation befindet, in dem ihm geholfen wird. Stimmlich unterstützt das Hilfs-Ich diese Geste, die anderen im Raum übertönend:

> Bleibt zurück! Schön zurück bleiben, ganz ruhig bleiben! Wir wollen hier erstmal ‘n bisschen Ruhe reinbringen …

Die Reaktion des Patienten ist:

> Genau, einfach hier mal … alle mal raus!

Es ist das erste Mal, dass ein Mitglied des Pflegeteams eine Zustimmung seitens des Patienten erfährt. Das eröffnet dem Hilfs-Ich die Möglichkeit einen neuen Verhandlungs- und Erfahrungsraum zu erschaffen. Zudem beginnt das Hilfs-Ich die Sprache des Patienten zu sprechen und dessen Perspektive auf die Situation einzunehmen:

> Das ist doch Scheiße, wegen einmal… hier Medis nicht einnehmen gleich verlegt werden. Das ist doch… ist doch nicht einzusehen.

Erst nachdem das Hilfs-Ich den Patienten in seiner Körperhaltung, seiner Sprache, seiner Interpretation der Situation und seinem Gefühlszustand imitiert und gedoppelt hat und sich der Patient zustimmend ihm gegenüber verhält, verändert das Hilfs-Ich seine Funktion und baut eine „Brücke“ zum Team:

> … ihr kennt den hier alle, ne? Ihr kennt euch, die andere Station kennt ihn nicht, wo ist der Sinn wieder vor vorne anzufangen?

Reaktion des Patienten:

> Genau. Richtig.

Gleichzeitig verbleibt das Hilfs-Ich in der Perspektive des Patienten:

> Gibt das ‚n Sinn? Nein!

Es entspinnt sich eine Verhandlungssituation zwischen Hilfs-Ich und Patient auf der einen und dem Team auf der anderen Seite. Die fortschreitende gegenseitige Annäherung zwischen Hilfs-Ich und Patienten gipfelt in dem Satz des Patienten:

> Wir wollen den Arzt sprechen.

Die Szene endet in einem Moment der Begegnung, der derart irritierend für beide ist, dass sie in ein befreiendes Lachen ausbrechen.

5.5 Diskussion: Warum scheitern die Versuche I und II? Und was geschieht Anderes im Versuch III?

In dem Moment, da eine Hilfs-Ich-Rolle übernommen wird, bedarf es eines spielerischen Momentes, welches das Hilfs-Ich in die Situation einführt. Kommt es aber zu gewaltsamen Auseinandersetzungen mit PatientInnen, dann finden sich die MitarbeiterInnen des Pflegeteams in eine sehr ernste Notlage gedrängt. Die berechtigte Sorge um die eigene körperliche und seelische Unversehrtheit (d. h. Organisationshandeln zur Aufrechterhaltung der Stationsordnung) steht im Fokus und nicht länger pflegerische oder therapeutische Hilfsangebote für PatientInnen. Aus dieser berechtigen Angst und Sorge (d. h. unter dem starken emotionalen Eindruck vom Unterlassungsgebot des Rollentauschs) vermag sich das Hilfs-Ich im ersten Versuch von seiner Rolle in der Weißen Wand nicht zu lösen. Unter den Bedingungen von Bedrohung und Angst ist die Einführung eines spielerischen Momentes überaus schwierig. Das Hilfs-Ich verlässt nicht den schützenden Ort der ‚Weißen Wand' und es spricht auch aus der Rolle heraus, mit der es als Pflegekraft am stärksten identifiziert ist. Und die Merkmale dieser Rolle sind eben ‚Freundlichkeit', ‚Zugewandtheit' und ‚Verständnis'.

Im zweiten Versuch schafft es das Hilfs-Ich eine Position neben dem Patienten einzunehmen, was die Herstellung einer gemeinsamen Perspektive auf die ‚Weiße Wand' ermöglichen würde. Aber das Hilfs-Ich stellt diese Perspektive nicht her, sondern wendet sich an den Patienten, um mit ihm in einen beruhigenden Dialog zu kommen. Überdies beginnt das Hilfs-Ich statt die Angst und Erregung des Patienten zu doppeln, diese zu deuten. Faktisch vollzieht das Hilfs-Ich den Rollentausch für den Patienten nur verbal erkennbar nicht aber körperlich-emotional.

Die drei Kernelemente eines möglichen Verständigungsprozesses, Spiegeln, Herstellung einer gemeinsamen Perspektive/Doppeln und Rollentausch, sind in den ersten beiden experimentellen Szene daher nicht realisiert. Vom Ort des therapeutischen Sprechens wird keine gemeinsame Perspektive auf etwas Drittes hergestellt, der vorherrschende Affekt wird nicht gespiegelt, sondern in sein Gegenteil gekehrt und die Sprachperspektive ‚ich' und ‚bei uns' offenbart, dass in diesem Moment das Hilfs-Ich nicht mit den Augen des Patienten auf die Szene schaut.

Im dritten Versuch nun agiert das Hilfs-Ich auf eine andere Weise. „Doppeln sollte vorwiegend mit Hilfe des Körpers erfolgen, nicht so sehr mittels kluger Worte" schreibt Zerka Moreno (2013, S. 320) in einer kleinen Notiz zu dieser psychodramatischen Technik. Und eben dies tut das Hilfs-Ich in unserer Filmszene. In all' seinen Gesten, Körperhaltungen und in der Lautstärke und dem Inhalt seiner Worte wird der Patient nachgeahmt. Zum Einstieg in die Szene nutzt das Hilfs-Ich ähnliche Worte und Gesten, die der Patient in der Ur-Szene gezeigt hatte. Dort hebt der Patient vorsichtig die Hände gegen die eindringenden und ihn umstellenden Pflegekräfte und sagt: *„Ey, draußen bleiben! Haut ab hier!"* Das Hilfs-Ich maximiert diese Geste, wodurch diese deutlicher und offensiver wirkt. Das ist der Moment, da sich der Patient das erste Mal in seinem Zustand verstanden fühlt. Und das ist auch der Moment, ab dem sich ein gemeinsamer Erfahrungsraum zwischen Hilfs-Ich und Patient entfaltet. Interessant ist die *Rückmeldung aus der der Rolle des Patienten zu lesen*:

> … erst hat er mich genervt … und dann fang ich an in der Wir-Person zu sprechen. Ich hab ihn als quasi jemand tatsächlich von mir gesehen und es ist wirk-

lich, obwohl ich wirklich eigentlich ja die ganze Zeit dagegen gesteuert habe, muss ich ehrlich zugeben ... Das war schon komisch zu spüren. Also ich hab mich ja selber erschrocken.

Erst in dem Raum des gemeinsamen ‚Wir‘ kann das Hilfs-Ich neue, andere eventuell hilfreichere Interventionen vorschlagen, zum Beispiel gemeinsame Überlegungen darüber anstellen, welche Auswirkungen es hätte, weiterhin Widerstand zu leisten und fixiert zu werden, oder welche Auswirkungen es hätte unter Protest die Station zu wechseln ohne Fixierungen. In einem gemeinsamen Denkraum könnten die Konsequenzen des einen oder anderen Verhaltens reflektiert werden.

6 Verschiedene Hilfs-Ich-Formen in den Ethnotheorien des Pflegepersonals

Im Forschungsprojekt wollten wir nun herausfinden, was die Teams, die über einen sehr langen Zeitraum Erfahrungen im Umgang mit PatientInnen gesammelt haben, über Hilfs-Ich-Rollen wissen. Dazu haben wir die Teams zu ExpertInnen-Gruppen-Diskussionen eingeladen. Die Ergebnisse dieser Diskussion sind in Abb. 3 zusammengefasst. Dabei zeigen sich zwei interessante Aspekte:

1. Die Teams unterscheiden 6 verschiedene Hilfs-Ich-Formationen mit Merkmalen, die in der Tabelle aufgeführt sind: Fürsprecher, Anwalt, Mediator, Verbündetes Double, Kopie und Mime. Zu diesen Hilfs-Ich-Formationen gibt es jeweils reflektierte Ethnotheorien: zur Wirkweise, zu den Risikofaktoren, zu den situativen Voraussetzungen und zu persönlichen Voraussetzungen, die Mitarbeiter sowie Patienten erfüllen müssen. Diese können hier aber aus Platzgründen nicht weiter ausgeführt werden.

Abb. 3 Arbeitshypothese: Ethnotheorien der MitarbeiterInnen des Pflegepersonals zu verschiedenen Formen des Hilfs-Ichs

Formen des Hilfs-Ichs

Ohne Rollen-/Seitenwechsel, ohne Perspektivübernahme

1. Fürsprecher
2. Anwalt

Mit neuer Rolle, ohne Perspektivübernahme

3. Situationsmanager/Mediator

mit Rollen-/Seitenwechsel, mit Perspektivübernahme

4. Verbündetes Double

Mit neuer Rolle, mit Perspektivübernahme

5. Kopie
6. Spiegel/Mime

2. Die Hilfs-Ich-Formen werden in der therapeutischen Interaktion äußert selten, eher zufällig und unsystematisch angewendet. Insbesondere in Zwangsbehandlungen kommen diese Hilfs-Ich-Formen (noch) nicht zum Einsatz.

7 Ausblick

Aus den Ergebnissen der ExpertInnen-Befragung haben wir für die weitere empirische Erforschung des interaktiven Geschehens vor, während und nach der Anwendung von Zwang die Arbeitshypothese entwickelt, dass insbesondere sehr erfahrene Teams einerseits über ein kreatives und reflektiertes therapeutisches Potential verfügen, welche andererseits aber durch konstitutive und regulative Regeln an seiner Entfaltung gehindert wird (Abb. 3).

Wir konnten aber unter Rückgriff auf genau dieses Potential der Pflege-Teams mit den genannten Kliniken vereinbaren, dass solche Hilfs-Ich-Formen zur Vermeidung von Zwangsbehandlungen eingesetzt werden dürfen. Als Erfolgskriterium dient dabei der Grundsatz: *Die Anwendung einer Hilfs-Ich-Form ist dann erfolgreich, wenn es gelingt, die physische Durchführung einer Zwangsmaßnahme zu verhindern (eskalationsvermeidend) oder zu reduzieren (eskalationsverringernd) und durch symbolische Interaktionsformen (z. B. neue Verhandlungen mit PatientInnen) zu ersetzen.* Im weiteren Verlauf des Forschungsprojektes „Simulation und Reduktion von Zwangsmaßnahmen in der Psychiatrie" werden wir die Erfahrungen des Pflegepersonals mit dem Einsatz von Hilfs-Ich-Formen detailliert untersuchen. Dabei wird uns die Methode des Psychodramas noch lange begleiten, die Regeln psychiatrischer Stationen zu rekonstruieren und symbolische Alternativen zur Zwangsbehandlung zu finden.

Anmerkungen

1 Das Forschungsprojekt ist angesiedelt an der Klinik für Psychiatrie, Sozialpsychiatrie und Psychotherapie der Medizinischen Hochschule Hannover (web: www.mh-hannover.de/psychiatrie.html und www.srzp.de) in Kooperation mit zwei allgemeinpsychiatrischen und forensischen Kliniken des Klinikums Region Hannover (KRH) sowie dem Institut für Kultursemiotik in Wennigsen (Web: www.x-kultursemiotik.de).

2 Bedeutet hier soviel wie „Retourkutsche".

Literatur

Ahrens, U. (2011). Psychodramatische Reinszenierung: Von Zwang und Gewalt in der Psychiatrie. *Zeitschrift für Semiotik, 33*(1–2), 55–78.

Bastiaan, P., Debus, S., & Haltenhof, H. (1998). Zwangsmabnahmen in der Psychiatrie. Fixierungen auf den psychiatrischen Stationen der Medizinischen Hochschule Hannover. *Psychiatrische Praxis, 25*(5), 231–234.

Debus, S. (2008). *Formen psychiatrischer Milieus – Semiotische Studien zur Methodologie der Milieuforschung*. Hannover: Medizinische Hochschule Hannover – Habilitationsschrift.

Debus, S. (2011). Zwangsanwendung im psychiatrischen Milieu – ein semiotisch fundiertes Forschungsprogramm. *Zeitschrift für Semiotik, 33*(1–2), 23–54.

Debus, S., & Eink, M. (Hrsg.). (2003). Semiotik und Sozialpsychiatrie. *Sozialpsychiatrische Informationen, 3*(2003), 1–64. (Bonn: Psychiatrie Verlag)

Debus, S., & Posner, R. (Hrsg.). (2011). Auf dem Weg zu einer semiotischen Kulturtheorie der Sozialen Psychiatrie. *Zeitschrift für Semiotik, 33*(1–2), 3–22.

Debus, S., Burmeister, H.-P., Floeth, T., & Zechert, C. (Hrsg.). (2005). *Semiotik und Sozialpsychiatrie – Über Sinn und Zeichen einer Fachsprache*. Pößneck: Bertelsmann.

Ketelsen, R., Schulz, M., & Driessen, M. (2011). Zwangsmaßnahmen im Vergleich an sechs psychiatrischen Abteilungen. *Gesundheitswesen, 73*(2), 105–111.

Klimitz, H., Uhlemann, H., & Fähndrich, E. (1998). Fixieren wir zu häufig? Indikation, Häufigkeit und Randbedingungen von Fixierungen in einer allgemeinpsychiatrischen Abteilung. Eine retrospektive Studie. *Psychiatrische Praxis, 25*(5), 235–239.

Laing, R. D. (1969). Mystifizierung, Konfusion und Konflikt. In G. Bateson, D. D. Jackson, R. D. Laing, T. Lidz, & L. C. Wynne (Hrsg.), *Schizophrenie und Familie* (S. 274–304). Frankfurt a. M.: Suhrkamp.

Laing, R. D. (1971). *Phänomenologie der Erfahrung*. Frankfurt a. M.: Suhrkamp.

Laing, R. D. (1994). *Das geteilte Selbst. Eine existentielle Studie über geistige Gesundheit und Wahnsinn.* Köln: Kiepenheuer & Witsch.

Martin, V., Kuster, W., Baur, M., Bohnet, U., Hermelink, G., Knopp, M., Kronstorfer, R., Martinez-Funk, B., Roser, M., Voigtländer, W., Brandecker, R., & Steinert, T. (2007). Die Inzidenz von Zwangsmassnahmen als Qualitätsindikator in psychiatrischen Kliniken. Probleme der Datenerfassung und -verarbeitung und erste Ergebnisse. *Psychiatrische Praxis, 34*(1), 26–33.

Martin, V., Bernhardsgrütter, R., Göbel, R., & Steinert, T. (2007). Ein Vergleich von Schweizer und deutschen Kliniken in Bezug auf die Anwendung von Fixierung und Isolierung. *Psychiatrische Praxis, 34*(suppl. 2), 212–217.

Moreno, J. L. (1959). *Psychodrama II.* New York: Beacon House.

Moreno, J. L. (1969). *Psychodrama III.* New York: Beacon House.

Moreno, Z. T. (2006). *The Quintessential Zerka.* London: Routledge.

Moreno, Z. T. (2012). *To dream again.* New York: Mental Health Resources.

Moreno, Z. T. (2013). Doubling should first be done with the body, not clever words. *Zeitschrift für Psycho-drama und Soziometrie, 2*, 319–321.

Nitschke-Janssen, M., & Brandik, E. (2006). Einflussfaktoren auf den Einsatz von Zwangsmassnahmen – Eine retrospektive Auswertung in einer schweizer kinder- und jugendlichen Versorgungsklinik. *Praxis der Kinderpsychologie und Kinderpsychiatrie, 55*(4), 255–270.

Posner, R., & Debus, S. (Hrsg.). (2011). *Semiotische Milieuforschung in der Sozialwissenschaft*. Tübingen: Stauffenburg Verlag.

Rytina, S. (2012). Zwang in der Psychiatrie. http://www.spiegel.de/gesundheit/psychologie/zwang-in-der-psychiatrie-das-letzte-mittel-a-836111.html. Zugegriffen: 6. Juni 2012.

Searle, J. R. (1997). *Sprechakte*. Frankfurt a. M.: Suhrkamp.

Serenari, M. (2011). Videoanalysen als Instrument der Datenerhebung und Datenanalyse am Beispiel von drei Karotisoperationen. *Zeitschrift für Semiotik, 33*(1–2), 79–110.

PD Dr. Stephan Debus, Hochschullehrer für Psychiatrische Methodenlehre, Medizinische Hochschule Hannover, Klinik für Psychiatrie, Sozialpsychiatrie und Psychotherapie, Leiter des Forschungsprojektes „Simulation und Reduktion von Zwangsmaßnahmen in der Psychiatrie“ (SRZP Website: www.srzp.de), Leiter des Forschungsinstituts für Kultursemiotik, langjähriger Sprecher des Fachausschuss Forschung der Deutschen Gesellschaft für Soziale Psychiatrie, Beiratsmitglied der Deutschen Gesellschaft für Semiotik, Mitherausgeber der Zeitschrift für Semiotik.

Dr. Ullrich Ahrens, Psychologe (M.A.) und Psychodramatherapeut, arbeitet als Leiter einer sozialpsychiatrischen Kontakt- und Beratungsstelle.

Z Psychodrama Soziometr (2016) (Suppl) 15:119–130
DOI 10.1007/s11620-015-0297-6

HAUPTBEITRÄGE

Zeitschrift für Psychodrama und Soziometrie

Veränderungsprozesse bei Psychiatrie-PatientInnen durch Psychodrama-Gruppentherapie im Rahmen einer psychiatrischen Ambulanzversorgung

Christian Fingerhut

Online publiziert: 27. November 2015

Zusammenfassung Vorliegende Arbeit befasst sich mit den Ergebnissen zweier Therapiegruppen, die der Autor zwischen April 2011 und Februar 2012 in der Ambulanz der Klinik für Psychiatrie am St. Marienhospital Hamm durchführte. Die aus initial jeweils zehn PatientInnen bestehenden zwei Gruppen fanden wöchentlich über jeweils vier Monate statt und wurden ko-therapeutisch durch pflegerische MitarbeiterInnen begleitet. Die eingesetzten Techniken werden dargestellt. Für einige PatientInnen wird exemplarisch die initial bestehende Konfliktsituation und das durch das Spiel erzielte Ergebnis dargestellt: Bei depressiven PatientInnen konnte durch Spiegeln bei arbeitsbezogenen Konflikten eine Abgrenzung oder Klärung erreicht werden. Bei PatientInnen mit Persönlichkeits- oder Angststörungen stand eine Stärkung der eigenen Identität im Vordergrund des Spiels. Abschließend werden Rückmeldungen von PatientInnen in einer Evaluation über einen Zeitraum von zwei Jahren dargestellt.

Schlüsselwörter Psychodrama-Gruppe · Psychiatrie · Psychotherapie · Ambulante Versorgung · ICD-10-Diagnosen · Anpassungsstörungen · Depression

Processes of change arising from psychodrama group therapy in a psychiatric outpatients' clinic

Abstract This article summarizes the results of two psychodrama groups, which took place in the psychiatric outpatients' clinic at the St. Marienhospital Hamm. Initially there were ten participants in each group, which ran weekly for four months (between April 2011 and February 2012). The Psychodrama techniques that were

Dr. med. C. Fingerhut (✉)
Drensteinfurt, Deutschland
E-Mail: christian.fingerhut@marienhospital-hamm.de
E-Mail: christianfingerhut@online.de

used will be explained. Case studies are used to illustrate the development from the initial conflict situation and which could be observed during role-play. Mirroring concerning work related conflicts was shown to be successful in enabling some depressive patients to reach discrimination or clarification. For patients with personality or anxiety disorders the emphasis was on the strengthening of their identity. Finally, the author presents a post-group evaluation of the patients over two years.

Keywords Psychodrama · Psychiatry · Psychotherapy · Outpatient's clinic · ICD-10-diagnoses · Adjustment disorders · Depression

1 Beschreibung der Klinik und des gruppentherapeutischen Settings

Die Klinik für Psychiatrie, Psychotherapie und Psychosomatik im westfälischen Hamm ist als Abteilungspsychiatrie eines Allgemeinkrankenhauses (Ärztliche Leitung Prof. Dr. Beine) zuständig für die regionale psychiatrische Pflichtversorgung.

Im Rahmen der Institutsambulanz findet werktäglich eine ärztlich geleitete allgemeinpsychiatrische Sprechstunde statt, womit ein kurzfristiges Gesprächsangebot vorgehalten wird.

Während bei Erstkontakten zunächst häufig Gruppenangebote wie Psychoedukation, Bewegung und Entspannung empfohlen werden, werden nach genauerer Einschätzung der Problematik oder stattgefundener Krisenbehandlung indikative oder problemorientierte Gruppen angeboten.

Voraussetzungen für die Teilnahme an der Psychodrama-Gruppe sind:
- ambulante Behandlungsstabilität
- erkennbare Reflexionsfähigkeit
- Eigenmotivation zur Bearbeitung von Konflikten.

Das auf der folgenden Seite abgedruckte Info-Blatt (Tab. 1) informierte geeignete und motivierte PatientInnen allgemeinverständlich über die Besonderheiten dieser Gruppentherapie.

Ab Mai 2011 wurden von mir in diesem Setting ambulante Psychodramagruppen angeboten und durchgeführt. Die ersten beiden fanden bis Februar 2012 statt und wurden im Rahmen meiner Abschlussarbeit zum Psychodramatherapeuten ausführlich dokumentiert. Der Artikel stellt eine gekürzte Fassung dieser Arbeit dar, erweitert allerdings um PatientInnenrückmeldungen aus späteren PatientInnengruppen.

Das neue Gruppenangebot wurde von mir als geschlossene Gruppe mit einer Größe von 10 bis 12 TeilnehmerInnen konzipiert, möglichst geschlechtsausgewogen. Hintergrund der geschlossenen Gruppenstruktur war die Überlegung einer zunehmenden Vertrauensbildung von TeilnehmerInnen, die absehbar eine längere Zeitspanne miteinander im Rollenhandeln verbringen.

Zum Konzept gehörte außerdem eine Begrenzung auf 10 bis 15 Sitzungen zu jeweils maximal 2 Zeitstunden, um einerseits allen TeilnehmerInnen die Möglichkeit zu geben mindestens einmal als ProtagonistIn ein Thema auf die Bühne zu bringen, andererseits aber auch durch die zeitliche Begrenzung die Fokussierung auf beson-

Tab. 1 Infoblatt

Psychodrama	
Zeit	Montags oder Donnerstags 16 bis maximal 18 Uhr
Treffpunkt	Therapieraum 3 Geronto-TK
Therapeuten	Dr. Fingerhut/Psychiatrische Fachpflege
Zielgruppe	Patienten mit Depressionen/ Persönlichkeitsstörungen
Nicht geeignet für	BPS, wahnhafte Störungen
Neueinstieg	Geschlossene Gruppe, jeweils ca.10–12 Sitzungen
Teilnehmerzahl	10 bis 12 Patienten, möglichst geschlechtsausgewogen

Psyche = Innenwelt/Drama = handelndes Erleben

Es geht darum, Verhaltensweisen in Szene zu setzen, Handlungen zu erproben, zu beobachten, zu vergleichen und in ihrer Wirkung zu erleben

Ablauf: Eine Psychodrama-Sitzung gliedert sich in eine Aufwärm-, Spiel- und Nachbesprechungsphase. Die Methode ist handlungsorientiert. Ein Patient spielt unter Anleitung und mit Hilfe von Mitspielern charakteristische für ihn problematische Situationen. Mit Hilfe von Rollentausch können Verzerrungen der Selbstwahrnehmung oder der Wahrnehmung von Beziehungen aufgedeckt werden, die Sichtweise des gespielten Gegenübers wird oft besser verstanden. Biografische Szenen oder in der Zukunft liegende Möglichkeiten können dargestellt und mit Requisiten ausgestaltet werden

Für viele Menschen ist es effektiver ein Problem zu spielen als darüber zu reden. Häufig ist ein im Psychodrama gelöstes Problem auch im realen Leben besser lösbar

Darüber hinaus gibt es je nach Gruppenzusammensetzung Möglichkeiten der Darstellung von vorgegebenen Themen (Soziodrama, Märchen) und Wünschen (z. B. Zauberladen)

Ein Vorgespräch ist i.R. der Ambulanzsprechstunde notwendig

Aktualisiert 10/11- Fingerhut

ders wichtige Themen zu fördern. Hierdurch sollte auch die Drop-Out-Rate reduziert werden.

Der Gruppenabschluss wurde mit den TeilnehmerInnen abgesprochen, wichtige Themen noch auf die Agenda gesetzt. In der letzten Gruppensitzung wurde am Ende eine Evaluation durchgeführt, Interessenten für eine Fortsetzung aufgenommen. Auf Evaluationsergebnisse wird am Ende des Artikels kurz eingegangen.

Grundzüge einer psychodramatisch orientierten Gruppentherapie wurden mit einem Team psychiatrischer Fachpflegekräfte vorab thematisiert, die im Wechsel als Ko-TherapeutInnen gewonnen werden konnten.

Deren Aufgaben bestanden insbesondere in:

- der Übernahme schwieriger AntagonistInnen-/Hilfs-Ichrollen
- dem Vorhalten von Einzelbetreuungskapazitäten bei vorübergehend labilisierten PatientInnen
- der Protokollführung der Spielsituation.

2 Eingesetzte Techniken

In der Erwärmungsphase:
Nach Kurt Lewin (1951), der Veränderungsprozesse als Abfolge der drei Phasen Auftauen, Verändern, Wiedereinfrieren charakterisiert, dient die Erwärmungsphase dem Auftauen der Strukturen des Systems.

Ziele der Erwärmung sind:

- emotionale Aktivierung
- emotionale Fokussierung auf ein einheitliches Aktivitätsniveau
- Fokussierung eines möglichst von allen getragenen Themas

Folgende Techniken wurden verwendet:

1. *Befindlichkeitsrunde*: Gegenseitige Vorstellung durch Zuwerfen eines Balls.
2. *Soziometrische Aufstellung* auf der Bühne nach Alter, Wohnort, Partnerschaft, stationären oder ambulanten Therapien etc. Patienten können auch eigene Fragen an die Gruppe stellen. Gegenseitiges Kennenlernen und Vertrauensbildung wird dadurch auf spielerische Weise umgesetzt.
3. *Stühle-Übung*: Auf dem Stuhl vor mir sitzt eine Person, die mir emotional wichtig ist, die ich anspreche und deren Rolle ich anschließend einnehme – Übung zur Rollenübernahme und zur thematischen Erwärmung.
4. *Zauberladen* (Magic Shop) als gruppenzentriertes Arrangement mit Käufer- und Verkäufergruppe zur Imagination von Wünschen.

In der Spielphase:

1. ProtagonistInnenspiel mit kurzer Anamneseerhebung auf der Bühne und Eindoppeln der AntagonistInnen/DoppelgängerInnen
2. Spiegeltechnik zur Betrachtung von Prozessen „von außen“
3. Freezing bzw. Zeitraffer zum Stoppen bzw. Beschleunigen von Spielabläufen
4. Play-Back-Theater: ProtagonistIn steuert das Spiel von außen, ist emotional weniger berührt
5. Schaffung eines sicheren Ortes (Angstabbau bei traumatisierten PatientInnen)
6. Doppeln zur Verstärkung/Korrektur von Aussagen
7. Soziometrische Spielelemente mit Hilfsmitteln (z. B. Seil zur Distanzermittlung)

In der Nachbesprechung:

1. Sharing: Was teile ich mit den jeweiligen ProtagonistInnen (Mitgefühl aus eigener Erfahrung)?
2. Rollenfeedback: Mitspieler/Antagonisten berichten, was sie in ihren Rollen gefühlt, erlebt haben
3. Zuschauerfeedback- keine Fragen!
4. „Letztes Wort“ der ProtagonistInnen über emotionale Bewegung und Befindlichkeit durch das eigene Spiel.

3 Diagnostische Zuordnung

Patienten mit folgenden ICD-10-Diagnosen wurden zur Gruppenteilnahme eingeladen:

1. Depressives Störungsspektrum, F32 bzw. F33
2. Anpassungsstörungen, F43

3. Persönlichkeitsstörungen mit Betonung dependenter Strukturen, F60.6 bzw. F60.7

Die im Folgenden exemplarisch dargestellten vier PatientInnenverläufe waren vordiagnostiziert als:

A) Frau B.: wahnhafte rezidivierende depressive Störung, derzeit remittiert, F33.3
B) Frau Sw.: schwere depressive Störung, F32.2, V.a. gemischte Persönlichkeitsstörung
C) Herr B.: Trennungskonflikt i.R. einer Anpassungsstörung, F43.2
D) Frau Se.: schwere depressive Störung, F32.2, V.a. gemischte Persönlichkeitsstörung

4 ProtagonistInnenspiele – Interpretation der Veränderungsprozesse

A) Frau B. möchte ihre erlebte Veränderung nach dem Aussteigen aus dem Beruf im Zusammenhang mit ihrer depressiven Erkrankung thematisieren.

In der Erwärmung berichtet sie über eine lange und intensive Berufstätigkeit im Krankenpflegebereich bis zu ihrer Erkrankung vor einigen Jahren. Jetzt schaffe sie auch im privaten Bereich nichts mehr, komme sich wie eine Versagerin vor. Mit dem Spiel wolle sie die Akzeptanz ihrer Störung verbessern.

1. Szene. Symbolisiert ihr früheres Leben mit „Zack-zack- bin immer unterwegs, mir macht es Spaß." Nach Eindopplung des Doppelgängers und Rollentausch stresst sie ihre Mitmenschen, durch Beschleunigung der Szene gerät sie außer Atem.

2. Szene. Krankheit wird eingedoppelt: „Habe sie lahmgelegt, zeige ihr die Grenzen auf, zur Not durch Klinikaufenthalte. Sie hat sich wie ein Hamster im Rad verausgabt." In der Szene wird sie durch ihre Krankheit gebremst. Im Spiegel: Die Erkrankung stützt auch.

3. Szene. Die Unsicherheit betritt die Bühne: „Wie soll es weitergehen mit Arbeit, Finanzen, Wohnung?" Mit Hilfe ihres Doppelgängers drängt die Unsicherheit die Krankheit von der Bühne. In ihrer eigenen Rolle erkennt sie den protektiven Aspekt der Krankheit: „Sie passt auf mich auf, ich kann mich mit ihr versöhnen."

Zur Unsicherheit: „Du bereitest mir jetzt keine schlaflosen Nächte mehr. ICH SCHAFFE DAS!"

Letztes Wort in der Nachbesprechung: „Früher konnte ich mich nur durch Auspowern wahrnehmen. Erkrankung schützt mich auch!"

Interpretation. Frau B. kehrte nach einer Trennung im Zusammenhang mit einer in Süddeutschland stationär behandelten *depressiven Phase* in ihre frühere Heimat zurück, stellte sich zur weiteren Medikamentenbehandlung in der Ambulanz vor, erlebte aber auch hier ihre verminderte Belastbarkeit die zu einer erneuten stationären Krisenintervention führte. Sie stellt das Thema Leistungsfähigkeit vor im Vergleich zu nach einer Depression in den Fokus. Im Spiel wird ihr klar, dass sie mit ihrer früheren Berufstätigkeit an ihre Grenzen gekommen ist, die sie vorher nicht beachtete. Indem sie die Krankheit personifiziert bekommt diese einen Sinn. Frau B. gibt an sich mit ihr versöhnen zu können, da sie sich nun besser wahrnehmen könne. Im weiteren Verlauf akzeptiert sie die Teilerwerbsfähigkeit nach erneuter Reha-Behandlung und teilt sich seitdem Teilzeit-Arbeitsangebote besser ein.

Die Veränderung bestand in der Klärung, neuer Prioritätensetzung, realistischerer Einschätzung der eigenen Möglichkeiten.

B) Frau Sw. möchte ihre durch ihre Erkrankung bedingte Talfahrt verstehen. Als *Ausgangsszene* dient ein beengtes Essen in einem Restaurant, welches inszeniert wird. Sie hatte sich auf den Abend gefreut. Dann aber durch längeres Warten und nahesitzende Tischnachbarn steigt zunehmend Panik auf, die sich bis zur Todesangst steigert. Sie gibt an diese zum ersten Mal nach dem Umzug in ihr jetziges Haus verspürt zu haben, kurz nach dem letzten persönlichen Kontakt zur Mutter.

Die zweite Szene spielt daher in der Tankstelle der Mutter, wo Frau Sw. ihr zum Geburtstag gratuliert. Diese nimmt die Gratulation wie einen Geschäftskontakt an, widmet sich unmittelbar danach wieder dem Kunden. Frau Sw. fühlt sich fehlplatziert, wie im falschen Film, wird von der Mutter nicht weiter beachtet.

In einer *Surplus-Szene* soll/will sie ihr Unwohlsein thematisieren, dies wird ihr zunächst von ihrem Doppelgänger vorgespielt. Erst als ihr Partner sie unterstützt, schafft sie es der Mutter zu sagen: Zeitlebens sei die Mutter/Tochter-Beziehung nur geschäftlich gewesen, emotional dem alles untergeordnet, sie habe sich immer nur benutzt gefühlt, sei daher froh von zuhause weg zu sein.

Im „letzten Wort“ gibt sie an, dass ihr einiges klar geworden sei, sie sich besser fühle.

Interpretation. Frau Sw. wurde aus der Tagesklinik in weitere ambulante und Gruppentherapie übernommen. Als *depressive Störung* vordiagnostiziert zeigt sie im Spiel die klassischen Symptome einer *Panikstörung* mit aufsteigenden Ängsten in beengten Situationen hier beim Essen im Restaurant. Die biografische Perspektive erscheint fruchtbar, es erfolgt auf Nachfrage die Angabe einer Schlüsselsituation, die der Patientin den Hintergrund bewusst macht.

Es gelingt ihr schließlich auch die fehlende emotionale Zuwendung – der imaginären Mutter gegenüber in einer Surplusszene – zu thematisieren, woraufhin sie im Spiel die Ängste ihr gegenüber verliert.

Eine weitere psychotherapeutische Bearbeitung sowie eine Fortsetzung der Gruppe waren geplant. Die erreichte Veränderung wurde nach Konfrontation mit den angstauslösenden Situationen, schließlich den Hintergründen im biografischen Kontext erkennbar. Durch Abnahme des Angstpegels konnte tendenziell eine Erweiterung der Interaktionsmöglichkeiten erreicht werden.

C) H. B. beschreibt sich als Mensch der dauernd unterwegs ist (D-U), *es allen recht machen will.* Er engagiert sich in seiner Freizeit überall, opfert auch seinen Jahresurlaub um dem Bruder bei der Ernte zu helfen: *Ich versuche mich zu zerreißen!*

Da er viele Aktivitäten beschreibt, wird die Szene durch einen Stuhlkreis mit vier Stühlen gestaltet, in dem sich die Freizeit, durch zwei Mitspielerinnen dargestellt, ständig weiterbewegt. Zusätzlich wird der Bruder und H.B.s Doppelgänger dargestellt.

Im Spielverlauf wird H. B. durch sich überschneidende Freizeitaktivitäten (Doppelkopf[1], Feuerwehr, Schützenverein, Fußball) zunehmend unter Druck gesetzt, da das Tempo im Sinne einer Maximierung vom Spielleiter gesteigert wird. Während er anfangs noch alles genießt, wird das Spiel daher hektisch, es gelingt ihm schließlich nicht mehr alle Aktivitäten zu koordinieren, es folgen Absagen. Schließlich sagt er alles ab, da die Hilfe für den Bruder bei der Ernte Vorrang hat.

Im Spiegel bzw. im Interview erlebt er sich *wie zwischen zwei Stühlen*. Schließlich sagt er dem Bruder zweimal ab und bekennt: *Ich brauche mehr Zeit für mich!* Seine Schlussfolgerung: „Muss mein Leben neu ordnen, Prioritätensetzung!"

Interpretation. H. B. war als *Trennungskonflikt/Anpassungsstörung* vordiagnostiziert: Als Sprechstundenpatient mit initialer Suizidalität war er knapp an einer stationären Aufnahme vorbeigeschrammt, hatte zeitweise Tranquilizer bekommen. Stand für ihn anfangs der Schmerz über die erlebte Trennung im Vordergrund, fokussierte er sein Spiel auf sein „Dauernd Unterwegssein." Hierdurch zerrissen blieb ihm nicht mehr genug Zeit für das wirklich Wichtige. Im Spiel wandeln sich die zuerst lustvoll erlebten vielfältigen Hobbies durch Maximierung zu einem „Hamsterradlauf", als dessen Konsequenz er der Beziehung zu seinem Bruder Vorrang gibt. Indirekt wird damit auch die Beziehungstrennung als Folge seiner Zeitproblematik angesprochen, als deren Konsequenz er zum Ende des Spiels seine Prioritäten neu setzen will. Im weiteren Behandlungsverlauf benötigte H. B. nur noch kurzfristige therapeutische Unterstützung.

D) Frau Se. benennt das Thema „Erwartungen", sie müsse immer die der anderen erfüllen. In der Erwärmung benennt sie verschiedene Situationen, in denen es ihr schwer fiel nein zu sagen. Aktuell geht es um Geld mit dem Hintergrund, dass die Familie von ihr erwarte z. B. den Neffen zu sponsern.

In der Szene spricht sie mit ihrem Mann, der dem Neffen das Geld für die Auto-Finanzierung geben würde. Sie benennt eigene Bedürfnisse aber auch verinnerlichte Erwartungen:

Von den Schwiegereltern fühle sie sich durch Missachtung bestraft, was sie kaum aushalte.

Die *Erwartung* wird auf die Bühne geholt, steht da mit breiter Brust: *Mir kann keiner was!* Die Protagonistin ist ratlos, fragt ihre Doppelgängerin, diese soll vorspielen. Die gibt vor: „Wir halten uns raus!" Das wird von ihr bestätigt: „Wir kümmern uns nur noch um uns!"

In der Nachbesprechung wird im Sharing große Betroffenheit deutlich: Nein sagen sei schwer! Im Schlusswort beschreibt sie ihre Verzweiflung im Konflikt zwischen eigenen Ansprüchen und Erwartungen. Klartext reden sei erforderlich!

In einem späteren *zweiten Spiel* möchte sie die Wut auf ihre Mutter darstellen: Im Gespräch beschreibt sie deutlich ein andauerndes Abhängigkeitsverhältnis, da sie bei ihr zur Miete wohne, man seit einigen Jahren nicht mehr miteinander rede, sie die Mutter trotzdem brauche.

In der ersten Szene äußert sich die Mutter abschätzig über die Tochter: Wegen der Misshandlungsvorwürfe spreche sie nicht mehr mit der Tochter. Im Weiteren findet keine Kommunikation statt! Um ihre Wut loszuwerden schlägt sie auf einen Stoffball neben der Mutter: „Ich will dir eine reinhauen, weil du mich schlecht behandelst, weil du mir meinen Sohn abspenstig gemacht hast!" Aus der Wut wird schließlich Trauer, sie erkennt, dass sie gehen muss, weil Respekt durch die Mutter nicht möglich ist. Im letzten Wort gibt sie an, gewachsen zu sein, ihre Stärke erkannt zu haben etwas zu beenden.

Interpretation. Frau Se. war als *schwere depressive Störung mit Verdacht auf Persönlichkeitsstörung* ambulant vordiagnostiziert. In den beiden Spielen (im Abstand von 1 Monat) nähert sie sich ihrer tieferliegenden Abhängigkeitsproblematik von der Oberfläche her an: Im ersten Spiel benennt sie Erwartungen der anderen an sich, von denen sie sich nicht distanzieren könne, zieht als Resümee Nein sagen lernen zu müssen, an sich zu denken. Als Hintergrund identifiziert sie in Einzelgesprächen ein andauerndes hochpathologisches dyadisches Abhängigkeitsverhältnis zur Mutter, da beide nicht mehr miteinander sprechen aber noch im gleichen Haus wohnen, schließlich wird zur Deeskalation ein stationärer Aufenthalt erforderlich.

Im zweiten Spiel verleiht sie ihrer Wut Ausdruck, erkennt ihre Trauer um das längst Verlorene und zieht den räumlichen Abstand in Betracht.

Hier hätte die Darstellung einer zeitlichen Zukunftsperspektive i.S. einer Surplusszene sicher noch verstärkend gewirkt.

Die Patientin bleibt noch länger in der Nachfolgegruppe, schätzt für sich auch die Ausdrucksmöglichkeit. Sie wird beim anstehenden Auszug einzeltherapeutisch begleitet, der schließlich auch stattfindet.

5 Methodenspezifische Veränderungsaspekte

Nach Moreno will der Mensch sich sinngemäß nicht gerne auf die Beweglichkeit und Unsicherheit des Augenblicks verlassen (1959). In dieser Angst ist die Basis gestörten Handelns zu sehen. Diese Formulierung bietet die Möglichkeit, Störungen als Ausdruck illusionärer Zielsetzungen, die der Abwehr dieser Angst dienen, zu begreifen.

Spontanes und kreatives Handeln erfordert aber – ebenfalls nach Moreno – AnhängerInnen des *wahrhaft Imperfekten* zu sein. Die Betroffenen können sich nur dann auf das Wagnis der Spontaneitätslage einlassen, wenn sie bereit sind, das Risiko eines Fehlers oder von Misslingen in Kauf zu nehmen.

In dem Maße wie Psychotherapie allgemein Veränderung (der Persönlichkeit) bedeutet, ist bei PatientInnen von einem Zögern auszugehen diese Veränderung zuzulassen, weil sie nicht wissen, was an Stelle der pathologischen Kompromissbildung stehen wird. Anders als bei verhaltenstherapeutischen Verfahren ist bei psychodynamischen/psychodramatischen Interventionen die Unsicherheit über Prozess und Ergebnis zu Recht deutlicher ausgeprägt, weil hier Schritte und Ziele vor Spielbeginn nur allgemein erläutert werden können.

Dies gilt zunächst für einen *Gruppenbeginn*, das Zögern entspringt der Befürchtung sich als erster verletzlich zu zeigen. Hier wurde durch Verwendung der *Aktionssozio-*

metrie mit Positionierung im Raum die Gruppe in Bewegung gebracht, spielerisch gegenseitig Informationen vermittelt über Herkunft, Alter, Lebenssituation, Therapieerfahrung etc. von Vorteil ist, dass sich die Gruppe gemeinsam öffnet, es gibt keinen Informationsvorsprung einzelner.

In der häufig in der zweiten Gruppenstunde praktizierten *Stühleübung* werden psychodramatische Basistechniken eingeübt: Nach Ansprache einer emotional nahestehenden Person werden durch Rollentausch vermutete Gedanken und Gefühle ausgedrückt, ein imaginärer Dialog in Gang gesetzt, der neben klärenden Aspekten bereits konflikthaft besetzte Beziehungen aufzeigt.

Analysiert man die unter Kapitel IV beschriebenen Spiele lassen sich die unter A und C beschriebenen arbeits- bzw. depressionsbezogenen Konflikte psychodramatisch überwiegend durch Rollentausch, Spiegelszenen oder Maximierung klären. Die erreichte Veränderung bestand in Abgrenzung, neuer Prioritätensetzung, realistischerer Einschätzung der eigenen Möglichkeiten.

Die unter B) und D) beschriebenen biografisch orientierten Spielverläufe wurden als konflikthaft ambivalente Eltern-Kind-Beziehungen ausgedrückt, die zu einer tiefgreifenden kindlichen Verunsicherung führten. Methodisch wichtig war die Schaffung eines sicheren Rückzugsraums, weiterhin die Darstellung der Ambivalenz durch Doppeln und die psychodramatische Darstellung einer möglichen Perspektive z. B. in Gestalt einer Surplusrealität.

Die Veränderung bestand in einer Stärkung der eigenen Identität und der Entwicklung von Ressourcen als Gegenentwurf.

Vor allem bei Angst- und Persönlichkeitsstörungen kann es sinnvoll sein über den biografischen Kontext in eine Auseinandersetzung mit der Angst zu gehen, wie es auch Bender und Stadler (2012) aufzeigen.

Analysiert man die beiden beschriebenen Gruppen weiter kann man zu dem Ergebnis gelangen, dass es bei den Spielen A und C eher um eine Begrenzung/Grenzsetzung bei Anpassungs- und depressiven Störungen ging, bei den Spielen B und D eher um eine Ausweitung der Interaktionsmöglichkeiten durch Erkenntnis/Entwicklung der Persönlichkeit bei Angst- oder Persönlichkeitsstörungen.

6 Kritische Einschätzung und Evaluation

Bei der Konzeption der Gruppe ging ich von einer engen Vernetzung zwischen stationären BehandlerInnen und der ambulant gesteuerten Einteilung in eine konfliktbearbeitende Psychodramabehandlung aus. Diese Vorstellung erwies sich als idealisiert. Stationäre PatientInnen wurden nur ausnahmsweise für die Gruppe angemeldet, die meisten PatientInnen aus ambulanter Behandlung heraus motiviert. Dies hatte einerseits zur Folge, dass die Motivation der als Ko-TherapeutInnen fungierenden Pflegekräfte im Lauf der Gruppe nachließ, zumal im gleichen Zeitraum deren stationäre Arbeitsbelastung durch Bettenausbau und Stellenkürzung zunahm.

Inzwischen wird die Ko-TherapeutInnenfunktion nach Vereinbarung mit der ärztlichen Leitung durch interessierte AssistenzärztInnen wahrgenommen, die dadurch neben dem bekannten psychotherapeutischen Weiterbildungscurriculum ein weiteres Psychotherapieverfahren kennenlernen. Die Gruppenzeiten wurden auf 2 Zeitstunden erweitert, der Beginn für die häufig berufstätigen PatientInnen auf den frühen Abend verlegt.

Auch zeigte sich, dass Psychodrama für (stationäre) ärztlich/therapeutische BehandlerInnen noch nicht als Option angekommen war, obwohl über das Angebot informiert worden war. Als Konsequenz organisierte ich mehrere Fortbildungen über das Thema. Eine regelmäßige Weiterbildung hätte das Ziel, dass dieses Angebot mittelfristig von weiteren Kollegen durchgeführt werden könnte. In Kurzseminaren könnten psychodramatische Techniken erlernt werden um berufsgruppenübergreifend Psychodrama zu verankern. Denkbar und bereits erprobt wäre auch die Teilnahme von MedizinstudentInnen im Rahmen des psychiatrischen Ausbildungsabschnitts oder im Praktischen Jahr. Bislang ist die Präsenz eines solchen Behandlungsverfahrens in einer Klinik jedoch in hohem Masse vom persönlichen Engagement Einzelner abhängig. Es gibt einfach zu wenige Vertreter die die Vielfalt dieser „Randgruppenmethode" darstellen.

Dabei scheint mir prinzipiell Psychodrama eine Behandlungsmethode zu sein, die richtig dosiert angewendet zur PatientInnenzufriedenheit beiträgt, weil in kurzen überschaubaren Behandlungsabschnitten den TeilnehmerInnen Erkenntnisse über sich vermittelt werden, aus denen heraus sie im wirklichen Leben Veränderungsschritte durchführen können.

Als Verfahren mit sog. „practice based evidence" bietet es psychodynamische, systemische und lösungsorientierte Sichtweisen. Es passt daher zu den Ansprüchen, die an moderne Therapieeinrichtungen gestellt werden, effektiv und Schulen übergreifend zu arbeiten.

Letztlich entscheiden heutzutage PatientInnen darüber, ob sie ein Psychotherapieverfahren annehmen. Dies schien mir sowohl bei der dargestellten als auch bei späteren Psychodrama-Gruppen in hohem Maß der Fall zu sein. Als ein Beleg mag die äußerst geringe Abbruchquote bei einer Gruppendauer von ca. 4 Monaten gelten:

Von 36 PatientInnen in 5 Gruppen zwischen 2011 und 2013 brachen 6 Teilnehmerinnen die Therapie ab was einer durchschnittlichen AbbrecherInnenquote von 17 % entspricht.

Zur Dokumentation dieses Eindrucks verfasste ich daraufhin auch für Weiterbildungszwecke eine Evaluation, deren Ergebnisse ich abschließend darstelle. Sie stellt inzwischen einen integralen Bestandteil des Gruppenabschlusses dar.

6.1 Evaluation/Bewertung ambulante Psychodrama-Gruppe

Zwischen Januar 2012 und November 2014 bewerteten 31 GruppenpatientInnen die erlebte Therapiegruppe.

Sie beantworteten folgende Fragen bzw. gaben offene Rückmeldungen:

1. Konnten Sie die für Sie relevanten Themen im Lauf der Sitzungen darstellen/spielen?

- 15 Mal wurde vollständig angekreuzt
- Offengeblieben seien familiäre Themen, Selbstabgrenzungsthemen, die Darstellung von Lebensangst.

2. Hat Ihnen die Methode „Psychodrama" zugesagt? Bitte markieren Sie auf einem Balken zwischen 100 und 0% den Grad der empfundenen Hilfe/ Zustandsverbesserung!

- Durchschnittlich wurden 75 % Zustandsverbesserung angekreuzt

3. Was war besonders hilfreich, was weniger?

- Hilfreich: Selbstbestimmung, Vergleiche ziehen, Erfahrungsaustausch, Gruppenvertrauen, Zusammenhalt, Aktionssoziometrie, Ansicht der eigenen Situation von außen, Aufzeigen von Lösungen durch Spiele, Sichtweise des Doppelgängers, Märchenspiel
- Weniger hilfreich: Fehlen des Ko-Therapeuten (Anmerkung: Stand zeitweise nicht zur Verfügung)

4. Konnten Sie in der Gruppe das erforderliche Vertrauen entwickeln?

- Ja: 25 Nennungen
- Später: 3
- Nein: 3

5. Würden Sie an einer neuen Gruppe teilnehmen wollen?

- Ja: 26 Nennungen
- Nein: 4
- Später: 1

6. Anregungen und Wünsche an die Gruppenleitung!

- Weiter mit 2 TherapeutInnen
- realistischere Requisiten
- längere Einführungsphase
- bessere Erläuterung der Gruppenregeln
- häufiger Gruppenspiele wie Zauberladen und Märchen

Anmerkungen

1 Bei Doppelkopf handelt es sich um ein Kartenspiel.

Literatur

Bender, W., & Stadler, C. (2012). *Psychodrama-Therapie. Grundlagen, Methodik, Anwendungsgebiete*. Stuttgart: Schattauer Verlag.

Lewin, K. (1951). *Field Theory in the Social Sciences*. New York: Harper & Row.

Zugrundeliegende und weiterführende Literatur

Moreno, J. L. (1959). *Gruppenpsychotherapie und Psychodrama*. Stuttgart: Thieme Verlag.
Schacht, M. (2003). *Spontaneität und Begegnung- Zur Persönlichkeitsentwicklung aus Sicht des Psychodramas*. Köln: Inscenario Verlag.
Von Ameln, F., Kramer, J. H., & Gerstmann, R. (Hrsg.). (2004). *Psychodrama*. Heidelberg: Springer Verlag.
Yablonski, L. (1998). *Psychodrama*. Stuttgart: Klett Cotta Verlag.
Yalom, I. D. (2010). *Theorie und Praxis der Gruppenpsychotherapie*. Stuttgart: Klett-Cotta.

Fingerhut Christian, geb. 1957, Dr. med., Facharzt für Psychiatrie, Zusatzbezeichnung Psychotherapie, Weiterbildung am Institut für soziale Interaktion (ISI) Hamburg zum Psychodrama-Therapeuten bis 2013, systemische Weiterbildung bei Dr. Aderhold. Seit 2010 Institutsambulanz der Klinik für Psychiatrie u. Psychotherapie am St. Marienhospital in Hamm/Westfalen (Klinik der Privaten Universität Witten/Herdecke), Arbeitsschwerpunkte Psychopharmakotherapie, Gruppentherapie, Psychiatrische Gutachten.

Z Psychodrama Soziometr (2016) (Suppl) 15:131–141
DOI 10.1007/s11620-015-0305-x

HAUPTBEITRÄGE

Zeitschrift für Psychodrama und Soziometrie

Psychodrama in the group of patients diagnosed with eating disorders

Simona Prosen

Published online: 26 November 2015

Abstract This article presents a case study showing a psychodramatic approach to treating patients diagnosed with eating disorders (anorexia and bulimia nervosa). Information from 196 psychodrama group meetings of patients diagnosed with eating disorders was collected and recorded, in a clinical setting over a period of 7 years from 2004 to 2010. The main themes were the patients' primary family relationships, recognition of, and exploring, emotions in the present situation and exploration of the eating disorder treatment process. Psychodrama facilitates the integration of emotional, cognitive and behavioural aspects of personal experience and it is a valuable psychotherapeutic modality in treating patients with eating disorders.

Keywords Eating disorders · Anorexia nervosa · Bulimia nervosa · Psychodrama · Group psychotherapy

Psychodrama in einer PatientInnengruppe mit Essstörungen

Zusammenfassung Der vorliegende Artikel beschäftigt sich mit einer Fallstudie, die einem psychodramatischen Zugang bei der Behandlung von Essstörungen (Anorexie und Bulimie) folgt. Die Daten wurden in 196 Psychodramatherapiegruppentreffen von PatientInnen mit einer Essstörungsdiagnose in einem stationären Setting zwischen 2004 und 2010 gesammelt und zusammengetragen. Die Hauptthemen dabei waren die Beziehungen der PatientInnen zu ihren Primärfamilien, das Erkennen und Erforschen von Emotionen in der Gegenwart und die Beschäftigung

S. Prosen (✉)
Faculty of Education,
University of Ljubljana,
Kardeljeva pl. 16,
1000 Ljubljana, Slovenia
e-mail: simona.prosen@pef.uni-lj.si

mit dem Prozess der Essstörungsbehandlung. Psychodrama fördert die Integration emotionaler, kognitiver und verhaltensbezogener Aspekte persönlicher Erfahrungen und es ist eine valide psychotherapeutische Methode bei der Behandlung von PatientInnen mit Essstörungen.

Schlüsselwörter Essstsselwör · Anorexia nervosa · Bulimie · Psychodrama · Gruppenpsychotherapie

There are several studies on the characteristics of people diagnosed with eating disorders (ED) (e.g., Cassin and von Ranson 2005; Fassino et al. 2004) and the factors that may contribute to ED development (e.g., Ketisch et al. 2014). However, studies on the role of psychotherapy with this group of people are less available. In this article, after describing the theoretical background of ED I will present the analysis of observations gathered from the psychodrama group of patients diagnosed with ED and reflect upon what it means in practice.

1 Definition and prevalence of ED

According to the fourth edition of Diagnostic and Statistical Manual of Mental Disorders (DSM-IV-TR, APA 2000, in: Thompson et al. 2007) ED include anorexia nervosa (AN), bulimia nervosa (BN), binge-eating disorder (BED) and eating disorders not otherwise specified (EDNOS). EDNOS provides a category for patients with clinically meaningful or sub-threshold symptoms of other established diagnoses. Cognitive, behavioural, emotional and motivational disturbances including abnormal eating behaviours, maladaptive weight control efforts and distorted self-evaluation of weight and shape contribute to the diagnosis of ED (Stice et al. 2006).

The prevalence rate for AN is approximately 0.5 % and between 1 and 3 % for BN (APA 2000, in: Stice et al. 2006). Gender differences in AN and BN are significant–women outnumber men by a 10:1 ratio. Patients with ED have the highest mortality rate among the psychiatric disorders (Fairburn et al. 2000) and as such, understanding ED from multiple perspectives is an important undertaking.

2 Aetiology of ED

The aetiology of ED has been the subject of research from the neuro-chemical and neuropsychiatric, as well as socio-cultural and psychological aspects. Many risk factors, including neurotransmitter abnormalities, sexual abuse in childhood, low self-esteem, perfectionism, need for control, dysfunctional family dynamics, internalization of the thin-ideal, dietary restraint, and mood disturbances have been considered in relation to ED (e.g., Wilson et al. 2003, in: Stice et al. 2006). Risk factors may be divided into several clusters, e.g. genetic, environmental—relational and cultural. Those more applicable for incorporation into psychotherapeutic work (i.e., family relations, attachment pattern, modelling, life events and gender role) will be described in greater detail.

Families play a central role in understanding a person with ED (e.g., Downs and Blow 2013; Ketisch et al. 2014). However, determining whether the family interactions are the cause or an effect of the person's ED can be difficult. Several family characteristics have been studied, including communication patterns within the family, parental modelling of eating, psychological functioning of the parents, and weight-related criticism or teasing the child (Thompson et al. 2007).

One of family problems is in establishing boundaries: it can appear not only at the family level but also at a dyadic level between a parent and child. Boundary dissolution can create *enmeshment* in which individuals lack differentiation and individuation (Minuchin et al. 1978, in: Rowa et al. 2001). Individuation from parents is a major developmental task in late adolescence and early adulthood (Puklek Levpušček 2006). It is likely to be very difficult for individuals whose parents are unable (or are perceived as such) to maintain adequate separation from their children. In Smolak and Levine's study (1993, in: Rowa et al. 2001) women with AN were less individuated than those in the control group. Bruch (1978, in: Broberg et al. 2001) was the first to propose a link between ED and fear of both abandonment and autonomy. She emphasized the importance of an individual's current interpersonal problems and their roots in the primary relationships. The link between ED and difficulties in close relationships becomes more evident, especially bearing in mind the findings from the attachment theory.

Attachment theory is applicable not only to the child-parent relationships but also to relationships with significant others throughout one's life. Individuals with the *secure* attachment pattern easily establish close relationships, trust others and have low separation anxiety. Individuals with the *avoidant* attachment pattern are cautious when entering intimate relationships and those with the *anxious-ambivalent* attachment pattern want to establishing intimacy but at the same time experience strong fear of rejection (Mikulincer and Shaver 2007). The attachment patterns show stability during a person's childhood, adolescence, and adulthood unless his/her environment undergoes major changes (Thompson 1999, in: Broberg et al. 2001). Insecure attachment patterns are significantly more prevalent in women with ED. They either precede the disorder or contribute to its development rather than merely being a result of the disorder (Broberg et al. 2001). Individuals with ED tend to perceive themselves as being personally and/or socially deficient (Guidano and Liotti 1983, in: Armstrong and Roth 1989). Lacking or underestimating their own resources, they depend excessively upon their significant others in order to feel safe and secure. This is characteristic of anxious-ambivalent attachment. Daughters with such attachment pattern described the nature of their attachment to their mothers as a push–pull relationship, hot and cold attachment, governed largely by their mothers' emotional demands. Such behaviour leads to the hyper-activating interpersonal strategies which keep the person in a state of dysfunctional anger toward the parents (Salzman 1997).

Within attachment framework bingeing can be explained as a method of self-soothing. Since the attachment figures are not always reliable, available or sensitive, there is a focus on maintaining control which may be understood as a reaction to the sense of being unable to influence the response that is needed. Even ED as a whole can be seen as maintaining connection while avoiding rejection.

Children learn from, and model themselves on, their parents and this could provide an explanation for ED. Significant connections have been made between comments from parents and a daughter's desire to lose weight, as well as her views on her body (e.g., Smolak et al. 1999, in: Thompson et al. 2007). However, media and peer influences are also powerful sources that can contribute to changes in eating patterns (e.g., Keery and van den Berg 2004, in: Thompson et al. 2007). Media project images and behaviours that imply the importance of appearance and thinness, whereas peers may tease or give negative comments related to appearance.

Life events, that explain ED, include a relatively heterogeneous list of influences, which have the power to radically affect an individual's psychological and possibly their physical state. Experiences such as: change of family home, loss of a loved one, and illness, can all initiate change in eating patterns that may evolve into an ED. Perhaps the most often cited and researched life events involve traumatic experiences related to sexual abuse (Thompson et al. 2007).

Another possible factor, influencing the onset of ED, is the issues of gender roles as adopted by the individual and/or promoted by society. The traditional feminine role included passivity, need for approval, dependence and focus on interpersonal relationships and was associated with an increased risk for eating problems, while masculinity was related to a decreased risk for eating problems (Murnen and Smolak 1998, in: Thompson et al. 2007). Also, one can speculate on the connection between gender and the expression of anger. As it is deemed less appropriate for a woman to show anger, this feeling may be turned inwards. This has been found to be the case in women with insecure attachment patterns and predominates in the group of women with ED (Calamari and Pini 2003).

As mentioned before, only about 10% of individuals with ED are men, with an exception of BED, where this ratio is roughly equal. The idealisation of thinness for women is paralleled by a relatively intense pressure on men to achieve a muscular ideal (e.g., Anderson 1995, in: Thompson et al. 2007). Homosexuality also appears to be associated with an elevated risk; 20% or more of men with ED state this as their sexual orientation (Anderson 1995, in: Thompson et al. 2007).

3 ED treatment and psychodrama

Different approaches to ED treatment have existed for some time, but it is generally thought that, even though the symptom maybe treated, the first relapse can only be prevented by psychotherapy, which involves an intrapersonal change. However, it is crucial that the psychotherapy process takes place within a secure therapeutic relationship that offers the person a different model for relationships than those previously experienced (Stice et al. 2006). To accomplish psychotherapeutic change, several approaches have been reported in treating ED, such as *interpersonal therapy, cognitive behavioural treatment, psychodynamic treatment* (e.g., Crow and Brandenburg 2010; Keel and McCormick 2010), and the subject of our interest, *psychodrama* (e.g., Meillo 1991; Pahole and Prosen 2010; 2011).

Psychodrama focuses on the healthy psychological processes of the individual and the dynamics of the group. It develops a conceptual frame of reference that explains the mechanisms for creating a corrective experience, either by rewriting painful and dysfunctional history or by supplying the experiences that are missing. Psychodrama also has the ability to address the sensory-motor level of functioning through concretisation and may become the treatment of choice for all psychological disorders that stem from unprocessed experiences and that are stored at that level (Kipper 1998)—ED being one.

Psychodrama enables a broad look at the events, emotions and relationship representations that one has, thus interrupting repetitions of unwanted experiences (Blatner and Blatner 1988). Meillo (1991) states that the particular value of psychodrama compared to verbal therapy is that it awakens more feelings in the group members. It offers the possibility of an actually felt, relived insight.

4 Methodology

4.1 Group description

The data presented in this article were gathered in the psychodrama group of patients diagnosed with ED at the University Psychiatric Hospital in Ljubljana. The ED inpatient group underwent several therapeutic modalities, (e.g., art therapy, psychodynamic therapy, education on diet and behavioural control techniques, family therapy), including psychodrama. The purpose of the psychodrama group was to enable the patients to work on their personal issues that maybe contributing to their ED. Psychodrama was led by two therapists; it took place once per week and lasted for an hour. All patients in the unit participated in the group during their stay in the hospital, which is approximately 4–5 months; they were in the group from admission until their discharge. The group operated on a semi-open basis; there were usually between 10 and 15 members. The majority of group members were women, and the female to male ratio was close to that reported in the literature—10:1.

4.2 Procedure

The psychodrama group observations were gathered continuously over a period of 7 years (2004–2010). Altogether, observations from 196 group meetings were included in the analysis gathered by one of the two therapists leading the group (the author of this article) at the end of each meeting. The observations included the *overall structure* of the psychodrama session: protagonist oriented psychodrama, group oriented psychodrama, groups not including psychodrama action and the *main theme* that was presented in the group. According to these two criteria the observations were classified into categories presented in the results and discussion section.

5 Results and discussion

Psychodrama values the *moment*, the here-and-now in which the past and the future meet to form highly significant experiences, and the *interpersonal interactions* among people who are related in meaningful ways. *Enactment*—personal issues are presented *via* role-playing, and *concretisation*—physical representations of persons, but also situations, feelings, ideas, personification of inanimate objects (Kipper 1998) are applied within the group. Psychodrama actually applies what is known as a state-dependent recall; the possibility of retrieving pieces of information if you return to the mental state you were in at the time these pieces of information were encoded (Rothschild 2000). That opens up the possibility, in the present situation, to encode them into a different context. An array of psychodrama techniques were used during the sessions, the most prevalent being role reversal with auxiliary egos representing parts of the protagonist's subjective reality (Dayton 1994; Yaniv 2012). Role reversal enables the protagonist to transcend the habitual limitations of a single perspective (Blatner and Blatner 1988).

In the psychodrama group of patients diagnosed with ED observations were gathered from 196 group meetings; as mentioned before, these observations included the *overall structure* of the psychodrama session and the *main theme* that was presented in the group. Observations were classified into categories according to these two criteria and are presented in Table 1.

Table 1 The structure and themes of the psychodrama group of patients diagnosed with ED (f=196)

	f	%
Protagonist oriented psychodrama	133	67.9
Primary–family relationships	75	56.4
Whole-family relationships	46	
Relationship with father	14	
Relationship with mother	9	
Relationship with siblings	6	
Emotions	20	15.0
Process of treatment	13	9.8
Relationship with partner	8	6.0
Self-image, identity	7	5.3
School and work	4	3.0
Training	3	2.3
Relationship with the group	2	1.5
Group oriented psychodrama	20	10.2
Imaginary roles	6	
Group relations	4	
Boundaries, responsibilities	4	
Emotions- trust and anger	3	
Food	2	
Family members	1	
Groups not including psychodrama action	43	21.9
Farewell to a group member	42	
Death of a group member	1	

f frequency, % percentage

The majority of the group members needed several weeks to warm up to the group process. They usually started with playing roles of auxiliary ego(s) and then proceeded to the role of protagonist. Often, being chosen for a particular role warmed them up to be the protagonist in the subsequent psychodrama group meeting. The majority of the group members were protagonist once or twice, with a few playing that role more often, usually working on one issue throughout several psychodrama sessions. Approximately one fifth of the group members never stepped into the role of the protagonist, which may have been due to their pre-timed discharge from the treatment or not feeling secure enough within the group. It is possible that they were resistant towards working on issues not directly connected to their symptoms, as Meillo (1991) observed in his group of girls with ED. Or, for them working on their issues through playing the roles of auxiliary ego(s) and being the audience for the work of other group members had been important enough. However, the possible consequences of being/not being a protagonist would need a further research, possibly through interviews with each group member.

The main issue that appeared in the protagonist oriented psychodramas was relationships within the primary family (56.4 %). In the majority of cases the whole family, i.e. all family members and their inter-relationships were represented; boundary enmeshment was often evident during these psychodramas. Also, the daughter (patient)–father relationship was a frequent theme in the psychodrama sessions. In accordance with the findings of Rowa et al. (2001) this relationship is more specifically connected to the ED. The daughter–mother relationship was explored, but less so; this is interesting, especially taking into account the higher level of boundary enmeshment present in a mother–daughter relationship (Ketisch et al. 2014; Rowa et al. 2001). There are several possible explanations of the described results.

1. The relationship with the father was perhaps more immediate, since it may have been easier for the patients to differentiate themselves from him, even to get angry with him in comparison with the mother; often a friendly relationship was reported with the mothers.
2. Sometimes an idealisation of the mother–daughter relationship appeared; perhaps also family therapy resulted in an improvement in their relationship. Maybe this newly improved relationship was subject to enjoyment rather than analysis.
3. Another possibility is that (taking into account the descriptions given by the patients) the daughter–father attachment pattern is closer to the avoiding pattern and the daughter–mother attachment pattern is closer to the anxious-ambivalent one. The avoiding pattern induces less separation fears while the ambivalent pattern induces more. The latter attachment pattern includes the experience of total closeness with the other person and striving for that closeness even when the experience is opposite. These observations need to be explored further in order to be confirmed.

The second theme in the protagonist oriented psychodrama was creating a so-called *emotiogram* (15 %): externalising and concretising protagonist's emotions. The emotiogram included identification of emotions in the present situation, looking at the connections between different emotional states and exploration of the function the emotions have in different relationships. The emotions were also located in the body.

Establishing physical awareness especially with people who may be alexithymic is important (Rothschild 2000). The most frequently mentioned emotions were anger, fear and anxiety, followed by loneliness and envy. Anger, when externalised was usually connected to the protagonist's relationship with either their father or abuser (in cases of physical or sexual abuse), but in many cases the anger was turned inwards. Directing anger internally maybe be connected to the insecure attachment patterns that prevail in women with ED (Armstrong and Roth 1989; Barone and Guiducci 2009, in: Tasca et al. 2011). It is interesting to note that in the process of exhibiting emotions on stage, food was–in approximately one quarter of times–mentioned alongside emotions; this may explain the actual role food plays in the ED psychodynamics—acting as a representative of certain (or even all) emotions. During the psychodrama action distinctions promoted by a therapist were made between emotions and food.

The process and progress of ED treatment was explored several times (9.8 %)—patients set out an imaginary time-line starting at the beginning of the treatment taking it to the present moment—in the context of what had happened, what were the important moments during that time, what new insights were gained.

Relationships between partners were not a frequent topic (6 %), this was probably due to the fact reported by Pahole (2005) that many women with AN, and about half the women with BN were not involved in a partnership. Self-image was also dealt with (5.3 %), usually in the form of a reflective dialogue with themselves. Two or more conflicting views were represented, symbolising the internal dynamics. Experiencing all these views through role-play made it possible to gain insight into how they interact. Sexual identity as a theme came up twice and both times it was males exploring their homosexual orientation. This is comparable to the data presented by Anderson (1995, in: Thompson et al. 2007), which showed that homosexuality appears to be associated with an elevated risk for developing ED in males.

At times (2.3 %) the psychodrama group worked more as a social skills training session where patients sought help regarding their behaviour in conflicted or a job interview situations. That is in accordance with Moreno's (1946/1987) statement that enactment comes first and re-training comes later. Social skills training is offered elsewhere in the unit and in psychodrama it was stressed that patients worked on their representations of people and situations, and that psychodrama enactments of their personal reality should not be directly copied into situations with real people.

In approximately 10 % of the psychodrama meetings group members chose to work in action on a theme that usually addressed the group dynamics (e.g., presenting–one at a time–their picture of boundaries between the group members). In 21.9 % of the meetings members of the group who completed their treatment (in accordance with the therapists' opinion or by deciding for themselves) were given a feedback by the group and *vice versa*. Often this presented a chance to specifically discuss feelings surrounding a person's departure from the group and in general about people entering and leaving their lives. In one instance the suicide of one of the members to whom the group was attached, proved to be a strong and painful experience for all members of the group. The themes were usually only discussed between the group members though in approximately a quarter of times the departure theme was addressed in action (e.g. sculpturing the group with and without a departing group member).

When considering the results discussed so far, it is important to stress that the working background is always the group as a whole—its safety and holding capacity. Experiencing painful emotions has healing properties and leads to change (Greenberg and Paivio 1998). However, the themes that were presented were often traumatic and special care had to be taken to prevent re-traumatisation (e.g., Kipper 1998; Rothschild 2000). Also it is important to pay attention to the personality of the protagonist and keep the action safe, allow them to go at their own pace of insight and change, not to push nor to jump ahead, and structure the theme into "small enough" bites that can be processed and integrated. Finally a necessary part of the process is deroling, stepping out of the enacted roles at the end of the psychodrama session, and sharing the experiences in role and from observing the drama.

Observations regarding different diagnoses of ED were that people with AN usually needed longer preparation time before taking on the role of protagonist. Sometimes even when they did, they had a very strong need to maintain control over the psychodrama action. Such need for control may be understood as a reaction to the sense of being unable to influence the attachment figures into responding (Broberg et al. 2001), or an inability to maintain the proper boundaries with them. Pitzele (1991) states that the therapist's directive leadership is important, especially in situations where a client has problems with control, but since it is not clear whether that refers to over or under-controlled behaviour, it is possible that too strong a push towards regaining control from the part of the therapist might be also contra-productive and counter-therapeutic. Frequently observed defence mechanisms were intellectualisation, negation, splitting, projection and reactive formation. Dissociation during the psychodrama action also appeared. In such cases several techniques had been applied, for example using a permanent double who was verbalising protagonist's possible sensations, feelings or/and thoughts to help a protagonist re-gain a contact with her/himself. Defence mechanisms such as dissociation are a protective response to severe trauma and helpful against overwhelming fear, anger, pain and helplessness (Singer 1995, in: Calamari and Pini 2003). Dissociation was reported more frequently in women with insecure, especially ambivalent attachment (e.g., Wallin 2007).

Sharing from the members was part of each session, as it allowed the protagonist to be re-introduced to the group. The feedback was usually rich, group members were responsive towards the themes presented and often referred to some unaddressed parts from the protagonist's work. Group members can offer a corrective emotional experience and confronting reality with the peer group is a powerful means in the struggle with internalised images (Pitzele 1991).

Conclusions

This article presents the psychodrama sessions of a group of patients diagnosed with ED. The main themes explored in the groups were the patients' primary-family relationships, recognition and exploration of emotions in the present situation and the process of ED treatment. Different factors that contributed to the ED problems emerged through the psychodrama sessions—for example family factors including modelling of dysfunctional eating and boundary problems, insecure attachment, traumatic experiences and gender role.

The progress of the group members was subjectively observed and discussed by the therapists as an increase in spontaneity that was evident through the enactment of a larger repertoire of roles, and through the changes that occurred in the existent roles. Such changes in role repertoire were facilitated by the fact that people could be more spontaneous enacting the role of someone else rather than their own (Blatner and Blatner 1988; Moreno 1953/1993).

The themes presented in the psychodrama group of patients with ED were gathered over a period of 7 years; we can conclude that the presented categorisation of themes provides a reliable portrayal of the personal issues that are crucial for patients with ED. As such, this categorisation may be used in the future for planning the ED treatment, especially regarding psychotherapy. Psychodrama's ability to facilitate the integration of emotional, cognitive and behavioural levels of personal experience suggests that it is a valuable psychotherapeutic modality in the treatment of ED. However, this needs to be systematically evaluated further.

References

Armstrong, J. G., & Roth, D. M. (1989). Attachment and separation difficulties in eating disorders: A preliminary investigation. *International Journal of Eating Disorders, 8*(2), 141–155.

Blatner, A., & Blatner, A. (1988). *Foundations of psychodrama* (3rd. edn.). New York: Springer Publishing Company.

Broberg, A. G., Hjalmers, I., & Nevonen, L. (2001). Eating disorders, attachment and interpersonal difficulties: A comparison between 18- to 24-year-old patients and normal controls. *European Eating Disorders Review, 9*(6), 381–396.

Calamari, E., & Pini, M. (2003). Dissociative experiences and anger proneness in late adolescent females with different attachment styles. *Adolescence, 38*(150), 287–303.

Cassin, S. E., & von Ranson, K. M. (2005). Personality and eating disorders: A decade in review. *Clinical Psychology Review, 25*, 895–916.

Crow, S. J., & Brandenburg, B. (2010). Diagnosis, assessment, and treatment planning for bulimia nervosa. In C. M. Grilo & J. E. Mitchell (Eds.), *The treatment of eating disorders: A clinical handbook* (pp. 28–43). New York: The Guilford Press.

Dayton, T. (1994). *The drama within: Psychodrama and experiential therapy*. Florida: Health Communications, Inc.

Downs, K. J., & Blow, A. J. (2013). A substantive and methodological review of family-based treatment for eating disorders: The last 25 years of research. *Journal of Family Therapy, 35*(1), 3–28.

Fairburn, C. G., Cooper, Z., Doll, H. A., Norman, P., & O'Connor, M. (2000). The natural course of bulimia nervosa and binge eating disorder in young women. *Archives of General Psychiatry, 57*(7), 659–665.

Fassino, S., Amianto, F., Gramaglia, C., Facchini, F., & Abbate Daga, G. (2004). Temperament and character in eating disorders: Ten years of studies. *Eating and Weight Disorders, 9*(2), 81–90.

Greenberg, L. S., & Paivio, S. C. (1998). Allowing and accepting painful emotional experiences. *The International Journal of Action Methods, 51*(2), 47–61.

Keel, P. K., & McCormick, L. (2010). Diagnosis, assessment, and treatment planning for anorexia nervosa. In C. M. Grilo & J. E. Mitchell (Eds.), *The treatment of eating disorders: A clinical handbook* (pp. 3–27). New York: The Guilford Press.

Ketisch, T., Jones, R., Mirsalimi, H., Casey, R., & Milton, T. (2014). Boundary disturbances and eating disorder symptoms. *The American Journal of Family Therapy, 42*, 438–451.

Kipper, D. A. (1998). Psychodrama and trauma: Implications for future interventions of psychodramatic role-playing modalities. *The International Journal of Action Methods, 51*(3), 113–121.

Meillo, J. (1991). Issues of milieu therapy: Psychodrama as a contribution to the treatment of a case of anorexia nervosa. In P. Holmes & M. Karp (Eds.), *Psychodrama: Inspiration and technique* (pp. 137–153). London: Tavistock/Routledge.

Mikulincer, M., & Shaver, P. R. (2007). *Attachment in adulthood.* New York: The Guilford Press.
Moreno, J. L. (1946/1987). Psychodrama and sociodrama. In J. Fox (Ed.), *The essential Moreno: Writings on psychodrama, group method, and spontaneity by J. L. Moreno* (pp. 13–19). New York: Springer Publishing Company.
Moreno, J. L. (1953/1993). *Who shall survive? Foundations of sociometry, group psychotherapy and sociodrama.* Virginia: Royal Publishing Company (students' edition).
Pahole, M. (2005). *Personality traits, attachment patterns and their inter-generational concordance in persons with eating disorders and their parents.* Unpublished doctoral thesis. Ljubljana: Faculty of Arts.
Pahole, M., & Prosen, S. (2010). Some aspects of attachment in the psychodrama group at the Eating Disorders Unit of the Psychiatry Clinics Ljubljana. In B. Škodlar (Ed.), *12th Bregant's days, [October 14–17, 2010, Rogaška Slatina]. Attachment* (pp. 107–118). Ljubljana: Združenje psihoterapevtov Slovenije.
Pahole, M., & Prosen, S. (2011). Understanding human in Morenian psychodrama. *Kairos, 5*(3–4), 77–84.
Pitzele, P. (1991). Adolescents inside out. In P. Holmes & M. Karp (Eds.), *Psychodrama: Inspiration and technique* (pp. 15–31). London: Tavistock/Routledge.
Puklek Levpušček, M. (2006). Adolescent individuation in relation to parents and friends: Age and gender differences. *European Journal of Developmental Psychology, 3*(3), 238–264.
Rothschild, B. (2000). *The body remembers.* London: W. W. Norton & Company.
Rowa, K., Kerig, P. K., & Geller, J. (2001). The family and anorexia nervosa: Examining parent-child boundary problems. *European Eating Disorders Review, 9*(2), 97–114.
Salzman, J. P. (1997). Ambivalent attachment in female adolescents: Association with affective instability and eating disorders. *International Journal of Eating Disorders, 21*(3), 251–259.
Stice, E., Peart, J., Thompson-Brenner, H., Martinez, E., & Westen, A. (2006). Eating disorders. In M. Hersen & J. C. Thomas (Eds.), *Comprehensive handbook of personality and psychopathology—Volume 2: Adult psychopathology* (pp. 389–408). USA: John Wiley & Sons Inc.
Tasca, G. A., Ritchie, K., & Balfour, L. (2011). Implications of attachment theory and research for the assessment and treatment of eating disorders. *Psychotherapy, 48*(3), 249–259.
Thompson, J. K., Roehrig, M., & Kinder, B. N. (2007). Eating disorders. In M. Hersen, S. M. Turner, & D. C. Beidel (Eds.), *Adult psychopathology and diagnosis, 5th ed* (pp. 571–600). USA: John Wiley & Sons Inc.
Wallin, D. J. (2007). *Attachment in psychotherapy.* New York: Guilford Press.
Yaniv, D. (2012). Dynamics of creativity and empathy in role reversal: Contributions from neuroscience. *Review of General Psychology, 16*(1), 70–77.

Simona Prosen, PhD, is a psychologist and psychodrama psychotherapist. Currently, she works at the University of Ljubljana, Faculty of Education, Slovenia. For ten years, she worked at the University Psychiatric Hospital in Ljubljana, where she ran in-patient and outpatient therapy groups, including psychodrama groups. She worked with various patient groups, her longest experience was with patients diagnosed with drug-addiction and patients diagnosed with eating disorders.

Z Psychodrama Soziometr (2016) (Suppl) 15:143–163
DOI 10.1007/s11620-015-0308-7

HAUPTBEITRÄGE

Zeitschrift für Psychodrama und Soziometrie

Vom Hai über den Neandertaler zum Bankangestellten – Experimentelle Annäherung an die Kinderpsychodrama-Forschung

Elisabeth Uschold-Meier · Rebecca Wagner

Online publiziert: 9. Dezember 2015

Zusammenfassung Beschrieben wird die Evaluation der Arbeit mit einer Psychodramakindergruppe in einer stationären Jugendhilfeeinrichtung. Fragestellung der Studie ist es, welche der angewandten Methoden (SDQ, OPD-KJ, Soziales Atom, Soziogramm, Rollentagebuch, RDI) zur Auswertung psychodramatherapeutischer Arbeit hilfreich sind. Kernpunkt ist der experimentelle Einsatz eines operationalisierbaren, psychodramaspezifischen Instrumentariums (RDI), das entwickelt wurde, um Entwicklungsfortschritte messbar zu machen. Ziel ist es, damit sowie mittels soziometrischer Testverfahren (Soziales Atom, Target Soziogramm) Veränderungen quantitativ sowie aus unterschiedlichen Perspektiven zu erfassen. Die Methoden können wissenschaftlich weiterentwickelt und differenziert werden. Da sie in ihrer Anwendung wenig Zeitaufwand benötigen und zudem der Selbstreflexion des Therapeuten/der Therapeutin dienen, sind sie in der beruflichen Praxis gut einzusetzen.

Schlüsselwörter Kinder · Kindertherapie · Psychodrama · Forschung

From the shark through the Neanderthal to the bank employee – an experimental approach to scientific research in psychodrama with children

Abstract The article describes the evaluation of the psychodramatic work with a group of children in a Children's Home. The research question is: which of the applied methods (SDQ, OPD-KJ, social atom, sociogram) are most suitable for

E. Uschold-Meier (✉) · R. Wagner
Gerchsheimer Str. 3,
97271 Kleinrinderfeld, Deutschland
E-Mail: praxis@uschold-meier.de

R. Wagner
E-Mail: rebecca.wagner@gmx.net

evaluating psychodrama therapy with children? The focus for this study is the experimental use of an operationalised psychodrama-specific method (RDI) that has been developed to make progress in development measureable. The goal is to quantify changes with it and, using sociometric tests (social atom, target sociogram), to measure change from different perspectives. These methods could be enhanced by science. Because they take a little time in their use and also support the self-reflection of the therapist. They are effective for use in professional practice.

Keywords Children · Psychotherapy with children · Psychodrama · Research

1 Die Rahmenbedingungen

Die Kinderpsychodramagruppe ist Teil des therapeutischen Angebots einer großen Jugendhilfeeinrichtung mit einem stationären, teilstationären und einem ambulanten Bereich, welche überregional tätig ist. Zu Beginn eines Schuljahres erhalten alle Abteilungen eine Art Katalog mit therapeutischen und heilpädagogischen Kursangeboten. Abhängig von der vorliegenden Diagnose und auf Grundlage des im Team ausgearbeiteten Erziehungsplanes werden jedem Kind für die Dauer eines Schuljahres in der Regel zwei bis drei Gruppenangebote vorgeschlagen oder zugewiesen.

2 Klientel

An der Gruppe nahmen zu Beginn acht Kinder teil, die zum ersten Messzeitpunkt (t1) zwischen acht und zwölf Jahre alt waren, drei Mädchen und fünf Jungen. Ein neunjähriger Junge wurde nach fünf Monaten aus der Einrichtung entlassen. Die Störungsbilder der Kinder waren sowohl nach der ICD-10 als auch mittels sozialpädagogischer Diagnosen im Rahmen von Erziehungsplänen klassifiziert. Bei allen Kindern lagen Mehrfachdiagnosen vor, von denen wir hier exemplarisch nur einige aufführen. Dem Verhalten von 70 % der Kinder lag eine Bindungsstörung (F 94) zugrunde, bei 40 % war eine hyperkinetische Störung des Sozialverhaltens (F 93), bei 20 % eine Störung im autistischen Formenkreis (F 84) und in einem Fall eine depressive Störung (F 3) erkannt worden. Zwei Kinder galten als lernbehindert, ein Mädchen als hochbegabt.

Nach kurzer Zeit stellte sich heraus, dass zwei Kinder mit der Gruppengröße überfordert waren. Wir teilten die Gruppe deshalb und arbeiteten für den Rest des Schuljahres mit diesen beiden Kindern in einem 1:1 Setting zusammen.

3 Das Gruppensetting

Die beiden Gruppen trafen sich mit Ausnahme der Ferienzeiten wöchentlich eine Stunde lang für die Dauer eines Schuljahres. Das Setting orientierte sich an den im Psychodrama üblichen Phasen *Warming up, Aktion, Rollenfeedback* und *Sharing* ergänzt durch verhaltenstherapeutische und hypnotherapeutische Elemente und solche aus der Energiearbeit und der systemischen Therapie.

4 Fragestellung und Ziele

Die Fragestellung bei der vorliegenden Studie ist, ob und welche der angewandten Methoden qualitativer Psychotherapieforschung sich als geeignet für die Evaluation psychodramatherapeutischer Arbeit mit Kindergruppen erweist.

Ähnlich wie Kirk und Dutton (2006, S. 34) die praxisbezogenen Ziele für ihre Arbeit mit autistischen Jugendlichen formulierten, war es unsere Intention, dass sich für die Kinder speziell folgende Bereiche zum Besseren verändern:

- die Zufriedenheit der Kinder mit ihrer Position innerhalb der Gruppe
- ihre Fähigkeiten zur Gestaltung sozialer Interaktionen
- ihre Empathie für sich selbst und andere (Auto-Tele und Telebeziehungen)
- ihr Erleben von Selbstwirksamkeit

Darüber hinaus richteten wir den Blick darauf, ob sich bei maladaptiven Beziehungsmustern der Kinder, sowohl im szenischen Spiel als auch in Beziehung zu den Therapeutinnen und zu anderen Kindern, Veränderungen in Richtung höherer Funktionalität in der Beziehungsgestaltung ergaben.

5 Untersuchungsmethoden

Bei der vorliegenden Arbeit handelt es sich um eine Pilotstudie. Die beschriebene Gruppe weist mit sieben Kindern eine kleine Gruppengröße auf, was nicht als repräsentative Stichprobe bezeichnet werden kann. Wir nahmen eine Vorher-Nachher-Messung relevanter Variablen innerhalb der Behandlungsgruppe vor. Pilotcharakter hat die Bandbreite an Erhebungsverfahren, die wir einsetzten und auf ihre Anwendbarkeit im Feld prüften. *Qualitativ beschreibende Elemente* wie z. B. das soziale Atom und gruppensoziometrische Verfahren und *Filmmaterial*, das z. T. zur Auswertung der Verhaltensbeobachtung während der Spielphase herangezogen wurde, kamen ebenso zum Einsatz wie *quantitative Verfahren*: der *SDQ* und der neu zusammengestellte *RDI*. Im Folgenden stellen wir unser Untersuchungsdesign vor. Unter der Überschrift „Untersuchungsergebnisse auf Gruppenebene" schildern wir weiter unten die dazugehörigen statistischen Auswertungsmöglichkeiten, anhand derer es möglich ist, die Wirksamkeit der Psychodramakindertherapie mit größeren Fallzahlen zu überprüfen.

Folgende Verfahren kamen jeweils *vor Beginn* der Gruppentherapie, in der *Mitte* und *am Ende* zur Anwendung (t1, t2 und t3):

- SDQ: Strengths and Difficulties Questionnaire
  Ein Fragebogen, der eher auf problematisches Verhalten fokussiert, weniger auf die Stärken eines Kindes. Er wurde sowohl von den jeweiligen Bezugserzieherinnen der Kinder ausgefüllt, als auch mit den Kindern gemeinsam im Einzelsetting in Interviewform durch die Therapeutinnen – die Problematik dieser Personalunion wird weiter unten im Diskussionsteil behandelt.

Wir wendeten ihn an, um herauszufinden, ob die Fortschritte, die wir im Rahmen der Therapiegruppe erlebten, auch im Gruppenalltag von den Kindern erlebt bzw. von den Erzieherinnen beobachtet wurden.

- OPD-KJ: „Operationalisierte psychodynamische Diagnostik für Kinder und Jugendliche“
  Angelegt als breit gefächertes Diagnosesystem, das seit Ende der 90er Jahre von tiefenpsychologisch orientierten PsychotherapeutInnen in Ergänzung zur psychiatrischen Diagnostik verwendet wird, um einzelne Aspekte seelischer Gesundheit zu beobachten und auszuwerten.
  Mit der OPD-KJ Achse II „Beziehung“ untersuchten wir qualitative Veränderungen in Bezug auf die Beziehungsgestaltung zwischen Therapeutin und Kind. Geratet wird auf einem Kreismodell mit zwei Achsen (x/y), wobei die x-Achse die Dimension zwischen *freundlicher Zuwendung und feindlicher Ablehnung*, die y-Achse die Dimension *Gewähren lassen vs. Kontrolle*, beurteilt.
- Soziales Atom
  Als aktionsbezogene Analyse arbeiteten wir mit diesem psychodramaspezifischen „Mehrschichtmodell“ (vgl. Cejka 2011, S. 157), und beabsichtigten damit, vom Kind subjektiv erlebte Veränderungen innerhalb der familiären Beziehungen zu erfassen.
- Soziometrie
  Zur Erstellung von Soziogrammen haben wir das *Target Diagramm* (Schlechtriemen 2013, S. 115) gewählt, da hier zu Forschungszwecken eine Berechnung der Punkte zwischen den Graphen möglich und es auf diese Weise mathematisch auswertbar (a. a. O., S. 114) ist.
  a) Um Veränderungen der Beziehungen der Kinder untereinander innerhalb der Psychodramagruppe zu erfassen, erstellten sowohl die Therapeutinnen als auch die Kinder selbst ein Gruppensoziogramm wie von Biegler-Vitek und Schorn (2013) beschrieben.
  b) Im Bereich der Wohngruppen untersuchten wir eine Veränderung der Beziehungen des Kindes zu den anderen Gruppenmitgliedern sowohl aus der Sicht des Kindes als auch aus der Perspektive der Bezugserzieherin.

Begleitend über den gesamten Verlauf wurde von den Therapeutinnen ein *Rollentagebuch* geführt, um die Rollenentwicklung der einzelnen Kinder zu dokumentieren.

Angeregt durch die Videodokumentation einer Einzelfallstudie, wie sie Krall im Rahmen eines Workshops beim Internationalen Psychologie Kongress an der Universität in Sibiu, Rumänien im Oktober 2013 vorgestellt hatte, wurden die Sitzungen über den gesamten Verlauf mittels *Videoaufzeichnungen* dokumentiert (vgl. Köfeler und Krall 2015, in diesem Band).

„*Was der PsychoanalytikerIn das ‚Narrativ‘ – ist der PsychodramatikerIn die ‚szenischeAktion*‘“ (Hintermeier 2011, S. 103). Um Entwicklungsfortschritte der Kinder, die in ihren szenischen Darstellungen beobachtbar waren, auswerten und erfassen zu können, entwickelten wir auf Grundlage der entwicklungspsychologischen Rollentheorie nach Schacht (2010, S. 22–63) als Kernpunkt unserer fortlaufenden Beobachtungen eine Tabelle, das *Role Development Inventory (RDI)*, in der das Verhalten der Kinder im szenischen Spielen nach jeder Sitzung skaliert werden kann.

6 Einzelfallstudie

Im Rahmen dieses Artikels legen wir den Fokus exemplarisch auf eine Einzelfallanalyse. In einer Fallstudie werden wir die Entwicklung eines Jungen im Verlauf der Kinderpsychodramagruppe beschreiben, ohne jedoch der Komplexität aller Lebensbereiche, der Gesamtheit der Person und ihrer lebensgeschichtlichen Hintergründe gerecht werden zu können, wie dies einer qualitativen Fallanalyse eigentlich angemessen wäre. Unser Interesse galt vielmehr der Frage, ob die eingesetzten Untersuchungsmethoden zu analogen Ergebnissen führten.

Aus Therapeutinnensicht wurde O. gewählt, weil seine Entwicklungsfortschritte innerhalb der Gruppe besonders evident waren. Auch seine Rolle innerhalb der Gruppenkonstellation hatte sich am augenfälligsten verändert. Als Kind, das sich zunächst sehr zurückhaltend präsentierte, erlangte er im weiteren Verlauf eine sehr integrative Funktion für die Gruppe.

Zu Beginn der Therapiegruppe war O. gerade 12 Jahre alt geworden. Er hatte folgende Diagnosestellungen nach dem ICD 10-Katalog: Atypischer Autismus (F 84.1), nicht organische Enuresis (F 98.0) und Enkopresis (F 98.1), einfache Aktivitäts- und Aufmerksamkeitsstörung (F 90.0), unterdurchschnittliche Intelligenz, rezidivierendes Erbrechen unklarer Genese, ernsthafte und durchgängige soziale Beeinträchtigung.

6.1 SDQ

Die Auswertung des SDQ (Abb. 1) erfolgte mittels der online ergänzend zum Fragebogen hinterlegten Auswertungsschablone[1]. Diese bildet aus den Rohwerten der beantworteten Items Scores auf sechs Skalen verschiedener Problembereiche der Kinder. In Abb. 2 sind die Scores für O. auf den sechs Skalen zu den drei Messzeitpunkten (t1–t3) dargestellt. Fett gedruckte Werte sind als auffällig zu sehen, die Pfeile geben jeweils an, ob der Wert als auffällig hoch oder auffällig niedrig zu bewerten ist.

Zu Beginn der Gruppe (t1) beschrieb O. sich selbst als Kind, das insgesamt viel Stress erlebt, Verhaltensschwierigkeiten aufweist und nur schwer mit anderen Kindern auskommt. Andererseits sei er nett zu andern Kindern und helfe ihnen auch. Zudem schilderte er sich als durchschnittlich emotional belastet und nicht einschrän-

	T1		T2		T3	
	selbst	fremd	selbst	fremd	selbst	fremd
Score for overall stress	↑ 19	16	15	↑ 17	12	↑17
Score for emotional distress	4	3	↑6	4	4	4
Score for behavioural difficulties	↑ 5	1	3	2	2	2
Score for hyperactivity and attentional difficulties	6	3	2	3	1	1
Score for difficulties getting along with other children	↓ 4	↓ 9	↑4	↑ 8	↑5	↓ 10
Score for kind and helpful behaviour	6	↓ 2	6	↓ 1	5	↓ 2

Abb. 1 Auswertung des SDQ in der Einzelfallanalyse

kend von Hyperaktivität betroffen. Über den Verlauf der Zeit schilderte O. positive Veränderungen: So ergaben sich an t2 und t3 aus O.s Selbstbeschreibungen unauffällige Werte für allgemeinen Stress sowie für Verhaltensprobleme, auch die Hyperaktivitätswerte nahmen weiter ab. O. beschrieb sich weiterhin als gleichbleibend hilfsbereit, sah aber auch zu allen drei Messzeitpunkten unverändert Probleme bei sich im Umgang mit anderen Kindern. An t2 schilderte er zunächst eine Zunahme von emotionalem Stress, was sich jedoch an t3 wieder normalisierte. Für O. selbst ergab sich somit über die Zeit hinweg ein deutlich positiverer Verlauf. Einzig seine Hauptproblematik als Autist, mit anderen Kindern gut auszukommen, war gleichbleibend negativ behaftet.

O.s Erzieher schilderten zu Beginn der Gruppe (t1) vor allem starke Probleme von O. mit anderen Kindern und auffällig mangelnde Hilfsbereitschaft anderen gegenüber. Auch zu den weiteren Messzeitpunkten (t2 und t3) wurden diese Aspekte bemängelt und keine positive Entwicklung verzeichnet. Der Wert für insgesamt erlebten Stress wurde von Seiten der Erzieher über die Zeit hinweg als auffälliger geschildert. Somit ergibt sich der interessante Befund, dass O. für sich Verbesserungen in verschiedenen Bereichen schildert, was von den ErzieherInnen seiner Wohngruppe so nicht oder konträr gesehen wird.

6.2 OPD-KJ

Die Auswertung des Beziehungsverhaltens (Abb. 2) erfolgte zu den drei Messzeitpunkten jeweils im Anschluss an die Einzelsitzungen, in denen O. von den Therapeutinnen zunächst zu den SDQ-Fragen interviewt wurde. In einem nächsten Schritt stellte er in Form eines sozialen „Familienatoms" dar, wie er sich selbst zum jeweiligen Zeitpunkt im Beziehungsgefüge seiner Familie erlebte. Schließlich legte er in einem Soziogramm seine Position in Bezug auf die anderen Kinder seiner Wohngruppe, wie er sie in diesem Moment empfand.

O. präsentierte sich als zurückhaltender, scheuer Junge mit einem auf den ersten Blick wenig anziehenden äußeren Erscheinungsbild. Sein Blick war häufig nach unten

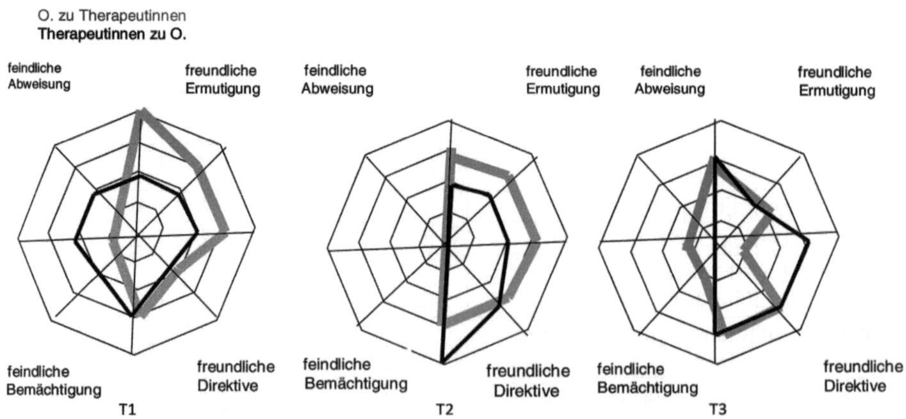

Abb. 2 OPD-KJ Einzelfallanalyse

gerichtet; wenn er ihn hob, neigte er dazu, nur kurz von schräg unten nach oben zu blinzeln, ohne direkt Augenkontakt aufzunehmen. Sein gesamtes Verhalten erweckte den Eindruck von vorsichtigem Misstrauen. Er wirkte in sich versunken, dachte lange über Fragen und Aufgabenstellungen nach, arbeitete jedoch bereitwillig mit.

Mit seinem sonderlich wirkenden Gebaren lud er zunächst nur mäßig zu freundlicher, zugewandter Offenheit auf Seite der Therapeutinnen ein. Die therapeutische Haltung im Erstkontakt (t1) war eher abwartend und neutral.

Eine deutliche Veränderung Richtung freundliche Ermutigung und Direktive sowohl auf Therapeutinnen- als auch auf Klientenseite wird bei t2 sichtbar.

Bei t3 expandiert die Graphik nach rechts unten stark zu freundlicher Direktive. Ursache dafür sehen wir in O.'s demonstrativer Lustlosigkeit und in seinen Versuchen, sich den Anforderungen und Fragestellungen immer wieder zu entziehen. Die Therapeutinnen interpretierten dieses für ihn unübliche Verhalten als den Versuch, mit dem bevorstehenden Abschied von der Gruppe umzugehen. Diese hatte ihm eine zunehmende Sicherheit ermöglicht, in der er frei agieren und neue Verhaltensmuster ausprobieren konnte (siehe dazu die graphische Auswertung seiner Entwicklungsfortschritte weiter unten unter Punkt 3 RDI-PDT und die soziometrische Erfassung der Gruppenkonstellation innerhalb der Kinderpsychodramagruppe). Andererseits sprach das Verhalten auch für die neu gewonnene Fähigkeit der Wahrnehmung seiner eigenen Befindlichkeit und dem Wagnis, seinen Bedürfnissen nachzugehen, auch wenn diese den Erwartungen des Gegenübers nicht entsprachen.

6.3 Soziales Atom

Zu O.s Aufnahme in die stationäre Jugendhilfe kam es, da die Familie mit seinem Autismus und den daraus resultierenden erheblichen Verhaltensauffälligkeiten überfordert war. O.s Mutter wies zudem eine psychische Erkrankung auf, die mit Neuroleptika behandelt werden musste. Sie war insgesamt in ihren Möglichkeiten, Emotionen O. gegenüber adäquat auszudrücken und auf sein Befinden einzugehen massiv eingeschränkt. O.s Vater trat sehr resolut und misstrauisch auf. Die Eltern standen den Hilfemaßnahmen zu Beginn eher ablehnend gegenüber. O. selbst zeigte sich misstrauisch schimpfend, emotional depriviert, niedergeschlagen und wenig kontaktfreudig. Es war ersichtlich, dass die Familienmitglieder aneinander hängen, aber aufgrund der akuten, vielfältigen Belastungen nicht mehr in der Lage waren, sich dies zu zeigen. Im Verlauf der Hilfemaßnahme kam es zu einer deutlichen Entspannung der Familienverhältnisse. Die Familienmitglieder gehen inzwischen freudig und liebevoll aufeinander zu.

Bei t1 (Abb. 3) fällt auf, wie weit O. die anderen Personen seiner Familie von sich entfernt empfindet. Auch wenn Mutter und Vater die Personen sind, die ihm am nächsten stehen, sind sie doch außerhalb des inneren Kreises. Mutter und Vater stehen relativ weit voneinander entfernt im Kreis der gewünschten Beziehungen. Bruder und Schwester stehen sich diametral gegenüber im Bereich des Bekanntschaftsvolumens. Auch der Großvater spielt eine wesentliche Rolle.

Bei der zweiten Erhebung sind die Eltern deutlich näher zueinander gerückt, wobei sich die Distanz zum Vater vergrößert hat. Es wirkt, als würde die Mutter die Sicht von Vater zu Sohn und vice versa verstellen. Die Entfernung zur Mutter ist im Vergleich zu

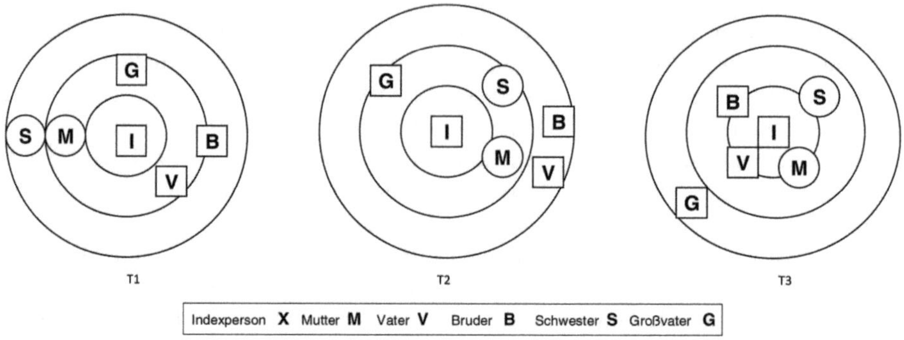

Abb. 3 Familienatom Einzelfallanalyse

t1 gleichbleibend. Die Schwester rückte näher zu O. und auch näher zu Vater und Bruder. Der Großvater wird mit mehr Distanz zu den anderen und isoliert stehend erlebt.

Beim dritten Messzeitpunkt besteht zwischen O. und seinen Eltern eine große Nähe. Sie sind im inneren Kern direkt hinter O. als dem jüngsten Kind der Familie positioniert und stehen als Elternpaar nebeneinander. Auch die älteren Geschwister sind auf dem Kreis des inneren Kerns. Der Großvater hat wieder dieselbe Distanz wie bei t1, jedoch nicht mehr so isoliert, sondern hat eine Nähe zum Vater. Es besteht nun eine direkte männliche Linie von Großvater über den Vater zu O. Auch der Bruder steht auf der „Männerseite" in seinem Blick. Die Konstante auf allen drei Abbildungen ist das Nähe-Distanz-Verhältnis zwischen Mutter und Schwester.

Die Abbildungen lassen die Interpretation zu, dass sich die familiären Beziehungen im Untersuchungszeitraum für O. in Richtung stärkerer Kohäsion in der Familie entwickelt haben. Die Eltern stehen nun hinter ihm. Auch die Beziehung zu seinen Geschwistern ist weniger distanziert. Insgesamt wirkt die familiäre Situation geordneter.

6.4 Soziogramme

Wie in Abb. 4 sichtbar ist, hat sich bei t2 die erlebte Distanz von O. zu den Kindern der Wohngruppe verringert. O. differenziert die Beziehungen zu den anderen Gruppenmitgliedern im Beobachtungszeitraum deutlich. Es gibt nun Kinder, die er mag und andere, mit denen er nicht gut auskommt. Dies ist mit einer Zunahme seiner Fremdwahrnehmungs- und Empathiefähigkeit erklärbar.

Bei t1 fällt auf, dass O. zu seinen MitbewohnerInnen keine Verbindung empfindet oder aber nicht in der Lage ist, diese wahrzunehmen. Die Distanz zu den Mädchen scheint er sehr groß und auch undifferenziert zu empfinden, während es bei den Jungen zumindest zwei zu geben scheint, zu denen die Distanz nicht ganz so groß ist. Interessanterweise unterscheidet sich diese Wahrnehmung nicht wesentlich von der der Bezugserzieherin (Abb. 5). Auch sie positioniert alle Mädchen bis auf eines in größerer Entfernung von O.; die Distanz ist in ihrem Erleben nicht ganz so gewaltig wie O. diese empfindet. Die Position von zwei männlichen Mitbewohnern ist abhängig von der insgesamt geringeren Distanz nicht erheblich anders.

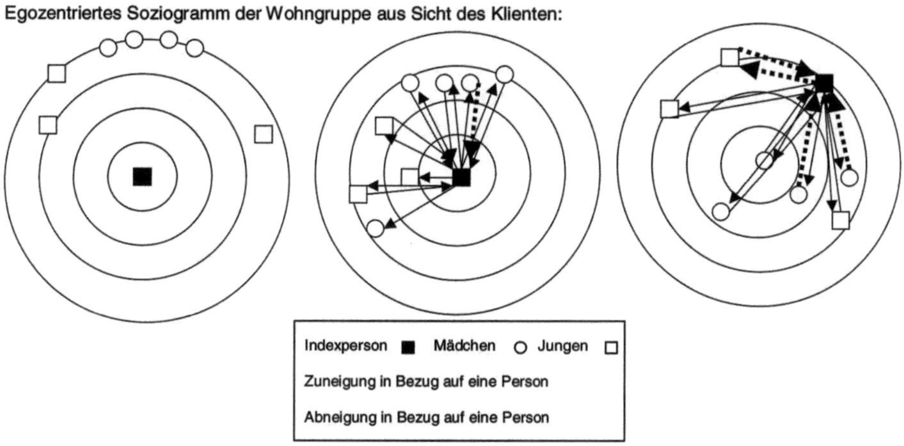

Abb. 4 Egozentriertes Soziogramm der Wohngruppe aus Sicht des Klienten

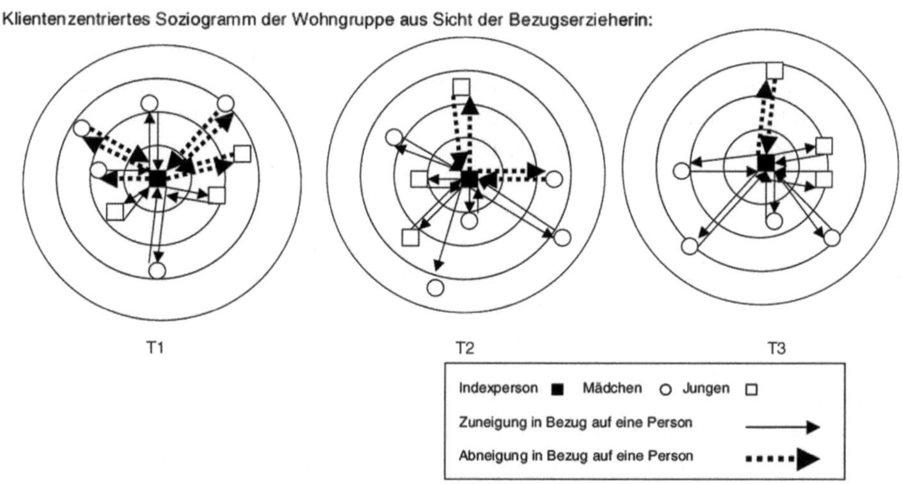

Abb. 5 Klientenzentriertes Soziogramm der Wohngruppe aus Sicht der Bezugserzieherin

Bei t2 kommt im subjektiven Erleben O.'s eine deutliche Verringerung der Distanz zu allen Gruppenmitgliedern zum Ausdruck. Die Beziehungen zu den Mädchen wirken bis auf die Antipathie, die O. von einem der Mädchen wahrnimmt, nach wie vor undifferenziert, während ein Junge dem inneren Kreis sehr nahe gerückt ist. Dies sowie die empfundene Ablehnung, die auf Gegenseitigkeit beruht, sieht die Bezugserzieherin ebenso. Sie positioniert die anderen Kinder der Wohngruppe deutlich differenzierter um O. als er das tut. Darüber hinaus registriert sie bereits eine gegenseitige Abstoßung zu einem Jungen der Wohngruppe, die sich in t3 fortsetzt und hier von O. ebenfalls so wahrgenommen und dargestellt wird.

Bei t3 ist gut erkennbar, wie differenziert O. die Beziehungen zu den einzelnen MitbewohnerInnen nun wahrnimmt und offenbar auch gestaltet. Auffallend ist, dass er sich selbst nach außen positioniert hat, während im Zentrum seiner Aufmerksamkeit ein älteres Mädchen der Gruppe steht, die er „sehr schön" findet.

6.5 Rollentagebuch

O. nahm im Lauf des Schuljahres die folgenden Rollen in dieser Reihenfolge ein: Hai, Tyrannosaurus Rex, Meerechse und Wolfshund, Amöbe, giftiger Katadromedar, Pottwal, Wolf im Rudel, Tod, Faultier, Star-Trek-Figur, Neandertaler, Krabatsohn, Superstar, Gorilla, Löwe, Ziege, Merlin, Schlafwandler, Posträuber, Bankangestellter, Urlauber, Wahrsager.

Im *Rollenatom*[2] wählte er von den bis dahin eingenommenen Rollen den Tod, das Faultier, die Star-Trek-Figur und den Neandertaler, denen er im Spiel vis-à-vis begegnen wollte. Umgekehrt wurde er im Rollenatom anderer Kinder als Gorilla und als Löwe ausgewählt und hatte sichtlich Spaß in diesen Rollen.

Ungefähr zu diesem Zeitpunkt änderte sich seine Funktion für die Gruppe. Er wirkte sehr integrativ, sowohl durch seine Rollenausgestaltung während des Spiels, als auch durch seine differenzierten Nachfragen und Rückmeldungen nach dem Spiel. Er trat empathischer und zugewandter in Beziehung, nahm Augenkontakt auf, lächelte viel, benannte, was er wahrnahm und fungierte in der Rollenfeedbackrunde für andere teilweise sogar als Hilfs-Ich.

6.6 RDI

Abbildung 6 zeigt exemplarisch einen Bewertungsbogen des *RDI* mit allen Variablen, die über den Verlauf der Kinderpsychodramagruppe jeweils am Ende einer Sitzung skaliert wurden. Eingetragen sind hier der Übersichtlichkeit halber drei Sitzungen aus O.s Bewertungsbogen. Höhere Skalenwerte stehen für eine höhere Ausprägung des Merkmals.

Es zeigt sich, dass O. über den Verlauf der Sitzungen hinweg immer komplexere Rollen wählte, die zunehmend mehr Interaktionen mit anderen erforderten. O.s Mut nahm zu, er trat im Spielverlauf weniger ängstlich auf. Der vermehrte Kontakt mit anderen barg auch mehr Konfliktpotential. Da jedoch seine Fähigkeiten zu Empathie und auch seine Achtsamkeit für sich selbst und für andere im Verlauf der Sitzungen anstiegen, gelang es ihm auch besser, diese Konflikte adäquat zu lösen. O. lernte zunehmend mit Feedback zielführend umzugehen. Er ging aus seiner Distanziertheit und Wortkargheit heraus und suchte vermehrt Kontakt und Nähe. Im Spiel zeigte sich dies durch erhöhten Aktionshunger.

Der RDI ermöglicht einerseits die rückschauende Schilderung des Entwicklungsverlaufs eines Kindes. Er stellte für uns im Verlauf der Sitzungen aber auch ein Diagnoseinstrument dar, um anhand der jeweiligen Befundlage gezielt Interventionen hin zu einem nächsten Entwicklungsschritt des jeweiligen Kindes zu planen.

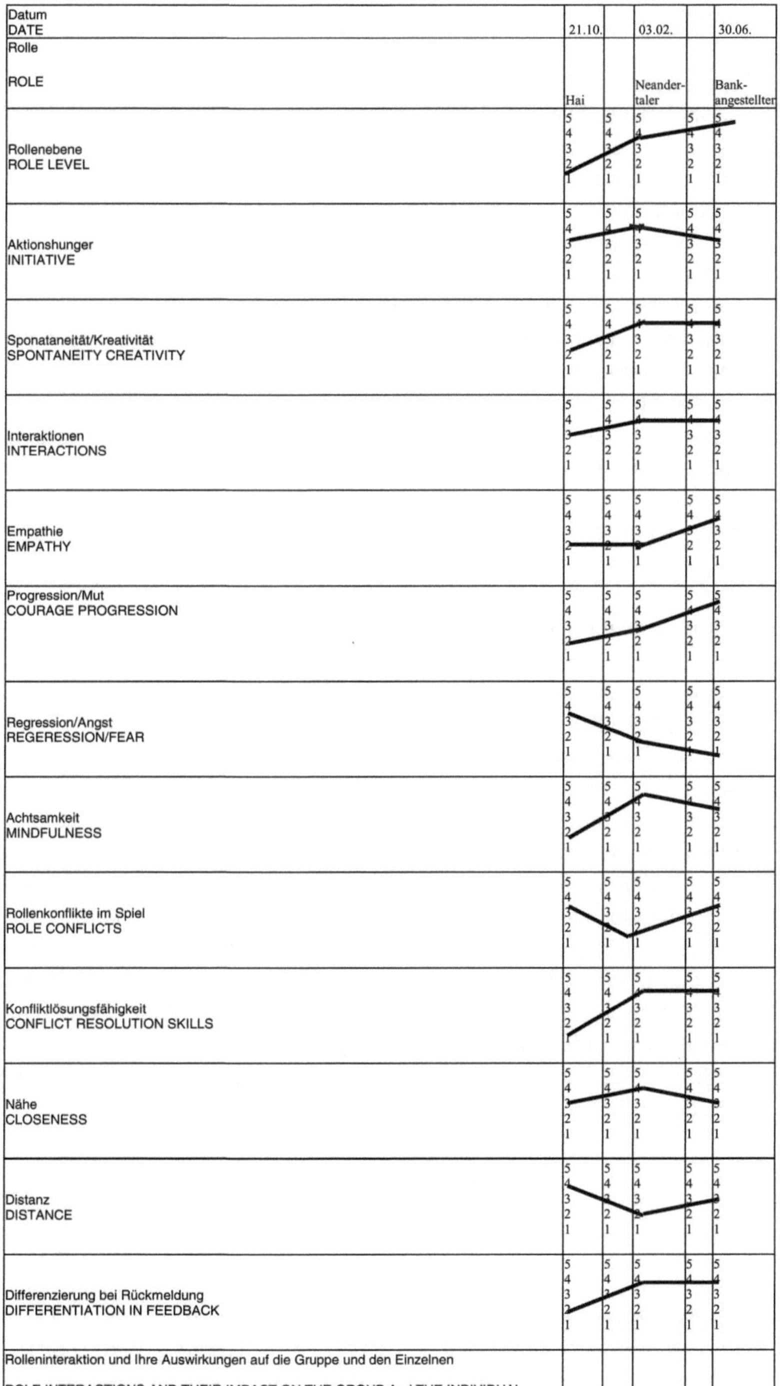

Abb. 6 Auswertung des RDI in der Einzelfallanalyse

7 Zusammenfassung

Die Ergebnisse des *SDQ* erlauben den Schluss, dass sich für O. insgesamt Vieles zum Positiven verändert hat. Dies und im Gegensatz dazu auch die Zunahme seiner Fähigkeit zur Gestaltung sozialer Interaktionen spiegeln sich sowohl in den Darstellungen des sozialen Atoms seiner Familie, in seinen eigenen soziometrischen Darstellungen wie auch in denen der Erzieherin wider. Letztere zeigen, dass O. besser in die Gruppe integriert ist und seine Position sich verbessert hat. Im *OPD-KJ* wird eine strukturelle Ausweitung beider Achsen sichtbar. Die Ergebnisse des *RDI* verweisen auf eine qualitative Veränderung in der Selbstwahrnehmung und in der Beziehungsgestaltung. Die Zunahme der Empathie für sich selbst und für andere, wie sie ihm *RDI* zum Ausdruck kommt, ermöglicht es ihm, zunehmend komplexere Rollen zu übernehmen und sein Potenzial zur Lösung von Konflikten zu steigern.

Bemerkenswert ist die Divergenz des Ergebnisses des *SDQ* in der Fremdeinschätzung und der im Soziogramm der Erzieherin dargestellten positiven Veränderungen seiner Position innerhalb der Wohngruppe, das analog zu allen Beobachtungen innerhalb der Therapiegruppe ist.

8 Untersuchungsergebnisse auf Gruppenebene

Im Folgenden werden die dazugehörigen statistischen Auswertungsmöglichkeiten geschildert (Abb. 8), anhand derer es mit größeren Fallzahlen möglich ist, die Wirksamkeit der Psychodramakindertherapie zu überprüfen. Um die Wirksamkeit therapeutischer Interventionen des Kinderpsychodramas darzustellen, gilt es nachzuweisen, dass beschriebene Schwierigkeiten und Verhaltensauffälligkeiten der Kinder im Verlauf der Behandlung statistisch bedeutsam abnehmen. Wie beschrieben erfolgte die quantitative Erfassung von Verhaltens-, emotionalen und Interaktionsproblemen der Kinder zu drei Messzeitpunkten (t1–t3). Die Messung zu t1 stellte eine grundsätzliche Erhebung der Verhaltensprobleme in der Gruppe dar. Die Messungen an t2 und t3 ermöglichten eine Aussage darüber, ob nach der Behandlung in einer Psychodramagruppe Verhaltensverbesserungen zu verzeichnen sind. Die quantitativen Messungen fanden mittels *SDQ* und dem *RDI* statt.

Die Tabelle in Abb. 7 zeigt die Mittelwerte der Gruppe auf den einzelnen Skalen des *SDQ*, jeweils in Selbst- und Fremdbeurteilung:

	t1		t2		t3	
	m selbst	m fremd	m selbst	m fremd	m selbst	m fremd
Score for overall stress	14	20	18,14	19,67	13,57	19,86
Score for emotional distress	5,29	4,89	5,71	4,17	3,29	4,43
Score for behavioural difficulties	3	4,86	3,29	4,33	2,86	4,86
Score for hyperactivity and attentional difficulties	5,14	4,71	5,14	4	3,71	3,71
Score for difficulties getting along with other children	4,43	5,86	4	7,17	3,71	6,86
Score for kind and helpful behaviour	7,71	5	8,29	3	7	4

Abb. 7 Auswertung des SDQ für die Gruppe

Abb. 8 Anzahl wechselseitiger Anziehungen zu den drei Messzeitpunkten

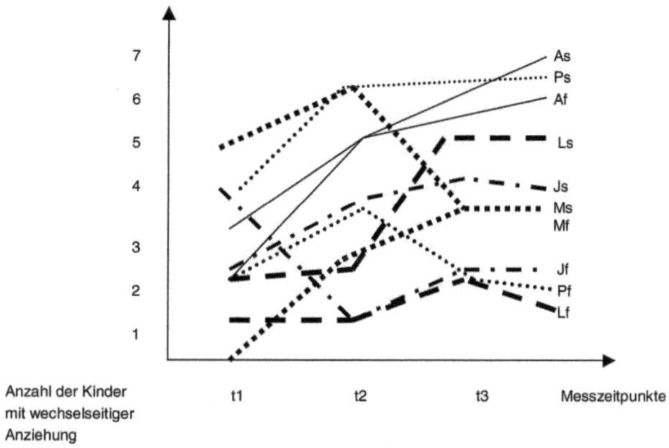

Es zeigen sich insgesamt geringe Veränderungen auf den einzelnen Skalen.

Auf eine statistische Auswertung des Verfahrens *OPD-KJ* für alle Kinder haben wir zum einen aus Gründen der Übersichtlichkeit verzichtet, zum anderen sind die Ergebnisse auf Gruppenebene in Bezug auf unsere Fragestellung wenig aussagekräftig. Insgesamt waren zum Zeitpunkt t1 bei allen Kindern deutlich ausgeprägte strukturelle Einschränkungen zu erkennen, die sich bei t3 deutlich Richtung „freundliche Zuwendung“ und auf der y-Achse in beide Richtungen ausgedehnt haben. Bei zwei Kindern fiel bei t1 ein starkes Bedürfnis nach Kontrolle bei gleichzeitig eher feindseligem Verhalten auf. Bei einem der beiden erfolgte bis t3 eine mäßige Erweiterung auf beiden Achsen, sowohl in Richtung Zuwendung als auch in die Fähigkeit von Gewährenlassen (y: Kontrolle vs. Gewähren lassen, x: Zuwendung vs. Feindliche Abwehr). Bei dem anderen fand bei gleichzeitig starker Veränderung Richtung „freundliche Zuwendung“ eine starke Ausprägung auf der y-Achse in beide Richtungen statt (Kontrolle und Gewährenlassen). Bei allen anderen war bei t1 die Ausprägung Richtung „freundliche Zuwendung“ schwach bis mäßig, das Bedürfnis nach Kontrolle mäßig bis stark vorhanden. Bei diesen Kindern waren bei t3 starke bis sehr starke strukturelle Ausdehnungen Richtung „liebevolle Zuwendung“, auf der y-Achse in beide Richtungen beobachtbar (Zuwendung und feindliche Abwehr), was als eine Erweiterung des persönlichen Handlungsspielraums interpretierbar ist.

Was die Auswertung der *sozialen Atome* im Bereich Familie anbelangt, haben wir sie unter den Gesichtspunkten *Kohäsion* innerhalb der Familie und der Fähigkeit zu *Differenzierter Wahrnehmung der innerfamiliären Beziehung* betrachtet. Hier zeigte sich, dass, während die Kohäsion innerhalb der Familien von den Kindern in der Regel durchgängig gleichbleibend gut erlebt wurde, die Differenzierung der Beziehungen bei den Kindern von t1 zu t3 deutlich zunahm.

Beim Blick auf die *Soziogramme* aller Kinder der Gruppe haben wir uns, um einen Überblick zu erhalten, auf zwei Fragestellungen beschränkt, die in Korrelation zu den vorab formulierten Zielen stehen. Wir wollten zum einen wissen, ob die Kinder sich im weiteren Verlauf in ihrer Wohngruppe integrierter fühlen, zum anderen interessierte uns, ob die Beziehungen mit gegenseitiger Anziehung zugenommen haben. Letzteres ist in den einzelnen Soziogrammen klar ersichtlich und numerisch erfassbar berechnet werden (Ausführungen dazu in der abschließenden Diskussion).

Das Verhalten bezüglich gegenseitger Anziehung stellt sich graphisch bei den fünf Kindern innerhalb ihrer Wohngruppe folgendermaßen dar:

Jedem Kind sind eine Farbe und ein Buchstabe zugeordnet. Das „s" hinter dem Buchstaben bezeichnet jeweils die Selbsteinschätzung der Kinder, „f" die Fremdeinschätzung der Erzieherin bezüglich der Position des Kindes. Bei A sind Selbst- und Fremdeinschätzung sehr nahe beieinander, phasenweise deckungsgleich. Die Beziehungen mit wechselseitiger Anziehung innerhalb der Wohngruppe haben deutlich zugenommen. Bei M haben Selbst- und Fremdeinschätzung sich angenähert. Bei L haben sowohl die ErzieherInnen eine Zunahme wechselseitiger Anziehung wahrgenommen, wie auch er selbst. Unterschiedliche Einschätzungen bestehen bezüglich der Quantität. Insgesamt kam es bei allen Kindern von t1 zu t3 zu einer Zunahme der von gegenseitiger Zuneigung geprägten Beziehungen innerhalb der Wohngruppe. Bei zwei Kindern, die ihre Gruppen ohne es zu wollen, oder zumindest mit ambivalenten Gefühlen, zum Ende des Schuljahres verlassen mussten, schlug sich dies auch in der Beziehungsgestaltung innerhalb der Wohngruppe nieder (P und J), wobei die Kinder dies subjektiv offenbar anders erlebten als die ErzieherInnen.

Um die Wirksamkeit der konkreten psychodramatischen Interventionen zu messen, erschien es uns insbesondere wichtig, die Veränderung psychodramaspezifischer Variablen quantitativ erfassbar und damit statistisch auswertbar zu machen. Wie eingangs bereits beschrieben, wurden die Items der *RDI* auf Grundlage der Rollentheorie nach Schacht (Schacht 2010, S. 21–63) zusammengestellt. Neben einigen deskriptiven Items (wie Rolle, Rollenebene und Auswirkung der Rolleninteraktion auf die Gruppe) finden sich psychodramaspezifische Items, die auf fünfstufigen Skalen erfasst werden. Jeweils am Ende einer Sitzung wird von den Therapeutinnen die Ausprägung der jeweiligen Variablen geratet. Es wurden Mittelwerte der Ausprägungen der jeweiligen Variablen für die gesamte Gruppe zu drei Messzeitpunkten im Jahresverlauf gebildet, jeweils aus 3 h zu Beginn, in der Mitte und am Ende.

Die Tabelle in Abb. 9 zeigt Mittelwerte der Kindergruppe bezüglich der einzelnen Variablen zu den drei Messzeitpunkten.

Die Mittelwerte zeigen an, dass sich die Ausprägungen der Variablen in die gewünschte Richtung entwickeln. Zur Feststellung statistisch bedeutsamer Mittelwertveränderungen der einzelnen Variablen der *RDI* in der Gruppe über die Zeit ist es möglich eine Varianzanalyse (*ANOVA*) mit Messwiederholung zu rechnen. Die Prüfung der Veränderung zwischen zwei Zeitpunkten der Gruppe ist mittels eines t-Tests für gepaarte Stichproben möglich. Da es sich um ein Pilotprojekt ohne Kontrollgruppe handelt, wurde davon abgesehen, da die Relevanz nicht gegeben ist.

Der *RDI* wäre zudem ein geeignetes Instrument, um das erhobene Filmmaterial statistisch auswertbar zu machen. Unabhängige BeurteilerInnen können anhand der aufgestellten Variablen des *RDI* die Filmsequenzen zu den drei Messzeitpunkten raten, so dass dann erneut die geschilderten Vorher-Nachher-Auswertungen möglich wären.

Zusammenfassend lässt sich für die gesamte Gruppe feststellen, dass die Erhebungen mit dem *SDQ* – ähnlich wie in der Einzelfallanalyse – nur geringfügige Veränderungen glauben machen. Im Gegensatz dazu stehen die Ergebnisse der anderen Testverfahren: die Anzahl der gegenseitigen Anziehungen innerhalb der Wohngruppe hat sich bei jedem Kind in der Selbst- und auch in der Fremdeinschätzung erhöht.

Abb. 9 RDI der Gruppe

Variable RDI	T1 Mittelwert	T2 Mittelwert	T3 Mittelwert
Rollenebene	1,52	2,33	2,81
Aktionshunger	2,81	2,95	3,52
Spontanität	2	2,95	3,9
Interaktionen	2,48	3,09	3,81
Empathie	1,81	2,43	3,76
Progression	2,14	2,93	3,76
Regression	2,76	2,38	2,05
Achtsamkeit	2,1	2,9	3,81
Konflikte	2,05	1,81	1,71
Konfliktlösungsfähigkeit	1,81	2,86	3,86
Nähe	2,38	2,81	3,24
Distanz	3,57	2,86	2,57
Differenzierung bei Rückmeldung	2,33	2,9	3,57

Dasselbe trifft auf den Grad der Integration des jeweiligen Kindes in der Wohngruppe zu. Die Gruppenkohäsion nahm von t1 bis t3 sukzessive zu, bis hin zu einem hohen Maß an Nähe zwischen den Kindern untereinander. Im RDI zeigte sich innerhalb der Kinderpsychodramagruppe eine Ausdehnung aller Variablen in die gewünschte Richtung.

9 Gruppenprozess

Um den Gruppenprozess innerhalb der Therapiegruppe zu erfassen, arbeiteten wir mit *Soziogrammen*, die von den Kindern (Abb. 10) und unabhängig davon von den Gruppentherapeutinnen (Abb. 11) gelegt wurden. Im ersten Soziogramm ist die Gruppe noch nicht geteilt, im weiteren Verlauf (t1 und t2) stellen wir lediglich die größere Gruppe soziometrisch dar. Während wir bei den Kindern untereinander ausschließlich die räumliche Zuordnung soziometrisch erfragten, unterschieden wir aus der Beobachterperspektive Anziehung, Ablehnung oder neutrale Beziehungen, um Veränderungen in den sozio-emotionalen Beziehungsstrukturen deutlich zu machen. So wird sichtbar, dass sich nicht nur insgesamt mehr Nähe innerhalb der Gruppe entwickelt hat, sondern auch die Beziehungen der Kinder untereinander von „eher

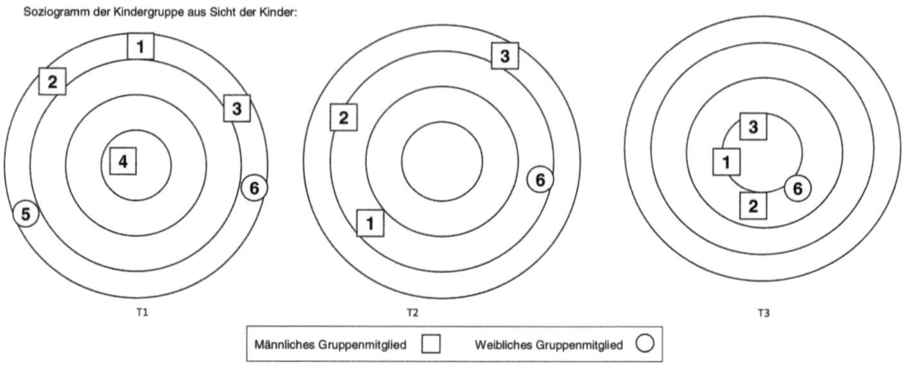

Abb. 10 Gruppensoziogramm aus Kindersicht

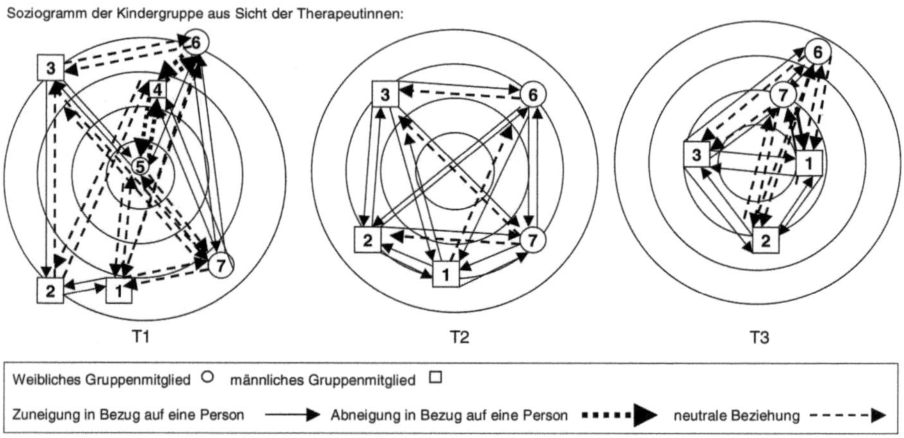

Abb. 11 Gruppensoziogramm aus Sicht der Therapeutinnen:

neutral" in von Gegenseitigkeit geprägte Anziehung umgeschlagen sind. Die Gruppenkohäsion nahm von t1 bis t3 sukzessive zu. Auf Grundlage des Kindersoziogramms sind alle integriert, es gibt keine AußenseiterInnen.

Dies und auch die Veränderungen in den Gruppensoziogrammen spricht für eine Zunahme der Fähigkeiten zur Gestaltung sozialer Interaktionen, die ohne eine Weiterentwicklung von Empathie nicht möglich gewesen wäre.

Das Ziel, dass sich die Position aller Kinder innerhalb der Gruppe verbessert, wurde erreicht. Wenngleich ein Mädchen, wie im Soziogramm der Therapeutinnen sichtbar, nach wie vor eher eine Sonderrolle inne hat, konnte doch die Nähe und das Empathievermögen der Kinder zu sich und untereinander gesteigert werden, und auch bei ihr entstand eine größere Nähe zu den anderen Kindern. Bei einem Jungen haben sich die Sympathien für die anderen, die zunächst nur von ihm ausgegangen sind, in gegenseitige Anziehung verändert.

10 Diskussion

Anhand eines Einzelfalls wie auch für die Gesamtgruppe haben wir die Auswertungsmethoden und Ergebnisse der angewendeten qualitativen und quantitativen Verfahren dargestellt. Ausgehend von der Fragestellung, welche Verfahren sich am besten eignen, um die Wirksamkeit der Kinderpsychodramatherapie nachzuweisen, sollen im Folgenden unsere Erkenntnisse zu den einzelnen Erhebungsverfahren zusammengestellt und diskutiert werden. Es handelt sich lediglich um eine experimentelle Studie, da die Auswertung bei allen genutzten Verfahren zum Einen in Ermangelung externer BeobachterInnen von den TherapeutInnen selbst und ohne Kontrollgruppe durchgeführt wurde. Zum anderen ist die Anzahl der untersuchten ProbandInnen keineswegs repräsentativ. Insofern werden bei der vorliegenden Arbeit klassische Kriterien empirischer Arbeit nicht erfüllt. Es handelt sich vielmehr um eine erste Annäherung, eine Studie, welche Verfahrensweisen sich als geeignet erweisen, um die Ergebnisse psychodramatherapeutischer Arbeit mit Kindern auszuwerten.

Für die Einzelfallanalyse wurde O. gewählt, da er sowohl in seiner Rollenentwicklung als auch in der Veränderung seiner Position innerhalb der Psychodramagruppe die augenscheinlichsten Veränderungen durchlebte.

Insgesamt fällt die Divergenz der Ergebnisse von *SDQ* und *RDI* auf. Während die Auswertungen des *RDI*, der soziometrischen Tests und der sozialen Atome durchgängig positive Veränderungen in den für die Zielsetzungen der Gruppe relevanten Bereichen verzeichnen, zeigen die Veränderungen, die mit dem *SDQ* messbar waren, – wenn überhaupt – lediglich geringfügige Verbesserungen.

Der *SDQ* ist ein einfach einsetzbarer und leicht auszuwertender Fragebogen, der statistisch überprüfbare Daten liefert. Soll eine störungsspezifische Auswertung erfolgen, erwies sich die Nutzung des SDQ für wahrnehmbare Veränderung in verschiedenen Lebensbereichen der Kinder jedoch nur als bedingt geeignet, da er sehr defizitorientiert ist und die Perspektive der Befragten entsprechend beeinflusst. Als eine mögliche Ursache für die Unterschiedlichkeit der Ergebnisse von *SDQ* und *RDI* sehen wir, dass eine Veränderung von Verhaltensmustern zunächst in einem sicheren, geschützten Rahmen erfolgt, wie ihn die Therapiegruppe für die Kinder darstellt, bevor sie in der Welt des Alltags umgesetzt werden kann. Da „symbolische Interaktion als wechselseitiges, aufeinander bezogenes Verhalten von Personen und Gruppen unter Verwendung gemeinsamer Symbole, wobei eine Ausrichtung an den Erwartungen der Handlungspartner aneinander erfolgt,“ (Lamnek zit. nach: Hintermeier 2011, S. 91) zu verstehen ist, sind vor allem Kinder auf die Unterstützung und den wachen Blick von Eltern, LehrerInnen und ErzieherInnen angewiesen, wenn sie es wagen, die Sicherheit vertrauter Muster zugunsten neuer, funktionaler Handlungsweisen aufzugeben. So ist es möglich, dass wir in unserer therapeutischen Haltung bewusst wohlwollend waren, während ErzieherInnen wie auch Eltern im Alltag vielleicht eher dazu neigen, auf dysfunktionale Verhaltensweisen einzugehen und diese den Kindern entsprechend zurückzumelden. Dies hat wiederum eine Wechselwirkung bezüglich der Selbstwahrnehmung der Kinder zur Folge. Insofern vertreten wir die Auffassung, dass der *SDQ* zur Abbildung von möglichen Veränderungen nur sehr bedingt geeignet ist.

Der *RDI* hingegen stellt ein Fragebogenverfahren für ressourcenorientierte Veränderungen innerhalb der Therapiegruppe dar, das nicht auf die Auswertung der Arbeit mit Kindergruppen beschränkt ist. Die einzelnen Items sind auf Grundlage der psychodramatischen Rollentheorie detailliert ausdifferenzierbar. Sie lassen sich aufgrund spezifischer Beobachtungskriterien zuordnen und raten. Hier verweisen wir auf die Arbeit von Köfeler und Krall (2015; in diesem Band). Neben der Messbarkeit des Therapieerfolgs geben die einzelnen Items Hinweise auf geeignete therapeutische Interventionen. Um eine Klarheit in Bezug auf Bewertungskriterien für das *RDI* zu erreichen, ist – analog zur Vorgehensweise bei der Nutzung der *OPD–KJ* ein entsprechendes Curriculum notwendig, in dem die BeobachterInnen vor der Anwendung ausgebildet werden. Insgesamt erwies sich das *RDI* als sehr praktikables Instrumentarium, mit dem Entwicklungsfortschritte der Kinder innerhalb der Therapiegruppe nach psychodramatischem Verständnis ohne großen Aufwand gemessen werden können. Auch eine Auswertung des *Videomaterials* ist auf Grundlage – des *RDI* – möglich.

Die *OPD-KJ* zeigte sich zur Messung qualitativer Veränderungen in der Interaktionsgestaltung sinnvoll (vgl. Bindernagel 2011, S. 116 ff.). Allerdings fehlt u. E. der Bezug zur Gestaltung der Alltagsbeziehungen der Kinder. Zudem ist seine Handhabung in der Praxis sehr aufwändig. In der Evaluation psychodramatischer Arbeit hat er unserer Erfahrung nach wenig Relevanz.

Zur Auswertung funktionaler oder dysfunktionaler Beziehungsgestaltung erwiesen sich soziometrische Verfahren wie das *Soziale Atom* und *Soziogramme* als hilfreich, da hier qualitative und quantitative Veränderungen auf einen Blick sichtbar werden. Es zeigte sich, dass die Kinder zu Beginn der Gruppe eine recht einfache, kaum differenzierte Sicht der Beziehungen hatten, die sie im weiteren Verlauf in allen Bereichen zunehmend differenzieren konnten. Bei den Verfahren *soziales Atom* und *Soziometrie*, die wir Individuum-orientiert anwendeten, beobachteten wir einen Zusammenhang zwischen der Zunahme von Empathie und damit einhergehender zunehmender Fähigkeit zur Differenzierung bei der Wahrnehmung in Beziehungen auf der einen Seite und der Gruppenintegration bzw. –kohäsion auf der anderen Seite. Daher scheint es lohnenswert, eine quantitative Auswertungsmöglichkeit für die Darstellungen von sozialen Atomen und Soziogrammen zu entwickeln. Variablen wie *Kohäsion* und *Differenzierung der Wahrnehmung von Beziehungen* können skaliert erfasst und damit statistisch ausgewertet werden. Aus den *sozialen Atomen und Soziometrien* ließen sich diese Variablen anhand der Darstellungen von Nähe und Distanz operationalisieren. Die Kreise im sozialen Atom und den Soziometrien entsprechen den Stufen auf einer Skala und können zu Mittelwerten zusammengefasst werden (Petzold 1979). Auf diese Weise ist es möglich, auszuzählen, wie viele Nennungen von Ablehnung und Anziehung zwischen Gruppenmitgliedern bestehen. Die Variablen können in ihren Veränderungen über die Zeit der Gruppentherapie ausgewertet werden. Von Vorteil ist, dass es sich im Vergleich zu anderen Untersuchungsmethoden bei *soziometrischen Testverfahren* um Messinstrumente und Interventionen in Einem handelt: sie laden sowohl zu Selbstreflexion als auch zu Visionalisierung gewünschter Beziehungen bzw. Veränderungen ein (Cejka 2011, S. 158). Die intensivere Arbeit mit dem *sozialen Atom*, wie es bei Cejka und Kirk (Kirk und Dutton 2006, S. 40) zur Anwendung kommt, ermöglicht einen Einblick sowohl in die soziale

Eingebundenheit, als auch in die Qualität der Beziehungen. In seiner ganzheitlichen Anwendung gibt *das soziale Atom A*ufschluss über das Ausmaß des Aktionshungers, also über Antrieb und Handlungsmotivation der ProbandInnen. Darüber hinaus stellen diese Verfahren ein operationalisierbares Instrumentarium dar, mit dem Veränderungen aus KlientInnen- und Elternsicht messbar sind.

Bei größeren Gruppen können statistisch bedeutsame Veränderungen innerhalb der Gruppe über die drei Messzeitpunkte hinweg für die Skalen des *SDQ* mittels Varianzanalyse (ANOVA) mit Messwiederholung erfasst werden. Vergleiche der Veränderungen zwischen zwei Zeitpunkten sind mittels t-Test für gepaarte Stichproben möglich. Um auszuwerten, inwieweit die Einschätzungen der Kinder mit denen ihrer BetreuerInnen übereinstimmen, könnten Pearson-Korrelationen errechnet werden. Dies ließe einen ersten Schluss zu, ob Verhaltensveränderungen, die in der Psychodramagruppe erlebt werden, auch einen Übertrag in den Lebensalltag der Kinder finden.

11 Ein guter nächster Schritt

Neurophysiologische Erkenntnisse über die Funktionsweise von Spiegelneuronen geben den Therapierichtungen Recht, die Erleben und Handeln aktiv mit einbeziehen. Bilder, sowohl die inneren, noch mehr die, die zur Darstellung kommen, bestimmen demnach unsere Sicht der Welt und unser Handeln (Hüther 2011). Forschungen belegen, dass neuropysiologische Veränderungen nachhaltig dann beobachtbar sind, wenn ein Mensch ganzheitlich, mit Leib und Seele, am therapeutischen Prozess beteiligt ist.

Während für Curricula wie z. B. „*Faustlos*" (Cierpka 2011, S. 57), mit dem auf systemischer Grundlage Konfliktmanagment mit Kindern trainiert werden soll, begleitende Evaluation zur Selbstverständlichkeit geworden ist, ist dies in der Psychodramatherapie noch nicht üblich.

Ich schließe mich Bindernagel an, der die Win-Win-Situation hervorhebt, die eine engere Zusammenarbeit zwischen Hochschulen und Praxis zu Forschungszwecken proklamiert (Bindernagel 2011, S. 22). Eine Ausweitung empirischer Forschung mit quantitativen und qualitativen Studien erfordert jedoch nicht allein eine Zusammenarbeit zwischen Hochschule und Praxis, sondern auch die Bereitschaft von PsychodramatikerInnen, über Länder- und Institutsgrenzen hinaus zu kooperieren. Im Rahmen des *FEPTO Research Commitees* wurde auf europäischer Ebene ein Anfang gemacht.

Unser Anliegen im vorliegenden Artikel ist es, durch die experimentelle Nutzung verschiedener Instrumentarien, einen Beitrag dazu zu leisten, welche Verfahren für die Evaluation (kinder)psychodramatischer Gruppentherapie geeignet sind. Unser Ziel ist es, dass Verfahren im (kinder)psychodramatherapeutischen Bereich entwickelt werden, die flächendeckend einsetzbar sind. Dazu braucht es die Zusammenarbeit von Menschen, die Interesse an Evaluation haben, und die Kooperation mit Hochschulen, denen vielfältige Möglichkeiten der Evaluation zur Verfügung stehen. Unseres Erachtens sollte sich die Evaluation (kinder)psychodramatischer Therapie sowohl psychodramaspezifischer Verfahren wie auch solcher bereits angewandter Forschungsmethoden bedienen.

Um einen kausalen Bezug zur Kinderpsychodramatherapie herstellen zu können, empfehlen wir resümierend ein Kontrollgruppendesign unter ähnlichen Bedingungen mit größeren Fallzahlen. Auf diese Weise könnte man mögliche Beeinträchtigungen der internen Validität kontrollieren. Auch der Einsatz *externer Beobachterinnen* trägt zur Validität einer Untersuchung in Vergleichsgruppen bei. Auf diese Weise würde eine kausale Interpretation der gewonnenen Ergebnisse deutlicher herausgearbeitet.

Erkenntnis entsteht durch Annäherung und Verdichtung, so Schätzing (2014). In diesem Sinn verstehen wir unsere Arbeit zum vorliegenden Artikel: „*In der Bewegung liegt die Veränderung, in der Veränderung die Chance, in der* Unschärfe die *künftige Wahrheit [...] Jeder ist eingeladen, diesen Prozess mitzuverfolgen – und mitzugestalten.*“ *(ebd. S. 19)*

Wir freuen uns über Rückmeldungen, Anregungen, Fragen und Diskussionen, vor allem jedoch über ein gemeinsames Weiterdenken und -entwickeln.

Denn, um mit Moreno zu schließen, „*von den sozialen Netzwerken und der Art der Kommunikation in den Netzwerken hängen nicht nur das Glück oder Unglück der einzelnen Menschen und ihr Weiterleben ab, sondern auch die Zukunft unserer Erde...* “ (Moreno zit. von Leutz, nach Pinter 2014).

Anmerkungen

1 www.sdqinfo.org.

2 Aus all seinen bisher in der Gruppe eingenommenen Rollen wählte O. vier aus, die er mit den anderen Kindern besetzte und soziometrisch im Raum verteilte. Er begegnete ihnen dann im gemeinsamen Spiel.

Literatur

Biegler-Vitek, G., & Schorn, B. (2013). „Die Eule liegt zwischen mir und dem Rudi und berührt jeden von uns mit einem Flügel ...“ – Anwendung und Bedeutung der Soziometrie in der psychodramatherapeutischen Arbeit mit Kindern und Jugendlichen. In C. Stadler (Hrsg.), *Soziometrie – Messung, Darstellung, Analyse und Intervention in sozialen Beziehungen* (S. 171–185). Wiesbaden: Springer VS.

Bindernagel, D., Scherrer, A., Winzeler, A. L., & Wyl, A. (2011). Psychodrama-Gruppentherapie mit Kindern – Anregungen für eine praxisorientierte Forschung. In C. Stadler & M. Wieser (Hrsg.), *Psychodrama – Empirische Forschung und Wissenschaft* (S. 109–125). Wiesbaden: VS Verlag für Sozialwissenschaften.

Cejka, S. (2011). Das soziale Atom als Anlyseinstrument sozialer Netzwerkforschung am Beispiel einer Projektevaluation innerhalb der Jugendwohlfahrt. In C. Stadler & M. Wieser (Hrsg.), *Psychodrama – Empirische Forschung und Wissenschaft* (S. 89–109). Wiesbaden: VS Verlag für Sozialwissenschaften.

Cierpka, M. (2011). *Faustlos – Mit Kindern Konflikte gewaltfrei lösen lernen*. Freiburg: Herder.

Hintermeier, S. (2011). Qualitative Psychodramaforschung. In C. Stadler & M. Wieser (Hrsg.), *Psychodrama – Empirische Forschung und Wissenschaft* (S. 89–109). Wiesbaden: VS Verlag für Sozialwissenschaften.

Hüther, G. (2011). *Die Macht der inneren Bilder. Wie Visionen das Gehirn, den Menschen und die Welt verändern*. Göttingen: Vandenhoeck & Ruprecht.

Kirk, K., & Dutton, C. (2006). „Nobody Nowhere“ to „Somebody Somewhere“: Researching the Effectiveness of psychodrama with young people with Asperger's syndrome. *British Journal of Psychodrama and Sociodrama, 21*(2), 31–53.
Köfeler, C., & Krall, H. (2015). Soziale Interaktion von Kindern mit Selektivem Mutismus. In C. Stadler, M. Wieser, & K. Kirk (Hrsg.), *Psychodrama. Empirische Forschung und Wissenschaft 2*. Wiesbaden: Springer VS.
Petzold, H. G. (1979). Zur Veränderung der sozialen Mikrostruktur im Alter: Eine Untersuchung von 40 „sozialen Atomen“ alter Menschen. *Integrative Therapie, 5*, 51–78.
Pintér, G. Homepage des Moreno Centrum in Budapest, 13.03.2014, http://www.morenocentrum.hu.
Schacht, M. (2010). *Das Ziel ist im Weg – Störungsverständnis und Therapieprozess im Psychodrama*. Wiesbaden: VS Verlag für Sozialwissenschaften.
Schätzing, F. (2013). *Nachrichten aus einem unbekannten Universum: Eine Zeitreise durch die Meere*. Fischer Verlag: Berlin.
Schlechtriemen, T. (2013). Morenos Soziogramme – Wie soziale Gruppenstrukturen grafisch dargestellt und analysiert werden können. In C. Stadler (Hrsg.), *Soziometrie – Messung, Darstellung, Analyse und Intervention in sozialen Beziehungen* (S. 101–121). Wiesbaden: Springer VS.
SDQ unter: www.sdqinfo.org.

Elisabeth Uschold-Meier, Diplom-Pädagogin, Psychodramaleiterin DFP. Initiatorin und Mitbegründerin der Studentischen Kinderkrippe Würzburg e. V. und des Familienzentrums e. V. in Würzburg, mehrjährige Tätigkeit in einer psychiatrischen Klinik und in der stationären Jugendhilfe. In freier Praxis tätig als Coach, Paar-, Eltern-, Familien- und Teamberaterin, in der Beratung und Therapie von Kindern und Jugendlichen, in der Fort- und Weiterbildung und als freie Autorin in Fachzeitschriften.

Rebecca Wagner, Diplom-Psychologin, Weiterbildung in pädagogisch-behavioristischem Psychodrama, Tätigkeit im Jugendstrafvollzug und der stationären Jugendhilfe.

Z Psychodrama Soziometr (2016) (Suppl) 15:165–177
DOI 10.1007/s11620-015-0303-z

HAUPTBEITRÄGE

Zeitschrift für Psychodrama und Soziometrie

Soziale Interaktion von Kindern mit Selektivem Mutismus

Christina Köfeler · Hannes Krall

Online publiziert: 8. Dezember 2015

Zusammenfassung In dem vorliegenden Beitrag wird der Frage nachgegangen, ob und in welcher Form soziale Interaktion und Rollenentwicklung von mutistischen Kindern in einer „Psychodrama Intensivgruppe“ (Biegler-Vitek und Wicher, 2014) gefördert werden können. Ein besonderer Schwerpunkt stellt dabei die Hilfs-Ich Funktion dar, die als einer von mehreren wesentlichen Einflussfaktoren vertiefend beschrieben werden soll. Die empirischen Daten, die im Rahmen dieses prozessorientierten Ansatzes gesammelt wurden, stützen sich auf videobasierte Beobachtungen, speziell entwickelte Fragebögen für Kinder und Hilfs-Ichs sowie Hilfs-Ich-Interviews. In einer Einzelfallstudie werden die Daten von insgesamt drei Kindern mit selektivem Mutismus schließlich analysiert und miteinander verglichen. Die aus dieser Auseinandersetzung abgeleiteten Hypothesen deuten an, dass die beobachteten Veränderungen von verbaler und nonverbaler Interaktionsfähigkeit wie auch Rollenerweiterungen mit der spezifischen Struktur des psychodramatischen Intensivsettings, spezifischen Hilfs-Ich-Funktionen sowie störungsspezifischen Charakteristiken der Kinder in Zusammenhang gebracht werden können.

Schlüsselwörter Psychodrama · Selektiver Mutismus · Soziale Interaktion · Hilfs-Ich-Funktionen · Videoanalyse

H. Krall (✉) · C. Köfeler
IfEB, Universität Klagenfurt,
Universitätsstraße 65–67,
9020 Klagenfurt, Österreich
E-Mail: Hannes.krall@aau.at

Social interaction of children with selective mutism

Abstract In this article the aim is to investigate whether, and in which way, social interaction and role development of children with Selective Mutism can be improved in a "Psychodrama Intensive Group" (Biegler-Vitek and Wicher Biegler-Vitek und Wicher 2014). A special emphasis is put on auxiliary ego functioning, which is considered to be one, out of a few, crucial influential factors that will be described in depth. The collected data of this process-oriented approach include video based observations, especially developed questionnaires completed by children and auxiliary egos and the transcripts of auxiliary ego interviews. In a case study empirical data of three children who suffered from Selective Mutism was analysed and compared. The findings of these investigations brought about hypotheses which suggest that the sighted variations of verbal and nonverbal interactions, as well as role extensions, can be associated with the particular structure of psychodramatic sessions and settings, intrinsic auxiliary ego functioning and disorder related characteristics.

Keywords Psychodrama · Selective mutism · Social interaction · Auxiliary ego functioning · Video analysis

Im Rahmen eines von Gabriele Biegler-Vitek und Monika Wicher entwickelten psychodramatischen Intensivsettings (Biegler-Vitek und Wicher 2014; Biegler-Vitek und Wicher 2012; Wicher 2007, 2012; Biegler-Vitek 2011a, 2011b) sollen soziale Interaktion und Rollenentwicklung von Kindern unterschiedlichen Alters, Geschlechts und Störungsbildes untersucht werden. Besonderer Berücksichtigung soll dabei der Herausarbeitung jener Einflussfaktoren zukommen, die in einem solchen therapeutischen Kontext zu hilfreichen Veränderungen von verbalen und nonverbalen Interaktionsverläufen beitragen. Insbesondere die Funktion des Hilfs-Ichs soll hierbei vertiefend herausgearbeitet werden.

Die psychodramatische Arbeit im angesprochenen Intensivsetting mit Kindern im Alter von 6 bis 12 Jahren läuft über jeweils 3 h an vier aufeinander folgenden Vormittagen. Die Kinder sind aufgrund unterschiedlicher Störungsbilder in laufender psychotherapeutischer Betreuung.

Die psychodramatische Gruppe, an der etwa 12 bis 14 Kinder teilnehmen können, wird von zwei Psychodramatikerinnen geleitet und von mehreren Hilfs-Ichs unterstützt. Jedes Kind hat also zusätzlich ein Hilfs-Ich zur Seite, das dieses über die vier Tage hinweg konstant begleitet. Die psychodramatische Arbeit ist über die jeweiligen Tage sowohl zeitlich, räumlich als auch im Ablauf strukturiert.

Jeder Tag beginnt mit einem Warm-up zum Kennenlernen bzw. zum Austausch der aktuellen Befindlichkeit. In weiterer Folge werden Rollen und Szenen von den Kindern mit Unterstützung ihres Hilfs-Ichs entwickelt und erprobt. Nach einer Pause werden die entwickelten Rollen und Szenen in der Gruppe vorgespielt. Im Anschluss folgen Rollenfeedback und Sharing, wobei die Leiterinnen gezielt bei den Kindern nachfragen. Im Sharing werden allgemeine Themen aufgegriffen, die von den Kindern im Spiel zum Ausdruck gebracht werden. Jeder Vormittag endet mit einem kurzen Abschluss- und Abschiedsritual.

Der Arbeitsraum ist klar strukturiert und mit Hilfe von Klebestreifen abgegrenzt. Die Gesamtgruppe wird von den Leiterinnen in drei Kleingruppen zu je etwa vier Kindern unterteilt, die alle wiederum einen eigenen Spielbereich vorfinden. Und schließlich hat in diesen Gruppenbereichen wieder jedes Kind einen individuellen Spielbereich, in dem zu Beginn mit Hilfe von Stühlen und Decken ein Rückzugsort bereitgestellt wird.

Die vier Tage folgen im Spielablauf einer festgelegten Struktur. Am ersten Tag wird zunächst mit Hilfe von Intermediärobjekten (Handpuppen) zwischen dem Kind und dem Hilfs-Ich und eventuell unter Einbeziehung der jeweiligen Kleingruppe gespielt. Am zweiten Tag wird von den Kindern mit Unterstützung der Hilfs-Ichs ein Schutzhaus aus bereitgestellten Kartons gebaut. Dieses Schutzhaus wird individuell eingerichtet und der Gruppe im Spiel vorgestellt. Des Weiteren folgt wiederum ein Spiel in der Kleingruppe, das dann am dritten und vierten Tag – je nach Interesse und Möglichkeiten des Kindes – zu einem offenen Spiel in der Großgruppe ausgedehnt wird.

Stadler und Spörrle (2008) haben hinsichtlich der Unterscheidung der in vielfältigster Form existierenden Rollenspiele in der Psychodramatherapie eine hilfreiche Kategorisierung vorgenommen. Demnach können Individuen in Rollenspielen in der eigenen Rolle, in der Rolle des anderen und in der Gruppe Handlungen durchführen. Diese drei Arten von Handlungsmöglichkeiten können entweder einem vorgegebenen Plot und festgelegtem Ablauf folgen oder gemäß Morenos Begriff des Stegreifspiels im Rahmen eines solchen zur Anwendung kommen (a. a. O., S. 182).

Die von Biegler-Vitek und Wicher (2014) entwickelte Form von Gruppenarbeit setzt auf eine Mischung unterschiedlicher Varianten des Rollenspiels und zielt so darauf ab, die Kinder in umfassender Weise in ihrer Rollenentwicklung und in der sozialen Interaktion in der Gruppe zu fördern. Die Kinder werden angeregt, in einer sicheren Umgebung und mit Unterstützung der Hilfs-Ichs ihre Spontaneität und Kreativität im Spiel zu entwickeln und in einer der jeweiligen sozialen Situation angemessenen Weise umzusetzen. Die Kinder werden mit Hilfe der Entwicklung von Rollen und Szenen auf spielerische Weise in ihrem Selbstwert und in ihren sozialen Kompetenzen gestärkt, um mit Anforderungen in ihren alltäglichen Lebenssituationen in konstruktiver Weise umgehen zu können.

Der vorliegende Beitrag untersucht im Speziellen die verbale bzw. nonverbale Kommunikation und Rollenentwicklung von mutistischen Kindern in der psychodramatischen Gruppenarbeit.

1 Selektiver Mutismus – „Ich kann und ich kann nicht. Ich will und ich will nicht."

Das Störungsbild des selektiven Mutismus zeichnet sich durch eine durchgängige und vorhersehbare Unfähigkeit zu sprachlichem Ausdruck in bestimmten sozialen Kontexten aus, während in anderen Kontexten eine gut ausgereifte und entwickelte Sprachkompetenz beobachtet werden kann. Diese „deutliche, emotional bedingte Selektivität des Sprechens" (Dilling et al. 2008, S. 334) einhergehend mit „abnormen Temperamentsmerkmalen" (a. a. O., S. 335) gilt demnach als Voraussetzung für eine profunde Diagnose.

„Wer sich mit Mutismus befasst, muss Ambivalenz, Zweideutigkeit, ja Spannungsbögen aushalten können. Nicht sprechen und darin gefangen sein, obwohl man eigentlich sprechen kann. Sprechen wollen und dabei doch die eigene Besonderheit in der Rolle der Nichtsprechenden so sehr genießen. Das ist Mutismus. Angst und Aggression – das ist er auch" (Köfeler 2014, S. 2).

Erstmals aufgetreten sind Begrifflichkeiten, die sich um dieses Phänomen zentrieren, bereits 1877 bei Kussmaul, der den Mutismus als aphasia voluntaria (Steinhausen et al. 2006, S. 751; Viana et al. 2009, S. 59), also als freiwilliges Schweigen, betitelte. Doch insbesondere der Aspekt der Freiwilligkeit bzw. Wahlfreiheit, der sich auch in dem von Tramer im Jahr 1934 geprägten Begriff des elektiven Mutismus festmachen lässt, erwies sich letztendlich als wissenschaftlich nicht haltbar, da den betroffenen Kindern die Freiheit der Wahl über sprechen oder nicht sprechen schlichtweg nicht zur Verfügung steht. Daher erscheint der Begriff des selektiven Mutismus adäquater und die dem Störungsbild immanente Problematik treffender abbildend (Katz-Bernstein 2011, S. 24 f.).

Neben einer völligen Stummheit bei Ansprache, also einer nicht vorhandenen sprachlichen Interaktion, lässt sich das klinische Erscheinungsbild auch auf nonverbaler Interaktionsebene durch eine Verweigerung des Blickkontakts, einer erstarrten, verschlossenen Körperhaltung, kaum vorhandener Gestik und beinahe maskenhafter Mimik fassen (Biegler-Vitek 2011a, S. 14).

Über die dem Mutismus immanenten Grundgefühle zwischen Angst einerseits, Aggression und oppositionellem Widerstand andererseits, wurde in der Literatur zuletzt immer wieder diskutiert. Dabei schienen Faktoren, wie beispielsweise eine stark ausgeprägte Komorbidität und Ähnlichkeit zu Angststörungen (Vecchio und Kearney 2005, S. 34; Carbone et al. 2010, S. 1065 f.), ähnliche Temperamentsmerkmale (Carbone et al. 2010, S. 1065) oder der ausgeprägte Hang zu internalisierenden Verhaltensmustern (Vecchio und Kearney 2005, S. 34 ff) der Konzeptualisierung des selektiven Mutismus als oppositionelle Störung des Sozialverhaltens deutlich entgegen zu treten.

Dieser Umstand führte zu einer neuen diagnostischen Klassifizierung in der fünften und neuesten Ausgabe des DSM unter die sogenannten klassischen Angststörungen (Wittchen et al. 2014, S. 549).

Jenen Befunden, wonach beispielsweise Bezugspersonen die Ängste der Kinder um ein vielfaches ausgeprägter einschätzen als Kinder dies selbst tun, das Schweigen und Rückzugsverhalten der Kinder als Ausdruck von Angst also überschätzt werden könnte, wurden demnach weniger Gewicht zugesprochen. Ebenso wenig wurde berücksichtigt, dass es neben selektiv mutistischen Kindern, die wie gelähmt und erstarrt vor Angst sind, auch solche gibt, die zwar nicht sprechen, aber sehr wohl über ausgeprägte nonverbale Kommunikationsformen verfügen, die lachen bzw. eine lebendige Mimik und Gestik aufweisen und damit so gar nicht ängstlich anmuten (Yeganeh et al. 2003, S. 1070 ff; Biegler-Vitek 2011a, S. 27 ff).

Eine solche Ausprägung des selektiven Mutismus ist häufig bei Kindern mit Migrationshintergrund vorzufinden, der durch andere Faktoren bedingt bzw. beeinflusst wird: „Immigration status – and the processes attached to it, such as acculturation, learning a second language, potential discrimination and peer ostracism, to name a few – may deserve unique attention in our efforts to understand SM." (Viana et al. 2009, S. 63)

Dies bringt unserer Ansicht nach trotz Zuordnung zu den Angststörungen die Notwendigkeit einer sehr differenzierten, unterschiedliche Einflussfaktoren berücksichtigenden Herangehensweise mit sich.

Auch was ätiologische Überlegungen betrifft, ist das Störungsbild des selektiven Mutismus keineswegs mittels einfacher Erklärungsmodelle fassbar. Hartmann zufolge müssen verursachende Faktoren von jenen unterschieden werden, die zu einer Aufrechterhaltung der Störung beitragen (2010, S. 23).

Als verursachend werden demzufolge die familiäre Prädisposition zu Angststörungen (Hartmann 2010, S. 12 ff; Steinhausen et al. 2006, S. 753 ff), organische Faktoren, wie beispielsweise eine Störung des serotonergen Neurotransmittersystems (Hartmann 2010, S. 28 ff), ein Migrationshintergrund (Steinhausen et al. 2006, S. 753 ff; Viana et al. 2009, S. 63) oder auch neurobiologische Entwicklungsverzögerungen (Oerbeck und Kristensen 2008, S. 548 f.) angesehen. Zu betonen ist hierbei, dass in den überwiegenden Fällen trotz gegenteiliger Mutmaßungen und dem geheimnisvoll anmutenden Charakter der Störung keine traumatische Genese vorliegt (Hartmann 2010, S. 21).

Zu den aufrechterhaltenden Faktoren der Störung zählt Edison et al. (2011) zufolge beispielsweise der häufig durch den Mutismus entstandene, stark kontrollierende elterliche Erziehungsstil, der insbesondere auch die so wesentliche Autonomieentwicklung der betroffenen Kinder einzuschränken vermag (S. 277 ff).

Nowakowski et al. (2011), die sich mit Prozessen rund um die „joint attention" (S. 78), also die gemeinsam geteilte, bewusst gelenkte Aufmerksamkeit befassen, konnten weiterhin zeigen, dass betreffende Kinder sich tendenziell eher aus herausfordernden Situationen zurückziehen, als sich diesen zu stellen. Diese verabsäumten Lern- und Entwicklungsmöglichkeiten tragen ebenfalls zur Aufrechterhaltung dieses so facettenreichen Störungsbildes bei (a. a. O., S. 87).

2 Forschungsdesign und Methodik

Das angewandte Forschungsdesign zur Untersuchung von sozialen Interaktionsprozessen lässt sich als Einzelfallstudie (Mayring 2002, S. 41 ff; Bohnsack et al. 2011, S. 60 ff) beschreiben, in der eine Triangulation (Flick 2011; Denzin 2009a, S. 297 ff) unterschiedlicher Erhebungs- und Auswertungsmethoden zur Anwendung kommt. Mit unterschiedlichen Verfahren werden im Forschungsprozess sowohl qualitative als auch quantitative Daten erhoben. Der Arbeitsprozess mit den Kindern wird mit Hilfe von Videoaufnahmen dokumentiert. Ein besonderes Augenmerk liegt dabei auf den Spiel- und Interaktionssequenzen zwischen den Kindern und ihren Hilfs-Ichs. Für jedes Kind wird eine Videodokumentation erstellt, die den gesamten Prozess des Kindes über die vier Vormittage zusammenfassend abbildet und für eine detaillierte Analyse zur Verfügung steht (Knoblauch et al. 2009).

Des Weiteren werden von den Hilfs-Ichs nach jedem Vormittag Fragebögen ausgefüllt, in denen Beobachtungen und Einschätzungen bezüglich der sozialen Interaktion und Rollenentwicklung des Kindes erhoben werden. Ebenso geben die Kinder mit Hilfe von Feedbackbögen Rückmeldungen, wie sie den jeweiligen Vormittag in der Gruppe erlebt haben, welche Unterstützung sie vom Hilfs-Ich erhalten haben und was das Hilfs-Ich in weiterer Folge anders machen soll.

Schließlich fanden nach jedem Vormittag strukturierte Reflexionsgespräche mit den Hilfs-Ichs statt, die sich den Entwicklungen des Kindes an dem jeweiligen Vormittag widmeten. Diese Gespräche wurden aufgezeichnet und standen für die weitere Auswertung als Transkript zur Verfügung.

Bei der Auswertung wird neben einer zusammenfassenden Darstellung der Daten aus den Fragebögen und einer textanalytischen Auswertung der Interviews in Anlehnung an Philipp Mayring (2008) eine Videoanalyse durchgeführt (Abb. 1).

Bei der Videoanalyse werden deduktive (Knoblauch 2009, S. 69; Tuma et al. 2013, S. 44 f) und interpretative (Reichertz und Englert 2011; Knoblauch 2009; Bohnsack 2011; Denzin 2009b) Ansätze miteinander verbunden.

Für jedes Kind wird zunächst eine Videodokumentation über aufgezeichnete Spiel- und Interaktionssequenzen erstellt, die als empirische Basis für die Auswertung dient. Danach folgt die Festlegung entsprechender Analyseeinheiten. In unserem Fall werden statt beispielsweise Minuteneinheiten ganze Handlungsakte bzw. Interaktionszüge, Reichertz und Englert (2011) zufolge als „turns" oder „moves" (S. 15) beschrieben, zu einer genaueren Analyse herangezogen.

Weiterführend wird das empirische Material nun mittels eines theoriegeleitet entwickelten, deduktiven Kategorienschemas (Köfeler 2014, S. 76 f.) analysiert. Da die einzelnen Auswertungsschritte aufgrund des Umfanges nicht im Detail dargestellt werden können, soll exemplarisch der verwendete Kodierleitfaden für die verbale Interaktion kurz vorgestellt werden.

Jede mit Hilfe dieses Kodierleitfadens getroffene Einschätzung wird genauestens begründet und wesentliche audiovisuelle Inhalte (Sprache, Mimik, Gestik, Blickkon-

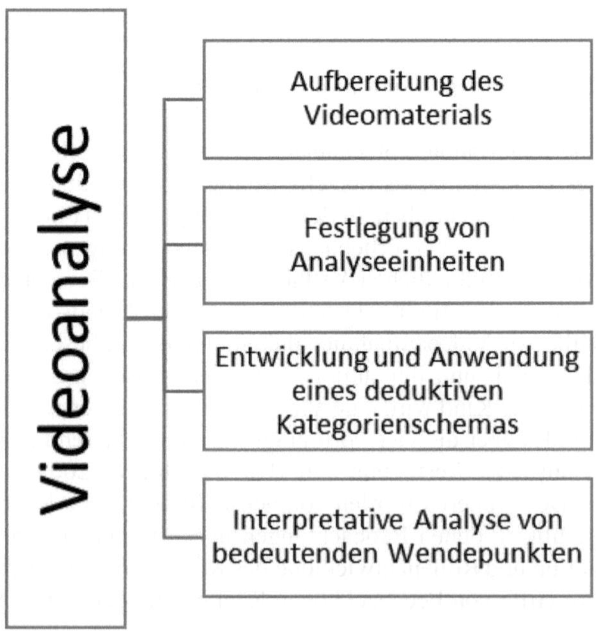

Abb. 1 Ablauf des videoanalytischen Vorgehens in der Untersuchung

takt, Handlungen, Rahmenbedingungen) gleich transkribiert. Diese Verschriftlichung fungiert weiterführend bereits als Basis für die interpretative Analyse, die sich auf besonders auffallende Interaktionszüge im Sinne von eklatanten, deduktiven Bewertungssprüngen bezieht.

Hinsichtlich interpretativer Analyse von herausgearbeiteten Veränderungsprozessen kommt insbesondere die sogenannte formulierende bzw. reflektierende Interpretation nach Bohnsack (2011, S. 17 ff) zur Anwendung.

3 Ergebnisse

Aus der so gesammelten Fülle an Auswertungsdaten über einen Fall (Interviewauswertungen, Fragebögen, Häufigkeitsschätzungen bzw. Interpretationen aus den Videos) werden schließlich Verläufe von insgesamt drei teilnehmenden Kindern hinsichtlich ihrer verbalen und non-verbalen Interaktion beschrieben.

Luisa ist ein fünfjähriges Mädchen mit nativem Mutismus, d. h. mit sehr wenigen Rollenskripts und einer grundsätzlich recht eingeschränkten nonverbalen Interaktionsfähigkeit. Bei Alexandra handelt es sich um ein zwölfjähriges Mädchen mit ausgeprägtem MigrantInnen-Mutismus, der durch ein nicht näher bekanntes traumatisches Ereignis zusätzlich erschwert wird. Valerie hingegen ist ein sechsjähriges Mädchen, das ebenfalls an MigrantInnen-Mutismus leidet, allerdings ohne traumatische Genese. Die Problematik ist daher vorwiegend auf eine ausgeprägte Sprechscheu fokussiert (Abb. 2).

In dem folgenden Diagramm werden die Häufigkeiten der Interaktionen im Verlauf über die vier Tage dargestellt:

3.1 Interaktionsfähigkeiten zu Beginn der Intensivwoche

Nimmt man den ersten Tag der Intensivwoche, der noch am ehesten Rückschlüsse auf den Ist-Stand des störungsimmanenten Erscheinungsbildes zuzulassen in der Lage ist, in den Fokus, so finden sich hinsichtlich verbaler Interaktion wie angenom-

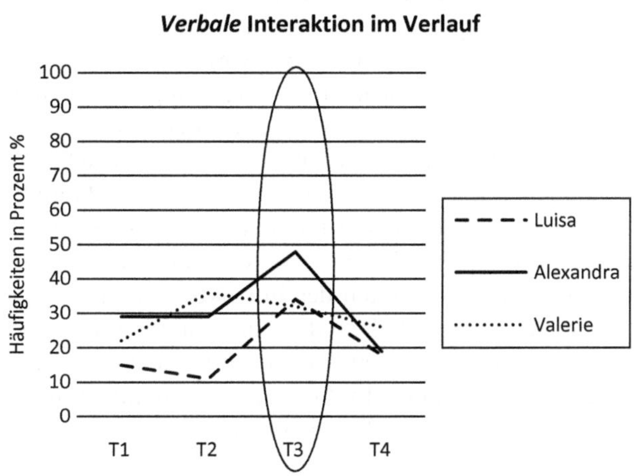

Abb. 2 Exemplarischer Auszug der Tabelle zur deduktiven und gleichzeitig interpretativen Auswertung der Videos. Für jeden „move" wird ein verbaler und nonverbaler Code vergeben. Diese Einschätzungen werden begründet. Entsprechende Veränderungsprozesse (grau unterlegt), die schließlich zu einem eklatanten Veränderungsmoment im Interaktionsverhalten führen (entsprechender Code hervorgehoben) werden im Anschluss einer interpretativen Analyse unterzogen

men niedrige Wertausprägungen zwischen 15 und 29 % bei allen drei analysierten Fällen. Am Beispiel Luisas erläutert bedeutet dies, dass das Mädchen in nur 15 % der beobachteten Analyseeinheiten Ja- und Nein-Antworten auf Ansprache gibt, somit in 85 % der Fälle keinerlei verbale Reaktionen zeigt.

Hinsichtlich nonverbaler Elemente zwischenmenschlicher Kommunikation (Blickkontakt, Mimik, Gestik, Körperhaltung, gesetzte Handlungen im Spiel) zeigen sich die Wertausprägungen zu Beginn der Intensivwoche breiter gestreut. Alexandra zeigt in nur 39 % der beobachteten „moves" zumindest wenig nonverbale Interaktion, d. h. Blickkontakt bei Ansprache, mimische Veränderungen, eine offene Körperhaltung sowie eine passive Beteiligung auf der Spielbühne mittels zusehen oder stereotyp anmutender Handlungen. Bei Valerie hingegen kann bereits in 93 % der beobachteten Analyseeinheiten zumindest derart nonverbales Interaktionsverhalten verbucht werden. Die weiterhin zu beobachtenden, durchgehend hohen Werte hinsichtlich ihres nonverbalen Ausdrucksvermögens untermauern die in der Literatur beschriebene Hypothese, wonach sich der selektive Mutismus im Falle eines Migrationshintergrunds einer deutlich anderen Dynamik und damit auch einem anderen, mehr auf Schwierigkeiten in der Sprache bezogenen Erscheinungsbild bedient.

3.2 Entwicklungen der Interaktionsfähigkeit im Verlauf der Intensivwoche

Was die Entwicklung der Interaktionsfähigkeit betrifft, so lässt sich aus angeführter Grafik (siehe Abb. 3) zunächst eine deutliche Differenzierung von verbaler und nonverbaler Ebene herausarbeiten.

Die Wertausprägungen nonverbaler Funktionen sind in einem deutlich höheren Bereich angesiedelt und zeigen in allen drei Fällen Verbesserungen bzw. ein gleichbleibend hohes Niveau an. Als besonders markant präsentiert sich der dritte Tag der Intensivwoche, der zumindest bei zwei mutistischen Mädchen sowohl hinsichtlich nonverbaler wie auch sprachlicher Interaktionen die höchsten Häufigkeiten beinhaltet. Dieser wird bei nachfolgenden Überlegungen zu wesentlichen Einflussfaktoren der psychodramatischen Therapie noch Gegenstand genauerer Analysen sein.

Hinsichtlich sprachlicher Funktion lassen sich aus der interpretativen Analyse der Videos und Interviews bei zumindest zwei Mädchen deutliche Verbesserungen qualitativer Aspekte herausarbeiten. Dies bedeutet, dass sich Ja/Nein Antworten auf Entscheidungsfragen zu Ein-Wort-Sätzen weiterentwickeln, Sprache auch ohne Erwärmungsphase mit dem Hilfs-Ich möglich ist und schließlich auch auf andere Personen in der Gruppe erweitert werden kann. Auch Lautstärke, Artikulation und Verständlichkeit des Gesprochenen verbessern sich.

Die Quantität sprachlichen Ausdrucks, die Häufigkeit verbaler Reaktionen also, erreicht am dritten Tag der Intensivwoche die höchste Wertausprägung, um am vierten Tag allerdings teils unter das Ausgangsniveau abzusinken (siehe Abb. 3). Dieses doch merkliche Absinken der Interaktionsfähigkeiten zum Abschluss der Intensivwoche hängt vermutlich an den langfristig gesehen doch sehr hohen sozialen Anforderungen in einer offenen Gruppensituation. Gleichzeitig steht der vierte Tag ganz im Zeichen der Themen Abschied und Autonomieentwicklung, die gerade bei selektiv mutistischen Kindern offensichtlich wiederum mit Rückzugsverhalten einhergehen.

Abb. 3 Häufigkeit der sozialen Interaktionen im Verlauf der vier Tage

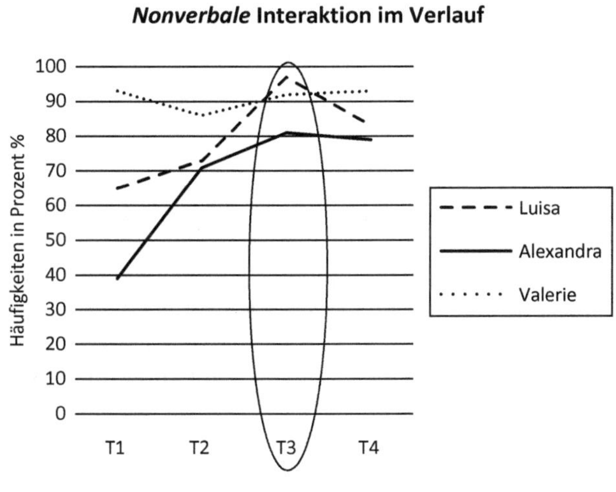

3.3 Einfluss- bzw. Wirkfaktoren

Im Rahmen der interpretativen Analyse der „moments of change" im Video lassen sich nun drei Einfluss- oder Wirkfaktoren innerhalb dieses sehr spezifischen Psychodrama-Settings herausarbeiten, die Erklärungsansätze der positiven Entwicklungen sozialer Interaktionsfähigkeit bereitstellen sollen.

3.3.1 Hilfs-Ich Funktionen

Was interaktionsfördernde Hilfs-Ich Funktionen anbelangt, so sind zunächst kreativitätsfördernde Maßnahmen mit dem Ziel der Erschließung neuer Handlungsmöglichkeiten wie auch der Erweiterung des Rollenrepertoires als für die Intensivwoche wesentlich anzuführen. Des Weiteren bergen adäquate Rückmeldungen des Hilfs-Ichs im Rollenfeedback eine den Handlungsspielraum des Kindes erweiternde Perspektive in sich und nehmen damit auch impulshaften Charakter an.

Als für die doch beträchtlich eingeschränkte Interaktionsfähigkeit des Störungsbildes „Selektiver Mutismus" besonders wesentliche Hilfs-Ich Funktionen lassen sich nunmehr neben einer „Sprachrohrfunktion" (doppelnd nach „innen", übersetzend nach „außen"), also einer Art Zwischenschaltung zur Außenwelt, vor allem immer wiederkehrende Interventionen mit impulshaftem, aufforderndem Charakter anführen. Trotz der Initiierung und Einforderung entsprechender Entwicklungsschritte sind aber auch die teils großen Ängste der Kinder mit zu bedenken, was eine ausreichende Bereitstellung von Schutz und Sicherheit in für die Kinder besonders stressbehafteten Situationen ebenso entsprechend notwendig erscheinen lässt. Um beide Interventionsformen in den therapeutischen Prozess integrieren zu können, hat sich aus den Analysen der Intensivwoche eine gut durchdachte und sensibel auf Spaltungstendenzen reagierende Rollendifferenzierung zwischen Therapeutinnen und Hilfs-Ich als unterstützend erwiesen. Während die Therapeutinnen von „außen" sachlich und klar an das Kind herantreten und entsprechende Entwicklungsschritte ein- bzw. herausfordern können, hat das Hilfs-Ich andererseits die Möglichkeit, sehr unterstützend, schützend und empathisch auf Seiten des mutistischen Kindes zu agieren.

Besonders am vierten Tag zeigt der Rückgang verbaler und nonverbaler Interaktionen möglicherweise auch aufgrund der in der offenen Gruppensituation erhöhten Anforderungen in der Interaktion mit anderen die Wichtigkeit der Unterstützung durch das Hilfs-Ich.

Zu schnelle Interaktionstempi gilt es in eine für die mutistischen Kinder passendere, verlangsamte Form zu transformieren. Außerdem können zu hohe Perfektionsansprüche der Kinder durch einen offenen, sehr transparenten Umgang mit eigenen Schwächen des Hilfs-Ichs ein Stück weit korrigiert werden.

Diese vielfältigen Funktionsmöglichkeiten und die daraus resultierenden interaktionsbezogenen Fortschritte der Kinder sprechen zusammenfassend deutlich für die Effizienz des Einsatzes von entsprechend störungsspezifischen Interventionen des Hilfs-Ichs in der psychodramatischen Gruppentherapie.

3.3.2 Struktur und Elemente der psychodramatischen Bühne

Dem Schutzhaus kommt in der psychodramatischen Gestaltung von Therapiesettings große Bedeutung zu. Neben der Regulation von Spannungszuständen unterstützen selbst konstruierte Bauwerke die Findung und Erweiterung von Rollen wie auch die Kontaktaufnahme zu anderen Kindern bzw. deren Hilfs-Ichs (Wicher 2012, S. 259 f.).

Im Falle mutistischer Kinder konnte im Rahmen der Intensivwoche der besondere Einsatz des Schutzhauses nicht nur als Rückzugsort, sondern auch als eine Art Intermediärobjekt zur Herstellung von Kommunikation und Dialog mit dem eigenen Hilfs-Ich und anderen Kindern in der Gruppe herausgearbeitet werden.

Wie bereits mehrfach erörtert, scheint der dritte Tag der Intensivwoche eine für die Interaktionsfähigkeit besondere Rolle einzunehmen, was durch die sehr hohen Wertausprägungen auf allen Ebenen untermauert wird. In den Analysen hierzu wird deutlich, dass die Hilfs-Ichs an diesem Tag besonders viele Handlungsimpulse setzen, in der Ambivalenz zwischen Forderung von Entwicklungsschritten einerseits, einer entsprechenden Schutzfunktion andererseits aber auch besonders stark hin und her gerissen sind.

Auf struktureller Ebene zeichnet sich der dritte Tag insbesondere durch eine Öffnung des Bühnenraums, der Entwicklung dreier Kleingruppen zu einer Großgruppe aus. Dies geht mit einer deutlichen Zunahme von sprachlichen und handlungsbezogenen Impulsen einher. Spielmöglichkeiten erweitern sich, gleichzeitig wird die exponierte Lage des Vorspielen-Müssens, so wie in den Kleingruppen gehandhabt, zugunsten eines verlängerten Spiels ein Stück weit aufgelöst. Der Gefahr, in der großen Gruppe unterzugehen oder mutismusspezifische Ängste zu verstärken, wird durch die Gruppenleitung und ein unterstützendes Hilfs-Ich entgegengewirkt. Als theoretisches Erklärungsmodell für diese Prozesse lässt sich der von Moreno entwickelte und von Hutter beschriebene „kreative Zirkel" (2000, S. 125) oder auch das „Doppeltheorem der Spontaneität – Kreativität" (a. a. O., S. 125) heranziehen. Die vorangegangenen zwei Tage der Intensivwoche bringen die Kinder mittels Initiierung entsprechender Spontaneitätsprozesse in die sogenannte Stegreiflage. Diese dient als idealer Nährboden für die Anstoßung der kreativen Potentiale des Individuums in der größeren Gruppe, was schließlich zur Entwicklung neuer Spielmöglichkeiten und einer Erweiterung des Rollenrepertoires führt. Dabei kommt es zum schrittweisen

Aufbau neuer Strukturen bzw. Rollenkonserven, die natürlich als besonders hilfreich bei der Veränderung störungsspezifischen Verhaltens erscheinen (a. a. O., S. 126 f).

3.3.3 Störungsspezifische Faktoren – Konkurrenzverhalten

In der Analyse zahlreicher Momente der Veränderung bzw. Verbesserung der Interaktionsfähigkeit fällt der Faktor Vergleich mit anderen mutistischen und nicht mutistischen Kindern auf. Die aus dem Perfektionismus heraus zu begreifende Tendenz, mit anderen zu konkurrieren, wirkt als unterstützender, extrinsischer Motivationsfaktor, was Sprache, aber auch Teilnahme an der Gruppe betrifft. Nachdem Valerie beispielsweise bei der Auswahl und Entgegennahme von Handpuppen für das Spiel von Alexandra beobachtet wird, wählt sich auch diese schließlich ein Intermediärobjekt aus.

4 Resümee und Ausblick

Die psychodramatische Gruppenarbeit geht von der Annahme aus, dass mutistische Kinder durch gezielte Impulse und Hilfestellungen in der psychodramatischen Gruppe zur Teilnahme an sozialen Interaktionen angeregt und gefördert werden können. Diese Erfahrungen sollen das Kind letztlich auch in sozialen Alltagssituationen befähigen, an sozialen Interaktionen teilzunehmen. In der Gruppe wird dies durch das spezifische Setting, den strukturierten Aufbau, eine strukturierende Leitung, die unterstützenden Hilfs-Ichs und vor allem auch mit Hilfe der psychodramatischen Arbeitsformen – wie den Warm-ups, der Arbeit mit den Intermediärobjekten, dem psychodramatischen Spiel in seinen unterschiedlichen Varianten (Stadler und Spörrle 2008), dem Rollenfeedback, Sharing und der nachfolgenden Integration des Erfahrenen – erreicht.

Die Fallanalysen von drei kontrastierend ausgewählten mutistischen Kindern zeigen, dass mit Hilfe der psychodramatischen Arbeit soziale Interaktion von mutistischen Kindern in einer Gruppe gefördert werden kann. Die Kinder lassen sowohl auf verbaler als auch auf nonverbaler Ebene eine Verbesserung hinsichtlich Häufigkeit als auch Differenziertheit der Interaktionen über den Gruppenverlauf erkennen. Allerdings ist dabei zu beachten, dass das Anforderungsniveau für soziale Interaktionen die Fähigkeiten der Kinder zum jeweiligen Zeitpunkt der Gruppenentwicklung nicht überfordern darf, da es sonst wieder zu einem Rückzug kommen kann.

Die Fallbeispiele weisen insgesamt in eine für das Psychodrama erfreuliche Richtung, können aber dennoch nur als explorierende deskriptive Analyse angesehen werden, die einer weiteren Überprüfung bedarf. Forschungsansätze mit einer Pre-Post-Erhebung über den gesamten Zeitraum der therapeutischen Arbeit – also nicht nur über die vier Tage in der Psychodrama Intensivgruppe – könnten in Verbindung mit einer Kontrollgruppe zum Einsatz kommen, um die vorliegenden Ergebnisse breiter abzusichern.

Literatur

Biegler-Vitek, G. (2011a). „*Reden ist Silber, Schweigen ist …* " Schlussfolgerungen für die Psychotherapie selektiv mutistischer Kinder aus der Sicht des Psychodramas. Unveröffentlichte Masterthesis. Donau-Universität Krems.

Biegler-Vitek, G. (2011b). „Wer ist in unserer Gruppe wohl der Stärkste, die Schönste, der Mutigste, ...“ Gruppendynamik und Soziometrie in psychodramatischen Psychotherapiegruppen für Kinder und Jugendliche. *Zeitschrift für Psychodrama und Soziometrie, 10*, 267–276. doi:10.1007/s11620-011-0105-x.

Biegler-Vitek, G., & Wicher, M. (2012). Psychodrama Intensivgruppe mit Kindern. Unveröffentlichtes Skriptum. Wien.

Biegler-Vitek, G., & Wicher, M. (Hrsg.). (2014). *Psychodrama-Psychotherapie mit Kindern und Jugendlichen*. Wien: Facultas.

Bohnsack, R. (2011). *Qualitative Bild- und Videointerpretation* (2. Aufl.). Opladen: Barbara Budrich.

Bohnsack, R., Marotzki, W., & Meuser, M. (2011). Fallrekonstruktion. In R. Bohnsack, W. Marotzki & M. Meuser (Hrsg.), *Hauptbegriffe qualitativer Sozialforschung* (3. Aufl., S. 60–62). Opladen: Barbara Budrich.

Carbone, D., Schmidt, L. A., Cunningham, C., McHolm, A. E., Edison, S., Pierre, J. St., & Boyle, M. H. (2010). Behavioral and socio-emotional functioning in children with selective mutism: A comparison with anxious and typically developing children across multiple informants. *Journal of Abnormal Child Psychology, 38*, 1057–1067. doi:10.1007/s10802-010-9425-y.

Denzin, N. K. (2009a). *The Research Act. A theoretical introduction to sociological methods*. Chicago: Aldine.

Denzin, N. K. (2009b). Reading Film – Filme und Videos als sozialwissenschaftliches Erfahrungsmaterial. In U. Flick, E. von Kardorff & I. Steinke (Hrsg.), *Qualitative Forschung. Ein Handbuch* (7. Aufl., S. 416–428). Reinbeck bei Hamburg: Rowohlt Taschenbuch Verlag.

Dilling, H., Mombour, W., & Schmidt, M. (2008). *Internationale Klassifikation psychischer Störungen. ICD-10 Kapitel V (F). Klinisch-diagnostische Leitlinien* (6. Aufl.). Bern: Hans Huber.

Edison, S. C., Evans, M. A., McHolm, A. E., Cunningham, C. E., Nowakowski, M. E., Boyle, M., & Schmidt, L. A. (2011). An investigation of control among parents of selectively mute, anxious, and non-anxious children. *Journal of Child Psychiatry and Human Development, 42*, 270–290. doi:10.1007/s10578-010-0214-1.

Flick, U. (2011). *Triangulation. Eine Einführung* (3. Aufl.). Wiesbaden: Verlag für Sozialwissenschaften.

Hartmann, B. (2010). Leben mit Mutismus – ein Schicksal? In B. Hartmann (Hrsg.), *Gesichter des Schweigens. Die systemische Mutismus-Therapie/SYMUT als Therapiealternative* (3. Aufl., S. 13–33). Idstein: Schulz-Kirchner.

Hutter, C. (2000). *Psychodrama als experimentelle Theologie. Rekonstruktion der therapeutischen Philosophie Morenos aus praktisch-theologischer Perspektive*. Münster: LIT.

Katz-Bernstein, N. (2011). *Selektiver Mutismus bei Kindern. Erscheinungsbilder, Diagnostik, Therapie* (3. Aufl.). München: Ernst Reinhardt.

Knoblauch, H. (2009). Videography. Focused ethnography and video analysis. In H. Knoblauch, B. Schnettler, J. Raab & H.-G. Soeffner (Hrsg.), *Video analysis: Methodology and methods. Qualitative audiovisual data analysis in sociology* (2. Aufl., S. 69–84). Frankfurt a. M.: Peter Lang.

Knoblauch, H., Schnettler, B., & Raab, J. (2009). Video – Analysis. Methodological aspects of interpretative audiovisual analysis in social research. In H. Knoblauch, B. Schnettler, J. Raab & H.-G. Soeffner (Hrsg.), *Video analysis: Methodology and methods. Qualitative audiovisual data analysis in sociology* (2. Aufl., S. 9–28). Frankfurt a. M.: Peter Lang.

Köfeler, C. (2014). *„Ich kann und ich kann nicht. Ich will und ich will nicht.“* Interaktion und Rollenentwicklung selektiv mutistischer Mädchen im Rahmen eines psychodramatischen Intensivsettings unter besonderer Berücksichtigung der Funktion des Hilfs-Ichs. Unveröffentlichte Diplomarbeit. Universität Klagenfurt.

Mayring, P. (2002). *Einführung in die qualitative Sozialforschung. Eine Anleitung zu qualitativem Denken* (5. Aufl.). Weinheim: Beltz.

Mayring, P. (2008). *Qualitative Inhaltsanalyse. Grundlagen und Techniken* (10. Aufl.). Weinheim: Beltz.

Nowakowski, M. E., Tasker, S. L., Cunningham, C. E., McHolm, A. E., Edison, S., Pierre, J. St., Boyle, M. H., & Schmidt, L. A. (2011). Joint Attention in parent-child dyads involving children with selective mutism: A comparison between anxious and typically developing children. *Journal of Child Psychiatry and Human Development, 42*, 78–92. doi:10.1007/s10578-010-0208-z.

Oerbeck, B., & Kristensen, H. (2008). Attention in selective mutism – An exploratory case-control study. *Journal of Anxiety Disorders, 22*, 548–554. doi:10.1016/j.janxdis.2007.04.008.

Reichertz, J., & Englert, C. J. (2011). *Einführung in die qualitative Videoanalyse. Eine hermeneutisch-wissenssoziologische Fallanalyse*. Wiesbaden: Verlag für Sozialwissenschaften.

Stadler, C., & Spörrle, M. (2008). Das Rollenspiel. Versuch einer Begriffsbestimmung. *Zeitschrift für Psychodrama und Soziometrie, 7*(2), 165–188. doi:10.1007/s11620-008-0018-5.

Steinhausen, H.-C., Wachter, M., Laimböck, K., & Winkler Metzke, C. (2006). A long-term outcome study of selective mutism in childhood. *Journal of Child Psychology and Psychiatry, 47*(7), 751–756. doi:10.1111/j.1469-7610.2005.01560.x.

Tuma, R., Schnettler, B., & Knoblauch, H. (2013). *Videographie. Einführung in die interpretative Videoanalyse sozialer Situationen*. Wiesbaden: Springer VS.

Vecchio, J. L., & Kearney, C. A. (2005). Selective mutism in children: Comparison to youths with and without anxiety disorders. *Journal of Psychopathology and Behavioral Assessment, 27*(1), 31–37. doi:10.1007/s10862-005-3263-1.

Viana, A. G., Beidel, D. C., & Rabian, B. (2009). Selective mutism: A review and integration of the last 15 years. *Clinical Psychology Review, 29*, 57–67. doi:10.1016/j.cpr.2008.09.009.

Wicher, M. (2007). *Erlebnis Gruppe. Psychodramagruppen für traumatisierte Kinder und Jugendliche im stationären Setting - unter besonderer Berücksichtigung von Bühnenaufbau, Nachnähren und Einsatz der Techniken Hilfs-Ich und Intermediär- bzw. Intraintermediärobjekten*. Unveröffentlichte Masterthesis. Donau Universität Krems.

Wicher, M. (2012). „Schutz: kenne ich nicht…“. Die drei-geteilte Bühne bzw. der speziell vorgegebene Bühnenaufbau als Intervention in der Psychodrama-Therapie mit Kindern und Jugendlichen. *Zeitschrift für Psychodrama und Soziometrie, 11*(2), 255–267. doi:10.1007/s11620-012-0149-6.

Wittchen, H.-U., Heinig, I., & Beesdo-Baum, K. (2014). Angststörungen im DSM-5 Ein Überblick über Änderungen in Struktur und Inhalt. *Der Nervenarzt, 85*, 548–552. doi:10.1007/s00115-013-3986-2.

Yeganeh, R., Beidel, D. C., Turner, S. M., Pina, A. A., & Silverman, W. K. (2003). Clinical distinctions between selective mutism and social phobia: An investigation of childhood psychopathology. *Journal of the American Academy of Child and Adolescent Psychiatry, 42*(9), 1069–1075. doi:10.1097/01.CHI.0000070262.24125.23.

Christina Köfeler, Jg. 1987, MMag.[a], Studium der Psychologie mit Schwerpunkt Klinisch-psychologische Interventionen und Psychotherapie sowie der Pädagogik mit Schwerpunkt Sozial- und Integrationspädagogik an der Universität Klagenfurt; dzt. i.A. zur Klinischen- und Gesundheitspsychologin; arbeitet in einer soziotherapeutischen Intensiv-Wohngemeinschaft für ältere Jugendliche mit komplexen Traumafolgestörungen. Forschungs- bzw. Interessenschwerpunkte: Psychodramatherapie mit Kindern und Jugendlichen mit Gewalt- und Traumatisierungserfahrungen, Mutismus, Autismus sowie Wirksamkeitsforschung.

Hannes Krall, 1963, ao. Univ.-Prof. Dr., arbeitet am Institut für Erziehungswissenschaft und Bildungsforschung an der Alpen-Adria-Universität Klagenfurt; Psychologe, Pädagoge, Psychotherapeut (Psychodrama), Supervisor, Lehrbeauftragung für Psychodrama an der Universität Innsbruck. Trainer für Supervision, Coaching und Organisationsberatung im ÖAGG. Vorsitz im FEPTO Research Committee (Federation of European Psychodrama Training Organizations). Mitglied der Society for Psychotherapy Research (SPR). Forschungsarbeiten und Publikationen in den Bereichen Psychodrama und Supervision, Ausbildungs- und Wirkungsforschung, Gewalt und Trauma bei Kindern und Jugendlichen.

Z Psychodrama Soziometr (2016) (Suppl) 15:179–196
DOI 10.1007/s11620-015-0315-8

HAUPTBEITRÄGE

Zeitschrift für Psychodrama und Soziometrie

Evaluation der Psychodramatherapie in einer Einrichtung für traumatisierte Jungen mit sexuell übergriffigem Verhalten

Kristina Scheuffgen[1] · Benjamin Pniewski[1] · Andrej König[1]

Online publiziert: 18. Januar 2016

Zusammenfassung Im Jahr 2010 wurde eine begleitende Behandlungsevaluation durch die Gesellschaft für Therapieevaluation und Qualitätssicherung (TEQS) für die Facheinrichtung Rumpelstilzchen installiert. In 6-monatigen Abständen werden die Jungen für ein Interview von einem TEQS-Mitarbeiter aufgesucht, um die Sicht des Jungen auf den Verlauf seiner Behandlung zu erheben. Parallel beantworten die behandelnden BezugspädagogInnen und BezugstherapeutInnen die gleichen standardisierten Fragen (Fragebogen) und geben ihre Einschätzung zum Verlauf der Behandlung der Jungen an. Das Ausmaß der Passung der Einschätzungen zwischen Klient, TherapeutIn und PädagogIn wird als Indikator für die Erfolgsaussicht der Behandlung gewertet. Bei Diskrepanzen in der Einschätzung wird fachspezifische Supervision angeregt, um ein gemeinsames Fallverständnis zu erlangen. Die ersten Ergebnisse von zwei Messzeitpunkten für die Behandlungsverläufe von 24 Jungen werden in diesem Artikel dargestellt. Zusätzlich hat ein wissenschaftlicher TEQS-Mitarbeiter zehn ehemalige Klienten in einem qualitativen Interview gezielt zu ihren Erfahrungen der Psychodramagruppentherapie befragt. Die Interviews wurden inhaltsanalytisch ausgewertet und werden ebenfalls dargestellt. Die Ergebnisse beider Erhebungen werden diskutiert.

Schlüsselwörter Sexuell übergriffiges Verhalten · Traumatisierung · Psychodramatherapie · Behandlungsevaluation

✉ Dr. Kristina Scheuffgen
Kristina.Scheuffgen@malteser.org

[1] MW Malteser Werke gGmbH, Geschäftssitz, Köln, Deutschland

Evaluation of psychodramatherapy in an institution for traumatised boys with sexually abusive behaviours

Abstract In 2010 a formal external treatment evaluation for the institution Rumpelstilzchen by the institute TEQS was installed. Every 6 months the boys are interviewed by a member of the institute staff and the view of each boy on the course of his treatment is examined in an interview. Parallel to this, the therapists and care staff answer the same questions and give their assessment to the course of each boy's treatment (questionnaire).The degree of the agreement of the assessments between clients, therapists and care staff is viewed as an indicator for the potential success of the treatment. In case of discrepancies between the assessments a process of supervision is recommended in order to gain a joint case understanding. The results of the first two points of measurement in the treatment evaluation for 24 boys are presented in this article. In addition a member of the institute's research staff interviewed 10 ex-clients with regards to their experiences of the psychodrama therapy group specifically (qualitative interview). The results were examined by content analysis and are presented as well. The results are discussed.

Keywords Sexually abusive behaviours · Traumatisation · Psychodrama therapy · Treatment evaluation

1 Sexuell übergriffige Kinder

Versucht man, die wesentlichen Ergebnisse internationaler Studien zusammenzufassen, dann finden sich in der Entwicklungsgeschichte sexuell übergriffiger Kinder verschiedene Faktoren und Auffälligkeiten, die das sexuelle Problemverhalten offensichtlich begünstigen können. Hierunter fallen zum Beispiel eigene sexuelle, körperliche und psychische Missbrauchserfahrungen (z. B. Silovsky und Niec 2002; Friedrich et al. 2003). Oft werden auch problematische Familienverhältnisse berichtet, wie häufig wechselnde Bezugspersonen oder eine Überforderung in der Elternrolle, die nicht selten zu Beeinträchtigungen der Eltern-Kind-Bindung führt (z. B. Pithers et al. 1998). Nach Johnson (1988) leben etwa 60 % der sexuell übergriffigen Kinder bei ihrer alleinerziehenden Mutter und nur etwa 15 % mit ihren biologischen Eltern in einem Haushalt. Viele der Kinder sind beispielsweise in Heimeinrichtungen oder Pflegefamilien untergebracht. Auch in einer aktuellen Studie (König et al. 2014) wurden sexuelle Übergriffe durch Minderjährige innerhalb von Einrichtungen der Kinder- und Jugendhilfe weitaus häufiger berichtet als beispielsweise sexuelle Gewalt durch pädagogische MitarbeiterInnen. Fortbildungskräfte aus spezialisierten Fachberatungsstellen gegen sexualisierte Gewalt beschrieben den Umgang mit einvernehmlicher Sexualität wie auch sexuellen Grenzverletzungen als die „brennenden Themen" pädagogischer Fachkräfte in Einrichtungen der Kinder- und Jugendhilfe.

Persönlichkeitsfehlentwicklungen zeigen sich bei sexuell übergriffigen Jungen vor allem in einer ängstlich-depressiven Symptomatik, in Minderwertigkeits- und Schuldgefühlen sowie in Gefühlen von Einsamkeit und sozialer Ablehnung. Aus dieser Problemkonstellation resultieren häufig soziale Probleme und sozialer Rückzug.

Auch die sozialen Kompetenzen der sexuell übergriffigen Jungen sind dadurch meist beeinträchtigt. Daneben zeigen sich aber auch aggressive und dissoziale Verhaltensweisen, die dann im sozialen Umfeld ausagiert werden (Elsner 2011).

2 Behandlungsevaluation

Ziel der vorliegenden Untersuchung ist es zum einen, Wirkmechanismen möglicher Veränderungen zu erfassen. Zum anderen sollen Sichtweisen auf Veränderungen aus der Perspektive der Bewohner sowie der pädagogischen und psychologischen Fachkräfte der spezifischen Facheinrichtung Rumpelstilzchen der Malteser Werke Köln abgebildet werden. Dabei stehen folgende zentrale Fragestellungen im Mittelpunkt: In welchen wichtigen Lebensbereichen (z. B. Ressourcen, aktuelle Belastungen, internalisierendes versus externalisierendes Problemverhalten) sehen Bewohner im Laufe der Hilfemaßnahme Veränderungen? Wie schätzen pädagogische und psychologische Fachkräfte die Veränderungen ihrer Bewohner ein? Stimmen die Sichtweisen der Bewohner mit den Sichtweisen der pädagogischen und psychologischen Fachkräfte überein? Haben pädagogische und psychologische Fachkräfte eine gemeinsame Sichtweise auf ihre Klientel?

In der Kinder- und Jugendhilfe erleben meist viele Institutionen und Personen (z. B. Jugendamt, Schule, Eltern, Fachkräfte in der Einrichtung etc.) Kinder in unterschiedlichen Kontexten und verfolgen häufig auch verschiedene kurz- und langfristige Ziele (z. B. Schutz vor Vernachlässigung, schulischer Erfolg, Rückkehr in die Herkunftsfamilie etc.). Eine gemeinsame Sichtweise i.S. einer guten therapeutischen Passung auf die aktuelle Lebens- und Problemlage von Klienten wird im Rahmen von Hilfemaßnahmen daher als wesentlicher positiver Wirkfaktor angesehen. Es ist anzunehmen, dass gemeinsame Ziele desto eher verfolgt und erreicht werden, je höher die Übereinstimmung (Passung) der einzelnen Sichtweisen zwischen Bewohnern, pädagogischen und psychologischen Fachkräften vorhanden ist. Voraussetzung hierfür ist die Transparenz unterschiedlicher bzw. gemeinsamer Sichtweisen aller beteiligten Personen, wozu gerade auch die Sichtweise der Kinder selber zählt.

Sowohl die mit den Malteser Werken Köln seit 2010 entwickelten Erhebungsinstrumente als auch die standardisierten Testverfahren (s. Methoden) dienen dazu, in der Facheinrichtung Rumpelstilzchen divergierende und gemeinsame Sichtweisen auf einzelne Klienten im Team transparent zu machen, und somit einen wichtigen Beitrag zur individuellen Prozessevaluation und Qualitätssicherung der spezifischen Hilfemaßnahme zu leisten. Bei der hier dargestellten Untersuchung handelt es sich also nicht um Ergebnisse aus einem kontrollierten empirischen Studiendesign (i. S. einer randomisierten Kohortenstudie), sondern um Behandlungsforschung, die aus der Praxis und für die Praxis entstanden ist.

3 Behandlungskonzept

In der Facheinrichtung Rumpelstilzchen werden Jungen aufgenommen, die nach ihrem 8. und vor der Vollendung ihres 14. Lebensjahres durch sexuell übergriffiges

Verhalten aufgefallen sind. Grundlage ist hier beobachtbares sexuell übergriffiges Verhalten, welches in seiner Ausprägung in der bisherigen Lebenssituation des Jungen nicht mehr tragbar und nicht mehr sicher begrenzbar ist. Die Behandlungsdauer variiert je nach Ausprägung der Symptomatik zwischen etwa einem, bis zu drei Jahren. Das Ziel ist es, die Jungen so früh wie möglich in ein weniger restriktives Setting zu verlegen. Dazu wurden bereits einige träger-interne Perspektiven entwickelt wie die Unterbringung in gemischtgeschlechtlichen Intensivgruppen oder in einer Kleinsteinrichtung mit Fortführung der störungsspezifischen Therapie durch die TherapeutInnen von Rumpelstilzchen.

Es leben insgesamt zehn Jungen in zwei Wohngruppen. Jede Wohngruppe wird von einem pädagogischen Team im Alltag betreut. Ein therapeutisches Team ist verantwortlich für die Gesamtbehandlung aller Jungen. Die therapeutisch-pädagogisch integrierte Behandlung bei Rumpelstilzchen basiert auf den aktuellen und internationalen Standards der stationären Jugendhilfe für Kinder mit sexuell übergriffigem Verhalten (Milner et al. 2006). Verzahnt sind hier die pädagogische Gestaltung des Lebens der Jungen in der Gruppe mit den in den formalen Behandlungsplänen und Therapiesitzungen festgelegten Interventionen und Zielen. In regelmäßigen Teamsitzungen mit den pädagogischen MitarbeiterInnen gilt es, eine hohe Transparenz des therapeutischen Prozesses zu erzielen, so dass das Gesamtteam die Dynamik von sexueller Übergriffigkeit und Traumatisierung, welche sich auch in Form von spezifischen Übertragungen und Gegenübertragungen zeigt für den pädagogischen Alltag reflektieren kann.

Das Team nimmt kontinuierliche Einschätzungen von Risikofaktoren, Risikosituationen, Traumatisierungen und Ressourcen zur Veränderung der bestehenden Problematiken vor und übersetzt diese Einschätzung in einen individualisiert festgelegten Erprobungsrahmen hinsichtlich Ausgang und sozialer Kontaktgestaltung. Dieser Rahmen definiert Grenzen im gemeinsamen Leben in der Gruppe und in der Gesellschaft. Das Behandlungsziel ist die langfristige Integration der Jungen in ein reguläres Umfeld bei einem möglichst geringen Gefährdungspotential für erneute sexuelle Übergriffe.

Das Besondere des therapeutischen Behandlungskonzepts liegt in der schwerpunktmäßigen Anwendung psychodramatischer Methoden. Jungen mit sexuell übergriffigem Verhalten sind in der Regel beziehungstraumatisiert und haben aufgrund dessen weitreichende Defizite in der Entwicklung ihrer Mentalisierungsfähigkeiten. Krüger (2015, S. 71) definiert die Psychodramatherapie als mentalisations-basierte Therapiemethode und schreibt: „Psychodrama hingegen ist inneres Mentalisieren und psychische Selbstorganisation durch äußeres Spielen auf der Zimmerbühne oder Tischbühne" (Krüger 2015, S. 20). Das Ziel der mentalisations-basierten Psychodramatherapie ist, „dass der Patient im psychodramatischen Spiel das Konflikthafte in seinen inneren Beziehungsbildern auflöst und in diesen inneren Bildern ein angemessenes Gleichgewicht zwischen Aktualisierung seines Selbst und Anpassung entwickelt" (Krüger 2014, Vortrag in Edenkoben, Moreno Institut). Dies gilt nach unserem Verständnis auch für Kinder.

Wöchentlich findet für jede der beiden pädagogischen Wohngruppen eine Psychodrama-Gruppentherapie statt. In der Wohngruppe der Jüngeren ist diese Gruppe überwiegend spieltherapeutisch gestaltet (Kinderpsychodramatisch) und dauert in etwa

60 min. Das heißt, dass die TherapeutInnen auf der Handlungsebene im spontanen Spiel aus ihren gewählten Rollen heraus notwenige Interventionen setzen (z. B. begrenzend, Halt gebend, versorgend, emotional korrigierend, etc., siehe hierzu Scheuffgen 2012).

In der Gruppe der älteren Jungen wird unter anderem auch mit dem protagonistInnenzentrierten Psychodrama (siehe hierzu Ameln et al. 2004; Bender und Stadler 2012) gearbeitet. Die Dauer dieser Psychodramagruppen beträgt mindestens 90 min. Dabei liegt ein besonderes Augenmerk auf dem Entwicklungsniveau der Jungen. Insbesondere in der Verwendung von Rollenspielern (Hilfs-Ichs) übernehmen in erster Linie die Therapeutinnen und Pädagoginnen die in einem ProtagonistInnenspiel zu besetzenden Rollen. Dies ist besonders wichtig, wenn missbräuchliche Dynamiken vorliegen. Zudem ist bei der Anwendung von ProtagonistInnenspielen in dieser Altersgruppe Gewicht zu legen auf die bei Kindern und Jugendlichen stärker ausgeprägten Selbstheilungskräfte in der symbolischen Bewältigung. Das heißt zum Beispiel, dass eine Verarbeitung von traumatischen Erlebnissen mit Hilfe von Fantasie und Imagination stattfinden kann und als wirksam erachtet wird.

Zusätzlich zu den psychodramatisch orientierten Gruppentherapien wird fall- und störungsspezifisch psychodramatisch im therapeutischen Tandem mit den Jungen einzeln gearbeitet; mit den jüngsten im monodramatischen Spiel, mit den Älteren zum Beispiel mit der psychodramatischen Stühlearbeit zu Selbstanteilen.

Neben dieser spezifischen psychodramatischen Arbeit wenden wir sowohl klassisch traumatherapeutische Interventionen an (z. B. Stabilisierungstechniken) als auch kognitiv-verhaltenstherapeutisch ausgelegte Programme zur Bearbeitung von Deliktszenarien, Verantwortungsübernahme und Entwicklung der Opferempathie. So findet die Deliktbearbeitung im engeren Sinne im Rahmen einer Präventionsgruppe statt, die sich an dem von Mielke (2009) entwickelten Programm orientiert, welches wir jeweils für unsere Altersgruppe und den Entwicklungsstand der Jungen adaptieren.

Zu Beginn der Behandlung stehen die Traumatisierungen der Jungen stärker im Vordergrund. Das Erreichen der innerpsychischen Stabilisierung, die Entwicklung der Differenzierung von Selbst- und Fremdwahrnehmung und eine gewisse Ich-Stärke wird als notwendige therapeutische und entwicklungsbedingte Voraussetzung für die Teilnahme an der stärker deliktbezogenen kognitiv-verhaltenstherapeutischen Arbeit in unserer Präventionsgruppe angesehen. Eine Risikoverminderung für erneute sexuelle Übergriffe ergibt sich aus der Kombination beider Ansätze.

Ein weiterer zentraler Bestandteil des Behandlungskonzepts ist die therapeutische Arbeit mit dem Bezugssystem des Jungen. Dabei ist es wichtig, die vorhandenen Bindungen, die diagnostisch als Ressourcen eingeschätzt werden, zu festigen und zu entwickeln, als auch bei früheren Beziehungsbelastungen diese mit den Bezugspersonen zunächst auf der Erwachsenenebene zu besprechen mit dem Ziel einer gemeinsamen Aufarbeitung mit dem Jungen. Gleichzeitig behalten wir immer den Blick auf potentiell missbräuchliche Bindungen, und veranlassen gegebenenfalls in Zusammenarbeit mit den Jugendämtern und Vormündern auch Kontaktsperren zu schädigenden Bezugspersonen.

4 Methodisches Vorgehen für die Behandlungsevaluation

4.1 Erhebungsinstrumente: TEQS Skalen und Psychometrische Tests

Zur Erfassung der drei Perspektiven (Selbsteinschätzung der Jungen vs. Fremdeinschätzung der BezugsbetreuerIn und der BezugstherapeutIn) wurde in Abstimmung mit dem Gesamtteam der Facheinrichtung Rumpelstilzchen ein auf die Klientel zugeschnittenes Evaluationsinstrument (TEQS-Skalen) entwickelt. Die Items der drei TEQS-Skalen (s. Tab. 1) beinhalten verschiedene Aspekte, die im Rahmen der spezifischen Hilfemaßnahme adressiert werden sollen (s. Behandlungskonzept). Jedes Item wird durch den Jungen, die BezugsbetreuerIn und die BezugstherapeutIn unabhängig voneinander auf einer Skala von 0 (= „trifft gar nicht zu“) bis 100 (= „trifft voll zu“) bewertet. Die Perspektive der Jungen wurde durch MitarbeiterInnen der TEQS im Rahmen eines halbjährlich durchgeführten strukturierten Interviews (Dauer ca. 15 bis 20 min pro Kind) erhoben, um weitgehend unabhängige Selbsteinschätzungen der Jungen zu erhalten. Für die folgenden statistischen Auswertungen (s. Ergebnisse) wurde für alle Jungen ($N=24$) der Mittelwert für jede der drei TEQS-Skalen bestimmt (Summenscore der Items/Anzahl der Items).

Neben den TEQS-Skalen wurden ebenfalls halbjährlich bei einigen Bewohnern ($n=14$) der Youth Self-Report (YSR 11–18; Selbsteinschätzung) und die Child Behavior Checklist (CBCL 4–18; Fremdeinschätzung) eingesetzt. Der YSR 11–18 konnte nicht bei allen Jungen durchgeführt werden, da Altersnormen erst ab dem 11. Lebensjahr vorliegen. Die CBCL 4–18 wurde durch die jeweiligen BezugsbetreuerInnen bearbeitet. Bei beiden Verfahren handelt es sich um normierte psychometrische Testverfahren zur Einschätzung der Symptombelastung in den letzten 6 Monaten. Der YSR 11–18 wurde von den Jungen selber ausgefüllt, wobei einige jüngere Bewohner Unterstützung bei Verständnisfragen durch die MitarbeiterInnen von Rumpelstilzchen erhielten. Die Subskalen „Sozialer Rückzug“, „Körperliche Beschwerden“, „Ängstlich/Depressiv“ werden zu der übergeordneten Skala „Internalisierende Probleme“ zusammengefasst. Die Subskalen „Dissoziales Verhalten“ und „Aggressives Verhalten“ bilden die übergeordnete Skala „Externalisierende Probleme“. Die Skala „Gesamtwert“ bildet die globale Symptombelastung auf der Grundlage aller 118 Items ab. Für die weiteren statistischen Analysen werden die T-Werte des YSR 11–18 sowie der CBCL 4–18 für die Skalen „Internalisierende Probleme“, „Externalisierende Probleme“ und „Gesamtwert“ genutzt.

Für insgesamt 24 Bewohner liegen die Daten der TEQS Skalen für zwei Messzeitpunkte vor, die Veränderungen in der Selbst- und Fremdwahrnehmung von behandlungsrelevanten Aspekten für die ersten ≈ 12 Monate der Hilfemaßnahme (s. Stichprobenbeschreibung) abbilden und deren Ergebnisse im folgenden Abschnitt dargestellt werden.

4.2 Qualitative Behandlungsevaluation der Psychodrama Gruppentherapie

Zur Evaluation der Psychodrama Gruppentherapie wurden insgesamt zehn ehemalige Bewohner aufgesucht und im Rahmen eines teilstandardisierten Leitfadeninterviews befragt. Alle ehemaligen Klienten, deren Anschriften ausfindig gemacht werden

Tab. 1 TEQS-Skalen und Items

Skalen	Items
Aktuelle Belastung durch negative Lebensereignisse (11 Items)	Wechsel von wichtigen Bezugspersonen
	Verlust wichtiger Bezugspersonen
	Psychische Erkrankung wichtiger Bezugspersonen
	Alkohol-/Drogenproblematik wichtiger Bezugspersonen
	Schwere körperliche Erkrankung wichtiger Bezugspersonen
	Wohnortwechsel
	Vorherige Unterbringung(en) in stationären Einrichtungen
	Erfahrung psychischer Gewalt
	Körperliche Misshandlungen
	Sexuelle Missbrauchserfahrungen
	Mobbing durch Gleichaltrige
Problematisches Verhalten während der Hilfemaßnahme (14 Items)	Körperlich gewalttätiges Verhalten gegen Andere
	Verbal aggressives Verhalten
	Sexuell übergriffiges Verhalten
	Sozialer Rückzug
	Selbstverletzendes Verhalten
	Regelwidriger Alkoholkonsum
	Regelwidriger Drogenkonsum
	Regelwidrige Entweichung aus der Einrichtung
	Schul-/Arbeitsverweigerung
	Widersetzen gegen Regeln der Einrichtung
	Diebstahl-/Betrugshandlungen
	Zerstören von Gegenständen
	Anstiften Anderer zu dissozialem Verhalten
	Mangelndes Gefühl für Nähe und Distanz in Beziehungen
Stärken und Ressourcen (13 Items)	Selbstständigkeit/Unabhängigkeit
	Positive Freizeitaktivitäten
	Tragfähige eigene Außenkontakte/Beziehungen
	Soziale Kompetenzen und Kommunikationsfähigkeit
	Selbstsicherheit und positives Selbstkonzept
	Gute Bewältigungsstrategien in schwierigen Situationen
	Anpassungsfähigkeit in Gruppen
	Gute Leistungsbereitschaft in Schule oder Arbeit
	Angemessenes Durchsetzen eigener Bedürfnisse und Ziele
	Realistische Einschätzung eigener Stärken und Schwächen
	Akzeptanz bestehender psychischer Probleme
	Verantwortungsvoller Umgang mit Geld
	Angemessene Körperhygiene

konnten, wurden kontaktiert. Die Teilnahme ergab sich aus der Einwilligung der ehemaligen Bewohner und ihrer Sorgeberechtigten, und der Möglichkeit eines Treffens. Zu Beginn der Psychodrama-Therapie waren die Bewohner (N = 10) im Mittel 10,9 (SD = 1,5; Alterspanne 8 bis 13 J.) Jahre alt. Bei der Durchführung der Interviews waren die ehemaligen Bewohner der Einrichtung Rumpelstilzchen im Mittel 14,5 (SD = 1,9; Altersspanne 10 bis 17 J.). Sechs der Bewohner befanden sich zum Zeitpunkt der Interviews in stationären Einrichtungen der Kinder- und Jugendhilfe, einer lebte in einer Pflegefamilie, und drei lebten wieder bei ihrer Herkunftsfamilie. Alle

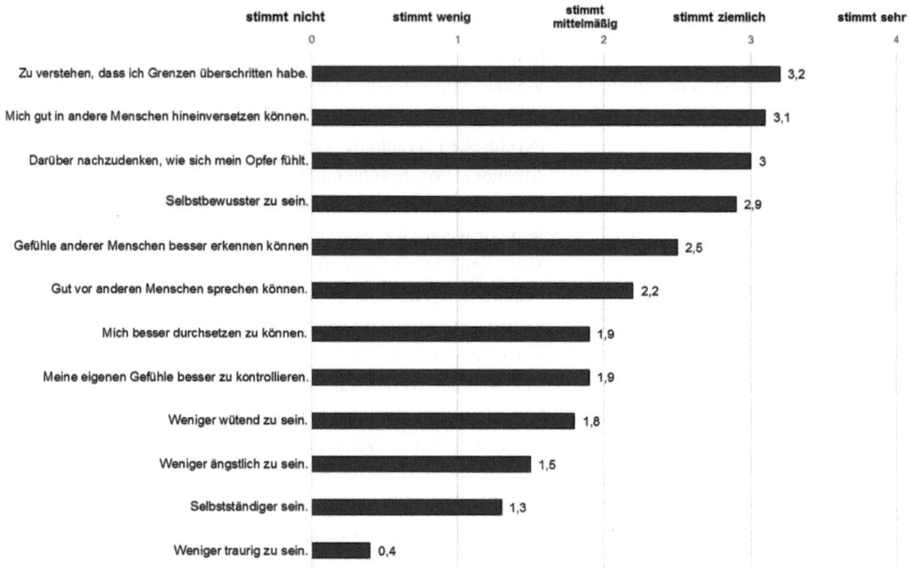

Abb. 1 Mittlere Zustimmung der Gruppenteilnehmer (*N*=10) zu Lernerfahrungen, die im Zusammenhang mit der Psychodramatherapie stehen

Interviews fanden im aktuellen Lebensumfeld der ehemaligen Bewohner statt und dauerten pro Jugendlichen etwa 20 min. Um sozial erwünschte Antworten zu minimieren wurden alle Interviews durch einen externen Interviewer, der nicht in den therapeutischen Prozess involviert war, geführt und aufgezeichnet. Die Interviews orientierten sich an folgenden fünf Leitfragen:

- Was hast du in der Psychodrama-Therapie erlebt?
- Wobei hat die Psychodrama-Therapie dir geholfen?
- Was hat dir an der Psychodrama-Therapie am besten gefallen?
- Was hat dir nicht gut an der Psychodrama-Therapie gefallen?
- Würdest du gerne noch mal diese Art von Gruppentherapie machen?

Abschließend füllten die Befragten noch einen standardisierten Fragebogen zu spezifischen Behandlungszielen der Psychodrama-Therapie aus (s. Abb. 1). Der Fragebogen wurde am Ende der Interviews bearbeitet, um während der Interviews möglichst freie Antworten der Jugendlichen zu erhalten. Die Auswertung des qualitativen Interviewmaterials erfolgte nach einem deduktiven inhaltsanalytischen Vorgehen (Mayring 2010).

5 Ergebnisse

5.1 Ergebnisse der Erhebungsinstrumente

In den folgenden Abschnitten sollen zunächst die Veränderungen auf den TEQS-Skalen (s. Tab. 1) für die beiden Messzeitpunkte der Hilfemaßnahme dargestellt werden.

Tab. 2 Unterschiede zwischen Selbst- und Fremdeinschätzungen

TEQS-Skalen	1. Messzeitpunkt *M (SE)*	2. Messzeitpunkt *M (SE)*	Signifikanz[a]	Effektstärke[b] ES_r
Bewohner				
Aktuelle Belastung durch negative Lebensereignisse	26,5 (3,7)	13,7 (2,7)	t(22)=2,662; $p<0,05$	0,49
Problematisches Verhalten während der Hilfemaßnahme	17,8 (2,3)	17,7 (2,8)	t(22)=0,023; $p=0,98$	-
Stärken und Ressourcen	63,3 (3,6)	66,8 (4,1)	t(22)=0,885; $p=0,39$	-
Pädagogische/r BezugsbetreuerIn				
Aktuelle Belastung durch negative Lebensereignisse	39,7 (4,1)	39,1 (3,1)	t(21)=0,133; $p=0,90$	-
Problematisches Verhalten während der Hilfemaßnahme	26,5 (2,0)	27,8 (2,8)	t(20)=−0,423; $p=0,68$	-
Stärken und Ressourcen	34,5 (3,3)	39,2 (3,5)	t(20)=−1,386; $p=0,18$	-
Psychologische/r BezugstherapeutIn				
Aktuelle Belastung durch negative Lebensereignisse	33,8 (3,2)	36,6 (3,7)	t(21)=−0,775; $p=0,45$	-
Problematisches Verhalten während der Hilfemaßnahme	22,9 (2,7)	26,1 (3,0)	t(18)=−1,426; $p=0,17$	-
Stärken und Ressourcen	38,1 (4,1)	43,5 (3,0)	t(17)=−1,304; $p=0,21$	-

N=24, *M* Mittelwert, *SE* Standardfehler

[a]zweiseitige Signifikanz

[b]$ES_r=0,10$ „geringer Effekt“, $ES_r=0,30$ „moderater Effekt“, $ES_r\geq0,50$ „deutlicher Effekt“ (Cohen 1992)

In Tab. 2 sind die Mittelwerte für die TEQS-Skalen „Aktuelle Belastung durch negative Lebensereignisse“, „Problematisches Verhalten während der Hilfemaßnahme“ sowie „Stärken und Ressourcen“ für beide Messzeitpunkte dargestellt. Der Wertebereich der drei Skalen reicht von 0 bis 100 und bildet das Ausmaß der Zustimmung ab. Der Wert 100 wäre für die TEQS-Skala „Stärken und Ressourcen“ maximal positiv, da viele Ressourcen bzw. Stärken bei dem Bewohner gesehen werden. Für die beiden anderen TEQS-Skalen entspricht der Wert 100 einer aktuellen maximalen Belastung durch negative Lebensereignisse bzw. einem maximalen Ausmaß an problematischen Verhaltensweisen des Bewohners. Betrachtet man die Veränderungen zwischen den beiden Messzeitpunkten aus den drei Perspektiven (Selbsteinschätzung der Jungen, Fremdeinschätzung durch die/den pädagogische/n BezugsbetreuerIn und die/den psychologische/n BezugstherapeutIn), so zeigt sich lediglich in der Selbsteinschätzung eine moderate bis deutliche Abnahme der aktuellen Belastung durch negative Lebensereignisse ($ES_r=0,49$). Dieser Befund korrespondiert mit den Ergebnissen der psychometrischen Testverfahren (vgl. Tab. 3). Hier zeigen sich ebenso eine deutliche Reduktion internalisierender Probleme aus Sicht der Bewohner sowie BezugsbetreuerInnen und keine Unterschiede im externalisierenden Problemverhalten.

In Tab. 3 werden die Ergebnisse der psychometrischen Verfahren Youth Self-Report (YSR 11–18; Selbsteinschätzung) und Child Behavior Checklist (CBCL 4–18; Fremdeinschätzung) dargestellt. T-Werte <60 entsprechen dem Normbereich, T-Werte ab 60 bis einschließlich 63 liegen im Grenzbereich und T-Werte >63 sind als

Tab. 3 Selbst- versus Fremdeinschätzung mit dem YSR und der CBCL (T-Werte)

Testskalen	1. Messzeitpunkt *M* (*SE*)	2. Messzeitpunkt *M* (*SE*)	Signifikanz[a]	Effektstärke[b] ES_r
YSR-Internalisierende Skalen	62,6 (2,9)	55,3 (2,8)	$t(13)=3{,}476$, $p<0{,}01$	0,69
YSR-Externalisierende Skalen	62,0 (2,3)	58,9 (2,3)	$t(13)=1{,}460$, $p=0{,}17$	–
YSR-Gesamtwert	70,5 (3,3)	63,6 (3,2)	$t(13)=2{,}874$, $p<0{,}05$	0,62
CBCL-Internalisierende Skalen	66,4 (1,5)	61,9 (1,3)	$t(13)=2{,}883$, $p<0{,}05$	0,62
CBCL-Externalisierende Skalen	68,0 (2,2)	69,7 (2,3)	$t(13)=-0{,}947$, $p=0{,}36$	–
CBCL-Gesamtwert	71,0 (1,6)	68,7 (1,8)	$t(13)=1{,}462$. $p=0{,}17$	–

Eine deutliche Reduktion zeigt sich in der Selbsteinschätzung der Jungen für die YSR-Internalisierende Skalen und den YSR-Gesamtwert. Aus Sicht der BezugbetreuerInnen ergibt sich ebenfalls eine signifikante deutliche Reduktion auf den CBCL-Internalisierenden Skalen, jedoch nicht im CBCL-Gesamtwert

$n=14$, *M* Mittelwert, *SE* Standardfehler

[a]zweiseitige Signifikanz

[b]$ES_r=0{,}10$ „geringer Effekt", $ES_r=0{,}30$ „moderater Effekt", $ES_r\geq 0{,}50$ „deutlicher Effekt" (Cohen 1992)

auffällig zu interpretieren. Es liegen lediglich für 14 Jungen Daten zu beiden Messzeitpunkten vor, da die psychometrische Testdiagnostik nicht obligatorisch war, und einige Jungen hinsichtlich ihres Alters nicht der Normierungsstichprobe entsprachen.

5.2 Ergebnisse der qualitativen Erhebung der Psychodramagruppentherapie

Die Auswertung des qualitativen Interviewmaterials erfolgte nach einem deduktiven inhaltsanalytischen Vorgehen (Mayring 2010). Entsprechende Ankerbeispiele für die einzelnen Kategorien finden sich in Tab. 4.

Im Rahmen der qualitativen Interviews wurde deutlich, dass die Kinder und Jugendlichen in ihrem retrospektiven Erleben der Psychodrama-Therapie sowohl positive als auch negative Aspekte benannt haben (s. Tab. 4). Insbesondere den kritischen Rückmeldungen soll nachgegangen werden, wobei bedacht werden muss, dass subjektiv negatives Erleben auch mit zum therapeutischen Prozess gehören kann, und gerade dann auch therapeutische Wirksamkeit vorliegen kann. Auf der Ebene der „Therapieinhalte und des therapeutischen Settings" wurden als zentrale positive Aspekte die Möglichkeit des „Vertrauensaufbaus zu Gruppenmitgliedern" und die „freie Themenwahl im Rollenspiel" benannt. Eben diese Aspekte bereiteten einigen Befragten hingegen auch Probleme. Ihnen fiel es schwer, sich in einem Gruppensetting zu schambesetzten Themen, wie den eigenen sexuellen Übergriffen oder eigenen Missbrauchserfahrungen zu öffnen. Auch das hohe Ausmaß an Freiheitsgraden bei der Themenfindung wurde teilweise als „chaotisch" und zu wenig zielorientiert wahrgenommen. Einer der Befragten wies darauf hin, dass eine altershomogenere Gruppenzusammensetzung, also eine Trennung von jüngeren (<12 J.) und älteren Kindern (>12 J.) für den Therapieprozess womöglich günstiger gewesen wäre.

Auch hinsichtlich der therapeutischen Lernerfahrungen zeigte sich zum Teil ein widersprüchliches Bild. So wurden als zentrale positive Aspekte die „Steigerung des eigenen Selbstwertgefühls", ein tieferes „Verständnis für die eigene Biografie und sexuelle Übergriffe" sowie der „Aufbau von Opferempathie" benannt. Gleichzeitig

Tab. 4 Erleben der Psychodrama-Therapie aus Sicht der Gruppenteilnehmer

Psychodrama-Therapie	Positive Aspekte	Negative Aspekte
Therapieinhalte u. Setting	**Vertrauensaufbau zu Gruppenmitgliedern** *„Das hilft einem wieder zurückzuschauen und Mut zu machen, dass man denkt: ok es ist passiert, ich kann darüber sprechen und mich lachen andere nicht aus." (A)* *„Ja dass offen über die Taten gesprochen wird, ja weil dann können auch die anderen Jugendlichen voneinander lernen."* (B) *„Deswegen ist das Spielen dann manchmal auch ein bisschen leichter* [als Reden]. *Damit alle mitspielen und alle auch einen guten Einblick davon habe, was passiert ist. Eigentlich wollte ich nie, dass andere Leute wissen was mir früher passiert ist, aber das war halt der Sinn so der Therapie."* (C) **Freie Wahl der Therapieinhalte** *„Das Gute war, dass du eigentlich machen konntest was du willst. Die Situation wurde nicht vorgegeben."* (D)	**Mangelndes Vertrauen im Gruppensetting** *„Es war schwierig vor vielen zu reden, weil weiß ich nicht, ich hatte einfach nicht so das Vertrauen in den anderen. Ich würde am Anfang nicht direkt so halt auf die Taten gehen, was passiert ist so. Dass man halt sich erstmal in den Gruppentherapien besser kennenlernt und so."* (F) *„Geholfen richtig hat's mir nicht. Das war für mich eher schlimmer, dass die anderen halt wussten jetzt so was da jetzt so los war und das mochte ich nicht."* (D) **Fehlende Struktur der Therapieinhalte** *„In der Gruppentherapie haben wir nie fast gearbeitet so richtig, über Sachen, sondern haben fast immer so gespielt." (G)* *„Ja sehr viel Streit auch und halt dieses Chaotische und dass es manchmal langweilig wurde." (A)*
Lernerfahrung	**Steigerung des Selbstwertgefühls** *„Was ich gelernt habe […] also erstmal einverstanden sein mit mir selber. Ich hab mich damals nicht so, ich war mit mir selber nicht zufrieden. Das ist jetzt komplett weg."* (E) *„Ich habe mich früher selber dafür gehasst, was ich getan habe und die haben mir hier beigebracht, dass also, dass ich dadurch halt kein schlechter Mensch bin und ich hab dann halt gelernt mit der Sache umzugehen und mich sozusagen nicht selber fertig zu machen."* (D) **Verständnis für die eigene Biografie und sexuelle Übergriffe** *„Um zu verstehen, was mir passiert ist. Wie gesagt, zum Beispiel mit den Eltern oder so, dass da was passiert ist, dass man das verstehen kann, weil manche Sachen versteht man einfach als kleines Kind einfach nicht. […] und guckt was war falsch, was könntest du besser machen oder was können deine Eltern besser machen."* (A) *„Ich war ja früher noch jünger und dann erst im Laufe der Zeit habe ich verstanden, was ich da wirklich gemacht habe. […] Dass es auch falsch war von mir, hab ich eingesehen."* (E) **Aufbau von Opferempathie** *„Wir haben im Rahmen der Therapie unsere Taten in Rollenspielen aufgearbeitet. Vielleicht ist es ja auch gerade deshalb gut, weil dann die Jugendlichen nochmal besser damit umgehen können, dass sie auch Opferanteile und Täteranteile haben. Einfach uns in die Opfer reinzuversetzen empathisch nennt man das ja, also einfühlsam. Vielleicht bestärkt das diese Empathie nochmal."* (B)	**Gedanken an eigene Opfererfahrungen** *„Ich bin froh, dass ich das komplett hier abgeschlossen habe. Weil dann einfach wieder die Angst ist, dass meine Gedanken halt wieder hoch kommen und die Erinnerung alle. Das ist so was mich halt ziemlich dann kränkt."* (F) *„Da es auch Jugendliche dort gab, die selber auch Opferanteile haben und wenn die dann halt als Opfer ausgewählt werden in diesem Spiel, glaube ich kann das auch schwierig sein und auch wieder schlechte Erfahrungen auslösen oder Gedanken auslösen."* (B) **Bagatellisierung von eigenen sexuellen Übergriffen** *„Der Missbrauch wurde nachgespielt und ich finde der Rahmen, das Nachspielen, das passt irgendwie finde ich nicht. Für mich war das dann nicht ernst. Ich habe das dann mit Spaß verbunden das aufzuarbeiten und ich finde das ist einfach kein Spaß, was wir gemacht haben."* (B)

wurden auch negative Gedanken und Ängste hinsichtlich eigener Opfererfahrungen, die durch Rollenspiele ausgelöst werden können, angeführt. Da es sich um Klienten handelt, die von missbräuchlichen und gewaltvollen Vorerfahrungen belastet sind, besteht die Gefahr, dass die Gruppe eine Retraumatisierung durch das Erleben eines Protagonistenspiels erfährt, auch wenn der Protagonist selbst in der Bearbeitung seines Themas geschützt wurde. Auf der anderen Seite, wurden Inszenierungen von Situationen, die im Zusammenhang mit übergriffigen Verhalten stehen oder das Benennen der übergriffigen Handlungen beinhalten zum Teil nicht ernst genommen, abgewehrt und bagatellisiert. Eine derartige Abwehr oder Abspaltung kann auch als Schutz vor Re-Traumatisierung verstanden werden.

Auf die Frage, ob sie sich vorstellen könnten nochmals an einer Psychodrama-Gruppe teilzunehmen, antwortete die Hälfte der Befragten mit „ja" und die andere Hälfte konnte sich eine erneute Teilnahme nicht vorstellen.

Die in Tab. 4 dargestellten qualitativen Befunde lassen sich durch die quantitativen Ergebnisse des Fragebogens bestätigen. In Abb. 1 wird die Zustimmung zu einer Reihe von Lernerfahrungen in Verbindung mit der Psychodramatherapie dargestellt. Auch hier beschreiben die Kinder und Jugendlichen, dass sie gelernt haben über ihre Grenzüberschreitungen zu reflektieren, sich in andere Menschen und ihre Opfer hineinzuversetzen, sich selbstbewusster zu erleben und Gefühle anderer besser zu erkennen. Die Zustimmung hinsichtlich der eigenen Emotionskontrolle sowie dem Umgang mit Wut, Angst und Trauer fällt dagegen geringer aus.

Zusammenfassend lässt sich festhalten, dass die Psychodrama-Therapie in einem stationären Gruppensetting für sexuell übergriffige Minderjährige ambivalent erlebt wird. Die qualitativen und quantitativen Ergebnisse der Befragung liefern jedoch erste wichtige Hinweise für die Optimierung der Psychodrama-Therapie mit dieser spezifischen Klientel. Eine altershomogenere Gruppenzusammensetzung, eine Phase der Vertrauensbildung unter den Gruppenmitgliedern (bevor über Missbrauchserfahrungen oder sexuelle Übergriffe gesprochen wird) sowie eine ausgewogene Mischung aus freiem und strukturierten Elementen des Rollenspiels stellen wesentliche Verbesserungsmöglichkeiten aus Sicht der Gruppenteilnehmer dar.

6 Diskussion

Wie in anderen Studien zu sexueller Übergriffigkeit in der Kindheit (z. B. Friedrich et al. 2003) zeigen sich auch in dieser Stichprobe bei nahezu allen Jungen belastende Lebensereignisse, häufig multiple Missbrauchserfahrungen, familiäre Probleme und psychische Auffälligkeiten bis hin zu schweren Traumatisierungen. Diese psychischen Belastungen bilden sich sowohl in den eingesetzten Selbstbeschreibungsskalen ab (s. Tab. 2), als auch in den psychometrischen Testverfahren (s. Tab. 3). Zu Beginn der Hilfemaßnahme liegen die mittleren T-Werte der Gesamtsymptombelastung in der Fremdeinschätzung (CBCL 4–18) durch die BezugsbetreuerInnen (M=71,0) und auch in der Selbsteinschätzung (YSR 11–18) der Jungen (M=70,5) deutlich über den altersentsprechenden Normwerten (s. Tab. 3). Neben internalisierenden Problemen, wie Ängsten, depressiven Symptomen und sozialen Problemen beschreiben die Jungen und BezugsbetreuerInnen ebenso externalisierende Probleme, wie dissoziales und aggressives Verhalten, die sich im Grenz- oder außerhalb des Normbereichs einordnen lassen (s. Tab. 3). Diese Befunde sind vergleichbar mit den Ergebnissen von Elsner und König (2010).

Spezifische Maßnahmen, die ausschließlich die Delikte der Jungen in den Vordergrund stellen, können den komplexen Problemlagen und Hilfebedarfen demnach nicht gerecht werden. Das Konzept von Rumpelstilzchen fokussiert deshalb gerade zu Beginn der Behandlung auf erlebte Traumatisierungen und fördert eine innerpsychische Stabilisierung und Ich-Stärkung der Jungen. Dies wird als Voraussetzung für die Teilnahme an eher deliktorientierten Präventionsmaßnahmen angesehen. Die dargestellten Ergebnisse umfassen ca. die ersten 12 Monate der Hilfemaßnahme, so dass sich entsprechend des Behandlungskonzepts insbesondere hinsichtlich internalisierender Probleme und der aktuellen psychischen Belastung Veränderungen in Selbst- und Fremdeinschätzung ergeben sollten.

Insbesondere in der Selbsteinschätzung der Jungen zeigt sich hier eine moderate bis deutlich signifikante Reduktion sowohl in der aktuellen Belastung durch negative Lebensereignisse ($ES_r = 0{,}49$) als auch hinsichtlich internalisierender Probleme ($ES_r = 0{,}69$; s. Tab. 2 und 3). Auch die BezugsbetreuerInnen sehen hier zumindest für internalisierende Probleme eine deutliche Verbesserung bei den Jungen ($ES_r = 0{,}62$; s. Tab. 3). Bemerkenswert ist, dass aus Sicht der psychologischen BezugstherapeutInnen eine geringfügige – allerdings nicht signifikante – Steigerung der aktuellen Belastung durch negative Lebensereignisse bei den Jungen beschrieben wird (s. Tab. 2). Hier lässt sich die Hypothese aufstellen, dass eine psychotherapeutische Bearbeitung belastender Lebensereignisse und Traumatisierungen (z. B. durch Methoden des Psychodramas) möglicherweise auch zu einer verbesserten Einschätzung durch die BezugstherapeutInnen führt. Betrachtet man die Gesamtsymptombelastung, so sehen ausschließlich die Jungen eine signifikante Symptomreduktion ($ES_r = 0{,}62$; s. Tab. 3). Dennoch befindet sich der mittlere T-Wert für die Gesamtsymptombelastung auch zum 2. Messzeitpunkt aus Sicht der Jungen außerhalb des Normbereichs.

Keine signifikanten Veränderungen zwischen den beiden Messzeitpunkten ergeben sich sowohl aus Sicht der Jungen als auch aus Sicht der BezugsbetreuerInnen und -therapeutInnen für die Skalen „Externalisierende Probleme“, „Problematisches Verhalten während der Hilfemaßnahme“ und „Stärken und Ressourcen“ (s. Tab. 2 und 3). Hier gibt es mehrere Erklärungsansätze. Da das Behandlungskonzept von Rumpelstilzchen zunächst vor allem auf internalisierende Problembereiche fokussiert ist, sind deutliche Veränderungen hinsichtlich dissozialer und aggressiver Verhaltensweisen bei den Jungen eher langfristig zu erwarten und lassen sich wahrscheinlich erst zu einem späteren Zeitpunkt der Maßnahme abbilden. Weitere Erhebungen sind notwendig, um diese langfristigen Entwicklungen zu überprüfen. Andererseits ist es auch denkbar, dass eine hohe Kumulation von Jungen mit externalisierendem Problemverhalten, wie sie in spezifischen stationären Einrichtungen gegeben ist, den Kindern kaum die Chance bietet, sich an positiven nicht-delinquenten Peers zu orientieren (i.S. vom Modelllernen). Der weitere Verlauf der Evaluation wird zeigen, ob sich in Zukunft auch für diese Problembereiche positive Veränderungen erzielen lassen oder eben nicht. Auch dieser Befund steht im Einklang mit den Ergebnissen von Elsner und König (2010).

Der systematischen Darstellung verschiedener Sichtweisen auf Ressourcen und Probleme sowie deren Entwicklung im Verlauf der Hilfemaßnahmen kommt eine eigene Bedeutung zu. Durch die Darstellung unterschiedlicher Perspektiven wird nicht nur die Transparenz und Nachvollziehbarkeit des Hilfeverlaufs erhöht, es entsteht dadurch auch eine wesentliche Voraussetzung dafür, die Sichtweisen und Interessen der Kinder angemessen in die Hilfemaßnahmen einzubeziehen.

7 Qualitative Untersuchung der Psychodramagruppentherapie

Die Rückmeldungen zur Psychodramatherapie sind vielseitig und aufschlussreich. Die ehemaligen Klienten nennen Aspekte, die mit den Zielen des Einsatzes der Methode übereinstimmen. Es geht um die Entwicklung der Mentalisierungsfähigkeit mit den Stichworten: Selbstwahrnehmung, Wahrnehmung von Grenzen und Grenzüberschreitung (sowohl ausgeübter als auch selbst erlittener), Perspektivwechsel (Wahrnehmung von Intentionen und mentalen Zuständen beim anderen), Empathie und Selbstreflektion. So beschrieben einige ehemaligen Klienten, dass sie durch die Psychodramagruppentherapie gelernt haben, über ihre Grenzüberschreitungen zu reflektieren, sich in andere Menschen und ihre Opfer hineinzuversetzen, sich selbstbewusster zu erleben und Gefühle anderer besser zu erkennen.

Einige der ehemaligen Klienten nennen negative Aspekte oder kritische Aspekte. So auf der einen Seite mangelndes Vertrauen in die Gruppe und ein zu schnelles Offenlegen von den eigenen begangenen Übergriffen oder selbst erlittenem Missbrauch.

Es handelt sich um eine Gruppentherapie, die fortwährend läuft und neue Jungen aufnimmt, und ältere entlässt, im direkten Zusammenhang mit ihrer Unterbringung in den beiden stationären Gruppen der Einrichtung. Es hat sich im Laufe der Jahre eine Gruppenkultur entwickelt, die die Erwartung beinhaltet, dass die Jungen zum Beispiel offen darüber reden, was zu ihrer Aufnahme in der Einrichtung geführt hat. Gerade die „Neuzugänge" zur Gruppe werden dies als Druck sich zu öffnen erleben. Im Verlauf ist das Thema ‚Vertrauen' in einer Gruppe von Jungen, die auch zusammen wohnen, ebenfalls immer wieder zentral. Zum einen ist der Satz „Ich spreche da nicht drüber, weil ich hier niemandem vertraue" auch ein immer anwendbares Argument, sich einer therapeutischen Bearbeitung der eigenen Themen im Gruppensetting zu entziehen. Auf der anderen Seite ist es für die weitere Entwicklung der Psychodramagruppentherapie ein wichtiger Hinweis, den Prozess der Vertrauensbildung in das therapeutische Arbeiten in der Gruppe ernst zu nehmen. Dies sollte zukünftig mit dem therapeutischen Team verstärkt reflektiert werden, um Veränderungen für das Psychodramatherapiekonzept daraus abzuleiten.

Einige ehemalige Klienten äußerten negative Gedanken und Ängste hinsichtlich eigener Opfererfahrungen.

Diese Äußerungen beziehen sich auf die Psychodramagruppentherapie mit den älteren Jungen, in der protagonistenzentriert gearbeitet wird, da in der Kinderpsychodramagruppe eine indirekte, symbolische Bearbeitung ohne Bezug zu biographischen Erlebnissen stattfindet. Besonders wichtig ist wie ein Protagonistenspiel auf die Gruppe (teilnehmende Beobachter und der Hilfs-Ichs) wirkt, da die Bearbeitung traumatischer Erfahrungen und von übergriffigem Verhalten eines

Jungen Auswirkungen auf das Erleben der anderen Jungen in der Gruppe haben. Diese Auswirkungen wurden bislang noch nicht genügend bedacht. Die Frage, welche Themen in einer Gruppentherapie bearbeitet werden können, und für welche Themen es sinnvoller wäre, ein gesondertes psychodramatherapeutisches Setting zu schaffen, sollte in den Behandlungsverläufen differenziert werden. Gesonderte Settings mit zwei TherapeutInnen, die einzeln mit einem Jungen und zusätzlichen erwachsenen RollenspielerInnen arbeiten, die gezielt zur Bearbeitung bestimmter Themen durchgeführt werden, werden bereits punktuell angeboten. In einigen Fällen ist es zum Beispiel so, dass eine psychodramatische Bearbeitung konkreter Themen nötig ist, und ein Klient dies auch gerne möchte, aber die Gruppe damit überfordert oder zu belastet wäre. In der Weiterentwicklung der Psychodramatherapie ist es möglich flexibel Settings zu schaffen, die parallel zur Psychodramagruppe angeboten werden.

Aussagen, dass negative Gedanken und Ängste zu eigenen Opfererfahrungen im Rahmen der Psychodramatherapie auftauchen, sind nicht nur negativ zu bewerten, wenngleich für das unmittelbare Erleben des Betroffenen unangenehm. Gerade bei sexuell übergriffigen Jungen ist die Dynamik oft in der Umkehr der Opfererfahrung zu verstehen. Das heißt, dass das Einnehmen der Machtposition (auch im Sinne des gezeigten sexuell übergriffigen Verhaltens) den Jungen einen Schutz vor den eigenen Ohnmachtsgefühlen ermöglicht. Wenn dann durch die Psychodramatherapie und andere Interventionen diese Abwehr nachlässt, dann führt das dazu, dass Beziehungstraumatisierungen und dazugehörende Affekte aktiviert werden. Dies ist therapeutisch gesehen ein Fortschritt, kann aber auch Gefühle von Ohnmacht, Vulnerabilität und Schwäche auslösen. Deshalb ist es nötig, dass stützende Maßnahmen über das Therapiesetting hinaus im stationären Rahmen individuell angeboten werden können, damit der Junge sich sicher fühlen kann (sicherer „Lebensort"). So ist beispielsweise eine regelmäßige Nachbesprechung der Gruppentherapie mit den PädagogInnen wichtig, damit zusätzliche stabilisierende Maßnahmen umgesetzt werden können. Eine Empfehlung der ehemaligen Klienten war auch, die Therapiegruppen altershomogen zusammenzusetzen. Dies ist inzwischen erfolgt, soweit die Aufnahmesteuerung dies zulässt. So gibt es eine Gruppe von etwa 8- bis 11-Jährigen, in der kinderpsychodramatisch gearbeitet wird, und eine Gruppe für die Älteren, etwa 12- bis 14-Jährigen, in der unter anderem protagonistenzentriert gearbeitet werden kann.

Kritisch wurden auch die Freiheitsgrade bei der Themenfindung betrachtet. In den Anfängen war die Psychodramagruppentherapie noch stärker an das protagonistInnenzentrierte Erwachsenenpsychodrama mit soziometrischer Protagonistenwahl angelehnt. Zum Teil waren dies schwierige Aushandlungsprozesse, in denen das Bedürfnis nach Aufmerksamkeit und Zuwendung durch starke Konkurrenzen und Rivalitäten ausagiert wurde. In den letzten Jahren wurde dazu übergegangen stärker im Voraus zu strukturieren. Zum Teil werden Themen im Einzelsetting mit den BezugstherapeutInnen gezielt für die Psychodramagruppentherapie vorbereitet und stärker eine „gerechte" Verteilung der Spielzeit auf die Klienten von den LeiterInnen festgelegt (die Erwachsenen setzen Regeln). Die Zeit, die für die Aushandlungsprozesse benötigt wurde, ist damit stark reduziert und die Gruppe reagierte darauf mit deutlicher Entlastung.

Die Einschätzung, dass die Psychodramagruppentherapie die eigene Emotionskontrolle verbessert habe, fiel in der Zustimmung der ehemaligen Klienten im Vergleich zu den anderen therapeutischen Zielen geringer aus. Bei diesem Ergebnis geht es um das subjektive Gefühl der Emotionskontrolle. Wenn Opfererfahrungen und Täterintrojekte sichtbar werden und integriert werden, dann gerät während dieses Prozesses das etablierte „Kontrollsystem“ ins Wanken. Emotionen, die mit Angst, Wut, Ohnmacht und Traurigkeit zu tun haben, können dann nicht mehr so „erfolgreich“ abgewehrt werden. Dies ist in einem Maße sinnvoll und notwendig für Veränderungsprozesse, aber bei Überflutung gegebenenfalls in der Wirkung auch re-traumatisierend. Die Jungen fühlen sich vulnerabel, verletzlich und von ihren Affekten überflutet. Im Grunde sind sie dem Ziel der Emotionskontrolle einen Schritt näher, dadurch, dass das bewusste Erleben von Emotionen und die Integration in einen nachvollziehbaren, narrativen Kontext erst die Möglichkeit für die Entwicklung einer stabilen Emotionskontrolle schafft. Wichtig ist, dass für diesen Prozess ein ‚Containment‘ angeboten werden kann. Diesem Punkt soll in der zukünftigen konzeptionellen Arbeit mehr Aufmerksamkeit geschenkt werden.

Der Umgang mit der Bearbeitung des Themas ‚Sexueller Übergriffigkeit‘ und dessen Störungsverständnis hat sich seit der Gründung der Einrichtung grundlegend geändert. Das Psychodrama-Konzept für die Einrichtung soll im weiteren Verlauf differenziert und verschriftlicht werden. Eine Grundannahme dazu ist, dass davon ausgegangen wird, dass die Jungen, die im Rumpelstilzchen aufgenommen werden, seit frühester Kindheit beziehungstraumatisiert sind und dazu meistens traumatische Erlebnisse in Form von körperlicher und sexueller Gewalt erfahren oder miterleben mussten. Deshalb stehen am Anfang der Behandlung die Stabilisierung und das Erleben eines sicheren Lebensortes im Vordergrund. Darauf aufbauend geht es um Körperwahrnehmung und das Erkennen von eigenen Grenzen und der Grenzen anderer Menschen. Diese Arbeit stellt eine Voraussetzung für die Möglichkeit einer Verarbeitung von eigenen Erfahrungen im Kontext von haltgebenden Beziehungen. Die Psychodramagruppentherapien wurden in ihrer Zusammensetzung differenziert nach Alter und Entwicklungsstand. Das heißt, dass die Jungen bis zum etwa 11. Lebensjahr ein kinderpsychodramatisches, sehr spielerisches Vorgehen in der Psychodramagruppe erleben, während mit den Jungen ab dem 12. Lebensjahr zum Teil protagonistenzentriert gearbeitet werden kann. In den Protagonistenspielen geht es um die Familie, die Lebenssituation des Kindes vor dem Zeitpunkt der Übergriffe, um besondere Lebensereignisse, die das Kind belasten und die es immer wieder erzählt oder in seinem aktuellen Erleben produziert. Hier wird im Surplus gearbeitet, und zum Teil mit der Bewältigung durch symbolische Inszenierung von Wünschen. Es gibt flankierende Psychodrama-Einzelsettings, jeweils zwei TherapeutInnen und gegebenenfalls zusätzliche erwachsene Hilfs-Ichs (z. B. BezugsbetreuerIn). In diesen Settings geht es in der Regel um Traumaverarbeitung, die in Anlehnung an Krüger (2015), adaptiert für die jeweilige Alters- und Entwicklungsstufe durchgeführt wird. Außerdem gibt es „Aufträge“ für die Bearbeitung bestimmter Themen aus den Einzeltherapien für die Psychodramagruppen, die mit den Jungen zusammen entwickelt wurden. Wir hoffen, durch die teilweise auch kritischen quantitativen und qualitativen Ergebnisse zur psychodramatischen Arbeit mit sexuell übergriffigen Minderjährigen einen ersten Beitrag zur Weiterentwicklung der Psychodramatherapie für eben diese spezifische Klientel geleistet zu haben. Die Befunde zeigen deutlich, dass eine kontinuierliche individuelle Prozessevaluation von Hilfemaßnahmen gerade in der pädagogisch-therapeutischen Arbeit mit delinquenten Minderjährigen essentiell ist, um iatrogene Effekte zu minimieren. Insbesondere der Blick der sexuell übergriffigen Jungen auf den eigenen Therapieprozess kann aus unserer Sicht einen wichtigen Beitrag für die Weiterentwicklung pädagogisch-therapeutischer Konzepte in stationären Settings der Kinder- und Jugendhilfe liefern.

Literatur

Ameln, Fv., Gerstmann, R., & Kramer, J. (2004). *Psychodrama*. Heidelberg: Springer.

Bender, W., & Stadler, C. (2012). *Psychodrama-Therapie: Grundlagen, Methodik und Anwendungsgebiete*. Stuttgart: Schattauer.

Cohen, J. (1992). A Power Primer. *Psychological Bulletin, 112*, 155–159.

Elsner, K. (2011). *Sexuell übergriffige Kinder – Biografien, Merkmale und Therapieverläufe im Vergleich mit aggressiv auffälligen und unauffälligen Kindern*. Unveröffentlichte Dissertation, Universität Duisburg-Essen.

Elsner, K., & König, A. (2010). Evaluation der Behandlung sexuell übergriffiger strafunmündiger Jungen. *Kindesmisshandlung und -vernachlässigung. Interdisziplinäre Fachzeitschrift für Prävention und Intervention, 13*, 20–43.

Friedrich, W. N., Davies, W., Fehrer, E., & Wright, J. (2003). Sexual behavior problems in preteen children: Developmental, ecological, and behavioral correlates. *Annals of the New York Academy of Sciences, 989*, 95–104.

Johnson, T. C. (1988). Child perpetrators – Children who molest other children: Preliminary findings. *Child Abuse & Neglect, 12*, 219–229.

König, A., Hülperath, S., & Elsner, K. (2014). *Abschlussbericht zur Evaluation der Bundesweiten Fortbildungsoffensive 2010–2014 zur Stärkung der Handlungsfähigkeit (Prävention und Intervention) von Mitarbeiterinnen und Mitarbeitern der Kinder- und Jugendhilfe zur Verhinderung von sexualisierter Gewalt*. Im Auftrag der Deutschen Gesellschaft für Prävention und Intervention bei Kindesmisshandlung und -vernachlässigung (DGfPI e. V.) mit Förderung des Bundesministerium für Familie, Senioren, Frauen und Jugend (BMFSFJ).

Krüger, R. (2014). *Störungsspezifische Psychodramatherapie in Theorie und Praxis*. Vortrag, Lehrbeauftragtentreffen Moreno Institut Edenkoben-Überlingen.

Krüger, R. (2015). *Störungsspezifische Psychodramatherapie*. Göttingen: Vandenhoeck & Ruprecht.

Mayring, P. (2010). Qualitative Inhaltsanalyse. In G. Mey & K. Mruck (Hrsg.), *Handbuch Qualitative Forschung in der Psychologie* (S. 601–613). Wiesbaden: VS Verlag für Sozialwissenschaften.

Mielke, F. (2009). *Behandlungsprogramm für die Arbeit mit jugendlichen Sexualtätern* (BMJS 12/21). Beratungsstelle im Packhaus, pro familia Landesverband Schleswig-Holstein e. V.

Milner, M., Borduin, C., Prescott, D., Bovensmann, H., Schepker, R., DuBois, R., Schladale, J., Eher, R., Schmeck, K., Langfedt, T., Smit, A., & Pfäfflin, F. (2006). Standards of care for juvenile sexual offenders of the international association for the treatment of sexual offenders. *Sexual Offender Treatment, 1*(3), 1–7.

Pithers, W. D., Gray, A., Busconi, A., & Houchens, P. (1998). Caregivers of children with sexual behavior problems: Psychological and familial functioning. *Child Abuse & Neglect, 22*, 129–141.

Scheuffgen, K. (2012). Kinderpsychodrama mit Jungen, die sexuell übergriffiges Verhalten zeigen. Psychodrama-Gruppentherapie in der stationären Jugendhilfe. *Zeitschrift für Psychodrama und Soziometrie, 11*(1), 107–123.

Silovsky, J. F., & Niec, L. (2002). Characteristics of young children with sexual behavior problems: A pilot study. *Child Maltreatment, 7*, 187–197.

Dr. Kristina Scheuffgen, geb. 1969: Psychodrama Therapeutin, Forensische Psychologin, Mitglied der British Psychological Society. Beschäftigt bei den Malteser Werken Köln seit 2009, dort Gründung und Therapeutische Leitung einer stationären Jugendhilfeeinrichtung für sexuell grenzverletzende Jungen. Promotion im Bereich kognitiver Entwicklungspsychologie (University College London) im Jahr 1998, Masters in Forensischer Psychologie (University of Leicester) im Jahr 2000. Anwendung von Psychodrama in der Therapie (Strafvollzug, Jugendforensik und Jugendhilfe) und in Beratungskontexten wie Supervision.

Benjamin Pniewski, geb. 1986: Psychologe (M. Sc.), Beschäftigt in der LVR-Klinik Viersen, dort im Bereich forensische Psychiatrie. Laufende Promotion im Bereich Behandlungsevaluation des Jugendmaßregelvollzugs (Universität Duisburg-Essen). Bis 2014 wissenschaftlicher Mitarbeiter in der LWL-Universitätsklinik Hamm für Kinder- und Jugendpsychiatrie und wissenschaftlicher Mitarbeiter bei TEQS GbR.

Andrej König, geb. 1978: Diplom-Psychologe, Vertretungsprofessor für Methodenlehre und Forensische Psychologie am Fachbereich Angewandte Sozialwissenschaften der Fachhochschule Dortmund. Bis 2012 wissenschaftlicher Mitarbeiter am Institut für Forensische Psychiatrie der Universität Duisburg-Essen. Promotion im Bereich der forensischen Risikoprognostik (Ruhr-Universität Bochum) im Jahr 2011. Seit 2006 Leitung ambulanter Sexualstraftätergruppen für das Institut für Opferschutz und Täterbehandlung (IOT e. V.) und wissenschaftlicher Mitarbeiter bei TEQS GbR.

Z Psychodrama Soziometr (2016) (Suppl) 15:197–215
DOI 10.1007/s11620-015-0299-4

HAUPTBEITRÄGE

Zeitschrift für Psychodrama
und Soziometrie

Effectiveness of psychodrama group therapy on pupils with mathematics anxiety

Gstrein Dorothea

Published online: 3 December 2015

Abstract The present study focuses on the effectiveness of psychodrama group therapy on adolescents suffering from mathematics anxiety. Five secondary school pupils in Merano, aged 17–19 years, took part in 10 group sessions of 90 min, held weekly over a period of about 3 months. The changes generated by psychodrama therapy in the pupils' problem areas, such as, high stress levels before tests, impaired working memory, low self-esteem and motivation to learn mathematics, were measured with the help of the Personal Questionnaire (Elliott and Shapiro, Simplified personal questionnaire procedure, 1999) and the Self-efficacy scale—Mathematics, two quantitative measuring instruments, and with the Client Change Interview, a qualitative measuring instrument. The results of the data collected indicate that psychodrama treatment brought forth significant changes in some pupils' problem areas.

Keywords Psychodrama · Mathematics anxiety · Mathematics self-efficacy · Working memory · Motivation to learn mathematics · Personal questionnaire · Self-efficacy scale—mathematics · Client change interview

Wirksamkeit der Psychodramagruppentherapie bei Schülern mit Angst vor Mathematik

Zusammenfassung Die vorliegende Studie beschäftigt sich mit der Wirksamkeit der Psychodramagruppentherapie bei Jugendlichen, die unter Angst vor Mathematik leiden. Fünf SchülerInnen einer Oberschule in Meran, Südtirol, im Alter von 17–19 Jahren, nahmen an 10 Gruppensitzungen von jeweils 90 Minuten

G. Dorothea (✉)
Winkelweg 4,
39012 Meran, Italy
e-mail: dorotheagstrein@hotmail.com

teil. Die Sitzungen wurden wöchentlich über einen Zeitraum von drei Monaten abgehalten. Die Veränderungen, die durch die Psychodramagruppentherapie in den von den SchülerInnen genannten Problembereichen, wie hohe Belastung vor Tests, beeinträchtigtes Arbeitsgedächtnis, geringer Selbstwert und mangelnde Motivation Mathematik zu lernen, erzielt wurden, wurden mit Hilfe des Personal Questionnaire (Elliott and Shapiro Simplified personal questionnaire procedure, 1999) und der Selbstwirksamkeitsskala—Mathematik, zwei quantitativen Messinstrumenten und mit dem Client Change Interview, einem qualitativen Messinstrument gemessen. Die Auswertung der gesammelten Daten deutet darauf hin, dass Psychodramagruppentherapie bei einigen SchülerInnen zu signifikanten Veränderungen in einzelnen Problembereichen geführt hat.

Schlüsselwörter Psychodrama · Angst vor Mathematik · Selbstwirksamkeit Mathematik · Arbeitsgedächtnis · Motivation Mathematik zu lernen · Personal Questionnaire · Selbstwirksamkeitsskala—Mathematik · Client Change Interview

1 Introduction

The topic of mathematics anxiety is receiving increasing attention within the psychological literature (Ma 1999; Ashcraft and Kirk 2001; Ashcraft and Krause 2007; Ashcraft and Moore 2009; Lyons and Beilock 2012), especially because of its often serious and detrimental influence on educational achievements. However, scientific papers investigating or showing the treatment effects of different kinds of therapies on mathematics anxiety are extremely rare if not inexistent. So far no study has been conducted on the effectiveness of psychodrama therapy on people suffering from this form of anxiety.

Mathematics anxiety seems to affect a notable proportion of the school age population and adults in post-secondary education (Ashcraft and Ridley 2005) and it does not appear to be restricted to specific parts of the world, since it is well-known both in western and in Asian countries. Mathematics seems to be the most feared and avoided subject among pupils in primary and secondary schools as well as among college students (Yeo 2004).

2 Mathematics anxiety

The first attempt to define and to deal with mathematics anxiety was made by M. F. Gough, an elementary school teacher. After seeing her students struggle with mathematics she wrote an article with the title "Mathemaphobia: Causes and Treatments" (1954). Since then mathematics anxiety has been studied more widely and various researchers have provided different definitions of this disorder. Richardson and Suinn (1972, p. 551), for instance, describe it as a state that involves "feelings of tensions and anxiety that interfere with the manipulation of numbers and the solving of mathematical problems in a wide variety of ordinary life and academic situations". They offered the first instrument that is specifically designed to measure mathematics anxiety, the "Mathematics Anxiety Rating Scale (MARS)", which is still in use today. Glen E. Hunt (1985, p. 32) describes mathematics anxiety as "the panic, helplessness, paralysis and mental disorganization that arises among some people when they are required to solve a mathematical problem". Ashcraft's (2002, p. 181) shorter and more recent definition of mathematics anxiety, reads as follows "a feeling of tension, apprehension, or fear that interferes with math performance".

Even if a notable proportion of the school age population and of adults suffers from mathematics anxiety, presently, it is not acknowledged by the Diagnostic and Statistical Manual of Mental Disorders (American Psychiatric Association 1994). Hopko et al. (1998) suggested that mathematics anxiety should be considered a genuine phobia and should be added to the category of specific phobias, since it meets all the standard diagnostic criteria for such reactions. An individual who suffers from mathematics anxiety is intent to avoid the phobic situation and if he cannot avoid it, he endures it with intense anxiety or distress. The avoidance of such a situation, anxious anticipation, or emotional stress in the feared situation, all significantly interfere with the individual's normal routine or academic functioning.

So far the most frequently investigated research questions regarding mathematics anxiety have been "How does mathematics anxiety develop?", "When does mathematics anxiety develop?", "Are there any gender differences in mathematics anxiety?", "Which role does working memory play in mathematics anxiety?", "Is there a correlation between mathematics anxiety and mathematics performance?".

The first research question, regarding the development of mathematics phobia, can be answered in two different ways. Maloney et al. (2010) have explored the extent to which anxiety and basic numerical abilities are present in adults. In their study they show that fundamental skills, like counting and number comparison, are correlated with mathematics anxiety also in adults. Also Rubinstein and Tannock (2010) have come to similar findings, namely that adults show deficiencies in basic mathematics abilities. Considering this, one could assume that if adults, children's role models, show base level process deficiencies, the effects may be exaggerated in children. In this way the presence of mathematics anxiety among adults could be seen as a possible reason for the development of math anxiety in children.

Another distinct possibility is that mathematic anxious teachers might convey their anxiety to their pupils. Hembree, (1990) when exploring societal roles in the development of mathematics anxiety, reported that college students who were preparing to be elementary teachers, showed a higher prevalence of mathematics anxiety than other students. Following this track and adding the hypotheses that in many western countries primary school teachers are almost exclusively female and form the group with the highest prevalence of math anxiety, Beilock et al. (2010) measured the mathematics anxiety of first and second grade teachers. They also studied the mathematics performance of their pupils at the beginning and end of the school year. Since children of this age are very susceptible to same-gender stereotypes, they predicted that girls would especially be affected by their female teachers' mathematics anxiety. The study's findings suggest that there is a strong correlation between the teachers' mathematics anxiety and the girls' mathematics performance, while the boys' performance kept unaltered.

Apart from this, relatively stable gender-related mathematics attitudes and stereotypes may also have an effect on females' mathematics performances. Gunderson et al. (2012) showed that both, teachers and parents, hold strong gender-related mathematics beliefs, especially emphasizing negative stereotypes for females. A continuous confrontation with this kind of stereotypes may additionally contribute to higher mathematics anxiety and lower mathematics achievements among females.

Two meta-analyses on mathematics anxiety have researched the relationships between mathematics anxiety and other personal and educational factors (Hembree 1990; Ma 1999). According to these studies mathematics anxiety is strongly correlated with mathematics performance and with other anxiety measures, in particular with test anxiety.

Liebert and Morris (1967) were the first to research test anxiety in general. According to them test anxiety consists of an emotional element and a cognitive element. A pupil or student, who reacts affectively to a test situation, may experience increased blood pressure and heart rate, sweaty palms, dizziness, dry mouth or trembling hands. A student, whose cognition is affected by a test situation, may have feelings of low self-efficacy, indecision, a sense of confusion, worry, poor concentration or defeatist self-talk. Their theory proposes an interference model of test anxiety. According to this theory the recall of prior learning is disturbed by test anxiety. If facts or in the case of mathematics, formulas, cannot be recalled, it is understandable that mathematics performance can be considerably degraded.

Eyseneck and Calvo (1992) proposed a model of the anxiety-to-performance relationship in cognitive tasks. Their theory has become known as the "processing efficiency theory". It claims that frequent intrusive thoughts and constantly present worry characteristics of high anxiety compete with the ongoing cognitive task for the limited processing resources of working memory. The result of such competition is either a slowing of performance or a decline in accuracy, both leading to performance deficits. The role of students' working memory, which seems to be particularly affected by mathematics anxiety, has been investigated by more recent studies (Ashcraft and Kirk 2001, Ashcraft and Krause 2007).

Ashcraft and Moore (2009) have studied the relationship between mathematics anxiety and desirable attitudes towards mathematics. The results of their research suggest that mathematics anxiety is strongly connected to avoidance strategies. An obvious but unfortunate consequence of continually avoiding math tasks is that students with high mathematics anxiety tend to end up with reduced math competence and lower achievement. In this way a vicious circle is preprogrammed since lower achievement will lead to lower enjoyment and lower self-confidence in math tasks and will finally result in poor motivation to learn math. The consequence of lower motivation may be inadequate progress, which could soon prompt negative feedback from parents and teachers resulting in negative self-perceptions.

A recent study by Lyons and Beilock (2012) shows the effect of mathematics anxiety on some regions of the human brain. The researchers have found out that this form of anxiety triggers the same brain activity like that of the physical sensation of pain. This study seems to provide the first neural evidence indicating the nature of the subjective experience of mathematics anxiety. The data collected suggest that simply by anticipating an unpleasant event, like an immediately forthcoming mathematics test, a math-anxious individual would show activation of neural regions that are involved in pain processing.

The list of negative effects and consequences of mathematics anxiety on the school age population is long. It ranges from lower enjoyment and lower self-confidence, avoidance tendencies, poor performance to negative feedbacks and even sensations of pain. It is no wonder that people experiencing these feelings and inadequacies are biased away from taking math classes or math-related career paths.

3 Psychodrama and mathematics anxiety

Research on different forms of therapy and their specific interventions, which are apt to alleviate pupils' and students' anxiety related to mathematics, are practically inexistent. Currently there are no studies that show the effectiveness of psychodrama as a treatment for adolescents who suffer from mathematics anxiety. This study can therefore be considered a first attempt to bring some light into a completely dark and unexplored area of research. The aim of this study is to investigate the effectiveness of psychodrama group therapy on adolescents who have mathematics anxiety.

Moreno (1946) provided some precious thoughts about anxiety. He was convinced that anxiety and spontaneity exist at opposite ends of the continuum, and that anxiety sets in because spontaneity is missing. When spontaneity is restrained our view of possibilities and choices is restricted. Within the perception of restricted choices and options we function in a robotic fashion with our creativity lying dormant. Creative acts, however, can generate changes, can produce unknown results. Moreno was convinced of "spontaneity-creativity as a propelling force in human progress" (1946, p. xv). Spontaneity would provide the energy that can help a person to respond adequately to a new situation, or would generate the capacity to respond in a new way to an old situation.

Pupils and students suffering from mathematics anxiety definitely lack spontaneity and experience limited choices of reactions. Especially before and in test situations, when their worrisome thoughts grow out of proportion; they are locked at one end of the continuum, at the anxiety end.

Prior to undertaking this study, the belief was that psychodrama group sessions would give the students the opportunity to enhance their creativity and to enable them to generate new responses to old and hindering situations. The basic concepts of psychodrama therapy, such as the re-enactment of a painful experience and a possible correction in the "surplus reality", or role reversal allowing a different perspective (Moreno and Moreno 1955) or feedback of fellow-students sharing the problem, should have healing effects on the participants. In the safe and supportive environment of the group sessions the participants would be encouraged to use their creative power and get the opportunity to try out new and more effective roles and behaviors.

4 Method

The aim of this study is to determine the effectiveness of psychodrama group therapy on adolescents who have mathematics anxiety.

In October 2013 I contacted some of my mathematics colleagues and asked them to inform their pupils about the study and to hand them out the recruitment letter explaining the aim and the procedure of the project. Seven pupils struggling with mathematics expressed their interest in participating in the study and were invited to a personal interview of about 60–90 min before the beginning of the group sessions. They stated their reasons for taking part in the study and they talked about their problems related to mathematics. This resulted in a very detailed, individualized list of problems forming their Personal Questionnaire (PQ), an expanded target complaint measure, developed by Robert Elliott (Elliott and Shapiro 1999). In order to guarantee the anonymity of the research participants they added their individual code consisting of their mothers' day and month of birth to their PQs (e.g. 1203).

The most frequently mentioned problems regarded their nervousness before a math test, their increased stress level, their inability to concentrate during the test, as well as continuous defeatist self-talk. Some pupils reported somatic disorders, stomach ache or headache or sleep disorders before a math test. All of the pupils interviewed said that their motivation to learn mathematics was rather low, that they often compared their performances with schoolmates and that their perceived self-efficacy related to mathematics was extremely low.

From this list of struggles, the following research questions were asked and formed the basis of the research, in relation to whether - psychodrama group therapy is effective:

1. in reducing somatic and physical symptoms
2. in reducing stress levels and promoting functioning of working memory to promote ability to ignore distracting and worrying thoughts.
3. in changing pupils' attitudes or relationship with mathematics
4. in promoting pupils' sense of self efficacy

4.1 Participants

Participants from the 3rd, 4th and 5th forms of the German-speaking high school, Fachoberschule für Tourismus und Biotechnologie "Marie Curie" in Merano (South Tyrol, Italy) were recruited for this study. The information about the project was passed on to the mathematics teachers and 7 pupils, 4 female and 3 male pupils aged between 17 and 19 volunteered to take part in the study and gave their informed consent. Parents' consent was needed for two participants, who had not been of legal age by the beginning of the project. Full data are available for 5 participants, 2 boys (all the students' names have been changed - Peter and Robert) and 3 girls (Monika, Caroline and Samantha) since two pupils, a girl and a boy did not come to the first two sessions and then decided not to take part in the project.

4.2 Procedure and measuring instruments

After the initial interviews the group sessions started. The first session took place on 20th November 2013. The meetings were held weekly on Wednesday afternoons, a school-free afternoon, in the school's art room and lasted about 90 min each. The only school-related advantage of the participants was the recognition of 4 h of "elective course". The group sessions were conducted within a time span of almost 3 months and ended on 12th February 2014. Only one pupil was present at all the ten meetings, the others attended six to eight sessions.

In this study three different instruments were used to measure possible changes due to psychodrama group therapy, Elliott's PQ and the Self-efficacy Scale—Mathematics, created by myself, based on the "General Self-Efficacy Scale (GSE)" by Schwarzer and Jerusalem (1999), two quantitative measurement tools, and the Client Change Interview (Elliott et al. 2003), a qualitative measuring instrument.

While the PQ is a widely used questionnaire concentrating on the problems of the participants on a 7-point Likert scale (1 = totally disagree to 7 = totally agree), the Self-efficacy Scale—Mathematics is a questionnaire consisting of positive statements on a 4-point Likert scale (1 = totally disagree to 4 = totally agree).

Typical statements in the pupils' PQs were "Before a math test I get very nervous", or "When I get a negative grade in a math test I would like to pack it all in" or "Some nights before a math test I find it hard to fall asleep". The four most frequently mentioned problem areas seemed to be impaired working memory due to high stress level, somatic disorders, low motivation to learn mathematics as well as low perceived self-efficacy and faith in oneself related to mathematics.

The Self-efficacy Scale Scale—Mathematics, on the other hand, includes only positive statements, such as "I can fully concentrate on the math test" or "I am highly motivated to understand and learn mathematics". The PQ was filled in at the beginning of every single group session as well as in the follow-up session by each participant, the Self-efficacy Scale—Mathematics at the first group meeting, at the very last and at the follow-up survey.

Follow-up data were collected in the second and third week of May 2014, generally known as a "hot" testing period at school. The students filled in their PQ, the Self-efficacy Scale—Mathematics for the last time, and were then invited to the Client Change Interview. In this semi-structured interview, lasting about an hour per participant, the pupils were asked about possible changes during or after the therapy, attributions to changes, helpful and non-helpful aspects of the therapy and possible suggestions for further improvement of psychodrama sessions.

The students were informed that the data collected with their PQs and their Self-efficacy Scale—Mathematics, would be analyzed and evaluated by a third person not involved either in the group sessions or in the study as a whole.

4.3 Group sessions

At the beginning of the group sessions a solid social framework was provided. This framework included a few simple rules, which were set up at the first meeting. The first rule regarded secrecy. Any disclosure made in the group would be considered privileged information. The respect for group members and for their privacy was of paramount importance. The second rule referred to the extent to which every group member would like to bring himself into play. Every member was given the right to decide individually how much of his feelings and thoughts he/she would like to share with others. Mutual respect and generally acknowledged communication rules made up the third basic rule, punctuality the fourth.

This social framework was set up in order to guarantee a safe environment in which pupils could begin their journey of personal empowerment, discovery of self-worth and expanding consciousness by using psychodrama. Especially in the first session personal exposure and risk taking of single members was to be avoided. None of the pupils had heard about psychodrama before and the idea of playing together or putting personal experiences on stage was something the participants felt rather embarrassed about.

At the beginning of each session the participants filled in their PQ, in the first and last session also their Self-efficacy Scale—Mathematics.

In the first session the pupils were given the opportunity to get to know each other as group members. This was done with the help of name games followed by some sociometric exercises, related to information about their family, age or hobbies. The last of these exercises included a visual presentation of the pupils' personal reflection on attitudes towards mathematics on a concretised 10-point line ranging from "very negative attitude towards mathematics"- 1 point marked by a chair in a corner of the room - to "totally positive attitude towards mathematics" – 10 points marked by another chair in the opposite corner. The session ended with the subjects' feedback about their immediate feelings and thoughts, first impressions and expectations for the coming sessions.

Subsequent sessions started with the pupils completing their PQs and individual statements to the group about their present states, mental and physical, and anything particular or important that may have happened during the previous week, be it something related to mathematics or not. The next stage of each session included a warm-up, which was followed by a group play, or a protagonist's play. If the session comprised a protagonist play, the group members involved in the play gave their role feedback, the others imparted the observations they had made. Then there was time for the participants' sharings, time for the exchange of similar experiences the single group members had made in their lives. The sessions always ended with a general feedback of the participants about the session and about their current state of mind.

A detailed description based on the minutes of two meetings follows in order to illustrate the work that has been done with the adolescents during the group sessions.

3rd Group Session—27th November 2013

At the beginning of the session all the participants fill in their PQs and speak about last week's experiences. While four students say that nothing particular has happened, Robert feels terribly frustrated because he just got back a maths test, very negative, grade 4 (Italian grades go from 3 to 10, 3 being totally negative and 10 excellent). An imaginary current "well-being line" related to mathematics is set up and all the pupils position themselves on a particular spot on the line from 1—very bad—to 10 extremely well. They all explain which point on the line they stand on and what they feel on this particular spot. Robert positions himself at "around 3", saying that he feels very bad there, his anger mounting. He describes the anger he felt when he saw his grade 4 on the on-line register. He says he was "so furious that he could have strangled someone". In a situation like this he would like to hit somebody or something, or he would like to do something totally crazy like riding his motorbike at breakneck speed or to race downhill on his bike. He could also pick something up and throw it against the wall. Robert chooses a participant to play the role of his anger. In the role of his anger he explores and tries out various ways that could reduce its impetus. He takes a pillow and as quick as lightening throws it on the floor, repeating this action several times. He is asked if there is anything else that could help him release his aggression. He would like to play the "downhill race". A course is established, chairs and benches marking the obstacles. Robert starts his downhill race, jumping over the obstacles and racing around. After three rounds he gives up, he feels exhausted, worn out. He watches his double repeating the actions and says "This looks silly".

When asked "What would be helpful for you now, what would do you good?" he answers "tranquility" and "time". He chooses two female participants, one of them representing "tranquility", the other "time" and places them about three meters behind his anger. In the role of "tranquility" Robert claims that he feels totally neglected and that would need much more attention. In the role of "time" he expresses his neutrality, "time" can wait, is in no hurry. Robert is rather surprised about these statements, since these qualities seem to be totally unknown to him. In the role of his anger he invites his newly discovered qualities "tranquility" and his "time" to come closer and he even turns round to look at them. In the last role reversal with his anger Robert states that he does not know the quality of these new characteristics very well, but they seem to be friendly and helpful and he would like to get to know them better. He seems calmer and more relaxed than at the beginning of the session.

After the protagonist's play the fellow-pupils give their role feedback and their sharing. They are encouraged to speak about their own experiences of anger related to mathematics or to other situations. The session is concluded enquiring about the protagonist's feelings and his present state of mind.

5th Group session—18th December 2013

First the participants fill in their PQs and inform the group about their condition in general and related to mathematics in particular. A warm-up focusing on feelings follows. The pupils are asked to walk through the room, to think first of a scene in which they felt sad, to adapt their posture, walking pace, gestures and facial expressions to this situation; scenes and situations related to other feelings, anger, joy and fear follow. Each group member briefly tells the others which scene has come to his mind. In the last situation the students are asked to remember a fearful situation they have experienced that has somehow to do with mathematics.

Caroline talks about a scene that happened 4 years ago, at the beginning of her first year of secondary education. Everything was new for her, new school, new classmates and she got back a math test and saw the mark on it, 3, totally negative. The teacher handed the paper out without any comment. She felt like crying then, but she did not, then she started feeling dizzy, everything around her was blurred. She felt sick and could not react.

The scene is put on the stage. The imaginary classroom is set up, Caroline chooses one participant to act as her double, another to play the teacher's role and a third to play her classmates. On stage, when playing the original scene, Caroline quickly feels the dizziness again and cannot understand the teacher, who just gives her back the paper, not saying a single word of encouragement. That is what she would have needed the most, a teacher comforting her, telling her that this is not the end of the world.

Caroline shows how the teacher should have reacted, how he should have comforted her, what he should have said, so that she would have felt better. The original scene is played again, this time incorporating the "corrections" proposed by Caroline. She gets the paper back, the teacher reacts supportively and encouragingly, comforts her and even offers her extra lessons. In this scene Caroline feels understood in her sorrow and does not feel dejected or low-spirited at all. In the role of her classmates she first feels terribly sorry for Caroline but unable to react, paralyzed. In the second scene when the teacher reacts sympathetically she does not feel any tension any more.

After concluding the scene the other participants give their role feedback and their sharing. All of them know the range of difficult feelings when seeing a totally negative mark on their test papers, when a teacher acts inappropriately and uncaringly, knowing that they just have to put away the feelings and come to terms with the frustration, sadness and grief.

5 Results

Full data are available for 5 participants, 2 male and 3 female pupils, all of whom have mathematics anxiety, their symptoms being present but transient. The symptoms are expected reactions to psychosocial stressors, namely solving mathematical problems, particularly in written forms of assessment, none of the participants shows any impairment in other school or social functioning.

5.1 Self-efficacy scale- mathematics

Data were collected on three different dates, on 20th November 2013, the first group session, on 12th February 2014, the tenth and last session, and in May 2014, the follow-up survey. In general the analysis of the data collected with this measuring instrument does not show clear trends or significant changes in the pupils' attitudes, feelings or behavior. Therefore only two exemplary graphs will be shown to illustrate the data of the Self-efficacy Scale—Mathematics.

The scores of the whole group regarding the pupils' motivation towards mathematics expressed by statement 8 "My motivation to understand and study mathematics is great" are represented in the graph below. It shows that the subjects have differently assessed their motivation at the three points of data collection, but no clear trend can be recorded (Fig. 1).

The next graph shows the scores related to statement 10 "If a mathematical problem arises, I can solve it by myself". This statement focuses on the pupils' rating of their ability to come to terms with mathematical problems. None of participants

Fig. 1 Trend motivation Statement 8

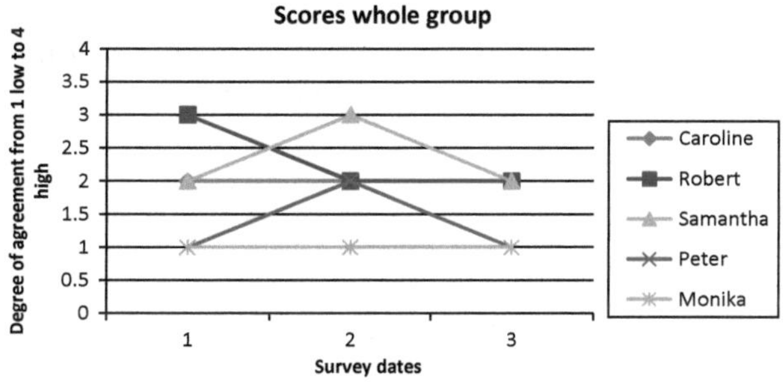

Fig. 2 Trend self-efficacy – faith in oneself Statement 10

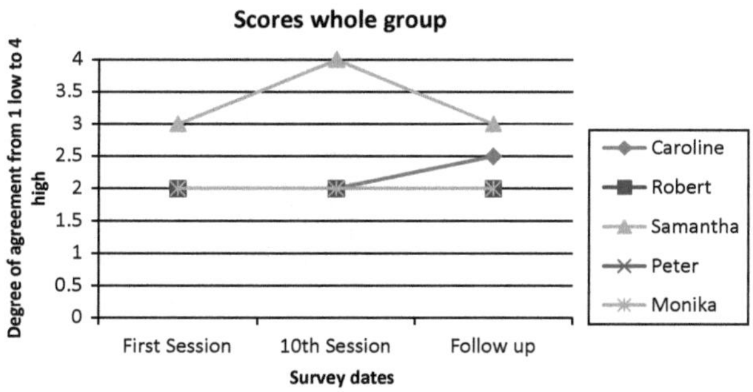

seems to feel that he has been able to increase his trust in himself related to the solution of mathematical problems. Only one pupil's scores have increased by 1 point at the 2nd measuring period but have decreased again in the follow-up survey (Fig. 2).

5.2 Personal questionnaire

In the PQs the pupils have made from 7 to 10 statements related to their problems connected with mathematics. The first data were recorded on 20th November 2013, further data followed weekly or whenever a group session was held until the end of the group sessions on 12th February 2014. Follow-up data were collected from 15th to 25th May, shortly before the Client Change Interview.

Since only one participant was present at the total number of group sessions, one attended only 6 sessions and others from 7 to 9, the number of measuring points varies. The analyses of the data collected by the PQ shows that no single problem stated in any of the participants' questionnaires has remained unaltered over the treatment period, some changes, even if small ones, can be found in all of them.

The statements that show only slight changes from the beginning of the group sessions to the follow-up survey, which make up the majority, will not be presented. The following graphs show considerable differences between the pupils' self-assessment recorded on the first session and the follow-up survey. The statements regard effects of psychodrama training on self-efficacy or belief in oneself, on somatic and sleep disorder, on working memory and on motivation.

Fig. 3 self-efficacy PQ Statement 7

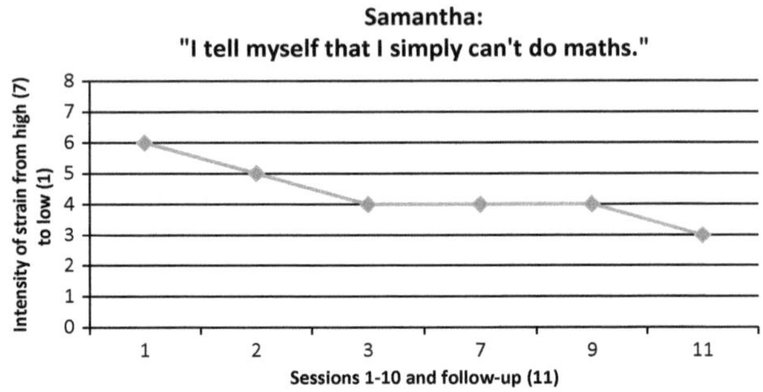

Fig. 4 Self-efficacy PQ Statement 9

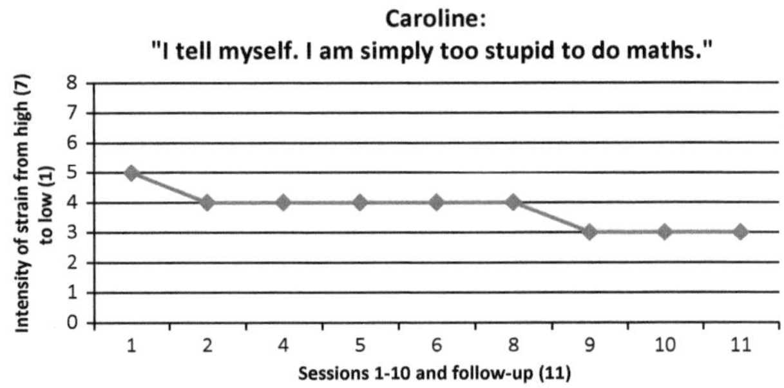

The following two graphs show the scores of Samantha and Caroline related to the evaluation of their self-efficacy in mathematics or their ability to deal with mathematical problems (Fig. 3, 4).

Both these graphs show significant changes in the pupils' perceived self-efficacy or trust in themselves. The scores related to the intensity of strain show a decrease of 3 points in one graph and of 2 points in the other.

In the next two graphs the changes recorded in the PQs of Samantha and Robert related to somatic and sleep disorders are shown. In the first, the stress caused by difficulties in falling asleep and by restless sleep is reduced by 2 points. In the second Robert, who mentioned strain because of a headache in combination with a math test, does not seem to consider this problem as seriously as before the psychodrama training (Fig. 5, 6).

The following graphs show the changes in the pupils' PQs related to the functioning of their working memory. In the course of the psychodrama group sessions the scores of these two pupils, mentioning first the risk of blackouts and second the difficulty to control impulses, show a noteworthy decrease from 5 to 3 points and from 5 to 2 points, respectively (Fig. 7, 8).

The following two graphs show the results of two pupils regarding their motivation to study mathematics. Both students seem to find it easier to study math or to be able to better cope with negative grades in this subject after the psychodrama group sessions. Samantha shows a decrease in the intensity of strain related to her motivation from 6 to 3 points, the other pupil's scores decrease from 5 to 2 regarding his negative perception of being motivated to study math (Fig. 9, 10).

Fig. 5 Sleep disorder PQ Statement 4

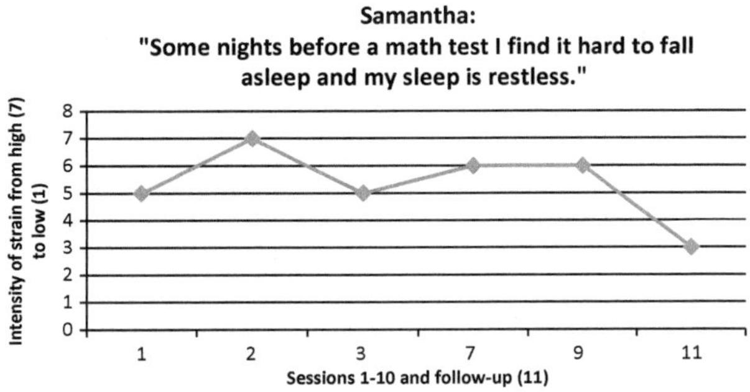

Fig. 6 Somatic disorder PQ Statement 4

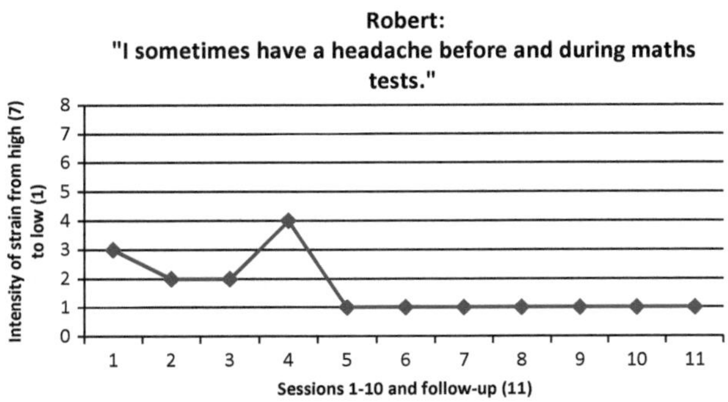

Fig. 7 Working memory PQ Statement 6

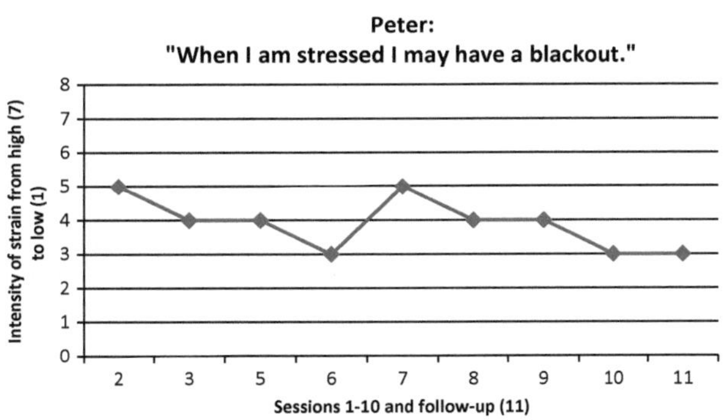

5.3 Client change interview

The Client Change Interview was conducted with the students in mid-May 2014. In the interviews the students all stated that the psychodrama group sessions had had some positive effects. The first positive effect mentioned was regarding their improved performance in mathematics, then the different attitude to mathematics, next their thoughts related to the subject and the reduced stress level experienced when sitting a mathematics exam.

All the participants reported that their grades had improved, some considerably. One participant, who had always got positive grades, but suffered from blackouts, stated that no blackout had occurred since the beginning of the sessions.

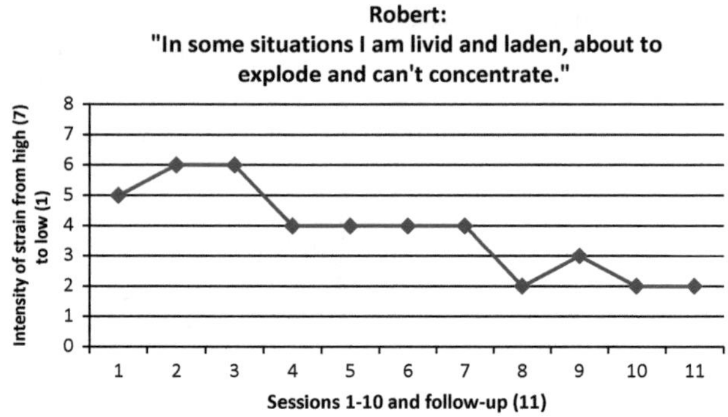

Fig. 8 Working memory PQ Statement 7

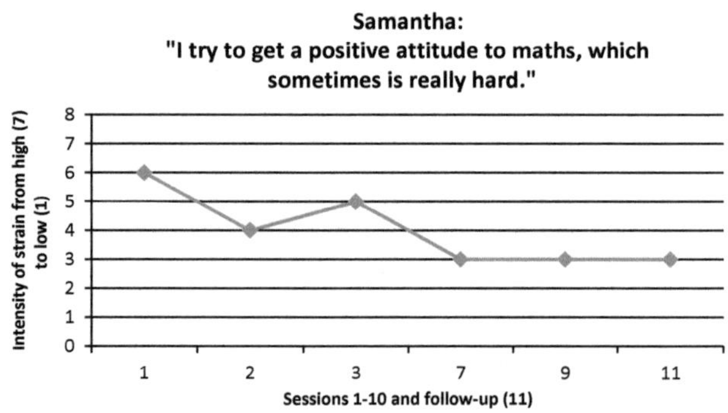

Fig. 9 Motivation PP Statement 1

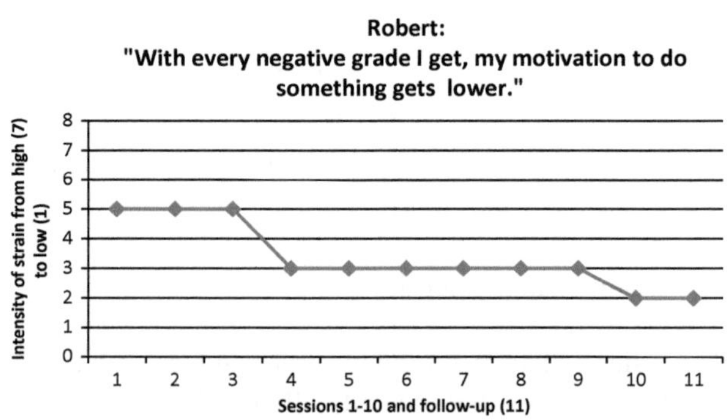

Fig. 10 Motivation PQ Statement 9

Regarding motivation to learn mathematics only one student convincingly declared that this goal had been reached. None of the other participants said that the psychodrama training had fundamentally changed their motivation to study mathematics, however, all the students reported that some changes in their attitude towards mathematics had occurred. They had the impression that the constant confrontation with their problems regarding mathematics seemed to have led to a new awareness and a more relaxed way of dealing with mathematics in general and that the pressure or the fear often felt before tests had become less. All the participants reported that negative and worrisome thoughts about tests, causing great distress before the psychodrama training had become less frequent now.

When asked about the reasons for these changes, four pupils said that the fact that they had got the opportunity to talk about their problem so openly with other people had been very helpful. They had become aware that others shared their difficulties.

None of the subjects could think of any important events in their private life, positive experiences, such as happy new relationships that could have been the cause of changes, or negative experiences, like the breaking-up of relationships or the loss of something or somebody, that could have contributed to the fact that they could not have made full use of the psychodrama training, respectively.

While two participants think that the changes could have occurred also without the psychodrama group sessions, three of them were convinced that without psychodrama the changes would not have happened. All of them confirmed that the changes were very important to them, one pupil considered them as extremely important.

When asked about the personal traits that may have helped the pupils make the changes, multiple answers were "will power", "patience", "positive thoughts", "open-mindedness" and "flexibility".

The most frequent answers to the question about non-helpful aspects of the psychodrama group training listed by the participants focused on framework conditions, especially limited time resources and school stress.

6 Discussion

This study is a modest contribution to the developing literature in adolescent psychodrama research. The pupils taking part in this study are functioning within the normal range therefore large effect sizes cannot be expected.

Apart from this, the study has several limitations, the first being the small experimental group size (5 participants). Another limitation is the low number of group sessions. 10 group sessions can hardly generate significant changes in all the participants' problem areas. A further weakness consists in the fact that only one follow-up survey was made. In this way it was not possible to establish the possible long-term effects of group participation benefits.

Another weak point is using the quantitative instrument of the Self-efficacy Scale—Mathematics used in this work. The questionnaire, specifically created especially for this work, lacks scientific validation and has not been able to show any significant changes in the pupils' problem areas. This may in part be due to the fact that on a 4-point Likert scale participants tend to choose central scores rather than scores on the extremes, in part it may be explained by the fact that pupils are definitely not used to thinking positively when assessing their mathematics abilities.

The statements made by the participants during the Client Change Interview must be considered with particular care. Firstly, because they may tend to please the person conducting the research, in this case probably even more since I am a teacher at the school; secondly, because they may have found it more appropriate to speak about positive aspects to please the interviewer, rather than pointing out negative aspects.

The analyses of the data collected with the PQs and the statements made in the Client Change Interview mostly correspond. A comparison of the data collected with the Self-efficacy Scale—Mathematics and the PQs shows that the results do not correspond, in particular as far as motivation is regarded. While in the Self-efficacy Scale—Mathematics no increase in the motivation can be noticed, in the PQs two students show a remarkable change in their attitude towards the subject.

The findings of the present work in relation to the research questions mentioned before can be summed up as follows.

As far as somatic problems, such as headache and sleep disorder, are concerned, the analyses of the PQs of two pupils shows that the intensity of strain has decreased from 3 to 1 and from 5 to 3 respectively, which can be considered significant changes.

The next research question was related to the effectiveness of psychodrama group therapy related to a reduction of the pupils' stress level, which would have positive effects on their working memory. The scores of the participant who mentioned the risk of blackouts in test situations in his PQ decreased from 5 to 3, another significant change. In the Client Change Interview he even said that no such blackout had occurred in the course of this school year.

Another pupil's scores, who according to statement 7 of his Personal Problem Questionnaire "feels livid and laden, about to explode", show a decrease of the stress level from 5 to 2. This change may be due to the protagonist play of this particular participant focusing on his aggression when getting a negative mark in a math test.

As far as positive effects of psychodrama group sessions on the pupils' motivation are concerned, two of them seem to have managed to increase their motivation of studying mathematics.

Statements in the PQs regarding the participants' self-efficacy in mathematics resulting in greater trust in their own ability were mentioned by two students. Both seem to have been able to reduce their lack of confidence and to increase their perceived self-efficacy.

Naturally other unknown factors not mentioned or considered by the participants may have influenced the outcomes of the pupils' scores in the PQs.

Although several improvements would be needed in future studies on the effectiveness of psychodrama on pupils with mathematics anxiety the results based on the data at hand are encouraging. The changes emerging from the PQs and the statements made in the Client Change Interview seem to support the initial hypotheses that psychodrama group sessions can have positive effects on the participants' motivation and on their physical well-being. Moreover, they seem to be able to enhance their self-efficacy related to mathematics and to improve their mathematics performance by reducing their stress levels.

The changes shown in the pupils' PQs and stated in the interviews suggest that the group therapy provided a medium in which the participants could expose their feelings, could share their partly traumatic early experiences with mathematics with other students. Through the frequent sharing given by other group members the participants definitely got the feeling that they were not alone with their specific problem, mathematics anxiety.

It can be assumed that re-enacting an stressful life experience has brought the pupils in contact with painful emotions, and this seems to be a crucial step to make corrective emotional experiences (Gassmann and Grawe 2006). Especially the technique of role reversal, of stepping into the role of someone else or into an element or quality unknown so far, seems to have been important for self-integration and for interpersonal socialization.

The representation of fantasies and real experiences on the psychodramatic stage seems to have offered them the opportunity to re-live and re-experience an unpleasant event in their life, offering a "correction" of the experience in the surplus reality. Through psychodrama their repeated worrisome thoughts, their fearful images and pictures, have been rendered alterable (Fürst 2004, p. 245).

Apart from these changes another goal of the study was reached, namely to enable the participants to gain insight in their personal problems and to get fully aware of them. During the group sessions, as some of them pointed out also in the Client Change Interview, they certainly became more aware of their strengths and weaknesses, in other words, they have got to know themselves better. In the Client Change Interview the pupils also stated that the feedback they got from their fellow-students improved their awareness of not seeing events, feelings and thoughts objectively and of not recognizing their own strengths. Sometimes this may have been painful, but it seems to have initiated a process of reflection, which allows the pupils to work on their behavioral weaknesses.

Another aim may have been achieved with this study. The presence of mathematics anxiety in classrooms and the variety of problems it causes can definitely be confirmed. Every mathematics teacher that recognizes this problem may get more and more aware of the influence of this specific anxiety on the pupils' mathematics performance. While the group sessions were being held I talked to the two mathematics teachers who were most helpful when recruiting pupils. By taking their pupils' anxiety seriously and offering them help they made a first step towards change. In the course of the treatment both teachers confirmed that some pupils' attitude towards mathematics had changed and that their performance had started to improve. Immordino-Yang and Damasio (2007, p. 9) have got to the heart of the issue stating "When we educators fail to appreciate the importance of students' emotions, we fail to appreciate a critical force in students' learning".

7 Outlook

The present study can be considered an exploratory case study showing the effects of psychodrama on adolescents with mathematics anxiety. The findings of this work highlight the need for further research in this field to clarify the conditions under which psychodrama group sessions are maximally effective. More refined measuring instruments should be developed and adopted in order to get more accordant results.

The number of subjects taking part in the group sessions should be increased, in this way the collected data would become more meaningful. More group sessions focusing on the participants' specific problems and experiences with mathematics could generate additional material for analyses.

In conclusion, it can be said that more time, more group sessions and a higher number of participants, would be needed to generate significant changes in deep-rooted convictions of the pupils' negative beliefs related to mathematics.

References

American Psychiatric Association (1994). *Diagnostic and statistical manual of mental disorders* (4th ed.). Washington, DC: American Psychiatric Association.

Ashcraft, M. (2002). Math anxiety: Personal, educational, and cognitive consequences. *Directions in Psychological Science, 11*, 181–185.

Ashcraft, M., & Kirk, E. (2001). The relationships among working memory, math anxiety, and performance. *Journal of Experimental Psychology: General, 130*(2), 224–237.

Ashcraft, M., & Krause, J. (2007). Working memory, math performance, and math anxiety. *Psychonomic Bulletin & Review, 3*(2), 243–248.

Ashcraft, M., & Moore, A. (2009). Mathematics anxiety and the affective drop in performance. *Journal of Psychoeducational Assessment, 27*, 197–205.

Ashcraft, M. H., & Ridley, K. S. (2005). Math anxiety and its cognitive consequences: A tutorial review. In: J. Campbell (Ed.): *The handbook of mathematical cognition* (pp. 315–327). New York: Psychology Press.

Beilock, S., Gunderson, E., Ramirez, G., & Levine, S. (2010). Female teachers' math anxiety affects girls' math achievement. *Proceedings of the National Academy of Sciences, 107*, 1860–1863.

Elliott, R., & Shapiro, D. (1999). *Simplified personal questionnaire procedure*. Toledo: University of Toledo.

Elliott, R., Slatick, E., & Urman, M. (2003). Qualitative change process research on psychotherapy: Alternative strategies. In J. Frommer & D. Rennie (Eds.), *The methodology of qualitative psychotherapy research*. Lengerich: Pabst Science Publishers.

Eyseneck, M., & Calvo, M. (1992). Anxiety and performance: The processing efficiency theory. *Cognition and Emotion, 6*, 409–434.

Fürst, J., Ottomeyer, K., & Pruckner, H. (Eds.). (2004). *Psychodramatherapie*. Wien: Facultas Verlag.

Gassmann, D., & Grawe, K. (2006). General change mechanisms: The relation between problem activation and resource activation in successful and unsuccessful therapeutic interactions. *Clinical Psychology and Psychotherapy, 13*, 1–11.

Gough, M. (1954). Mathemaphobia: Causes and treatment. *The Clearing House, 28*(5), 290–294.

Gunderson, E., Ramirez, G., Levine, S., & Beilock, S. (2012). The role of parents and teachers in the development of gender-related math attitudes. *Sex Roles, 66*, 153–166.

Hembree, R. (1990). The nature, effect and relief of mathematics anxiety. *Journal for Research in Mathematics Education, 21*, 33–46.

Hopko, D., Ashcraft, M., Gute, J., Ruggiero, K., & Lewis, C. (1998). Mathematics anxiety and working memory: Support for the existence of a deficient inhibition mechanism. *Journal of Anxiety Disorders, 12*(4), 343–355.

Hunt, G. E. (1985). Math anxiety – where do we go from here? *Focus on Learning Problems in Mathematics, 7*(2), 29–40.

Immordino-Yang, H., & Damasio, A. (2007). We feel, therefore we learn: The relevance of affective and social neuroscience to education. *Mind, Brain, and Education, 1*(1), 3–10.

Liebert, R., & Morris, L. (1967). Cognitive and emotional components of test anxiety: A distinction and some initial data. *Psychological Reports, 20*, 975–978.

Lyons, I., & Beilock, S. (2012) When Math Hurts: Math Anxiety Predicts Pain Network Activation in Anticipation of Doing Math. http://www.plosone.org/article/info:doi/10.1371/journal.pone.0048076. Accessed 14 April 2014.

Ma, X. (1999). A meta-analysis of the relationship between anxiety toward mathematics and achievement in mathematics. *Journal for Research in Mathematics Education, 30*, 520–541.

Maloney, E., Ansari, D., & Fugelsang, J. (2010). The effect of mathematics anxiety on the processing of numerical magnitude. *Quarterly Journal of Experimental Psychology, 64*, 10–16.

Moreno, J. L. (1946). *Psychodrama* (Vol. I. p. xii). New York: Beacon House.

Moreno, J. L., & Moreno, Z. (1955). Discovery of the spontaneous man with special emphasis upon the technique of role reversal. *Group Psychotherapy, 8, 103–129.* (Reprinted in 1959, Psychodrama, Vol. 2, New York: Beacon House, 135–158.).

Richardson, F., & Suinn, R. (1972). The mathematics anxiety rating scale: Psychometric data. *Journal of Counseling Psychology, 19*(6), 551–554.

Rubinstein, O., & Tannock, R. (2010). Mathematics anxiety in children with developmental dyscalculia. *Behavioral and Brain Functions,6: 46.* http://www.ncbi.nlm.nih.gov/pmc/articles/PMC2913999/. Accessed 15 May 2014.

Schwarzer, R., & Jerusalem, M. (1999). *Skalen zur Erfassung von Lehrer- und Schülermerkmalen. Dokumentation der psychometrischen Verfahren im Rahmen der Wissenschaftlichen Begleitung des Modellversuchs Selbstwirksame Schulen.* Berlin: Freie Universität.

Yeo, K. (2004). Do high ability students have mathematics anxiety? *Journal of Science and Mathematics Education in S.E. Asia, 27*(2), 135–152.

Gstrein Dorothea, 1958, Psychologist, Psychodramatist, Teacher of English at “Fachoberschule für Tourismus und Biotechnologie – Marie Curie” Merano

Z Psychodrama Soziometr (2016) (Suppl) 15:217–233
DOI 10.1007/s11620-015-0304-y

HAUPTBEITRÄGE

Zeitschrift für Psychodrama und Soziometrie

Wirksamkeitsuntersuchung zur Selbstsupervision mit Rollentausch unter Angehörigen helfender Berufe

Zsuzsa Marlok · Gábor Török · Tamás Martos · Czigány László

Online publiziert: 17. Dezember 2015

Zusammenfassung In der vorliegenden Studie untersuchen wir die Wirksamkeit der Technik der Selbstsupervision mit Rollentausch im Sinne von R. Krüger. Eine zentrale Frage war, wie sich diese Selbstsupervision auf die Beziehung des oder der HelferIn zum oder zur KlientIn auswirkt. Wir haben die Selbstsupervision mit Rollentausch in einer experimentellen Wirksamkeitsuntersuchung in ihren Auswirkungen mit einer auf dem Schreibparadigma von Pennebaker beruhenden Selbstsupervisionstechnik verglichen, um zu prüfen, ob der Rollentausch im Kontext der Selbstsupervision einen besonderen Gewinn aufweisen kann.

Nach den Ergebnissen der Untersuchung haben beide Techniken zur Abnahme der Gefühle von emotionaler Belastung und Blockade beigetragen. Bei der Selbstsupervision mit Rollentausch verbesserte sich aber die Fähigkeit, sich dem oder der KlientIn zuzuwenden, ihn oder sie wirklich hilfreich zu beraten, signifikant stärker.

Schlüsselwörter Psychodrama · Selbstsupervision · Rollentausch · Expressives Schreiben · Wirksamkeitsuntersuchung

Selbstsupervision mit Rollentausch wird allein durchgeführt, keine andere Person, kein Hilfs-Ich ist anwesend, deswegen sollte definitonsgemäß der Begriff Rollenwechsel benutzt werden. Es handelt sich dabei um ein klassisches monodramatisches Vorgehen. Da aber in der Selbstsupervision zahlreiche, sequentielle Rollenwechsel vorgenommen werden, um damit die Beziehung zwischen SupervisandIn und KlientIn deutlich ins Erleben zu bringen, wird diese Form der Selbstsupervision idelatypisch von den SupervisandInnen wie ein Rollentausch erlebt.

Der Einfachheit halber benutzen wir in der Studie den Begriff KlientIn, der sowohl für einen oder eine EinzelklientIn in einer helfenden oder therapeutischen Beziehung als auch für ein Psychodramagruppenmitglied stehen kann.

Dr. Zs. Marlok, PhD (✉) · Dr. G. Török, PhD · T. Martos, PhD · C. László
Semmelweis Egyetem Egészségügyi Közszolgálati Kar Mentálhigiéné Intézet,
1428 Pf.: 370, Budapest, Ungarn
E-Mail: marlok.zsuzsa@public.semmelweis.univ.hu;
zsmarlok@gmail.com

Efficacy study on self-supervision with role-reversal among helping professionals

Abstract In the present study we tested the efficacy of the technique of 'self supervision with role reversal' according to R. Krüger. The key question was whether this kind of self supervision has an effect on the relationship of a helper with her client. In an experimental efficacy study we compared the effect of two self supervision techniques: the SSRR technique and a version of the writing paradigm of Pennebaker. We sought to investigate whether role reversal can be of added value in the context of self supervision.

Results showed that the use of both techniques contributed to decreased feeling of emotional overload and blockades in the helper. Moreover, SSRR produced a significant higher increase in the capacity of turning towards the clients and to advise them in a helpful manner.

Keywords Psychodrama · Self supervision · Role reversal · Expressive writing · Efficacy study

1 Einleitung – über uns

Als Mitglieder des AutorInnenteams arbeiten wir am Institut für Mentalhygiene der Semmelweis-Universität Budapest[1]. Das Institut bietet Angehörigen helfender Berufe (ÄrztInnen, LehrerInnen, SozialarbeiterInnen, PfarrerInnen, Ordensleuten, KindergärtnerInnen, HeilpädagogInnen usw.) einen postgradualen Weiterbildungsstudiengang in Mentalhygiene[2] sowie in Seelsorge, und einen MA-Studiengang in Sozialarbeit sowie in Familientherapie an. Als Lehrende leiten wir unter anderem zum Pflichtstudium gehörende Selbsterfahrungs-Psychodramagruppen sowie Seminare zum Helfenden Gespräch nach Rogers (Faber und van der Schoot 1965). Als PsychologInnen, Fachleute für Mentalhygiene, bzw. SeelsorgerInnen bieten wir KlientInnen im Einzelsetting helfende Gespräche an, z. B. in der Seelsorge und Lebensberatung. Darüber hinaus sind wir in unserem Institut auch an Forschungsprojekten beteiligt.

Die Selbstsupervision ist für jeden Bereich unserer Arbeit von Relevanz, deswegen sind wir an deren Anwendung und Erforschung als PsychodramaleiterInnen, Lehrende und auch als HelferInnen interessiert.

Reinhard Krüger kommt auf Einladung von Teodóra Tomcsányi, der Gründerin unseres Instituts, Psychodrama-Psychotherapeutin und -ausbilderin, seit 2009 zweimal pro Jahr nach Budapest, um die Mitarbeitenden des Instituts in Anwendung von Psychodrama-Techniken im Einzel- und Gruppensetting weiterzubilden. Im Rahmen dieses Curriculums haben wir den ‚fiktiven'[3] psychodramatischen Dialog mit Rollentausch zur Selbstsupervision kennenlernen können.

Die Technik hat sofort unser Interesse geweckt. Wir hatten das Gefühl, ein effektives Instrument zur Verbesserung unserer Arbeit in die Hand bekommen zu haben. Das ist uns zum Teil daher so wichtig, weil wir aufgrund bestimmter Umstände nur in großen Abständen Einzel- und/oder Gruppensupervision wahrnehmen können. Das regelmäßige Treffen mit KlientInnen/Gruppenmitgliedern macht es aber notwendig, den Grund für mögliche Blockaden, persönliche Betroffenheiten und emotionale Belastungen sowie für die Übertragungs- und Gegenübertragungsprozesse möglichst schnell zu verstehen. Ausgehend von dieser Erfahrung haben wir die Wirksamkeitsuntersuchung der Selbstsupervision mit Rollentausch in Angriff genommen. Es ist uns erst später bewusst geworden, dass dadurch die Wirksamkeit von Rollentausch als einer Psychodrama-Grundtechnik per se – losgelöst vom multifaktoriellen System von Psychodrama – in den Fokus unserer Aufmerksamkeit geraten ist.

2 Begriffsklärung – Selbstsupervision

Vor der Darstellung der Untersuchung möchten wir zuerst kurz darauf eingehen, wie sich die Selbstsupervision als selbstständige Methode zu den allgemein bekannten Supervisionsformen (Einzelsupervision, Gruppensupervision) verhält. Zum Begriff der Selbstsupervision kann mit Recht die Frage gestellt werden, ob Supervision ohne Supervisor In und/oder Gruppe überhaupt möglich ist, weil die Außensicht als wesentliches Element der Supervision fehlt.

Wir verstehen Selbstsupervision als ein Reflexionsinstrument, bei dem nicht eine andere Person (der oder die SupervisorIn) oder die Gruppe den methodischen Rahmen zum Verstehen und Überwinden der Blockade sowie zum Perspektivenwechsel vorgibt. Vielmehr tritt die Person selbst, die den Fall und das Problem „bringt", allein in einen strukturierten und aus vorgegebenen Schritten bestehenden Prozess ein. Deshalb wird diese allein ausführbare systematische Tätigkeit zur Auflösung von inneren Blockaden als Selbstsupervision bezeichnet.

Wie bereits erwähnt, ist der Begriff und die Psychodrama-Methodik des ‚fiktiven' psychodramatischen Dialogs mit Rollentausch zur Selbstsupervision, im weiteren Selbstsupervision mit Rollentausch[4] (SmR) genannt, mit dem Namen des deutschen Psychotherapeuten Reinhard Krüger verbunden (Krüger 2010; 2015). Diese Methode kann die traditionelle Praxis von Supervision erweitern. Sie zielt ab auf die Auflösung innerer Blockaden in der therapeutischen, psychodramatischen und helfenden Arbeit, auf die Wiedererlangung und Effektivitätssteigerung der beruflichen Handlungsfähigkeit, auf die Vorbeugung von Überbelastung und auf die Bewahrung der seelischen Gesundheit des Helfers oder der HelferIn – dies sind Ziele, die auch in anderen Supervisionsformen grundlegend sind.

Die Selbstsupervision ersetzt jedoch nicht die Anwendung der üblichen Supervision mit Hilfe eines oder einer SupervisorIn. Aber wir sind der Ansicht – und werden es anhand der von uns ermittelten empirischen Ergebnisse nachstehend nachweisen –, dass die Selbstsupervision bei der Weiterbegleitung von KlientInnen und bei der emotionalen Entlastung der HelferInnen eine Hilfe darstellen kann. In einzelnen Fällen kann sie allein zu einer ausreichenden Lösung führen, in anderen Fällen kann sie bei der Vorbereitung der Einzel- oder Gruppensupervision, bei einer deutlicheren Formulierung der Fragen oder genaueren Beschreibung der inneren Blockade eine wichtige Rolle spielen.

Im Folgenden stellen wir kurz das Wesen der von uns untersuchten Selbstsupervision mit Rollentausch und die in der empirischen Untersuchung als Kontrollverfahren zur SmR eingesetzte, auf dem Schreibparadigma von Pennebaker („Writing Paradigm", Pennebaker 1997), beruhende Selbstreflexionstechnik, das Expressive Schreiben[5], dar.

2.1 Selbstsupervision mit Rollentausch

Die SmR ist ein ‚fiktiver' psychodramatischer Dialog mit zahlreichen, aufeinanderfolgenden Rollenwechseln. Er kann nach Krüger (2010; 2015) zum Zweck der Selbstsupervision in der Arbeit mit KlientInnen oder auch zur Instandhaltung und Bewahrung der seelischen Gesundheit eingesetzt werden.

Das ‚fiktive' Gespräch mit ständigem Rollenwechsel nimmt in etwa 15–20 min in Anspruch. Es ist wichtig, dass man während der Arbeit ungestört allein ist. Das Ziel ist nicht, ein therapeutisches Gespräch mit dem oder der jeweiligen KlientIn zu führen. Man soll sich in der Begegnung nicht als HelferIn, sondern als „fühlender Mensch" verhalten, der seinen Gefühlen und Gedanken freien Lauf lässt, und über die Realität hinaus alles laut sagt, was er dem oder der KlientIn gegenüber fühlt oder über ihn oder sie denkt. Es ist dabei wichtig, nicht auf den oder die KlientIn Rücksicht zu nehmen, sondern Gefühle wie die Wut, Ohnmacht, Frust, Traurigkeit, usw. loszuwerden. In der Rolle des Klienten oder der Klientin soll man zuerst das in der eigenen Rolle als HelferIn Gesagte innerlich aufnehmen und dann aus der KlientInrolle heraus über die Realität hinaus frei und ohne Kontrolle darauf reagieren.

Bei der Selbstsupervision ist der häufige Rollenwechsel von großer Bedeutung, der so lange wiederholt werden sollte, bis man nichts mehr zu sagen hat. Am Ende des Gesprächs soll man über das Gesagte nachdenken und darum bemüht sein, das Geschehene zu verstehen. Mithilfe dieser Arbeit kann man die angesammelten bedrückenden Gefühlen loswerden und durch die daraus resultierende innere Freiheit, die Handlungsfähigkeit und Neugier auf den oder die KlientIn zurückgewinnen. Diese Befreiung kann schon allein dadurch erfolgen, dass der oder die HelferIn in der Klientenrolle am eigenen Körper spürt, dass der oder die KlientIn einfach nicht versteht, was der oder die HelferIn will, und bloß den Wunsch hat, in seinem oder ihrem Leiden ernst genommen zu werden.

Es ist äußerst wichtig, nach der SmR das dabei Erlebte bewusst zu machen. Da jede Erkenntnis, auch die kleinste und auf den ersten Blick scheinbar bedeutungslose Idee wichtig sein kann, ist es sinnvoll, alles nach dem Abschluss der Arbeit zu notieren. Nach Krügers Empfehlung kann die SmR bei jeder Art Beziehungsblockade – bei Spannungen in der Partnerschaft oder am Arbeitsplatz – sowie zur Vorbereitung von Gruppensupervision eingesetzt werden.

Der Rollentausch scheint zwar eine sehr einfache Technik zu sein, ist aber in der Tat ein hoch komplexes Verfahren. Durch den äußeren Wechsel auf den Stuhl des Konfliktpartners tritt man anders als im bloßen Denken jeweils ganz in die innere Welt des anderen ein, und wechselt dann durch einen erneuten Rollenwechsel wieder zurück in die eigene Rolle, ganz zurück in die eigene Welt. Dadurch erkennt man über sein vorheriges Wissen hinaus klarer von innen her die innere Wirklichkeit seines Konfliktpartners, und aber auch seine eigene Wirklichkeit.

2.2 Selbstsupervision durch Expressives Schreiben

Die als Kontrollverfahren angewandte Technik, die unseres Erachtens auch zur Selbstsupervision eingesetzt werden kann, bedient sich dem Schreibparadigma von Pennebaker (1997), das im Wesentlichen ein automatisches, unkontrolliertes Schreiben bedeutet. Es kann einmal, aber auch an mehreren aufeinander folgenden Tagen in einem Zeitrahmen von 15–20 min erfolgen. Beim sog. Expressiven Schreiben (Pennebaker 2004; Pennebaker und Chung 2011) soll nicht auf Rechtschreibung, Satzbau oder Grammatik geachtet werden, das Schreiben selbst ist das Ziel. Man soll den Gefühlen und Gedanken freien Lauf lassen und sie zu Papier bringen, sogar auch mehrmals in der fürs Schreiben vorgesehenen Zeiteinheit.

Nach J. W. Pennebaker wirken die schriftlich ausgedrückten Gefühle und Gedanken ihrerseits auf uns zurück. Schreiben ist eine Form von Selbstausdruck, und kann sich in emotional belastenden Situationen und bei der Verarbeitung schmerzvoller Erinnerungen und traumatischer Lebensereignisse heilend auswirken. Als Sozialpädagoge und Forscher an der Universität Texas untersucht er seit Jahrzehnten die Auswirkungen des Selbstausdrucks auf die Gesundheit. Im Fokus seiner Untersuchungen steht die Analyse der Effekte ehrlichen Redens und Schreibens, die zur Auflösung der inneren Gehemmtheit führen und dadurch heilende Auswirkungen entfalten können. Pennebaker hat in zahlreichen Bereichen den Nutzen und das Selbstheilungspotenzial des Mitteilens von persönlichen Geschichten aufgedeckt. Seine zentrale Ausgangsthese ist es, dass die Hemmung des freien Ausdrucks von Gefühlen zu erlebten Lebensereignissen und die daraus resultierende Unabgeschlossenheit unserer Geschichten der Gesundheit schaden. „Schweigen" ist eine innere physische Arbeit, die einen Stressfaktor darstellen kann – umso mehr, je mehr bedrückende Gefühle wir erleben. Pennebaker kam zu dem Schluss, dass uns die Sprache durch ihre systematisierende Kraft in emotional belastenden Situationen zur Hilfe kommen kann, da sich durch freies Schreiben oder Erzählen unsere Erlebnisse zu kohärenten Geschichten ausgestalten, wodurch wiederum Auflösung, Sinngebung und Neuorientierung erzielt werden. Nach den Ergebnissen seiner Untersuchungen kann diese Methode unabhängig von der Intensität der Erlebnisse zur Verarbeitung jeder unabgeschlossenen und emotional bewegenden Situation benutzt werden. Als Psychologe und Therapeut betont er freilich, dass in vielen Fällen diese Art auf Selbstausdruck basierte „selbstständige Arbeit" nur ein Teil eines komplexen, z. B. therapeutischen Prozesses sein kann, in dem Hemmungen aufgelöst und emotional belastende Situationen verarbeitbar werden. Sie kann aber nach seiner Empfehlung als leicht zugängliches und anwendbares Verfahren sowohl in der helfenden oder therapeutischen Arbeit als auch außerhalb dieser Settings allein eingesetzt werden.

3 Die Untersuchung

3.1 Die Ausgangshypothese

Eine zentrale Hypothese unserer Untersuchung ist es, dass die SmR den oder die HelferIn emotional entlasten kann, d. h. die Intensität der dem oder der KlientIn gegenüber erlebten belastenden Gefühle – wie z. B. Wut, Ohnmacht, Kraftlosigkeit – mildern kann. Wir nahmen ferner an, dass über die emotionale Entlastung hinaus auch die kognitive Einsicht der Helfenden gesteigert wird, was wiederum zu einem besseren Verstehen der Gründe für die innere Blockade führen und dadurch zu deren Auflösung beitragen kann. Wir unterscheiden dabei drei Ebenen der kognitiven Einsicht:

Die HelferInnen können erstens einen tieferen Einblick in die inneren Geschehnisse und Reaktionsmotive der KlientInnen bekommen, zweitens ihre blockierten Funktionsweisen tiefer verstehen und drittens einen besseren Überblick über die Dynamik der HelferIn-KlientIn-Beziehung sowie über deren Übertragungs- und Gegenübertragungskomponente gewinnen.

3.2 Methodik – Experiment

Die Untersuchung wurde in einer randomisierten Versuchsanordnung unter Teilnahme einer Versuchsgruppe und einer Kontrollgruppe durchgeführt. Zur Untersuchung der Wirksamkeit der SmR haben wir anhand der Gemeinsamkeiten und Differenzen der zwei Techniken das SES als Kontrollverfahren geeignet gefunden. Beide Techniken können selbstständig in Einzelarbeit als Selbstreflexionstechnik angewandt werden, was den experimentellen Vergleich ermöglichte.

3.3 Die untersuchte Population

Zur Studienteilnahme wurden AbsolventInnen und Studierende der Weiterbildungsstudiengänge für Mentalhygiene (HelferInnen aus unterschiedlichen Bereichen), für Seelsorge und des Masterstudienganges für Sozialarbeit sowie GruppenleiterInnen des Ungarischen Psychodramavereins eingeladen. Im Aufruf zur Teilnahme an der Untersuchung wurden die Teilnehmenden darüber informiert, dass dabei eine in Ungarn bisher unbekannte, ohne Supervisionsgruppe und SupervisorIn allein ausführbare, zur inneren Reflexion dienende Supervisionstechnik auf ihre Wirksamkeit hin geprüft wird. Sie wurden ferner auch darüber informiert, dass diese Methode im Lichte der auf diese Weise gewonnenen Ergebnisse in unsere Weiterbildungsstudiengänge eingeführt und für Angehörige helfender Berufe in Ungarn bekannt und zugänglich gemacht wird.

Der Aufruf wurde per E-Mail und auf Flyern auf der vom Institut veranstalteten Jahresfachtagung bekanntgegeben und hat so annähernd 300 Personen erreicht.

Voraussetzung für die Studienteilnahme war eine aktuell vorhandene emotional belastende Beziehung – mit einem oder einer EinzelklientIn oder einem Psychodramagruppenmitglied. Die Untersuchung wurde auch auf HelferInnen ausgeweitet, die zwar keine aktuell belastende KlientInnenbeziehung aufzuweisen vermochten, dafür aber auf dem Arbeitsplatz oder im Bekanntenkreis (nicht in der Familie!) eine emotional belastende Beziehung z. B. mit einem oder einer KollegIn, ChefIn, MitarbeiterIn, FreundIn oder NachbarIn erleben. Die Anmeldung erfolgte per E-Mail. Auf den Aufruf hin haben sich etwa 100 Personen angemeldet, von denen 83 Personen ($N=20$ Männer, Durchschnittalter $37{,}6 \pm 13{,}8$ Jahre, und $N=63$ Frauen, Durchschnittalter $42{,}2 \pm 10{,}2$ Jahre) tatsächlich an der Untersuchung teilgenommen haben.

3.4 Ablauf der Untersuchung

Zur Abwicklung der Untersuchung benötigten wir pro TeilnehmerIn einen leeren Raum, so dass wir angesichts der Raumkapazität der Universität zu den einzelnen Erhebungszeitpunkten nur jeweils 10 Personen eingeladen haben. Die zur Durchführung der Selbstsupervision notwendigen, sehr kleinschrittig beschriebenen, vorformulierten Anweisungen wurden vor der Untersuchung in geschlossene, von 1 bis 100 nummerierte Briefumschläge gesteckt. In die Briefumschläge mit einer ungeraden Kodeziffer wurden die Instruktionen für die SES, in die Briefumschläge mit einer geraden Kodeziffer die Anweisungen für die SmR gelegt.

Die Umschläge enthielten folgende Unterlagen.

1. Informationsschreiben über den Verlauf und Schritte der Untersuchung.
2. Fragebogen zu persönlichen Angaben des oder der ProbandIn (Geschlecht, Alter, Beruf, GruppenleiterIn/HelferIn seit…)
3. Fragebogen zur ausgewählten Person: Art (Gruppenmitglied), (Einzel-)KlientIn, andere Person) und Dauer der Beziehung
4. Fragebogen zur Klientenbeziehung (Skala ‚A')[6]– Was denkt und fühlt der oder die HelferIn in dem Moment, also *vor* der Selbstsupervision gegenüber der von ihm ausgewählten Person?
5. Schritte der jeweiligen Selbstsupervision und der dafür vorgesehene Zeitrahmen – (mindestens 15, höchstens 30 min)
6. Fragebogen zur Klientenbeziehung (Skala ‚B') – Was denkt und fühlt der oder die HelferIn *unmittelbar nach* der Selbstsupervision gegenüber der von ihm ausgewählten Person?
7. Fragebogen mit offenen Fragen – Psychodramaerfahrung, Gefühle und Gedanken während der Selbstsupervision, eventuell aufgetretene hindernde und/oder störende Umstände.

Zunächst haben wir die ProbandInnen über den Ablauf der Untersuchung informiert. Ihnen wurde mitgeteilt, dass sie nach der Verteilung der Umschläge mit den Instruktionen einzeln in einem Raum für 45–50 min arbeiten sollen. Sie wurden gebeten, die Anweisungen genau durchzulesen und sie zu befolgen, damit die Aufgabe für sie durchführbar wird. Wir baten sie weiterhin nach dem Abschluss der selbstständigen Arbeit in den gemeinsamen Raum zurückzukehren.

Sie wurden darüber nicht aufgeklärt, dass es um zwei verschiedene Verfahren geht. Die Umschläge wurden jedes Mal per Zufallsprinzip unter den jeweils erschienenen 10 ProbandInnen verteilt. Jedes Mal wurden je zur Hälfte Umschläge mit der Versuchsbedingung SmR und SES verteilt.

Nach der Durchführung der Selbstsupervision wurden die ProbandInnen gebeten, im dritten Schritt der Untersuchung die Skala ‚C' und einen Fragebogen mit offenen Fragen zur KlientInnenbeziehung sowie einen ans Institut adressierten Umschlag mitzunehmen. Sie wurden gebeten die Skala und den Fragebogen innerhalb von 24 h nach dem nächsten Treffen mit der zur Supervision ausgesuchten Person auszufüllen und an uns zurückzuschicken, möglichst innerhalb eines Monats, aber nicht direkt in den darauffolgenden Tagen nach der Selbstsupervision.

4 Methodik

4.1 Entwicklung des Fragebogens zur KlientInnenbeziehung

Da uns zur Durchführung der Untersuchung kein Messinstrument zur Verfügung stand, konzipierten wir zunächst eine für unsere Forschungszwecke geeignete Skala. Im ersten Schritt hat das aus den AutorInnen gebildete ExpertInnenteam dazu ca. 50 Items generiert. Der wichtigste Anhaltspunkt bei der Generierung der Items war es, dass sie möglicherweise ein breites Spektrum an Helfereinstellungen den KlientInnen gegenüber abdecken. Die Zusammenstellung umfasste dementsprechend sowohl emotionale und mit der Emotionsregulierung verbundene als auch kognitive sowie Verhaltensmerkmale, die in der ersten Person Singular als eine persönliche Erfahrung mit einem oder einer konkreten KlientIn formuliert wurden.

Die so gesammelten Items wurden vom Team überprüft und von ihnen 29 Items ausgewählt, die verschiedene Erfahrungen und innere Zustände in KlientInbeziehungen erfassten und nicht zu große Ähnlichkeiten (z. B. in der Formulierung) zueinander aufwiesen. Die auf diese Weise ausgewählten Items haben wir in Form eines Online-Fragebogens mit dem Ziel veröffentlicht, dass aufgrund der von möglichst vielen HelferInnen ausgefüllten Fragebögen die Items herausgefiltert werden können, die emotionale Erlebnisse und Einstellungen der HelferInnen gegenüber ihren KlientInnen möglichst genau und differenziert zu beschreiben vermögen. Unter den 29 Items haben wir insgesamt 22 gefunden, die sich sowohl mathematisch (hohe Ladung auf einer Komponente und niedrige Ladung auf den anderen Komponenten) als auch aus der Sicht der Interpretierbarkeit als geeignet zur Aufnahme in den endgültigen Fragebogen erwiesen haben. Nachdem wir die 22 Items vier Subskalen zugeordnet und an den Ergebnissen der ersten Datenerhebung geprüft hatten, fanden wir die so gebildeten Subskalen reliabel. Dann wurden die von uns ausgewählten Items einer sprachlichen Überprüfung unterzogen, und wo es notwendig schien, kleine Änderungen an der Formulierung vorgenommen. So wurde eine 22 Items und 4 Subskalen umfassende Einschätzungsskala gebildet (Martos et al. 2014). Wir haben mit diesem „Fragebogen zur Klientenbeziehung" als eigens entwickeltem Messinstrument die subjektiven Erlebnisse und Einstellungen der HelferInnen den jeweiligen KlientInnen gegenüber zu erfassen gesucht.

4.2 Messinstrumente – Fragebogen zur KlientInnenbeziehung

Der *Fragebogen zur KlientInnenbeziehung* besteht aus 22 Items, die sich auf 4 Subskalen verteilen (siehe Anlage 1). Sie messen vier emotionale oder kognitive Merkmale, welche die HelferInnen in der Beziehung zum ihren KlientInnen erfahren können:

1. *Innere Blockade*, d. h. die im helfenden Prozess gemachte Erfahrung, dass z. B. „Meine bisher benutzten Instrumente sind in der Beziehung gar nicht oder nur wenig wirksam", oder „Ich bin blockiert in dieser Beziehung."

2. *Neugierige Zuwendung*, d. h. die Erfahrung, dass z. B. „Ich könnte dieser Person beistehen und sie unterstützen." oder „Ich habe den Wunsch, mich nicht wieder mit dieser Person treffen zu müssen."
3. *Emotionale Belastung*, d. h. die Erfahrung, dass z. B. „Wenn ich an diese Person denke, erlebe ich intensivere Gefühle als in anderen ähnlichen Beziehungen." oder „Ich habe das Gefühl, dass diese Person zu stark meine Aufmerksamkeit und Gefühle in Anspruch nimmt."
4. *Kognitive Einsicht*, d. h. die Erfahrung, dass z. B. „Ich kann ganz genau formulieren, was zwischen uns abläuft." oder „Ich sehe meinen Anteil an den Geschehnissen zwischen uns."

In der Untersuchung sollen die einzelnen Aussagen auf einen oder eine konkrete KlientIn bezogen bewertet werden, inwieweit sie zum jeweiligen Zeitpunkt für den oder die ProbandIn zutreffend sind. Die Bewertung erfolgte über eine 7-stufige Likert-Skala, die von 1 = „trifft gar nicht zu" bis 7 = „trifft voll zu" reichte. Die bei der Reliabilitätsanalyse der vier Subskalen gefundenen Cronbachs Alpha-Werte lagen bei der Erhebung vor der Untersuchung zwischen 0,618 und 0,717, bei der Erhebung danach zwischen 0,618 und 0,808 und bei der Nachfolgeerhebung zwischen 0,701 und 0,864, was darauf hindeutet, dass die Skalen des Fragebogens hinreichende Reliabilität haben. Die Interkorrelationen zwischen den Subskalen reichten in Absolutwert von 0,02 bis 0,50 (zwischen Emotionaler Blockade und Zuwendung) und das zeigt, dass die Subskalen ausreichend independent sind.

4.3 Stichprobe

An der Untersuchungsreihe haben insgesamt 83 Personen teilgenommen, von denen 45 zufällig zu der Versuchsbedingung „SmR" und 38 zu der Versuchsbedingung „SES" zugewiesen wurden (54,2 und 45,8 %).[7]

Die im Fragebogen abgefragten wichtigsten persönlichen Angaben der ProbandInnen werden in Tab. 1 je nach Versuchsbedingung einzeln dargestellt.

Bezüglich der von uns gemessenen und analysierten Merkmale zeigte sich nur eine einzige signifikante Differenz zwischen den Gruppen: ProbandInnen in der Versuchsbedingung SmR haben nachher in größerer Zahl die Situation als störend erlebt als die Personen in der Versuchsbedingung SES. Dies ist mit der einfachen Tatsache zu erklären, dass die SmR spezifischere Bedingungen wie z. B. größere Ungestörtheit und mehr Organisation voraussetzt.

5 Ergebnisse

Wir haben an den vier Subskalen je einzeln zwei verschiedene grundlegende Analysen vorgenommen:

1. einen Vergleich zwischen den Werten vor und nach der Untersuchungssituation über GLM-Verfahren ($N=83$)

Tab. 1 Vergleich der ProbandInnen der beiden Versuchsbedingungen

	SmR	SES	Bemerkung
Geschlecht			
Männer	10 (22,2 %)	10 (26,3 %)	
Frauen	35 (77,8 %)	28 (73,7 %)	Chi-Quadrat = 0,189, df = 1, p = 0,664
Durchschnittsalter (in Jahren)	42,2 ± 10,2	39,7 ± 12,4	t = 1,02, df = 81, p = 0,313
HelferIn seit (in Jahren)			
0–3	11 (24,4 %)	11 (28,9 %)	
3–10	12 (26,7 %)	9 (23,7 %)	
> 10	20 (44,4 %)	13 (34,2 %)	
Nicht als HelferIn tätig	2 (4,4 %)	5 (13,2 %)	Chi-Quadrat = 2,627, df = 3, p = 0,453
Dauer der helfenden Beziehung (in Jahren)			
weniger als 1 Jahr	16 (39,0 %)	14 (138,9 %)	
zwischen 1 und 3 Jahren	13 (31,7 %)	9 (25,0 %)	
mehr als 3 Jahre	12 (29,3 %)	13 (36,1 %)	Chi-Quadrat = 0,578, df = 2, p = 0,784
Psychodramaerfahrung			
Ja	36 (80,0 %)	26 (74,3 %)	
Nein	9 (20,0 %)	9 (25,7 %)	Chi-Quadrat = 0,369, df = 1, p = 0,544
Während der Untersuchung empfundene Gefühle			
Langeweile			
Ja	0 (0,0 %)	0 (0,0 %)	
Nein	45 (100,0 %)	35 (100,0 %)	(Nicht berechenbar)
Irritationen			
Ja	2 (4,4 %)	4 (11,4 %)	
Nein	43 (95,6 %)	31 (88,6 %)	Chi-Quadrat = 1,384, df = 1, p = 0,239
Freude/Spaß			
Ja	21 (46,7 %)	19 (54,3 %)	
Nein	24 (53,3 %)	16 (45,7 %)	Chi-Quadrat = 0,457, df = 1, p = 0,499
Störende Umstände während der Untersuchung			
Es gab keine.	27 (62,8 %)	29 (85,3 %)	
Es gab welche.	16 (37,2 %)	5 (14,7 %)	Chi-Quadrat = 4,85, df = 1, p = 0,028

Wo die Gesamtzahl der ProbandInnen nicht 83 ist, sind die Angaben unvollständig und zeigen die Prozentzahlen das Verhältnis innerhalb der jeweiligen Versuchsbedingungen

2. einen Vergleich von den Werten vor und nach der Untersuchungssituation mit den Werten der in der Nachfolgeerhebung gegebenen Antworten – diese ergänzende Analyse wurde notwendig, da nur ein Teil der ProbandInnen im Rahmen der Nachfolgeuntersuchung die Skala ‚C' zurückgeschickt hat (N = 61). Daher mussten die ProbandInnen, die die Nachfolgeerhebung nicht mitgemacht und den Antwortbriefumschlag nicht an uns zurückgesendet haben, mit ihren zu allen Messzeitpunkten mitgeteilten Angaben in der Analyse weggelassen werden.

Da der Vergleich der ProbandInnen der beiden Versuchsbedingungen das Ergebnis brachte, dass die Personen in der Versuchsbedingung SmR signifikant häufiger über die Wahrnehmung von störenden Umständen berichtet haben, haben wir die obigen Analysen unter Kontrolle der möglichen Störvariable „Wahrnehmung störender Umstände" wiederholt. Da jedoch diese ergänzende Analyse an den Ergebnissen nichts geändert hat, werden hier die Ergebnisse der ursprünglichen Analyse bekannt gegeben (siehe Tab. 2, 3, 4, 5).

Aufgrund der Analysen lässt sich zu den Auswirkungen der beiden ausprobierten Techniken und zu deren Verhältnis zueinander Folgendes festhalten:

1. Beide Techniken erwiesen sich unter dem Aspekt als wirksam, dass sich die Wahrnehmung aller ProbandInnen durch die mit den KlientInnen gemachten Erfahrungen in eine positive Richtung veränderte: nach der Anwendung der Techniken sind die emotionale Belastung und das Gefühl der inneren Blockade im Vergleich zum Zustand davor erlebnismäßig geringer und die Fähigkeit zur neugierigen Zuwendung und die kognitive Einsicht stärker geworden. Diese Veränderungen erwiesen sich auch in der Nachfolgeuntersuchung als nachhaltig, bei der inneren Blockade und emotionalen Belastung war sogar danach eine weitere Abnahme zu verzeichnen, während die Merkmale „kognitive Einsicht" und „Zuwendung" sich im Vergleich zur Situation nach der Untersuchung nicht signifikant veränderten.
2. Die Versuchsbedingungen, d. h. die beiden verschiedenen Selbstsupervisionstechniken zeigten im Allgemeinen keinen Unterschied im Ausmaß der mit ihnen einhergehenden Veränderungen: beide Techniken erwiesen sich wie oben beschrieben als wirksam. Wir fanden nur eine Ausnahme: das Ausmaß von neugieriger Zuwendung nahm bei der SmR signifikant stärker zu als bei der SES. Diese Differenz blieb auch bei der Nachfolgeuntersuchung bestehen.
3. Da im Vergleich von SmR und SES auf der Subskala „Neugierige Zuwendung" ein signifikanter Unterschied erschien, haben wir die Items der Subskala eingehender analysiert. Die Analyse zeigte, dass die Tendenz zur Vermeidung der Begegnung mit den KlientInnen nach der Anwendung beider Selbstsupervisionstechniken signifikant abnahm und die Vorfreude auf das nächste Treffen stärker wurde. Das bedeutet, dass sich die Fähigkeit zur Zuwendung zu den KlientInnen verbesserte und die Neigung zur Abwendung zurückging. Die eindeutige Differenz zwischen den Techniken zeigte sich zugunsten der SmR in der Fähigkeit zur Zuwendung und Unterstützung der KlientInnen, sowie in der Neugier und Offenheit für diese bzw. für die Beziehung.

6 Diskussion

Oben haben wir den theoretischen Hintergrund von Selbstsupervision geschildert und zwei für die Selbstsupervision geeignete Verfahren vorgestellt: die Selbstsupervision mit Rollentausch und das Expressive Schreiben. Um die zwei Techniken auf ihre Wirksamkeit hin miteinander vergleichen zu können, haben wir ein Experiment konzipiert und durchgeführt.

Nach den Ergebnissen der Studie haben beide Selbstsupervisionstechniken einen unmittelbaren und über mehrere Wochen anhaltenden positiven Einfluss auf die subjektiven Erlebnisse und Einstellungen der teilnehmenden HelferInnen dem oder der KlientIn gegenüber. Die Anwendung beider Techniken führte zu einer Abnahme der Gefühle der emotionalen Belastung und der inneren Blockade und Zunahme der Fähigkeit zur Zuwendung und der kognitiven Einsicht.

Tab. 2 Punktzahlen der Subskala „Innere Blockade" zu den einzelnen Messzeitpunkten (T1-T2-T3) und nach der jeweiligen Versuchsbedingung (SmR vs. SES)

Innere Blockade	T1	T2	T3
	MW (STA)	MW (STA)	MW (STA)
SmR	4,86 (0,96)[a]	4,02 (1,11)[b]	3,39 (1,01)[c]
SES	5,15 (0,90)[a]	4,38 (1,16)[b]	3,24 (1,27)[c]

$F=54{,}22$ ($N=83$, $df=1$, $p<0{,}001$) für T1-T2; und $F=162{,}16$ ($N=61$, $df=1$, $p<0{,}001$) für T1-T2-T3 Vergleiche. Unterschiede zwischen SmR und SES sind nicht signifikant ($p>0{,}1$)

Mittelwerte mit verschiedenen Buchstaben sind signifikant unterschiedlich ($p<0{,}05$) nach Bonferroni Korrektur in post hoc Test

Tab. 3 Punktzahlen der Subskala „Neugierige Zuwendung" zu den einzelnen Messzeitpunkten (T1-T2-T3) und nach der jeweiligen Versuchsbedingung (SmR vs SES)

Zuwendung	T1	T2	T3
	MW (STA)	MW (STA)	MW (STA)
SmR	3,74 (1,51)[a]	4,58 (1,36)[b]	4,18 (1,33)[bc]
SES	3,78 (1,20)[a]	4,02 (1,30)[c]	4,03 (1,03)[c]

$F=12{,}16$ ($N=83$, $df=1$, $p<0{,}001$) für T1-T2; und $F=7{,}26$ ($N=61$, $df=1$, $p<0{,}01$) für T1-T2-T3 Vergleiche. Unterschiede zwischen SmR und SES sind nicht signifikant ($p>0{,}1$). Interaktion zwischen Erhebung (T1-T2) und Bedingung (SmR und SES) ist signifikant: $F=8{,}13$ ($N=83$, $df=1$, $p<0{,}01$)

Mittelwerte mit verschiedenen Buchstaben sind signifikant unterschiedlich ($p<0{,}05$) nach Bonferroni Korrektur in post hoc Test

Tab. 4 Punktzahlen der Subskala „Emotionale Belastung" zu den einzelnen Messzeitpunkten (T1-T2-T3) und nach der jeweiligen Versuchsbedingung (SmR vs SES)

Emotionale Belastung	T1	T2	T3
	MW (STA)	MW (STA)	MW (STA)
SmR	5,29 (1,08)[a]	4,50 (1,25)[b]	3,80 (1,24)[c]
SES	5,12 (0,93)[a]	4,71 (1,1)[b]	3,61 (1,4)[c]

$F=25{,}87$ ($N=83$, $df=1$, $p<0{,}001$) für T1-T2; und $F=73{,}37$ ($N=61$, $df=1$, $p<0{,}001$) für T1-T2-T3 Vergleiche. Unterschiede zwischen SmR und SES sind nicht signifikant ($p>0{,}1$)

Mittelwerte mit verschiedenen Buchstaben sind signifikant unterschiedlich ($p<0{,}05$) nach Bonferroni Korrektur in post hoc Test

Tab. 5 Punktzahlen der Subskala „Kognitive Einsicht" zu den einzelnen Messzeitpunkten (T1-T2-T3) und nach der jeweiligen Versuchsbedingung (SmR vs SES)

Kognitive Einsicht	T1	T2	T3
	MW (STA)	MW (STA)	MW (STA)
SmR	3,96 (1,08)[a]	4,88 (0,84)[b]	4,71 (1,16)[b]
SES	4,04 (1,14)[a]	4,81 (1,16)[b]	5,25 (0,77)[b]

$F=47{,}97$ ($N=83$, $df=1$, $p<0{,}001$) für T1-T2; und $F=44{,}72$ ($N=61$, $df=1$, $p<0{,}001$) für T1-T2-T3 Vergleiche. Unterschiede zwischen SmR und SES sind nicht signifikant ($p>0{,}1$)

Mittelwerte mit verschiedenen Buchstaben sind signifikant unterschiedlich ($p<0{,}05$) nach Bonferroni Korrektur in post hoc Test

Stimmt gar nicht zu	Stimmt völlig zu					
1 2 3 4 5 6 7							
Die Beziehung zu dieser Person stellt für mich eine emotionale Belastung dar	1	2	3	4	5	6	7
Ich habe den Wunsch, mich nicht wieder mit dieser Person treffen zu müssen	1	2	3	4	5	6	7
Mich beschäftigt, was diese Person über unsere gemeinsame Arbeit denkt	1	2	3	4	5	6	7
Ich fühle mich ohnmächtig in der Beziehung mit dieser Person	1	2	3	4	5	6	7
Ich könnte dieser Person beistehen und sie unterstützen	1	2	3	4	5	6	7
Nach dem Treffen mit dieser Person fühle ich mich erschöpft	1	2	3	4	5	6	7
Meine bisher benutzten Instrumente sind in der Beziehung gar nicht oder nur wenig wirksam	1	2	3	4	5	6	7
Ich erlebe mich in dieser Beziehung als inkompetent	1	2	3	4	5	6	7
Ich habe das Gefühl, dass diese Person zu stark meine Aufmerksamkeit und Gefühle in Anspruch nimmt	1	2	3	4	5	6	7
In der Begegnung mit dieser Person muss ich stärker als gewöhnlich auf meine Gefühle achten	1	2	3	4	5	6	7
Ich muss mit anderen über diese Person reden	1	2	3	4	5	6	7
Ich kann ganz genau formulieren, was zwischen uns abläuft	1	2	3	4	5	6	7
Ich kann einsehen, warum ich gerade jetzt diesem Problem begegnet bin	1	2	3	4	5	6	7
Ich verstehe nicht, warum unsere Beziehung nicht funktioniert	1	2	3	4	5	6	7
Ich kann für mich die inneren Gefühle und Gedanken dieser Person formulieren	1	2	3	4	5	6	7
Wenn ich an diese Person denke, erlebe ich intensivere Gefühle als in anderen ähnlichen Beziehungen	1	2	3	4	5	6	7
Ich bin in dieser Beziehung gefühlsmäßig und gedanklich frei	1	2	3	4	5	6	7
Erwartungsvoll sehe ich unserem nächsten Treffen entgegen	1	2	3	4	5	6	7
Ich sehe meinen Anteil an den Geschehnissen zwischen uns	1	2	3	4	5	6	7
Ich habe schon daran gedacht, dass sich diese Person so verhält, weil ich etwas falsch mache	1	2	3	4	5	6	7
Ich bin blockiert in dieser Beziehung	1	2	3	4	5	6	7
Mich würde interessieren, was diese Person von mir denkt	1	2	3	4	5	6	7

In den Ergebnissen zeigte sich ein markanter Unterschied zugunsten der *Selbstsupervision mit Rollentausch: das Ausmaß von neugieriger Zuwendung* nahm signifikant im Vergleich zum Kontrollverfahren zu. Es taucht die Frage auf, warum Selbstsupervision mit Rollentausch in diesem Kontext mehr leisten kann.

Zur Erklärung dieser Ergebnisse bietet sich die Theorie zum Rollentausch an (Krüger 2003; 2015). Im psychodramatischen Dialog mit mehreren Rollenwechseln handelt es sich um eine Beziehungsklärung, bei der durch den Tausch der Rollen in den Aktionen und Reaktionen Ursache und Wirkung in der Beziehung erkundet werden. Durch das wechselweise Spielen in der Rolle der SupervisandInnen und der KlientInnen kann das innere Bild von der Beziehung und die innere Wirklichkeit der KonfliktpartnerInnen erkundet werden, wodurch auch Projektionen aufgelöst werden können. Bei Empathie nimmt man den anderen in seine eigene „Seele" mit hinein, beim psychodramatischen Dialog mit Rollenwechseln bringt man den anderen aus der „Seele" heraus und setzt ihn auf den anderen Stuhl. So werden Ich und Du getrennt. „In dem fiktiven psychodramatischen Dialog erweitern sich auf der äusseren Bühne die altgewohnten Bahnen des inneren Denkens gezielt über die alte Realität hinaus und werden ggf. in der Beziehung vorhandene Übertragungs- und Gegenübertragungsreaktionen durch die offenen Mitteilungen bewusst ausser Kraft gesetzt." (Krüger 2015, S. 15) SmR kann also eine Idee über Ursache und Wirkung in einem Beziehungskonflikt vermitteln, und so wird die Vermischung von Ich und Du mit Hilfe der Ich-Erfahrung, der Du-Erfahrung und der Erfahrung der Beziehung durch Interaktion getrennt.

Bei drei der vier untersuchten Merkmale – innere Blockade, emotionale Belastung und kognitive Einsicht – bewirkten beide Techniken eine positive Veränderung. Dies lässt sich damit erklären, dass in beiden Techniken eine undifferenzierte emotionale und kognitive Innenwelt durch das Aussagen oder Niederschreiben nach außen gebracht, geformt und artikuliert wird. Dadurch verwirklicht sich ein Grundsatz psychodramatischer Arbeit, nämlich dass die innere Welt nach außen gebracht wird („inner world outside") (Holmes 1992).

Die Ergebnisse der Studie lassen sich aber auch so deuten, dass Selbsthilfe und HelferInnenautonomie als mögliche gültige Prinzipien in der Supervision berücksichtigt und angewandt werden könnten. TeilnehmerInnen eines Workshops zum Thema Selbstsupervision, wo wir beide Techniken eingeführt haben, gaben uns die Rückmeldung– unabhängig von der jeweiligen Technik -, dass ihnen die Selbstsupervision einen Anstoß zur inneren Arbeit gab. Wieder andere berichteten davon, dass die Selbstsupervision einen Erkenntnissprung für sie brachte. Eine Teilnehmerin teilte mit, dass sie die Blockade einer KlientInnenbeziehung, an der sie schon seit langem und mehrmals in Gruppensupervision gearbeitet hat, mithilfe der SmR endlich gefühlsmäßig aufheben konnte. Sie hat diesen Durchbruch damit begründet, dass sie dadurch, dass sie frei und ohne Kontrolle ihre angehäuften negativen Gefühle herauslassen und in der Rolle ihres Gegenübers nachvollziehen konnte, eine körperlich-seelische Entlastung erfahren hat.

Unseres Erachtens könnten diese Erkenntnisse weitere – sogar auch internationale – Untersuchungen zum Vergleich von Supervision mit SupervisorInnen und Selbstsupervision anstoßen.

Aus unserer Sicht gilt selbst die Entwicklung des *Fragebogens zur Klientenbeziehung* als ein weiteres wichtiges Ergebnis der Untersuchung. Viele ProbandInnen signalisierten uns, dass allein die Ausfüllung des Fragebogens ihnen einen ersten Anstoß zur Reflexion und tieferer Einsicht gab. Ähnliche Feedbacks haben wir auch von den TeilnehmerInnen des Seminars zur Selbstsupervision erhalten. Der Fragebogen kann unserer Erfahrung nach effektiv als Reflexionsinstrument eingesetzt werden, da sie die aktuelle Befindlichkeit des oder der HelferIn erfassen, sein oder ihr persönliches und interpersonales Bewusstsein steigern und die innere persönliche Reflexion und Verstehen fördern kann. Eine Weiterentwicklung des Fragebogens ist unsererseits vorgesehen.

Durch unsere Untersuchung hat sich ferner auch bestätigt, dass einerseits die Erforschung der Psychodrama-Methode und die Entwicklung ihrer Theorie und Praxis entscheidend für die Zukunft von Psychodrama sein kann und andererseits es nicht genügt, in Psychodrama ausgebildet zu werden und die Methode anzuwenden. Die Reflexion unserer Arbeit ist unverzichtbar, damit die Grundprinzipien des Psychodramas in Fachkreisen anerkannt werden und in möglichst viele helfende Tätigkeiten oder Berufe Eingang finden.

Anmerkungen

1 http://www.mental.semmelweis.hu/de/.

2 Der Begriff Mentalhygiene wird in der Bedeutung Psychohygiene benutzt.

3 Mit dem Begriff 'fiktives Gespräch' soll ausgesagt werden, dass dieser psychodramatische Dialog nicht direkt übend eine Anleitung erarbeiten soll, wie mit dem Konfliktgegner gegebenenfalls zu sprechen wäre. Es geht vielmehr darum, durch diese Arbeit innerlich in dem Beziehungskonflikt die eigene Hypothese über die Realität in der Beziehung zu überprüfen oder gegebenenfalls eine neue Hypothese über die Beziehung zu erarbeiten. Diese Hypothese der Beziehungswirklichkeit ergibt sich aus dem Erkennen der beziehungsbezogenen inneren Realität des Konfliktgegners und der beziehungbezogenen inneren Realität des Protagonisten selbst. Im Psychodrama wird die Veränderung und Erweiterung des inneren Beziehungsbildes durch das psychodramatische Spiel 'Surplus Reality' genannt.

4 In der Studie benutzen wir des Weiteren die Verkürzung SmR für die Selbstsupervision mit Rollentausch.

5 In der Studie benutzen wir des Weiteren die Verkürzung SES für die Selbstsupervision durch Expressives Schreiben.

6 Die Skala A, B, und C sind identisch. Siehe Anlage.

7 Die Differenz in der Zahl der zu den beiden Versuchsbedingungen zugewiesenen Personen ist darauf zurückzuführen, dass nicht immer alle 10 eingeladenen Personen zur Erhebung erschienen sind und bei einer ungeraden Teilnehmerzahl war aufgrund der Zufallsverteilung der Umschläge die Zahl der zu den beiden Versuchsbedingungen zugewiesenen Personen nicht identisch. Da wir aber leider auf diese Tatsache nicht aufmerksam wurden, konnten wir diese Differenz zu den verschiedenen Zeitpunkten nicht ausgleichen.

7 Anlage 1

Fragebogen zur Klientenbeziehung

Denken Sie an die von Ihnen ausgewählte Person und füllen Sie mithilfe der unten stehenden Skala den Fragebogen aus.

Geben Sie Ihre Antwort dementsprechend an, was Sie dieser Person gegenüber JETZT fühlen und von ihm JETZT denken. Sie sollen in Ihren Antworten auf Ihre aktuellen Gefühle und Gedanken der jeweiligen Person gegenüber achten. Wir bitten Sie, ehrlich zu sich selbst zu sein und nicht daran zu denken, was Sie fühlen und denken sollten.

Sie können anhand der unten stehenden 7-stufigen Skala durch Markierung der für die jeweilige Aussage zutreffenden Ziffer angeben, insofern Sie mit der Aussage einverstanden sind.

Literatur

Faber, H., & van der Schoot, E. (1965). *The art of pastoral conversation*. New York: Abingdon Press.

Holmes, P. (1992). *The inner world outside. Object relations theory and psychodrama*. London: Routledge.

Krüger, R. T. (2003). Indikationen und Kontraindikationen für den Rollentausch in der psychodramatischen Psychotherapie. *Zeitschrift für Psychodrama und Soziometrie, 2*, 91–115.

Krüger, R. T. (2010) *Der psychodramatische Dialog mit Rollentausch zur Selbstsupervision ohne Supervisorin*. Unveröffentlichtes Manuskript.

Krüger, R. T. (2015). *Störungsspezifische Psychodramatherapie. Ein Lehrbuch. Unveröffentlichtes Manuskript*. Göttingen: Vandenhoeck & Ruprecht.

Martos, T., Marlok, Z., & Török, G. (2014). *A Klienskapcsolati Kérdőív: alkalmazási útmutató és pszichometriai adatok. Kézirat*. Budapest: Mentálhigiéné Intézet.

Pennebaker, J. W. (1997). *The healing power of expressing emotions*. New York: Guilford Press.

Pennebaker, J. W. (2004). Theories, therapies, and taxpayers: On the complexities of the expressive writing paradigm. *Clinical Psychology: Science and Practice, 11*, 138–142.

Pennebaker, J. W., & Chung, C. K. (2011). *Expressive writing: Connections to physical and mental health*. The Oxford handbook of health psychology, 417–437.

Zsuzsa Marlok, Dr. (PhD Erziehungswissenschaft.), 1964. Sie arbeitet als Dozentin an der Semmelweis Universität Budapest, im Institut für Mentalhygiene. Lehrerin, Fachfrau für Mentalhygiene, Psychodramaleiterin und Bibliodramaleiterin, seit 2013 Lehr-Psychodrama- und Lehrbibliodrama Leiterin in der Ungarischen Gesellschaft für Psychodrama, Familientherapeutin. Arbeitsschwerpunkte: Psychodrama-Selbsterfahrungs- und Ausbildungsgruppen, Psychodrama im Einzelsetting, Beratung, Familientherapie, Fortbildungen und Workshops zum Thema Psychodrama in Gruppen und im Einzelsetting.

Gábor Török, Dr. (PhD), Lehrer, Seelsorger, Psychodramaleiter, Assistenzprofessor im Institut für Mentalhygiene, Semmelweis Universität, Ungarn; torok.gabor@public.semmelweis-univ.hu.

Tamás Martos, PhD. Psychologe, 1968, Dozent am Institut für Mentalhygiene der Semmelweis-Universität, Psychodrama-Leiter. Schwerpunkte: Forschung auf den Gebieten der Persönlichkeits-, Familien- und Religionspsychologie, Leitung von Psychodrama-Selbsterfahrungsgruppen.

Czigány László, 1970, Germanist, Deutschlehrer, Übersetzer.

Z Psychodrama Soziometr (2016) (Suppl) 15:235–253
DOI 10.1007/s11620-015-0295-8

HAUPTBEITRÄGE

Zeitschrift für Psychodrama und Soziometrie

The usefulness of role reversal in one-to-one supervision: a qualitative research project using heuristic enquiry

Sue Daniel

Published online: 26 November 2015

Abstract I conducted a qualitative phenomenological investigation with three participants into the application of a specific psychodrama production technique; namely Role Reversal—in one-to-one supervision. Role reversal increases therapists' ability to empathize with their clients, to individuate from any projective tendencies, to be more aware of what they are doing and it also serves to raise consciousness in therapists. This paper explores the usefulness of role reversal in one-to-one supervision. It showed that there was an increase in spontaneity and a corresponding decrease in anxiety, which led to an expansion in the therapists' consciousness and confidence. There is a reflection on the role of the researcher-practitioner and a comparison between this and a similar project, which demonstrates comparable results.

Keywords Role reversal · One-to-one supervision · Qualitative phenomenological investigation · Heuristic enquiry · Psychodrama

Die Wirksamkeit des Rollenwechsels in der Einzelsupervision. Ein qualitatives Forschungsprojekt auf der Grundlage einer heuristischen Untersuchung

Zusammenfassung Es wurde eine qualitativ phänomenologische Untersuchung mit einer Stichprobe von drei Personen zu einer spezifischen Psychodrama-Technik, dem Rollenwechsel, im Rahmen eines Einzelsupervisionssettings durchgeführt. Der Rollenwechsel fördert die Empathiefähigkeit der TherapeutInnen für ihre

S. Daniel (✉)
Psychodrama Institute of Melbourne,
1/10–12 Adolph Street,
3121 Cremorne, Victoria, Australia
e-mail: suedan@netspace.net.au

KlientInnen; insbesondere vermindert er projektive Tendenzen, schärft die Wahrnehmung für das eigene Handeln und dient grundsätzlich dazu, das Bewusstsein der TherapeutInnen zu erweitern. Der vorliegende Beitrag untersucht die Wirksamkeit des Rollenwechsels in der Einzelsupervision. Es wird gezeigt, dass es einen Zuwachs an Spontaneität und eine korrespondierende Abnahme an Angst bei den TherapeutInnen gibt, die zur Steigerung von Selbstbewusstsein und Selbstvertrauen führen. Darüber hinaus wird die Rolle des Forscher/Praktikers reflektiert, und ein Vergleich mit Resultaten dieses Forschungsprojektes und den Ergebnissen einer ähnlichen Studie gezogen, um Zusammenhänge zu zeigen.

Schlüsselwörter Rollenwechsel · Einzelsupervision · Qualitative phänomenologische Untersuchung · Heuristische Forschung · Psychodrama

Role reversal is one of several classical psychodramatic production techniques that are central to the psychodrama method. It involves getting into another person's shoes; a person takes up the role of 'the other' usually in action, but also mentally to see the world from their viewpoint and to experience the world of 'the other'. To role reverse, you have to put your own views and ideas aside and concentrate on being in another person's shoes. Zerka Moreno (1991, personal conversation, Holwell, UK) called it "the *sine qua non* of psychodrama", the essence of the method. Although this technique belongs to psychodrama, the concept is universal. Henry David Thoreau (1854) once remarked: "Could a greater miracle take place than for us to look thru each other's eyes for an instant." Similarly heard in this Algonquin Native American prayer, courtesy of Young 1946: "Oh Great Spirit, grant that I may not judge my neighbor, before I have walked for a day in his moccasins". Harper Lee (1960) wrote, "You never really know a man until you understand things from his point of view, until you climb into his skin and walk around in it."

Introduction

This paper investigates the efficacy of role reversal in one-to-one supervision. Many articles and research projects have focused on the use of psychodrama in various settings and the use of various techniques in such settings, (Kipper and Ritchie 2003; Van der May and Peake 1980; Lippitt 1958; McVie et al. 2011; Daniels 2008; Gimenez Hinkle 2008; Moreno and Moreno 1959/1975). As far as I can ascertain, there are no published replications of research into any one specific technique or replications of research into the application of psychodrama in a particular field with a particular group.

The results of this study revealed four emergent themes:

1) Doubts about therapist competency
2) Experiencing emotion of client and self in the role reversal
3) Role reversal as a mechanism for change
4) Understanding the client-therapist relationship.

These are discussed, as are the participants' reflections after the role reversal session. A brief comparison is made with the work of Maxine Daniels (2008), who recorded approximately the same four themes. From the comparison it is concluded that, regardless of the individual person of the researcher or participant, role reversal has an ameliorating and immediate effect in one-to-one supervision.

1 Background to the study

In July 2011, at a British Psychodrama Association conference in London, Maxine Daniels presented a phenomenological research study, which was part of her doctoral thesis, "What do supervisees experience when role reversing with their clients in the supervision session?" For this project Maxine conducted a qualitative phenomenological investigation into the application of role reversal in one-to-one supervision. She constructed a questionnaire, which formed the basis for semi-structured interviews using Interpretive Phenomenological Analysis (IPA) with three qualified psychotherapists. The focus of her study was on the outcomes of the therapists' role reversal with their clients in order to gain a deeper understanding of their experience in both their own role and their client's role during the role reversal. My aims, in repeating Maxine's study, were to reduce the difference between supervision interventions, to allow a meaningful comparison of the findings of the research and to undertake additional formal exploration on the effects of role reversal.

2 Brief historical perspective of psychodrama and role reversal

Psychodrama was created and developed by Jacob Levy Moreno (1889–1974). Moreno's view was "that spontaneity and creativity were the characteristics of a 'healthy personality, healthy relationships and a healthy society' and that problems occurred for people when they "failed to be creative and spontaneous to the extent that they were unable to resolve internal and external problems in effective ways" (Moreno 1934). Moreno created the psychodrama method with the twin axis of spontaneity/creativity at its core and developed a spontaneity theory of child development, a general spontaneity theory, a personality theory and a theory of roles (Moreno 1946/1972). He also developed techniques for the purpose of empowering people to be more fully themselves and to aid them in their development. These techniques have stood the test of time and have been employed in a range of settings.

2.1 What is psychodrama?

Psyche = self (or soul), o = of, and drama = a happening. Therefore it can be read literally as 'the drama of the soul' or more simply and factually it is something that happens to a person in relation to the world around them. It is an interpersonal (sociometric) method and involves relationship with self and the everyday world of people, objects and animals. Psychodrama can be about exploring a problem, celebrating something or going on a journey of discovery; all in action. It is not about problem solving yet it can be used to investigate a problem and a person may arrive at a solution or discover a truth.

2.2 The method of role reversal in one-to-one supervision

In this one-to-one environment there is no auxiliary ego with whom to role reverse, except perhaps, the supervisor. They can take up a role for their supervisee; however due to these dual roles of *supervisor* and *auxiliary-ego* great care must be taken for accuracy and role separation. This means that a supervisor must have the capacity to take on roles with alacrity and be spontaneous. This is why the supervisor needs to have training and supervision in the psychodrama method. It is quite an art to take up a role for another person. It has nothing to do with acting per se but rather the ability to listen and observe body language and nuances like tone of voice and changes in skin tone and to be aware of your own feeling and thought processes when in role.

It may be best if the supervisee takes up all the roles themselves (self and client), as in a monodrama, with only the empty chair as a prop. After they have addressed the empty chair they can then role reverse and as the 'other', respond to themselves, or they can set out the client's system using cushions and/or chairs and then role reverse through the system. A cushion or another chair is chosen to represent himself or herself as 'the therapist'. The supervisee then goes back and forth changing roles, usually when there is a role change noted by the supervisor, or when a question is asked from any of the role positions. Other techniques can be used such as concretisation (Daniel 2006), maximisation, the aside and the soliloquy (Daniel 2007) and also doubling and mirroring. All of the above apply in the one-to-one psychotherapy milieu.

3 Qualitative research: some history and fit with the psychodrama method

William James (1902) in 'The Variety of Religious Experiences' contributed to qualitative psychological thought by his descriptions of the field of thought and his analogies of the idea of the self. Qualitative Research (QR) lends itself nicely to psychodrama because of the descriptive component. It fits the '*here and now*' ethos of psychodrama and the notion of the self. The basic tenet of psychodrama is: that a person always lives and moves in a relationship network. This includes the person of the researcher. The researcher is not outside the relationship of the people or events being researched. The relationship therefore between any given subject in an experiment and the researcher is as relevant as the data being collected. What he sees, thinks and dreams about is all fodder for the research.

4 Interpretative phenomenological analysis (IPA) and heuristic enquiry

The researcher is considered to be part of the whole process and not an outside observer of static data, which means, that the person will be influenced by the session, the interview process and affected through the experience of working with the participants. It is therefore valuable for a researcher to think about the nature of the data being collected and how it is collected. I made a point of transcribing the data myself to keep as close as possible to the experience of the participants and my own ongoing reflective experience and process. This process so named, 'Heuristic Enquiry' by Clark Moustakas (1990, 1994) comes from the Greek word *heuriskein*, meaning 'to discover' or 'to find'. Basically it implies a process of internal searching through reflecting on one's thoughts and feelings. Given the subjective nature of such a process, questions can arise about the existence of global themes in our work and whether all people experience similar things? Would different supervisors with different training, skill sets, ethics, philosophy of life, ability to be empathic or theoretical bases find the same results? Other influences might affect these results; including the length of time working as fully accredited professionals, different clients, cultures, environments and epochs.

5 Methodology

5.1 The subjects

Three participants, one female and two males, aged between 30 and 40 responded positively to my invitation to voluntarily participate in this research project. It is not unusual to use three people for a qualitative research study, as found by Kelly (1969). He discovered that it was comparatively easy to manage data by finding the common denominator in two subjects and comparing that with a third. My participants were registered psychologists, skilled and competent therapists with a wealth of training and experience, in their fourth year of psychodrama training at the time of the study. Each were employed as psychologists in organizations, were supervisors themselves, and in private practice. Two participants were born in other countries and although fluent in English, it was their second language. In addition to being the researcher-practitioner for this project, I was also their primary psychodrama trainer and supervisor. Our tele was mutually positive and we embarked on this project with much enthusiasm. For the purpose of anonymity I have renamed my participants Lola, Manfred and Joseph. They chose clients they currently found difficult. There was no payment involved from them or me for this research project.

5.2 Research methodology

An interpretative Phenomenological Analysis (IPA) was used to:

1. Ascertain the efficacy of role reversal in one-to-one supervision.
2. Gain insight into how the participants perceived their client's world through the technique of role reversal and to encapsulate their experiences in the session and the interview phase 1 month later.
3. Replicate the study of Maxine Daniels (2008).

5.3 Measures

The study consisted of a constructed situation in which each of the participants had a 1 h supervision session. Directly after the session they filled in a questionnaire, which was then sealed in an envelope. One month later they relooked at this in a 1 h interview session. Both sessions were recorded on a mobile and then transcribed. The texts were analyzed one at a time.

5.4 Brief structured recall (BSR)

The questionnaire that each participant filled in immediately after the supervision session consisted of five questions, which formed the basis for the semi-structured interview 1 month later:

1. What feelings did you experience during the role reversal?
2. What thoughts can you recall from the activity?
3. What are you thinking about your client now?
4. What thoughts do you have about yourself as a therapist?
5. Anything else you want to add about this experience?

For information on BSR processes, the reader may find the work of Smith (2008), Willig (2008), Elliott et al. (2001), Kvale (1996) and Greenberg et al. (1993) of use.

6 Ethics

6.1 Purpose of supervision

One purpose of supervision is that a person will get clear about something and be able to bring forward what they want to get out of the session. The warm-up to a role reversal session is therefore significant and likewise the warm-up to an interview session. At the beginning of each session, I made sure the participants were comfortable. I was particularly mindful in doing this because the first participant, Lola, expressed fears of being judged by me. All people want to feel good about themselves and what they do; as do I. We want to be affirmed in ourselves. As supervisees we want to go into supervision confident that we will come away with something for our clients, trainees or trainers. This could be either an insight into our roles, or our growing edges or to find out what blocks we might be experiencing. We want to feel confident that we will be able to have insight into our own functioning and roles and get some accurate mirroring, doubling and role reversal.

The supervision process is revealing and we can feel very vulnerable, not only regarding, what might be revealed to our own selves but to the 'other'. The supervisor/supervisee relationship is *complementary*. That is, it is marked by difference. A *symmetrical* role relationship is marked by similarity (supervisee/supervisee for example). These two types of role relationships are not good or bad, or weak or strong – this analysis would be dependent on the individual situation; they are just different. The function of each person in the supervisor/supervisee complementary role relationship is different. It is important that the researcher-practitioner is able to be empathic in their role as the supervisor. For example, Lola confided to me, "*It is like you being in the room with me and my client so I feel closely watched, this is a bit daunting.*" I felt touched, that she shared this experience with me and became even more sensitive to her after that[1].

6.2 Interventions

In the enactment phase, I mainly used the technique of role reversal; but when relevant included the techniques of soliloquy, the aside, mirroring and doubling. At the end of the interview session, following psychodrama protocol, I shared with the participants some things that had touched me in their sessions related to my work and life. Sharing helps the supervisee to see the supervisor as a person like himself or herself, grappling with similar issues and problems in their work life.

6.3 Letter of consent

Each participant signed and dated a letter of consent, which became the written agreement between them to be involved in this study. They knew they could withdraw from the research at any time, that the data would be anonymous and that I would screen sensitive material from the public arena. Whilst I reminded them of that at the beginning of both sessions, they laughed and said, "Carry on".

7 Data collection for the supervision session

7.1 Outline of the conduct of the supervision session

All participants were familiar with the surroundings for the study. I welcomed each one, reminding them, that their session was part of a research study. An interview phase took place to ascertain the particular client or issue they wanted to focus on and confirm what they wanted. Their responses made up the supervisory contract. This interview was crucial to establish the purpose of the session and to gain some knowledge about what they had done so far with their clients. While each participant was already warmed up to the session and their client, the interview deepened this warm up. Once the interview concluded we moved onto setting the scene. Then there was an enactment in which the technique of role reversal was employed along with other relevant techniques. I interviewed the participants in their roles as therapists and as they took up the role of their clients. I continued interviewing for role as new roles emerged in the session; either when they were *in their own roles* or *in their client's roles*. At the conclusion of the session I turned off the phone, gave the participants a questionnaire to fill in and left the room so that they could have extra privacy. We then arranged a time to meet for the Interview Session.

8 Data collection for the interview session held 1 month later

8.1 Outline of the conduct of the semi-structured interview

I restated the purpose of the 1 h interview phase. I informed them that the transcripts and data would be protected and that the raw data on the phone would be deleted after transcription. I reminded them that they could withdraw from the research study if they chose to and I asked if they had any questions about the procedure. They read the consent letter again and I handed them the envelope, which had not been opened since they sealed it. They read aloud each written response to the questionnaire. I asked open-ended questions based on each answer, going with the information they gave me and responding where necessary to gain more information and also to assist them to make sense of what they had experienced or were now experiencing. I chose to mirror their responses and double them at times and shared my observations and reflections with them.

9 Analysis of the data

I read through the transcripts and recorded general notes using a drawn left hand column for easy reading of data and themes. Next I identified themes and wrote these down in a right hand column. I gathered the themes into a cluster of core themes (also known as master or superordinate themes) and as the clustering was done I checked with the transcript for the accurate words used by the participants to analyze the themes in relation to both psychological and psychodramatic concepts. I then created a table of core themes (see Table 1 as an example). This process enabled me to keep in contact with the original data and the language used by each participant. To illustrate the themes and clusters I used certain dialogue from the participants and this was highlighted under each cluster. The data was then cross referenced to show how each participant contributed to the analytic outcome. As well as jotting down notes and themes as they emerged, I wrote a sentence of what struck me the most about each participant and in so doing discovered numerous common themes.

Results

Examples of both core and subthemes are in Tables 1–5. The four core themes that emerged from the study are set out in the following order:

1. Doubts about therapist competency
2. Experiencing emotion of client and self in the role reversal
3. Role reversal as a mechanism for change
4. Understanding the client-therapist relationship.

These are the same themes recorded by Maxine Daniels except for the second theme where I added, '*and self*' because the role reversal actually made the participants more aware of their own feelings and emotions. This was an important factor for the

Table 1 Core Theme 1: Doubts about therapist competency

Lola	Manfred	Joseph
Subtheme 1:Feeling doubtful of ability as therapist		
Lola	**Manfred**	**Joseph**
"If I get something wrong that means I'm not a good psychologist, I'm not a competent therapist, I'm a fake, clearly not good enough. Needing to fix and do the work of the client."	"I felt very uncomfortable at the time; I was worried about my competence and the ability to meet this client's needs. Fearful of being wrong, need to get client to work."	"I wanted certainty and guarantee. Cautious of the pace of the client. I was ambivalent, which may have been related to competence or right method."
Subtheme 2: Feeling stuck		
Lola	**Manfred**	**Joseph**
"I don't know what to say or do here. There's that stuckness. I need to solve it, so I'm stuck but I can't solve it, so it's all related."	"What is it that is stopping me responding, what's the block that stops me from being able to respectfully challenge him and why is it that I get stuck?"	"I was concerned and cautious about what my client needed to the point of going slow, holding back."
Subtheme 3: Frustrations, dissatisfactions and struggles		
Lola	**Manfred**	**Joseph**
"Anger and fury at myself, frustrated and teary. There is a blankness, stuckness and feelings of hopelessness. I'm pushing my client because he presents as an educated, smart person but also he is passive, plays, "Poor me, I'm depressed." Maybe that's got to do with my own frustration about his depression."	"Initially I was dissatisfied with myself. My client is so intelligent and so good at making arguments. I'm not good at making arguments. If he comes up with something like an assertion towards me or about something and I want to challenge it, I find it very difficult to actually put that out there."	"I have a struggle, maybe the struggle in her, maybe that moment for her that I fear change, because I think that's kind of the foundation of change for her."
Subtheme 4: Anxiety, shame and guilt		
Lola	**Manfred**	**Joseph**
"Then there's the anxiety sitting underneath all that anger and frustration. The anxiety of not knowing things, the anxiety about not doing it right, the anxiety of getting it wrong."	"I actually feel quite anxious when working with him. It's partially about his high expectations and his demands on what I do and how I do it, but also anxiety around my concern that although he says to hit him with anything, he won't be able to take it."	"I am anxious that if I move too quickly, say what I think, I would scare her and maybe she'd feel hopeless. There is a role in me that is showing her where to go, so in doing that, it validates both my role and my part of my anxiousness."

change process, which emerged in the 3rd core theme: Role reversal as a mechanism for change. Further results stemming from both sessions are in Table 5: An overview of participants' realizations after the role reversal session.

10 Doubts about therapist competency

Table 1 reveals the 4 subthemes that emerged and made up Core theme 1:

1) *Feeling doubtful of ability as therapist*
2) *Feeling stuck*

3) *Frustrations, dissatisfactions and struggles*
4) *Anxiety, shame and guilt.*

All three therapists had doubts about their ability and were able to clearly identify what was at the root of this. They were all feeling stuck in relation to their clients and did not know what to do or say at particular moments. Each was concerned for their client and also themselves; feeling that what was going on with their client was a direct reflection on themselves. All demonstrated a fear of the unknown. Manfred and Joseph were afraid of what would happen if they made certain interventions. Lola realized that outcome was important for her and to feel that she had done a good job. She wanted to solve her client's situation and did not know what to say or do because of not knowing. Manfred said he wasn't good at making arguments and holding ground with his client and became stuck in expressing himself. Joseph was reflecting on whether it was he that feared change and was feeling stuck at the point his client was about to change; her struggle mirroring his own. All therapists were endeavoring to control their clients because they were anxious about getting things wrong. The problem with this was that they were stuck. They had to dare to be wrong to move.

A common theme, which emerged in all three participants, was anxiety around the nature and timing of their interventions. Each had grappled with pace, when to push, when to challenge or whether to challenge and were slightly too moderately anxious about this. Lola realized that she was pushing her male client because of her own frustration about his "depression". If he wasn't moving then it was her lack of competence. Manfred and Joseph were afraid to challenge their clients and were anxious about this. Manfred's client was male and Joseph's was female. Manfred experienced his client as having high expectations on him, wanting him to be more active, but Manfred was afraid that if he did act, then the client might not have been able to deal with it. However, maybe it was that Manfred, who would have trouble with that. How would he deal with the anger, pain, sadness and guilt of his client? Would he feel responsible for his client's pain? Joseph was anxious about challenging his client, preferring to go at her pace, to go slow and not push. He was unsure whether he or she was frightened of change. He spoke about his ambivalence. Lola was also unsure of what to do, anxious about getting "it" wrong and this came over as impatience with her client. She voiced doubts about her ability as a therapist and said that she felt hopeless. All three participants were in the role of the 'Clear Seer'; able to see relatively clearly what was going on for themselves with their chosen clients with some awareness, but not able to shift roles at this time.

11 Experiencing emotion of client and self in the role reversal

All therapists realized what it was like to be in their client's shoes. This meant first of all that they could role reverse. Some people can't, which may mean that they haven't been confirmed in themselves enough. If a client or supervisee cannot role reverse, then mirroring may assist them to be clearer about their functioning and if mirroring doesn't work, then doubling can be used. This will assist a person to be more fully confirmed in him or herself (Daniel 2007). The question about whether role rever-

Table 2 Core theme 2: Experiencing emotion of client and self in the role reversal

Subtheme 1: Experiencing emotion of client in the role reversal		
Lola	**Manfred**	**Joseph**
"When I was being him, I was just there experiencing what I was experiencing. As my client I just was telling the therapist (me) about what's happening. There was no, "Well, so what are you going to do, are you going to fix me," there was nothing like that. I realized my client was experiencing a lot of pressure."	"When I was in the role of the client, I experienced discomfort, mistrust and frustration. I know him well enough to know that's what he feels. I realized that he (the client) doesn't want to hurt me."	"In the client's role I felt ambivalence in the change, "Is this a good thing, can I do it?" As the client, I felt nervous, relieved and positive, saw therapist as trustworthy but most of all, I was ready for change."
Subtheme 2: Empathy for client through role reversal		
Lola	**Manfred**	**Joseph**
"When I was in the role of my client there were no expectations on me (the therapist) to fix the client. And that pain or that feeling that the client has, that's their feeling, that's what it is at that moment for them, I can't, and it's not about, taking those feelings away."	"When I was being the client, I was just being conscious of him by being him. He loves to be challenged and if he doesn't have a significant amount of challenge then he gets bored and that's when he gets more disruptive. Probably I feel a little bit more attuned to his battle with engagement and sabotage, that he wants me to confirm his unhelpful world view by betraying or abandoning him, sometimes, not all the time, it's not what he really wants, it's what he expects because he's had a lifelong of bad or absent mirroring."	"As my client I felt relief, some ambivalence in the change, some confusion and I felt pleased and happy. The insight came through being in both her and my roles, through the role reversal process. She is a strong and courageous client. She is ready for change maybe I am not. It's a good supervision technique to get another angle on clients that therapists see; yeah it's a good supervision technique. I need to do more of it."
Subtheme 3: Experiencing emotion of self in the role reversal		
Lola	**Manfred**	**Joseph**
"I felt a lot of emotion when I was myself being confronted by my own self. Like bang, it all flooded in. It was pretty much the frustration, the fist tightening, I wanted to stamp my leg and say come on, to myself."	"When I was being myself but in the role of my double, I felt initially dissatisfied with myself and then I had some clarity around the interpersonal relationship. Then through the process of the role reversal, I worked out, 'Just keep doing what you are doing'."	"Being in her role and experiencing those roles as in a real situation gave me the insight into my own feelings of relief, pleasure and ambivalence and the insight was linking; by increasing my openness to it, the openness gave me more insight as well."

sal increased empathy has been answered through the comments of the participants (Table 2). Each of them became clearer about what the client actually felt instead of what they had *thought* he or she felt and thereby gained some major insights into their clients and themselves.

Lola experienced a lot of feeling in her body during the supervision session. This emerged strongly when she was talking about her encounter with herself in the supervision session. I had taken up her role as therapist and Lola was in a mirror position observing herself in relation to her client. Seeing herself had a big impact (See Table 2). When I asked her where in her body she felt it she realized it was in her stomach and legs. Mirroring her I stated that the battle was going on in her and she quickly agreed. In the interview phase Lola said "I think the most useful thing was when you pointed out merely what was going on is happening within myself and when you asked me that just now it's become much clearer than before". Manfred also experienced a lot in the mirror position; seeing himself (me, as his auxiliary) in the role of the double (him) he achieved some clarity around the interpersonal relationship from this mirror position. Joseph felt that by being in his client's role and experiencing those roles as in a real situation gave him insight into his own feelings. This insight increased his openness to feeling and that openness gave him more insight as well.

12 Role reversal as a mechanism for change

All participants reported significant changes when they next met with their clients. Lola found that when she was aware of her feelings she could change her role and sit back rather than be at the mercy of her 'Critical Judge'. This was a big change for her. Manfred made a therapeutic decision to keep on doing what he was doing as he understood the client-therapist relationship a lot more and was not concerned by the client's criticisms. This meant basically that he was reconfirmed in his own self. Joseph found that he could relax and enjoy his clients and had an increased ability to reflect on his sessions with his clients. He felt more able to go with the flow in himself and his clients and felt prepared for whatever may emerge. All participants reported changes in how they were working with their clients and also with a range of other clients such was the radiating effect of the role reversal. Lola was more aware of what she was experiencing in her body, more spontaneous and relaxed and more able to go with what was in herself, rather than letting her anxiety dictate. She was also aware of the effect she was having on several of her clients with these changes—a couple and with her team. In her words, "I am more aware of my own expectations on myself, which has always been there but it crops up once in a while and I think with this research study it cropped up here and so the expectation that I should solve the problem was high. Now that I am the team leader the girls are coming to me a bit more and that theme came up today, about the fixer role, parents leaving their kids here and expecting us to fix them, that sort of thing, and I said to myself that when I am feeling anxious that's when I have that expectation, that I should be doing something here". Lola said that she could let it go or just be more aware of it and was able to sit back and did not need to jump in and solve it. She said: "Just as soon as I recognize it, I say, well hang on, I'm doing this, sit back". She found she was more able to reflect on her feelings.

Manfred was reflective about several of his clients with whom he has had difficulty. In the interview session he really opened up about his clients and what he does with them. He spoke about a third client who has particular worldviews and values and doesn't know how to handle these. Manfred worked out that he just had to sit there and be with her and let her talk. He reported that after 2 weeks of him doing that, his client's affect (her mood) changed. Whilst he didn't know yet whether she had been able to maintain that from their last session he thought that through just being able to sit with someone, who is having suicidal feelings and no plans to do anything for themselves, is useful.

Joseph was very excited to notice new things in the following weeks after our supervision session; not only with his research client but also with other clients. He said: "There seemed like a shift deeply in the clients and I was quite intrigued with that and found it quite unusual in a way; unusual because it was a cluster, like three or four in a row and I thought, 'Wow!' I was surprised and intrigued and I thought is it something that I am kind of doing, because I think I remember mentioning in the supervision session, that I would like to 'bottle that up'[2]. I didn't know what *that* was but at the same time knowing and feeling that it was a result of a process for me of the way that I'm being".

13 Understanding the client-therapist relationship

All participants reported being more conscious of themselves and their clients; each had greater individuation and clarity about him or herself as a person separate from their clients. They had become more aware of the functioning, thoughts and feelings of themselves and their clients; not just the clients that they presented in the role reversal but with several of their clients. There was a radiating effect from the role reversal whereby they all felt more at ease with themselves in their work practice in general; their spontaneity increased and there was a corresponding decrease in anxiety. All participants came to the realization that being 'with' their clients rather than what they do or don't do with the client was important and subsequently they all became more aware of the client's needs. Through role reversal and experiencing being in the role of her client Lola realized her client just needed her to be there for him. Manfred realized he just needed to be present to his client. Joseph realized he could be himself with his clients and that was sufficient. Role reversal certainly helped in the participants feeling more separate from their clients and having different feelings. As Lola read out and talked about her responses in the questionnaire she reported that it was like looking at herself as a separate being like in a mirror. She could see herself being frustrated in the supervision session and she did not feel frustrated any more. She realized the client wasn't criticizing her rather that she had been critical of herself. During the action phase of the supervision session Lola became more connected with her self and her body. This was significant for her. She identified the strong somatic role of anxiety in her body. She was conscious of where it lay in her body, when it emerged with subsequent clients, what was going on, she was able to note when it lifted. The individuation occurred on a somatic level. Manfred did say he felt a bit vulnerable toward the end of the experience of role reversal. Joseph increased his auto-tele through the role reversal, that is, his relationship with himself. He was able to discern the meaning of ambivalence for himself he reframed it from something negative to something positive; he could see its function in his role system.

Through the experience of being involved in this study, the relationship with 'self' changed for all three participants and they became more confident. Role reversal improved each participant's relationship with his or her own self, that is to say, his or

Table 3 Core Theme 3: Role reversal as a mechanism for change

Subtheme 1: The radiating effect of the role reversal		
Lola	**Manfred**	**Joseph**
"I've seen my client after our session here and I find that I'm more able to be relaxed, be a bit more provocative, rather than, "I shouldn't say that, that's a bit wrong, or that's not appropriate", and to be able to sort of express what is it inside me in that way. I'm a bit more challenging for them all (her clients)I think and it probably shakes them up a bit."	"I have more clarity overall because whenever I'd see this other client I'd always leave those sessions feeling very angry because of his lack of remorse. After I left the session with him yesterday the funniest things came out of my mouth, quite Fawltyesque, (reference to Basil Fawlty in the TV series 'Fawlty Towers'). I can see that he doesn't understand his emotions very well and he doesn't want to; he's not interested in connecting."	"There was a marked change in our relationship when I saw her after the supervision session, like an elevation, I think she was already in that transition to change already, but at the same time I was more open too because of the experience of that role reversal, which gave me more preparedness to being open to whatever was to come in that session."

her auto-tele became more positive. Lola and Manfred had 'critical' role relationships with themselves in the beginning; being very self-critical and judgmental, however this changed as a result of the supervision. Joseph was not so much outwardly critical of himself, instead he expressed ambivalence about his functioning and ability.

All participants reported being more able to express themselves with their clients through their experience in the role reversal. Lola felt more able to challenge her client and express what was in her. Manfred became clearer about his clients' feelings and problems, his clients' needs and his own process. In the end he said he was happy to keep on doing what he does and being himself with his clients. He developed more confidence through this process. He also reached out to his work supervisor and shared his feelings with her about the client and she in turn was able to validate that it wasn't him but rather the client who plays games and attempts to sabotage the sessions. Since the client had refused to work with his supervisor he felt quite good that he was staying in the saddle; at least so far. Joseph identified with his early cultural upbringing and a way of viewing the world. I observed in him an integration of many of his roles from the past, the present and for the future. The following table is a summary of the participants' realizations from the whole research experience.

14 Researcher's reflections on holding multiple roles with participants

My participants were a little anxious in the beginning. Lola expressed this right at the start of the action part of her session. She said it was daunting having me there because she felt as if I was in the therapy session with her and her client. Manfred wrote that he felt more vulnerable after his supervision session. To some degree this may have been because I was also their psychodrama trainer and supervisor. However, in Manfred's case I think that it was because he actually felt more confident in himself and realized that he was working well; a new experience for him. He called it weird (see Table 4).

I think, that my multiple roles significantly increased each person's anxiety as to their competency as therapists. They wanted to do well with their clients and be seen

Table 4 Core Theme 4: Understanding the client-therapist relationship

Subtheme 1: Being aware of the client's needs		
Lola	**Manfred**	**Joseph**
"I think being true to what I feel is important rather than that sort of projection, of my need to solve it for him."	"I realized that I just needed to be present to him."	"I was concerned and cautious about what my client needed, I did get clear about that. I can be myself with her."
Subtheme 2: Greater individuation and awareness of self as therapist		
Lola	**Manfred**	**Joseph**
"I feel like I am wiser. I'm wiser and she (my old self) is learning, she's frustrated and she is learning. I am the future and she is the past. He (the client) isn't criticizing me. One thing I have gained from this, which is good is that I don't feel I have to do a whole drama. The role reversal is effective and quick. The emotion was so strong and it went so deep."	"I felt some clarity about my role, what I need to do, which is to just keep doing what I'm doing. I suppose the stuff that comes from him trying to make me be a different kind of therapist doesn't matter, I just have to do what I am doing, because you know it is working on some level. I also wrote don't try and change your personal style to one that doesn't suit you and be transparent and measured because that is what you are good at."	"To some extent I feel some sense of security now. There is still uncertainty but the ambivalence is not negative, it's not fear, and it's not being really scared. The uncertainty is skewed towards, it's a good thing, so this means that I'm not going to get lost, there is some stability in that uncertainty, there is security in that uncertainty and there is a sense of motivation, an interest in the change that is pleasing."
Subtheme 3: Greater confidence in self		
Lola	**Manfred**	**Joseph**
"The processing has been good too. With my emotions I have more awareness in my body. I recognized the signs early and that tapped me into what is going on when I am with clients. It was really good, really helpful that the anxiety that was on my chest lifted and I felt relief. I have a strong 'fix it' role and I have a battle between 'I have to know' versus 'I don't have to know.' I don't need to hide behind the superficial things because I don't know what to do. I just need to be curious with the client."	"I noticed at the time that it wasn't until I was in that mirror position that I could identify what I needed to do, so the stuff around just keeping doing what I am doing wasn't clear until I was in that mirror and it's weird because that mirror started off as quite a critical role. I'm speaking a little bit more confidently than I was at the start of this. It's weird reading something that tells me this is what you are good at (smiling)."	"I read something about the identity of the mountain people today…there is a part of me that considers myself as that particularly because I resided and studied there…proud of being that…irrespective of what other people may think or people may criticize it, so they are accepting of that identity…they don't try to become anything else…they are authentic and I like that."

as competent; the truth was they had some doubts about their functioning. They did however become more real with me through the whole process, more transparent and open and, equally, I with them. I modeled this way of being throughout the study and especially in the interview phase when I shared my feelings and thoughts as a fellow practitioner and supervisor. They felt more comfortable being vulnerable with me and opened up more as a result. Manfred reached out and confided in his supervisor at work about a client that he had previously felt very vulnerable about. He spontaneously did this after the supervision session. This encounter helped him considerably because he was able to see he wasn't the only one having a particular problem with the client. Joseph felt more at ease with himself and with his cultural heritage.

Table 5 Overview of participants realizations and actions after role reversal

Lola	Manfred	Joseph
More aware of her expectations on herself	Felt more ok being himself, no other changes necessary	More conscious of his reflection process during next session with client
Realized her own expectations that she should solve the client's problem	Needed to just keep doing what he was doing. To continue to be transparent and measured because that is what he is good at	Comfortable with being conscious of his private reflections in session with his client
Realized her tense feelings, that her body language was tense and that she was frustrated	Valued talking to his work supervisor who shared her feelings of incompetence, which were triggered by the same client	Marked change noticed in himself, like an elevation in relationship with his client to a closer relationship
Connected her feelings of anxiety to her expectation that she should be doing something	Realized that the client is not purposeful about sabotaging the session but rather is limited by his (the client's) roles	Role reversal made him more prepared for session with his client and to being open to whatever emerged
Insight into new behavior, sitting back in chair, feeling calmer	Insight into the value of sitting with a client regardless of the content of the material	Felt competent and aware whether he was helping or not helping the client. Competency needed to be maintained, like self- actualization, not to be complacent
Able to challenge client but not push	More open to provoking client	More flow in him, more open to that flow
Able to express more what is inside of her. Being true to herself.	Realized his respect for his client and was concerned to portray the client accurately. Thought his client was one of the most ethical people he had ever come across, even though the client had done such a terrible thing (a particular crime).	Always eager to learn. Felt ok as a therapist, meaning that he felt confident to do the job. He stopped being self-conscious about how he was performing or doing the right thing.

15 A brief comparison with Maxine Daniels' research and discussion

Maxine concluded in her study, that it would be valid to conduct a further study to ascertain whether participants with different supervisors gain the same results with the emergent themes. My study reflects her findings to a large degree as I did discover similar and strong emergent core themes. The subthemes differed in two respects: none of my participants experienced feeling trapped, stuck yes but not trapped: none felt like giving up on the client despite the frustration and various fears that they had. Maxine stated that her participants might have been biased towards a positive outcome in their answers. I don't think that my participants were biased particularly because they know that the more open they are to revealing and exploring their difficulties, the more we can trust them as ethical professional people capable of independently doing their work. For example, Manfred wrote that being in the mirror position first enabled him to discover something and after that he was able to work out what to do through the role reversal process. There is a possibility that participants may have had a desire to please me and if so this may have swayed results. However a fourfold process was in place, which allowed a tight scrutiny of the whole process to see if there was bias. Firstly there was the experience of being with them in the supervision session; secondly the data from the supervision session (the transcripts); thirdly their answers to the questionnaire; and fourthly the interview session the following month included the conversation and discussion coming from that. Each one of these things allowed for a cross referencing of experiences.

A further finding of Maxine's was that her participants felt deskilled as therapists (core theme 1, subtheme 1). My participants expressed some doubts that they had about what they were doing or not doing and I put this down to being doubtful or critical about their competence rather than them thinking they were *not* skilled enough. They wanted to explore their doubts in supervision to see what was blocking them or what else may have been affecting their work with their clients; so doubts were a motivating force for each.

Maxine stated, that all therapists reported a positive outcome of working with clients since experiencing the role reversal in the supervision session. I also found this to be so. My participants reported they also had positive outcomes with a number of other clients during the month after the supervision session. Thus I concluded that the role reversal experience had a radiating effect.

Maxine's participants all reported feeling more motivated and looking forward to working with their clients. This was also the case with my participants who were forward looking and feeling curious about how their clients would be the next time they saw them. They were all much more outward looking and not so introspective and critical of themselves. And finally Maxine reported that she learnt some things from her research, which were useful for her practice. I did too and that was to put myself more often in the shoes of my supervisees as they express themselves in relation to me. I can always learn something new about my clients and myself, which will benefit everyone. Learning is ongoing. There is something lovely and heartwarming about that.

16 Recommendations

1. I strongly recommend for any phenomenological enquiry such as this that an interview phase be incorporated. In the interview session the participants became clearer about their clients, their own process and other clients. The beauty of the session was it gave them a chance to process and discuss further what they wrote and experienced in their supervision session. Talking it through with me was important because it brought out more. Particularly it showed the changes they had experienced in the way they were now working and thinking about themselves. It also gave them an opportunity to have closure from the study and time to reflect on their own self-evaluation. This was significant for maintaining their autonomy, confidence and sense of self. In a repeated study it may be worthwhile to do another follow up session to see if the learning continued or how it was integrated further.
2. Role reversal would be a good technique for training psychotherapists in developing empathy toward themselves and their clients. In fact it would be a good training tool for a host of people in the health and welfare sectors, business and the education systems. However, the judicious use of role reversal is called for

because some people may require doubling first or need some mirroring before the role reversal. Being in another's shoes is a very powerful experience with many feelings arising from it; so training in psychodrama and supervision is recommended for those who want to use this technique.

Conclusions

I found that role reversal is an effective and economic technique in one-to-one supervision. Each participant showed a marked increase in consciousness and demonstrated that they felt more confident and confirmed in themselves and their abilities through the role reversal. The participants saw themselves and their clients more clearly and understood that not only what they do but also how they are in themselves (their being-ness) is integral to their practice as therapists. This latter fact helped considerably in reducing their anxiety around being competent. Each had more empathy for their clients and this occurred through being in the shoes of the clients. This excerpt from a popular Country and Western song, "Walk a Mile in My Shoes" (South 1970) perhaps sums it up:

> If I could be you, if you could be me for just one hour, If we could find a way to get inside each other's mind, If you could see you through my eyes instead of your ego, I believe you'd be surprised to see that you've been blind, Walk a mile in my shoes, walk a mile in my shoes, Hey, before you abuse, criticize and accuse, Walk a mile in my shoes (Chorus).

Notes

1 For more information on symmetrical and complementary role relationships, as coined by the anthropologist, Gregory Bateson, see: Bateson in: Watzlawick (1967/2011) and Daniel (2013).

2 Australian slang meaning something is so good we want to put it in a bottle and keep it so we can have it again.

References

Daniel, S. (2006). Day by day: Role theory, sociometry and psychodrama with adolescents and young women. *Journal of Group Psychotherapy, Psychodrama and Sociometry, 58*, 195–205.

Daniel, S. (2007). Psychodrama, role theory and the cultural atom: New developments in role theory. In C. Baim, J. Burmeister & M. Maciel. (Eds.), *Psychodrama: Advances in theory and practice*. London: Routledge.

Daniel, S. (2013). The supervisory relationship in psychodrama training: More than a process. In H. Krall, J. Fürst & P. Fontaine. (Eds.), *Supervision in psychodrama: Experiential learning in psychotherapy and training*. Germany: Springer VS.

Daniels, M. (2008). What do supervisee's experience when role reversing with their clients in the supervision session? *Practice evaluation project*. Doctorate in psychotherapy by professional studies. Cohort 10, (DPY 4443). Paper delivered at the British Psychodrama and Sociodrama Conference, "Embodiment of Change." July 2011.

Elliott, R., Slatick, M., & Urman, M. (2001). Qualitative change process research on psychotherapy: Alternative strategies. *Psychologische Beiträge, 43*(3), 69.
Gimenez Hinkle, M. (2008). Psychodrama: A creative approach for addressing parallel process in group supervision. *Journal of Creativity in Mental Health, 3*(4). doi:10.1080/15401380802527464. (Haworth Press)
Greenberg, L., Rice, S., & Elliott, R. (1993). *Process-experiential therapy: Facilitating emotional change*. New York: Guilford.
James, W. (1902). *The variety of religious experiences*. Longman Publishing. Group. (Wikipedia).
Kelly, G. A. (1969). Humanistic methodology in psychological research. *Journal of Humanistic Psychology, 11*(1), 53–65.
Kipper, D. A., & Ritchie, T. D. (2003). The effectiveness of psychodramatic techniques: A meta-analysis. *Group Dynamics: Theory and Practice, 7*(1), 13–25.
Kvale, S. (1996). *Interviews: An introduction to qualitative research interviewing*. Thousand Oaks: Sage.
Lee, H. (1960/2010). *To kill a mockingbird*. USA: Hachette Book Group: Grand Central Publishing.
Lippitt, R. (1958). The auxiliary chair technique. *Group Psychotherapy, 11*, 8–23.
McVea, C. S., Gow, K., & Lowe, R. (2011). Comprehensive interpersonal experience in psychodrama group therapy: A comprehensive process analysis of significant therapeutic events. *Psychotherapy Research*, 1–14. http:/dx.doi.org/10.1080/10503307.2011.577823.
Moreno, J. L. (1934/1953). *Who shall survive? Foundations of sociometry, group psychotherapy and sociodrama*. Beacon: Beacon House Inc. (Wikipedia).
Moreno, J. L. (1946/1972). *Psychodrama. Vol.1: Fourth edition with new introduction*. Ambler: Beacon House, Inc.
Moreno, J. L., & Moreno, Z. T. (1959/1975). "Universal peace in our time." *Psychodrama. Vol. 3: Action therapy and principles of practice* (2nd ed.). Beacon: Beacon House, Inc.
Moustakas, C. (1990). *Heuristic research: Design, methodology and applications*. London: Sage Publications, Inc.
Moustakas, C. (1994). *Phenomenological research methods*. London: Sage Publications, Inc.
Smith, J. A. (2008). *Qualitative psychology: A practical guide to research methods* (2nd ed.). London: Sage Publications.
South, J. (1970). *Walk a mile in my shoes*. Wikipedia.
Thoreau, H. J. (1854). *Walden*. Boston: Ticknor and Fields.
Van der May, J., & Peake, T. (1980). Psychodrama as a psychotherapy supervision technique. *Journal of Group Psychotherapy, Psychodrama and Sociometry, 33*, 25–32.
Watzlawick, P., Beavin Bavelas, J., & Jackson, D. D. (1967/2011). *Pragmatics of human communication: A study of interactional patterns, pathologies and paradoxes*. London: W. W Norton & Co.
Willig, C. (2008). *Phenomenological methods: Introducing qualitative research in psychology* (2nd ed.). England Open University Press.
Young, E. (1946). *Algonquin Indian tales*. Boston: Indy Publishing.

Sue Daniel is a Trainer, Educator and Practitioner (TEP) in psychodrama, a consulting psychologist, supervisor, organisational consultant, and individual and group psychotherapist in private practice, living in Melbourne, Australia. Honorary Visiting Professor, Muroran Institute of Technology, Hokkaido, Japan. Director, Psychodrama Institute of Melbourne, Australia.

Z Psychodrama Soziometr (2016) (Suppl) 15:255–274
DOI 10.1007/s11620-015-0309-6

HAUPTBEITRÄGE

Zeitschrift für Psychodrama und Soziometrie

The influence of psychodrama on promoting self-disclosure in groups of university students

Olcay Çam

Published online: 10 December 2015

Abstract The purpose of this study was to investigate the influence of psychodrama on self-disclosure, which is an important skill of interpersonal relationships.

It was carried out with a group of university students (5 females, 3 males) and comprised 13 psychodrama sessions. Each session lasted for 4 h and all the members were unmarried. Two psychodrama psychotherapists participated in the sessions alternating their therapist and co-therapist roles each session. Six of the sessions were group plays or sociodrama, five of the sessions were protagonist plays. One of the sessions explored "the meaning of the life" by using the objects in the room; each member explained the reason why s/he had chosen a certain object and what it meant to her/him. The last session was the "magic shop" game.

"Jourard Self-Disclosure Inventory" (Selçuk, İnsan İlişkilerinde Kendini Açma (Self-disclosure in Interpersonal Relationships), Vadi Yayıncılık, Ankara, 1992; Öner, Türkiye'de Kullanılan Psikolojik Testler. (Psychological Tests Used in Turkey) 3. Baskı, Boğaziçi Üniversitesi Yayınları, İstanbul, pp 398–399, 1997) and "The Communication Skills Evaluation Scale" (Korkut, The Journal Of Psychological Counselling And Guidance, 2(7)18–23, 1996a) were applied to the students at the beginning of the sessions. These tests were repeated at the end of the psychodrama process in order to observe the influence of psychodrama on the scores. It was confirmed that university students' self-disclosure scores were increased by psychodrama. As the students evaluated their interpersonal communication skills during this period, they became aware of their need for developing higher communication skills. The author concludes that awareness of communication skills was raised via psychodrama and that psychodrama is a useful method for increasing and developing self-disclosure.

Prof. Dr. O. Çam (✉)
Nursing Faculty, Ege University,
35100 Bornova-Izmir, Turkey
E-Mail: olcaycam@gmail.com

Keywords Self-disclosure · Psychodrama · University student · Communication skills

Der Einfluss des Psychodramas auf die Förderung der Selbstoffenbarung innerhalb einer Gruppe von StudentInnen

Zusammenfassung Die Selbstauskunft ist eine wichtige Fähigkeit der zwischenmenschlichen Beziehungen. Das Ziel dieser Studie war den Einfluss von Psychodrama auf die Selbstauskunft zu untersuchen.

Die Studie, die aus 13 Psychodramasitzungen bestand, wurde mit einer Gruppe von UniversitätsstudentInnen (5 weiblich, 3 männlich) durchgeführt. Jede Sitzung dauerte vier Stunden. Alle Teilnehmerinnen und Teilnehmer waren ledig. Zwei Psychodrama-TherapeutInnen leiteten die Sitzungen, bei der sie die TherapeutInnen- und Co-TherapeutInnen-Rollen abwechselnd übernommen haben. Sechs der Sitzungen waren Gruppenspiele oder Soziodramen und fünf davon waren ProtagonistInnen-Spiele. Eine der Sitzungen war dem Thema „Der Sinn des Lebens" gewidmet. In dieser Sitzung hat sich jede Teilnehmerin und jeder Teilnehmer einen Gegenstand im Raum ausgesucht. Sie erläuterten jeweils warum sie den jeweiligen Gegenstand auswählten und was dieser Gegenstand ihnen bedeutete. Die letzte Sitzung war das Spiel „Der Zauberladen".

„Jourard Selbstauskunft Fragebogen" (Selçuk, İnsan İlişkilerinde Kendini Açma (Self-disclosure in Interpersonal Relationships), Vadi Yayıncılık, Ankara, 1992) und „The Communication Skills Evaluation Scale" (Korkut, The Journal Of Psychological Counselling And Guidance, 2(7)18–23, 1996a) wurden vor dem Beginn der Psychodrama Sitzungen angewandt. Diese wurden nach der letzten Sitzung wiederholt, um den Einfluss von Psychodrama auf die Scores zu untersuchen. Es wurde bestätigt, dass die Selbstauskunft-Scores der StudentInnen durch Psychodrama gestiegen sind. Dadurch dass die StudentInnen in diesem Zeitraum eigene zwischenmenschliche Kommunikationsfähigkeiten selbst bewerten mussten, wurde ihnen der Bedarf bewusst, diese Fähigkeiten weiter zu entwickeln. Die Schlussfolgerungen der Studie sind folgende: a) Das Bewusstsein für die Kommunikationsfähigkeiten erhöht sich durch das Psychodrama, und b) das Psychodrama ist ein wirksamer Ansatz, die Selbstauskunft zu entwickeln und zu steigern.

Schlüsselwörter Selbstoffenbarung · Psychodrama · StudentInnen · Kommunikationsfähigkeiten

1. Introduction

On psychodrama stage, people gain their own methods of expressing themselves in accord with their own developmental process and their own personality. In brief, psychodrama is the transformation of the person's inner world into action (Dökmen 1995).

Moreno admits that there are two basic features of personal development; the first being the development of interpersonal skills socio-emotional development and the second being the experience gained while acquiring roles (role development). He asserts that the concept of role can be seen in every phase of life. In all his thoughts on development, his point of departure is the concept of spontaneity. He claims that a person is not pushed into his own existence blindfoldedly; on the contrary, even in the embryonal stage, s/he forms a spontaneous relationship with his/her own world. From the very beginning, the human is a being who takes action and manifest behaviours. The human being is in interaction with the cosmos even in predevelopment stages (Özbek and Leutz 1987; Schützenberger-Ancelin 1995).

In adolescence, while reviewing the people whom s/he identified himself with in his childhood, the young person tries new roles with the new people identified. S/He tries to make a choice among these roles and construct a plan for his future. Determining how and as whom the young person will proceed in his/her life, these roles have a binding effect. The adolescent has difficulty feeling himself as whole person not only because of the question of how much the choices waiting for him in the future are in accord with the adolescent's past and wishes, but also because of the variety of roles and people identified both in the past and at present (Bakar 1996). In order for the young person to develop new behaving patterns, to understand, present, work on and experiment solutions to the problems he faces with-in interpersonal relationships, the psychodrama group psychotherapy creates a suitable environment. It is accepted in psychodrama that both the physical and the social environment are important factors to affect the individuals' feelings and behaviours. It is also known that techniques in psychodrama group psychotherapy requiring actions such as playing a role are helpful in developing ego identity, thus helping the young person to have a chance to experience different feelings and experiment different behaviours and roles (Öztürk-Kılıç 1990).

Given the chance of experimenting a variety of roles (the role of a father, son, friend, lover, etc.), the young individual can learn how to express himself within these roles and deal with these different roles. He can apply what he has learned within a particular role to different situations. In other words, when he achieves more, he can overcome more difficulties and he can create new patterns without being stuck to the usual (Blatner 1973).

What bases the interpersonal relationships is the ability to express one's ideas and feelings to the others. In most of those relationships, one is expected to make a judgement on a subject, to give his opinions and to disclose himself. While being about objective situations related with different people, places and events, these judgements can also be related with the personal subjective situations (Hargie et al. 1981).

As it was cited by Durak-Batıgün (1998) one of the effective therapeutic factors was self-disclosure. Self-disclosing behaviour is also a pre-requisite for the other therapeutic factors to emerge. The more the individuals disclose of themselves, the more they can benefit from the group therapy (Durak-Batıgün 1998).

Self-disclosure can involve past and present events in the life of the individual, his fantasies and dreams, his future hopes and wishes and present feelings towards others (Yalom 1992).

Self-disclosure had been defined as: "The act of verbally and non-verbally sharing with another some aspects of what makes you a person, aspects the other individual would not be likely to recognize or understand without your help. The importance of self-disclosure, as a social skill, is usually associated with the work of Sidney Jourard who emphasised the value of this skill in interpersonal communication" (Cited in Selçuk 1992). Jourard stressed the need for a high degree of openness between individuals in many contexts, and illustrated the potency of self-disclosure as a technique for encouraging deep levels of interpersonal sharing. Self-disclosure becomes conspicuous the nature of the interaction (Hargie et al. 1981).

Valued by the participants although they are sometimes afraid of doing, self-disclosure is a complementary part of all group therapy practices. It has been indicated by many studies that as the amount of self-disclosure in the group increases, the bond within the group gets stronger (Göka 1998; Naar 1987; Öztürk-Kılıç 1990; Öztürk Kılıç and Özbay 1993; Yalom 1992; Gökler 1998.)

During the process of gaining roles, the individual starts to get socialized through language while forming self-evaluations. During the process of socialization, in interpersonal relationships, the individual has to express and disclose himself. Meanwhile, the individual constructs his own individual world. Through this world, he gets into relationships with others. Within these relationships, expressing and disclosing himself helps him get feedback from the others, which, in turn, helps him improve his individually-constructed world.

In the line of this information, the aim of this study is to show how psychodrama carried out with a group of university students' affects self-disclosure, or the ability of self-expression, one of the skills in interpersonal relationships.

2 Method

The group sessions ran during an academic year, excluding the semester holiday and the exam periods. The 4-hour long group studies were carried out on Fridays afternoons. The place for the group meeting was in the Department of Psychological Guidance, Counselling and Rehabilitation at Ege University Directorate of Health, Culture and Sports. The group sessions were held by two directors alternately and they changed their therapist and co-therapist roles every following session. A psychologist was included in the session in order to record the data. At the beginning and end of the group sessions, group members were administered two different scales: Self-Disclosure Inventory and The Communication Skills Evaluation Scale. Considering its importance in terms of interpersonal relationships, we formed mixed groups of male and female students.

Eight of the sessions were group play or sociodrama; five were protagonist centred; one of the sessions explored the "meaning of the life" by using the objects in the room. Each of the members explained why she/he chose that object and what was the meaning of the whole and parts of the object. The last session was "magic shop".

3 Instruments (scales used in the study)

Two scales, Self-Disclosure Inventory and The Communication Skills Evaluation Scale, were applied to the students at the beginning and end of the group sessions.

Self-disclosure inventory. Self-Disclosure Inventory was developed by Jourard and Lasakow. Feriha Baymur translated it into Turkish and Doğan (1983) adapted it for Turkey (Öner 1997). This version was also validated by Selçuk (1992) and is proved to have high validity.

The inventory has 6 subscales: self-disclosure regarding:

1. Ideas and opinions,
2. The school or occupation,
3. The family,
4. Personality,
5. Body,
6. Sexuality.

There are 5 components of the inventory which identifies the people to whom the individual discloses himself: to mother, to father, to a friend of the same sex, to a friend of the opposite sex and to an educator/a teacher. For each part, the choices differ as "2", "1", and "0"; "2" being "self-disclosure without any hesitation", "1" being "giving a general opinion when asked, a bit hesitating", "0" being "keeping silent" and "X" being "giving an incorrect information about a subject". The participants are asked to choose one of those choices for each part. While "0" and "X" do mean no points, "2" means 2 points and "1" means 1 point. The total scores are calculated for each subscale. Moreover, the scores are also calculated for each part regarding the recipients of the self-disclosure. In consequence, each individual has a total score for each 6 subscales and 5 components (showing to whom and how much the individual discloses himself). The higher the total score, the higher the self-disclosure (Beydoğan 1994; Öner 1997; Selçuk 1992).

Communication skills evaluation scale. This 25-item scale was developed by Korkut (1996a), to understand how individuals evaluate their own communication skills on gradual scale from 0 to 5. The highest score to be obtained in the scale is 100 and a high total score indicates that the individual evaluates his communication skills in a positive way. The validity and reliabilityof the scale were also tested by Korkut (1996a, b).

4 Information about the group

Group members. 12 students participated in each of the two introductory meeting. 7 members from one group and 8 from the other decided to participate to the groups. We gave them a period of three weeks of trial. So, after those weeks, we started with 10 members to the continuous sessions. Until the end, with 2 drop outs, 8 members were left. However, because of the inconsistencies with the others' schedules, a total

Table 1 Participants' Characteristics

Member No	Gender/Age	School/Degree	The reason for applying
1	Male/21	Faculty of Science, 3rd year	Having difficulties in interpersonal relationships, lack of self-confidence, difficulty expressing his feelings
2	Female/22	Faculty of Medicine, 3rd year	Having difficulty with concentrating on lessons, discomfort, sadness, and communication problems
3	Male/22	Faculty of Arts, 4th year	Having difficulties in relationships, desire to be relaxed and safe, worries about her future
4	Female/21	School of Languages, 3rd year	Adaptation problems, desire for self-exploration, boredom and discomfort.
5	Female/18	School of Nursing, 1st year	Distrust, being extremely emotional, touchiness, not being able to get into different environments
6	Female/22	Faculty of Engineering, 4th year	Not being able to behave independently, extreme attachment to the family, inability to express ideas and feelings, concerns about academic success, fear of being unsuccessful
7	Male/22	Faculty of Agriculture, 4th year	Discomfort, boredom, having problems with friends, decrease in academic success
8	Female/21	School of Teacher, 4th year	Lack of self-confidence, disinterest to the environment, concentration problems, and shy

of 8 students, 3 males and 5 females, continued the sessions until the end. For ethical reasons, their names and surnames are not revealed in this study (Table 1).

5 Group process

When the group members were asked about the therapists' participation in the sessions, they revealed the negative effect of one director missing a session.

Session one. In the first group session after the director therapist gave an example, the members stood behind their chairs and introduced a seated member as if they were someone else for the purpose of introducing group members. After all the group members were introduced, the therapist had the group move with the suggestion, "everyone will become a flower in the place and shape that they want." All the members chose a flower from nature, which included, difenbachia, small daisy, rose bud, large red rose, large daisy, sea water lily, pond water lily and ivy. The therapist chatted with each flower with questions like what state they were in, why, and how they felt.

Session two. In the second group session, after talking with the group members about general topics, they were divided into groups of two for warm-up games. Each couple pair was asked to choose the best place for them and explain to the other person for 10 min an event that affected them the most, then the other member did the same for a total of 20 min. After this activity they played the "Puss-In-The-Corner" game. At the end the most successful group member was applauded and announced as leader. The therapist asked, "Since you have a leader, what would you like to do with her/him?" After the members discussed different ideas it was decided to enact a parliament. The parliament was enacted as a group game.

Session three. In the third session, the focus was their relationships with members of the opposite sex. Two group members wanted to act out a problem they had experienced with their boyfriends. The group chose a protagonist. During the action phase relationships were enacted on three separate stages and the protagonist's intense and mixed feelings were made clear during the play. The member understood how negatively these feelings affected the relationship. The therapist asked what could have been done differently in these situations and these changes were tried. The most appropriate one was repeated. At the end of the play the member was exhausted but more at ease (member number eight was the group protagonist).

Session four. In the fourth session a member who had lost an uncle wanted help coping with this loss. The protagonist had just learned that she was pregnant and while she was thinking about telephoning her mother who lived in another city and telling her, the telephone rang and she learned about his death. In the play this telephone conversation was enacted. The member realized during the play that she feared losing her mother more than her uncle and together with this concern she had a deep need for support from her mother. The auxiliary who acted as her mother during the play embraced her with positive words and this emotional support started to meet her need for support. The same auxiliary had recently fear of lose her own mother, and merely by acting like a secret protagonist in this role she herself needed support and stated that this communication was good for her. At the end of the session both protagonist and auxiliary thanked the group for helping her understand her relationship with her mother and her needs; she emerged with a plan to resolve.

Session five. In the fifth session a member wanted to explore the consequences of losing a semester due to failing and then not telling her parent; she was in her final year and anxious. The protagonist said that it would be enough for her father to know. She said that she would want to be alone with her father when she told him and added that a situation had occurred when she could have told her father. One of the group members took on the role of her father. The father came into room and the protagonist did not speak with the father then went into another room and talked to herself. Then the protagonist gained insight saying, "I want to talk with my father, but again I can't do it," "I'm afraid," and tried to show the difference in the situation. Then the therapist, supporting the protagonist, encouraged her by saying, "You can try to do now what you could not do there." On the stage that had been set the protagonist tried to talk with her father. During the play the therapist frequently changed the protagonist and father's roles. During these role changes the protagonist said, "Now I really want my father to hug me and hold me," and verbalized the need that she felt to be loved by her father.

The therapist encouraged the protagonist to act in accordance with her need. The protagonist cried and hugged her father and stayed like that for a while. The protagonist said that she realized she had a need for a warm relationship with her father and they hugged. After the play ended a group circle was formed for sharing. The protagonist stated that first she wanted to listen to the group. When all the members actively participated and she realized that a child needs to feel close to their father. Sharing took place with examples of what other group members had experienced.

Feedback was received that her father did not know any other attitude other than being authoritarian in the role of a father and that she was bothered by that. The therapist said, "Our mothers and fathers may not have had close relationships with their own mothers and fathers. Maybe they do not know any other attitudes to have. They may have missed an opportunity to experience a closer relationship with their parents. With support we might be able to get our parents used to different attitudes." One of the members said, "One day I was going on a long holiday. I said good-bye to my mother but I forgot my father. My mother reminded me not to forget my father. When I turned and said good-bye to my father as well I will never forget my father's joy." The protagonist said, "During the play I saw clearly that it was not important whether or not I told him that I had failed my classes. I understood what my real need was. Next week when I go home I am going to act differently." In this play it was seen that a problem that arose when a family was not told about a lost semester turned out to be, in actuality, a need for a father's love.

Here the protagonist can use external cases to reflect internal feelings and bring to the surface the internal reflection (need for love and acceptance) of the external problem (not saying that she had lost a semester). Psychodrama can not only help individuals gain insight about themselves but can also help them make changes in their internal lives. Internal life that is reflected in the process is made concrete in a visual way and enacted on stage. An individual relives their internal world that is made concrete on stage, perceives it, remembers it and then internalizes it again. This is now a changed and new internal feeling (Gökler 1998).

Session six. In the next meeting one of the members who was quiet said, "I have been thinking about the play last week of hugging a father, as a result of an event I experienced when I was a child, I avoid physical contact with people, and I realized this last week when I took the role on stage of hugging a father. When I was in my role in the play I realized I had an intense need to be hugged." She became the chosen protagonist.

While the protagonist walked on the stage together with the therapist remembered an occasion recently when she was able to comfortably hug his closest girlfriend. During the action she realized that the person she need to be hugged by the most was her boyfriend, in fact she was not wanted by her boyfriend, and because this relationship continued this way she was very angry at both herself and at her boyfriend. At the end of this scene, we moved to a scene where protagonist experienced the emotion the most of not being needed by her boyfriend. When this scene was enacted during the protagonist role she perceived the moment when she felt the need the most to be close emotionally was the most she was not wanted.

At the end of the play most of the group members met the protagonist's need to be sincerely close, hugged her and acted in ways she needed. During sharing the member who had taken the role of the boyfriend gave feedback that he was very bothered that the protagonist did not act sincerely like she was afraid of ending her relationship with her boyfriend and because she kept this relationship suspended. One of the female members (member number five, female, 18 years old) explained an event when she had experienced an attack when she was eight years old, and said, "I understand this for the first time in my life." This member stated that the scene that was enacted had a part in her making connections with her relationships with boyfriends that were uneasy. It was seen that this protagonist scene helped the group members to see how they could have tied their problems with having trusting, physical contact with the opposite sex to events that had happened previously (with negative experiences, in particular).

A member that had been protagonist in a previous group stated that she had clarified her relationship with her boyfriend and decided to stay friends and that this put her at ease. Group members began to talk about how to start a special relationship, end it, and, after ending it, to continue to be friends. Because the group members were showing an inclination to talk and being indecisive about a play to enact, the therapist decided to do something about their indecision and to cause them to make an appropriate decision. The group members accepted her recommendation and decided to enact a group play about indecision and deciding whether or not to start a relationship with someone of the opposite sex. The group played an improvisation group scene of a meeting of a group of friends in a university cafeteria. During the scene some members, on the subject of making a decision, chose roles appropriate to their real situations, and some members took opposite roles.

While enacting this improvisation the group members made connections between their real life situations and the process of decisiveness and indecision that was experienced in the play. For example a member who experienced a situation of advising another member in this role, and who had made an offer of friendship stated that he understood her and her family's behaviors better that he had experienced in his own life. Some members also while thinking they were decisive realized that in reality they were indecisive. In addition in relationships with the opposite sex they saw the effect the decision making process leaves on them and their awareness on this subject was broadened.

Session seven. In this session as well the group members warmed up by talking. While they were talking the themes that arose that had not been addressed were the meaning of life, feelings of loneliness, and unwanted states in life. The therapist said, "Everyone can use objects in the room to express the 'meaning of life' to them." To accomplish this, the group members were told to move around the room and warm up well. Using objects in the room they chose a place and put themselves into an appropriate posture. In this way they created situations that they wanted to change in their lives and the meaning of life. The therapist, after a certain amount of time, went around to the group members who were ready. The first member who was ready (member number eight) had taken a certain posture in a chair in the room. "This is the meaning of my life," he said. The therapist put herself into the role of every part of the chair. The member said, "I am on this chair, people come and pass by. Sometimes unimportant people come as well. Should I stop them? I think. The chair's cover is unraveling. I'm aware of this. I need to repair it but I am postponing it for now. This unraveling isn't interfering with much of anything, it is noticed from the outside but it isn't something that needs to be taken care of right away. It is just something that needs to be repaired; it can be repaired when the time comes." Then, as the legs of the chair, "I am carrying him." There is a lot here, acquaintances, family, friends, loved ones, "We are what keeps you on your feet," they are saying. The therapist corresponding with him said, "He needs us. He learns a lot from us. We are a part of him." The therapist noticed the colors of the protagonist. The protagonist said, "It is mixed but lively colors." The protagonist took a corresponding seating place and said, "This place gives security and trust. I am in harmony with the environment. " Then supporting the back, for the back of the chair, he said, "It gives strength and support."

Another member (second member) became a vase with a wide base and narrow top that was supported on a cupboard next to the wall. One member (member number six) first became a book, then a flower and then different objects. In this process his meaning of life was asked. The therapist helped the group member clarify what his meaning in life was and what it was that he wanted to change in his life by changing roles with each object and when necessary becoming his own protagonist. This member realized that he was concentrating on the subject of how he was of benefit to others as every object and was not able to think what he himself was to others thinking that he was useful.

After a similar process was completed with all members, in the sharing and feedback stage it was observed that all members began to have broader understanding about what could and could not be done in real life, and what they could be, and they began to notice what their life limitations were at this time.

Session eight. At the beginning of the session the member number two verbalized that she was experiencing an urgent problem in her relationship with her fiancée. Member number seven also shared two poems he had written with the group. There was a common theme from both members about love and lovers. The group members were first inclined to the member with a stated need and when the other member accepted this, the member experiencing a problem with her fiancée became the protagonist. The first scene of the play was a home and family setting. The protagonist was warmed up with role changes. Then under these conditions the other members acted as if it had been them and showed her. The first scene that was enacted by the protagonist herself was followed by a fellow ego using the same technique for the protagonist. In this was the protagonist behaved differently than her own behaviors and was able to have an idea about how her relationship was formed. At the end of the play the feedback of the member who had the role of her fiancée was particularly important for the protagonist. The feedback and sharing from the other members gave support and confidence to the protagonist.

Session nine. The group members were happy to be together again in this first session after a long semester break. In their first conversations after the holiday the subjects they discussed were about what they experienced when they met with their friends from school and meeting with friends of the opposite sex. After this discussion the therapist divided the group into two, half of the group was to be girls and half was to be boys. She told the members that they could be in the place they wanted and could interact however they wanted. The members decided how they would compare together with couples that they formed. After every couple confronted each other the command was given, "now boys are girls and girls are boys" and the game was repeated. After this warm-up it was decided that every member would briefly explain one story, the other members would become the people explained in the story according to the places and an improvisation of the story would be made. While one member was explaining her story the others acted it out. With this technique (play-back) while explaining stories members who were ready would act out the story at the same time. The places where the stories took place were a school, laboratory, canteen, cafe and classrooms. The contents included same sex and opposite sex relationships and some competitors. After a certain interval the group members got together and enjoyed each other.

Session ten. Group members at the beginning of the group were talking about the holiday in the days ahead, how the weather was getting warmer and the intensity of classes. The therapist, for the purpose of getting the group to get used to warming up while talking, had the group stand up, and according to their level of energy and need, to take their own place and position in the room. As a result of this the group was seen to get at ease, rest and have fun together. It became clear that the group had a shared need for a holiday. Based on the leaning of the group the therapist recommended to the group that they could play a holiday fantasy, the members quickly made a holiday play and prepared to go on a holiday. Being given attention and feeling of closeness by the owner of the guest-house where they went (who was a co-therapist) they had fun and a good time (group play).

In the role feedback and sharing time the group members verbalized that they were pleased that they did something together. All members participated actively in this play. One of the members tried to do something for others and shared that she was happy that she was able to meet others' needs.

Penultimate session. The psychodrama group work had come to an end. To end the group at the first of the last two sessions the decision was made according to the wishes of the group members that a group play, "daydream," would be enacted. Daydream was a group study using imagination and visualization of their life. Opportunity was provided for relationships in the group to be seen as how other group members perceived them. At the same time provision was made for conflicts that members expect to be solved in their lives to be brought up. The therapist had the group members lie on their backs on the floor with their heads in the middle in a circle and their feet extending in a star fashion. The room lights were dimmed. The group members were asked to close their eyes. The members were allowed time to relax. The therapist asked the members to focus on an image that came to their mind or to take a recommendation that she gave (grass, mountain, etc.) The members shared with each other when their images were clarified. A sheet was placed on the floor to prepare the stage. The group members were arranged in a star fashion on the floor. After the therapist had them relax the group was told to put themselves in a grassy green field. The members discussed one by one what they saw there and where they were and what they were doing there. One member was a shepherd, another member saw herself as a child playing there, another that there were car noises in the distance, that she was a child running like she was escaping from something in the green field, then she got confused and saw herself in front of a deep ditch and saw herself fall into the ditch. The ditch was made of soil. The child was stuck and felt like she couldn't get out. People came from nearby and threw a rope to the child. The child didn't want to take the rope but the people convinced her. The child took the rope and left herself to the initiatives of those above. At first the child could not be brought out but then the child was thoroughly encouraged and came out on her own. The child was confused, the surroundings were very bright. When she saw herself there she saw a cabin. She went there and saw her mother. The child was put at ease.

In this session there was no group writer. Later in interviews with the members to remember what happened in this session the member who had the best memory of the daydream was the member who saw the child.

In the sharing phase of this session there was a feeling of peace in the members as those who saved the child who fell into the ditch that they had been successful saving a child. This session was planned to unite the group as a part of group psychotherapy with universal feelings of altruism or loneliness. The member who was the child, prior to this group work, had felt isolated and insecure in relationships with friends, that these feelings had changed completely since these groups and this play and felt lucky and special that she had had this chance to participate in psychodrama in her university years and wanted to thank all of the members and therapists. It is believed that this member, who was the last to open up to the group and experienced difficulties when she opened up, was benefited by the group acceptance and support.

The final session. Psychodrama was the last session of the group psychotherapy group. The group members, while warming up even though this was the last group session, discussed that they were close to every member who talked about things that they could not do and that there were other problems that they could not solve. In this context they were stating their resistance to the group ending. The therapist however recommended the game, "magic store," thinking that it would be a part in helping them see what they had obtained and the strength they had. "Magic store-shop" is a psychodramatic technique that moves from fantasy to symbolism and from there to the truth. The play begins with the question, "What object, what value, and what virtue would you most like to buy?" The individual, in comparing what s/he will take, finds opportunity to observe the value in what s/he will give to get something else. The individual realizes what this change or exchange that s/he wants symbolizes for him/herself and tries to connect it to what is true in his/her current life (Schützenberger-Ancelin 1995; Gökler 1998).

The magic shop was an activity in which the therapist works primarily one to one and at times together with the members and increases the individuals' awareness of their characteristics and the function of these characteristics. In the magic shop a person finds everything that they can add to the world spiritually. Group members can buy from the store any value that they want to have. However they have to exchange something for everything they want to buy. When members want to buy something they decide what they want to give in exchange. The wise elderly store owner does not want the store or the customer to be harmed and it is very important that everything that is given and taken be of the same value. The store owner needs to understand well what the member wants and why. The characteristic that the customer requests needs to be something that increases the awareness of or benefit of understanding more deeply the characteristic that they are requesting to buy from the store. In advanced stages of group work a better result is obtained. The leader needs to be able to play well, needs to be knowledgeable about transfers and well-prepared. To prevent potential problems it is explained that the store is always open, that things purchased can be given back and that different things can be taken and given.

In the play the therapist became a wizard and the co-therapist was a helper who worked next to him and made decisions with him. While doing this the therapists were warming themselves up while they explained the store to the members and helped them to warm-up. Every member wanted to shop separately. When they felt they were ready they entered the store in turn to give the decisions they had made. However the store owner was bargaining strictly by asking the member who came in whether or not what they wanted was in the store and what they would give in exchange for it.

The things that those who went into the magic store wanted to buy and what they were willing to give in exchange were these:

- For being able to enjoy life, to lose physical health and be bedridden (member number two).
- For having confidence, to give youth and lose the years gained with confidence (member number two).
- For being successful at work, to not have a social life (member number five).
- For being able to take a one month time package, to not have a vacation for two years (member number eight).
- For having a happy and peaceful family life, not having a career and work life (member number four).
- For having a perfect physical appearance, not having intelligence and intellectual ability (member number seven),
- For having courage, to not have feelings of desire (member number six).

The most common state in coming to the magic shop and the last member's request was for "courage."

None of the members refused to make an exchange. Their areas of awareness increased about values and what they would take and give by talking during the shopping. In the feedback phase, when the group members were told that this store was not opened for selling but for not selling they laughed. At the end of the game all of the members were thoroughly exhausted. However they were more relaxed than they had been at the beginning of the game. They shared the fear and concern they felt for their friends while watching them bargain with each other and decide whether or not to give up something.

During the sharing phase the members stated that it was good to be able to trade back the time or thing that they had exchanged for something they got from the magic shop, and that even if they had done something wrong they could get rid of it and they focused on the importance of being able to change. Because it was the last session the group members held hands together standing in a circle. They closed their eyes and made wishes for each other. Then they opened their eyes and shot off rockets into the sky that had their wishes.

6 Commentary

The unity and togetherness of the group was more evident with the going on a holiday together, and playing daydream and magic shop games. In the group holiday game the role of guest house therapist portrayed by the co-therapist showed that the co-therapist was understood both as having something to manage and as being a group member spending time together. In the daydream game the members experienced positive and unified support from each other and at the same time they worked to help her overcome her feelings of loneliness that had been made clear as the same as the child who had fallen. This situation at the end of the group is thought to have been beneficial in the process of the members making an effort to develop individual coping. In the final session in which the magic shop was played every member came, one by one, to shop, and at the end of the group stage the group members were able to evaluate the game as they gave individual feedback about everyone's personal characteristics and tried to determine direction for themselves. In addition this situation could be evaluated as the group's preparation for ending and being able to accept this conclusion.

7 Results and discussion

The distributions between the scores gained from the subscales of the Self-Disclosure Inventory given at the beginning and the end of the group process are shown in Table 2. The results of the Self-Disclosure Inventory and The Communication Skills Evaluation Scale of given to the group members at the beginning and end of the process of group sessions are shown in the Table 3. Finally in Table 4, the differences in group members' disclosing themselves are summarized.

The results of the Self-Disclosure Inventory, given before and after the group meetings, indicated that 5 members' self-disclosure scores had increased, while the 3 members' had decreased. Member 1 had a dramatic decreased. He had lack of self confidence and difficulty in expressing his feelings. In the magic-shop game he asked for-self-confidence. After psychodrama, he wanted individual therapy. We can be thinking, the period studied is not enough time to treat serious problems.

As the results of the subscales of the Self-Disclosure Inventory and the people to whom the members choose to disclose themselves in Table 4 are studied, a total of 90 changes can be observed. Among these changes, 60 of them (two-third of the total) indicated an increase in self-disclosure, and 30 showed a change in self-disclosing rates or no self-disclosure at all. When the results of the scales are considered, while most of the changes were positive, there were negative changes as well. However, those negative changes are, in fact, considered significant in the sense that they helped the members' self-awareness to increase; those members recognized that they needed to improve their communication skills. Group psychotherapy has had an effect on the group members' self-disclosure abilities and it was also observed that this effect was mostly a positive one.

Table 2 The distributions of the subscale scores in self-disclosure inventory before and after psychodrama

Self-disclosure inventory and its subscales	Members															
	1. member		2. member		3. member		4. member		5. member		6. member		7. member		8. member	
	Before Psychd.	After Psychod.	Before Psychod.	After Psychod.	Before Psychod.	After Psychod.	Before Psychod.	After Psychod.	Before Psychod.	After Psychod.	Before Psychod.	After Psychod.	Before Psychod.	After Psychod.	Before Psychod.	After Psychodr.
Self-disclosure to the mother	43	**20**	36	**29**	91	**93**	37	**89**	78	**73**	76	**77**	36	**51**	42	**67**
Self-disclosure to the father	9	**2**	18	**6**	4	**23**	7	**45**	62	**62**	59	**61**	36	**51**	28	**45**
Self-disclosure to a friend of the same sex	90	**60**	63	**55**	86	**88**	85	**94**	77	**75**	72	**83**	48	**50**	56	**71**
Self-disclosure to a friend of the opposite sex	71	**43**	57	**64**	82	**85**	67	**92**	68	**67**	46	**47**	48	**50**	54	**69**
Self-disclosure to the teacher	39	**7**	9	**11**	20	**13**	66	**92**	41	**40**	6	**8**	20	**37**	18	**24**
Self-disclosure about the ideas and opinions	52	**34**	42	**41**	54	**54**	62	**72**	59	**61**	50	**53**	52	**56**	49	**53**
Self-disclosure about the school or job	46	**28**	35	**42**	55	**57**	50	**72**	56	**58**	56	**65**	11	**33**	49	**50**

Table 2 (continued)

Self-disclosure inventory and its subscales	Members															
	1. member		2. member		3. member		4. member		5. member		6. member		7. member		8. member	
	Before Psychd.	After Psychod.	Before Psychod.	After Psychod.	Before Psychod.	After Psychod.	Before Psychod.	After Psychod.	Before Psychod.	After Psychod.	Before Psychod.	After Psychod.	Before Psychod.	After Psychod.	Before Psychod.	After Psychodr.
Self-disclosure about the family	40	**20**	40	**28**	35	**41**	58	**70**	47	**48**	46	**54**	32	**24**	24	**43**
Self-disclosure about sexuality	33	**15**	13	**5**	42	**48**	47	**64**	50	**36**	28	**28**	22	**28**	10	**29**
Self-disclosure about personal issues	36	**14**	24	**24**	42	**47**	9	**63**	36	**38**	28	**15**	4	**28**	12	**39**
Self-disclosure about hobbies and interests	40	**21**	29	**25**	55	**55**	36	**71**	78	**76**	60	**64**	67	**70**	34	**62**
Total change	247	**132**	183	**165**	283	**302**	262	**412**	326	**317**	268	**278**	188	**239**	188	**276**

Table 3 The distribution of the group members' total scores in self-disclosure inventory and communication skills evaluation scale before and after psychodrama

Group members	Scale scores			
	Total score in jourard self-disclosure inventory		Total score in communication skills evaluation scale	
	Before psychodrama	After psychodrama	Before psychodrama	After psychodrama
Member 1	247	132	67	59
Member 2	183	165	62	61
Member 3	283	302	85	84
Member 4	262	412	84	79
Member 5	326	317	67	69
Member 6	268	278	79	60
Member 7	188	239	60	68
Member 8	188	276	63	65

As Tables 2, 3 and 4 studied together in detail in consideration of each member's scores before and after the group sessions, the results obtained in regard to the reasons and the directions of the differences in self-disclosure scores can be as follows:

* Member 1 was the member whose self-disclosure score had decreased most (115 points). When the member was interviewed about the reason for this situation, he stated that he had separated from his girlfriend during the period just before the last tests, which had a significant effect on his decreasing self-disclosure scores. He also revealed that he was upset because the group sessions had come to an end. In the magic shop game, he asked for the self-confidence. After the group meetings ended, this member continued to one-to one therapy.

* Member 2's total self-disclosure score had decreased (18 points). However, as it can be seen in Table 4, her playing the protagonist game about her boyfriend caused her scores in self disclosure to the teacher and a friend of the opposite sex to increase. Compared to her scores before psychodrama, her evaluation of her interpersonal communication skills did not change much after psychodrama. She asked for the joy of life in the magic shop game.

* Member 3's self-disclosure score had increased after psychodrama group psychotherapy (19 points). His score in self-disclosure to the father had significantly increased. Besides, his score in self-disclosure to a friend of the same sex as well as the opposite sex had also increased. Since some of his reasons for applying were problems with the family, the fact that his scores in self-disclosure to the mother and the father had significantly increased can be considered as a positive influence of the group sessions in terms of the relationship among the family members. His scores in self-disclosure about sexuality and personal issues to the family had also increased. There was no significant change in his evaluation of his interpersonal communication skills. He did not join the magic shop game.

* Member 4 was the one whose self-disclosure score had increased most when her scores before and after the psychodrama group sessions are examined (150 points). Her scores in self-disclosure to the father, the mother, a friend of the opposite sex and the teacher were the ones that showed the most increase. Likewise, her scores in self-disclosure about sexuality, personal issues, school, family, hobbies and interests had increased as well. The member played a protagonist game. This game was beneficial

Table 4 The results of the self-disclosure inventory

Self-disclosure and its subscales	Changes
Self-disclosure (Total score)	Increased in 5 members Decreased in 3 members
Self-disclosure to the mother	Increased in 5 members Decreased in 3 members
Self-disclosure to the father	Increased in 5 members Decreased in 2 members No change in 1 member
Self-disclosure to a friend of the same sex	Increased in 5 members Decreased in 3 members
Self-disclosure to a friend of the opposite sex	Increased in 6 members Decreased in 2 members
Self-disclosure to the teacher	Increased in 5 members Decreased in 3 members
Self-disclosure about the ideas and opinions	Increased in 4 members Decreased in 2 members No change in 2 members
Self-disclosure about the school or job	Increased in 7 members Decreased in 1 member
Self-disclosure about the family	Increased in 5 members Decreased in 3 members
Self-disclosure about sexuality	Increased in 4 members Decreased in 3 members No change in 1 member
Self-disclosure about personal issues	Increased in 5 members Decreased in 2 members No change in 1 member
Self-disclosure about hobbies and interests	Increased in 4 members Decreased in 3 members No change in 1 member
Total change	60 changes as increase in self-disclosure (positive) 30 changes as decrease in self-disclosure (negative or partly negative) 6 unchanged status in self-disclosure

for her in the sense that she noticed that she was in need of love and gained insight on what to do about it. After psychodrama, she evaluated her interpersonal communication skills a bit negatively, compared to her evaluation before psychodrama. In the magic shop game, she asked for a happy and peaceful life.

* Member 5's self-disclosure score indicated a small amount of decrease after psychodrama (9 points). When her scores in the subscales of the Self-Disclosure Inventory were examined, no significant difference was observed. Her evaluation of her interpersonal communication skills was a bit more positive after psychodrama. She did not join any of the protagonist games. She asked for the success in business life in the magic shop game.

* Member 6's self-disclosure score had increased a bit after psychodrama (10 points). There was also an increase in her self-disclosure to a friend of the same sex. The school and family-related issues of self-disclosure also indicated a bit of increase. However, her self-disclosure score about personal issues had decreased with a small amount. Her evaluation of her interpersonal communication skills was more negative

after psychodrama. She was a protagonist in one game and in the magic shop game, she was the last person to come and she asked for courage.

* Member 7 was one of the members whose self-disclosure score indicated a significant increase after psychodrama group psychotherapy. The people to whom there was an increase in his self-disclosure scores were his father, his mother and his teacher. His self-disclosure scores about personal issues and the school were also ones that showed the highest increase, whereas his scores in self-disclosure to the family had decreased. After psychodrama, he evaluated his interpersonal communication skills more positively. In the magic shop game, he asked for a perfect physical appearance.

* Member 8 was also one of the members whose self-disclosure score had increased most in general (88 points). Her scores in self-disclosure to her father, her mother, a friend of the same and opposite sex and her scores in self-disclosure about hobbies and interests, personal issues, family and sexuality had also indicated an increase. After psychodrama, her evaluation of her interpersonal communication skills was a bit more positive (Table 2). She played one protagonist game during the psychodrama group sessions and in the magic shop game, she asked for "a 2-month time package".

It can be claimed that the group sessions helped the group members to evaluate their past, present and future interpersonal relationships objectively by the help of doubling and role reversal techniques. The group sessions gave the members courage by giving them the opportunity to experience and express different feelings and ideas and to experiment different behaviours. Therefore, the sessions made a contribution to the members' ability to overview and discuss the problems they experience in all aspects of their lives.

At the end of the period, when the things experienced through the group process and the results obtained from the scales are evaluated together, it can be asserted that the psychodrama group psychotherapy carried out with these young people was beneficial for them and gave them the opportunity to experience new roles and express themselves within these roles, which, in turn, helped them to improve their interpersonal communication skills and their ability to disclose and express themselves. We aware that a number of 13 sessions is not long enough to see serious symptomatic and developmental changes. And also, it is difficult to measure therapeutic changes with scales. Our aim to discuss the scores in detail was just to emphasize that there is a start of change in self-disclosure and expression. Such a short period of group experience, transferential problems to be solved cannot even be evoked. In addition, it is just a honeymoon period yet. For the new beginning psychodramatists, it is motivating to experience and prove that a kind of therapeutic change is starting.

Conflict of interest The author declares that there are isn't any actual or potential conflicts of interest in relation to this article.

References

Bakar, D. (1996). Üniversite Öğrencilerinde Benlik Sisteminin İncelenmesi, E.Ü. Sosyal Bilimler Enstitüsü, Psikoloji Anabilim Dalı, Yayınlanmamış Yüksek Lisans Tezi, İzmir.

Beydoğan, M. (1994). Buca Eğitim Fakültesi ve Eğitim Yüksek Okulu Öğrencilerinin Kendini Açma Davranışları. VIII. Ulusal Psikoloji Kongresi Bildirisi.

Blatner, A. H. (1973). *Acting in practical applications of psychodramatic methods*. New York: Springer.

Dökmen, Ü (1995). *Sosyometri ve Psikodrama*. 2. Baskı, Istanbul: Sistem Yayıncılık.

Durak-Batıgün, A. (1998). Comparison of the methods in process and outcome studies of group therapies. *Turkish Psychological Review, 1*(2), 63–82.

Göka, A. (1998).Therapeutic factors in group psychotherapy. *Journal of Psychiatriy, Psychology Psychopharmacology, 6*(2);19–26.

Gökler, B. (1998). *Psikodrama Yoluyla Tedavi Gören Bir Ergen Grubunun Süreç Analizinde Simgelerin Kullanımı* (The Usage Of Symbols In The Process Analysis Of An Adolescent Group Treated With Psychodrama). Dr. Abdülkadir Özbek Psikodrama Enstitüsü, Psikodrama Terapisti Tezi, Ankara.

Hargie, A., Saunders, C., & Dickson, D. (1981). *Social skill in interpersonal communication* (2nd edn., pp. 209–227). London: Croom Helm Ltd.

Jourard, S. M. (1971). *Self-disclosure: An experimental analysis of the transparent self.* New York: Wiley-Interscience.

Korkut, F. (1996a). The development of 'the communication skills scale' and it's reliability and validity studies. *The Journal Of Psychological Counselling And Guidance, 2*(7), 18–23.

Korkut, F. (1996b). Effects of the communication skill training program on the high school students evaluation communication skills they possess. *Journal of Psychiatriy, Psychology, Psychopharmacolgy, 4*(3), 191–198.

Moreno, J. L. (1964). *Psychodrama* (Vol. 1, 3rd ed.). Beacon: Beacon House.

Naar, R. (1987). *Grup Psikoterapisine İlk Adım*. Çev.: Nesrin Hişli Şahin, Istanbul: Erdem Kitabevi.

Öner, N. (1997). Türkiye'de Kullanılan Psikolojik Testler. (Psychological Tests Used in Turkey) 3. Baskı, Boğaziçi Üniversitesi Yayınları, İstanbul, pp. 398–399.

Özbek, A., & Leutz, G. (1987). *Psikodrama Grup Psikoterapisinde Sahnesel Etkileşim (On-Stage Interaction in Psychodrama Group Psychoterapy)*. Ankara: Has-soy Matbaası.

Öztürk-Kılıç, E. (1990). *Ergen Etkileşim Grubunda Terapötik Faktörler*. S.S.K. Ankara Hastanesi Psikiyatri Polikliniği, Uzmanlık Tezi, Ankara.

Öztürk Kılıç, E., & Özbay, H. (1993). Group psychotherapy practice with adolescents. *Journal of Psychiatriy, Psychology, Psychopharmacolgy, 1*(4), 338–343.

Schützenberger-Ancelin, A. (1995). *Psikodrama Yöntemlerin Bir Özet Sunumu*. (Precis de psychodrame) Translated by Abdulkadir Özbek, Ankara: Varan Matbaası.

Selçuk, Z. (1992). *İnsan İlişkilerinde Kendini Açma (Self-disclosure in Interpersonal Relationships)*. Ankara: Vadi Yayıncılık.

Yalom, I. D. (1992). *The Theory And Practice of Group Psychotherapy*. Çev: Ataman Tangör, Özgür Karaçam, Istanbul: Nobel Tıp Kitabevleri.

Prof. Dr. Olcay Çam is a professor of psychiatry nursing and a psychodramatist. She completed her bachelor's in nursing at the Ege University in 1982. Prof. Çam received her master's and PhD degrees in psychiatry nursing from the same university in 1984 and 1991, respectively. Her dissertation was on burn-out syndrome in nurses, which pioneered the discussion of the topic in Turkey.

Z Psychodrama Soziometr (2016) (Suppl) 15:275–288
DOI 10.1007/s11620-015-0298-5

HAUPTBEITRÄGE

Zeitschrift für Psychodrama und Soziometrie

Integration von Forschung in der Psychotherapieausbildung – Erfahrungen von Studierenden mit forschungsorientierten Inhalten und Tätigkeiten im Projekt TRAIN

Jutta Fürst · Hannes Krall

Online publiziert: 4. Dezember 2015

Zusammenfassung Eine verstärkte Forschungsorientierung in der Psychotherapie sollte bereits in der Ausbildung ansetzen. In dem Projekt TRAIN – Towards Research Applied in an International Network of Trainees – werden forschungsorientierte Inhalte und Tätigkeiten verstärkt in bestehende Ausbildungscurricula integriert. Ziel des Forschungs- und Entwicklungsprojektes ist es, Forschungskompetenzen bei Studierenden von Lehrgängen im Bereich der Beratung und Psychotherapie aufzubauen.

In dem vorliegenden Beitrag werden Erfahrungen von neun Studierenden mit forschungsorientierten Inhalten und Tätigkeiten in der Psychotherapieausbildung untersucht. Studierende eines Lehrganges werden befragt, wie sie die Integration von Forschung in ihrer Ausbildung erlebt haben, was sie als hilfreich bzw. hinderlich einschätzen und welche Verbesserungsmöglichkeiten sie für zukünftige Lehrgänge sehen.

Die Ergebnisse zeigen, dass die Studierenden insgesamt Forschung als sehr bedeutsam für die gesellschaftliche Akzeptanz der Methode und die Qualität der eigenen Arbeit ansehen. Dennoch stehen der Neugier und dem Interesse an Forschung auch belastende und frustrierende Erfahrungen gegenüber. Vorschläge zu Verbesserungen werden von den Studierenden genannt und in dem Beitrag beschrieben.

Schlüsselwörter Ausbildungsforschung · Psychodrama · Projektevaluation

Dr. J. Fürst (✉)
Salvatorgasse 2a,
6060 Hall i.T., Österreich
E-Mail: jutta.fuerst@uibk.ac.at

Ao. Univ.-Prof. H. Krall
IfEB, Alpen-Adria-Universität Klagenfurt,
Universitätsstr. 65–67,
9020 Klagenfurt, Österreich
E-Mail: hannes.krall@aau.at

Integration of research into psychotherapy training – experiences of trainees with research oriented content and activities within the project TRAIN

Abstract Enhanced orientation towards research in psychotherapy should be present from the very beginning of the training process. The TRAIN project – Towards Research Applied in an International Network of Trainees – focuses on a better integration of research oriented contents and skills in the training curriculum. This research and development project aims to strengthen research competencies of trainees in counselling and psychotherapy training.

In the present study experiences of trainees with research oriented contents and skills in the training process are investigated. Trainees of one training group are interviewed as to how they experienced research oriented aspects of their training, what they see as helpful or hindering in their learning and what improvements they propose for the future.

The results show that in general trainees see research as very important for the acceptance of the method in society as well as for the quality of their work. Nonetheless interest and motivation to learn about research is often accompanied by distress and frustration. Suggestions how to improve the integration of research for future training groups are made by the trainees and summarized in this article.

Keywords Training research · Psychodrama · Project evaluation

1 Einleitung

In den Bereichen Beratung und Psychotherapie gibt es ein häufig konstatiertes Defizit an Forschung. Die mangelnde Forschungspraxis in einer psychotherapeutischen Methode führt oft auch zu dem Umstand, dass sich PraktikerInnen distanzierend oder sogar ablehnend gegenüber Forschung äußern und damit die Kluft zwischen Praxis und Forschung aufrechterhalten (Widdowson 2012). Umgekehrt kann aber auch die Forschungspraxis kritisiert werden, zu sehr von eigenen Forschungsansätzen und – intentionen auszugehen und zu wenig zu unternehmen, um eine bessere Kooperation zwischen psychotherapeutischer Praxis und Forschung zu entwickeln. Praxisorientierte Psychotherapieforschung (Castonguay et al. 2013) und Praxisforschungsnetzwerke (Castonguay 2011) scheinen diesbezüglich ein vielversprechender Ansatz zu sein.

Studien belegen jedoch auch, dass PsychotherapeutInnen gegenüber Forschung grundsätzlich aufgeschlossen sind (Felber und Margreiter 2007). Für das Psychodrama zeigen internationale Erhebungen zum Stellenwert von Forschung ebenso ein durchaus positives Bild (Krall 2012a, b). Forschung wird als etwas sehr Förderliches für die Qualität psychotherapeutischer Arbeit und die Weiterentwicklung der Methode angesehen. Des Weiteren wird deutlich, dass bei vielen TrainerInnen, PraktikerInnen und Studierenden die Bereitschaft groß ist, sich weiterzubilden und sich in Forschungsaktivitäten zu engagieren. Dennoch finden sich bisher vergleichsweise in nur geringem Ausmaß entsprechende Forschungserfahrungen und aktuell laufende Projekte. Um überhaupt die Grundlagen für vermehrte Partizipation im Forschungsbereich nachhaltig zu verankern, sind Entwicklungsschritte jedoch auf mehreren Ebenen zu setzen. Die Integration von Forschung in die Ausbildung hat dabei einen zentralen Stellenwert.

2 Wissenschafts- und Forschungskultur als Herausforderung für die Ausbildung

Im Psychodrama besteht seit Anfang der 1990er Jahre in Form der FEPTO (Federation of European Psychodrama Training Organizations) ein professionelles Netzwerk, das Trainingsstandards in Europa festsetzt und den jeweiligen neuen Erfordernissen anpasst. In den letzten Jahren hat in der FEPTO vor allem die Frage an Aufmerksamkeit gewonnen, wie Forschung im Psychodrama gestärkt werden könne. In vielen Bereichen sind mittlerweile Initiativen zur Entwicklung und Förderung von Forschungsaktivitäten entstanden (Krall 2013, 2014). Dabei wird versucht, eine Wissenschafts- und Forschungskultur schrittweise stärker in den Ausbildungsinstitutionen und den jeweiligen Curricula zu verankern.

3 TRAIN – Towards Research Applied in an International Network of Trainees

In dem internationalen Ausbildungsprojekt TRAIN – Towards Research Applied in an International Network of Trainees – wird unter Beteiligung von Österreich, Portugal und der Türkei ein gemeinsames ausbildungsbegleitendes Programm durchgeführt, das die Forschungskompetenz der Studierenden in der Ausbildung zur PsychotherapeutIn in der Methode Psychodrama verbessern soll. Außerdem zielt es darauf, eine positive Grundhaltung der Studierenden und das Interesse für Forschung zu stärken (Fürst und Krall 2011a, b). Aus diesem Grund wurde auch der Begriff Forschung für die Studierenden sehr weit gefasst und schließt bei diesem Projekt die Evaluierung der eigenen psychotherapeutischen Tätigkeit ein.

In dem Projekt TRAIN werden Studierende über einem Zeitraum von vier bis sechs Jahren schrittweise an theoretische und praktische Aspekte der Forschung herangeführt, indem sie die verschiedenen Rollen aus unterschiedlichen Perspektiven wahrnehmen und erfahren. Unter Verwendung qualitativer und quantitativer wissenschaftlicher Verfahren erlernen die Studierenden deren Anwendung, Auswertung und Interpretation.

Die Idee zu diesem Projekt wurde im FEPTO Research Committee 2009 (Moita 2009) entwickelt und 2010 mit einem neu startenden Lehrgang erstmals praktisch umgesetzt. TRAIN zielt darauf ab, Forschung in die jeweiligen Curricula als Ausbildungsinhalt zu integrieren, Motivation und Interesse an Forschung zu fördern, die Kompetenz zur Durchführung kleinerer Studien zu steigern und die Kooperation mit KollegInnen im internationalen Bereich anzuregen.

Einige Grundprinzipien, ein grob strukturiertes Manual und die Verwendung einheitlicher Messinstrumente sollen dazu dienen, diese Ziele zu erreichen. Zu den Prinzipien zählen

- Forschen wird als ein Teil der PsychotherapeutInnenidentität betrachtet und ist damit ein immanenter Teil der Lehre.
- Die Erprobung der Messinstrumente im Selbstversuch geht dem Einsatz in der eigenen praktischen Arbeit mit KlientInnen voran.
- Die Anwendung gemeinsamer einfacher Messinstrumente und die Erweiterung des Basisinstrumentariums je nach Fragestellung werden empfohlen.
- Die Ausbildung stützt sich auf eine mehrdimensionale Konzeption in Bezug auf Inhaltsvermittlung (theoretisch-praktisch), verwendete Messverfahren (quantitativ-qualitativ), Forschungsfragen (allgemein-speziell) und Setting (Einzel- oder Gruppensetting).

Da es sich bei den von den Studierenden durchführbaren Projekten zumeist um Einzelfallstudien handelt, erfolgt die Vorgangsweise in Anlehnung an das von Robert Elliott (2002) vorgeschlagene Hermeneutic Single Case Efficacy Design (HSCED), das durch die Verwendung verschiedenster Verfahren (qualitativ und quantitativ) und unter Einbeziehung verschiedener Perspektiven (PatientIn, TherapeutIn, ForscherIn) eine Analyse und Interpretation der therapeutischen Prozesse und Ergebnisse gestattet.

Die Auswahl der Messinstrumente erfolgt nach den Kriterien: einfache und praxisnahe Handhabung, Einsatzmöglichkeit in verschiedenen Sprachen und kostenfreie bzw. kostengünstige Verfügbarkeit. Aus diesen Gründen wird den Studierenden der Einsatz der folgenden Instrumente und Verfahren empfohlen:

CORE-OM (Clinical Outcome in Routine Evaluation – Outcome Measure), ein in seiner Langform 34 Fragen umfassender Fragebogen, der die Befindlichkeit auf vier Skalen (well-being, symptoms, functioning und risks) misst (Gray und Mellor-Clark 2007).

Der PQ (Personal Questionnaire) ist ein individualisierter Fragebogen, der gezielt die individuellen Problemlagen von einzelnen KlientInnen erfasst und die über die Zeit erfolgten Veränderungen dokumentiert (Elliott et al. 1999).

Mit dem HAT (Helpful Aspects of Therapy) werden schließlich jene Aspekte in einer therapeutischen Sitzung erfasst, die von den KlientInnen als hilfreich oder hinderlich empfunden wurden (Elliott 2012).

In größeren Abständen und am Ende einer Therapie wird das Client Change Interview (CCI) eingesetzt. In Form eines strukturierten Interviews werden in systematischer Form die für die KlientInnen wesentlichen Veränderungen und Einflussfaktoren im Laufe der Therapie erhoben (Elliott 2012).

Die Studierenden werden angeleitet, die eigene therapeutische Arbeit mithilfe der Messinstrumente zu evaluieren und für ihre Abschlussarbeit zu verwenden. Dabei können je nach Fragestellung die forschungsmethodischen Verfahren und die Verwendung der Forschungsinstrumente auch abgeändert und den spezifischen Bedingungen des jeweiligen Projektes angepasst werden. Alle diese Verfahren werden durch eine detaillierte Falldokumentation ergänzt, in der die Diagnose nach ICD 10 bzw. DSM IV, gesetzte Interventionen und der Therapieablauf für jede Sitzung dargestellt werden.

Die bereits vorliegenden Arbeiten von Studierenden zeigen ein durchwegs erfreuliches Bild. Für die Abschlussarbeiten werden Themen gewählt, die weitgehend durch das Arbeitsfeld der Studierenden bestimmt sind. Um exemplarisch einige Arbeiten zu nennen, soll auf nachfolgende Projekte verwiesen werden:

Gstrein (2014) untersuchte in ihrer Abschlussarbeit die „Wirksamkeit von Psychodrama bei Gymnasialschülern mit Mathematikängsten“ (siehe auch Beitrag in diesem Band). In einer Pre-post Studie, in der die TeilnehmerInnen einer Psychodramagruppe mit Hilfe des PQ (Elliott et al. 1999), einer modifizierten Form der Selbstwirksamkeitsskala – Mathematik von Schwarzer und Jerusalem (1999) und dem CCI (Elliott 2012) untersucht wurden, zeigten sich bemerkenswerte Veränderungen. Steinmair (2015) ging der Frage nach, ob Psychodrama als handlungsorientierte Gruppentherapieform die Selbstwirksamkeitserwartung von psychiatrischen Patientinnen erhöht. Die eingesetzten Messverfahren waren die Symptomcheckliste von Derogatis (Franke 2002), die Selbstwirksamkeitsskala von Schwarzer und Jerusalem (1999) und das CCI (Elliott 2012). Obwohl die Kurzeittherapie von 8 Gruppensitzungen keine wesentlichen Veränderungen erwarten ließen, berichteten die PatientInnen positive Reaktionen auf den Einsatz psychodramatischer Techniken. Allgemeine Veränderungen und jene im relevanten Beziehungsfeld von PatientInnen einer ambulanten PatientInnengruppe untersuchte Ellensohn (2014) in seiner Abschlussarbeit. Er verwendete neben den Basisverfahren CORE-OM, HAT und CCI noch zwei psychodramatische Verfahren zur Erfassung der Beziehungssituation von PatientInnen, den SNI (Social Network Inventory von Treadwell) und den MSAPT (Moreno Social Atom Projectiv Test). Auch in seiner Untersuchung wurden von den PatientInnen psychodramatische Techniken als wirksam beschrieben.

Die Abschlussarbeiten der Studierenden zeigen, dass sie in der Lage sind, ihre praktische Arbeit empirisch zu evaluieren und die Ergebnisse kritisch zu interpretieren. Sie sind in der Lage durch den Einsatz verschiedenster Methoden eine mehrperspektivische Beschreibung ihrer Fallarbeit zu liefern und sich kritisch mit dem Einsatz von Methoden auseinanderzusetzen.

Im Rahmen der Ausbildungsforschung wird begleitend untersucht, welche Haltungen und Einstellungen Studierende gegenüber forschungsorientierten Inhalten und Tätigkeiten in der Ausbildung einnehmen und was sie als förderlich und hinderlich bei der Entwicklung von Forschungskompetenzen im Rahmen ihrer Psychotherapieausbildung ansehen.

3.1 Methode

Um festzustellen, wie die Studierenden des Lehrganges die Integration von Forschung in die Ausbildung erlebten und in welcher Weise dieser Schwerpunkt ihre Einstellung beeinflusst hat, wurden nach Absolvierung des Lehrganges – aber noch vor Abgabe der Abschlussarbeit – Interviews durchgeführt.

Die Interviews, die für jeweils 60 min anberaumt waren, wurden von der Leiterin des Lehrganges durchgeführt, mit Hilfe eines Tonbandgerätes aufgezeichnet, von einer institutsfernen Person transkribiert und von der Interviewerin analysiert. Alle Interviews folgten einem Leitfaden, der folgende Fragen beinhaltete:

- Woran erinnerst du dich, wenn du an Forschung in der Ausbildung und Praxis denkst?
- Welche Elemente bzw. Erfahrungen haben deine Einstellung zur Forschung während der Ausbildung positiv beeinflusst? (Seminare, Lehrende, Lehrinhalte…)

- Welche Elemente bzw. Erfahrungen haben deine Einstellung zur Forschung während der Ausbildung negativ beeinflusst?
- Wie ist das Thema Forschung derzeit in deiner alltäglichen Praxis vertreten? (Projekte, Literatur, Fortbildung…)
- Wenn du die Gesamtentwicklung in deiner Ausbildung und Praxis betrachtest, was waren die ein bis drei wichtigsten Punkte im positiven Sinn und welche ein bis drei im negativen Sinn?

Die Gespräche wurden im Hinblick auf folgende deduktive Kategorien analysiert: Einstellungen und Haltungen bezüglich Forschung, hilfreiche und hinderliche Aspekte der Vermittlung von Forschung in der Ausbildung, emotionale Reaktionen auf Inhalte und Tätigkeiten im Zusammenhang mit Forschung, sowie Verbesserungsvorschläge für zukünftige Lehrgänge. Alle entsprechenden Äußerungen wurden vermerkt, den jeweiligen Kategorien zugeordnet und ausgezählt.

Alle neun Studierenden – acht Frauen und ein Mann – eines Lehrganges nahmen freiwillig an dieser Studie teil. Sie hatten durchwegs dieselben Lehrveranstaltungen im selben Zeitraum besucht und befanden sich nach Absolvierung des Lehrganges, aber noch vor Abgabe der Abschlussarbeit. Das gemittelte Alter betrug zum Zeitpunkt des Interviews 42,8 Jahre ($s=7{,}8$). Vier Personen hatten ein abgeschlossenes Studium in Psychologie, zwei in Pädagogik, eine in Medizin, eine in Wirtschaft, sowie eine Person hatte eine Ausbildung zum Lebens- und Sozialberater.

3.2 Ergebnisse

Alle Studierenden wurden vor Beginn der Ausbildung darüber informiert, dass Forschung als ein integraler Teil der Ausbildung zu betrachten ist und sie sich mit Unterzeichnung des Vertrages damit einverstanden erklärten. Aufgrund unterschiedlicher persönlicher Zugangsweisen und unterschiedlicher Vorerfahrungen mit Forschungsarbeiten – beispielsweise im Zusammenhang mit Ausbildungen in den verschiedenartigen Herkunftsberufen – war anzunehmen, dass sich auch die Einstellung und Haltung der Studierenden zum Thema Forschung in der Ausbildung stark unterscheiden. Nicht zuletzt ist anzunehmen, dass die in der Psychotherapieausbildung vermittelten forschungsorientierten Inhalte und Tätigkeiten bei den Studierenden ihre Spuren hinterlassen haben.

3.2.1 Einstellungen und Haltungen gegenüber Forschung

Die Auswertung der Interviews zeigt zunächst, dass Forschung und Psychotherapie als sehr unterschiedlich erlebt werden. Beiden Tätigkeiten werden grundsätzlich andere Qualitäten zugeordnet. Forschung und Psychotherapie scheinen einander als unvereinbares Gegensatzpaar gegenüber zu stehen. Ein paar Beispiele aus den Interviews:

Forschunge	Psychotherapie
„…ist das Exakte, Genaue.“	„…heißt, dass man manchmal nicht weiß, wohin man geht.“
„…ist kompliziert.“	„…da muss man nicht immer denken.“
„…ist unemotional.“	„…da ist mehr Spielraum für Interpretation.“
„…ist ein großes Gebäude.“	„…ist praktisch.“
„…versucht nicht wirklich greifbare Dinge in Zahlen zu fassen.“	„…ist intuitiver.“
„…braucht Zeit und Energie.“	„…ist weniger distanziert.“
„…Forscher sind die mit den Fragebögen.“	„…Psychotherapeuten sind die, die handeln.“

Die Studierenden halten Forschung aus unterschiedlichen Gründen für sinnvoll. Einzelne fanden Forschung persönlich interessant, um Antworten für sich stellende Fragen zu finden. Anderen erschien, dass der Einsatz von Forschungsinstrumenten eine positive Auswirkung auf den Therapieprozess habe. Sie hatten den Eindruck, dass sich PatientInnen mehr Zeit für sich selbst und den therapeutischen Prozess auch außerhalb der Therapie nahmen. Die PatientInnen hätten geäußert, dass sie sich wichtiger vorkamen und ihre Gefühle besser wahrnehmen konnten.

Manche Studierende sahen auch Forschung und Monitoring des psychotherapeutischen Prozesses als eine Möglichkeit zur persönlichen Weiterentwicklung.

Die beiden meistgenannten Argumente für Forschung waren deren Bedeutung für die Qualitätssicherung der praktischen therapeutischen Arbeit und deren Beitrag für die Akzeptanz der Methode. Die Bewertung dieser Argumente verteilte sich wie folgt.

Die folgende Abbildung (Abb. 1) zeigt, dass die Studierenden Forschung als wesentlich für die Verbesserung der Methode sehen und diesem Aspekt eine höhere Bedeutung beimessen als der Beweisführung zur Wirksamkeit der Methode.

Die Rolle der Forschung für die Akzeptanz der Methode wurde wie folgt zum Ausdruck gebracht:

- *„Es (Forschung) ist wichtig, um uns nach außen zu präsentieren.“*
- *„…auch wissenschaftlich belegen können gegenüber anderen Fachgruppen.“*
- *„Wenn eine Therapierichtung eine Legitimation weiter haben will, dann braucht sie einfach Forschung.“*
- *„…Der Beweis läuft nun einmal über die Forschung.“*

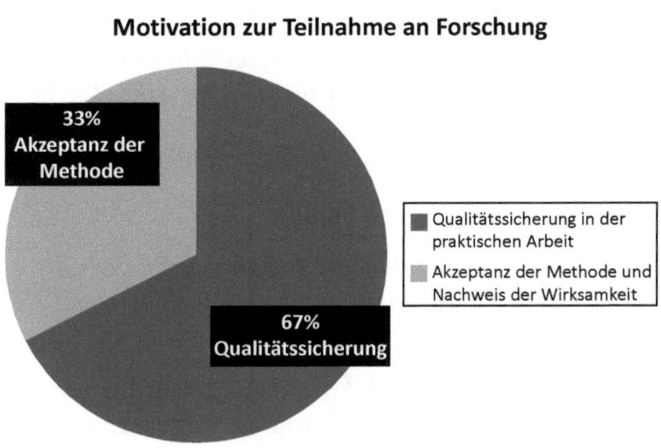

Abb. 1 Forschungsmotivation bezüglich Akzeptanz der Methode und allgemeinem Wirksamkeitsnachweis vs. Qualitätssicherung in der praktischen Arbeit

- *„Forschung unterstützt unser Recht (als Psychodramatikerinnen) zu existieren."*

Im Konkreten wurden zur Qualitätssicherung beispielsweise folgende Äußerungen gemacht:

- *„Es ist schon wichtig, eine Rückmeldung zu kriegen und zu schauen, was hilft und was nicht."*
- *„Ich kann mir nicht vorstellen, dass ich Klienten über Jahre behandle ohne zu evaluieren, was ich da mache."*
- *„Ich erkenneauch viel mehr den Nutzen und dass es hilfreich ist, also nicht nur für mich, sondern auch für die beforschte Person im Therapieprozess."*
- *„Forschung ist wichtig um eine andere Sichtweise zu bekommen."*

3.2.2 Emotionale Reaktionen auf forschungsorientierte Inhalte und Tätigkeiten

Obwohl alle Studierenden vor Beginn der Ausbildung informiert wurden, dass Forschung als ein integraler Teil der Ausbildung zu betrachten ist und sie sich mit Unterzeichnung des Vertrages damit einverstanden erklärten, lösten doch verschiedene Lehrinhalte, Ankündigungen, Hinweise und praktische Übungen zur Forschung unterschiedliche Gefühle aus. Die Anzahl, der in den Interviews geäußerten Gefühle, war nur unwesentlich geringer als Einstellungen und Meinungen zur Forschung.

Es wurden folgende emotionale Reaktionen auf forschungsorientierte Inhalte und Tätigkeiten in der Ausbildung genannt: Stress, Unsicherheit und Panik, Enttäuschung, Frustration, Ärger, Neugier, Freude und Spaß. Einige Beispiele aus den Interviews sollen das veranschaulichen.

Unsicherheit, Stress, und Ängste:

- *„Also für mich war es ein großes Gebilde, an das man sich ein bisschen schwer herantraut."*
- *„Am Anfang habe ich gedacht, eine wissenschaftliche Arbeit schreiben, wie soll das funktionieren. Es war einfach Stress."*
- *„Also jetzt ist es nicht mehr so, dass ich das Ganze mit Panik angehe."*

Enttäuschung, Frustration und Ärger:

- *„Es ist einfach frustrierend wenn man nicht die Artikel bekommt, die man sucht."*
- *„Es war zwei-dreimal, wo ich Ideen gehabt habe, was dann gescheitert ist. Viel Enttäuschung."*
- *„Die Fragebögen waren vielleicht lästig in diesem Moment."*

Interesse, Neugierde und Freude:

- *„Durch die Ausbildung ist auch wieder die Lust gekommen... mehr zu machen, um auch Effekte besser nachweisen zu können."*
- *„Forschung ist spannend"*

Unsicherheit, Stress und Ängste wurde am Beginn der Ausbildung unabhängig von der Vorbildung verspürt. Frustration, Enttäuschung und Ärger hingegen wurden eher

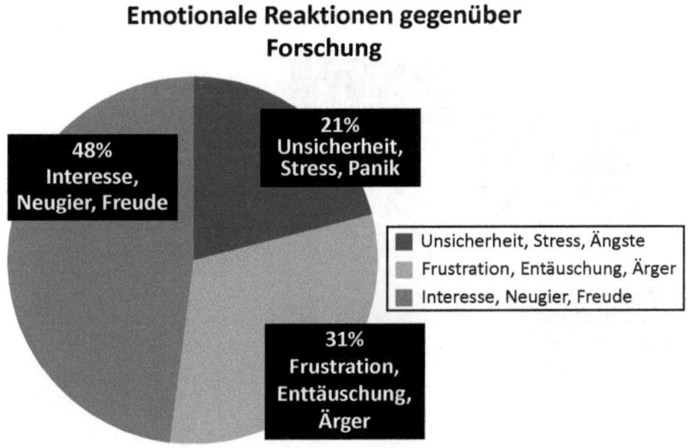

Abb. 2 Emotionalen Reaktionen auf Forschung

im Zusammenhang mit den Herausforderungen gegen Ende der Ausbildung genannt. Interesse, Neugier und Freude an der Forschung wurde zu unterschiedlichen Zeitpunkten und in verschiedenen Zusammenhängen genannt (Abb. 2).

Unsicherheit, Stress und Ängste umfassten 21 % der genannten Gefühle, Frustration, Enttäuschung und Ärger 31 % und Interesse, Neugier und Freude 48 %. Im Gesamten hielten sich positive und belastende Gefühle die Waage.

3.2.3 Hilfreiche und hinderliche Aspekte für die Integration von Forschung

Als hilfreiche Aspekte in der Integration von Forschung in die Psychotherapieausbildung wurden an erster Stelle die praktischen Übungen genannt, die von den Selbsterprobungen der verschiedenen Erhebungsmethoden wie CORE-OM, PQ, HAT usw. über die Literaturrecherchen, bis zu den praktischen Dateneingaben in ein Statistikprogramm reichten. An zweiter Stelle der Nennungen standen die Informationen, die zur Verfügung gestellt wurden. Dazu gehörten die Informationen, die auf der universitären online Plattform angeboten wurden, wie jene Forschungsbeispiele, die in den Literaturseminaren durchgearbeitet wurden.

Es wurden des Weiteren die Beziehungsqualität der Studierenden untereinander und zu den Lehrenden, die Motivierung durch die positive Einstellung der Lehrenden zur Forschung, die Rückmeldungen an die Studierenden und die Wiederholung genannt (Abb. 3).

Dazu noch einige Formulierungen der Studierenden:

- *„...die Literaturrecherche – ich finde das war sehr gut, also sehr praktisch einfach."*
- *„...dass wir uns von Block zu Block herangetastet haben an das Ganze."*
- *„Ich finde es ganz wichtig, dass man das selber auch gemacht hat."*
- *„...mich selbst beforschen."*
- *„Er hat gesagt, wir sollen uns trauen und probieren."*
- *„... das mit der Direktverbindung mit der Arbeit, zu dem Projekt, das ich dann für die Abschlussarbeit mache."*
- *„...Artikel unter dem Forschungsaspekt zu lesen."*
- *„Die Haltung der Lehrenden zur Forschung"*

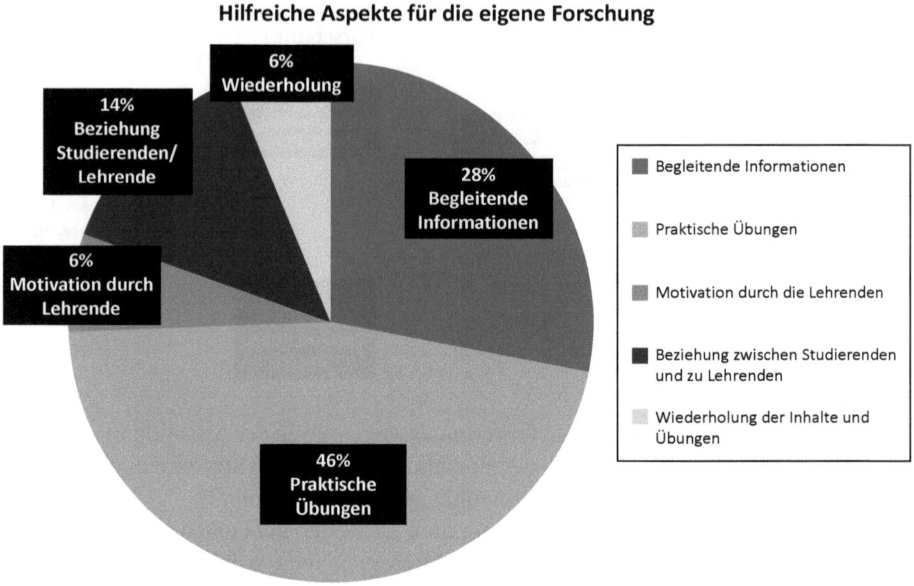

Abb. 3 Hilfreiche Aspekte

Es gab 81 Nennungen zu hilfreichen Aspekten und 14 Nennungen zu hinderlichen Aspekten. Als hinderlich erwies sich für einzelne der Umstand, dass ein bestimmtes Forschungsprojekt nicht in die alltägliche Praxis zu übertragen war, da einige psychosoziale Einrichtungen, in denen Studierende arbeiteten, nicht die entsprechenden Voraussetzungen boten. Auch die Richtlinien von Ethikkommissionen erschwerten einzelne Projekte. Die große Anzahl an auszufüllenden Fragebögen am Beginn, die geringe Anzahl an guten nachahmenswerten Forschungsbeispielen im Bereich Psychodrama und Beziehungskonflikte in der Gruppe wurden ebenfalls von einigen als hinderlich genannt. Überraschend war der Punkt, dass auch die Freiwilligkeit sich dem Thema Forschung zu stellen, von den TeilnehmerInnen als hinderlich betrachtet wurde.

Von den Studierenden wurden auch einige Vorschläge gebracht. Es sollte mit noch kleineren Schritten von Beginn an Forschung herangeführt und von Beginn an noch mehr Informationen gegeben werden.

Information:

- *„...am Beginn genau zu wissen, was für die Abschlussarbeit notwendig ist."*
- *„...vielleicht wären ein paar 'Konserven' gut... 'Forschungskonserven'."*

Didaktik:

- *„...kleine Schritte von Beginn an."*
- *„Ein bisschen mehr Informationen wären hilfreich."*

Motivation:

- *„Es sollte nicht so viel Aufwand sein."*
- *„Es ist wichtig, (Forschung) von Anfang an als Teil der des Lehrplans zu vermitteln."*

3.3 Diskussion

Die Integration von forschungsorientierten Inhalten und Tätigkeiten im Projekt TRAIN zielt darauf, eine grundsätzlich positive Haltung gegenüber Forschung zu stärken und Interesse und Kompetenzen für die Teilnahme an Forschungsprojekten zu fördern. Castongay et al. (2013) sehen die eher distanzierte Haltung von PsychotherapeutInnen gegenüber Forschung zum Teil dadurch bedingt, dass die wissenschaftlichen Ergebnisse nur geringe praktische Relevanz haben. Gerade um diesem Aspekt Rechnung zu tragen, sollte Forschung an die praktische Arbeit der Studierenden gekoppelt werden.

Die Forschungsarbeiten der Studierenden sind daher als Aktions- und Praxisforschungsprojekte angelegt und ermöglichen eine wissenschaftlich fundierte Reflexion der eigenen Praxis. Wissenschaftstheoretische und forschungsmethodologische Inhalte werden in die Ausbildung integriert, um die Studierenden dieser Lehrgänge zu befähigen, eigene Forschungsarbeiten in Arbeitsfeldern der Beratung und Psychotherapie mit Hilfe grundlegender qualitativer und quantitativer Verfahren durchzuführen.

Bisherige Studien (Krall 2014) zeigen, dass ein großer Prozentsatz der PsychodramatikerInnen ein grundsätzliches Interesse an Forschung ausdrückt, ohne selbst an Studien teilgenommen zu haben oder aktiv in Forschung involviert zu sein. Aufgrund der vorliegenden Aussagen der Studierenden in dieser Studie lässt sich das möglicherweise dadurch erklären, dass PsychodramatikerInnen Forschung als andersartig und im Vergleich zur psychotherapeutischen Tätigkeit als fremd erleben. Sie empfinden Forschung als nicht zur PsychotherapeutInnenidentität gehörend. Das würde bedeuten, dass in Zukunft diesem Aspekt in der Ausbildung mehr Bedeutung beigemessen und überlegt werden muss, einerseits die Gemeinsamkeiten dieser beiden Identitäten herauszuarbeiten und andererseits Forschung als integralen Bestandteil der Psychotherapeutenidentität erlebbar werden zu lassen.

Forschung wird von den Studierenden als besonders wichtig für die Verbesserung der Qualität der psychotherapeutischen Arbeit (67 %) gesehen, während Forschung zur Bestätigung der Wirksamkeit der Methode (33 %) vergleichsweise geringere Bedeutung zukommt. Auch aus diesem Befund lässt sich schließen, dass bei den Studierenden die unmittelbare praktische Relevanz von Forschungsergebnissen für die eigene Arbeit im Vordergrund steht.

Überraschend ist das Ergebnis, dass die auftretenden Ängste und Stresserlebnisse im Zusammenhang mit Forschung unabhängig von den Vorerfahrungen mit wissenschaftlichen Arbeiten sind. Es wäre naheliegend anzunehmen, dass ein bereits absolviertes Studium und die dabei erworbenen Kompetenzen im wissenschaftlichen Arbeiten den Stress reduzieren würden, was sich jedoch nach den Aussagen der Studierenden nicht bestätigt.

Grundsätzlich ist davon auszugehen, dass Studierende Unterstützung und stressreduzierende Information besonders am Beginn der Ausbildung benötigen. Dazu ist eine aufbauende didaktische Planung in kleinen Schritten erforderlich, die Beispiele guter, einfacher und machbarer Forschungspraxis beinhaltet und Kompetenzerwerb durch praktische Übungen in den Vordergrund stellt.

Frustration und Ärger bei der Planung und Ausführung der empirischen Abschlussarbeit ist häufig verursacht durch zu hoch gesteckte Ziele, praktische Probleme am Arbeitsplatz, organisatorische Schwierigkeiten und Beziehungskonflikte. Die Erwartungen an die Forschungsleistungen der Studierenden dürfen nicht realitätsfern sein, da sonst unnötigerweise Frustrationen und Enttäuschungen entstehen. Da generell in dem Projekt die Förderung eines positiven Zuganges zu Forschung im Vordergrund stehen soll, müssen die Vorgehensweisen und Zielsetzungen maßgeschneidert an die jeweiligen Voraussetzungen angepasst werden.

Die Rückmeldungen zu den hilfreichen Aspekten in der Ausbildung der Studierenden zeigen, dass vor allem die Verbindung von Praxis und Theorie an erster Stelle steht. Im Speziellen wurden dabei die Erfahrungen mit den quantitativen und qualitativen Messinstrumenten genannt, die von den Studierenden zunächst selbst ausgefüllt (z. B. CORE-OM, MSAPT, HAT) oder deren Erarbeitung mit den KlientInnen in Paarübungen erprobt wurden (z. B. PQ). Auch die praktischen Übungen zur Literaturrecherche, Eingabe der Daten in ein Statistikprogramm, Auswertung und Darstellung der Daten und nicht zuletzt das Lesen und die Auseinandersetzung mit ausgewählten empirischen Studien wurden als hilfreich genannt.

Ein weiterer wichtiger Faktor für die Entwicklung der Forscherrolle ist die Beziehung der Studierenden zu den Lehrenden und zu den KollegInnen. Konflikte und Störungen auf der Beziehungsebene scheinen sich insgesamt negativ auf die Einstellung zur Forschung auszuwirken. In der Forschungsarbeit sind einige Konfliktquellen vorhanden, die bereits im Vorfeld berücksichtigt werden müssen.

Nicht zu unterschätzen ist die Bedeutung laufender Information, die den Studierenden über entsprechende universitätsinterne Internetplattformen zur Verfügung gestellt wird. Aber auch die Nutzung dieser Medien muss gelernt und geübt werden. Darüber hinaus sollten aber auch aktuelle Informationen direkt per Handout oder Emails an Studierende ausgegeben werden. Diesem Zweck dient beispielsweise ein monatliches Informationsblatt, das Antwort auf laufende Fragen gibt und Struktur anbietet, wenn aufgrund der Anforderungen Stress entsteht.

Nicht zu Letzt spielt die Einstellung der Lehrenden zur Forschung eine bedeutende Rolle. Lehrende sind für die Studierenden Modelle und deren Einstellung zur Forschung wirkt sich unmittelbar motivierend oder demotivierend aus. Deshalb müsste in Folge wohl noch mehr Augenmerk auf die Ausbildung der Lehrenden gelegt werden, um in Zukunft TrainerInnen zur Verfügung zu haben, die mit ihrer Haltung die Bedeutung der Forschung in der Psychotherapie vermitteln können.

Als wesentliche Kritikpunkte an der vorliegenden Erhebung sind die geringe Anzahl der Interviewten zu nennen, sowie die Durchführung der Interviews durch die Leiterin der Ausbildung und der Zeitpunkt vor der Zertifizierung. Zudem fehlt die Unabhängigkeit zwischen Interviewerin und Interpretin des Datenmaterials, was die Aussagekraft der Ergebnisse einschränkt. Vorsichtig interpretiert kann die Studie jedoch Hinweise geben, in welche Richtungen Veränderungen stattfinden müssten.

Für zukünftige Lehrgänge sollte nach Sichtweise der Studierenden Forschung als integraler Bestandteil der Ausbildung für alle Studierenden von Beginn an sichtbar sein. Dazu sind im Besonderen Beispiele notwendig, in denen für Studierende machbare Psychotherapieforschung in nachvollziehbarer Weise praktisch und anschaulich demonstriert wird. Es erscheint den Studierenden unerlässlich, dass die Lehrenden selbst, Forschung als Teil ihrer Psychotherapeutenidentität wahrnehmen und dies auch vermitteln.

Literatur

Castonguay, L. G. (2011). Psychotherapy, psychopathology, research and practice: Pathways of connections and integration. *Psychotherapy Research, 3*(2), 125–140.

Castonguay, L., Barkham, M., Lutz, W., & McAleavey. (2013). Practice-oriented research. Approaches and applications. In M. M. Lambert. (Hrsg.), *Bergin and Garfield's handbook of psychotherapy and behavior change* (S. 85–108). New Jersey: John Wiley.

Ellensohn, T. (2014). Beforschung einer psychotherapeutischen Kleingruppe im ambulanten Setting: Veränderungen im Allgemeinen und Entwicklung von Beziehungen im relevanten Beziehungsfeld. Unveröffentlichte Abschlussarbeit. Universität Innsbruck.

Elliott, R. (2002). Hermeneutic single case efficacy design. *Psychotherapy Research, 12*(1), 1–21.

Elliott, R. (2012). Qualitative methods for studying psychotherapy change processes. In A. Thompson & D. Harper (Hrsg.), *Qualitative research methods in mental health & psychotherapy: An introduction for students & practitioners* (S. 69–81). Chichester: Wiley-Blackwells.

Elliott, R., Mack, C., & Shapiro, D. A. (1999). Simplified Personal Questionnaire Procedure. Verfügbar unter: http://www.experiential-researchers.org/instruments/elliott/pqprocedure.html. Zugegriffen: 26. Jan. 2015.

Felber, M., & Margreiter, U. (2007). Einstellung von Psychotherapeut(inn)en zu Psychotherapieforschung. *Psychotherapie Forum, 15,* 192–196.

Franke, G. H. (2002). *SCL-90-R. Symptomcheckliste von L. R. Derogatis – deutsche Version.* Göttingen: Beltz Test.

Fürst, J., & Krall, H. (2011a). Train – Project. Tools and procedures (unveröffentlichtes Konzept).

Fürst, J., & Krall, H. (2011b). „Towards research applied in international networks of trainees- the TRAIN project". Presentation at the FEPTO research committee meeting, Douglas (Isle of Man), 18.–20. 2. 2011.

Gray, P., & Mellor-Clark, J. (Hrsg.). (2007). Core: A Decade of Development. Rugby: Core IMS. Verfügbar unter: http://www.coreims.co.uk/index.html. Zugegriffen: 26. Jan. 2015.

Gstrein, D. (2014). Effectiveness of psychodrama on secondary students with mathematics anxiety. Unveröffentlichte Abschlussarbeit. Universität Innsbruck.

Krall, H. (2012a). Practitioner research in psychodrama: Strengthening the researcher's role. In I. Testoni, M. S. Guglielmin I., M. Wieser, G. Tarashoeva, G. Moita & M. D. Bucuţă (Hrsg.): Ending gender violence in the family and in the society. Empirical research in psychodrama, group psychodynamic therapy and group processes. *Interdisciplinary Journal of Family Studies* (2), 261–265.

Krall, H. (2012b). Research in Psychodrama – FEPTO-Trainers and their view about research. *FEPTO News, 2,* 16–20.

Krall, H. (Hrsg.). (2013). Ending Gender Violence – Empirical Research in Psychodrama Group Therapy and Group Processes. Report of the FEPTO Research Committee Meeting in Padua.

Krall, H. (2014). Psychodrama research: The perspective of trainees, practitioners and trainers. Konferenzpräsentation: Integrating Research in Training – Improving Research Competencies of Trainers in Psychodrama. Budapest.

Krall, H. (Hrsg.). (2014). Integrating Research in Training – Improving Research Competencies of Trainers in Psychodrama. Report of the FEPTO Research Committee Meeting in Budapest.

Moita, G. (2009). Catania FEPTO research meeting. *FEPTO News, 9*(3), 17–25.

Schwarzer, R., & Jerusalem, M. (1999). *Skalen zur Erfassung von Lehrer- und Schülermerkmalen. Dokumentation der psychometrischen Verfahren im Rahmen der Wissenschaftlichen Begleitung des Modellversuchs Selbstwirksame Schulen.* Berlin: Freie Universität Berlin.

Steinmair, E. (2015). Psychodrama und Selbstwirksamkeit. Unterstützt das Psychodrama als handlungsorientierte Gruppentherapieform die Erhöhung der Selbstwirksamkeitserwartung bei psychiatrischen Patientinnen? Unveröffentlichte Abschlussarbeit. Universität Innsbruck.

Widdowson, M. (2012). Perception of psychotherapy trainees of psychotherapy research. *Counselling and Psychotherapy Research*, 1–9. http://dx.doi.org/10.1080/14733145.2012.697473.

Jutta Fürst, Dr., 1953, Klinische Psychologin, Psychotherapeutin für Psychodrama und Katathym Imaginative Psychotherapie, sowie für Kinder und Jugendlichenpsychotherapie, Freie Praxis in Hall i.T., Supervisorin und Lehrtherapeutin für Psychodrama am Institut für psychosoziale Intervention und Kommunikation an der Universität Innsbruck. Wissenschaftliche Leitung des Universitätslehrganges für Psychodrama an der Universität Innsbruck. Publikationen im Bereich Supervision und Ausbildungsforschung.

Hannes Krall, 1963, ao. Univ.-Prof. Dr., arbeitet am Institut für Erziehungswissenschaft und Bildungsforschung an der Alpen-Adria-Universität Klagenfurt; Psychologe, Pädagoge, Psychotherapeut (Psychodrama), Supervisor. Lehrbeauftragung für Psychodrama an der Universität Innsbruck. Trainer für Supervision, Coaching und Organisationsberatung im ÖAGG. Präsident der Federation of European Psychodrama Training Organizations (FEPTO) und Co-Chair im FEPTO Research Committee. Mitglied in der Society for Psychotherapy Research (SPR). Forschungsarbeiten und Publikationen in den Bereichen Psychodrama und Supervision, Ausbildungs- und Wirkungsforschung, Gewalt und Trauma bei Kindern und Jugendlichen.

Z Psychodrama Soziometr (2016) (Suppl) 15:289–296
DOI 10.1007/s11620-015-0306-9

HAUPTBEITRÄGE

Zeitschrift für Psychodrama und Soziometrie

Wege zur Evaluation psychodramatischer Ausbildungen

Konrad Schnabel · Johannes Reif

Online publiziert: 25. November 2015

Zusammenfassung Im Vergleich zu den vermehrten Anstrengungen bei der Evaluation psychodramatischer Interventionsansätze gibt es bisher nur relativ wenig Forschung zur Qualität und zum Erfolg psychodramatischer Ausbildungen. Der Artikel gibt einen kurzen Überblick über bisherige Forschungsansätze und stellt Ergebnisse einer eigenen Studie vor. Dabei wurde deutlich, dass die Bereitschaft zur Einlassung auf psychodramatische Selbsterfahrung bereits früh für die Ausbildungsleitung identifizierbar ist und darüber hinaus klar damit zusammenhängt, ob die Ausbildung nach dem ersten Ausbildungsjahr fortgesetzt wird oder nicht. Diskutiert werden die Wichtigkeit der Verwendung von nicht nur selbstbeurteilten sondern auch fremdeingeschätzten Evaluationskriterien sowie die Bedeutung von Studien, die auch langfristige Ausbildungseffekte erfassen.

Schlüsselwörter Ausbildungsevaluation · Therapeutische Kompetenz · Qualitätssicherung · Lebenszufriedenheit · Psychodrama

Ways to evaluate psychodrama training

Abstract Compared to increased efforts in the field of evaluation of psychodrama oriented interventions, research on the quality and success of psychodrama training is relatively scarce. The article provides a short overview of previous research approaches and presents results of our own study. Our findings indicate that training supervisors are able to identify the readiness of trainees to engage in psychodramatic self-experience at an early stage and that this predicts whether the education

K. Schnabel (✉) · J. Reif
International Psychoanalytic University,
Stromstraße 1,
10555 Berlin, Deutschland
E-Mail: konrad.schnabel@ipu-berlin.de

is continued after the first year or not. Discussion focuses on the importance of using self-, as well as observer, judgments as evaluation criteria and the significance of measuring long term training effects.

Keywords Education evaluation · Therapeutic competence · Quality assurance · Satisfaction with life · Psychodrama

1 Evaluation psychotherapeutischer Ausbildungen

In Bezug auf die beiden in der Bundesrepublik Deutschland sozialrechtlich anerkannten psychotherapeutischen Verfahren (Verhaltenstherapie und tiefenpsychologisch orientierte bzw. psychoanalytische Psychotherapie) wird immer wieder kritisiert, dass zwar vergleichsweise viel Forschung zur Effektivität und zum Prozess von Psychotherapie aber nur wenig Forschungsaktivität zur Qualität der Ausbildung existiert (Strauß und Kohl 2009). Die Situation der Evaluation psychodramatischer Ausbildungen gestaltet sich ähnlich und erst in den letzten Jahren wurde damit begonnen, Instrumente zur Ausbildungsevaluation zu entwickeln und anzuwenden (Stadler und Wieser 2011). Dabei liegt die Notwendigkeit der Sicherung hoher Qualitätsstandards bei der Psychodrama-Ausbildung auf der Hand, da die Ausbildungsqualität selbstverständlich einen maßgeblichen Einfluss auf die Qualifikation der aus ihr hervorgehenden psychotherapeutisch Tätigen nimmt.

In Deutschland wurde der Kenntnisstand zur Ausbildungsevaluation – zumindest was die sozialrechtlich anerkannten Verfahren betrifft – insbesondere durch das vom Bundesministerium für Gesundheit in Auftrag gegebene Forschungsgutachten zur Ausbildung von psychologischen PsychotherapeutInnen sowie Kinder- und Jugendlichen-psychotherapeutInnen entscheidend verbessert (Strauß et al. 2009a). Dabei berichteten Ausbildungsteilnehmende verbreitet den Wunsch nach mehr praxisrelevantem Wissen und nach einer praxisnäheren Wissensvermittlung (Sonntag et al. 2009). Außerdem beschrieben sie praktische Ausbildungsinhalte sowie Supervision als die wichtigsten Ausbildungsbestandteile. Von Seiten der AbsolventInnen wurde neben der schwierigen finanziellen Situation vor allem die mangelnde fachliche Anleitung während der zu absolvierenden praktischen Tätigkeit kritisiert (Glaesmer et al. 2009). Lehrkräfte betonten ebenfalls die Bedeutung von praxisbezogenem Wissen und von der Ausbildung in konkreten Behandlungstechniken sowie von Supervision und Selbsterfahrung (Kohl et al. 2009). Außerdem forderten sie zur vermehrten Evaluation nicht nur des theoretischen Unterrichts sondern auch der praktischen Ausbildungsbestandteile auf.

Insgesamt lassen sich unterschiedliche Ebenen der Ausbildungsforschung voneinander abgrenzen (Strauß und Kohl 2009). Erstens die Input-Ebene, die zu Beginn der Ausbildung den Status quo der Ausbildungsteilnehmenden einerseits und der Ausbildungseinrichtung andererseits beschreibt. Hierzu zählen Vorerfahrungen der Ausbildungsteilnehmenden aber auch ihre Persönlichkeitseigenschaften inklusive persönliche Stärken sowie Vulnerabilitätsfaktoren. Ebenso werden hierzu Aspekte der Struktur und Organisation des Ausbildungsprogrammes und beispielsweise den Teilnehmenden bereits bekannte, redundante Ausbildungsinhalte gezählt. Zweitens werden auf der Prozess-Ebene Aspekte untersucht, die die Ausbildungsforschung im engsten Sinne betreffen. Hierzu gehört die Entwicklung von spezifischen therapeutischen Fertigkeiten, wie der Aufbau einer therapeutischen Beziehung, die Herstellung von Rapport, die Ermutigung zur Selbstoffenbarung und zum Zulassen von Emotionen, die Einsichtsförderung bei KlientInnen und das Erreichen von Verhaltensänderungen. Darüber hinaus zählen zu den Prozess-Variablen der Erwerb fachlich-theoretischer Kompetenzen, aber auch die Einschätzung von Supervision und Selbsterfahrung genauso wie die Zufriedenheit mit den unterschiedlichen Ausbildungsbestandteilen. Dabei wird bemängelt, dass es zwar verbreitet Ansätze zur Evaluation der theoretischen Ausbildungseinheiten und der Zufriedenheit der Ausbildungsteilnehmenden gibt, dass aber die Ausbildung von den zu vermittelnden psychotherapeutischen Fertigkeiten, die Kompetenzentwicklung und deren Determinanten insgesamt zu wenig beforscht wird (Strauß und Kohl 2009). Drittens lassen sich auf der Output-Ebene kurz- und langfristige Ergebnisse des Ausbildungsprozesses analysieren. Dazu gehören positive Aspekte wie die Entwicklung individueller Kompetenzen ebenso wie negative Aspekte in Form von beeinträchtigenden Konsequenzen für das Privatleben. Prüfungsergebnisse, weitere professionelle Entwicklungen und Ergebnisse der kontinuierlichen Supervision zählen ebenfalls zu den Output-Variablen. Der folgende Abschnitt fasst die vorliegenden Forschungsergebnisse zu diesen drei Evaluations-Ebenen in Bezug auf die Ausbildung im Psychodrama zusammen.

2 Ausbildungsevaluation im Psychodrama

Andreatta et al. (2011) verwendeten einen Fragebogen zur Erfassung von interpersoneller Problemlösekompetenz und untersuchten Teilnehmende über den gesamten Verlauf einer vierjährigen Psychodrama-Ausbildung. Das verwendete Verfahren erfasste im Selbsturteil auf insgesamt acht Skalen unterschiedliche Aspekte von Schwierigkeiten bezüglich interpersoneller Beziehungsparameter (z. B. „zu autokratisch/dominant“ oder „zu fürsorglich/freundlich“). Zum Abschluss der Ausbildung zeigte sich auf sieben der acht Skalen eine signifikante Verbesserung und somit eine höhere selbstbeurteilte Problemlösekompetenz der Ausbildungsteilnehmenden. Das Verfahren eignet sich gleichermaßen zur Input-, Prozess- und Output-Forschung und untersucht mit den erfassten Beziehungskompetenzen ein zentrales Element psychotherapeutischer Kompetenzen.

Krall und Fürst (2011) analysierten die Wirksamkeit psychodramatischer Ausbildungssupervision durch Befragung von Ausbildungsteilnehmenden und ihren Supervisor Innen. Dabei ging es vor allem um Fragen, inwiefern Supervision dazu beiträgt, dass die Ausbildungsteilnehmenden ihre psychotherapeutische Praxis weniger belastend erleben, methodisches und theoretisches Wissen verinnerlichen und ein vertieftes Verständnis für ihre KlientInnen entwickeln. Die durchgeführten Befragungen erfolgten unmittelbar nach der Supervision sowie nach einem zeitlichen Abstand von mehreren Wochen. Die Ergebnisse zeigten, dass Supervision nachhaltig zur Belastungsreduktion beiträgt und dass die Supervisionsziele in einem hohen Maße erreicht wurden. Insbesondere die szenische Bearbeitung von Fallbeispielen wurde als unterstützend erlebt. Insgesamt schätzten die Teilnehmenden die Supervisionsergebnisse tendenziell sogar noch etwas positiver ein als die Supervisor Innen selbst. Eine positive Einschätzung der Supervisionsziele zeigte sich nicht nur unmittelbar nach Abschluss der Supervision sondern auch noch nach einem zeitlichen Abstand von mehreren Wochen.

Stippler und Möller (2011) untersuchten quantitative und qualitative Veränderungen der Konzeptkompetenz während der Psychodrama-Ausbildung anhand der Bearbeitung von Fallvignetten. Konzeptkompetenz beschreibt die Fähigkeit zur Erstellung eines sinnvollen Behandlungskonzeptes und beinhaltet diagnostische Kompetenzen, die ein Erklärungsmodell für die Beschwerden eines Patienten erarbeiten, ebenso wie die Fähigkeit zur Entwicklung eines Therapiekonzeptes, um diese Beschwerden zu lindern. Maßgebliche Kriterien der Konzeptkompetenz sind das Erkennen von Komplexität (Berücksichtigung vieler unterschiedlicher Facetten einer aktuellen Problematik), das Herstellen von Kohärenz (Anzahl der Verknüpfungen zwischen den unterschiedlichen Problemfacetten) und das Schaffen von zirkulärer Vernetztheit (Verknüpfungen die über einfache Wenn-dann-Zusammenhänge hinausgehen). Insgesamt weisen die Ergebnisse auf einen Ausbildungserfolg in Bezug auf die Entwicklung der Konzeptkompetenz der Ausbildungsteilnehmenden hin. So zeigen sich nach Abschluss der theoretischen Ausbildung im Vergleich zum Ausbildungsbeginn deutliche Verbesserungen in Bezug auf die Kriterien Komplexität, Kohärenz und zirkuläre Vernetztheit.

Mitterhofer et al. (2011) untersuchten mit Hilfe des Diagnostic Role-Playing Tests den Kompetenzerwerb in der Psychodramaausbildung. Dabei wurde die Rollenausgestaltung zu Beginn und Ende der Ausbildung hinsichtlich der Aspekte Spontaneität und Kreativität miteinander verglichen. Im Rahmen des Diagnostic Role Playing Test wurde die Übernahme der sozialen Rollen „Großeltern" und „Obdachlose" beobachtet. Als Ergebnis zeigten sich deutliche Veränderungen bei der Ausgestaltung der Rollen, die als eine Zunahme von Spontanität und Kreativität im Verlauf der Ausbildung interpretiert werden.

Bemerkenswert an den Studien von Stippler und Möller (2011) und von Mitterhofer et al. (2011) ist, dass Ausbildungserfolgskriterien nicht in subjektiver Selbsteinschätzung sondern durch objektivierbare Fremdurteile erfasst wurden. Dadurch wird ein wichtiger Schritt in Richtung praktischer Relevanz unternommen, da für den Erfolg als Psychotherapeutin oder Psychotherapeut die Fremdeinschätzung der eigenen Kompetenzen schlussendlich von höherer Bedeutung ist als das subjektive Selbsturteil. Dennoch sollten weitere Studien untersuchen, in welchem Umfang Veränderungen in der Konzeptkompetenz und bei der Rollenausgestaltung tatsächlich mit verbesserten Fertigkeiten in der psychotherapeutischen Praxis in Zusammenhang stehen. In diesem Zusammenhang wären Studien wünschenswert, die Veränderungen der psychodramatischen Leitungskompetenz im Verlauf der Therapieausbildung untersuchen. Da das Doppeln eine zentrale Technik psychodramatischer Ansätze ist, könnten Studien, die Veränderungen bei der Fähigkeit zum Doppeln bei den Ausbildungsteilnehmenden erfassen, einen ersten wichtigen Beitrag leisten.

3 Affektivität, Lebenszufriedenheit und fremdbeurteilte psychodramatische Kompetenzen als Evaluationskriterien

In einer eigenen Studie untersuchten wir zwei aufeinanderfolgende Jahrgänge im ersten Jahr ihrer Psychodrama-Ausbildung (Grundstufe I) am Psychodramaforum Berlin. Das erste Ausbildungsjahr erstreckt sich über insgesamt 12 Wochenend-Module im monatlichen Abstand. Dabei wurden in einem Längsschnitt-Design zu vier unterschiedlichen Messzeitpunkten (2., 4., 8. und 12. Modul) Daten erhoben. Die Stichprobe bestand aus insgesamt 27 Teilnehmenden (16 Frauen, 11 Männer) im Alter von 22 bis 63 Jahren (Durchschnittsalter 42,1 Jahre). Sechs Teilnehmende beendeten die Ausbildung nach dem ersten Jahr und 19 Teilnehmende setzten ihre Ausbildung danach mit der Grundstufe II fort.

Zur Selbstbeurteilung verwendeten wir die Wohlbefindensmaße Lebenszufriedenheit (deutsche Version der Satisfaction with Life Scale von Glaesmer et al. 2011) und positiver sowie negativer Affekt (deutsche Version der Positive and Negative Affect Schedule von Krohne et al. 1996). Varianzanalysen mit Messzeitpunkt als messwiederholtem Faktor (4 Messzeitpunkte) und Fortsetzung der Ausbildung nach dem ersten Ausbildungsjahr (ja/nein) als Gruppenfaktor zeigten keinerlei signifikanten Haupt- und Interaktionseffekt für die abhängigen Variablen positiver Affekt, negativer Affekt und Lebenszufriedenheit. Lediglich deskriptiv zeigte sich ein leichter Anstieg der mittleren Lebenszufriedenheit vom ersten bis zum dritten Messzeitpunkt.

Zusätzlich wurden beim ersten der beiden Ausbildungsjahrgänge Fremdurteile der Ausbildungsleitung und Co-Leitung erfasst. Diese Ausbildungsgruppe bestand aus 16 Teilnehmenden, von denen 5 die Ausbildung nach dem ersten Jahr beendeten und 11 mit dem zweiten Ausbildungsjahr fortführten. Zur Fremdeinschätzung der Ausbildungsteilnehmenden wurden zunächst zwei Items aus der Beobachtungsskala Therapierelevante Interpersonelle Verhaltensweisen (Eversmann et al. 2011) ausgewählt und anschließend durch vier selbstgenerierte Items ergänzt. Eingeschätzt wurden „Übliches Verhalten gegenüber anderen" auf einer Likert Skala von 1 = kühl bis 7 = freundlich sowie „Empathiefähigkeit (Verständnis für die Gefühle anderer)", „Authentische Rollendarstellung und Einfühlung in Rollen", „Spielfreude", „Bereitschaft zur Auseinandersetzung mit eigenen Themen" und „Realitätsgerechte Selbstwahrnehmung" jeweils auf einer Likert Skala von 1 = trifft gar nicht zu bis 7 = trifft genau zu. Ausbildungsleitung und Co-Leitung beurteilten unabhängig voneinander die Teilnehmenden zu den vier unterschiedlichen Messzeitpunkten jeweils am Ende der Ausbildungswochenenden. Dabei gab sich eine befriedigende Beurteiler Übereinstimmung (rs >.70) für die sechs Items.

Zur Prüfung signifikanter Effekte wurden Varianzanalysen mit Messzeitpunkt als messwiederholtem Faktor (4 Messzeitpunkte) und Fortsetzung der Ausbildung nach dem ersten Ausbildungsjahr (ja/nein) als Gruppenfaktor gerechnet. Dabei zeigten sich auf vier der fremdeingeschätzten Items (Freundlichkeit des Verhaltens gegenüber anderen, authentische Rollendarstellung, Spielfreude, Auseinandersetzung mit eigenen Themen) signifikante Haupteffekte der Gruppenzugehörigkeit, Fs(1, 11) > 4.96, ps < .05. Ausbildungsteilnehmende, die nach dem ersten Ausbildungsjahr die Ausbildung fortsetzten, hatten hier durchgängig höhere Werte als Teilnehmende, die nach dem ersten Ausbildungsjahr ausstiegen. Ausschließlich beim Item „authentische Rollendarstellung“ zeigte sich außerdem ein signifikanter Haupteffekt des Messzeitpunkts, $F(3, 33)=8.70$, $p=.001$. Dabei wurde insbesondere eine Abnahme vom ersten auf den zweiten Messzeitpunkt ersichtlich, der sich möglicherweise durch strenger werdende Beurteilungskriterien bei den beiden Beurteilenden erklären lässt. Es ergaben sich keine signifikanten Interaktionseffekte.

Wichtig erscheint, dass sich signifikante Unterschiede zwischen Teilnehmenden, die die Ausbildung fortsetzten versus nach einem Jahr beendeten, ausschließlich in den fremdbeurteilten Variablen, nicht jedoch bei der selbstbeurteilten Lebenszufriedenheit und Affektivität ergaben. Ebenso zeigten sich keine signifikanten Interaktionen mit dem Messzeitpunkt. Demzufolge sind für die Ausbildungsleitenden Teilnehmende, die sich engagiert und mit persönlichem Einsatz an der psychodramatischen Selbsterfahrung beteiligen, bereits früh identifizierbar. Entgegen unseren Erwartungen zeigten sich im Verlauf des ersten Ausbildungsjahres keine positiven Veränderungen bei der Lebenszufriedenheit und im Affekt. Ebenso ergaben sich keine Veränderungen bei den fremdeingeschätzten Kompetenzen. Dies dürfte höchstwahrscheinlich damit zu erklären sein, dass eine einjährige Ausbildung noch nicht ausreicht, um deutliche Veränderungen beim selbsteingeschätzten Wohlbefinden herbeizuführen. In Bezug auf die Fremdurteile wäre wünschenswert, dass die Beurteilenden blind gegenüber dem Messzeitpunkt wären, was nur aufwändig durch Videomitschnitte und eine zufällige Reihenfolge bei der Beurteilung ermöglicht werden könnte. So ist denkbar, dass die Ausbildungsleitung ihre Beurteilungsansprüche mit dem Fortschreiten der Ausbildung erhöhte, was dann in der Folge einem Anstieg der Mittelwerte bei den Fremdurteilen entgegenlief.

4 Ausblick

Mindestens ebenso wichtig wie die Prüfung der Effektivität psychodramatischer Interventionen ist die Evaluation psychodramatischer Ausbildungen. Schließlich vermitteln und schaffen sie die notwendigen Kenntnisse und Fertigkeiten für erfolgreiches psychotherapeutisches Arbeiten. Ergebnisse aus Evaluationsstudien von nicht-psychodramatischen, psychotherapeutischen Ausbildungen betonen die Bedeutung von praxisnahem Wissen und von Selbsterfahrung in der Ausbildung (Strauß und Kohl 2009). Damit sind Aspekte genannt, die erfreulicherweise in psychodramatischen Ausbildungen besondere Berücksichtigung finden. Insgesamt sollten aber auch Psychodramatikerinnen und Psychodramatiker noch mehr die verschiedenen Instrumente nutzen, die bereits zur Evaluation psychotherapeutischer Ausbildungen verwendet werden (z. B. Strauß et al. 2009b). Dies gilt insbesondere, weil bisher vor allem Fragen zum Kompetenzerwerb in der psychotherapeutischen Praxis große Forschungslücken aufweisen. Damit wird ein Bereich umschrieben, für den Psychodrama-Ansätze aufgrund ihrer ausgeprägten Handlungsorientierung mit an erster Stelle prädestiniert sind.

Ausbildungsevaluationen können auch auf Ablehnung stoßen. Für Ausbildungsteilnehmende und die Leitung bedeuten sie zusätzlichen Arbeitsaufwand. Mitunter sind Teilnehmende besorgt, in den Evaluationsfragebögen etwas von sich preiszugeben. Diesen Sorgen sind wir in unserer Studie mit einem eindeutig zuordenbaren, aber anonymen Code begegnet. Umgekehrt liegen die Vorzüge der Ausbildungsevaluation auf der Hand. Evaluationen können zur Qualitätssicherung und als Feedback-Instrument sowohl von Leitungs- als auch von Teilnehmendenseite eingesetzt werden. In unserer Studie wurde deutlich, dass es zur Auswahl von geeigneten Ausbildungskandidatinnen und –kandidaten Sinn machen würde, vorab die Spielfreude und das sich Einlassen auf psychodramatische Selbsterfahrung über ein Wochenende zu beobachten und daraufhin entsprechende Empfehlungen abzugeben.

Ebenso ist es unbedingt erforderlich, auch verstärkt Studien durchzuführen, die die langfristigen Konsequenzen einer Ausbildungsteilnahme auf den Kompetenzerwerb und die Persönlichkeitsentwicklung untersuchen. Hier liegen bislang überhaupt keine Untersuchungen vor. Gerade im Vergleich der unterschiedlichen psychotherapeutischen Ansätze könnten hier wichtige Erkenntnisse über die spezifischen Qualitätsmerkmale psychodramatischer Ausbildungen und ihres in Bezug auf die anderen Verfahren komplementären Potentials gewonnen werden. Dabei erscheint der Aufwand im Gegensatz zu Studien zur Effektivität von psychotherapeutischen Interventionen noch vergleichsweise einfacher handhabbar. Die Ausbildungsteilnehmenden sind über einen längeren Zeitraum an den Ausbildungsinstituten anwesend und die Einschätzungen können unmittelbar vor Ort abgegeben werden. Wünschenswert wäre zumindest eine Kooperation innerhalb der psychodramatischen Ausbildungsinstitute aber natürlich auch über die Grenzen der unterschiedlichen therapeutischen Verfahren hinweg.

Literatur

Andreatta, P., Drexler, A., Pauza, E., & Möller, H. (2011). Entwicklung interpersoneller Problemlösekompetenz während psychotherapeutischer Ausbildung in Psychodrama. *Zeitschrift für Psychodrama und Soziometrie, 10*(1), 213–223.

Eversmann, J., Schöttke, H., Wiedl, K. H., & Rogner, J. (2011). Die Beobachtungsskala „Therapie-relevante interpersonelle Verhaltensweisen" (TRIB) in der Auswahl von Teilnehmern der Psychotherapieausbildung. *Zeitschrift für klinische Psychologie und Psychotherapie, 40*(1), 11–21.

Glaesmer, H., Sonntag, A., Barnow, S., Brähler, E., Fegert, J. M., Fliegel, S., Freyberger, H. J., Goldbeck, L., Kohl, S., Lebiger-Vogel, J., Leuzinger-Bohleber, M., Michels-Lucht, F., Willutzki, U., Spröber, N., & Strauß, B. (2009). Psychotherapeutenausbildung aus Sicht der Absolventen. *Psychotherapeut, 54*(6), 437–444.

Glaesmer, H., Grande, G., Braehler, E., & Roth, M. (2011). The German version of the satisfaction with life scale (SWLS). *European Journal of Psychological Assessment, 27*(2), 127–132.

Kohl, D. P. S., Barnow, S., Brähler, E., Fegert, J. M., Fliegel, S., Freyberger, H. J., Goldbeck, L., Lebiger-Vogel, J., Leuzinger-Bohleber, M., Michels-Lucht, F., Sonntag, A., Spröber, N., Willutzki, U., & Strauß, B. (2009). Die Psychotherapieausbildung aus Sicht der Lehrkräfte. *Psychotherapeut, 54*(6), 445–456.

Krall, H., & Fürst, J. (2011). *Supervision in der Psychodrama-Psychotherapieausbildung. Zeitschrift für Psychodrama und Soziometrie, 10*(1), 253–266.

Krohne, H. W., Egloff, B., Kohlmann, C. W., & Tausch, A. (1996). Untersuchungen mit einer deutschen Version der Positive and Negative Affect Schedule (PANAS). *Diagnostica, 42*, 139–156.

Mitterhofer, H., Andreatta, P., & Seewald, M. (2011). Das Rollenspiel in der Psychodramaausbildung im Fokus der Sozialforschung. *Zeitschrift für Psychodrama und Soziometrie, 10*(1), 225–237.

Sonntag, A., Glaesmer, H., Barnow, S., Brähler, E., Fegert, J. M., Fliegel, S., Freyberger, H. J., Goldbeck, L., Kohl, S., Lebiger-Vogel, J., Leuzinger-Bohleber, M., Michels-Lucht, F., Spröber, N., Willutzki, U., & Strauß, B. (2009). Die Psychotherapeutenausbildung aus Sicht der Teilnehmer. *Psychotherapeut, 54*(6), 427–436.

Stadler, C., & Wieser, M. (2011). Vorwort der Herausgeber. *Zeitschrift für Psychodrama und Soziometrie, 10*(1), 1–7.
Stippler, M., & Möller, H. (2011). Die Entwicklung der Konzeptkompetenz in der Psychodrama-Ausbildung. *Zeitschrift für Psychodrama und Soziometrie, 10*(1), 239–251.
Strauß, B., & Kohl, S. (2009). Themen der Ausbildungsforschung in der Psychotherapie. *Psychotherapeut, 54*(6), 411–426.
Strauß, B., Barnow, S., Brähler, E., Fegert, J., Fliegel, S., Freyberger, H. J., Goldbeck, L., Leuzinger-Bohleber, M., & Willutzki, U. (2009a). Forschungsgutachten zur Ausbildung von Psychologischen Psychotherapeuten und Kinder- und Jugendlichenpsychotherapeuten. https://www.bundesgesundheitsministerium.de/fileadmin/redaktion/pdf_publikationen/forschungsberichte/Forschungsgutachten-Ausbildung-Psychologische-Psychotherapeuten.pdf.
Strauß, B., Barnow, S., Brähler, E., Fegert, J., Fliegel, S., Freyberger, H. J., Goldbeck, L., Leuzinger-Bohleber, M., & Willutzki, U. (2009b). Begleitband zum Forschungsgutachten zur Ausbildung von Psychologischen Psychotherapeuten und Kinder- und Jugendlichenpsychotherapeuten. http://www.mpsy.uniklinikum-jena.de/mpsy_media/Downloads/Begleitband_Forschungsgutachten_Psychotherapieausbildung_300409.pdf.

Konrad Schnabel, Jg. 1971, Diplompsychologe, Professor für Persönlichkeitspsychologie und Diagnostische Psychologie an der International Psychoanalytic University Berlin, 2009-2014 Ausbildung zum Psychodrama-Therapeuten am Psychodramaforum Berlin. Forschungsschwerpunkte sind spontanes Verhalten und unbewusste Persönlichkeitsanteile.

Johannes Reif, Jg. 1990, studiert an der Freien Universität im Masterstudiengang Arbeits-, Organisations- und Wirtschaftspsychologie. B.Sc. in Psychologie an der Universität Potsdam. Reif absolvierte die Grundstufe I der Psychodrama-Weiterbildung „Szenisch Arbeiten“ am Psychodramaforum Berlin und arbeitet freiberuflich als Einzelfallhelfer mit behinderten Jugendlichen zusammen.

Z Psychodrama Soziometr (2016) (Suppl) 15:297–321
DOI 10.1007/s11620-015-0300-2

HAUPTBEITRÄGE

Zeitschrift für Psychodrama und Soziometrie

Psychodramaforschung in Form von Masterthesen – ein Überblick über Themen und Methoden der ersten 8 Jahrgänge der Masterthesen der Universitätslehrgänge Psychodrama Psychotherapie des ÖAGG

Sonja Hintermeier

Online publiziert: 9. Dezember 2015

Zusammenfassung Eine Variante psychodramatischer Psychotherapieforschung besteht in Masterthesen, welche im Kontext von Fachspezifika-Masterlehrgängen und aufbauenden Universitätslehrgängen erstellt werden. Die Autorin hat die in den ersten 8 Jahren der universitären Psychodrama-Lehrgänge des ÖAGG abgefassten Masterarbeiten gesichtet und als Ergebnis ihrer Arbeit einen detaillierten Überblick über die in diesem Zeitraum bearbeiteten Themen und verwendeten Methoden geschaffen. In diesem Artikel wird anhand von Klassifizierungen und Kategorisierungen der Masterthesen ein Ordnungssystem geboten, das eine rasche Orientierung ermöglicht, zu welchen Themenbereichen es bereits Masterarbeiten gibt, welche Forschungsmethoden verwendet wurden und zu welchen Themenbereichen und Fragestellungen noch Forschungslücken existieren. Die gefundenen Häufigkeiten werden diskutiert und mögliche Weiterentwicklungen angedacht.

Schlüsselwörter Psychodramatherapie · Psychotherapieforschung · Masterthesen · Überblicksartikel · Psychodrama Theorie · Praxis · Empirische Studien

veröffentlicht in der Online-Bibliothek der Donauuniversität Krems: http://www.donau-uni.ac.at/de/service/bibliothek/index.php

Mag[a]. S. Hintermeier, MSc (✉)
Praxis für Psychotherapie und Supervision,
Dürergasse 14–16/6,
1060 Wien, Österreich
E-Mail: praxis@sonjahintermeier.at

Psychodrama research in the form of master theses – an overview of subjects and methods in the first 8 years of the master theses of the university courses psychodrama psychotherapy of the ÖAGG

Abstract One form of psychodramatic psychotherapy research is undertaken for master theses in the context of master courses and upgrading university courses for psychotherapy. The author has researched a majority of master theses drawn up in the first 8 years of university courses of the ÖAGG and as a result created a detailed and complete overview of the processed topics and methods used. In this article based on classifications and categorizations of the master theses, a classification system is offered that allows a rapid orientation about the existing topics in master theses, the methods that have been used and what subjects and issues are absent or gaps in research. The frequencies found are discussed and possible developments are anticipated.

Keywords Psychodrama therapy · Psychotherapy research · Master theses · Survey article · Psychodrama theory · Practice · Empirical studies

1 Einleitung

Masterthesen entstehen im Rahmen des Ausbildungsinstitutes der Fachsektion Psychodrama im ÖAGG[1] in zweierlei Settings:

1. Als Abschlussarbeit des 2005 implementierten Masterlehrgangs Fachspezifikum Psychodrama, das der ÖAGG in Kooperation mit der Donau-Universität Krems anbietet.
2. Als Abschluss des 2006 gestarteten Universitätslehrganges Psychotherapie – Master of Science – Upgrade für graduierte Psychodrama-PsychotherapeutInnen – ebenfalls an der Donau-Universität Krems – welches eingetragene Psychodrama-PsychotherapeutInnen absolvieren können, die vor der Implementierung der akademischen Ausbildung ihr Fachspezifikum Psychodrama absolviert haben und nun auf den Masterlehrgang upgraden wollen.

Seit Start dieser Lehrgänge 2005 bzw. 2006 bis zum Ende des Untersuchungszeitraumes ist die beeindruckende Menge von insgesamt 82 Arbeiten entstanden. Trotz ihrer zum Teil sehr hohen Qualität sind diese Arbeiten dem breiteren psychodramatischen KollegInnenkreis kaum bekannt. Daher entstand bei mir die Idee diese Masterthesen systematisch auf Inhalte und Methoden zu untersuchen und in aufbereiteter Form überblicksartig vorzustellen. Meine Forschungsfragen waren: Welche Themen wurden bearbeitet und welche Forschungsmethoden verwendet? Zeigen sich deutliche thematische Schwerpunkte (Clusterbildungen) bzw. auffällige thematische Lücken? Zeigen sich deutliche Bevorzugungen hinsichtlich bestimmter Forschungsmethoden? Welche Möglichkeiten und Empfehlungen lassen sich daraus für weitere Masterthesen ableiten?

Es wurden alle Arbeiten in die Untersuchung einbezogen, welche zum Stichtag 24. Jänner 2015 im Online-Katalog der Bibliothek[2] der Donauuniversität Krems (in weiterer Folge als DUK abgekürzt) zum Download vorlagen. Da 3 Masterarbeiten für den Download „gesperrt" waren, wurden nur die verbleibenden 79 Masterthesen in die Untersuchung einbezogen. Diese 79 Arbeiten wurden von mir in den letzten zwei Jahren gelesen und hinsichtlich der folgenden Merkmale analysiert und entsprechenden Kategorien zugeordnet:

- nach dem thematischen Fokus (Theorie- vs. Praxis-Bezug)
- nach Forschungsdesigns und Forschungsmethoden
- nach dem untersuchten Setting (Einzel, Paare, Familie, Soziales Atom, Gruppe) und
- nach den behandelten KlientInnen/PatientInnen-Gruppen (Alter, Geschlecht)

Während die Kategorien bei den Forschungsmethoden vorgegeben waren, mussten sie in Bezug auf den thematischen Fokus erst am Material entwickelt werden. Die Kategorienbildung erfolgte im Rahmen eines systematischen, regelgeleiteten Vorgehens. Die Arbeiten wurden von mir zur Gänze gelesen, zu jeder Arbeit ein „Kurzdossier" mit markanten Beschreibungsmerkmalen verfasst und auf dieser Basis übergeordnete Kategorien entwickelt. Hier wird nun das Ergebnis meiner Analyse vorgestellt, die gefundenen Clusterbildungen und Forschungslücken diskutiert und auch auf die Qualität der Arbeiten Bezug genommen.

Ziel dieses Beitrages ist es,

- Psychodrama-KollegInnen und andere Interessierte zu informieren, über welche Themen im Rahmen des Universitätslehrganges Psychotherapie/Psychodrama im ÖAGG Masterthesen verfasst wurden;
- Studierenden Orientierung zu bieten, zu welchen Fragestellungen geforscht werden kann, welche Designs und Forschungsmethoden genutzt werden können und wo es noch „unerforschtes Land" gibt.
- den AutorInnen auf diesem Weg die „spiegelende" Wertschätzung zu bieten, die Schreibende erst bei einer Veröffentlichung erhalten.

2 Kategorisierung der Masterthesen nach dem thematischen Fokus

Die untersuchten Masterthesen lassen sich nach ihrem Fokus grob in zwei Gruppen einteilen: In solche mit Theorie- und solche mit Praxis-Bezug (Tab. 1):

2.1 Arbeiten zu Theorie-Themen

Maria-Theresia Schönherr (2008) interpretiert in ihrer Arbeit den Entwicklungsprozess einer Romanfigur als Beispiel für jenen von Ottomeyer (2004) als

Tab. 1 Theorie-/Praxisbezug

Masterthesen gesamt	79	100 %
Theorie-Themen	6	8 %
Praxis-Themen	73	92 %

„Regenerationsdrama“ bezeichneten Vorgang, wenn „eingeklemmtes Leben befreit wird“. Regina Bulian (2009) behandelt das Thema *Begegnungsszenen* (in der Psychotherapie) nach den theoretischen Konzepten von Stern, Lorenzer und des Psychodramas. Silvia Franke (2011) analysiert in ihrer metatheoretischen Arbeit den psychodramatischen *Begriff des Tele* hinsichtlich möglicher Parallelen in Philosophie, Psychotherapie und Naturwissenschaften. Kerstin Karlhuber (2011) untersucht das Phänomen des *„Stimmenhören“ aus Sicht der psychodramatischen Entwicklungstheorie* nach Schacht. Doris Tornow (2013) beforscht das Thema *biografische Entstehungsbedingungen von Burnout* aus psychodramatischer Sicht. Manfred Stelzig (2014) leistet in seiner Arbeit ausgehend von aktuellen Erkenntnissen der Säuglingsforschung Theorieentwicklung zu der *biologischen Verankerung von Elternrollen.*

2.2 Arbeiten zu Praxis-Themen[3]

Diese große Gruppe von Arbeiten mit praxisbezogenen Fragestellungen lässt sich nach dem thematischen Fokus in folgende Untergruppen unterteilen (Tab. 2):

2.2.1 Arbeiten mit Fragestellungen zu bestimmten institutionellen Kontexten

Bei dieser Gruppe von Arbeiten stehen bestimmte institutionelle Kontexte/Bühnen psychodramatherapeutischen Arbeitens im Fokus der interessierenden Fragestellung:

Zwei Arbeiten beschäftigen sich mit psychotherapeutischen Interventionen im Schul-Kontext: Gabriele Fercher (2012) schildert, wie sie in ihrer Schule parallel zu ihrer Rolle als Lehrerin psychodramatherapeutische Angebote implementieren konnte und reflektiert über das mit dieser *Doppelrolle Lehrerin – Psychotherapeutin* verbundene Spannungsfeld. Elisabeth Grosinger-Spiss (2013) stellt ein von ihr entwickeltes Konzept für *Rollenerweiterung von* (entwicklungsverzögerten) *Vorschulkindern* in der Volksschule vor.

Die Arbeit von Christa Bauer (2012) befasst sich mit Psychotherapie im Rahmen *beruflicher Rehabilitation*, und zwar mit der Frage, ob und wie Psychodramatherapie die Entwicklung/Rückgewinnung der Rolle der „Arbeitenden“ fördern kann.

Folgende Arbeiten befassen sich mit psychotherapeutischen Interventionen auf der Bühne spezieller Krankenhaus-Stationen: Hannelore Houdek (2011) stellt die von ihr entwickelte Anwendung von Intermediärobjekten bei der *Operationsvorbereitung von Kindern* vor. Sabine Feuerstein (2009) beschreibt ihre Arbeit mit Eltern (Müttern) auf der *Kinder-Intensivstation* und wie diese in solch einer Krisensituation mit psychodramatherapeutischer Begleitung adäquat unterstützt werden können.

Tab. 2 Thematischer Fokus

Praxisbezogene Masterthesen	73
Fragestellungen zu bestimmten institutionellen Kontexten (Bühnen)	8
Fragestellungen zu speziellen Settings	5
Methodenbezogene Fragestellungen	20
Fragestellungen zu speziellen KlientInnengruppen	1
Störungsspezifische Fragestellungen	24
Fragestellungen zu speziellen Therapiethemen	15

Psychotherapie im Rahmen einer stationären Psychiatriebehandlung bildet den thematischen Fokus folgender Arbeiten: Ursula Apolloner (2010) untersucht inwieweit Ressourcenarbeit die *Ablösung von Kindern aus dem stationären Setting* einer kinderpsychiatrischen Station erleichtern kann. Kristin Scharfetter (2013) beforscht die *Rahmenbedingungen stationärer Gruppentherapie* aus theoretischer Sicht und stellt ein von ihr entwickeltes Konzept dafür dar. Helmut Kronberger (2014) untersucht, wie die Gestaltung des therapeutischen Umfelds in einem stationären Setting *Wendepunkte in den Therapieprozessen* der PatientInnen begünstigen kann.

2.2.2 Arbeiten mit Fragestellungen zu spezifischen Therapie-Settings

Spezielle Settings sind bei folgenden Arbeiten der Gegenstand des Forschungsinteresses:

Hannelore Stollewerk (2007) stellt die Möglichkeit der *Einbindung des realen sozialen Atoms* in einen (stationären) Therapieprozess von Kindern und Jugendlichen dar. Franz Lechner (2010) beforscht die Möglichkeit einer *Einbindung der Eltern in den (ambulanten) Gruppentherapie-Prozess* ihrer Kinder in Form einer begleitenden Eltern-Gruppe. Karin Kölbl-Fischer (2011) untersucht das Setting psychodramatischer *Paartherapie* auf seine *Möglichkeiten zur Konflikt- und Krisenbewältigung*. Hilde Gött (2012) beschreibt den Prozess *soziodramatischer Begegnungsgruppen von Nachkommen von NS-Opfern und NS-Tätern*. Regina Beer (2013) behandelt die Möglichkeiten und Voraussetzungen einer *geschlechtshomogenen Mädchen-Gruppe* für die Entwicklung von Rollenerweiterung.

2.2.3 Arbeiten mit methodenbezogenen Fragestellungen

In dieser Gruppe von Arbeiten lassen sich folgende Untergruppen unterscheiden:

- Fragestellungen zu speziellen Interventionsformen:

In folgenden Masterarbeiten werden Präventionsprojekte beforscht: Kurt Fellöckers (2008) Masterarbeit basiert auf der Analyse eines – auf psychodramatherapeutischen und psychodramapädagogischen Theorien aufbauenden – *Theater-Projekts im Rahmen schulischer Suchtprävention*. Eva Breuß-Purtscher (2013) betrachtet die Vorgangsweise bei *Nachschulungskursen für alkoholauffällige LenkerInnen* als Beispiel von Sekundärprävention von Alkoholabhängigkeit aus psychodramatischer Sicht. Christine Klimt (2013) analysiert ein von ihr mitbegründetes *Präventionsprojekt gegen sexuelle Gewalt an Kindern* unter psychodramatischen Gesichtspunkten.

Andrea Nindler (2013) beschreibt ein von ihr entwickeltes Konzept für *Krisenintervention/Trauerbegleitung für Kinder und Jugendliche* in der Schule.

- Fragestellungen zu speziellen (Gruppen-) Arrangements:

Roswitha Riepl (2011) geht in ihrer Arbeit der Frage nach, welche theoretischen *Grundlagen psychodramatischer Aufstellungsarbeit* zugrundeliegen und worin sich psychodramatische Aufstellungsarbeit von den anderen Formen der Aufstellungsarbeit unterscheidet. Barbara Pfaffenwimmer (2011) charakterisiert den *therapeutischen Handlungsraum des Bibliodrama* im Hinblick auf ihre These, dass die Bewältigung spirituell-religiöser Rollenkonflikte die Erweiterung der eigenen Rollenressourcen fördert. Elisabeth Schöpfer (2013) beschreibt in ihrer Arbeit die *Möglichkeiten therapeutischen Stegreiftheaters in der Rehabilitation* langzeithospitalisierter PsychiatriepatientInnen.

- Fragestellungen zu speziellen methodischen Strategien/Handlungstechniken:

Markus Canazei (2007) behandelt den Themenkomplex rund um den Begriff *Anwärmung in Gruppen* metatheoretisch und in Bezug auf Implikationen für die Praxis. Christoph Zauner (2010) erkundet die *Wirkungen des Einsatzes (selbst) gebastelter Heldenfiguren als Intermediärobjekte* in der Einzeltherapie eines Jugendlichen. Astrid Amann (2013) analysiert die *Möglichkeiten und Bedeutungen des Spiegelns*, Robert Kasper (2013) *jene der Technik der Zukunftsprojektion* im Rahmen psychodramatischer Prozesse. Silvia Weigl (2014) bearbeitet die Frage nach der *Wirkung und den Einsatzmöglichkeiten des Sozialen Atoms* in den unterschiedlichen Phasen des Therapieprozesses.

- Fragestellungen zum Einbezug „fremder" (Therapie-) Methoden/Techniken:

Um den Einsatz von Computer-Technik in psychodramatischen Therapie- und Beratungsprozessen geht es bei Sabine Spitzer-Prochazka (2008): Sie erläutert die *Möglichkeiten des Einsatzes computervermittelter Kommunikation* im Sinne psychodramatischer Online-Beratung.

Um diagnostische Methoden geht es bei folgenden Arbeiten: Therese Kasper (2013) analysiert die Verwendbarkeit der *„Handlungsliste" als Instrument der Selbststeuerung* im Prozess der Selbsterkenntnis bei der Reorganisation einer störenden Handlungsstruktur. Eva Wanderer (2014) untersucht die *Kompatibilität von OPD2-Diagnostik für Psychodrama-Therapien* und entwickelt psychodramatische Checklisten, in die die OPD-2 einfließt.

Folgende Arbeiten behandeln den Einsatz fremder Therapie-Techniken: Isabella Lenz (2013) stellt dar, wie ausgewählte Techniken aus *Körpertherapie-Verfahren* für die *Nachnährung der psychosomatischen Rollenebene* in Psychodramatherapie integriert werden können. Martin Geiger (2012) reflektiert in seiner Arbeit die *Verwendung von Musik als Intermediärobjekt* in der PD-Einzel-Therapie, Angelika Hagenbichler (2013) beschreibt die *Verwendung von Musikinstrumenten* in der PD-Gruppentherapie.

- Fragestellungen zur therapeutischen Rollen- und Beziehungsgestaltung:

Renate Hochgerner (2006) charakterisiert in ihrer Arbeit die *Funktionen der therapeutischen Beziehung* in der Arbeit mit einem strukturell beeinträchtigten Kind in instabilen sozialen Beziehungen. Karl-Ernst Heidegger (2011) behandelt die im Kinderpsychodrama kontrovers diskutierte *Frage des „körperlichen Mitspielen" des/der TherapeutIn und* bietet theoretische Begründungen für die von ihm vertretene Position.

2.2.4 Arbeiten mit klientInnenspezifischen Fragestellungen

Bislang existiert nur eine Arbeit mit einer explizit auf eine KlientInnengruppe bezogene Fragestellung: Hildegard Pruckner (2006) stellt in ihrer umfangreichen Grundlagenarbeit ihr *Konzept psychodramatischer Kindertherapie* dar.

2.2.5 Arbeiten mit störungsspezifischen Fragestellungen

Bei dieser Untergruppe von Arbeiten geht es um Fragestellungen rund um bestimmte Störungsbilder, meist mit dem Ziel der Entwicklung störungsspezifischer Modifikationen von Psychodramatherapie. Da von den Krankenkassen die Internationale Klassifikation psychischer Störungen in der Version 10 (ICD 10) verwendet wird, stelle ich die störungsspezifischen Masterthesen den jeweiligen F-Kapiteln zugeordnet dar:

- F0 Organische Störungen:

Birgit Rotter (2012) stellt in ihrer Arbeit die bei *Altersdemenz (F 02)* notwendigen Adaptionen und Modifikationen der Psychodramatechniken im Rahmen von Psychodrama-Gruppentherapie vor.

- F1 Psychische und Verhaltensstörungen durch psychotrope Substanzen:

Bernhard Starzer-Eidenberger (2013) untersucht die Wirkung einer *psychodramatischen Raucherentwöhnungs-Maßnahme auf Störungen durch Tabak (F17)*. Elisabeth Grissenberger (2014) beforscht den *Einfluss der Gestaltung sozialer Beziehungen auf den Behandlungserfolg von stationärer Alkoholtherapie.*

- F4 Neurotische, Belastungs- und Somatoforme Störungen:

Katharina Chalupsky (2012) stellt in ihrer Arbeit einen von ihr entwickelten kurzzeittherapeutischen Ansatz zur Behandlung *von Flugangst* (F40) vor. Barbara Schorn (2012) behandelt in ihrer Arbeit die Behandlung von *Sozialangst* bei *Kindern* (F 93.2) *und Jugendlichen* (F40.1). Karl Grimmer (2007) entwickelt in seiner Grundlagenarbeit sein *Konzept einer störungs-spezifischen Psychodrama-Therapie von Angststörungen* (F41). Irmtraud Langer (2012) beleuchtet die Diagnose *Panikattacken* (F41.0) aus biologischer bis weltanschaulicher Sicht und verweist auf Techniken, die in der Therapie hilfreich sind. Sigrid Bachler-Klein (2010) stellt in ihrer Arbeit psychodramatische Behandlungszugänge zu *Zwangsstörungen bei Kindern* (F42) dar. Gabriele Kastner (2011) fragt in ihrer Arbeit über *dissoziative Störungen* (F44) bei Frauen, was früh und komplex traumatisierten Frauen helfen kann, therapie- und begegnungsfähig zu werden. Isolde Amon (2011) beschreibt theoretische Konzepte bezüglich *psychosomatischer und somatoformer Erkrankungen* (F45) und ihr darauf aufbauendes psychodramatisches Behandlungskonzept für diese Störungen.

- F5 Verhaltensauffälligkeiten mit körperlichen Störungen oder Faktoren:

Sabine Kern (2008) entwickelt in ihrer Masterthese ein Konzept zur Entstehung und Aufrechterhaltung von *Anorexie (F50.0) und Bulimie (F50.2) aus der Sicht des „Spontaneitäts-Kreativitäts-Zyklus“* und darauf aufbauend störungsspezifische Interventionen für die einzeltherapeutische Arbeit. Birgit Etlinger (2012) untersucht in ihrer Arbeit zu *Bulimie (F50.2) aus rollentheoretischer Sicht* eine Behandlung im homogenen Gruppensetting als unterstützenden Rahmen des Aufgebens der bulimischen Rollenkonserve und für Rollenerweiterung. Barbara Haid (2014) beforscht, welche psychodramatischen Interventionen im Gruppensetting die *(gestörte) Körperwahrnehmung bulimischer Frauen* verbessern helfen.

Wolfgang Hofer (2013) reflektiert die Kompatibilität klassisch *sexualtherapeutischer Ansätze für Sexualstörungen* (F52) mit dem Psychodrama und entwickelt auf dieser Basis das Fundament einer Psychodrama-Sexualtherapie im Paar-Setting.

- F6 Persönlichkeits- und Verhaltensstörungen:

Sonja Hintermeier (2008) stellt in ihrer Arbeit auf der Basis von Psychodramatheorie und Praxisbeispielen ihr entwicklungsförderndes Modell für Einzeltherapie mit *Borderline-PatientInnen* (F 60.31) dar. Christine Pichlhöfer (2010) erläutert in ihrer Arbeit *Übereinstimmungen und Unterschiede zwischen der abhängigen Persönlichkeitsstörung (F60.7) und Co-Abhängigkeit.* Doris Nowak-Schuh (2013) stellt theoretische Ansätze zur *Therapie des Narzissmus* (F60.8) und neurotischer narzisstischer Mechanismen dar und entwickelt ein Konzept für einen psychodramatherapeutischen Ansatz.

- F8 Entwicklungsstörungen:

Claudia Pfohl (2012) untersucht in ihrer Arbeit zum *Asperger-Syndrom* (F84), ob Psychodrama-Gruppentherapie geeignet ist, die für Asperger typische Symptomatik einer mangelnden Gefühlswahrnehmung und Begegnungsfähigkeit zu verbessern.

- F9 Verhaltens- und emotionale Störungen mit Beginn in Kindheit und Jugend:

Maria Schatovich-Kiss (2009) erarbeitet in ihrer Arbeit zu *ADHS (F90.0) bei Kindern* ein psychodramatisches Verständnis für die Entwicklung von ADHS und darauf aufbauend ein Konzept störungsspezifischer Interventionen im Gruppensetting. Eva Sakrausky (2013) beforscht in ihrer Arbeit, ob die Psychodramagruppe dem „*aggressiven Kind*" (F91 und F92) einen geeigneten Rahmen zur Rollenentwicklung zur Verfügung stellen kann. Helene Bader (2011) stellt den Monodrama-Therapieprozess eines Mädchens mit *Sozialangst* (F93.2) dar. Gabriele Biegler-Vitek (2011) entwickelt in ihrer Arbeit ein Ätiologie-Konzept und darauf aufbauend ein *störungsspezifisches Behandlungs-Konzept für* Mutismus (F94.0).

Zusätzlich zu diesen störungsspezifischen Arbeiten gibt es solche, die ihren Fokus nicht auf eine bestimmte Störung (Differenzialdiagnose) sondern allgemeiner auf ein deutlich niedriges Strukturniveau gelegt haben, welches sowohl bei schweren affektiven Störungen als auch bei Persönlichkeits-Entwicklungsstörungen vorliegt: Irmgard Grauf (2010) untersucht die Möglichkeiten der *stationären Behandlung struktureller Störungen mit Gruppentherapie.* Gerda Trinkel (2013) stellt ihr Konzept einer *ambulanten Psychodramagruppe für Menschen mit strukturellen Störungen* dar und evaluiert, ob strukturbezogene Interventionen ein Nachreifen struktureller Fähigkeiten bewirkt haben.

2.2.6 Arbeiten zu speziellen Therapie-Themen

Diese sehr große Gruppe an Masterthesen lässt sich in folgende Themengruppen unterteilen:

- Arbeiten zu bestimmten psychischen Phänomenen:

Elke Ehrlinger (2011) untersucht in ihrer Arbeit zu *Emotionen*, inwieweit Psychodrama-Therapie das Wahrnehmen von Gefühlen fördern kann und welche Techniken dazu besonders hilfreich sind. Martin Krautschneider (2012) vergleicht in seiner Arbeit zum *Flow in der Psychodrama-Therapie* PatientInnen-Gruppen mit und ohne begleitendes Yogatraining.

- Arbeiten zu Rollenentwicklung/Persönlichkeitsreifung:

Elisabeth Zahrl-Weis (2012) reflektiert anhand einer Einzeltherapie mit einem Vorschulkind die Bedeutung der *Entwicklung des Als-ob und der Spielfähigkeit* als Basis für die Entwicklung der Fähigkeit zur Rollendistanz und der spielerischen Handlungsfähigkeit. Cornelia Kühtreiber (2012) untersucht im Rahmen einer Evaluationsstudie einer Kinder-Psychodramagruppe die in diesem Zeitraum erfolgte *Rollenentwicklung der Kinder*.

- Arbeiten zu Beziehungsfähigkeit/Beziehungsgestaltung:

Reinhilde Reinthaler (2011) befasst sich in ihrer Arbeit mit dem Konstrukt des *„Helfer-Syndroms" nach Schmidbauer* und versucht es in das Psychodrama zu übertragen.

Erika Brandstetter (2013) erkundet in ihrer Arbeit, wie sich die *Liebes-Fähigkeit in psychodramatischer Begrifflichkeit* verstehen lässt und welche Defizite Menschen mit pseudoautonomer und abhängiger Beziehungsgestaltung aufweisen.

- Arbeiten zu sozialer Zugehörigkeit/Integration:

Susanne Blachowsky (2010) schildert in ihrer Arbeit den *Weg aus der sozialen Isolation* im Rahmen einer Gruppentherapie für *Eltern hörbehinderter Kinder*. Daniela Trattnigg (2011) geht in ihrer Arbeit der Frage nach, welche speziellen psychodramatischen Arrangements die *Bewältigung von Einsamkeit* fördern. Monika Mürzl (2013) beschreibt in ihrer Arbeit die Möglichkeit der *Integration von Migrantinnen-Kindern* mit massiven sprachlichen Defiziten in Kinder-Psychodrama-Gruppen.

- Arbeiten zu Stress/Belastung/Überlastung:

Hannes Goditsch (2007) behandelt in seiner Arbeit die *Auswirkungen von in der Kindheit erlebter Überforderung durch die Eltern* auf das Wohlbefinden im Erwachsenenalter. Irmgard Ressl (2009) evaluiert die *Wirksamkeit psychodramatherapeutischer Interventionen bei Burnout* anhand eines Therapieprozesses eines Patienten mit dieser Problematik. Sonja Frank (2014) untersucht die *Auswirkungen des Burnout-Syndroms auf das soziale Atom*.

- Arbeiten zu Trauma/Traumaverarbeitung:

Monika Wicher (2007) stellt die Entwicklung ihres Gruppentherapiekonzeptes und spezielle *Interventionsformen für traumatisierte Kinder* vor. Hildegard Knapp (2011) analysiert *geschlechtsspezifische Verarbeitungsweisen von traumatischen Ereignissen* im Erwachsenenalter. Karin Leitgeb (2013) beforscht eine *Psychodramagruppe von Frauen mit Gewalterfahrungen* hinsichtlich der Frage, welche Interventionen für die Frauen hilfreich sind, um aus der Opferrolle auszusteigen.

3 Kategorisierung der Masterthesen nach Forschungsdesigns und –Methoden[4]

Hinsichtlich der Forschungs-Methodik lassen sich 3 Gruppen von Arbeiten unterscheiden: Literatur- Arbeiten, Empirische Arbeiten und Theorieverschränkte Praxisberichte:

3.1 Literatur-Arbeiten

Bei Literatur-Arbeiten wird die interessierende Fragestellung ausschließlich anhand von einschlägiger Theorie/Literatur bearbeitet (eventuelle Praxisbeispiele dienen ausschließlich der Illustration theoretischer Inhalte) und diese dann ausführlich diskutiert. Nur folgende Arbeiten wurden als Literaturarbeiten verfasst: die Arbeit von Canazei zu Anwärmung in Gruppen (2007), die von Schönherr über das „Regenerationsdrama" (2008), die von Bulian zu Begegnungsszenen in der Psychotherapie (2009), die von Franke zum Telebegriff (2011), die von Langer über Panikattacken (2012), jene von Reinthaler zum Helfersyndrom (2011), die von Riepl über Aufstellungsarbeit (2011) und jene von Stelzig (2014) über biologisch verankerte Elternrollen.

3.2 Empirische Arbeiten

Bei empirischen Arbeiten kann der Forschungsprozess nach einem (rein) quantitativen, (rein) qualitativen oder einem Mix Method Design erfolgen:

3.2.1 Arbeiten nach einem quantitativen Design

In dieser Untergruppe gibt es nur folgende Arbeiten: Grauf (2010) evaluiert eine stationäre Therapiegruppe von Frauen mit strukturellen Störungen mittels BSI (Brief Symptom Inventory), BDI (Beck- Depressions-Inventar) und WHOQOL-BREF (World Health Organisation Quality of Life). Trinkel (2013) verwendet für die Evaluation ihrer ambulanten Therapiegruppe für Menschen mit strukturellen Störungen ebenfalls das BSI.

3.2.2 Empirische Arbeiten nach einem qualitativen Design

Die als qualitative Forschungsarbeit verfassten Masterthesen lassen sich aufgrund der verwendeten Forschungsdesigns folgenden Untergruppen zuordnen:

- Dokumentenanalysen:

Fellöcker (2008) analysiert ein suchtpräventives Theaterstück für Volkschulkinder, anhand des zugrundliegenden Textbuches, mittels der qualitativen Inhaltsanalyse nach Mayring, im Hinblick auf die dargestellten theoretischen Grundlagen von Suchtprävention.

- Einzelfallanalysen:

Bachler-Klein (2010) beschreibt in ihrer Arbeit über die Entwicklung eines störungsspezifischen Konzeptes für die Behandlung kindlicher Zwangsstörungen den Behandlungsprozess eines Buben. Karlhuber (2011) nutzt für ihre qualitative Untersuchung von „Stimmenhören" problemzentrierte Interviews von StimmenhörerInnen, die sie mithilfe der qualitativen Inhaltsanalyse nach Mayring analysiert. Amann (2013) integriert in ihre theoretische Untersuchung zur „Bedeutung des Spiegeln im Psychodrama-Prozess" eine einfache Befragung von PsychodramaleiterInnen. Tornow (2013) verwendet für ihre qualitative Untersuchung der biografischen Bedingungen von Burnout narrative Interviews mit Patientinnen, die sie mithilfe der Inhaltsanalyse nach Mayring auswertet.

- Feldforschung:

Kastner (2011) nutzt für die Beforschung ihrer Fragestellung zum Thema therapeutische Unterstützung früh und komplex traumatisierter Frauen (mit dissoziativer Identitätsstörung) die Grounded Theory zur Hypothesengenerierung.

- Qualitative Evaluationsstudien:

Ressl (2009) analysiert für ihre Evaluationsstudie eines Therapieprozesses eines Patienten mit Burnout den schriftlichen Therapiebericht des Patienten mittels qualitativer Inhaltsanalyse. Ehrlinger (2011) verwendet für die Untersuchung zur Wirkung von Psychodrama-Techniken auf die Gefühlswahrnehmung Gruppentherapieprotokolle einer Frauengruppe, Aussagen der Patientinnen aus einer Gruppendiskussion und anschließenden Einzelinterviews. Etlinger (2012) benutzt für ihre Evaluation einer Therapiegruppe für Frauen mit Bulimie problemzentrierte Interviews der Teilnehmerinnen, die sie mittels Inhaltsanalyse nach Mayring auswertet. Krautschneider (2012) verwendet für seine Vergleichs-Untersuchung von Flow-Erleben bei PatientInnen mit und ohne begleitenden Yogatrainings als Erhebungsinstrument teilstrukturierte Interviews mit den PatientInnen, die dann mittels der Grounded Theory ausgewertet wurden.

3.2.3 Empirische Arbeiten nach einem Mixed Method Design

- Feldforschung:

Lechner (2010) befragt für seine Untersuchung (der Möglichkeit der Einbeziehung von Eltern in den Therapieprozess ihrer Kindern) Eltern mithilfe von Fragebögen, die sowohl quantitativ (geschlossene Fragen) wie qualitativ (offene Fragen) ausgewertet werden. Grissenberger (2014) setzt in ihrer Studie über die Auswirkung der Gestaltung sozialer Beziehungen in der Alkoholtherapie (zu 4 Zeitpunkten hergestellte) soziale Atome, welche quantitativ und qualitativ ausgewertet werden, als Untersuchungs-Material ein.

- Evaluationstudien:

Kühtreiber (2012) nutzt für ihre Untersuchung (der Rollenentwicklung der Kinder einer Kindergruppe) Beobachtungsprotokolle aus den Gruppentherapiesitzungen, die sie in quantitative Daten operationalisiert, und Interviewprotokolle mit den Eltern, die sie frei qualitativ auswertet. Pfohl (2012) dienen für ihre Evaluation der Sozialkompetenzgruppe adoleszenter Asperger-PatientInnen der FEEL Test als quantitatives Erhebungsinstrument und Leitfadeninterviews mit den (männlichen) Teilnehmern und Beoachtungen aus dem Gruppenprozess als qualitative Daten. Starzer-Eidenberger (2013) verwendet in seiner Evaluationsstudie über psychodramatische Raucherentwöhnung in der Gruppe quantitative Erhebungsinstrumente (FTND, einen Test zur Messung der Nikotinabhängigkeit, die Messung der Anzahl der täglich gerauchten Zigaretten und den 6MWD) und qualitative Daten zum Therapieprozess (HAT, Therapietagebuch). Zauner (2010) analysiert für die Evaluation eines Therapieprozesses mit einem depressiven Jugendlichen sowohl quantitative Daten (der klinisch-psychologischen Diagnostik) als auch qualitative Daten (Beobachtungsprotokolle, visuelles Therapiematerial und ein Experteninterview).

3.3 Theorieverschränkte Praxisberichte

Den Großteil der Masterthesen stellen sogenannte „Theorieverschränkte Praxisberichte" dar. Das ist ein Typ qualitativer Praxisforschung, der von der Donauuniversität Krems für die Masterlehrgänge als Design qualitativer Forschungsarbeit vorgeschlagen wird und in zwei Formen durchgeführt werden kann:

Beim *prozessgeleiteten theorieverschränkten Praxisbericht* steht ein Fall im Fokus der Untersuchung. Zu diesem Fall wird (ähnlich den Frühformen psychoanalytischer Hermeneutik) über den gesamten Therapieverlauf der Therapieprozess dargestellt und dieser (allgemein und methodenspezifisch) in Bezug auf das interessierende Thema theoretisch reflektiert.

Beim *themengeleiteten theorieverschränkten Praxisbericht* steht ein Thema (z. B. Therapie bei Angststörungen, Trauerarbeit, o.ä.) im Fokus der Untersuchung, zu dem einzelne Aspekte in mehreren Kapiteln theoretisch beleuchtet und anhand von Praxisbeispielen mehrerer Fälle illustriert werden.

3.3.1 Prozessgeleitete theorieverschränkte Praxisberichte

14 von 53 Praxisberichten sind als prozessgeleitete Praxisberichte abgefasst. Diese lassen sich danach unterscheiden, was als „Fall" exemplarisch untersucht wird:

Von Spitzer-Prochazka (2008) wurde die Entwicklung eines psychodramatischen Online-Angebotes im Einzelsetting theoretisch reflektiert.

Einzeltherapieprozesse wurden bei folgenden Praxisberichten untersucht: von Hochgerner (2006) der eines strukturell beeinträchtigten Buben mit instabilen Beziehungen; von Amon (2011) der einer erwachsenen Klientin mit somatoformen Störungen; von Bader (2011) der eines sozialängstlichen Mädchens; von Bauer (2012) der einer Klientin im Rahmen einer beruflichen Rehabilitationsmaßnahme; von Zahrl-Weis (2012) der eines „früh gestörten" Vorschulkindes und von Frank (2014) der einer Patientin mit Burnout.

Von Stollewerk (2007) wurden als Fall ein Therapie-Kind und sein soziales Atom untersucht, von Hofer (2013) ein Paar in psychodramatischer Sexualtherapie.

Gruppenprozesse standen im Fokus folgender Praxisberichte: bei Wicher (2007) die Entwicklung ihres Konzepts einer Gruppe für traumatisierte Kinder im heilpädagogischen Setting; bei Blachowsky (2010) der Prozess einer Eltern- (bzw. Mütter-) Gruppe hörbehinderter Kinder; bei Gött (2012) der Prozess einer Begegnungsgruppe von Nachkommen von NS-Opfern und Tätern; bei Leitgeb (2013) der Prozess einer Empowerment-Gruppe für Frauen mit Gewalterfahrungen; von Klimt (2013) ein Präventionsprojekt gegen sexuelle Gewalt an Kindern.

3.3.2 Themengeleitete theorieverschränkte Praxisberichte

39 von 53 Praxisberichten wurden als themengeleitete Praxisberichte abgefasst. Bei diesen steht ein interessierendes Thema im Fokus des Interesses, das theoretisch beleuchtet und anhand von Praxisbeispielen aus mehreren Therapien illustriert wird:

Bei der Arbeit von Apolloner (2010) ist das die Unterstützung des Abschiedes von Jugendlichen aus der Psychiatrie, bei Beer (2013) Rollenerweiterung in der Mädchengruppe, bei Biegler-Vitek (2011) die Behandlung von Mutismus, bei Brandstetter (2013) Liebe, Bindung und Partnerschaft, bei Breuß-Purtscher (2013) Nachschulung als Sekundärprävention bei alkoholauffälligen LenkerInnen, bei Chalupsky (2012) die Behandlung von Flugangst, bei Fercher (2012) das Spannungsfeld in der Doppelrolle Lehrerin und Psychotherapeutin, bei Feuerstein (2009) die therapeutische Betreuung auf einer pädiatrischen Intensivstation, bei Geiger (2012) der Einbezug von Musik, bei Goditsch (2007) Auswirkungen von Überforderung in der Kindheit, bei Grimmer (2007) Psychodramatherapie bei Angststörungen, bei Grosinger-Spiss (2013) Rollenerweiterung von Vorschulkindern, bei Hagenbichler (2013) der Einbezug von Musizieren in die Psychodramatherapie, bei Haid (2014) Gruppen-Interventionen zur Verbesserung der Körperwahrnehmung bulimischer Patientinnen, bei Heidegger (2011) die Frage der Beziehungsgestaltung auf der Spielbühne, bei Hintermeier (2008) entwicklungsfördernde Interventionen in der Borderline-Therapie, bei Houdek (2011) die Möglichkeiten des Einsatzes von Psychodramatechniken bei der Operations-Vorbereitung von Kindern, bei Kasper (2013) die Technik der Zukunftsprojektion, bei Kasper (2013) die Technik der Handlungsliste, bei Kern (2008) ein psychodramatischer Behandlungsansatz für Anorexie und Bulimie, bei Knapp (2011) geschlechtsspezifische Verarbeitungsweisen traumatischer Erlebnisse, bei Kölbl-Fischer (2011) Paartherapie, bei Kronberger (2014) die Bedingungen stationärer Behandlungs-Settings in ihrer Wirkung auf individuelle Therapieprozesse, bei Lenz (2013) der Einbezug körpertherapeutischer Techniken, bei Mürzl (2013) Gruppenarbeit mit Kindern mit Migrations-Thematik, bei Nindler (2013) Trauerbegleitung in der Schule, bei Nowak-Schuh (2013) Narzissmus, bei Pfaffenwimmer (2011) Bibliodrama, bei Pichlhöfer (2010) abhängige Persönlichkeitsstörung und Coabhängigkeit, bei Pruckner (2006) psychodramatische Kinder-Psychotherapie, bei Rotter (2012) Gruppentherapie bei Altersdemenz, bei Sakrausky (2013) eine Psychodrama-Gruppe für aggressive Kinder, bei Scharfetter (2013) stationäre Gruppentherapie, bei Schatovich-Kiss (2009) ADHS-Kinder in der Gruppentherapie, bei Schöpfer (2013) Stegreiftheater mit langzeithospitalisierten PatientInnen, bei Schorn (2012) Gruppen-

Tab. 3 Forschungsmethodik

Masterthesen gesamt	79	100 %			
Literatur-Arbeiten	8	10 %			
Empirische Arbeiten	18	23 %	Quantitativ	2	2,5 %
			Qualitativ	10	13 %
			Mixed Method	6	7,5 %
Praxisberichte	53	67 %	Prozessgeleitet	14	18 %
			Themengeleitet	39	49 %

therapie bei sozialängstlichen Kindern und Jugendlichen, bei Trattnigg (2011) die Überwindung von Einsamkeit, bei Weigl (2014) die Verwendung des sozialen Atoms in unterschiedlichen Phasen des Therapieprozesses und bei Wanderer (2014) die Gegenüberstellung und Verknüpfung von Psychodrama und OPD-2-Diagnostik.

4 Interpretation der Ergebnisse und Schlussfolgerungen

4.1 Zur Verteilung der Themen-Cluster

4.1.1 Masterthesen zu Theorie-Themen

Wie gezeigt wurde, liegen bis heute nur einige wenige Masterthesen (8 %) über Theorie-Themen vor. Behandelt wurden die Themen: Begegnungsszenen in der Psychotherapie, das Tele, das „Regenerationsdrama" (Ottomeyer), Burnout, Stimmenhören und die biologische Verankerung von Elternrollen. Hier gibt es also noch große Spielräume für weitere Arbeiten zu den theoretischen Grundlagen von Psychodrama: zur Philosophie, zum Menschenbild, zur Rollentheorie, zur Entwicklungstheorie, dem Störungsmodell oder zu allgemeinen psychotherapierelevanten Themen, die aus psychodramatischer Sicht beforscht werden könnten.

4.1.2 Masterthesen zu Praxis-Themen

Der überwiegende Teil der Masterthesen (92 %) beforscht praxisbezogene Fragestellungen. Diese können – wie dargestellt – in übergeordnete Kategorien zusammengefasst werden. Nach den gefundenen Häufigkeiten lässt sich folgendes Ranking erstellen (Tab. 4):

Am häufigsten wurden also störungsspezifische Fragestellungen gewählt, knapp gefolgt von methodenspezifischen Fragestellungen, dann Fragestellungen zu bestimmten Therapiethemen und schon seltener kontextbezogene und settingspezifische Fragestellungen. Nur eine Masterthese widmete sich einer klientInnenspezifischen Fragestellung.

- Beforschung störungsspezifischer Fragestellungen:

Gleich ein Drittel aller praxisbezogenen Masterthesen behandeln störungsspezifische Fragestellungen. Auch innerhalb dieser großen Gruppe gibt es deutliche Häufungen (Tab. 5):

Tab. 4 Kategorien der Praxisthemen

Praxis-Themen	73	100 %
Störungsspezifische Fragestellungen	24	33 %
Methodenspezifische Fragestellungen	20	27 %
Fragestellungen zu Therapiethemen	15	21 %
Fragestellungen zu institutionellen Kontexten	8	11 %
Setting-spezifische Fragestellungen	5	7 %
KlientInnenspezifische Fragestellungen	1	1 %

Tab. 5 Einteilung Störungen

Störungsspezifische Masterthesen	24
F4: Neurotische, Belastungs- und Somatoforme Störungen	7
F9 Verhaltens- und emotionale Störungen mit Beginn in Kindheit und Jugend	4
F5 Verhaltensauffälligkeiten mit körperlichen Störungen oder Faktoren	4
F6 Persönlichkeits- und Verhaltensstörungen	3
F1 Psychische und Verhaltensstörungen durch psychotrope Substanzen	2
F0 Organische Störungen	1
F8 Entwicklungsstörungen	1
Strukturelle Störungen	2

Die meisten störungsspezifischen Masterthesen befassten sich mit Störungen der Kapitel Gruppe F4 gefolgt von Störungen der Kapitel F5, F9 und F6. Bei genauer Betrachtung zeigen sich Clusterbildungen von Arbeiten zu Angststörungen, Essstörungen, Verhaltens- und emotionale Störungen bei Kindern und Jugendlichen und zu Persönlichkeitsstörungen. Auffällig ist weiters eine kategorienübergreifende Häufung von Arbeiten zu strukturellen Störungen[5].

Zu folgenden Kategorien des ICD10 wurden bis dato noch keine störungsspezifischen Masterthesen verfasst: zu F2 Schizophrenie, schizotype und wahnhafte Störungen, F3 Affektive Störungen und F7 Intelligenzminderung.[6] Spielräume für störungsspezifische Arbeiten gibt es noch innerhalb folgender Störungskategorien: F1 in Bezug auf Sedativa und die verschiedene illegalen Suchtmittel; F4 in Bezug auf F43 Reaktionen auf schwere Belastungen und Anpassungsstörungen; F5 in Bezug auf F51 Schlafstörungen und F53 psychische Störungen im Wochenbett; F60 in Bezug auf weitere spezifische Persönlichkeitsstörungen wie z. B. die histrionische, zwanghafte, ängstlich-vermeidende usf. und F61 kombinierte Persönlichkeitsstörungen, F62 andauernde Persönlichkeitsänderungen, F63 abnorme Gewohnheiten und Störungen der Impulskontrolle, F64 Störungen der Geschlechtsidentität, F65 Störungen der Sexualpräferenz und F66 psychische und Verhaltensstörungen in Verbindung mit der sexuellen Entwicklung und Orientierung; F8 in Bezug auf F80 Entwicklungsstörungen der Sprache und F81 Entwicklungsstörungen schulischer Fertigkeiten; F90 in Bezug auf F95 Ticstörungen und F98 sonstige Verhaltens– und emotionale Störungen mit Beginn in der Kindheit und Jugend;

- Beforschung methodischer Fragestellungen:

Ein wenig mehr als ein Viertel aller praxisbezogenen Masterthesen behandeln methodenbezogene Fragestellungen (Tab. 6):

Tab. 6 Einteilung Methodik

Methodenbezogene Masterthesen	20
Einbezug fremder Methoden und Techniken	6
Methodische Strategien/Handlungstechniken	5
Spezielle Interventionsformen	4
Spezielle (Gruppen-)Arrangements	3
Therapeutische Rollen- und Beziehungsgestaltung	2

In Summe beforschen 14 Arbeiten den Einsatz psychodramatischer Methoden: Dass so viele Arbeiten auf methodisches Handeln in der Psychodramatherapie fokussieren, erklärt sich dadurch, dass das Psychodrama „in methodischer Hinsicht zweifellos zu den komplexesten Verfahren der Therapie und Beratung“ zählt (von Ameln 2005, S. 10) und der Beherrschung des psychodramatischen Handwerkskoffers im Rahmen der Ausbildung ein hoher Stellenwert beikommt. Dass bei immerhin 6 Arbeiten der Einbezug fremder Techniken beforscht wird, zeigt die Integrationsbereitschaft der AutorInnen und die Flexibilität und Kompatibilität des psychodramatischen Methodenpools.

Trotz der hohen Anzahl von Arbeiten zu methodischen Fragestellungen, gibt es aber auch hier noch Spielräume für weitere Forschungstätigkeit: Zusätzlich zu den bereits beforschten Gruppen-Arrangements (psychodramatische Aufstellungsarbeit, Bibliodrama und Stegreiftheater) und Handlungstechniken (Arbeit mit Intermediärobjekten, Spiegeln, Zukunftsprojektion und die Arbeit mit dem sozialen Atom) finden sich in der Literatur (z. B. in von Ameln 2005 und Bender und Stadler 2012) viele weitere Arrangements und Handlungstechniken, deren Einsatz beforscht werden könnte: z. B. Vignetten, Rollentraining, das gruppenzentrierte Spiel (z. B. Märchenspiele), spezielle gruppenzentrierte Arrangements wie Clap-Theater, Playback-Theater, ebenso wie die Handlungstechniken Szenenaufbau, Doppeln, Rollenwechsel, Rollentausch, Szenenwechsel und Sharing u.v.m.[7]

Für weitere methodenbezogene Masterthesen könnten störungsspezifische und methodische Fragestellungen kombiniert werden, also die Verwendung bestimmter Settings, Arrangements oder Handlungstechniken bei unterschiedlichen Störungen untersucht werden. Passend zum aktuellen Diskurs in der Psychotherapieforschung zur Bedeutung der therapeutischen Beziehung wären auch weitere Forschungen zur therapeutischen Rollen- und Beziehungsgestaltung und zu telischen Prozessen zwischen TherapeutIn und PatientIn interessant.

- Beforschung spezieller Therapieanlässe/Themen:

15 Arbeiten behandelten spezielle Therapiethemen. Wie dargestellt, konnten folgende untersuchte Themenfelder gefunden werden (Tab. 7):

In den gefundenen Themenclustern spiegeln sich die Kernthemen des Psychodramas: der Mensch als Actor und soziales Wesen, Rollenhandeln und -Entwicklung, Spontaneität und Spiel, Begegnung und Tele, soziale Integration, aber auch die Beschäftigung mit marginalisierten Gruppen, die schon Moreno intensiv gepflegt hat Auffällig ist die Häufigkeit der Beschäftigung mit Themen rund um Traumatisierung, die deutlich wird, wenn man hier auch jene Arbeiten einordnet, die Trauma als (prominentes) Nebenthema behandeln.[8]

Tab. 7 Therapiethemen

Therapiethemen		15
Psychische Phänomene	Emotionen und Flow	2
Rollen-/Persönlichkeitsentwicklung	Als-ob/Spielfähigkeit, Rollenentwicklung,	2
Beziehungsfähigkeit/Beziehungsgestaltung	Liebe-Bindung-Partnerschaft, Helfer-Syndrom	2
Soziale Zugehörigkeit/Integration	Soziale Isolation von Eltern behinderter Kinder, Einsamkeit, Integration von MigrantInnenkindern	3
Stress und Belastungen	Überforderung, Burn out	3
Trauma/Traumaverarbeitung	Gruppe für traumatisierte Kinder, geschlechtsspezifische Verarbeitungsweisen, Gewalterfahrungen von Frauen	3

Interessant ist, dass bisher keine Therapiethemen rund um Körpererleben und Körperlichkeit beforscht wurden. Hier zeigt sich aus meiner Sicht eine deutliche Forschungslücke! Denkbar wären Fragestellungen zur psychodramatischen Behandlung (nicht störungsspezifischer) körperbezogener Therapiethemen, wie z. B. der Bewältigung von Krankheiten, Behinderung(en) oder altersbedingten körperlichen Veränderungen, dem Umgang mit (chronischem) Schmerz, aber auch rund um Sexualität (sexuelle Lust, sexuelle Orientierung, sexuelle Identität, Pubertät) und Fortpflanzung (Kinderwunsch, Schwangerschaft bzw. –Schwangerschaftsabbruch, Klimakterium usf.).

- Beforschung bestimmter „Bühnen":

8 Praxis-Arbeiten fokussieren in ihrer Fragestellung auf die Beforschung der institutionellen Kontexte psychotherapeutischer Behandlung: Die hier beforschten „Bühnen" spiegeln einerseits die Anpassungsfähigkeit des Methodenpools von Psychodramatherapie, andererseits die Kreativität der PsychodramakollegInnen in der Implementierung von Psychodramatherapie in ihren Arbeitsbereichen wider. So wird Psychodramatherapie nicht nur im bekannten stationären Psychotherapiesetting beschrieben und beforscht, sondern auch in Schule und beruflicher Rehabilitation und – für mich persönlich besonders überraschend – auch im Operationssaal und in der Intensivstation.

Ich bin gespannt, welche weitere Bühnen psychodramatherapeutischen Handelns in zukünftigen Masterthesen vorgestellt werden: bekannte Bühnen, auf denen bereits therapeutisch gearbeitet wird, wie z. B. Betriebe, Alters- und Pflegeheime, Gefängnisse oder auch weitere, erst zu erobernde, „neue" Bühnen.

- Beforschung bestimmter Settings:

Das Setting selbst war nur bei 5 Arbeiten im Fokus des Forschungsinteresses, was nicht erstaunt, da es nur eine begrenzte Anzahl von Settings und zu den häufigsten (Einzel- und Gruppen-) Settings mittlerweile unzählige Publikationen gibt. Erfreulich ist aus meiner Sicht die Beforschung psychodramatischer Paartherapie, da diese oft eher mit systemischer Therapie assoziiert, aber von vielen PsychodramatherapeutInnen angeboten wird. Ebenso spannend wäre die Beforschung des – in psychodramatischen Publikationen – eher selten berücksichtigten Familientherapie-Settings im Rahmen von Masterthesen.

- Beforschung klientInnenspezifischer Fragestellungen:

Nur eine Masterthese beschäftigt sich mit einer auf eine ganze KlientInnengruppe bezogene Fragestellung. Da diese Grundlagenarbeit ausführlich die Grundsätze psychodramatischer Kindertherapie behandelt und Erwachsenentherapie in unzähligen Publikationen dargestellt wurde, lässt sich hier aber keine Forschungslücke wahrnehmen.

4.2 Zur Häufigkeit der verschiedenen Typen von Forschungsarbeit

Wie dargelegt, besteht der größte Teil (71 von 79, das sind 90 %) der bisherigen Masterthesen aus empirischen Arbeiten oder theorieverschränkten Praxisberichten (siehe Tab. 3).

4.2.1 Theorieverschränkte Praxisberichte

Mit 53 von insgesamt 79 Masterarbeiten (67 %) stellen theorieverschränkte Praxisberichte den größten Teil der Masterthesen dar. Erklären lässt sich das möglicherweise dadurch, dass diese – fälschlicherweise – den Ruf haben einfacher zu sein als empirische Arbeiten, was nicht den Tatsachen entspricht. Theorie-Praxisverschränkung erfordert Denken auf einem hohen Abstraktionsniveau und eine gute Text-Organisation. Ein großer Teil der theoretischen Arbeit bei Praxisberichten besteht darin, fremde Theorie ins „Psychodramatische" zu übersetzen. Diese Übersetzungsarbeit ist meist sehr aufwändig und erfordert viel Denkarbeit (Tab. 8).

4.2.2 Empirische Arbeiten

Empirische Forschung hat den Ruf, schwierig zu sein und besonderes Forschungswissen zu erfordern. Umso erfreulicher, dass es mittlerweile dennoch bereits 18 Beispiele empirischer Masterthesen (23 % aller Masterthesen) gibt. Auffällig ist, dass qualitative Arbeiten und solche mit Mixed Method-Designs gegenüber Arbeiten mit rein quantitativen Designs bevorzugt werden. Möglicherweise werden diese als dem kreativen, verspielten Charakter psychodramatischen Arbeiten als angemessener erlebt als rein quantitative Designs oder letzere – zu Unrecht – als schwieriger und unkreativer eingeschätzt. Dass quantitative Methoden aber nicht per se unkreativ sein müssen, lässt sich bei einigen der vorgestellten Masterarbeiten gut feststellen.[9]

Innerhalb der Gruppe der qualitativen Untersuchungen fällt eine Häufung von Einzelfallstudien und Evaluationsstudien auf, welche für Psychotherapieforschung auch besonders geeignet sind. Als häufigste Auswertungsmethode sticht die qualitative Inhaltsanalyse nach Mayring ins Auge, welche sich für Interpretation sprachlichen Materials gut eignet und auch für Forschungsneulinge relativ einfach anwendbar ist.

Tab. 8 Empirische Arbeiten

Empirische Arbeiten	18	23 %
Quantitativ	2	2,5 %
Qualitativ	10	13 %
Mixed Method	6	7,5 %

Tab. 9 Altersgruppen

Empirische Arbeiten und Praxisberichte	71	100 %		
Kinder/Jugendliche	23	32 %	Kinder	23
			Jugendliche	1
Erwachsene	48	68 %	Erwachsene	47
			Hochbetagte	1

Tab. 10 Geschlechtereinteilung

Empirische Arbeiten und Praxisberichte	71	100 %		
Mädchen/Frauen	17	24 %		
			genderspezifisch	5
Burschen/Männer	7	10 %		
			genderspezifisch	1
Beide Geschlechter	47	66 %		
			genderspezifisch	2

Wenngleich bei einzelnen empirischen Arbeiten auch aktionsbezogene Erhebungs-Methoden verwendet werden[10], zeigt sich bezüglich des untersuchten Materials insgesamt eine deutliche Bevorzugung sprachlichen Untersuchungs-Materials gegenüber visuellem Material wie Fotos und Zeichnungen oder aktionsbezogenem und Material wie Videos etc. Aus meiner Sicht wäre es für die Psychodramaforschung bereichernd, wenn häufiger aktionsbezogene Erhebungsmethoden verwendet würden, wie soziometrische Techniken, Aufstellungsarbeit oder Stegreifspiele im Sinne von Handlungsforschung (Tab. 9)[11].

4.3 Zur Häufigkeitsverteilung der untersuchten Personengruppen und Settings[12]

4.3.1 Verteilung nach Altersgruppen

Auffallend ist die hohe Anzahl von Masterthesen zu psychodramatischen Kinder- und Jugendlichentherapien.[13] In all diesen Arbeiten zeigt sich die besondere Eignung von Psychodrama für die Arbeit mit Heranwachsenden, welche auch für viele Studierende das Kriterium der Entscheidung für Psychodrama als Therapieverfahren war (Tab. 10).

4.3.2 Verteilung nach Geschlecht

Beim Großteil der praxisbezogenen Masterarbeiten (66 %) wurden Personen beiderlei Geschlechts untersucht, bei 17 Arbeiten nur weibliche[14], bei 7 Arbeiten nur männliche Untersuchungspersonen[15]. Bei 8 Arbeiten wurde die Fragestellung auch genderspezifisch untersucht.[16] In Bezug auf Genderfragen lässt sich der (zeitgemäße) Trend feststellen, der Geschlechtszugehörigkeit – anders als Moreno dies getan hat – Bedeutung zuzumessen und entsprechende Fragestellungen genderspezifisch zu beforschen. Wie die bisherigen genderspezifischen Arbeiten zeigen, hat das Psychodrama in der Rollentheorie eine gute theoretische Basis für die Beforschung von Fragen zum „Doing gender" und der Rolle des Geschlechts bei der Rollenentwicklung, die noch weiterentwickelt werden könnte (Tab. 11).

4.3.3 Verteilung der Untersuchungs-Settings

Bei der Häufigkeitsverteilung der untersuchten Settings fällt auf, dass die Fragestellung bei mehr als der Hälfte der empirischen Arbeiten und Praxisberichte ausschließlich oder zumindest auch im Gruppensetting untersucht wurde. Während sich bei der Altersgruppe der Erwachsenen die untersuchten Settings Gruppentherapie und Einzeltherapie in etwa die Waage halten, war bei Kindern und Jugendlichen die Gruppe als beforschtes Setting dominanter!

Diese Verteilung erinnert an die historischen Wurzeln von Psychodramatherapie in der Arbeit mit Kindern und in der Arbeit mit Gruppen – beides sind wesentliche Qualitäten, die Psychodrama auch heute noch besonders auszeichnen.

5 Resümee

Wie deutlich geworden sein wird, zeigt diese große Gruppe der - in den ersten 8 Jahren der Universitätslehrgänge Psychodrama des ÖAGG abgefassten - Masterthesen eine beeindruckende inhaltliche und methodische Vielfalt. Dasselbe gilt auch für Qualität der Arbeiten:

Einige der Masterthesen brillieren meines Erachtens nach mit einem hohen wissenschaftlichen Niveau: z. B. die Arbeiten von Franke über Tele, von Canazei über Anwärmung in Gruppen, von Brandstetter über Liebe und Partnerschaft, von Fellöcker über Suchtprävention, von Grissenberger über Alkoholtherapie, von Heidegger über die Frage des körperlichen Mitspielens des/der TherapeutIn, von Kronberger über Wendepunkte in stationären Therapieprozessen, von Lenz über die psychosomatische Rollenebene, von Kastner über dissoziative Störungen bei Frauen, von Scharfetter über stationäre Gruppentherapie, von Starzer-Eidenberger über Raucherentwöhnung, von Stelzig über biologisch verankerte Elternrollen und von Trattnigg über die Bewältigung von Einsamkeit.

Andere Arbeiten punkten aus meiner Sicht mit einem starken Praxisbezug, der v. a. für NeueinsteigerInnen in die Psychodramatherapie mit einem bestimmten Klientel oder einer bestimmten Störung hilfreich sein kann: z. B. die Arbeiten von Biegler-Vitek über Mutismus, von Chalupsky über Flugangst, von Grimmer über Angststörungen, von Hintermeier über die Borderlinestörung, von Hochgerner

Tab. 11 Settings

Untersuchungs-Settings	71	100 %		
Einzelsetting	30	42 %	Kinder/Jugendliche	6
			Erwachsene	24
Paarsetting	2	3 %	Erwachsene	2
Soziales Atom	1	1,5 %	Kinder	1
Gruppensetting	32	45 %	Kinder/Jugendliche	13
			Erwachsene	19
Einzel + Gruppe	6	8,5 %	Kinder/Jugendliche	3
			Erwachsene	3

über Kinder mit strukturellen Störungen, von Hofer über Sexualtherapie, von Kern über Anorexie und Bulimie, von Kölbl-Fischer über Paartherapie, von Nowak-Schuh über Narzissmus, von Pruckner über Kindertherapie, von Riepl über psychodramatische Aufstellungsarbeit, von Schatovich-Kiss über ADHS-Kinder, von Schöpfer über Stegreiftheater in der psychiatrischen Rehabilitation, von Trinkel über Gruppentherapie bei strukturellen Störungen, von Wicher über Gruppentherapie mit traumatisierten Kindern und von Zahrl-Weis über die Förderung der Entwicklung der kindlichen Spielfähigkeit.

Und zu guter Letzt gibt es Arbeiten, die eigens kreierte Arbeitsbereiche beforschen und damit aufzeigen, wie spontan und kreativ Psychodrama dem interessierenden Feld angepasst werden kann: z. B. Geigers Arbeit über den Einbezug von Musik, Götts Arbeit über eine Begegnungsgruppe von Nachkommen von NS-Opfern und –TäterInnen, Houdeks Arbeit über OP-Vorbereitung von Kindern, Nindlers Arbeit über Trauerbegleitung in der Schule und Spitzer-Prochazkas Arbeit über psychodramatische Onlineberatung.

Bei allen Arbeiten lässt sich durch die Zeilen erspüren, dass das Forschen und Verfassen einer Masterarbeit – bei aller Mühe und Anstrengung – viel Freude machen und Befriedigung bringen kann. Forschen bedeutet Kommunikation mit anderen ForscherInnen. Dabei ist es nicht nur erlaubt, selbstständig zu denken, einen Standpunkt zu vertreten und sich auf andere zu beziehen, sondern sogar gefordert. Während für erfahrene PsychodramatherapeutInnen die Weitergabe von Wissen im Vordergrund stehen mag, kann das Verfassen einer akademischen Abschlussarbeit für Studierende als „Erwachsenwerden" in der gelernten Methode betrachtet werden. Diese Freude, dieser Stolz, dieses neu gewonnene Selbstbewusstsein Psychodrama- KollegInnen Wissenswertes zu bieten zu haben, wird in vielen Arbeiten deutlich spürbar und erscheint angesichts der hohen Qualität vieler Arbeiten auch durchaus gerechtfertigt!

Anmerkungen

1 Der Österreichische Arbeitskreis für Gruppentherapie und Gruppendynamik ist der Trägerverein der Fachsektion Psychodrama, welche seit 1978 Psychodrama-Ausbildungen anbietet.

2 http://www.donau-uni.ac.at/de/service/bibliothek/index.php

3 Hier geht es nur um die Unterscheidung des thematischen Fokus, noch nicht um die Forschungsmethode. Praxisbezogene Arbeiten können methodisch auch Theoriearbeiten sein.

4 Die hier von mir erfolgte Einordnung kann in Einzelfällen von jener der AutorIn abweichen.

5 Zu diesem Cluster können zusätzlich zu den Arbeiten von Grauf und Trinkel nämlich auch jene von Hintermeier, Kastner, Hochgerner, Pichlhöfer und Zahrl-Weis gezählt werden.

6 Zwar werden implizit bei Karlhuber schizophrenogene Störungen (F2), bei Goditsch, Trinkel, Grauf und Zauner affektive Störungen (F3), bei Knapp und Wicher Reaktionen schwere Belastungen und Anpassungsstörungen (F4) angesprochen, aber eben nicht gezielt störungsspezifisch beforscht. Dass es zu Intelligenzminderung (F7) bis dato noch keine Masterthesen gibt, erklärt sich daraus, dass Intelligenzminderung kein klassisches Einsatzgebiet psychotherapeutischer Behandlung ist.

7 Da die verschiedenen AutorInnen die methodischen Instrumente unterschiedlich einordnen, wird hier auf den Verweis zu einem Werk verzichtet.

8 Zu diesem Cluster können zusätzlich zu den Arbeiten von Knapp, Leitgeb und Wicher auch die von Gött, Kastner und Mürzl gezählt werden.

9 z. B. die Arbeiten von Grissenberger, Lechner, Kühtreiber, Starzer-Eidenberger oder Zauner.

10 Bei den Arbeiten von Grissenberger, Weigl, und Zauner.

11 siehe Hintermeier 2011.

12 Die genannten Häufigkeiten beziehen sich nur auf die empirischen Arbeiten und Praxisberichte.

13 Dies sind die Arbeiten von Apolloner, Bachler-Klein, Bader, Beer, Biegler-Vitek, Fellöcker, Fercher, Grosinger-Spiss, Heidegger, Hochgerner, Houdek, Heidegger, Klimt, Kühtreiber, Mürzl, Nindler, Pruckner, Sakrausky, Schatovich-Kiss, Schorn, Stollewerk, Wicher, Zahrl-Weis und Zauner. Da Lechner Eltern befragt, wird er hier nicht mitgezählt, obwohl seine Arbeit um Kindertherapie geht.

14 Dies waren die Arbeiten von Amon, Bader, Bauer, Beer, Brandstetter, Chalupsky, Ehrlinger, Etlinger, Feuerstein, Grauf, Kastner, Kern, Leitgeb, Pichlhöfer, Schorn, Spitzer und Trinkel.

15 Das waren die Arbeiten von Bachler-Klein, Hochgerner, Mürzl, Ressl, Sakrausky, Zahrl-Weis und Zauner.

16 Die Rede ist hier von Beer, Kern, Kastner, Knapp und Leitgeb (frauenspezifisch), Zauner (männerspezifisch) und Apolloner und Knapp für beide Geschlechter.

Literatur

Die untersuchten Masterthesen

Amann, A. (2013). Die Bedeutung des Spiegelns im Psychodrama-Prozess.

Amon, I. (2011). Psychosomatik im Psychodrama. Die Behandlung von somatoformen Symptomen in der Einzeltherapie.

Apolloner, U. (2010). Am Ende der Kindheit – wo ist mein Zuhause? Geschlechtsspezifische Ressourcenarbeit in der Psychodramagruppe mit Mädchen und Buben zur inneren Stabilisierung und Entwicklung einer Bereitschaft sich aus dem geschützten Kontext der Psychiatrie zu verabschieden.

Bachler-Klein, S. (2010). Begegnung in einer undurchschaubaren Welt. Ein psychodramatisches Konzept der Entstehung und Behandlung von Zwangsstörungen im Kindes- und Jugendalter.

Bader, H. (2011). Die gute und die schlechte Antonia sollen eine Person werden. Theorieverschränkter Praxisbericht über eine Psychodramatherapie mit einer kindlichen Angstpatientin vor dem Hintergrund aktueller Forschungsergebnisse.

Bauer, C. (2012). Berufliche Rehabilitation aus der Sicht der Psychodrama Psychotherapie. Szenen auf dem Weg zu einer beruflichen Identität.

Beer, R. (2013). Rollenerweiterung von zehn – zwölfjährigen Mädchen in der geschlechtshomogenen Gruppe.

Biegler-Vitek, G. (2011). „Reden ist Silber, Schweigen ist …“ Schlussfolgerungen für die Psychotherapie selektiv mutistischer Kinder aus der Sicht des Psychodramas.

Blachowsky, S. (2010). Wege aus der Isolation über eine therapeutische Gruppe. Theoretische Reflexion und Begründung eines psychodramatischen, gruppentherapeutischen Ansatzes in der Arbeit mit Eltern von behinderten Kindern unter besonderer Berücksichtigung der Erwärmungsphase.

Brandstetter, E. A. (2013). Liebe – Bindung-Partnerschaft. Implikationen für die Förderung der Liebesfähigkeit bei abhängiger und pseudo-autonomer Beziehungsgestaltung.

Breuß-Purtscher, E. (2013). Psychodramatische Kernanahmen und Methodiken in der Verkehrssicherheitsarbeit am Beispiel Nachschulung für alkoholauffällige LenkerInnen.

Bulian, R. (2009). Die Begegnung und das Szenische bei Daniel Stern, Alfred Lorenzer und im Psychodrama.

Canazei, M. (2007). Anwärmung in psychodramatisch geführten Gruppen.

Chalupsky, K. (2012). Psychodramatisches Verständnis und Therapie von Angststörungen am Beispiel der Flugangst.

Ehrlinger, E. (2011). Bedeutung von Emotionen im Psychodrama.

Etlinger, B. (2012). Das bin nur ich und mein Essen – nur wir zwei. Vom Wirken einer Psychodrama-Psychotherapiegruppe für an Bulimia nervosa leidenden Frauen.

Fellöcker, K. (2008). Suchtprävention und Psychodrama. Zur Bedeutung psychodramatischer Theorie für die Praxis der Suchtprävention anhand des suchtpräventiven Theaterstücks „Traust Du Dich?“.

Fercher, G. (2012). Die Doppelrolle einer Pädagogin und Psychotherapeutin auf der Bühne einer Schule. Ein Spannungsfeld.

Feuerstein, S. (2009). Psychodrama auf der pädiatrischen Intensivstation. Eine theorieverschränkte Praxisreflexion.

Frank, S. (2014). Burnout im Spiegel des sozialen Atoms.

Franke, S. (2011). Metaphern der Bezogenheit. Der Begriff des „Tele" im Psychodrama und seine Parallelen in Psychotherapie, Philosophie und Naturwissenschaft.

Geiger, M. (2012). Psychodramatherapie in der Begegnung mit Musik. Zur Wirkung von Musik im Psychotherapieprozess.

Goditsch, H. H. (2007). Überforderung in der Kindheit durch die Eltern und deren Auswirkungen im Erwachsenenalter anhand von 4 Fallbespielen.

Gött, H. (2012). Die Schatten der Vergangenheit in der Gegenwart. Aufarbeitung der Folgen von Auschwitz in realer Begegnung von Nachkommen der NS-Opfer und der NS-Täter.

Grauf, I. (2010). Strukturelle Störungen und die Möglichkeiten einer therapeutischen Begleitung mit Hilfe des Psychodramas.

Grimmer, K. (2007). Psychodrama bei Angststörungen – Überlegungen und Techniken zur Therapie von Angststörungen.

Grissenberger, E. (2014). Wie beeinflusst die Gestaltung der sozialen Beziehungen den Behandlungserfolg alkoholsuchtkranker Menschen?

Grosinger-Spiss, E. M. (2013). „Ich-Du-Gruppe" Ein Projekt mit (Vor-)Schulkindern nach Moreno – Ein begleitetes Spiel im Focus der Rollenebenen nach M. Schacht – eine „theoretische Praxisreflexion".

Hagenbichler, A. (2013). Die Bedeutung der Arbeit mit Musikinstrumenten im Psychodrama.

Haid, B. (2014). Bodysatisfaction. Behandlung der Körperwahrnehmungsstörung und Steigerung der Körperzufriedenheit bei Frauen mit Bulimia nervosa durch die Psychodramagruppe BAWADE.

Heidegger, K. (2011). Beziehungsgestaltung auf der Spielbühne. Zur Theorie und Praxis des körperlichen Mitspielens im Kinderpsychodrama.

Hintermeier, S. (2008). Vom Chaos zur Individuation. Entwicklungsfördernde Interventionen in der psychodramatherapeutischen Einzelarbeit mit Borderline-PatientInnen.

Hochgerner, R. (2006). Halt geben im haltlosen Leben. Funktionen psychotherapeutischer Arbeit mit strukturell beeinträchtigten Kindern in instabilen sozialen Beziehungen.

Hofer, W. (2013). Psychodrama-Sexualtherapie im ambulanten Setting.

Houdek, H. (2011). Die Anwendung von Intermediärobjekten zur Vorbereitung von Kindern auf eine Operation.

Karlhuber, K. (2011).Stimmenhören aus der Sicht der Psychodramatischen Entwicklungstheorie.

Kasper, T. G. (2013). Die Handlungsliste. Ein Instrument der Selbststeuerung im Prozess der Selbsterkenntnis bei der Reorganisation einer störenden Handlungsstruktur im Kontext psychodramatischer Arbeit.

Kasper, R. (2013). Die Arbeit mit Zukunftsprojektion im Psychodrama – Theoretische Grundlegung und Anwendung.

Kastner, G. (2011). Das verletzte Selbst. Eine „grounded theory" zum psychodramatischen Störungs- und Therapieverständnis früh und komplex traumatisierter Frauen.

Kern, S. (2008). Anorexia und Bulimia als rigide Rollenkonserven. Magersucht und Bulimie aus dem Blickwinkel des Modells der Spontaneität-Kreativität.

Klimt, C. (2013). Analyse angewandter Präventionsarbeit gegen sexuelle Gewalt an Kindern unter dem Gesichtspunkt der psychodramatischen Kernthemen Soziales Atom und Rollenkonfiguration.

Knapp, H. (2011). Geschlechtsspezifische Verarbeitungsweisen von traumatischen Ereignissen im Erwachsenenalter.

Kölbl-Fischer, K. (2011). Paartherapie und ihre Möglichkeiten zur Konflikt- und Krisenbewältigung. Entwicklungsmöglichkeiten von PartnerInnen unter besonderer Berücksichtigung von Theorie und entwicklungspsychologischer Begründung psychodramatischer Interventionstechniken.

Krautschneider, M. (2012). Flow in der psychotherapeutischen Praxis.

Kronberger, H. (2014). Wendepunkte. Selbstorganisationsprozesse in der Stationären Psychotherapie.

Kühtreiber, C. (2012). Rollenentwicklung in der Psychodramagruppe und Transfer in den Alltag. Fallstudien zur Psychodrama-Therapie mit Kindern.

Langer, I. (2012). Panikattacken psychodramatisch behandeln.

Lechner, F. (2010). Die Einbindung der Eltern in den Psychodrama-Gruppentherapieprozess ihrer Kinder. Erhebung über die Zufriedenheit der Eltern mit der Arbeit des Therapeuten/der Therapeutin ihres Kindes und über ihre Bereitschaft an einer begleitenden Elterngruppe teilzunehmen.

Leitgeb, K. (2013). Themenzentrierte Psychodrama-Gruppe für Frauen mit (häuslichen) Gewalterfahrungen unter Berücksichtigung der psychodramatischen Entwicklungstheorie.

Lenz, I. (2013). Konzept der psychosomatischen Rollenebene: Theoretische und praktische Ergänzungen durch körpertherapeutische Konzepte und Methoden.

Mürzl, M. (2013). Gelebte Integration. Psychodrama, Soziometrie und Rollenspiel mit mehrsprachigen, kulturell heterogenen Kindergruppen.

Nindler, A. (2013). „Wenn eine Welt zusammenbricht … unterstützt die ‚Care-Box', eine psychodramatische Soforthilfe, in der Akutsituation und begleitet umsichtig und tröstend den Trauerprozess". Krisenintervention und Begleitung für Kinder und Jugendliche bei Tod und Trauer.

Nowak-Schuh, D. (2013). Narzissmus- Ansätze eines psychodramatischen Störungsverständnisses.

Pfaffenwimmer, B. (2011). Konservierte Rollen lebendig machen. Bibliodrama mit Erwachsenen. Ein psychotherapeutischer Handlungsraum.

Pfohl, C. (2012). Mosaik Autismus. Psychotherapie/Psychodrama bei Menschen mit Asperger-Syndrom.

Pichlhöfer, C. (2010). Abhängige Persönlichkeitsstörung und andere Nähe-Störungen in Zusammenhang mit Co-Abhängigkeit.

Pruckner, H. (2006). Das Spiel ist der Königsweg der Kinder. Psychodrama, Soziometrie und Rollenspiel mit Kindern.

Reinthaler, R. (2011). Hilfe für Helfer im Psychodrama. Problembereiche der helfenden Dienstleistung und ihre Übertragung ins Psychodrama am Beispiel des psychoanalytischen Konstrukts „Helfer-Syndrom" von Wolfgang Schmidbauer.

Ressl, I. (2009). Burn-On statt Burn-Out. Evaluation eines psychodramatischen Therapieprozesses zur Behandlung des Burnout Syndroms.

Riepl, R. (2011). Homo Metrum. Die Grundlagen der psychodramatischen Aufstellungsarbeit.

Rotter, B. (2012). Adaptionen und Besonderheiten der Psychodrama-Gruppentherapie bei altersdementen Menschen.

Sakrausky, E. (2013). „Ein Hai verlässt sein Riff" – Das „aggressive Kind" und was ihm die Kinder-Psychodramagruppe bieten kann.

Scharfetter, K. (2013). In Strukturen wachsen. Rahmengestaltung stationärer Gruppenpsychotherapie.

Schatovich-Kiss, M. (2009). ADHS-Kinder in der Psychodrama-Kinderspielgruppe.

Schönherr, M. (2008). Die veruntreute Lebensfreude, eingeklemmtes Leben befreien.

Schöpfer, E. (2013). Möglichkeiten des Stegreiftheaters in der Rehabilitation von langzeithospitalisierten PsychiatriepatientInnen.

Schorn, B. (2012). Von der Erstarrung zum Rollenspiel. Psychodramatische Behandlung von sozialängstlichen Kindern und Jugendlichen.

Spitzer-Prochazka, S. (2008). „CvK4PD2" Eine spontan-kreative Annäherung an psychodramatisches Online-Setting.

Starzer-Eidenberger, B. (2013). Der Rollenwechsel und der Rollentausch, eine Methode zur Dissonanzreduktion bei der Änderung des Rauchverhaltens.

Stelzig, M. (2014). Biologisch verankerte Rollen und die befriedigende Interaktion zwischen Säugling und Eltern als Teil des impliziten Wissens des Neugeborenen und wieweit diese Erkenntnis das psychodramatische Handeln beeinflusst.

Stollewerk, H. (2007). Das Netz des Akrobaten. Zum Umgang mit dem realen sozialen Atom in der Psychodrama Kinder- und Jugendlichentherapie unter Einbeziehung der speziellen Thematik von „Bindung und Bindungsstörungen".

Tornow, D. (2013). Ich leiste, also bin ich. Biografische Bedingungen bei einer Burnout Erkrankung.

Trattnigg, D. (2011). Der Weg der Einsamen auf der Suche nach dem Du – Eine psychodramatische Wegbeschreibung.

Trinkel, G. (2013). Psychodramatische Gruppentherapie unter Beachtung struktureller Interventionen. Evaluation einer ambulant durchgeführten psychotherapeutischen Gruppe.

Wanderer, E. (2014). Psychodrama und OPD–2.

Weigl, S. (2014). Wirkung und Einsatzmöglichkeiten des Sozialen Atoms in den unterschiedlichen Phasen des Therapieprozesses.

Wicher, M. (2007). Erlebnis Gruppe. Psychodramagruppen für traumatisierte Kinder und Jugendliche im stationären Setting – unter besonderer Berücksichtigung von Bühnenaufbau, Nachnähren und Einsatz der Techniken Hilfs- Ich und Intermediär- bzw. Intraintermediärobjekte.

Zahrl-Weis, E. (2012). Frühe Störungen-frühe Behandlung. Psychodrama-Einzelpsychotherapie im Vorschulalter mit besonderem Augenmerk auf die Entwicklung des Als-ob und der Spielfähigkeit als Basis von Rollendistanz und der Fähigkeit zum spontan kreativen Handeln.

Zauner, C. (2010). Selbstgestaltete Heldenfiguren als intraintermediäre bzw. intermediäre Objekte in der psychodramatischen Arbeit mit einem depressiven Jugendlichen im monodramatischen Setting.

Sonstige Literatur

Bender, W., & Stadler, C. (2012). *Psychodrama-Therapie. Grundlagen, Methodik und Anwendungsgebiete*. Stuttgart: Schattauer.
Hintermeier, S. (2011). Qualitative Psychodramaforschung. *Zeitschrift für Psychodrama und Soziometrie, 3*, 89–107. doi:10.1007/s11620-011-0125-6.
Ottomeyer, K. (2004). Das Psychodrama zwischen Psychoanalyse und kritischer Gesellschaftstheorie. Manuskript, in gekürzter Form publiziert In J. Fürst, K. Ottomeyer & H. Pruckner H. (Hrsg.), *Psychodrama-Therapie. Ein Handbuch*. Wien: Facultas.
Von Ameln, F. Gerstmann, R., & Kramer, J. (2005). *Psychodrama*. Heidelberg: Springer.

Mag[a]. Sonja Hintermeier, Jg. 1965, Mag. phil., MSc, Klinische Psychologin und Gesundheitspsychologin, Psychodrama-Therapeutin in eigener Praxis, Lehr-Psychotherapeutin und Lehrsupervisorin der Fachsektion Psychodrama im ÖAGG, Lehrbeauftragte an der Donau-Universität Krems für Seminare rund ums Erstellen wissenschaftlicher Arbeiten im Rahmen des Fachspezifikums Psychodrama (Literatur und Psychotherapieforschung, Masterthesenseminar).

Z Psychodrama Soziometr (2016) (Suppl) 15:323–325
DOI 10.1007/s11620-015-0302-0

HAUPTBEITRÄGE

Zeitschrift für Psychodrama und Soziometrie

Grasping the tail of a comet: researching and writing about psychodrama in the 21st century

Kate Kirk

Published online: 9 December 2015

Abstract By way of a letter to J. L Moreno, this short article explores the trials and tribulations of researching psychodrama as a practitioner. The trials are related to the predominance of positivist quantitative research that seems apparently at odds with the philosophy and tenets of psychodrama.

Keywords Psychodrama · Research · Research standards · Practitioner · Researchers

Der Griff nach dem Kometenschweif: Forschen und Schreiben zum Psychodrama im 21. Jahrhundert

Zusammenfassung In Form eines Briefes an J.L. Moreno untersucht dieser kurze Beitrag die Irrungen und Wirrungen, Psychodrama als PraktikerIn zu beforschen. Die Versuche sind bezogen auf die Dominanz der positivistischen, quantitativen Forschungstradition, die scheinbar im Widerspruch zur Philosophie und den Grundsätzen des Psychodramas steht.

Schlüsselwörter Psychodrama · Forschung · Forschungsstandards · PraktikerInnen · ForscherInnen

This article is the slightly revised version of Kirk, K. (2008) *Grasping the tail of the comet: researching and writing about psychodrama in the 21st century. British Journal of Psychodrama and Sociodrama* 23 (1), 7–9

K. Kirk (✉)
CAMHS Noble's Hospital,
IM4 4DG Braddan, Douglas, Isle of Man, British Isles
e-mail: Kate.Kirk@gov.im

Dear Dr. Moreno,

Psychodramatists find themselves in changing times; we are in danger of being beleaguered by managers, statisticians and accountants. Their voices demand value for money, with cost-effectiveness and evidence-based practice. They often pay lip-service to the clients: the too hungry consumers of their services. Their eyes are firmly fixed on profit margins as they skilfully manipulate the objects that form the organisation's assets (their staff) to keep them from 'feeding' the 'hungry' too well. This bleak introduction may be a bit Orwellian, especially as we are well away from 1984, but there are many workers who will recognise some of its truth.

The final demand, evidence-based practice, has become the great catch-phrase of the past decades, at least, in the context of health and social care. Practitioners understandably can feel oppressed by these number crunchers who know little of the vulnerable nature of client work in, say, mental health, child protection, or criminal justice systems. Practitioners see and hear the stories of their clients as they work tentatively and, more often than not, intuitively with shattered lives and fragile minds. The division between the worker's view and the bureaucrat's view is wide; the wedge is formed by the competing philosophies of marketplace versus psychotherapy.

Similar struggles exist in writing about psychodrama. If it is not highly stylised, representative of some arcane academic structure, it is often judged to be too anecdotal and so denied access to 'proper' journals. Ordinary practitioners rarely risk putting pen to paper for fear of falling at the first fence of not being 'proper'. Yet so much excellent and innovative practice is lost—what happens to practice wisdom when it is neither described nor discussed? Does it vaporise like a comet's tail?

I chose the title of this letter to you because it connects a phenomenon of the cosmos (albeit an astronomical aspect) with your own cosmic visions. I wondered how it might be to grasp metaphorically the tail of a comet, to describe it, to decipher its nature, to understand its relationship to its ever-changing environment as it goes through space. I believe that this metaphor captures the intricacies of psychodrama research: process, content, personnel, theory, practice etc. etc. Because, despite the push in this currently audit minded world, psychodrama continues to be largely made up of the phenomena found in therapeutic encounter; the I—Thou relationships within a group.

As a qualitative researcher it is phenomenally (please excuse the pun) difficult to gain acceptance and legitimacy in this scientific, positivist and, largely, quantitative world of research. In some ways, thankfully, there are some psychodramatists who have made it their business to straddle these two diverse worlds in a way that I have yet to achieve. This can be seen in Michael Wieser's dedication to systematically collecting and collating hard based research evidence into the treatment effects of psychodrama (see Wieser 2007).

I believe that there are many practitioners who struggle with a stereotypical image of research, which is that it is for scientific "egg-heads" in white coats. The good news is that there is a move towards constructivism—where all knowledge regardless of source is pooled and can be drawn from to inform practice. Importantly for psychodramatists, the 'new paradigm' research is a search for meaning, a capturing of the essence of human experience. The focus is on meaning not measurement.

Peter Reason, one of the proponents of co-operative inquiry, emphasises the empowerment of the human participant and promotes the participatory nature of research where researcher is also subject and subject is also researcher. Research becomes a collaborative endeavour, in actual fact a lot like psychodrama. I think you would appreciate Reason's words on this process:

> Through a process of human inquiry we may learn to walk in spirit, walk in beauty, walk in wisdom, walk in skill, and we may through this learn what we mean by spirit, beauty, wisdom, truth and skill ... maybe that is one way of seeing the quest. (Reason 1993, p. 273)

Perhaps we all need to see ways to walk in peace and collaborate more fully in our own research and writing quests. If we don't, as we ride this comet, how else can we establish what this comet actually is and how it works: your legacy, the one we call 'psychodrama'.

All the very best

Kate

Postscript This letter was part of the British Journal of Psychodrama and Sociodrama (BJP&S), which was dedicated to writing letters to Dr Moreno about what was happening at that point in time, 2008, in psychodrama practice. It was surplus reality, in print, intended to address our founding father; it was fun too.

So here we are in 2015 and here is a journal full of international articles dedicated to research into psychodrama and all its riches. Perhaps the comet has landed and we can see it, touch it and describe it in ways that make sense to our psychodrama colleagues, other psychotherapists and researchers.

References

Reason, P. (1993). Reflections of sacred experience and sacred science. *Journal of Management Inquiry, 2*(3), 273–283.

Wieser, M. (2007). Studies on treatment effects of psychodrama psychotherapy. In C. Baim, C. J. Burmeister, & M. Maciel (Eds.), *Psychodrama: Advances in theory and practice* (pp. 271–292). Hove: Routledge.

Kate Kirk, has worked for the Isle of Man CAMHS (Child and Adolescent Mental Health Service) as a psychodrama psychotherapist since 2001, prior to that she worked in palliative care with children and adults. Her special interests are using psychodrama in Paediatric Liaison with young people who present with physical illness and with young people with Asperger's Syndrome. She worked for two years as research and development co-ordinator for a local UK NHS Trust in the North West of England. She has undertaken a number of research projects including her Master's research which explored how psychodramatists work safely with clients who have been sexually abused and her PhD research on the impact of working therapeutically with clients who have experienced sexual trauma as adults or children. She has explored the effectiveness of psychodrama with young people who have Asperger's syndrome. She has been known to run workshops entitled Befriending the Research Monster to warm psychodramatists up to researching their practice.

MIX
Papier aus verantwortungsvollen Quellen
Paper from responsible sources
FSC® C105338

If you have any concerns about our products,
you can contact us on
ProductSafety@springernature.com

In case Publisher is established outside the EU,
the EU authorized representative is:
Springer Nature Customer Service Center GmbH
Europaplatz 3, 69115 Heidelberg, Germany

Printed by Libri Plureos GmbH
in Hamburg, Germany